Programming Languages
for Parallel Processing

Programming Languages
for Parallel Processing

David B. Skillicorn
Domenico Talia

IEEE Computer Society Press
Los Alamitos, California

Washington • Brussels • Tokyo

Library of Congress Cataloging-in-Publication Data

Skillicorn, David B.
Programming languages for parallel processing /
    David B. Skillicorn, Domenico Talia.
        p.   cm.
    Includes bibliographical references (p .) and index.
    ISBN 0-8186-6502-5 (paper).
    1. Parallel programming (Computer science)   2. Programming languages (Electronic computers)
    I. Talia, Domenico.   II. Title.
    QA76.642.S62   1995
    005.2—dc20
                    94-41230
                    CIP

Published by the
IEEE Computer Society Press
10662 Los Vaqueros Circle
P.O. Box 3014
Los Alamitos, CA 90720-1264

IEEE Computer Society Press Order Number 6502-01
IEEE Catalog Number EH0412-7
Library of Congress Number 94-41230
ISBN 0-8186-6502-5 (paper)

Additional copies can be ordered from

IEEE Computer Society Press Customer Service Center 10662 Los Vaqueros Circle P.O. Box 3014 Los Alamitos, CA 90720-1264 Tel: (714) 821-8380 Fax: (714) 821-4641 Email: cs.books@computer.org	IEEE Service Center 445 Hoes Lane P.O. Box 1331 Piscataway, NJ 08855-1331 Tel: (908) 981-1393 Fax: (908) 981-9667	IEEE Computer Society 13, avenue de l'Aquilon B-1200 Brussels BELGIUM Tel: +32-2-770-2198 Fax: +32-2-770-8505	IEEE Computer Society Ooshima Building 2-19-1 Minami-Aoyama Minato-ku, Tokyo 107 JAPAN Tel: +81-3-3408-3118 Fax: +81-3-3408-3553

Technical Editor: Pradip Srimani
Copy Editor: Phyllis Walker
Production Editor: Lisa O'Conner
Computer-based cover art by Hans & Cassady, Inc.—Westerville, Ohio
Printed in the United States of America by McNaughton & Gunn, Inc.

 The Institute of Electrical and Electronics Engineers, Inc.

Contents

Preface

The needs of parallel computing power will bring many changes in software design and development in the coming years. This book presents and discusses programming languages for parallel-processing architectures. Its aims are to overview the most important parallel-programming languages designed in the last decade and to introduce issues and concepts related to the development of parallel software. The book surveys parallel languages currently being used to develop parallel applications in many areas, from numerical to symbolic computing, and new parallel-programming languages that will be used in the next 10 years to program parallel computers.

The text is written primarily for computer scientists, programmers, and students who need to study, design, and implement parallel applications. A large investment has been made in the design of parallel hardware. However, to ensure the success of parallel computation, investment must be made in the development of parallel-software tools and methodologies. Moreover, many people must be trained to write parallel software. This book is a contribution in this direction. It is a survey containing, in some cases, papers that are influential in the parallel-programming area and, in other cases, tutorial papers on parallel-programming languages that have a significant effect on the spread of parallel programming as a way of implementing high-performance applications.

The high-quality papers included in this book describe various paradigms that have been defined and implemented to support various models of parallelism. The papers represent a balance of practical approaches that are currently used by many practitioners—for example, C*, Occam, the Parallel Virtual Machine (PVM), High Performance Fortran (HPF), Linda, and Sisal—and research proposals that will be fruitful in the near future—for example, Orca, Concurrent Aggregates (CA), Program Composition Notation (PCN), concurrent constraint languages, CC++, and the Bulk Synchronous Parallelism (BSP) language.

Chapter 1 is an introduction that overviews parallel-programming paradigms and discusses the major properties of several parallel-programming languages. The next six chapters include papers that describe parallel-programming languages. Papers are grouped into the following chapters according to the paradigm used to express parallelism:

- Chapter 2: languages based on the shared-memory model,

- Chapter 3: languages based on the distributed-memory model,

- Chapter 4: parallel object-oriented languages,

- Chapter 5: parallel functional-programming languages,
- Chapter 6: concurrent logic languages, and
- Chapter 7: more innovative approaches to parallel programming.

A list of references cited is provided at the end of each chapter. At the end of the book is an extensive bibliography.

David B. Skillicorn and Domenico Talia

December 1994

Chapter 1:
Introduction

Parallel computers represent a great opportunity to develop high-performance systems and to solve large problems in many application areas. During the last few years, highly parallel computers, ranging in size from hundreds to thousands of nodes, have become commercially available. They continue to gain recognition as powerful tools for scientific research, information management, and engineering applications. This trend is driven by parallel-programming languages and tools that contribute to making parallel computers useful in supporting a broad range of applications.

Parallel computers are composed of several computing elements connected by means of a shared-memory space (in *multiprocessors*) or by means of a communication network (in *multicomputers*). Both types of parallel computers support the execution of more than one operation at a given time, allowing parallel execution of the activities that must be performed in solving a problem. In a multiprocessor, the computing elements cooperate using shared memory to read and write data. In a multicomputer, the computing elements cooperate by means of the communication structure, which has a regular topology—such as a hypercube, mesh, or tree—and which guarantees that messages can be passed between two generic computing nodes.

Many concurrent models and languages have been designed to develop applications on parallel computers. Concurrent programming languages allow the design of parallel algorithms as a set of concurrent actions mapped onto different computing nodes. The cooperation between two actions can take place in many ways, according to the selected language.

The design of programming languages and software tools for parallel computers is essential for wide diffusion and efficient utilization of these novel architectures. The use of high-level languages decreases both the design time and the execution time of parallel applications and makes it easier for new users to approach parallel computers.

This book overviews the major concurrent programming paradigms designed in the last decade for programming parallel computers and introduces issues and concepts related to the development of parallel software. It surveys parallel languages currently being used to develop parallel applications in many areas, from numerical to symbolic computing, and new parallel-programming languages that will be used in the next 10 years to program parallel computers.

Chapter 1 introduces parallel-programming paradigms and discusses the major properties of several parallel-programming languages. The next six chapters include representative papers describing various paradigms designed to support various models of parallelism, with papers grouped

1

into chapters according to the paradigm they use to express parallelism. Chapters 2 and 3 include papers on languages that follow the imperative paradigm and that express parallelism at the *process* or *statement* level. In particular, Chapter 2 discusses languages based on the *shared-memory model*. These programming languages present a view of memory as if it were shared, although the implementation may or may not be. Processes communicate and synchronize through the use of *shared data*. Chapter 3 discusses concurrent languages based on the *distributed-memory model*. A distributed concurrent program consists of a set of *processes*, located on one or many computers, that cooperate by *message passing*. This paradigm reflects the model of distributed-memory architectures composed of a set of processors connected by a communication network. Chapter 4 describes parallel object-oriented languages. Objects and parallelism can be integrated since the modularity of *objects* makes them a natural unit for parallel execution. The papers included in this chapter show how this integration can be successful. Chapter 5 examines parallel functional-programming languages. They express a fine-grain parallelism at the level of *expressions*. The papers included in this chapter discuss the main problems involved in the parallel implementation of functional programs and the range of proposed solutions to these problems. Chapter 6 examines concurrent logic languages that express parallelism at the *clauses* level. The aim of concurrent logic languages, which offer another declarative approach to programming parallel computers, is to exploit the parallelism inside logic programs by means of a parallel proof strategy. Finally, Chapter 7 presents a collection of more innovative approaches to parallel programming. Compared to the languages discussed in Chapters 2 through 6, the languages presented in Chapter 7 tend to have been designed with stronger semantics, directed toward software construction and correctness. Some of these programming languages may be the ones to be used for the development of parallel applications in the next decade.

Background

Parallelism in programming languages was originally studied as a branch of operating system programming. The first concepts were aimed at providing synchronization primitives for concurrent processes. These concepts were introduced by Dijkstra [DIJ68], Brinch Hansen [BRI73], and Hoare [HOA74], who proposed primitive mechanisms such as *semaphores, conditional critical regions,* and *monitors*.

Semaphores are a simple mechanism for the implementation of synchronization between processes that access the same resource. A semaphore is a nonnegative integer variable on which two operations are defined: P (wait) and V (signal). Each access to a shared resource must be preceded by a P operation and followed by a V operation on the same semaphore. Conditional critical regions overcome some of the difficulties of using semaphores by providing a structured mechanism to implement synchronization. Each shared resource can be accessed only by using conditional critical region statements that guarantee mutual exclusion on the resource. Finally, monitors encapsulate both a resource and the operations that manipulate it. Resources defined in a monitor must be accessed only by using the operations defined by the monitor itself. Thus, a monitor guarantees mutual exclusion on the resource, and a programmer may ignore the implementation details of the resource handling.

The above mechanisms were included in sequential programming languages. For example, the *monitor* concept was introduced by Brinch Hansen [BRI75] in Concurrent Pascal, an extension of the Pascal language. In 1978, Hoare published a paper [HOA78] proposing the Communicating Sequential Processes (CSP) model, which strongly influenced the design of several other programming languages for message-passing parallel architectures. As a consequence of these early research activities, several high-level parallel-programming languages were designed and implemented on the parallel computers that were commercially available. These languages, based mainly on the conventional imperative approach, began to be used to express and develop parallel programs, thus extending their application area from that of operating systems to many other areas.

The design of parallel programs requires facing problems that are not present in sequential programming. Typical issues in parallel programming are synchronization, process creation, communication handling, deadlock, and process termination. These issues arise mainly because, when a concurrent program is running, there are many flows of control through the program, one for each process. Thus, a designer of parallel applications is concerned with the problem of ensuring the correct behavior of all the processes that the program comprises. The aim of designing parallel-programming languages was to help programmers cope with these problems, thus allowing the programming of parallel computers to be not much more difficult than that of sequential computers.

In the last decade, an enormous number of parallel-programming languages that provide high-level constructs and better mechanisms have been designed. They reflect many paradigms and architectural models and cover a wide range of goals, performance, and applications. Many programmers are using them, and many researchers are experimenting with them in new application areas.

Parallelism today

The state of parallel computing today can be summed up as follows:

- Architecture-specific programming of parallel machines is mature, and the tools used for it are becoming sophisticated.

- Architecture-independent programming of parallel machines is beginning to be seriously thought about as a plausible long-term approach.

3

Commercial parallel computers exist in each of Flynn's [FLY72] architecture classes: single-instruction, multiple-data (SIMD) machines; multiple-instruction, multiple-data (MIMD) multicomputers using many different interconnection networks, such as the Intel iPSC [CLO88], the Ncube [HAY86], the Transputer-based machines [INM91], and the J-Machine [DAL92]; and some shared-memory machines [GOT83a], most with modest parallelism. Many systems are available in configurations of about a thousand processors, although most delivered systems are not this large.

Massive parallelism is well on the way to becoming a reality. Research versions of more unusual architectures exist: for example, multithreaded machines and dataflow architectures. New ideas for parallel hardware appear regularly, and a significant fraction of these ideas come to some kind of commercial fruition.

The basic idioms for programming each architectural style are widely understood. For example, SIMD machines use data-parallel programming languages and clever algorithms to exploit parallelism. Mechanisms such as *test&op* or monitors have been developed to handle contention in shared-memory MIMD architectures. Message passing and remote procedure calls (RPCs) are used in distributed-memory MIMD architectures.

Single-assignment languages have been developed for dataflow architectures. Parallelizing compilers have been developed to prolong the life span of existing sequential code and to provide an easy way of developing new code for parallel architectures. Applications have been built to take advantage of all these architectural and programming styles, and they are in production use to solve problems requiring high-performance computing.

Second-generation abstractions have also been developed for several architectures. For example, it has been widely appreciated that the mental model of SIMD programming is useful, even for programming a machine that does not require it. This has led to the single-program, multiple-data (SPMD) programming model, in which synchronization between the program pieces executing on different processors is relaxed. In the SPMD model, an application is composed of n similar processes, with each one operating on a different set of data. The processes cooperate and synchronize not after each operation, as in the SIMD model, but when they need to.

The requirements of explicit message passing have been weakened by concepts such as *tuple space*, which decouples the *send* and *receive* of communication actions, and *channel* implementation by (the appearance of) variable references. Both dataflow and process-structured programming styles have converged on systems of lightweight processes, communicating using active messages.

Tools for parallel programming are available and are becoming rapidly more sophisticated. These tools include

1. *graphical user interfaces (GUIs)* for constructing programs for constructing programs by interconnecting processes diagrammatically rather than by explicitly writing a message-passing harness [LOB92];

2. *assistants* for parallelizing existing code, including profiling tools to determine where the potential for parallelism exists [BLO93], [LEV93]; and

3. *debuggers* for tracking the state of any process or thread, using techniques including those that make monitoring minimally intrusive and that use graphical displays to present large volumes of data in useful ways [PAN93].

The above discussion of the state of parallelism today might suggest that parallel computation is well on its way to becoming a major part of ordinary computation. Such a scenario can become a reality if some of the problems of parallel computation are solved. The main problem preventing the widespread, mainstream use of parallel computation is the mismatch between the development of parallel architectures and the needs of potential users. Parallel architectures, as we have seen, come in a wide variety of arrangements.

New parallel architectures continue to be developed, with significantly new ideas appearing in them. We expect this trend to continue with the integration of optical devices, first into interconnects and then into processors themselves. Thus, parallel machines have life spans measured in years; every few years, another, more powerful architecture is developed. The kind of architecture that is the performance leader at any moment in time is unlikely to retain its position in a few years, and predicting future favorites seems a hopeless task. This creates a difficult problem for the user who wants a parallel machine as a tool that runs software, because the software typically has a life span of decades. The software developed today for a parallel machine ought to be able to continue to be run as the parallel platforms underneath are replaced. We are far from being able to do this. Developing parallel software is expensive, and maintaining it and migrating it to new platforms are major efforts, often requiring almost complete reconstruction for each move. Clearly, for all but the most performance-driven, any moment looks like the wrong moment to make a move to parallel computation. So, many have decided to wait until a viable growth path has been developed, and they have been waiting for several years. A tremendous pent-up demand for parallelism has thus been created, along with a frustration with the possibilities of parallelism as they exist today.

A great part of the problem is the tight connection between software and programming style and the architecture that executes it. As long as software contains embedded assumptions about properties of the architecture, migrating it from one architecture to another is difficult. This tight connection also makes software development difficult for programmers, since using a different style of architecture means learning a whole new style of writing programs and a new collection of programming idioms. Those who require high performance live with these difficulties and pay the enormous price required to keep software running as architectures change. However, there are reasons other than high performance to use parallelism. Such reasons will lead to a mass market in parallel computation, if the software problems can be overcome. Some reasons to use parallelism are listed below.

- It can deliver high performance when necessary.

- A multiprocessor can be cheaper per computation than the leading-edge uniprocessor, especially as development costs increase for each new generation of processors.

- Many real-world problems are naturally parallel and can be modeled more naturally and directly in a parallel way.

- The speed of light is a bound on the speed that can be achieved by a single processor, so ultimately there is no choice but to use parallelism.

Desirable properties of parallel models

A successful model of parallel computation should provide the right abstraction of the computation steps of which architectures are capable. If the model is too concrete and low-level, it becomes outdated as architectures change in unforeseen ways. If it is too abstract, adequate performance is hard to obtain. Thus, a model requires a careful balancing of different needs. A model for parallel computation should have the properties listed below. These are listed in decreasing order of importance for general-purpose parallel computation. Of course, these properties are very much in tension with each other, and the important goal is to find the best balance between them.

1. The model should be *architecture-independent*; that is, the source of a program should not need to be altered for the program to run on different architectures or configurations. This implies that the model should abstract from all the features that are specific only to particular architectures.

2. The model should be *intellectually abstract*. Machines with a thousand processors usually have many more threads active to hide latency—perhaps 10 times as many. The state of the computation depends on the state of 10,000 active threads and potential or actual communications between them. This kind of complexity is beyond human capacity to comprehend in detail. A model should conceal most of this complexity if humans are to understand and reason about programs. In particular, a model should conceal

    - *decomposition* into parallel threads—that is, the way in which the work to be done is divided up and allocated to processors;

- *communication* between threads—that is, the actions taken to send and receive each individual communication between threads; and

- *synchronization* between threads, because in general this requires understanding the global state of the computation.

3. The model should have a *software development methodology* that allows programs to be developed in a structured way from specifications. The complexity of a large parallel program requires a controlled way of developing it. This controlled development is essential, first to produce correct programs and then to allow them to be maintained. The post hoc verification strategy suggested for sequential software is not very useful in a parallel setting, because it does not help with the actual construction of the software and because the verification proofs depend on the program structure, which can be arbitrarily awkward. Building programs using a calculus is a much more attractive approach, because it provides a structured way of building programs, documents the choices made during development, and builds only correct programs.

4. The model must possess *cost measures* or, preferably, a *cost calculus*. Derivations cannot be sensibly carried out in the absence of information about the cost of making decisions at choice points. Thus, the model must make it possible to compute the cost of the program at early stages in the derivation, in ways that do not depend in detail on the target architecture. If the cost system makes it possible to determine the cost of changing a part of a program independently of the rest of it, then it is even more useful.

5. The model must have *no preferred scale of granularity* for the units of work assigned to individual processors. Uniprocessors are becoming powerful and often internally use small amounts of parallelism. A model that limits the maximum grain of work that can be allocated to each processor may find that computations require many processors, each of which is underutilized. Also, many systems make use of parallelism at two different levels, so some flexibility in deciding how to break up a computation into parallel streams is required.

6. The model should be *efficiently implementable* on a wide variety of architectures. We can classify architectures by power—that is, by their ability to execute arbitrary computations—as follows:

- The most powerful class of architectures comprises shared-memory MIMD machines and distributed-memory MIMD machines [DUN90] with an interconnect volume that grows as $p \log p$, where p is the number of processors. On such machines, an arbitrary computation with parallelism p, taking time t, can be executed in such a way that the product *pt* is preserved [VAL90b]. Doing so requires using parallel *slackness*—that is, using fewer physical processors than the parallelism *p* present in the computation. This allows latency to be hidden by multiplexing threads onto processors. Such architectures are very powerful but do not scale well because of the interconnect volume required.

- The second most powerful class of architectures comprises distributed-memory MIMD machines in which the interconnect volume grows only linearly with the number of processors. Such machines are scalable, because they require only a constant number of communication links per processor; hence, the local neighborhoods of processors are unaffected by scaling. Implementing arbitrary computations on such machines cannot be achieved without loss of efficiency on the order of the diameter *d* of the interconnect; that is, a computation that apparently requires time *t* on *p* processors will in fact do work on the order of *ptd*. A direct emulation of an arbitrary computation requires time whose growth is proportional to the diameter of the interconnect, because mapping to achieve locality generally cannot be done. Using multiplexing also fails, because the amount of communication generated can overrun the capacity of the interconnect.

- The third most powerful class of architectures comprises SIMD machines, which, though scalable, very inefficiently emulate arbitrary computations. This is because of their inability to do more than a small, constant number of different actions on each step [SKI90].

The above discussion of machine power and scalability implies that for a model to be efficiently implementable over scalable architectures, it must reduce the volume of communication that it carries out. The volume can be reduced either by reducing the *number* of communication actions or by reducing the *distance* that each action travels. Models that do not limit the volume of communication cannot be efficiently implemented on the architectures of most long-term interest: the scalable ones. Efficient implementation on SIMD architectures requires even further restrictions on a programming model, since some regularity in time is necessary.

Different properties may be of interest in different application domains. For example, many scientific computations have time complexity that is quadratic or worse. For these, an extra factor caused by communication bandwidth limitations may be acceptable if it allows arbitrary computations to be written.

Overview of models and languages

This section uses the above-listed properties of a successful model of parallel computation to assess the models and languages for parallel processing presented later in this book, as well as others. Many of these models were not developed with the ambitious goal of incorporating these properties, so we are not being critical of them if they fail to have some of the properties. Nevertheless, this assessment provides a clear picture of the current situation.

As we have seen, the most important determinant of the possibility of efficiently implementing a program on the full range of parallel architectures is how much communication takes place. If the volume of communication is more than linear in the number of threads, the program will not be efficiently implementable on a distributed-memory machine with constant valence. Thus, we can classify parallel models into two groups: *arbitrary-computation structures*, which allow arbitrary computations to be written, and *restricted-computation structures*, which restrict the form of computations so as to restrict communication volume. Table 1 shows this classification of models.

Table 1. Classification of parallel models.

Arbitrary-computation structures
Abstract models
Higher order functional-programming models
Logic-programming models
Interleaving languages
Partly abstract models
Coordination languages
Concurrent logic languages
Process nets
Active messages
Low-level models
Architecture-independent models
Architecture-specific models
Restricted-computation structures
Vertical-tiling models
Block-tiling models
Horizontal-tiling models
Algorithmic skeletons
Data-type-specific models
Data-type-independent models

Arbitrary-computation structures

We begin by considering models that allow arbitrary computations. In these languages, any program can be written in any way that appears appropriate to the programmer. These languages can be further classified into *abstract models, partly abstract models,* and *low-level models,* according to how well they hide decomposition and communication.

Abstract models. In the first category of arbitrary-computation structures are models that require neither decomposition into threads nor explicit communication between threads. In such models, a description of a computation says what is to be done but does not say how, in what pieces, how the pieces are to interact, or where the pieces are to execute. Of course, these details must then be inferred by the compiler. Below, we consider three kinds of such models: *higher order functional-programming models, logic-programming models,* and *interleaving languages.*

Higher order functional-programming models. Higher order functional programming and logic programming (discussed next) are two declarative approaches to parallel programs, concentrating on what is to be done rather than how it is done. Programs do not specify in any direct way how they are to be executed in parallel, so that decomposition does not need to be explicit. Communication and synchronization take place as needed during the execution of a computation and are not visible, or even predictable, by the programmer. Thus, higher order functional programming satisfies quite well the model requirements for software development. Developing cost measures for it is not easy, precisely because so much of what happens at runtime is hidden at the software level. How efficiently this approach can be implemented is still an open question.

Parallel graph reduction, which is the usual implementation technique for functional programming, has been only a limited success, particularly when implemented on distributed-memory machines [DAR87], [KEL89], [PEY87], [RAH93].

Logic-programming models. Parallel execution models for logic languages can be divided according to whether they exploit

- parallelism expressed by means of annotations: parallelism is specified explicitly in programs by programmers (see the discussion below of *concurrent logic languages*), or

- parallelism implicit in the program and extracted by the language support both during static analysis and at runtime (*parallel logic models*).

Well-known parallel logic models based on implicit parallelism are Parallel Prolog Processor (PPP) [FAG90], the And/Or Process model [CON87], and the Reduce/Or model [KAL91]. These models provide an automatic decomposition of the execution tree of a logic program into parallel processes by the language support [TAL94]. Some of these models have been implemented on parallel architectures, and performance results are available.

Interleaving languages. Interleaving approaches build on ideas from Dijkstra's guarded command language and CSP [HOA78]. The logical view of a program's execution is as an infinite number of repetitions of a step in which a set of *guards* is evaluated, one is selected from among those guards that evaluate as *true*, and the corresponding statement is executed. If the statements corresponding to true guards are independent, they can be concurrently evaluated, without altering the program's semantics. This idea lies behind Unity [CHA88]. This model abstracts completely from decomposition and communication, but determining costs and efficiently implementing the model seem difficult and so far have not been achieved.

Partly abstract models. In the second category of arbitrary-computation structures are models that require the software to explicitly state what the decomposition will be but that then abstract from some of the complexity of communication. Several levels of effectiveness in hiding this complexity are found in the models in this category, which are *coordination languages*, *concurrent logic languages*, *process nets*, and *active messages*.

Coordination languages. Coordination languages make decomposition explicit but hide some of the details of communication. They are called "coordination languages" because they provide the connections between threads written in any sequential programming language and are thus in some sense orthogonal to the underlying language.

The best-known example of a coordination language is Linda [AHU88], [CAR87], [CAR88], [CAR93], which is discussed in Chapter 2. Linda decouples the *send* and *receive* parts of a communication by providing the abstraction of a *tuple space*. Tuple space can be associatively accessed to retrieve values placed in it earlier by other threads. The "sending" thread does not need to know the "receiving" thread, nor does it even need to know if the "receiving" thread exists. This is a useful abstraction, because it removes the need to match sends and receives that may be widely separated in programs. The abstraction need not be too inefficient, if accesses to the tuple space can be compiled into message transfers most or all of the time. However, programmers are completely responsible for decomposition and must manage large numbers of simultaneously active threads.

A language that improves Linda by adding to it some ideas from Occam is the language Ease [ERI91a], [ERI91b], [ERI91c], [ERI93]. Ease threads communicate by means of *contexts*, which are shared-data areas that are hybrids of Occam *channels* and Linda *tuple spaces*. Threads read and write data to contexts; however, they may use a second set of primitives that move a data item to a context and relinquish ownership of it or retrieve a data item from a context and remove it from the context. Such operations can use pass-by-reference, since they can guarantee that the data will be referenced by only one thread at a time. Although Ease has many of the same properties that Linda has, it makes building efficient implementations easier and helps with decomposition by using process structuring in the style of Occam.

Other related languages relieve the complexity of communication by making it appear more like memory reference. For example, Program Composition Notation (PCN) [FOS93] and Compositional C++, both discussed in Chapter 7, hide communication by single-use variables. An attempt to read from one of these variables blocks the thread if a value has not already been placed in it by another thread. Since variables can be used only once, the effect of stream communication is achieved by recursively calling threads, so that each new context uses each variable once. PCN uses a process-structuring approach like Occam's to help with decomposition complexity.

Concurrent logic languages. Concurrent logic languages use variable annotations and the *guard* concept to specify synchronization among concurrent activities. The best-known concurrent logic languages are Concurrent Prolog, Parlog, and Guarded Horn Clauses (GHC). The last two are presented in Chapter 6. Using these concurrent logic languages, a user establishes—by means of *annotations*—the direction of communications between two subgoals having shared variables.

Concurrent logic languages extend the application areas of logic programming from expert systems, natural languages, and databases to system-level applications. Program annotation requires a different style of programming in Prolog. However, they make the compiler's task easier. In fact, parallel implementations of concurrent logic languages are the most efficient of the implementations of parallel logic-programming models.

Process nets. Another class of languages is based on process nets, which are networks of more or less autonomous computations that communicate using message passing that is usually asynchronous and one-directional. Message passing is more explicit for process nets than for the other partly abstract models considered above, and decomposition is still mostly the responsibility of the programmer.

The best-known model of this kind is *dataflow* [HER87]. Dataflow graphs show only the data dependencies between operations, so that any two operations that are not directly connected are potentially concurrently executable. Decomposition need not be explicitly specified in dataflow systems, although some kind of configuration language is sometimes used. Communication between operations is not done by explicit sends and receives but rather by the use of a variable name on the left-hand side of an assignment in one place and on the right-hand side of an assignment in another place.

While dataflow permits reasonably efficient implementations, it provides a fairly abstract view to the programmer. However, scheduling is underspecified in the sense that much information known at compile time about the ordering of operations is unavailable at execution time. This makes problematic any determination of the cost of a computation.

Other models of this kind are the Actors model [AGH86], [BAU91a], [BAU91b] and models based on object-oriented languages that are discussed in Chapter 4. Again, decomposition is quite explicit; however, in message passing, the emphasis is on the *send* step rather than the *receive* step. Actors is the "natural" model for distributed-memory MIMD architectures. Parallel object-oriented languages such as An Object-Based Concurrent Language (ABCL/1) and Concurrent Smalltalk are based on active objects as the unit of parallelism. Each process is bound to a particular object for which it is created.

Active messages. A variant approach is based on active messages. Here, messages are conceived not as data objects passed between threads but rather as active agents in their own right. A message is sent by a thread to another processor, where it transmutes into an active thread on that processor. The active-messages approach reduces the complexity of communication, because it removes altogether the need for a *receive* operation and because decomposition follows from the communication structure rather than requiring a separate set of decisions. This approach is embodied in the Movie system [FAI92] and in Concurrent Aggregates (CA) [CHI90], a language designed for the J-Machine [DAL92], [NOA90] that is described in Chapter 4.

Low-level models. In the third category of arbitrary-computation structures are languages that do not hide much detail of decomposition and communication. Many of today's architecture-specific models are at this detailed level. We can distinguish between those models that are *architecture-independent*—that is, those that try to provide enough facilities to use any architecture—and those that are *application-specific*—that is, those that are tightly tied to a particular style of architecture.

Architecture-independent models. Architecture-independent languages are represented by systems that provide a rich set of primitives to allow any architecture to be programmed effectively without the need to worry about the specific mechanisms that each architecture uses. Languages of this general kind are the programming languages Ada, Concurrent C, Orca [BAL90], and Synchronizing Resources (SR) [AND93]. These languages provide mechanisms for decomposition, communication, and synchronization—but in the context of an imperative programming language. Several different mechanisms are provided to achieve each possible effect, but there is no specific attempt to make these languages simultaneously architecture-independent and efficient.

In another set of architecture-independent models are those developed primarily to harness the unused power of networks of workstations. Since such networks tend to be heterogeneous, these models are forced to be architecture-independent. They include systems such as the Parallel Virtual Machine (PVM) [BEG92], [BEG93], presented in Chapter 3, and p4 [BUT92]. They are basically message-passing systems with very large grain processes, and so they suffer from drawbacks: explicit message passing and decomposition, inefficiencies, and the need for tuning in order to get even reasonable performance. Matters are further complicated by the need to set up configurations, which can often require operating system familiarity. Nevertheless, networks of workstations are by far the most common type of parallel system installed today, so these models have become very popular.

Architecture-specific models. Architecture-specific low-level models cover all the programming approaches that are specific to a particular architectural style. These models include most of the programming systems in production use today. A survey of such systems is given by Bal, Steiner, and Tanenbaum [BAL89]. Other interesting references are [GOT83a] and [GOT83b]. One system of particular interest is Occam [JON88], which made parallel processing common in most of Europe. May, Shepherd, and Keane [MAY87] describe this language in a paper that is included in Chapter 3. Occam has a sufficiently strong semantic foundation that reasoning about programs and transforming them are possible, so that some of the software development issues are addressed by the language. Nevertheless, the consensus is that Occam's low-level treatment of process decomposition and communication is too awkward to make it practical for developing large software systems.

Restricted-computation structures

In the second major subdivision of models are those that restrict the form in which computations may be written. Sometimes, these restrictions are imposed in the interest of intelligibility. Also, the results on communication volume that are cited earlier provide good reasons for being careful about the occurrences of communication permitted in a computation (see item (6) in the section entitled "Desirable properties of parallel models").

Since all the models classified as restricted-computation structures restrict the form of a computation, it is useful to think of these models as requiring the trace of a computation to be made up from some set of tiles, templates, or dominoes. In some models, there is assumed to be a fixed set of such tiles, but this need not be the case. Tiles are chosen to achieve the goals outlined in the section referred to above: to allow a new level of abstraction in thinking about the computation and to restrict the amount of communication that can occur within each tile.

We can classify models by the shape of tile that they use. There are three possible tile shapes: vertical, block, and horizontal. *Vertical tiles* describe the actions of a single processor (and thus are equivalent to part of a thread), *block tiles* describe the actions of a cluster of processors, and *horizontal tiles* describe the actions of all the processors for some time period.

Vertical-tiling models. In vertical-tiling models, tiles limit communication actions to one per tile, but that one action is a global one. Thus, these models reduce the number of communication actions initiated by a computation but do not limit the distance these actions might travel in the interconnect. Since the only requirement is to reduce the total volume, this approach works to prevent interconnect overload.

14

Valiant [VAL89], [VAL90a] suggested the Bulk Synchronous Parallelism (BSP) model, in which computations are divided into *phases*, alternating global communication and local computation. The interval between global communication steps is determined by the delivery capability of the interconnect of the target machine. A paper presenting GL [MCC93], a programming language that implements this approach, is included in Chapter 7. The BSP approach reduces the amount of global communication so that computations can be efficiently implemented on the full range of architectures. However, the interval between communication steps depends on target properties—mainly, the size of the target—so that there is still some architectural dependence. This approach does not provide much abstraction from decomposition and communication, nor is there any software development methodology.

A related approach is LogP [CUL93]. In this approach, vertical tiles similar to those used in GL are used, but there is no requirement to have all the global communication occur in a synchronous way. Instead, the tiles are restricted to a single global communication action each, and the size of tiles is determined by properties of the target architecture. Thus, a machine with slow communication or little interconnect bandwidth must use large tiles.

For both GL and LogP, it may happen that a particular algorithm cannot be expressed using tiles large enough to conceal all the communication latency of a target machine. When this happens, efficient implementation is not possible. However, determining exactly how inefficient the implementation will be is possible.

Block-tiling models. Block tiles limit communication to within each block. Establishing global communication requires having an occasional block that covers the full width of the machine. The assumption is that a smaller block can be allocated to a submachine. Because this submachine has fewer processors, communication with any of these processors may be faster than a global communication in the machine as a whole. For example, in the hypercube, a submachine of size a power of two can be allocated as a block. The only model of this kind is the Hierarchical Parallel Random Access Machine (Hierarchical PRAM [HPRAM]), developed by Heywood and Ranka [HEY91a], [HEY91b], [HEY91c].

Horizontal-tiling models. Horizontal tiling uses the full width of the machine for each tile. However, the tile may be internally structured and may contain significant internal communication and computation. It must restrict communication, either in frequency or, more commonly, in the distance traveled by each message. Because the programmer can choose how to organize the internal structure of the tile, subcomputations that need to communicate are placed in processors that are close to each other.

Horizontal tiling is a much more popular strategy for restricting computations than either of the other two forms of tiling. Horizontal-tiling models can be subdivided into groups according to how the tiles are chosen and what kind of operations they capture. Horizontal tiles are often called *skeletons* in a functional setting and *data-parallel operations* in an imperative setting.

Algorithmic skeletons. Some skeletons are based on popular algorithms or common program structures. We might call them "algorithmic skeletons" since they are the parallel analogs of control structures and library routines.

The Pisa Parallel Programming Language (P^3L) [BAI91], [DAN90], [DAN92], discussed in Chapter 7, uses a set of algorithmic skeletons that capture common parallel-programming paradigms such as pipelines, worker farms, and reductions. Similar skeletons were developed by Cole [COL89], [COL90], who computed cost measures for them on a parallel architecture. Work in a similar direction is being done by a group at Imperial College, in London, headed by Darlington [DAR93].

The KIDS system [SMI90], [SMI91] contains a powerful software development tool that is capable of completely deriving a program, given some knowledge of the application domain and information about what kind of algorithm is needed. Some of the algorithm styles this system can build are divide-and-conquer, greedy optimization, and dynamic programming. The KIDS system has deep knowledge of such program templates, and it is probably the most advanced program derivation system in the world today. It satisfies most of the requirements for a model, particularly those relating to software development. However, it does not address efficiency of implementation in an architecture-independent way, and the system does not include cost measures.

Data-type-specific models. Other skeletons are based on operations that are *data-type-specific.* Most such models restrict themselves to a particular data type.

The construction of the Connection Machine CM-2 provided a huge impetus to programming models based on lists, since this was the natural data type supported by the architecture. A wide variety of languages were soon developed whose basic operations were data-parallel list operations. These operations usually included a map operation; some form of reduction, perhaps using only a fixed set of operators; and, later, scans (parallel prefixes) and permutation operations.

In approximately chronological order of their development, data-type-specific models are Scan [BLE87], Multiprefix [SHE92], Paralations [GOL89], [SAB89], Data-Parallel C [HAT91], [QUI90], the Scan-Vector Model and the Nested Data-Parallel Language (NESL) [BLE88], [BLE90], [BLE92], and the Data-Parallel Categorical Abstract Machine (DP-CAM) [HAI93]. Their operations are usually relatively easy to efficiently implement on different architectures, and costs often can be calculated for these operations. Also, their operations conceal much of the complexity of the underlying computation, as for all data-parallel models, because they present only a single thread at the software level. However, they do not provide any assistance with software development, and the data-parallel operations provided are often chosen because these operations are easy to implement, rather than because they are useful for software development.

The following similar models have been developed, based on *sets* and/or *bags*: Gamma [BAN91], [CRE91], [MUS91], the Parallel Set-Based Language (Parallel SETL) [FLY93], [HUM91], and Parallel Sets [KIL92a], [KIL92b].

Data-type-independent models. A *data-type-independent* approach to data-parallel programming can also be taken. This approach, represented by the model based on the Bird-Meertens Formalism [BIR87], discussed in Chapter 7, began as a derivational style for the development of functional programs. A Bird-Meertens theory begins with base types and extends them to new data-parallel types (*categorical data types*) using *type functors*. The derived model is architecture-independent in the sense that it can be immediately implemented on any architecture into which the standard topology for each data type can be embedded. For lists, such architectures include all the standard architectural classes, including SIMD machines. For other types, standard topologies are not yet understood well enough to assess architecture-independence. Efficient implementations depend on being able to reasonably emulate standard topologies on real machines. While how to reasonably emulate standard topologies on real machines is still an open question, the implementation of parallel computations on lists has been quite successful [CAI92]. Finally, there are models based on the data type of arrays. These include languages that derive from A Programming Language (APL)—such as Mathematics of Arrays (MOA) [MUL88]—and languages developed from Fortran—such as High Performance Fortran (HPF) [HIG93], [STE93], presented in Chapter 3, and Pandore II [AND92]. The data-parallel language C*, presented in Chapter 3, is slightly more general but could also be included here.

References cited

* *Those references marked with an asterisk are included in this book as reprinted papers.*

[AGH86] G. Agha, *Actors: A Model of Concurrent Computation in Distributed Systems*, MIT Press, Cambridge, Mass., 1986.

[AHU88] S. Ahuja et al., "Matching Languages and Hardware for Parallel Computation in the Linda Machine," *IEEE Trans. Computers*, Vol. 37, No. 8, Aug. 1988, pp. 921–929.

[AND92] F. Andre, O. Cheron, and J.-L. Pazat, "Compiling Sequential Programs for Distributed Memory Parallel Computers with Pandore II," May 1992.

[AND93] G.R. Andrews and R.A. Olsson, *The SR Programming Language*, Benjamin/Cummings Pub. Co., Inc., Menlo Park, Calif., 1993.

[BAI91] F. Baiardi et al., "Architectural Models and Design Methodologies for General-Purpose Highly-Parallel Computers," *Proc. Advanced Computer Technology, Reliable Systems and Applications: 5th Ann. European Computer Conference (CompEuro '91)*, IEEE CS Press, Los Alamitos, Calif., 1991, pp. 18–25.

[BAL89] H.E. Bal, J.G. Steiner, and A.S. Tanenbaum, "Programming Languages for Distributed Computing Systems," *ACM Computing Surveys*, Vol. 21, No. 3, Sept. 1989, pp. 261–322.

[BAL90] H.E. Bal, A.S. Tanenbaum, and M.F. Kaashoek, "Orca: A Language for Distributed Processing," *ACM SIGPLAN Notices*, Vol. 25, No. 5, May 1990, pp. 17–24.

[BAN91] J.P. Banâtre and D. Le Metayer, "Introduction to Gamma," in *Lecture Notes in Computer Sci.—Research Directions in High-Level Parallel Programming Languages*, J.P. Banâtre and D. Le Metayer, eds., Vol. 574, Springer-Verlag, New York, N.Y., June 1991, pp. 197–202.

[BAU91a] F. Baude, *Utilisation du Paradigme Acteur pour le Calcul Parallèle*, doctoral thesis, Université de Paris-Sud, Paris, France, 1991.

[BAU91b] F. Baude and G. Vidal-Naquet, "Actors as a Parallel Programming Model," *Lecture Notes in Computer Sci.—Proc. 8th Symp. Theoretical Aspects Computer Sci.*, 480, Springer-Verlag, New York, N.Y., 1991.

[BEG92] A. Beguelin et al., "PVM Software System and Documentation," 1992 (available by e-mail from netlib@ornl.gov).

[BEG93] A. Beguelin et al., "PVM and HeNCE: Tools for Heterogeneous Network Computing," in *Software for Parallel Computation*, J.S. Kowalik and L. Grandinetti, eds., NATO ASI Series F, Vol. 106, Springer-Verlag, New York, N.Y., 1993.

[BIR87 R.S. Bird, "An Introduction to the Theory of Lists," in *Logic of Programming and Calculi of Discrete Design*, M. Broy, ed., Springer-Verlag, New York, N.Y., 1987, pp. 3–42.

[BLE87] G. Blelloch, "Scans as Primitive Parallel Operations," *Proc. 1987 Int'l Conf. Parallel Processing*, The Penn. State Univ. Press, University Park, Pa., 1987, pp. 355–362.

[BLE88] G.E. Blelloch and G.W. Sabot, "Compiling Collection-Oriented Languages onto Massively Parallel Computers, *Proc. 2nd Symp. Frontiers Massively Parallel Computation*, IEEE CS Press, Los Alamitos, Calif., 1988, pp. 575–585.

[BLE90] G.E. Blelloch, *Vector Models for Data Parallel Computing*, MIT Press, Cambridge, Mass., 1990.

[BLE92] G.E. Blelloch, "NESL: A Nested Data Parallel Language," Tech. Report CMU-CS-92-103, School of Computer Sci., Carnegie Mellon Univ., Pittsburgh, Pa., Jan. 1992.

[BLO93] U. Block, F. Ferstl, and W. Gentzsch, "Software Tools for Developing and Porting Parallel Programs," in *Software for Parallel Computation*, J.S. Kowalik and L. Grandinetti, eds., NATO ASI Series F, Vol. 106, Springer-Verlag, New York, N.Y., 1993, pp. 62–75.

[BRI73] P. Brinch Hansen, *Operating Systems Principles*, Prentice-Hall, Inc., Englewood Cliffs, N.J., 1973.

[BRI75] P. Brinch Hansen, "The Programming Language Concurrent Pascal," *IEEE Trans. Software Eng.*, Vol. SE-1, No. 2, June 1975, pp. 199–207.

[BUT92] R. Butler and E. Lusk, "User's Guide to the p4 Programming System," Tech. Report ANL-92/17, Math. and Computer Sci. Division, Argonne Nat'l Laboratory, Argonne, Ill., Oct. 1992.

[CAI92]   W. Cai and D.B. Skillicorn, "Evaluation of a Set of Message-Passing Routines in Transputer Networks," *Proc. World Transputer Users Group (WoTUG '92 Transputer Systems—Ongoing Research*, IOS Press, Amsterdam, The Netherlands, 1992, pp. 24–36.

[CAR87]   N. Carriero, "Implementation of Tuple Space Machines," Tech. Report YALEU/DCS/RR-567, Dept. of Computer Sci., Yale Univ., New Haven, Conn., Dec. 1987 (research report).

[CAR88]   N. Carriero and D. Gelernter, "Application Experience with Linda," *Proc. ACM/SIGPLAN Symp. Parallel Programming*, ACM Press, New York, N.Y., 1988, pp. 173–187.

[CAR93]   N. Carriero and D. Gelernter, "Learning from Our Success," in *Software for Parallel Computation*, J.S. Kowalik and L. Grandinetti, eds., NATO ASI Series F, Vol. 106, Springer-Verlag, New York, N.Y., 1993, pp. 37–45.

[CHA88]   K.M. Chandy and J. Misra, *Parallel Program Design: A Foundation*, Addison-Wesley Pub. Co., Reading, Mass., 1988.

[CHI90]   A.A. Chien and W.J. Dally, "Concurrent Aggregates," *Proc. 2nd SIGPLAN Symp. Principles and Practice Parallel Programming*, ACM Press, New York, N.Y., 1990, pp. 187–196.

[CLO88]   P. Close, "The iPSC/2 Node Architecture," *Proc. 3rd Conf. Hypercube Concurrent Computers and Applications*, Society for Industrial and Applied Mathematics (SIAM), Philadelphia, Pa., 1988.

[COL89]   M. Cole, *Algorithmic Skeletons: Structured Management of Parallel Computation*, Research Monographs in Parallel and Distributed Computing, Pitman, London, United Kingdom, 1989.

[COL90]   M. Cole, "Towards Fully Local Multicomputer Implementations of Functional Programs," Tech. Report CS90/R7, Dept. of Computing Sci., Univ. of Glasgow, Glasgow, United Kingdom, Jan. 1990.

[CON87]   J.S. Conery, *Parallel Execution of Logic Programs*, Kluwer Academic Pub., Norwell, Mass., 1987.

[CRE91]   C. Creveuil, "Implementation of Gamma on the Connection Machine," in *Lecture Notes in Computer Sci.—Research Directions in High-Level Parallel Programming Languages*, J.P. Banâtre and D. Le Metayer, eds., Vol. 574, Springer-Verlag, New York, N.Y., June 1991, pp. 219–230.

[CUL93]   D. Culler et al., "LogP: Toward a Realistic Model of Parallel Computation," *Proc. ACM SIGPLAN Symp. Principles and Practice Parallel Programming*, ACM Press, New York, N.Y., 1993, pp. 1–12.

[DAL92]   W.J. Dally et al., "The Message-Driven Processor," *IEEE Micro*, Vol. 12, No. 2, Apr. 1992, pp. 23–39.

[DAN90]   M. Danelutto et al., "High Level Language Constructs for Massively Parallel Computing," Tech. Report HPL-PSC-90-19, Hewlett-Packard Pisa Sci. Center, Pisa, Italy, 1990.

*[DAN92] M. Danelutto et al., "A Methodology for the Development and the Support of Massively Parallel Programs," *Future Generation Computer Systems*, Vol. 8, Nos. 1–3, July 1992, pp. 205–220.

[DAR87]   J. Darlington et al., "The Design and Implementation of ALICE: A Parallel Graph Reduction Machine," in *Selected Reprints on Dataflow and Reduction Architectures*, S.S. Thakkar, ed., IEEE CS Press, Los Alamitos, Calif., 1987.

[DAR93]   J. Darlington et al., "Parallel Programming Using Skeleton Functions," *Lecture Notes in Computer Sci.—Proc. Parallel Architectures and Languages Europe (PARLE '93)*, Vol. 694, Springer-Verlag, New York, N.Y., 1993.

[DIJ68]   E.W. Dijkstra, "Co-Operating Sequential Processes" in *New Programming Languages*, F. Genyus, ed., Academic Press, New York, N.Y., 1968, pp. 43–112.

[DUN90]   R. Duncan, "A Survey of Parallel Computer Architectures," *Computer*, Vol. 23, No. 2, Feb. 1990, pp. 5–16.

[ERI91a]   S. Ericsson Zenith, "The Axiomatic Characterization of Ease," in *Linda-Like Systems and Their Implementation*, Tech. Report TR91-13, Edinburgh Parallel Computing Centre, Edinburgh, United Kingdom, 1991, pp. 143–152.

[ERI91b]   S. Ericsson Zenith, "A Rationale for Programming with Ease," in *Lecture Notes in Computer Sci.—Research Directions in High-Level Parallel Programming Languages*, J.P. Banâtre and D. Le Metayer, eds., Vol. 574, Springer-Verlag, New York, N.Y., June 1991, pp. 147–156.

[ERI91c]   S. Ericsson Zenith, "Programming with Ease," Centre de Recherche en Informatique, Ecole Nationale Supérieure des Mines de Paris, Paris, France, Sept. 20, 1991.

[ERI93]   S. Ericsson Zenith, "Ease: The Model and Its Implementation," *Proc. Workshop Languages, Compilers and Run-Time Environments Distributed Memory Multiprocessors*, ACM SIGPLAN Notices, Vol. 28, No. 1, Jan. 1993, p. 87.

[FAG90]   B.S. Fagin and A.M. Despain, "The Performance of Parallel Prolog Programs," *IEEE Trans. Computers*, Vol. 39, No. 12, Dec. 1990, pp. 1434–1445.

[FAI92]   C. Faigle et al., "MOVIE Model for Open Systems Based High Performance Distributed Computing," *Proc. 1st Int'l Symp. High-Performance Distributed Computing*, IEEE CS Press, Los Alamitos, Calif., 1992, pp. 37–56.

[FLY72]   M.J. Flynn, "Some Computer Organizations and Their Effectiveness," *IEEE Trans. Computers*, Vol. 21, No. 9, Sept. 1972, pp. 948–960.

[FLY93]   S. Flynn Hummel and R. Kelly, "A Rationale for Parallel Programming with Sets," *J. Programming Languages*, Vol. 1, 1993, pp. 187–207.

[FOS93]   I. Foster and S. Tuecke, "Parallel Programming with PCN," Jan. 1993 (available by ftp from info.mcs.anl.gov).

[GOL89]   K.J. Goldman, "Paralation Views: Abstractions for Efficient Scientific Computing on the Connection Machine," Tech. Report MIT/LCS/TM398, MIT Laboratory for Computer Sci., Cambridge, Mass., 1989.

[GOT83a]   A. Gottlieb et al., "The NYU Ultracomputer—Designing an MIMD Shared Memory Parallel Computer, *IEEE Trans. Computers*, Vol. C-32, No. 2, Feb. 1983, pp. 175–189.

[GOT83b]   A. Gottlieb, B. Lubachevsky, and L. Rudolph, "Basic Techniques for the Efficient Coordination of Large Numbers of Cooperating Sequential Processes," *ACM Trans. Programming Languages and Systems*, Vol. 5, No. 2, Apr. 1983.

[HAI93]   G. Hains and C. Foisy, "The Data-Parallel Categorical Abstract Machine," *Lecture Notes in Computer Sci.—Proc. Parallel Architectures and Languages Europe (PARLE '93)*, Vol. 694, Springer-Verlag, New York, N.Y., 1993.

[HAT91]   P.J. Hatcher and M.J. Quinn, *Data-Parallel Programming on MIMD Computers*, MIT Press, Cambridge, Mass., 1991.

[HAY86]   J.P. Hayes et al., "A Microprocessor-Based Hypercube Supercomputer," *IEEE Micro*, Vol. 6, No. 5, Oct. 1986, pp. 6–17.

[HER87] J. Herath, T. Yuba, and N. Saito, "Dataflow Computing," in *Lecture Notes in Computer Sci.—Parallel Algorithms and Architectures*, Vol. 269, Springer-Verlag, New York, N.Y., May 1987, pp. 25–36.

[HEY91a] T. Heywood and S. Ranka, "A Practical Hierarchical Model of Parallel Computation: Binary Tree and Fft Graph Algorithms," Tech. Report SU-CIS-91-07, School of Computer and Information Sci., Syracuse Univ., Syracuse, N.Y., 1991.

[HEY91b] T. Heywood and S. Ranka, "A Practical Hierarchical Model of Parallel Computation: The Model," Tech. Report SU-CIS-91-06, School of Computer and Information Sci., Syracuse Univ., Syracuse, N.Y., 1991.

[HEY91c] T.H. Heywood, *A Practical Hierarchical Model of Parallel Computation*, doctoral thesis, School of Computer and Information Sci., Syracuse Univ., Syracuse, N.Y., Nov. 1991 (also published as Tech. Report SU-CIS-91-39, School of Computer and Information Sci., Syracuse Univ., Syracuse, N.Y., Nov. 1991).

[HIG93] "High Performance Fortran Language Specification," Jan. 1993 (available by ftp from titan.cs.rice.edu).

[HOA74] C.A.R. Hoare, "Monitors: An Operating System Structuring Concept," *Comm. ACM*, Vol. 17, No. 10, Oct. 1974, pp. 549–557.

[HOA78] C.A.R. Hoare, "Communicating Sequential Processes," *Comm. ACM*, Vol. 21, No. 8, Aug. 1978, pp. 666–677.

[HUM91] R. Hummel, R. Kelly, and S. Flynn Hummel, "A Set-Based Language for Prototyping Parallel Algorithms," *Proc. Computer Architecture Machine Perception Conf. '91*, 1991.

[INM91] Inmos Ltd., *The T9000 Transputer*, 1st ed., Inmos, Bristol, United Kingdom, 1991.

[JON88] G. Jones and M. Goldsmith, *Programming in Occam2*, Prentice-Hall, Inc., Englewood Cliffs, N.J., 1988.

[KAL91] L.V. Kale, "The REDUCE-OR Process Model for Parallel Execution of Logic Programs," *J. Logic Programming*, No. 11, July 1991, pp. 55–84.

[KEL89] P. Kelly, *Functional Programming for Loosely-Coupled Multiprocessors*, Pitman, London, United Kingdom, 1989.

[KIL92a] M.F. Kilian, "Can O-O Aid Massively Parallel Programming?," *Proc. Dartmouth Inst. Advanced Graduate Study Parallel Computation Symp.*, 1992, pp. 246–256.

[KIL92b] M.F. Kilian, *Parallel Sets: An Object-Oriented Methodology for Massively Parallel Programming*, doctoral thesis, Harvard Univ., Cambridge, Mass., 1992.

[LEV93] J.M. Levesque, "FORGE90 and High Performance Fortran (HPF)," in *Software for Parallel Computation*, J.S. Kowalik and L. Grandinetti, eds., NATO ASI Series F, Vol. 106, Springer-Verlag, New York, N.Y., 1993, pp. 111–119.

[LOB92] G. Lobe et al., "The Enterprise Model for Developing Distributed Applications," Tech. Report 92-20, Dept. of Computing Sci., Univ. of Alberta, Edmonton, Canada, Nov. 1992.

*[MAY87] D. May, R. Shepherd, and C. Keane, "Communicating Process Architecture: Transputers and Occam," in *Lecture Notes in Computer Sci.—Future Parallel Computers*, P. Treleavan and M. Vanneschi, eds., Vol. 272, Springer-Verlag, New York, N.Y., 1987, pages 35–47, 81.

*[MCC94] W.F. McColl, "Bulk Synchronous Parallel Computing," draft of a paper to be published in *Proc. 2nd Workshop Abstract Models Parallel Computation*, Oxford Univ. Press, New York, N.Y., 1994.

[MUL88]   L.M.R. Mullin, *A Mathematics of Arrays*, doctoral thesis, Syracuse Univ., Syracuse, N.Y., Dec. 1988.

[MUS91]   L. Mussat, "Parallel Programming with Bags," in *Lecture Notes in Computer Sci.—Research Directions in High-Level Parallel Programming Languages*, J.P. Banâtre and D. Le Metayer, eds., Vol. 574, Springer-Verlag, New York, N.Y., June 1991, pp. 203–218.

[NOA90]   M.O. Noakes and W.J. Dally, "System Design of the J-Machine," *Proc. 6th MIT Conf. Advanced Research VLSI*, MIT Press, Cambridge, Mass., 1990, pp. 179–194.

[PAN93]   C. Pancake, "Graphical Support for Parallel Debugging," in *Software for Parallel Computation*, J.S. Kowalik and L. Grandinetti, eds., NATO ASI Series F, Vol. 106, Springer-Verlag, New York, N.Y., 1993, pp. 216–230.

[PEY87]   S.L. Peyton Jones, C. Clack, and N. Harris, "GRIP—A Parallel Graph Reduction Machine," tech. report, Dept. of Computer Sci., Univ. of London, London, United Kingdom, 1987.

*[QUI90]   M.J. Quinn and P.J. Hatcher, "Data-Parallel Programming on Multicomputers," *IEEE Software*, Vol. 7, No. 5, Sept. 1990, pp. 69–76.

[RAH93]   F.A. Rahbi and G.A. Manson, "Experiments with a Transputer-Based Parallel Graph Reduction Machine," *Concurrency Practice and Experience*, 1993.

[SAB89]   G. Sabot, *The Paralation Model: Architecture-Independent Parallel Programming*, MIT Press, Cambridge, Mass., 1989.

[SHE92]   T.J. Sheffler, Match and Move, An Approach to Data Parallel Computing, doctoral thesis, Carnegie Mellon Univ., Pittsburgh, Pa., Oct. 1992 (also published as Tech. Report CMU-CS-92-203, Carnegie Mellon Univ., Pittsburgh, Pa., Oct. 1992).

*[SKI90]   D.B. Skillicorn, "Architecture-Independent Parallel Computation," *Computer*, Vol. 23, No. 12, Dec. 1990, pp. 38–50.

[SMI90]   D.R. Smith, "KIDS: A Semiautomatic Program Development System," *IEEE Trans. Software Eng.*, Vol. 16, No. 9, Sept. 1990, pp. 1024–1043.

[SMI91]   D.R. Smith, "KIDS—A Knowledge-Based Software Development System," in *Automating Software Design*, American Assoc. for Artificial Intelligence (AAAI) Press, Menlo Park, Calif., 1991.

[STE93]   G.L. Steele, Jr., "High Performance Fortran: Status Report," *Proc. Workshop Languages, Compilers and Run-Time Environments Distributed Memory Multiprocessors*, ACM SIGPLAN Notices, Vol. 28, No. 1, Jan. 1993, pp. 1–4.

[TAL94]   D. Talia, "Parallel Logic Programming Systems on Multicomputers," *J. Programming Languages*, Vol. 2, No. 1, Mar. 1994, pp. 77–87.

[VAL89]   L.G. Valiant, "Bulk Synchronous Parallel Computers," Tech. Report TR-08-89, Computer Sci., Harvard Univ., Cambridge, Mass., 1989.

[VAL90a] L.G. Valiant, "A Bridging Model for Parallel Computation," *Comm. ACM*, Vol. 33, No. 8, Aug. 1990, pp. 103–111.

[VAL90b] L.G. Valiant, "General Purpose Parallel Architectures," in *Handbook of Theoretical Computer Science*, Vol. A, J. van Leeuwen, ed., Elsevier Sci. Pub., New York, N.Y., and MIT Press, Cambridge, Mass., 1990.

Chapter 2:
Shared-Memory Paradigms

The concept of *shared memory* is useful for decoupling issues of program control flow from issues of data mapping, communication, and synchronization. Providing physical shared memory on parallel architectures, especially massively parallel ones, is probably too difficult, but it is a useful abstraction, even if the implementation it hides is distributed.

The Parallel Random Access Machine (PRAM) models share memory directly, but programming in this style is difficult because programmers are responsible for ensuring that simultaneous memory references to the same location do not occur. One way to make programming easier is to use techniques adapted from operating systems to enclose accesses to shared data in *critical sections*. These critical sections can then be further modified to make them lightweight enough to be used for single memory references.

Some machines provide *test&op* instructions in the hardware. The first paper included in this chapter, "Synchronization Algorithms for Shared-Memory Multiprocessors," by Graunke and Thakkar, examines techniques for implementing mutual exclusion in software. This paper presents several such techniques and gives performance data for each of them.

Another approach to shared memory provides a high-level abstraction of shared memory. One way to do this uses what is called *virtual shared memory*. The programming language presents a view of memory as if it were shared, but the implementation may or may not be. The goal of such an approach is to emulate shared memory well enough that the same number of messages travel around the system when a program executes as would have traveled if the program had been written to explicitly pass messages. In other words, the emulation of shared memory imposes no extra message traffic.

One way to emulate shared memory is to extend techniques for cache coherence in multiprocessors to software memory coherence [GOO89]. This involves weakening the implementation semantics of coherence as much as possible to make the problem tractable and then managing memory units at the operating system level. The other way is to build a system based on a useful set of sharing primitives. This approach, used in Orca, is described in the second paper included in this chapter, "Orca: A Language for Parallel Programming of Distributed Systems," by Bal, Kaashoek, and Tanenbaum. The Orca system is a hierarchically structured set of abstractions. At the lowest level of abstraction, reliable broadcast is the basic primitive, so that writes to a replicated structure can rapidly take effect throughout a system. At the next level of abstraction, shared data are encapsulated in passive objects that are replicated throughout the system. Orca itself provides an object-based language to create and manage objects. Rather than providing a strict coherence, Orca provides serializability: If several operations execute concurrently on an object, they affect the object as if they were being executed serially in some order. Orca has been implemented only on small parallel machines, and because its performance depends on the relative infrequency of writes compared to reads, its scalable performance presents a question mark.

A second orthogonal approach to providing high-level abstractions of shared memory is embodied in Linda, which provides an associative memory abstraction called *tuple space*. Threads communicate with each other only by placing tuples in and removing tuples from this shared associative memory. As a result, programs written in any imperative language can be augmented with tuple space operations to create a new parallel-programming language. These languages are called *coordination languages* because the tuple space abstraction coordinates, but is orthogonal to, the computation activities. This chapter's final paper, "How to Write Parallel Programs: A Guide to the Perplexed," by Carriero and Gelernter, describes the Linda approach.

In Linda, tuple space is accessed by four actions: one that places a tuple in tuple space, two that remove a tuple from tuple space—one of these by copying and the other by destroying, and one that evaluates its components before storing the results in tuple space (allowing the creation of new processes). The efficient implementation of tuple space depends on distinguishing tuples by size and component types at compile time and compiling them to message passing whenever the source and destination can be uniquely identified and to hash tables when they cannot.

In distributed-memory implementations, the use of two messages per tuple space access is claimed, which is not an unreasonable overhead. There are two difficulties with Linda, which have been addressed by two extensions of it. The first difficulty is that a single, shared, associative memory does not provide any way of structuring the processes that use it, so that Linda programs have no natural higher level structure. The second is that as programs get larger, the lack of scoping in tuple space makes the optimizations of tuple space access described above less and less efficient. For example, two sets of communications in different parts of a program may, by coincidence, use tuples with the same type signature. They will tend to be implemented in the same hash table and their accesses will interfere. One extension of Linda, the Shared Dataspace Language (SDL) [ROM88], extends tuple space with actions that allow a piece of tuple space to be removed from the whole, treated by a set of processes as if it were the whole tuple space, and then reinserted into the global tuple space. Another extension, Ease [ERI91], provides process structuring in the style of Occam, allowing processes to be hierarchically separated into parallel or sequential groups; also, it provides a new set of primitives to access tuple space.

References cited

[ERI91]   S. Ericsson Zenith, "A Rationale for Programming with Ease," in *Lecture Notes in Computer Sci.—Research Directions in High-Level Parallel Programming Languages*, J.P. Banâtre and D. Le Metayer, eds., Vol. 574, Springer-Verlag, New York, N.Y., June 1991, pp. 147–156.

[GOO89]   J. Goodman, M. Verson, and P. Worst, "Efficient Synchronization Primitives for Large-Scale Cache-Coherent Multiprocessors," *Proc. 3rd Int'l Conf. Architectural Support Programming Languages and Operating Systems*, 1989, pp. 64–75.

[ROM88]   G.-C. Roman, H.C. Cunningham, and M.E. Ehlers, "A Shared Dataspace Language Supporting Large-Scale Concurrency," *Proc. 8th Int'l Conf. Distributed Computing Systems*, IEEE CS Press, Los Alamitos, Calif., 1988, pp. 265–272.

Synchronization Algorithms for Shared-Memory Multiprocessors

Gary Graunke and Shreekant Thakkar

Sequent Computer Systems

Synchronization on a shared-memory system is an important operation, since an application's speedup or throughput depends on the operation's efficiency. Synchronization controls access to a shared resource, usually some data structure shared between processes. Fast synchronization mechanisms and shared memory have ensured the success of shared-memory multiprocessors over distributed-memory systems for many applications. Higher level synchronization mechanisms such as counting semaphores, barrier synchronization, and fetch-and-operation are often built on top of the hardware mechanism in most bus-based shared-memory systems.[1]

While software locking algorithms behave reasonably efficiently in the absence of contention,[2] systems with more than a few processors often provide sufficient contention to significantly decrease system performance. The basic mechanism provided in hardware is an atomic memory read-write capability often associated with a test-and-set instruction on the processor. The synchronization mechanism provided on most shared-memory machines is a hardware lock. Some implementations support only a test-and-set operation, while others allow arbitrary read-modify-write operations.

Only New York University's Ultra[3] and IBM's RP3[4] support fetch-and-operation-type mechanisms in hardware as part of the

Knowing the right type of locking algorithm to use when multiple processes contend for a single lock can prevent performance degradation in shared-memory multiprocessor systems.

combining network. Other interesting hardware schemes have been suggested for shared-memory multiprocessors.[5]

Our study resulted from a performance evaluation of the Symmetry multiprocessor system. This evaluation revealed that the synchronization mechanism on Symmetry did not perform well for highly contested locks, as found in certain parallel applications. These applications are as diverse as parallel scientific codes and commercial database systems.

Several software synchronization mechanisms were developed and evaluated using a hardware monitor on the Symmetry multiprocessor system. The purpose of these mechanisms was to reduce contention for the lock. The mechanisms remain valuable even when changes are made to the hardware synchronization mechanism to improve support for highly contested locks.

After a brief look at the Symmetry architecture, we describe a number of lock algorithms and their use of hardware resources. We then observe the performance of each lock from the perspective of both the program itself and the total system performance.

Architecture

Sequent's Symmetry series is a bus-based shared-memory multiprocessor[6] (see Figure 1). A machine can contain from two to 30 CPUs with an aggregate performance of around 150 million instructions per second. Each processor subsystem contains a 32-bit microprocessor, a floating-point unit, an optional floating-point accelerator, and a private cache. The system features a 53-megabyte-per-second pipelined system bus, up to 240 megabytes of main memory, and a diagnostic and console processor. A Symmetry Model C system with a 20-megahertz Intel 80386/

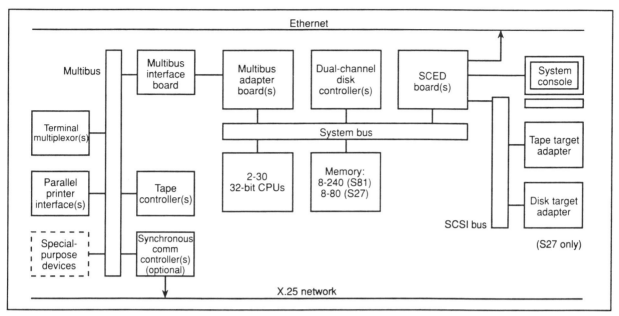

Figure 1. Sequent Symmetry hardware.

80387 and 128-kilobyte local caches was used for the experiments. Each processor also has a 32-bit private counter incremented every microsecond. The counters, synchronized when the hardware is initialized, serve as a global time-of-day clock that every processor can access simultaneously. The microsecond clock can be accessed in an amount of time comparable to that for accessing cached memory, and without using the system bus.

The Dynix operating system is a parallel version of Unix designed and implemented by Sequent for the Balance and Symmetry machines. It provides all services of AT&T System V Unix as well as those of Berkeley 4.2 BSD Unix.

Symmetry coherence protocols. The Symmetry system supports the Symmetry copy-back cache coherence protocol.[6] This protocol supports four cache states: invalid, private, shared, and modified. Private and modified are both exclusive states. The private state is read-exclusive and the modified state is write-exclusive. The cache coherence protocol is based on the concept of ownership. To perform a write operation, a cache must first perform an exclusive read operation on the bus (assuming a cache miss) to gain ownership of the block. Only then can the block be updated in the cache. Thus, if another cache holds the block in a modified state, it must respond to the read-exclusive request

and invalidate its copy. The responding cache asserts the "owned" line on the bus, indicating to memory not to respond to that request. For a nonexclusive read request on the bus, all caches that hold the block in a shared state will assert the "shared" line on the bus. The memory responds and the block is loaded into the requesting cache as "shared."

Coherent cache protocols such as this have the consequence that after the first read, subsequent reads will be satisfied in the cache with no bus traffic until the cache block is modified. This consequence is exploited in most spin locks.

Synchronization mechanisms. The synchronization mechanism on the Symmetry model uses cache-based locks. The locks are also ownership based; that is, a locked read from a processor is treated like a write operation by the cache controller. The cache controller performs an exclusive read operation on the bus (assuming a cache miss) to gain ownership of the block. The atomic operation is then completed in the cache. These locks are optimized for multiuser systems where locks are lightly contended and the critical sections are short. They are cache-based so that when these conditions exist, the lock and unlock operations can be done without any further bus access. They do not work well in some parallel applications where a lock is heavily contended. Several other software syn-

chronization schemes can reduce contention for the locks in the hardware. Independent studies by Anderson[7] and Sequent evaluated the performance of these schemes. This article describes the Sequent study.

Response latency. In general, caches in multiprocessor systems serve two masters, the processor and the bus. A cache must respond to bus requests when it owns a dirty block, and also to processor requests. The memory responds to only one processor access at a time; hence, it can respond much faster. Therefore, a cache-to-cache transfer is usually slower than a memory-to-cache transfer. The Symmetry multiprocessor system follows this pattern.

Sequent's system bus is a split-transaction bus. A fixed number of requests are allowed on the bus, and responses to requests are strictly ordered. Responses to earlier requests must occur before responses to later requests are allowed on the bus.

The number of requests allowed on the bus is optimized for the number of cycles required by a memory response, because memory responds to most bus requests. Cache responses, having longer latency, require more bus cycles than memory responses. The additional bus cycles spent waiting for nonoptimal, slower-than-memory response are wasted, since no further requests can be put on the bus.

```
To lock:

    for (;;) {
        while (*lock == LOCKED);
        if (atomic_exchange_byte(lock, LOCKED) != LOCKED)
            break;
    }
```

Figure 2. Pessimistic variation of the snooping lock.

```
To lock:

        static private unsigned maxdelay = 0;
    { int count, delay;
        if (lock == UNLOCKED &&
                atomic_exchange_byte(lock, LOCKED) != LOCKED) {
            for (maxdelay /= 2; ; maxdelay = 2 * maxdelay + 1) {
                do {
                    while (lock != UNLOCKED);     /* spin until unlocked */
                    delay(irand() & maxdelay);    /* delay using clock */
                } while (lock != UNLOCKED);   /* check again */
            if (atomic_exchange_byte(lock, LOCKED) != LOCKED)
                break;
            }
        }
    }
```

Figure 3. Delay-after-release variation of the collision avoidance lock.

These cycles are called "hold" cycles. Thus, if a cache responds to a bus request, potentially useful bus cycles are wasted as hold cycles.

Only the caches respond when a highly contested lock is accessed. Thus, many bus cycles during this operation are hold cycles, observed using the hardware monitor. We evaluated the software synchronization schemes by observing these cycles during the test.

Algorithms

We investigated a simple test-and-set lock, locks with read snooping, collision avoidance locks, tournament locks, and a queuing lock.

The algorithms are given here in the C language, although the actual measurements reported later were made on a hand-coded Intel 80386 assembly language version of each algorithm. We used the "asm function" capability to allow the assembly language to be expanded in line in the test program.

Several functions require explanation. The atomic_exchange functions exchange the second argument with the memory value indicated by the first argument. The latter value is returned as the function result. The *myid* variable, a unique process identification value, is a small positive integer.

Simple lock. The simplest test-and-set-lock data structure can be a byte having two values: locked and unlocked. To initialize a lock,

```
char *lock;
*lock = UNLOCKED;
```

To lock, an atomic instruction is used to implement a test-and-set operation. Each process continues to test and set a byte in shared memory until it finds that the previous value was zero.

```
while (atomic_exchange_byte
        (lock, LOCKED) == LOCKED);
```

Unlocking is done by clearing the byte to unlocked.

```
(void) atomic_exchange_byte
        (lock, UNLOCKED);
```

On the Sequent Symmetry this is done via an atomic exchange instruction to prevent the unlocking write from occurring between a read and write of another process' test-and-set instruction. It is done for compatibility with preceding write-through models where the lock only prevents two atomic instructions from occurring at the same time. It does not exclude other read and write requests from occurring. The instruction often used, the exchange instruction, is implicitly atomic in the Intel 80386 instruction set.

Under contention, each waiting process continuously requests to read and modify the shared byte with a lock. The unlock operation must compete with lock operations to access the byte.

Snooping locks. Snooping locks take advantage of cache coherency to eliminate bus transactions by waiting processes until the lock is released.[8] They have the same data structure and values as the simple lock. In fact, data structure, initialization, and unlocking are identical to those of the simple lock. Since only one cache block is involved, snooping locks present minimal bus traffic when an uncontested lock changes owners. On the other hand, the $O(n^2)$ rush of bus traffic when the lock is released is still present. If caches are updated instead of invalidated, the $O(n)$ lock attempts will still generate some bus traffic that will interfere with the process in the critical section as well as with other processes not involved in the lock.

Optimistic variation. The optimistic variation of this algorithm improves the simple lock by limiting bus activity of waiting processes to times when they have a chance of getting the lock.

To lock, each waiting process attempts a test-and-set on a shared byte, as before. If unlocked, it has obtained the lock. Otherwise, it reads the byte until it becomes unlocked before attempting another test-and-set. The cache satisfies further read requests until another process unlocks the lock or attempts a test-and-set, invalidating the cache copy of the lock.

The C code to lock is

```
while (atomic_exchange_byte
        (lock, LOCKED) == LOCKED)
    while (*lock == LOCKED);
```

This version produces no bus requests while a number of processes wait for the lock. When the lock is released, however, a flurry of competing test-and-sets — and later reads — flood the bus. If the lock is held a long time, the impact is unimpor-

28

tant. However, for short critical sections, the lock is released before the last spurt of activity has subsided, resulting in continuous bus saturation.

Pessimistic variation. A pessimistic variation is identical to the optimistic snooping lock except that it begins by reading the lock byte rather than by attempting an initial test-and-set. This is useful under contention, since it prevents the initial test-and-set of an arriving process from disturbing the waiting processes in the same way an unlock disturbs them. However, it increases the latency for noncontended locks, and it does nothing to solve the problem of contention that occurs when the lock is released. (See Figure 2.)

Collision avoidance locks. After studying the effects of snooping locks, Anderson[7] proposed collision avoidance as a way to reduce contention. With this method, each waiting process delays a different amount of time before rechecking and attempting to obtain the lock. This reduces the number of unsuccessful test-and-set instructions and the resulting reads by other waiting processes.

There are many possible variations of collision avoidance locks. In some the initial attempt may vary, as in the snooping locks. In others the initial delay parameter may be a constant, or a value determined by experience. Anderson showed that exponential increases, preferred over linear increases, allow newly arriving processes to adjust rapidly to the optimal delay. He also found that the delay should not be increased when the lock is busy, but only when it is unlocked and a subsequent attempt to obtain it fails. Various combinations of spinning and/or polling can be used, either before or after the delay.

We encountered several pitfalls in evaluating collision avoidance locks. If the maximum delay is inadequate and the delay is not increased exponentially, the performance may degenerate suddenly as the number of processes increases. The delay should be a function of bus speed, not processor speed. As we ran earlier algorithms parameterized for the slower processors existing at that time, we found that delays were inadequate. Moreover, Sequent supports systems with mixed-speed processors. Our solution uses the microsecond clock to count out the delays. This allows the parameterization to span several generations of processors and reduces the effect of locking out slower processors.

On the other hand, using too large a delay

produces an extreme bias toward newly arriving processes. By storing the delay value in the lock, we found in one lock that newly arriving processes obtained 97 percent of the lock acquisitions. This short-term unfairness was masked by the fact that every tenth of a second Symmetry processors must process an unmaskable day-clock interrupt. This allows processes with a large delay to obtain the lock and switch roles with the previously dominant processes. The repeated switching of roles gives the appearance of fairness over the long term. A second method of counting the lock acquisitions in each 32-microsecond time interval for each process also identified grossly unfair locks.

We chose two implementations based on Anderson's work. Both check the lock each time before attempting to obtain it. Both initialize their maximum delay to half of its value when they last acquired the lock. Both increase the maximum delay by doubling and adding 1 (1, 3, 7, 15, 31...). Both increase the delay only after failed attempts to obtain the lock via a test-and-set, but not after a check of the lock using a read finds it busy. Both use a random number generator to compute the delay.

The maximum delay was chosen to be 127 microseconds, so that one to two processes, on the average, would check the lock in a near-empty critical section. This is adequate for rapid response to an unlock operation while also providing good contention relief. In checking the delays of 16 processes obtaining the locks, we found that 22 percent were newly arriving processes, 38 percent had a maximum delay of 63 microseconds, and 40 percent had the maximum delay of 127 microseconds.

The lock data structure, initialization, and unlock operations are the same as those for the simple lock algorithm. One private cell per process holds the maximum delay, and another cell is used by the random number generator.

Delay-after-release variation. The first variation waits for the lock to be released

before delaying. The function irand() returns an integer. The delay(x) function uses the microsecond clock to delay for x microseconds. (See Figure 3.)

Delay-between-reference variation. The second variation merely polls the lock after each delay. The tight spin is omitted from the previous algorithm.

Both locks avoid a rush of bus activity as a lock is released. On systems that update stale values rather than invalidate them, the first variation would do slightly better. The second variation may be useful on systems without cached locks, since the rate of polling is already low enough that it doesn't significantly affect bus operations.

Collision locks have all the advantages of snooping locks and none of the disadvantages. For uncontested locks, they have minimal latency. As contention increases, they still save plenty of bandwidth for processes not involved in the lock.

Tournament locks. A second approach to reducing contention is to have a tree of locks of radix B and height H. The tree forms a tournament wherein winners of leaf lock contests become contestants at the next level. The winner of the root lock has permission to enter the critical section protected by the tree of locks.

Each process uses its process identity to choose a random path from the root to a leaf lock. The process may contend only for locks on that path. While every process may contend for the root lock, the number of processes eligible to contend for a lock decreases by the radix of the tree at each level as we proceed toward the leaves. Thus, contention at the leaf locks can be made arbitrarily small as the number of leaves approaches the number of processes.

Each lock must be allocated to a separate cache block to prevent interference between processes manipulating different locks. The data structure for $B = 2$ and $H = 5$ is shown in Figure 4. (Array element zero is wasted for convenience but need not be

---

```
struct tlock {
    struct cache_block {
        char slock;      /* snooping lock */
        char pad[15];    /* 16-byte cache block */
    } blk[32];           /* B^H */
};
```

Figure 4. Example data structure for a tournament lock.

```
struct q_lock {          /* the lock */
        char bytes[NPROCS];
        int who_was_last;
        char this_means_locked;
} the_lock;
```

Figure 5. The queuing lock data structure.

in practice.)

The tournament lock is initialized by setting each snooping lock in the tree to unlocked:

```
for (i = 1; i < (1<<(H-1)); i++)
    lock->blk[i].slock = UNLOCKED;
```

The tournament lock is unlocked by unlocking the snooping root lock in the usual manner:

```
(void) atomic_exchange_byte
    (lock->blk[1].slock, UNLOCKED);
```

Pessimistic variation. The pessimistic version of the tournament lock assumes that there is high contention and enters competition at its leaf lock. Once it obtains the leaf lock, it can proceed toward the root lock.

After a process obtains an interior lock, it releases the last lock it previously obtained. This allows another waiting process to follow the first process up the tree.

Each lock in the tree is the pessimistic snooping lock. The snooping lock is used because of greatly reduced contention at the leaf-level locks. (We have omitted the C code for this lock, since it does not contribute to clarity.)

Assuming that the distribution of the process identity to leaves is random, each lock in the tree reduces contention by a factor of B. The overall reduction for the entire tree is B^H.

We can expect this lock variation to have a latency of H times the cost of the optimistic snooping lock with at most B processes contending. So there is a substantial minimum cost even if the lock is not contested.

Optimistic variation. The optimistic version attempts to make the cost of contention relief and the latency proportional to the base B logarithm of the number of contending processes. It has two phases. In the first phase a newly arriving process uses a read to determine whether the root lock is free. If it is, it will try to obtain the lock via a test-and-set. If not, or if the test-and-set fails, it moves one step toward its leaf node (unless already at the leaf node) and tries to obtain that lock. Once it obtains a lock in this manner, it enters the next phase.

The second phase is identical to the pessimistic tree lock. The process works its way back to the root lock.

Each lock in the tree may be either an optimistic or a pessimistic snooping lock, since the initial phase provides the initial read that distinguishes one from the other. The version we tested used pessimistic snooping locks. (Again, we omit the C code for clarity.)

Contention for the root lock is limited to B processes plus lucky newly arriving processes whose initial read determines that the root lock is in its unlocked state. This version has nearly the same contention relief as the pessimistic version but much lower costs in terms of processing and bus transactions when the lock is not highly contested. The costs are comparable to the pessimistic snooping lock for no contention, and they grow proportionally with the logarithm of the number of waiting processes. However, the worst-case performance may be slightly worse than with the pessimistic variation when that pessimism is justified. At that point the optimistic version will do extra work, which may increase the latency. Partially offsetting this is the fact that newly arriving processes may get lucky and obtain the lock with relatively little work.

Queuing lock. A tree of locks can reduce contention to two processes when $B = 2$. But what if $B = 1$? Assuming that H is sufficiently large, the contention is limited to a single enqueue operation, performed by new processes as they arrive. This permits the hand-off of the lock to be free of contention. With a little more optimization on the intermediate locks, we have a queue lock. Anderson arrived at a similar queue lock independently.

This lock requires a more complex data structure. Instead of a single byte to indicate whether the lock is locked or unlocked, we now have one such byte per process. The identity of the process that last attempted to acquire the lock is recorded in the lock. Finally, instead of the fixed values locked and unlocked, we have the last process that attempted to acquire the lock deciding what value represents "locked." (See Figure 5.)

A newly arriving process sets a hardware lock (see Figure 6). It reads the identity of the process that arrived ahead of it and the value the previous process chose to represent "locked." It then places its own identity and its own byte's value into the lock and releases the hardware lock. Using the locked value of the previous process, it then waits for the byte value of that process to differ from locked.

To free the lock, the process simply changes the value in its own byte. To ini-

```
to_lock(lock)
struct q_lock *lock;
{ char who_is_ahead_of_me, what_is_locked;
        hardware_lock();
                who_is_ahead_of_me = lock->who_was_last;
                what_is_locked = lock->this_means_locked;
                lock->who_was_last = myid;
                lock->this_means_locked = lock->bytes[myid];
        hardware_unlock();
        while (lock->bytes[who_is_ahead_of_me] == what_is_locked)
                /* spin in cache */ ;
}

to_unlock(lock)
struct q_lock *lock;
{
        lock->bytes[myid] ^= 1;
}
```

Figure 6. The algorithms used to lock and free the queuing lock.

tialize the lock, we simply set the process identity to any process and set the "this_means_locked" value unequal to the value of that process' byte:

```
lock->who_was_last = 0;
lock->this_means_locked =
    lock->byte[0] ^ 1;
```

This alternation of "locked" values prevents a race condition. If a process were to set the value of its cell to locked before trying for the lock, and to unlocked afterward, the process behind it might not "see" the unlocked value before attempting to acquire the lock again — setting the value back to locked. This commonly occurs when the lock is acquired by the same process twice in a row.

On the Symmetry system the atomic portion of the lock algorithm can be performed with a single 32-bit integer exchange instruction. Of course, the byte values are placed in separate cache blocks to avoid unwanted interference from adjacent bytes. Also, the address of a process' lock byte serves as its identity. By allocating the bytes to even addresses and using only one bit for the value, both values can be packed into a word. This allows the number of processes to be determined dynamically.

This lock has some favorable properties under contention. The number of bus transactions for a contested lock is four. One less read will be done in the uncontested case because the read that "sees" the lock in its locked state will not occur. Furthermore, only one process, the "next" process, will do the read after an unlock, and it will have no competition. The remaining waiting processes are safely off the bus and out of the way. The absence of a write to relock the lock during the hand-off means that the contribution of the lock to the critical section is minimal.

This queued lock has the disadvantage that it does not trivially provide for a true conditional lock. A conditional lock function either acquires the lock or returns a failure result if the lock was already locked. It does not wait. While it is easy to return failure if the lock is already locked, there is no guarantee that a process that fails its initial attempt will return quickly. Also, if a process wishes to reclaim its cell but was the last to obtain a lock, it must obtain the lock merely to substitute a public cell for its own cell.

Comparisons. The algorithms present various trade-offs in terms of their memory

Table 1. Communication operations to lock and unlock a contended lock.

Algorithm	Noncritical		Critical Section	
	Arrival	Failure/Wait	Success	Unlock
Simple	–	$k*n*M$	M	M or W
Snoop1(O)	M	$n*(M+n*R)$	R+M	M or W
Snoop2(P)	R	$(n-1)*(M+n*R)$	R+M	M or W
Back_rel	M or R	$n/c*n/c(R+M/c)$	R+M	M or W
Back_ref	M or R	$n/c(R+M/c)$	R+M	M or W
Tournament(P)	$(2*h-1)*(R+M)$	R+M	R+M	M or W
Tournament(O)	$(2*\log(n)-1)*(R+M)$	R+M	R+M	M or W
Queue	M+R	–	R	W

Key:
R read access
W write access
M read-modify-write access

n is the number of processes
c is the ratio of the average delay time to the critical-section time for n processes
k is the number of attempts that can be made in the critical-section time
h is the height of the tree of locks

requirements, impact on communication resources, uncontested latency, and contribution to the critical-section time.

Memory requirements of the simple, snooping, and collision avoidance locks are minimal — a single byte. Tournament locks require multiple cache blocks to perform well. Queue locks require memory in proportion to the number of processes, and the processes must act to reclaim memory after using the lock.

The impact of communication operations is heavily architecture dependent. Some systems may allow only one atomic read-modify-write operation, making these operations significantly more costly than writes. Systems with cache invalidation may perform significantly more reads for some algorithms than systems with write-broadcast-update coherency.

Table 1 summarizes "rule of thumb" estimation formulas for a single lock and unlock operation on a lock with N contending processes. The formulas are meant to show the growth of operations as the number of processes increases; they are not meant to be predictors of performance, even when properly parameterized. The costs are labeled in terms of read (R), write (W), and atomic read-modify-write (M) operations. The operations performed in the arrival and wait stages may affect uncontested latency and total system performance. Operations performed in suc-

cessfully obtaining a lock and releasing it add to the duration of the critical section.

The simple lock clearly floods the communication network. The contested snooping lock also has unsatisfactory worst-case behavior when the critical section is short. Collision avoidance and tournament locks seem promising. The queue lock should perform optimally in the contested case, but in the uncontested case it will move three cache blocks from processor to processor while the other locks will move only one. That is, the "success" and "unlock" operations are free when the lock is uncontested for the byte locks.

As the number of processes becomes large, the simple and snooping locks become unreasonable, requiring $O(N^2)$ operations for each release with N processes contending. The collision avoidance algorithms using exponential delay growth can adjust to a growing number of processes, keeping the bus activity fairly linear. Tournament locks slow the growth to $O(\log N)$, increasing in value as the number of processes becomes larger. Finally, the queue lock remains unaffected by the number of processes.

The uncontested latency of the simple, optimistic snooping, and collision avoidance lock algorithms is optimally short. The pessimistic snooping, optimistic tournament, and queue lock algorithms are not far behind. The pessimistic tournament

```
#include "parallel.h"
#include <stdio.h>
#define M 10000000
shared slock_t l;   /* the lock */
int np;                     /* the number of processes */
int count;                  /* a private counter */

doit()
{
        register int i, j;
        j = M / np;         /* allocate the iterations evenly */
        for (i = 0; i < j; i++) {
                S_LOCK(&l);
                count++;
                S_UNLOCK(&l);
                delay(1);         /* use microsecond clock */
        }
}

main(argc, argv)
int argc;
char *argv[];
{
        S_INIT_LOCK(&l);
        if (argc != 2) {
                fprintf(stderr,"usage: test np\n");
                exit(1);
        }
        sscanf(argv[1], "%d", &np);
        m_set_procs(np);
        m_fork(doit);
}
```

Figure 7. Test code for the simple, snooping, and collision avoidance algorithms.

lock is extremely bad for uncontested locks, requiring the same amount of work in the best and worst cases.

The queue lock contributes the least to the critical section. The simple lock would also be good except that the atomic-modify requests of waiting processes often delay the unlock operation, adding time to the critical section. The other algorithms are all equal and reasonable.

Performance results

Several experimental tests analyzed the behavior of high-contention locks on the system bus. A pathological case causing worst-case behavior on the system bus was devised. The program was designed to increment a counter N times, dividing the work evenly among the processes. The counter is incremented only once inside the critical section protected by the lock.

The amount of computation in the critical section is small compared with the amount required for synchronization. While the counter would be shared in actual applications, a private counter was used for this test so that the bus activity observed would be totally attributable to the lock/unlock operations. This also had the effect of making the critical section shorter than it would be otherwise, particularly when the bus is heavily used.

Each process enters the critical section a predetermined number of times. A 1-microsecond delay is inserted after the lock is released. This allows other processes to obtain the lock and the cache block the lock is in. The releasing process, therefore, can be considered a newly arriving process with no special access to the lock in its next attempt. We also tried a 10-microsecond delay, but the results did not differ significantly from those of the 1-microsecond delay, taking into account the

fact that the delay effectively removes one to two processes from contention.

Test code for the simple, snooping, and collision avoidance algorithms appears in Figure 7. The test code for the other algorithms was identical except for substitution of the more complex lock data structures. The shared keyword indicates variables in shared memory. The others are per-process variables copied upon fork. The program does approximately the same amount of "useful work" regardless of the number of processes.

The caches become the sole responders when a highly contested lock is accessed. Thus, during this operation many bus cycles are hold cycles, since caches are responding to the requests for the lock.

We analyzed system behavior by examining the number of hold cycles on the bus caused by excessive cache-to-cache traffic on the bus. This traffic is caused by the locking activity. We wanted to determine which of the software mechanisms for synchronization produced hold cycles on the bus. The other metrics used for measuring performance were the real time for the test to complete and the total bus use.

The Symmetry multiprocessor has built-in, nonintrusive performance instrumentation for measuring both hardware and operating system performance. The hardware instrumentation measures performance of the cache and bus protocols. The software instrumentation measures utilization of processor, disk, and other operating system functions.

Using the hardware monitor, we observed the hold cycles caused by the locking activity. We evaluated the software synchronization schemes by observing the hold cycles during the test.

The Symmetry Model C system used in this experiment was configured with 30 processors. Model C is a copy-back system with a two-way set-associative cache of 128 kilobytes. Model C supports the Symmetry coherence protocol, as described earlier. Two processors were not used in the measurements. One was dedicated to the performance monitor; the other was reserved to handle interrupts and periodic chores of the operating system. The monitor does not cause any intrusion on the bus. No other activity was present on the system.

Performance analysis. Figures 8-10 show the performance of simple, snooping, collision avoidance (two variations), tournament, and queue-based synchronization mechanisms. Figure 8 shows real time for all tests except for one using the simple lock algorithm. We do not present the simple lock results beyond eight processors because we already know that lock to be the poorest performing mechanism. In fact, the test using simple locks would take a very long time to complete. The two snooping locks are indistinguishable and are therefore presented as one curve.

The initial decrease in real time from one to two processes results from the delay after unlocking in the test driver. Without the delay after unlocking, only the pessimistic tree lock and the queue lock have an initial decrease in execution time. This is due to their strict first-in, first-out properties and to the fact that only a relatively small portion of the locking time is in the critical section.

This delay removes one process from contention. A separate test using the microsecond clock should be used to time lock acquisition for uncontested locks not in cache.

Figure 9 shows hold cycles generated by all tests. Figure 10 shows all bus cycles, including hold cycles, generated by each test.

The hold cycles introduced by contention for locks start to inhibit the performance of these tests. The useful bus utilization for some tests is dwarfed by the hold cycles. We must remember, though, that this is a pathological case. In real parallel applications the amount of computation is much higher than in these tests. The shared-memory architecture of Symmetry supports medium- or large-grain parallelism well, as the results described here indicate.

Tests on the simple lock and the snooping locks saturate the bus after five and 10 processes, respectively. As expected, the simple lock generates the most hold cycles. However, the snooping locks provide only minimal relief, since practically no bus bandwidth is available for other processes.

The next poorest performing algorithms are the tournament algorithms. This is surprising, since the additional delay introduced reduces the number of hold cycles. However, this delay (computation) generates a lot of activity. This can be seen by the increase in bus use. Thus, the total number of bus cycles consumed is greater than the number consumed by collision avoidance locks.

The test using bottom-up (pessimistic) tournament locks takes significantly less time than the one using snooping locks. However, this test takes much longer in real time than one using top-down (opti-

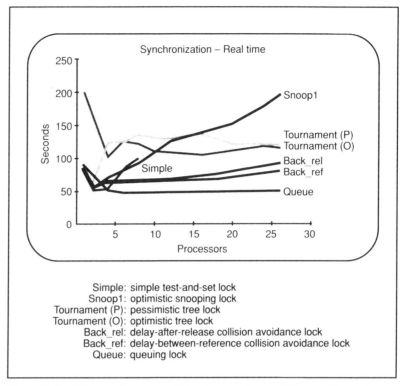

Simple: simple test-and-set lock
Snoop1: optimistic snooping lock
Tournament (P): pessimistic tree lock
Tournament (O): optimistic tree lock
Back_rel: delay-after-release collision avoidance lock
Back_ref: delay-between-reference collision avoidance lock
Queue: queuing lock

Figure 8. Real-time performance of simple, snooping, collision avoidance, tournament, and queue-based locks.

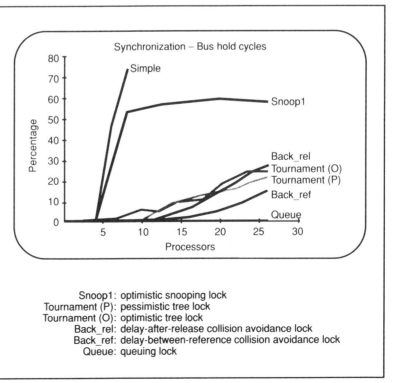

Snoop1: optimistic snooping lock
Tournament (P): pessimistic tree lock
Tournament (O): optimistic tree lock
Back_rel: delay-after-release collision avoidance lock
Back_ref: delay-between-reference collision avoidance lock
Queue: queuing lock

Figure 9. The bus hold cycles generated in testing the various locks.

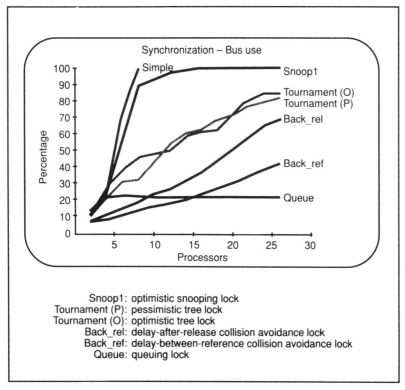

Snoop1: optimistic snooping lock
Tournament (P): pessimistic tree lock
Tournament (O): optimistic tree lock
Back_rel: delay-after-release collision avoidance lock
Back_ref: delay-between-reference collision avoidance lock
Queue: queuing lock

Figure 10. The bus cycles and hold cycles generated in the tests.

mistic) tournament locks, until sufficient processes are available to overcome the latency of going through the levels. This occurs at about four processes. Periodically, between four and 10 processes and between 20 and 26 processes, the optimistic tournament generates more hold cycles than the pessimistic version. However, the smaller amount of work that it does allows it to execute faster for smaller numbers of processes. The trend indicates that as the number of processes increases, the difference between the two tests becomes smaller. This is understandable, since contention for the lock increases. Actually, the pessimistic version will probably take less time beyond 30 processes, the point at which the extra work in the optimistic version no longer pays off.

Bus use is higher for the test using the optimistic tournament locks than for that using the snooping locks. This is because more work is done to reduce contention for the main lock. The hold cycles on the bus significantly decrease with the test using the optimistic tournament locks. However, the hold cycles are not completely gone, since some contention still occurs.

Note that collision avoidance locks perform well across the entire range of pro-

cesses. They have the least amount of bus traffic for small numbers of processes and reasonably flat actual time curves. The difference in execution time is negligible, but bus use differs significantly. And while the delay-after-release version has greatly reduced bus traffic after the lock is released, the polling version eliminates that read altogether. Caches that update rather than invalidate would probably make this difference negligible.

The test using the queue-based locks shows the best performance at the high end. The real time for the test is identical after two processes because the algorithm ensures that one process is always contending for the lock. The hold cycles for this test are negligible. Bus use for these locks is constant as the number of processes increases.

While the queue lock is comparable to the collision avoidance locks for small numbers of processes, it consumes more bus bandwidth than the backoff-reference lock for up to 15 processes. This suggests that the backoff-reference lock is preferred when, instead of just one, several locks are contested simultaneously. For large scalable systems, queue locks would be better.

locks rather than shared data represent the real hot spots in these systems for some parallel applications. We observed a problem with highly contested locks on the present Symmetry system for such applications. Several software synchronization schemes were developed and evaluated to reduce the bus traffic caused by this synchronization mechanism under high contention. We used a hardware monitor to observe and evaluate performance of these schemes. Each scheme showed markedly different effects in both the number and kind of requests generated under contention.

The simple lock algorithm should never be used on systems with support for cache coherence. Locks that may encounter contention should be protected with some form of collision avoidance. Snooping locks are probably inadequate for all but modest numbers of processes. The backoff-reference lock is recommended for general use, where contention for multiple locks is common. Due to its low bus use, more bus bandwidth remains for processes not participating in the contested locks.

When many processes contend for a single lock, a queue lock gives the best execution time. The queue lock makes a small contribution to the critical section as a result of its one-to-one interprocess communication, and it is totally insensitive to the number of processes. An example of this might be a parallel loop, where the number of processes used from loop to loop is unchanged.

The hardware mechanism should support highly contested locks more efficiently, but not at the expense of increasing latency for lightly contested locks. This can be done by adding a write-broadcast capability on bus-based systems. This allows the process that releases the lock to update other caches spinning on the lock without bus activity. Further bus activity resulting from the acquisition of locks can be reduced by read snooping. Even systems with broadcast capabilities require the proper software algorithms. Polling locks require only primitive test-and-set support, although other locks and other synchronization operations benefit from additional hardware support. More elaborate hardware schemes are unnecessary even when considering larger nonbus-based shared-memory multiprocessor systems. ■

Acknowledgments

We would like to thank the referees and Ed Lazowska and Tom Anderson for their feedback and many suggestions. We also thank Betty Fuller for her administrative assistance.

References

1. A. Dinning, "A Survey of Synchronization Methods for Parallel Computers," *Computer*, Vol. 22, No. 7, July 1989, pp. 66-77.

2. L. Lamport, "A Fast Mutual Exclusion Algorithm," *ACM Trans. Computer Systems*, Vol. 5, No. 1, 1987, pp. 1-11.

3. A. Gottlieb et al., "The NYU Ultracomputer — Designing an MIMD Shared-Memory Parallel Machine," *IEEE Trans. Computers*, Vol. C-22, No. 2, Feb. 1983, pp. 175-189.

4. G. Pfister et al., "The RP3 System," *Proc. Int'l Conf. Parallel Processing*, Pennsylvania State Univ. Press, University Park, Pa., 1986, pp. 764-771.

5. J. Goodman, M. Verson, and P. Worst, "Efficient Synchronization Primitives for Large-Scale Cache-Coherent Multiprocessors," *Proc. Third Int'l Conf. Architectural Support for Programming Languages and Operating Systems*, CS Press, Los Alamitos, Calif., Order No. 1936, Apr. 1989, pp. 64-75.

6. T. Lovett and S.S. Thakkar, "The Symmetry Multiprocessor System," *Proc. Int'l Conf. Parallel Processing*, Pennsylvania State Univ. Press, University Park, Pa., 1988, pp. 303-310.

7. T. Anderson, "The Performance of Spin Lock Alternatives for Shared-Memory Multiprocessors," *IEEE Trans. Parallel and Distributed Systems*, Vol. 1, No. 1, 1990, pp. 6-16.

8. Z. Segall and L. Rudolph, "Dynamic Decentralized Cache Schemes for an MIMD Parallel Processor," *Proc. 11th Ann. Int'l Symp. Computer Architecture*, CS Press, Los Alamitos, Calif., Order No. 538, June 1984, pp. 340-347.

Gary Graunke is a software design engineer at Sequent Computer Systems in Beaverton, Oregon. His interests include parallel algorithms, computer architectures, and programming languages.

Graunke received a BS in computer science with distinction from the University of Wisconsin at Madison. He is a member of the IEEE and ACM.

Shreekant Thakkar is a guest editor of this special issue. His photograph and biography appear on page 11.

The authors can be contacted at Sequent Computer Systems, 15450 SW Koll Parkway, Beaverton, OR 97006.

Orca: A Language For Parallel Programming of Distributed Systems

Henri E. Bal, M. Frans Kaashoek, *Student Member, IEEE*, and Andrew S. Tanenbaum, *Member, IEEE*

Abstract— Orca is a language for implementing parallel applications on loosely coupled distributed systems. Unlike most languages for distributed programming, it allows processes on different machines to share data. Such data are encapsulated in data-objects, which are instances of user-defined abstract data types. The implementation of Orca takes care of the physical distribution of objects among the local memories of the processors. In particular, an implementation may replicate and/or migrate objects in order to decrease access times to objects and increase parallelism. This paper gives a detailed description of the Orca language design and motivates the design choices. Orca is intended for applications programmers rather than systems programmers. This is reflected in its design goals to provide a simple, easy to use language that is type-secure and provides clean semantics. The paper discusses three example parallel applications in Orca, one of which is described in detail. It also describes one of the existing implementations, which is based on reliable broadcasting. Performance measurements of this system are given for three parallel applications. The measurements show that significant speedups can be obtained for all three applications. Finally, the paper compares Orca with several related languages and systems.

Index Terms—Amoeba, broadcasting, distributed systems, distributed shared memory, Orca, parallel programming, shared objects.

I. INTRODUCTION

AS communication in loosely coupled distributed computing systems gets faster, such systems become more and more attractive for running parallel applications. In the Amoeba system, for example, the cost of sending a short message between Sun workstations over an Ethernet is 1.1 ms [1]. Although this is still slower than communication in most multicomputers (e.g., hypercubes and transputer grids), it is fast enough for many coarse-grained parallel applications. In return, distributed systems are easy to build from off-the-shelf components by interconnecting multiple workstations or microprocessors through a local area network (LAN). In addition, such systems can easily be expanded to far larger numbers of processors than shared-memory multiprocessors.

In our research, we are studying the implementation of parallel applications on distributed systems. We started out

Manuscript received December 20, 1989; revised December 6, 1991. Recommended by C. Ghezzi. This work was supported in part by The Netherlands organization for scientific research (NWO) through Grant 125-30-10. A preliminary version of this paper was published in the *Proc. 1st Usenix/SERC Workshop on Experiences with Building Distributed and Multiprocessor Systems* (Ft. Lauderdale, FL), October 1989.

The authors are with the Department of Mathematics and Computer Science, Vrije Universiteit, Amsterdam, The Netherlands.

IEEE Log Number 9106477.

by implementing several coarse-grained parallel applications on top of the Amoeba system, using an existing sequential language extended with message passing for interprocess communication [2]. We felt that for parallel applications, both the use of message passing and a sequential base language have many disadvantages, making them complicated for applications programmers to use.

Since then, we have developed a new language for distributed programming, called *Orca* [3]–[5]. Orca is intended for distributed applications programming rather than systems programming, and is therefore designed to be a simple, expressive, and efficient language with clean semantics. Below, we will briefly discuss the most important novelties in the language design.

Processes in Orca can communicate through shared data, even if the processors on which they run do not have physical shared memory. The main novelty of our approach is the way access to shared data is expressed. Unlike shared physical memory (or distributed shared memory [6]), shared data in Orca are accessed through user-defined high-level operations, which, as we will see, has many important implications.

Supporting shared data on a distributed system imposes some challenging implementation problems. We have worked on several implementations of Orca, one of which we will describe in the paper. This system uses a reliable broadcast protocol. Both the protocol and the integration with the rest of the system are new research results.

Unlike the majority of other languages for distributed programming, Orca is not an extension to an existing sequential language. Instead, its sequential and distributed constructs (especially data structures) have been designed together, in such a way that they integrate well. The language design addresses issues that are dealt with by few other languages. Most distributed languages simply add primitives for parallelism and communication to a sequential base language, but ignore problems due to poor integration with sequential constructs. A typical example is passing a pointer in a message, which is usually not detected and may cause great havoc. Orca provides a solution to this problem and keeps the semantics of the language clean. At the same time, the Orca constructs are designed to have semantics close to conventional languages, thus making it easy for programmers to learn Orca.

An important goal in the design of Orca was to keep the language as simple as possible. Many interesting parallel applications exist outside the area of computer science, so the language must be suitable for general-applications programmers. Orca lacks low-level features that would only be useful for systems programming. In addition, Orca reduces complexity by avoiding language features aimed solely at increasing efficiency, especially if the same effect can be achieved through an optimizing compiler. Language designers frequently have to choose between adding language features or adding compiler optimizations. In general, we prefer the latter option. We will discuss several examples of this design principle in the paper. Finally, the principle of orthogonality [7] is used with care, but it is not a design goal by itself.

Another issue we have taken into account is that of debugging. As debugging of distributed programs is difficult, one needs all the help one can get, so we have paid considerable attention to debugging. Most important, Orca is a type-secure language. The language design allows the implementation to detect many errors during compile-time. In addition, the language run-time system does extensive error checking.

The paper gives an overview of Orca, a distributed implementation of Orca, and its performance. It is structured as follows. In Section II we will describe the Orca language and motivate our design choices. In Section III we will present an example application written in Orca. In Section IV we will discuss one implementation of Orca, based on reliable broadcast. We will also describe how to implement this broadcast primitive on top of LAN's that only support unreliable broadcast. We will briefly compare this system with another implementation of Orca that uses Remote Procedure Call [8] rather than broadcasting. In Section V we will give performance measurements for several applications. In Section VI we will compare our approach with those of related languages and systems. Finally, in Section VII we will present our conclusions.

II. ORCA

Orca is a procedural, strongly typed language. Its sequential statements and expressions are fairly conventional and are roughly comparable (although not identical) to those of Modula-2. The data structuring facilities of Orca, however, are substantially different from those used in Modula-2. Orca supports records, unions, dynamic arrays, sets, bags, and general graphs. Pointers have intentionally been omitted to provide security. Also, the language lacks global variables, although such variables can be simulated by passing them around as reference parameters.

The rest of this section is structured as follows. We will first motivate our choice for shared data over message passing. Next, we will look at processes, which are used for expressing parallelism. Subsequently, we will describe Orca's communication model, which is based on shared data-objects. Synchronization of operations on shared objects is discussed next, followed by a discussion of hierarchically used objects. Finally, we look at Orca's data structures.

A. Distributed Shared Memory

Most languages for distributed programming are based on message passing [9]. This choice seems obvious, since the underlying hardware already supports message passing. Still, there are many cases in which message passing is not the appropriate programming model. Message passing is a form of communication between two parties, which interact explicitly by sending and receiving messages. Message passing is less suitable, however, if several processes need to communicate indirectly by sharing global state information.

There are many examples of such applications. For example, in parallel branch-and-bound algorithms the current best solution (the bound) is stored in a global variable accessed by all processes. This is not to say the algorithms actually need physical shared memory: they merely need *logically* shared data. Such algorithms are much harder to implement efficiently using message passing than using shared data.

The literature contains numerous other examples of distributed applications and algorithms that would greatly benefit from support for shared data, even if no physical shared memory is available. Applications described in the literature include: a distributed speech recognition system [10]; linear equation solving, three-dimensional partial differential equations, and split-merge sort [11]; computer chess [12]; distributed system services (e.g., name service, time service), global scheduling, and replicated files [13].

So the difficulty in providing (logically) shared data makes message passing a poor match for many applications. Several researchers have therefore worked on communication models based on *logically shared data* rather than message passing. With these models the programmer can use shared data, although the underlying hardware does not provide physical shared memory. A memory model that looks to the user as a shared memory but is implemented on disjoint machines is referred to as *Distributed Shared Memory* (DSM).

Many different forms of DSM exist. Li's Shared Virtual Memory (SVM) [6] is perhaps the best-known example. It simulates physical shared-memory on a distributed system. The SVM distributes the pages of the memory space over the local memories. Read-only pages may also be replicated. SVM provides a clean simple model, but unfortunately there are many problems in implementing it efficiently.

A few existing programming languages also fall into the DSM class. Linda [14] supports a globally shared Tuple Space, which processes can access using a form of associative addressing. On distributed systems Tuple Space can be replicated or partitioned, much as pages in SVM are. The operations allowed on Tuple Space are low-level and built-in, which, as we will argue later, complicates programming and makes an efficient distributed implementation difficult.

The Emerald language [15] is related to the DSM class, in that it provides a shared name space for objects, together with a location-transparent invocation mechanism. Emerald does not use any of the replication techniques that are typical of DSM systems, however.

The most important issue addressed by Orca is how data can be shared among distributed processes in an efficient way. In languages for multiprocessors, shared data structures are stored in the shared memory and accessed in basically the same way as local variables; namely, through simple load and store instructions. If a process is going to change part of a shared data structure and it does not want other processes to interfere, it locks that part. All these operations (loads, stores, locks) on shared data structures involve little overhead, because access to shared memory is hardly more expensive than access to local memory.

In a distributed system, on the other hand, the time needed to access data very much depends on the location of the data. Accessing data on remote processors is orders of magnitude more expensive than accessing local data. It is therefore infeasible to apply the multiprocessor model of programming to distributed systems. The operations used in this model are far too low-level and will have tremendous overhead on distributed systems.

The key idea in Orca is to access shared data structures through higher level operations. Instead of using low-level instructions for reading, writing, and locking shared data, we let programmers define composite operations for manipulating shared data structures. Shared data structures in our model are encapsulated in so-called *data-objects*[1] that are manipulated through a set of user-defined operations. Data-objects are best thought of as instances (variables) of *abstract data types*. The programmer specifies an abstract data type by defining operations that can be applied to instances (data-objects) of that type. The actual data contained in the object and the executable code for the operations are hidden in the implementation of the abstract data type.

B. Processes

Parallelism in Orca is explicit, because compilers currently are not effective at generating parallelism automatically. Implicit parallelism may be suitable for vector machines, but with the current state of the art in compiler technology, it is not effective for distributed systems.

Parallelism is expressed in Orca through explicit creation of sequential processes. Processes are conceptually similar to procedures, except that procedure invocations are serial and process invocations are parallel.

Initially, an Orca program consists of a single process, but new processes can be created explicitly through the **fork** statement:

fork name(actual-parameters) [**on** (cpu-number)];

This statement creates a new anonymous child process. Optionally, the new process can be assigned to a given processor. Processors are numbered sequentially; the **fork** statement may contain an **on**-part with an expression that specifies the processor on which to run the child process. If the **on**-part is absent, the child process is created on the same processor as its parent. The system does not move processes around on its own initiative, since this is undesirable for many parallel applications.

A process can take parameters, as specified in its definition. Two kinds are allowed: input and shared. A process may take any kind of data structure as value (input) parameter. In this case, the process gets a copy of the actual parameter. The parent can also pass any of its *data-objects* as a shared

[1] We will sometimes use the term "object" as a shorthand notation. Note, however, that this term is used in many other languages and systems, with various different meanings.

Fig. 1. Specification part of an object type *IntObject*.

Fig. 2. Implementation part of an object type *IntObject*.

parameter to the child. In this case, the data-object will be shared between the parent and the child. The parent and child can communicate through this shared object by executing the operations defined by the object's type, as will be explained later. For example, if a process *child* is declared as

process child(Id: integer; X: **shared** AnObjectType);
begin. . .**end**;

a new child process can be created as follows:

MyObj: AnObjectType;   # declare an object
. . .
        # create a new child process, passing the constant 12 as
        # value parameter and the object MyObj as shared
            parameter.
    fork child(12, MyObj);

The children can pass shared objects to *their* children and so on. In this way the objects get distributed among some of the descendants of the process that created them. If any of these processes performs an operation on the object, they all observe the same effect as if the object were in shared memory, protected by a lock variable.

C. Shared Data-Objects and Abstract Data Types

A shared data-object is a variable of an abstract data type (object type). An abstract data type definition in Orca consists of two parts: a *specification* part and an *implementation* part. The specification part defines the operations applicable to objects of the given type. As a simple example, the specification part of an object type encapsulating an integer is shown in Fig. 1.

The implementation part contains the data used to represent objects of this type, the code to initialize the data of new instances of the type, and the code implementing the operations. Part of the implementation of type *IntObject* is shown in Fig. 2.

An operation implementation is similar to a procedure. An operation can only access its own local variables and parameters and the local (internal) data of the object it is applied to.

Once an object type has been defined, instances (objects) of the type can be created by declaring variables of the type. When an object is created, memory for the local variables of the object is allocated and the initialization code is executed. From then on operations can be applied to the object. The Orca syntax to declare an object and apply an operation to it is illustrated below:

```
X: IntObject;
tmp: integer;

X$Assign(3);        # assign 3 to X
X$Add(1);           # increment X
tmp := X$Value( );  # read current value of X
```

Orca supports a single abstract data type mechanism, which can be used for encapsulating shared and nonshared data. In other words, the mechanism can also be used for regular (sequential) abstract data types. Even stronger, the same abstract type can be used for creating shared as well as local objects. Neither object declarations nor object-type declarations specify whether objects will be shared. This information is derived from the usage of objects: only objects that are ever passed as shared parameter in a **fork** statement are shared. All other objects are local and are treated as normal variables of an abstract data type.

Most other languages use different mechanisms for these two purposes. Argus [16], for example, uses clusters for local data and guardians for shared data; clusters and guardians are completely different. SR [17] provides a single mechanism (resources), but the overhead of operations on resources is far too high to be useful for sequential abstract data types [18].

The fact that shared data are accessed through user-defined operations is an important distinction between our model and other models. Shared virtual memory, for example, simulates physical shared memory, so shared data are accessed through low-level read and write operations. Linda's Tuple Space model also uses a fixed number of built-in operations to add, read, and delete shared tuples. Having users define their own operations has many advantages, both for the ease of programming and for the implementation, as we will discuss shortly.

Although data-objects logically are shared among processes, their implementation does not need physical shared memory. In the worst case, an operation on a remote object can be implemented using message passing. The general idea, however, is for the implementation to take care of the physical distribution of data-objects among processors. As we will see in Section IV, one way to achieve this goal is to replicate shared data-objects. By replicating objects, access control to shared objects is decentralized, which decreases access costs and increases parallelism. This is a major difference with, say, monitors [19], which centralize control to shared data.

D. Synchronization

An abstract data type in Orca can be used for creating shared as well as local objects. For objects that are shared among multiple processes the issue of synchronization arises. Two types of synchronization exist: mutual exclusion synchronization and condition synchronization [20]. We will look at them in turn.

1) Mutual Exclusion Synchronization: Mutual exclusion in our model is done implicitly by executing all operations on objects *indivisibly*. Conceptually, each operation locks the entire object it is applied to, does the work, and releases the lock only when it is finished. To be more precise, the model guarantees *serializability* [21] of operation invocations: if two operations are applied simultaneously to the same data-object, then the result is as if one of them is executed before the other; the order of invocation, however, is nondeterministic.

An implementation of the model need not actually execute all operations one by one. To increase the degree of parallelism it may execute multiple operations on the same object simultaneously as long as the effect is the same as for serialized execution. For example, operations that only read (but do not change) the data stored in an object can easily be executed in parallel.

Since users can define their own operations on objects, it is up to the user to decide which pieces of code should be executed indivisibly. For example, an abstract data type encapsulating an integer variable may have an operation to increment the integer. This operation will be done indivisibly. If, on the other hand, the integer is incremented through separate read and write operations (i.e., first read the current value, then write the incremented value back), the increment will be done as two separate actions and will thus not be indivisible. This rule for defining which actions are indivisible and which are not is both easy to understand and flexible: single operations are indivisible; sequences of operations are not. The model does not provide mutual exclusion at a granularity lower than the object level. Other languages (e.g., Sloop [22]) give programmers more accurate control over mutual exclusion synchronization.

Our model does not support indivisible operations on a collection of objects. Operations on multiple objects require a distributed locking protocol, which is complicated to implement efficiently. Moreover, this generality is seldom needed by parallel applications. We prefer to keep our basic model simple and implement more complicated actions on top of it. Operations in our model therefore apply to single objects and are always executed indivisibly. However, the model is sufficiently powerful to allow users to construct locks for multioperation sequences on different objects so arbitrary actions can be performed indivisibly.

2) Condition Synchronization: The second form of synchronization is condition synchronization, which allows processes to wait (block) until a certain condition becomes true. In our model, condition synchronization is integrated with operation invocations by allowing operations to block. Processes synchronize implicitly through operations on shared objects. A blocking operation consists of one or more guarded commands:

```
operation op(formal-parameters): ResultType;
begin
```

guard condition$_1$ **do** statements$_1$ **od**;

   ...

   guard condition$_n$ **do** statements$_n$ **od**;
end;

The conditions are Boolean expressions, called *guards*. To simplify the presentation we will initially assume that guards are side-effect free. The problem of side effects will be considered later, when discussing hierarchically used objects.

The operation initially blocks until at least one of the guards evaluates to "true." Next, one true guard is selected nondeterministically and its sequence of statements is executed.

The Boolean expressions may depend on the parameters and local data of the operation and on the data of the object. If a guard fails it can later become true after the state of the object has been changed. It may thus be necessary to evaluate the guards several times.

We have chosen this form of condition synchronization because it is highly simple and fits well into the model. An alternative approach that we considered and rejected is to use a separate synchronization primitive, independent of the mechanism for shared objects. To illustrate the difference between these two alternatives, we will first look at a specific example.

Consider a shared *Queue* object with operations to add elements to the tail and retrieve elements from the head:

operation Add(x: item);   # add to tail
operation Get( ): item;   # get from head

A process type to fetch an element from an empty queue should not be allowed to continue. In other words, the number of *Get* operations applied to a queue should not exceed the number of *Add* operations. This is an example of a *synchronization constraint* on the order in which operations are executed. There are at least two conceivable ways for expressing such constraints in our model:

1) Processes trying to execute *Get* should first check the status of the queue and block while the queue is empty. Doing a *Get* on an empty queue results in an error.
2) The *Get* operation itself blocks while the queue is empty. Processes executing a *Get* on an empty queue therefore block automatically.

In both cases a new primitive is needed for blocking processes. In the first case this primitive is to be used directly by user processes; in the second case only operations on objects use it. Also, the first approach calls for an extra operation on queues that checks if a given queue is empty. (For both approaches, unblocking the process and removing the head element from the queue should be done in one indivisible action to avoid race conditions.)

The first approach has one major drawback: the *users* of an object are responsible for satisfying synchronization constraints. This is in contrast with the general idea of abstract data types to hide implementation details of objects from users. The second approach is much cleaner, as the *implementer* of the object takes care of synchronization and hides it from the users. We therefore use the second approach and do

condition synchronization inside the operations. The model allows operations to block; processes can only block by executing operations that block.

An important issue in the design of the synchronization mechanism is how to provide blocking operations while still guaranteeing the indivisibility of operation invocations. If an operation may block at any point during its execution operations can no longer be serialized. Our solution is to allow operations only to block *initially*, before modifying the object. An operation may wait until a certain condition becomes true, but once it has started executing it cannot block again.

E. Hierarchical Objects

Abstract data types are useful for extending a language with new types. This method for building new types is hierarchical: existing abstract data types can be used to build new ones. The internal data of an object can therefore themselves be objects. Note that hierarchical objects are not derived from the constituent objects by extending them (as can be done in object-oriented languages). The old and new objects have a "use" relation, not an "inheritance" relation.

This nesting of objects causes a difficult design problem, as we will explain below. Suppose we have an existing object type *OldType*, specified as follows:

object specification OldType;
   operation OldOperation1( ): boolean;
   operation OldOperation2( );
end;

We may use this object type in the implementation of another type (we omit the specification of this type):

object implementation NewType;
   NestedObject: OldType;   # a nested object
   operation NewOperation( );
   begin
      guard NestedObject\$OldOperation1( ) **do**
        ...
        NestedObject\$OldOperation2( );
      od;
   end;
end;

Objects of the new type contain an object, *NestedObject*, of type *OldType*. The latter object is called a *nested* object, because it is part of another object. Note that instances of *NewType* are still *single* objects whose operations are executed indivisibly. The nested object is invisible outside its enclosing object, just like any other internal data.

The implementer of *NewType* can be seen as a *user* of *OldType*. So the implementer of *NewType* does not know how *OldType* is implemented. This lack of information about the *implementation* of the operations on *OldType* causes two problems.

The first problem is illustrated by the use of *OldOperation1* in the guard of *NewOperation*. We need to know whether the guard expressions have side effects, as they may have to be evaluated several times. Unfortunately, we do not know whether the invocation of *OldOperation1* has any side effects. If the operation modifies *NestedObject* it does have side effects. We can only tell so, however, by looking at the *implementation* of this operation, which goes against the idea of abstract data types.

The second problem is more subtle. Suppose a process declares an object *NewObject* of type *NewType* and shares it with some of its child processes. If one of the processes invokes *NewOperation* on *NewObject*, the implementation of this object will invoke *OldOperation2* on the nested object. The problem is that the latter operation may very well *block*. If so, we violate the rule that operations are only allowed to block *initially*. In this situation there are two equally unattractive options:

1) Suspend the process invoking *NewOperation*, but allow other processes to access the object. This means, however, that the operation will no longer be indivisible.
2) Block the calling process, but do not allow any other processes to access the object. This implies that the process will be suspended forever, because no other process will be able to modify *NestedObject*.

One could solve this problem by disallowing blocking operations on nested objects, but again this requires looking at the *implementation* of an operation to see how it may be used.

Cooper and Hamilton have observed similar conflicts between parallel programming and data abstraction in the context of monitors [23]. They propose extending operation specifications with information about their implementation, such as whether or not the operation suspends or has any side effects. We feel it is not very elegant to make such concessions, however. The specification of an abstract data type should not reveal information about the implementation.

We solve these two problems by refining the execution model of operations. Conceptually, an operation is executed as follows. The operation repeatedly tries to evaluate its guards, and then tries to execute the statements of a successful guard. Before evaluating a guard, however, the operation (conceptually) creates a copy of the entire object, including any nested (or deeply nested) objects. This copy is used during the evaluation of the guard and execution of the statements. The operation *commits* to a certain alternative, as soon as both:

1) The guard succeeds (evaluates to true), and
2) The corresponding statements can be executed without invoking any blocking operations on nested objects.

As soon as a guard fails or the statements invoke a blocking operation, the copy of the entire object is thrown away and another alternative is tried. So an operation does not commit until it has finished executing a successful guard and its corresponding statements without invoking any blocking operations on nested objects. If all alternatives of an operation fail, the operation (and the process invoking it) blocks until the object is modified by another process. If an operation commits to a certain alternative, the object is assigned the current value of the copy (i.e., the value after evaluating the selected guard and statements).

This scheme solves both of the above problems. An operation on a nested object used inside a guard (e.g., *OldOperation1* in the code above) may have side effects; these side effects will not be made permanent until the guard is actually committed to. An operation on a nested object may also block. As long as all guards of that operation fail, however, the alternative containing the invocation will never be committed to. The operation has no effects until it commits to a certain alternative. Before commitment it may try some alternatives, but their effects are thrown away. If the operation commits to an alternative, both the guards and statements of the alternative are executed without blocking. Therefore operation invocations are still executed indivisibly.

The key issue is how to implement this execution model efficiently. It is quite expensive to copy objects before trying each alternative. In nearly all cases, however, the compiler will be able to optimize away the need for copying objects. Many object types will not have any nested objects, so they do not suffer from the problems described above. Also, an optimizing compiler can check if an operation used in a guard or body is side-effect free and nonblocking. To do so, it needs to access the implementation code of nested objects. This is not any different from other global optimizations (e.g., inline substitution), which basically need to access the entire source program. Also, the same mechanism can be used to test for circularities in nested object definitions.

Our solution therefore preserves abstraction from the programmer's point of view, but sometimes requires global optimizations to be efficient. The current Orca compiler performs these optimizations. This approach keeps the language simple and relies on optimization techniques for achieving efficiency.

F. Data Structures

In most procedural languages data structures like graphs, trees, and lists are built out of dynamically allocated and deallocated blocks of memory, linked together through *pointers*. For distributed programming this approach has many disadvantages. The main difficulty is how to transmit a complex data structure containing pointers to a remote machine. Pointers, if implemented as addresses, are only meaningful within a single machine, so they need special treatment before being transmitted. Even more important, most languages do not consider such graphs to be first-class objects, so it is hard to determine *what* has to be transmitted.

In addition to these problems, giving the programmer explicit control over allocation and deallocation of memory usually violates type security. A programmer can deallocate memory and then use it again, leading to obscure bugs.

In Orca these problems are solved through the introduction of a *graph* data type. A graph in Orca consists of zero or more *nodes*, each having a number of *fields*, similar to the fields of a record. Also, the graph itself may contain *global fields*, which are used to store information about the entire graph (e.g., the root of a tree or the head and tail of a list). Individual nodes within a graph are identified by values of a *nodename* type. A variable or field of a *nodename* type is initialized to NIL, which indicates it does not name any node yet. As an example, a binary-tree type may be defined as follows:

```
type node = nodename of BinTree;
type BinTree =
    graph       # global field;
      root: node;      # name of the root of the tree
    nodes   # fields of each node:
      data: integer;
      LeftSon,
      RightSon: node;      # names of left and right sons
    end;
```

This program fragment declares a graph type *BinTree*. Each node of such a graph contains a data field and fields identifying the left and right sons of the node. Furthermore, the graph has one global field, identifying the root node of the tree.

A tree data structure is created by declaring a variable of this type. Initially, the tree is empty, but nodes can be added and deleted dynamically as follows:

```
t: BinTree;
n: node;
n := addnode(t);      # add a node to t, store its name in n
deletenode(t, n);      # delete the node with given name from t
```

The construct **addnode** adds a new node to a graph and returns a unique name for it, chosen by the run-time system. The run-time system also automatically allocates memory for the new node. In this sense, **addnode** is similar to the standard procedure *new* in Pascal [24]. As a crucial difference between the two primitives, however, the **addnode** construct specifies the data structure for which the new block of memory is intended. Unlike in Pascal, the run time system of Orca can keep track of the nodes that belong to a certain graph. This information is used whenever a copy of the graph has to be created—for example, when it is passed as a value parameter to a procedure or remote process. Also, the information is used to delete the entire graph at the end of the procedure in which it is declared.

The global fields of a graph and the fields of its nodes are accessed through designators that are similar to those for records and arrays:

```
t.root := n;                  # access the global field of t
t[n].data := 12;              # access data field of node n
t[n].LeftSon := addnode(t);   # create left son of n
n := t[n].LeftSon             # store name of left son in n
```

Note that the designator for the field of a node specifies the name of the node as well as the graph itself. This notation differs from the one in Pascal, where nodes are identified by pointers only. The notation of Orca may be somewhat more cumbersome, but it has the advantage that it is always clear which data structure is accessed. Also, it makes it possible to represent a nodename as an index into a graph, rather than as a machine address. Nodenames can therefore be transmitted to remote machines without losing their meaning.

Graphs in Orca are type-secure. If a certain node is deleted from a graph and one of its fields is subsequently accessed, a run-time error occurs, as illustrated by the following piece of code:

```
n := addnode(t);
deletenode(t, n);
t[n].data := 12;      # causes a run-time error
```

The run-time system checks whether the graph *t* contains a node with the given name. Furthermore, each invocation of **addnode**(t) returns a different name, so the same nodename will not be reused for denoting a different node. Whenever a node has been deleted from a graph, any future references to the node will cause a run-time error.

The data structuring mechanism of Orca has some properties of arrays and some properties of pointer-based data structures. The mechanism supports dynamic allocation of memory through the **addnode** primitive. Graphs, like arrays, are first-class entities in Orca. This design has several advantages: they can easily be passed to remote processes; assignment is defined for graph variables; functions may return a value of a graph type; and graphs are automatically deallocated at the end of their enclosing procedure. The latter feature reduces the need for automatic garbage collection of nodes. Nodenames in Orca have the safety advantages of both pointers and array indices. Like pointers, they cannot be manipulated through arithmetic operations; like array indices, any illegal usage of a nodename will be detected at run time.

The graph type of Orca also has some disadvantages compared to pointers. With pointers, for example, any two data structures can be hooked together through a single assignment statement. With graphs this is more difficult. If the programmer anticipates the join the data structures can be built using a single graph. If separate graphs are used, one will have to be copied into the other.

Another disadvantage is the run-time overhead of graphs. A graph is represented as a table with pointers to the actual nodes, so the nodes are accessed indirectly through this table [3]. Also, there is a cost in making graphs type-secure, since each node access has to be validated. We are currently working on decreasing these costs through global optimizations.

III. AN EXAMPLE OBJECT TYPE AND APPLICATION

In this section we will give an example of an object type definition in Orca, and of a parallel application that uses this object type. The object defines a generic job queue type, with operations to add and delete jobs. It is used in several parallel programs based on the replicated workers paradigm. With this paradigm a master process repeatedly generates jobs to be executed by workers. Communication between the master and workers takes place through the job queue. One such application, parallel branch-and-bound, will be discussed.

A. An Example Object Type

The specification of the object type GenericJobQueue is shown in Fig. 3. The formal parameter T represents the type of the elements (jobs) of the queue.

Three different operations are defined on job queues. *AddJob* adds a new job to the tail of the queue. The operation *NoMoreJobs* is to be called when no more jobs will be added to the queue (i.e., when the master has generated all the jobs).

```
generic (type T)
object specification GenericJobQueue:
    operation AddJob(job: T);            # add a job to the tail of the queue
    operation NoMoreJobs();              # invoked when no more jobs will be added
    operation GetJob(job: out T): boolean;
        # Fetch a job from the head of the queue. This operation
        # fails if the queue is empty and NoMoreJobs has been invoked.
end generic;
```

Fig. 3.   Specification part of the object type definition *GenericJobQueue*.

```
generic
object implementation GenericJobQueue:
    type ItemName = nodename of queue;
    type queue =
        graph # a queue is represented as a linear list
            first, last: ItemName;           # first/last element of queue
        nodes
            next: ItemName;                  # next element in queue
            data: T;                         # data contained by this element
        end;

    done: boolean; # set to true if NoMoreJobs has been invoked.
    Q: queue;      # the queue itself

    operation AddJob(job: T);
        p: ItemName;
    begin # add a job to the tail of the queue
        p := addnode(Q);              # add a new node to Q, return its name in p
        Q[p].data := job;             # fill in data field of the new node; next field is NIL
        if Q.first = NIL then         # Is it the first node?
            Q.first := p;             # yes; assign it to global data field
        else
            Q[Q.last].next := p;      # no; set predecessor's next field
        fi;
        Q.last := p;                  # Assign to "last" global data field
    end;

    operation NoMoreJobs();
    begin        # Invoked to indicate that no more jobs will be added
        done := true;
    end;

    operation GetJob(job: out T): boolean;
        p: ItemName;
    begin        # Try to fetch a job from the queue
        guard Q.first /= NIL do       # A job is available
            p := Q.first;             # Remove it from the queue
            Q.first := Q[p].next;
            if Q.first = NIL then Q.last := NIL; fi;
            job := Q[p].data;         # assign to output parameter
            deletenode(Q.p);          # delete the node from the queue
            return true;              # succeeded in fetching a job
        od;

        guard done and (Q.first = NIL) do
            return false;             # All jobs have been done
        od;
    end;

begin        # Initialization code for JobQueues ; executed on object creation.
    done := false;  # initialize done to false
end generic;
```

Fig. 4.   Implementation part of the object type definition *GenericJobQueue*.

Finally, the operation *GetJob* tries to fetch a job from the head of the queue. If the queue is not empty, *GetJob* removes the first job from the queue and returns it through the **out** parameter *job*; the operation itself returns "true" in this case. If the queue is empty and the operation *NoMoreJobs* has been applied to the queue, the operation fails and returns "false." If none of these two conditions—queue not empty or *NoMoreJobs* invoked—holds, the operation blocks until one of them becomes true.

The implementation part is shown in Fig. 4. Objects of this type contain two variables: a Boolean variable *done* and a variable *Q* of type *queue*. The latter type is defined as a **graph** with two global fields, identifying the first and last element of the queue. Each element contains the **nodename** of the next element in the queue and data of formal type *T*.

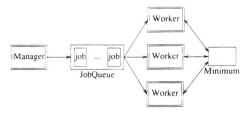

Fig. 5.   Structure of the Orca implementation of TSP. The Manager and Workers are processes. The *JobQueue* is a data-object shared among all these processes. Minimum is a data-object of type *IntObject*; it is read and written by all workers.

The implementation of *AddJob* uses straightforward list manipulation. The *GetJob* operation is more interesting. It contains two **guards**, reflecting the two conditions described above.

B. An Example Parallel Application in Orca

We will now look at one example application in Orca: the traveling salesman problem (TSP). A salesman is given an initial city in which to start and a list of cities to visit. Each city must be visited once and only once. The objective is to find the shortest path that visits all the cities. The problem is solved using a parallel branch-and-bound algorithm.

The algorithm we have implemented in Orca uses one *manager* process to generate initial paths for the salesman, starting at the initial city but visiting only part of the other cities. A number of *worker* processes further expand these initial paths, using the "nearest-city-first" heuristic. A worker systematically generates all paths, starting with a given initial path, and checks if they are better than the current shortest full path. The length of the current best path is stored in a data-object of type *IntObject* (see Fig. 1). This object is shared among all worker processes. The manager and worker processes communicate through a shared job queue, as shown in Fig. 5.

The Orca code for the master and worker processes is shown in Fig. 6. The master process creates and initializes the shared object *minimum* and forks one worker process on each processor except its own one. Subsequently, it generates the jobs by calling a function *GenerateJobs* (not shown here) and then forks a worker process on its own processor. In this way job generation executes in parallel with most of the worker processes. The final worker process is not created until all jobs have been generated, so job generation will not be slowed down by a competing process on the same processor.

Each worker process repeatedly fetches a job from the job queue and executes it by calling the function *tsp*. The *tsp* function generates all routes that start with a given initial route. If the initial route passed as parameter is longer than the current best route *tsp* returns immediately, because such a partial route cannot lead to an optimal solution. If the route passed as parameter is a full route (visiting all cities), a new best route has been found, so the value of *minimum* should be updated. It is possible, however, that two or more worker processes simultaneously detect a route that is better than the current best route. Therefore the value of *minimum* is updated

```
type PathType = array[integer] of integer;
type JobType =
    record
        len: integer;        # length of partial route
        path: PathType;      # the partial route itself
    end;
type DistTab = ...;          # distances table
object TspQueue = new GenericJobQueue(JobType);
    # Instantiation of the GenericJobQueue type


process master();
        minimum: IntObject;        # length of current best path (shared object)
        q: TspQueue;               # the job queue (shared object)
        i: integer;
        distance: DistTab;         # table with distances between cities
begin
        minimum$assign(MAX(integer));        # initialize minimum to infinity
        for i in 1..NCPUS() - 1 do
            # fork one worker per processor, except current processor
            fork worker(minimum, q, distance) on(i);
        od;
        GenerateJobs(q, distance);  # main thread generates the jobs
        q$NoMoreJobs();             # all jobs have been generated now
        fork worker(minimum, q, distance) on(0);
            # jobs have been generated; fork a worker on this cpu too
end;


process worker(
        minimum: shared IntObject;        # length of current best path
        q: shared TspQueue;               # job queue
        distance: DistTab)                # distances between cities

        job: JobType;
begin
        while q$GetJob(job) do  # while there are jobs to do:
            tsp(job.len, job.path, minimum, distance);
            # do sequential tsp
        od;
end;
```

Fig. 6. Orca code for the master and worker processes of TSP.

through the indivisible operation *Min*, which checks if the new value presented is actually less than the current value of the object.

If the job queue is empty and no more jobs will be generated the operation *GetJob* will return "false" and the workers will terminate.

IV. A DISTRIBUTED IMPLEMENTATION OF ORCA

Although Orca is a language for programming distributed systems, its communication model is based on shared data. The implementation of the language therefore should hide the physical distribution of the hardware and simulate shared data in an efficient way. We have several implementations of the language [3]. The implementation described in this paper is based on *replication* and *reliable broadcasting*. We will briefly discuss a second implementation in Section IV-D.

Replication of data is used in several fault-tolerant systems (e.g., ISIS [25]) to increase the availability of data in the presence of processor failures. Orca, in contrast, is not intended for fault-tolerant applications. In our implementation replication is used to decrease the access costs to shared data.

Briefly stated, each processor keeps a local copy of each shared data-object. This copy can be accessed by all processes running on that processor (see Fig. 7). Operations that do not change the object (called *read* operations) use this copy directly, without any messages being sent. Operations that do change the object (called *write* operations) broadcast the new values (or the operations) to all the other processors, so they are updated simultaneously.

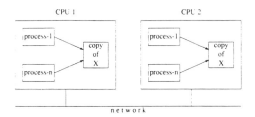

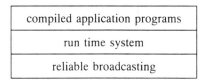

Fig. 7. Replication of data-objects in a distributed system.

The implementation is best thought of as a three-layer software system, as shown below:

| compiled application programs |
| run time system |
| reliable broadcasting |

The top layer is concerned with applications, which are written in Orca and compiled to machine code by the Orca compiler. The executable code contains calls to the Orca run-time system; for example, to create and manipulate processes and objects.

The middle layer is the run-time system (RTS). It implements the primitives called by the upper layer. For example, if an application performs an operation on a shared data-object, it is up to the RTS to ensure that the system behaves as if the object was placed in shared memory. To achieve this the RTS of each processor maintains copies of shared objects, which are updated using reliable broadcasting.

The bottom layer is concerned with implementing the reliable broadcasting so that the RTS does not have to worry about what happens if a broadcast message is lost. As far as the RTS is concerned, broadcast is error free. It is the job of the bottom layer to make it work.

Below, we will describe the protocols and algorithms in each layer. This section is structured top-down: we first discuss the applications layer, then the RTS layer, and finally the reliable broadcast layer.

A. Top Layer: Orca Application Programs

Application programs are translated by the Orca compiler into executable code for the target system.[2] The code produced by the compiler contains calls to RTS routines that manage processes, shared data-objects, and complex data structures (e.g., dynamic arrays, sets, and graphs). In this paper we will only discuss how operation invocations are compiled.

As described above, it is very important to distinguish between *read* and *write* operations on objects. The compiler therefore analyzes the implementation code of each operation and checks whether the operation modifies the object to which

---

[2] We assume the target system does not contain multiple types of CPU's. Although a heterogeneous implementation of Orca is conceivable, we do not address this issue here.

it is applied.[3] In most languages this optimization would be difficult to implement. Consider, for example, a Pascal statement containing an indirect assignment through a pointer variable:

p^.f := 0;

It is hard to determine which data structure is affected by this statement. Orca does not have this problem, since the name of the data structure is given by the programmer. The Orca equivalent of the Pascal code given above would look like:

G[n].f := 0;

which explicitly specifies the name of the data structure that will be modified. So in Orca the compiler can determine which operations modify the object's data structures and which do not.

The compiler stores its information in an *operation descriptor*. This descriptor also specifies the sizes and modes (input or output) of the parameters of the operation. If an Orca program applies an operation on a given object the compiler generates a call to the RTS primitive *INVOKE*. This routine is called as follows:

INVOKE(object, operation-descriptor, parameters . . .);

The first argument identifies the object to which the operation is applied. (It is a network-wide name for the object.) The second argument is the operation descriptor. The remaining arguments of *INVOKE* are the parameters of the operation. The implementation of this primitive is discussed below.

B. Middle Layer: The Orca Run-Time System

The middle layer implements the Orca run-time system. As mentioned above, its primary job is to manage shared data-objects. In particular, it implements the *INVOKE* primitive described above. For efficiency, the RTS replicates objects so it can apply operations to local copies of objects whenever possible.

There are many different design choices to be made related to replication, such as where to replicate objects, how to synchronize write operations to replicated objects, and whether to update or invalidate copies after a write operation. We have looked at many alternative strategies [26]. The RTS described in this paper uses full replication of objects, updates replicas by applying write operations to all replicas, and implements mutual exclusion synchronization through a distributed update protocol.

The full replication scheme was chosen for its simplicity and good performance for many applications. An alternative is to let the RTS decide dynamically where to store replicas. This strategy is employed in another implementation of Orca [26].

We have chosen to use an update scheme rather than an invalidation scheme for two reasons. First, in many applications objects contain large amounts of data (e.g., a 100 Kb

vector). Invalidating a copy of such an object is wasteful, since the next time the object is replicated its entire value must be transmitted. Second, in many cases, updating a copy will take no more CPU time and network bandwidth than sending invalidation messages.

The presence of multiple copies of the same logical data introduces the so-called *inconsistency problem*. If the data are modified, all copies must be modified. If this updating is not done as one indivisible action, different processors will temporarily have different values for the same logical data, which is unacceptable.

The semantics of shared data-objects in our model define that simultaneous operations on the same object must conceptually be serialized. The exact order in which they are to be executed is not defined, however. If, for example, a read operation and a write operation are applied to the same object simultaneously, the read operation may observe either the value before or after the write, but not an intermediate value. However, all processes having access to the object must see the events happen in the same order.

The RTS described here solves the inconsistency problem by using a distributed update protocol that guarantees that all processes observe changes to shared objects *in the same order*. One way to achieve this would be to lock all copies of an object prior to changing the object. Unfortunately, distributed locking is quite expensive and complicated. Our update protocol does not use locking. The key to avoid locking is the use of an *indivisible, reliable broadcast* primitive, which has the following properties:

- Each message is sent reliably from one source to all destinations
- If two processors simultaneously broadcast two messages (say m_1 and m_2), then either all destinations first receive m_1, or they all receive m_2 first. Mixed forms (some get m_1 first, some get m_2 first) are excluded by the software protocols.

This primitive is implemented by the bottom layer of our system, as will be described in Section IV-C. Here, we simply assume that the indivisible reliable broadcast exists.

The RTS uses an *object-manager* for each processor. The object-manager is a light-weight process (thread) that takes care of updating the local copies of all objects stored on its processor. Objects (and replicas) are stored in an address space shared by the object-manager and user processes. User processes can *read* local copies directly, without intervention by the object-managers. Write operations on shared objects, on the other hand, are marshaled and then broadcast to all the object-managers in the system. A user process that broadcasts a write operation suspends until the message has been handled by its local object-manager. This is illustrated in Fig. 8.

Each object-manager maintains a queue of messages that have arrived, but that have not yet been handled. As all processors receive all messages in the same order, the queues of all managers are the same, except that some managers may be ahead of others in handling the messages at the head of the queue.

---

[3]The actual implementation is somewhat more complicated, since an operation may have multiple guards (alternatives), some of which may be read-only.

```
INVOKE(obj, op, parameters)
    if op.ReadOnly then              # check if it's a read operation
        set read-lock on local copy of obj;
        call op.code(obj, parameters);    # do operation locally
        unlock local copy of obj
    else
        broadcast GlobalOperation(obj, op, parameters) to all managers;
        block current process;
    fi;
```

Fig. 8. Implementation of the *INVOKE* run-time system primitive. This routine is called by user processes.

```
receive GlobalOperation(obj, op, parameters) from W →
    set write-lock on local copy of obj;
    call op.code(obj, parameters);    # apply operation to local copy
    unlock local copy of obj
    if W is a local process then
        unblock(W);
    fi;
```

Fig. 9. The code to be executed by the object-managers for handling *GlobalOperation* messages.

The object-manager of each processor handles the messages of its queue in strict FIFO order. A message may be handled as soon as it appears at the head of the queue. To handle a message *GlobalOperation(obj, op, parameters)*, the message is removed from the queue, unmarshaled, the local copy of the object is locked, the operation is applied to the local copy, and finally the copy is unlocked. If the message was sent by a process on the same processor, the manager unblocks that process (see Fig. 9).

Write operations are executed by all object-managers in the same order. If a read operation is executed concurrently with a write operation, the read may either be executed before or after the write, but not during it. Note that this is in agreement with the serialization principle described above.

C. Bottom Layer: Reliable Broadcast

In this section we describe a simple protocol that allows a group of nodes on an unreliable broadcast network to broadcast messages reliably. The protocol guarantees that all of the receivers in the group receive all broadcast messages, and that all receivers accept the messages in the same order. The main purpose of this section is to show that a protocol with the required semantics is feasible, without going into too much detail about the protocol itself.

With current microprocessors and LAN's, lost or damaged packets and processor crashes occur infrequently. Nevertheless, the probability of an error is not zero, so they must be dealt with. For this reason our approach to achieving reliable broadcast is to make the normal case highly efficient, even at the expense of making error-recovery more complex, since error recovery will not be done often.

The basic reliable broadcast protocol works as follows. When the RTS wants to broadcast a message M, it hands the message to its kernel. The kernel then encapsulates M in an ordinary point-to-point message and sends it to a special kernel called the *sequencer*. The sequencer's node contains the same hardware and kernel as all the others. The only difference is that a flag in the kernel tells it to process messages differently. If the sequencer should crash, the protocol provides for the election of a new sequencer on a different node.

The sequencer determines the ordering of all broadcast messages by assigning a *sequence number* to each message. When the sequencer receives the point-to-point message containing M, it allocates the next sequence number s, and broadcasts a packet containing M and s. Thus all broadcasts are issued from the same node by the sequencer. Assuming that no packets are lost, it is easy to see that if two RTS's simultaneously want to broadcast, one of them will reach the sequencer first and its message will be broadcast to all the other nodes first. Only when that broadcast has been completed will the other broadcast be started. The sequencer provides a global ordering in time. In this way we can easily guarantee the atomicity of broadcasting.

Although most modern networks are highly reliable, they are not perfect, so the protocol must deal with errors. Suppose some node misses a broadcast packet, either due to a communication failure or lack of buffer space when the packet arrived. When the following broadcast packet eventually arrives the kernel will immediately notice a gap in the sequence numbers. It was expecting s next, and it got $s + 1$, so it knows it has missed one.

The kernel then sends a special point-to-point message to the sequencer, asking it for copies of the missing message (or messages, if several have been missed). To be able to reply to such requests, the sequencer stores old broadcast messages in its *history buffer*. The missing messages are sent directly to the process requesting them.

As a practical matter the sequencer has a finite amount of space in its history buffer, so it cannot store broadcast messages forever. However, if it could somehow discover that all machines have received broadcasts up to and including k, it could then purge the first k broadcast messages from the history buffer.

The protocol has several ways of letting the sequencer discover this information. For one thing, each point-to-point message to the sequencer (e.g., a broadcast request) contains, in a header field, the sequence number of the last broadcast received by the sender of the message. In this way the sequencer can maintain a table, indexed by node number, showing that node i has received all broadcast messages 0 up to T_i, and perhaps more. At any moment the sequencer can compute the lowest value in this table, and safely discard all broadcast messages up to and including that value. For example, if the values of this table are 8, 7, 9, 8, 6, and 8, the sequencer knows that everyone has received broadcasts 0 through 6, so they can be deleted from the history buffer.

If a node does not need to do any broadcasting for a while, the sequencer will not have an up-to-date idea of which broadcasts it has received. To provide this information, nodes that have been quiet for a certain interval Δt can just send the sequencer a special packet acknowledging all received broadcasts. The sequencer can explicitly ask for this information if it runs out of history space.

Besides the protocol described above (Method 1), we have designed and implemented another protocol (Method 2) that does not send messages to the sequencer first. Instead, the kernel of the sender immediately broadcasts the message. Each receiving kernel stores the message, and the sequencer broadcasts a short acknowledgment message for it. These acknowledgments again carry sequence numbers, which define the ordering of the original messages. If a kernel receives an acknowledgment with the right (i.e., next in line) sequence number, it delivers the original message to the application.

Both protocols guarantee the same semantics, but have different performances under different circumstances. With Method 1, each message is sent over the network twice (once to the sequencer and once from the sequencer to the other kernels). Method 2 uses less bandwidth than Method 1, (the message appears only once on the network) but generates more interrupts, because it uses two broadcast messages (one from the sender to the other kernels and one short message from the sequencer to all kernels). For the implementation of the Orca run-time system we use Method 1, because the messages generated by the run-time system are short and because Method 1 steals less computing cycles from the Orca application to handle interrupts.

In philosophy, the protocol described above somewhat resembles the one described by Chang and Maxemchuk [27], but they differ in some major aspects. With our protocol, messages can be delivered to the user as soon as one (special) node has acknowledged the message. In addition, fewer control messages are needed in the normal case (no lost messages). Our protocol therefore is highly efficient, since, during normal operation, only two packets are needed (assuming that a message fits in a single packet)—one point-to-point packet from the sender to the sequencer, and one broadcast packet from the sequencer to everyone. A comparison between our protocol and other well-known protocols (e.g., those of Birman and Joseph [28], Garcia-Molina and Spauster [29], and several others) is given in [30].

D. Comparison with an RPC-Based Protocol

We have described above one implementation of Orca, based on full replication of objects and on a distributed update protocol using indivisible broadcasting. Below, we will compare this implementation with another one based on partial replication and Remote Procedure Call (RPC).

Updating replicas with RPC is more complicated than with indivisible broadcast. The problem is that all replicas must be updated in a consistent way. To assure consistency, the RPC system uses a two-phase update protocol. During the first phase all copies are updated and locked. After all updates have been acknowledged the second phase begins, during which all copies are unlocked.

This protocol is much more expensive than the one based on broadcasting. The time for an update to complete depends on the number of copies. It therefore makes sense to use a *partial* replication strategy, and only replicate objects where they are needed. The RPC system maintains statistics about the number of read and write operations issued by each processor for each object. Based on this information it decides dynamically where to store the object and where to keep copies. The system can dynamically migrate the object or create and delete copies.

The statistics impose some overhead on the operations, but in general the savings in communication time are well worth this overhead. Still, in most cases, the RPC system has more communication costs than the broadcast system. For the TSP program, for example, it is far more efficient to update the global bound variable through a single broadcast message than through multiple RPC's.

The RPC system is more efficient if the read/write ratio of an object is low. In this case the broadcast system will needlessly replicate the object, but the RPC system will observe this behavior and decide dynamically not to replicate the object.

V. Performance of Example Applications

In this section we will take a brief look at the performance of some example Orca programs. The main goal of this section is to show that, at least for some realistic applications, good speedups can be obtained with our approach.

The prototype distributed implementation we use is based on the layered approach described in the previous section. The prototype runs on top of the Amoeba system, which has been extended with the broadcast protocol described earlier.

The implementation runs on a distributed system containing 16 MC68030 CPU's (running at 16 MHz) connected to each other through a 10 Mb/s Ethernet [31]. The implementation uses Ethernet multicast communication to broadcast a message to a group of processors. All processors are on one Ethernet, and are connected to it by Lance chip interfaces.

The performance of the broadcast protocol on the Ethernet system is described in [30]. The time needed for multicasting a short message reliably to two processors is 2.6 ms. With 16 receivers a multicast takes 2.7 ms.[4] This high performance is due to the fact that our protocol is optimized for the common case (i.e., no lost messages). During the experiments described below the number of lost messages was found to be zero.

We have used the implementation for developing several parallel applications written in Orca. Some of these are small, but others are larger. The largest application we currently have is a parallel chess program consisting of about 2500 lines of code. In addition to TSP, smaller applications include matrix multiplication, prime number generation, and sorting. Below, we will give performance measurements of three sample programs running on the Ethernet implementation.

A. Parallel Traveling Salesman Problem

The first application, the Traveling Salesman Problem (TSP), was described in Section III-B. The program uses two shared objects: a job queue and an IntObject containing the length of the current best path (see Fig. 5). It should be clear that reading of the current best path length will be done very often, but since this is a local operation there is no communication overhead. Updating the best path happens much less often, but still only requires one broadcast message.

Although updates of the best path happen infrequently, it is important to broadcast any improvements immediately. If a worker uses an old (i.e., inferior) value of the best path, it

---

[4] In an earlier implementation of the protocol [32] the delay was 1.4 ms. The difference is entirely due to a new routing protocol on which the group communication protocol is implemented. (The Amoeba kernel can now deal with different kinds of networks and route messages dynamically over multiple networks.)

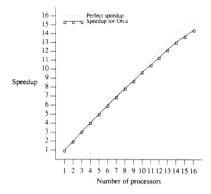

Fig. 10. Measured speedup for the Orca implementation of the Traveling Salesman Problem.

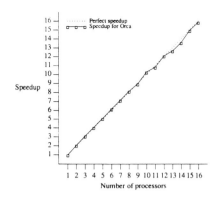

Fig. 11. Measured speedup for the Orca implementation of the All-pairs Shortest Paths problem.

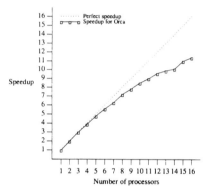

Fig. 12. Measured speedup for the Orca implementation of Successive Overrelaxation.

will investigate paths that could have been pruned if the new value had been known. In other words, the worker will search more nodes than necessary. This *search overhead* may easily become a dominating factor and cause a severe performance degradation.

The performance of the traveling salesman program (for a randomly generated graph with 12 cities) is given in Fig. 10. The implementation achieves a speedup close to linear. With 16 CPU's, it is 14.44 times faster than with 1 CPU.

B. Parallel All-Pairs Shortest Paths Problem

The second application we describe here is the All-pairs Shortest Paths problem (ASP). In this problem it is desired to find the length of the shortest path from any node i to any other node j in a given graph. The parallel algorithm we use is similar to the one given in [33], which is a parallel version of Floyd's algorithm. The distances between the nodes are represented in a matrix. Each processor computes part of the result matrix. The algorithm requires a nontrivial amount of communication and synchronization among the processors.

The performance of the program (for a graph with 300 nodes) is given in Fig. 11. The parallel algorithm performs 300 iterations; after each iteration, an array of 300 integers is sent from one processor to all other processors. In spite of this high communication overhead the implementation still has a good performance. With 16 CPU's, it achieves a speedup of 15.88. One of the main reasons for this good performance is the use of broadcast messages for transferring the array to all processors.

C. Successive Overrelaxation

Both TSP and ASP benefit from the use of broadcasting. We will now consider an application that only needs point-to-point message passing. The application is successive overrelaxation (SOR), which is an iterative method for solving discretized Laplace equations on a grid. During each iteration the algorithm considers all nonboundary points of the grid. For each point, SOR first computes the average value of its four neighbors and then updates the point using this value.

We have parallelized SOR by partitioning the grid into regions and assigning these regions to different processors. The partitioning of the grid is such that at the beginning of an iteration, each processor needs to exchange values with only two other processors. The parallel algorithm therefore only needs point-to-point message passing. With our current prototype implementation of Orca, however, all communication is based on broadcasting. The message passing is simulated in Orca by having the sender and receiver share a buffer object. Since shared objects are updated through broadcasting, all processors will receive the update message. So SOR is a worst-case example for our system.

The measured speedup for SOR is shown in Fig. 12. Despite the high communication overhead, the program still achieves a reasonable speedup. The speedup on 16 CPU's is 11.4.

VI. RELATED WORK

In this section we will compare our language with several related languages and systems. In particular, we will look at objects (as used in parallel object-based languages), Linda's Tuple Space, and Shared Virtual Memory.

A. Objects

Objects are used in many object-based languages for parallel or distributed programming, such as Emerald [15], Amber [34], and ALPS [35]. Objects in such languages typically have two parts:

1) Encapsulated data
2) A *manager process* that controls access to the data.

The data are accessed by sending a message to the manager process, asking it to perform a certain operation on the data. Since such objects contain a process as well as data, they are said to be *active*.

Although, in some sense, parallel object-based languages allow processes (objects) to share data (also objects), their semantics are closer to message passing than to shared variables. Access to the shared data is under full control of the manager process. In ALPS, for example, all operations on an object go through its manager process, which determines the order in which the operations are to be executed. Therefore the only way to implement the model is to store an object on one specific processor, together with its manager process, and to translate all operations on the object into remote procedure calls to the manager process.

Our model does not have such centralized control. Objects in Orca are purely passive—they contain data, but no manager process. Access control to shared data-objects is distributed; it is basically determined by only two rules:

1) Operations must be executed indivisibly
2) Operations are blocked while their guards are false.

Therefore the model can be implemented by replicating data-objects on multiple processors, as we discussed in Section IV. Read operations can be applied to the local copy without any message passing being involved. Moreover, processes located on different processors can apply read operations simultaneously, without losing any parallelism.

B. Linda's Tuple Space

Linda [14] is one of the first languages to recognize the disadvantages of central manager processes for guarding shared data. Linda supports so-called *distributed data structures*, which can be accessed simultaneously by multiple processes. In contrast, object-based languages typically serialize access to shared data structures. Linda uses the Tuple Space model for implementing distributed data structures.

In general, distributed data structures in Linda are built out of multiple tuples. Different tuples can be accessed independently from each other, so processes can manipulate different tuples of the same data structure simultaneously. In principle, multiple **read** operations of the same tuple can also be executed simultaneously. Tuples are (conceptually) modified by taking them out of Tuple Space first, so modifications of a given tuple are executed strictly sequentially.

Although the idea of distributed data structures is appealing, we think the support given by the Tuple Space for implementing such data structures has important disadvantages. For distributed data structures built out of single tuples, mutual exclusion synchronization is done automatically. Operations on complex data structures (built out of multiple tuples), however, have to be synchronized explicitly by the programmer. In essence, Tuple Space supports a fixed number of built-in operations that are executed indivisibly, but its support for building more complex indivisible operations is too low-level [36].

In Orca, on the other hand, programmers can define operations of arbitrary complexity on shared data structures; all

these operations are executed indivisibly, so mutual exclusion synchronization is always done automatically by the run-time system. This means it is the job of the implementation (the compiler and run-time system) to see which operations can be executed in parallel and which have to be executed sequentially. As discussed above, one way of doing this is by distinguishing between read and write operations and executing reads in parallel on local copies; more advanced implementations are also feasible.

C. Shared Virtual Memory

Shared Virtual Memory (SVM) [6] simulates physical shared memory on a distributed system. It partitions the global address space into fixed-sized pages, just as with virtual memory. Each processor contains some portion of the pages. If a process tries to access a page that it does not have, it gets a page-fault, and the operating system will then fetch the page from wherever it is located. Read-only pages may be shared among multiple processors. Writable pages must reside on a single machine—they cannot be shared. If a processor needs to modify a page it will first have to invalidate all copies of the page on other processors.

There are many important differences between the implementation of our model and SVM. SVM is (at least partly) implemented inside the operating system, so it can use the MMU registers. In Orca, everything except for the broadcast protocol is implemented in software outside the operating system. This difference gives SVM a potential performance advantage.

Still, our model has important advantages over SVM. First, shared data-objects are accessed through well-defined high-level operations, whereas SVM is accessed through low-level read and write instructions. Consequently, we have a choice between invalidating objects after a write operation or updating them by applying the operation to all copies (or, alternatively, sending the new value). With SVM there is no such choice; only invalidating pages is viable [6]. In many cases, however, invalidating copies will be far less efficient than updating them.

Several researchers have tried to solve this performance problem by relaxing the consistency constraints of the memory (e.g., [37], [38]). Although these weakly consistent memory models may have better performance, we fear that they also ruin the ease of programming for which DSM was designed in the first place. Since Orca is intended to simplify applications programming, Orca programmers should not have to worry about consistency. (In the future, we may investigate whether a compiler is able to relax the consistency transparently, much as is done in the Munin system [39]).

A second important difference between Orca and SVM is the granularity of the shared data. In SVM, the granularity is the page-size, which is fixed (e.g., 4K). In Orca, the granularity is the object, which is determined by the user. So with SVM, if only a single bit of a page is modified, the whole page has to be invalidated. This property leads to the well-known problem of "false sharing." Suppose a process P repeatedly writes a variable X and process Q repeatedly writes Y. If X and Y happen to be on the same page, this page will continuously be moved between P and Q, resulting in thrashing. If X and Y

are on different pages, thrashing will not occur. Since SVM is transparent, however, the programmer has no control over the allocation of variables to pages. In Orca this problem does not occur, since X and Y would be separate objects and be treated independently.

A more detailed comparison between our work and SVM is given in [40].

VII. CONCLUSION

We have described a new model and language for parallel programming of distributed systems. In contrast with most other models for distributed programming, our model allows processes on different machines to share data. The key idea in our model is to encapsulate shared data in data-objects and to access these objects through user-defined operations. The advantages of this approach for the programmer and implementer are summarized below.

Since operations on objects are always executed indivisibly, mutual exclusion synchronization is done automatically, which simplifies programming. Condition synchronization is integrated into the model by allowing operations to suspend. The mechanism for suspending operations is easy to use and is only visible to the implementer of the operations and not to their users.

The implementation of our model takes care of the physical distribution of shared data among processors. In particular, the implementation replicates shared data, so each process can directly read the local copy on its own processor. After a write operation, all replicas are updated by broadcasting the operation. This update strategy is only possible because shared data are accessed through user-defined operations. SVM, for example, cannot efficiently update replicas after a write operation, since a logical write operation may require many machine instructions, each modifying memory. Updating the memory by broadcasting the machine instructions would be highly inefficient, since the communication overhead per instruction would be enormous.

We have also defined a language, Orca, based on shared data-objects. The design of Orca avoids problems found in many other distributed languages, such as pointers and global variables. A major goal in the design was to keep the language simple. In particular, we have given several examples of simplifying the language design by having the compiler do certain optimizations.

We have studied one distributed implementation of Orca. This implementation runs on a collection of processors connected through a broadcast network. We have not looked at implementations of Orca on other systems, such as hypercubes. Such an implementation would be feasible, however, since the Orca language itself does not depend on the network topology. To port Orca to other architectures, a new run-time system (probably with a new replication strategy) would be needed, but the language and its application programs would not have to be changed.

Our approach is best suited for moderate-grained parallel applications in which processes share data that are read frequently and modified infrequently. A good example is the TSP program, which uses a shared object that is read very frequently and is changed only a few times. This program shows an excellent performance. The applications also benefit from the efficient broadcast protocol used in our implementation. The usefulness of broadcasting was demonstrated by the ASP program.

In conclusion, we think that Orca is a useful language for writing parallel programs for distributed systems. Also, we have shown that the language is efficient for a range of applications.

ACKNOWLEDGMENT

The authors would like to thank W. van Leersum for implementing the Orca compiler, and E. Baalbergen, F. Douglis, A. Geels, and the anonymous referees for giving useful comments on the paper.

REFERENCES

[1] A. S. Tanenbaum et al., "Experiences with the Amoeba distributed operating system," Comm. ACM, vol. 33, no. 2, pp. 46–63, Dec. 1990.

[2] H. E. Bal, R. van Renesse, and A. S. Tanenbaum. "Implementing distributed algorithms using remote procedure calls," in Proc. AFIPS Nat. Computer Conf. (Chicago, IL), June 1987, pp. 499–506.

[3] H. E. Bal, Programming Distributed Systems. Summit, NJ: Silicon, 1990.

[4] H. E. Bal and A. S. Tanenbaum, "Distributed programming with shared data," in Proc. IEEE CS 1988 Int. Conf. on Computer Languages (Miami, FL), Oct. 1988, pp. 82–91.

[5] H. E. Bal, M. F. Kaashoek, and A. S. Tanenbaum, "Experience with distributed programming in Orca," in Proc. IEEE CS 1990 Int. Conf. on Computer Languages (New Orleans, LA), Mar. 1990, pp. 79–89.

[6] K. Li and P. Hudak, "Memory coherence in Shared Virtual Memory systems," in Proc. 5th Ann. ACM Symp. on Princ. of Distr. Computing (Calgary, AB, Can.), Aug. 1986, pp. 229–239.

[7] C. Ghezzi and M. Jazayeri, Programming Language Concepts. New York: Wiley, 1987.

[8] A. D. Birrell and B. J. Nelson, "Implementing remote procedure calls," ACM Trans. Comp. Syst., vol. 2, no. 1, pp. 39–59, Feb. 1984.

[9] H. E. Bal, J. G. Steiner, and A. S. Tanenbaum, "Programming languages for distributed computing systems," ACM Comput. Surveys, vol. 21, no. 3, pp. 261–322, Sept. 1989.

[10] R. Bisiani and A. Forin, "Architectural support for multilanguage parallel programming on heterogenous systems," in Proc. 2nd Int. Conf. on Architectural Support for Program. Languages and Operating Syst. (Palo Alto, CA), Oct. 1987, pp. 21–30.

[11] K. Li, "IVY: a Shared Virtual Memory system for parallel computing," in Proc. 1988 Int. Conf. Parallel Process. (St. Charles, IL), Aug. 1988, pp. 94–101.

[12] E. W. Felten and S. W. Otto, "A highly parallel chess program," in Proc. Int. Conf. on 5th Generation Computer Syst. 1988 (Tokyo), Nov. 1988, pp. 1001–1009.

[13] D. R. Cheriton, "Preliminary thoughts on problem-oriented shared memory: a decentralized approach to distributed systems," ACM Oper. Syst. Rev., vol. 19, no. 4, pp. 26–33, Oct. 1985.

[14] S. Ahuja, N. Carriero, and D. Gelernter, "Linda and friends," IEEE Computer, vol. 19, no. 8, pp. 26–34, Aug. 1986.

[15] E. Jul, H. Levy, N. Hutchinson, and A. Black, "Fine-grained mobility in the Emerald system," ACM Trans. Comput. Syst., vol. 6, no. 1, pp. 109–133, Feb. 1988.

[16] B. Liskov, "Distributed programming in Argus," Commun. ACM, vol. 31, no. 3, pp. 300–312, Mar. 1988.

[17] G. R. Andrews et al., "An overview of the SR language and implementation." ACM Trans. Program. Lang. Syst., vol. 10, no. 1, pp. 51–86, Jan. 1988.

[18] H. E. Bal, "An evaluation of the SR language design," Vrije Univ., Amsterdam, Rep. IR-219, Aug. 1990.

[19] C. A. R. Hoare, "Monitors: an operating system structuring concept," Commun. ACM, vol. 17, no. 10, pp. 549–557, Oct. 1974.

[20] G. R. Andrews and F. B. Schneider, "Concepts and notations for concurrent programming," ACM Comput. Surveys, vol. 15, no. 1, pp. 3–43, Mar. 1983.

[21] K. P. Eswaran, J. N. Gray, R. A. Lorie, and I. L. Traiger, "The notions of consistency and predicate locks in a database system," *Commun. ACM*, vol. 19, no. 11, pp. 624–633, Nov. 1976.

[22] S. E. Lucco, "Parallel programming in a virtual object space," *SIGPLAN Notices (Proc. Object-Oriented Program. Syst., Languages and Appl. 1987*, Orlando, FL). vol. 22, no. 12, pp. 26–34, Dec. 1987.

[23] R. C. B. Cooper and K. G. Hamilton, "Preserving abstraction in concurrent programming," *IEEE Trans. Software Eng.*, vol. 14, pp. 258–263, Feb. 1988.

[24] N. Wirth, "The programming language Pascal," *Acta Inform.*, vol. 1, no. 1, pp. 35–63, 1971.

[25] T. A. Joseph and K. P. Birman, "Low-cost management of replicated data in fault-tolerant distributed systems," *ACM Trans. Comput. Syst.*, vol. 4, no. 1, pp. 54–70, Feb. 1986.

[26] H. E. Bal, M. F. Kaashoek, A. S. Tanenbaum, and J. Jansen, "Replication techniques for speeding-up parallel applications on distributed systems," Vrije Univ., Amsterdam, Rep. IR-202, Oct. 1989.

[27] J. Chang and N. F. Maxemchuk, "Reliable broadcast protocols," *ACM Trans. Comput. Syst.*, vol. 2, no. 3, pp. 251–273, Aug. 1984.

[28] K. P. Birman and T. A. Joseph, "Reliable communication in the presence of failures," *ACM Trans. Comput. Syst.*, vol. 5, no. 1, pp. 47–76, Feb. 1987.

[29] H. Garcia-Molina and A. Spauster, "Message ordering in a multicast environment," in *Proc. 9th Int. Conf. on Distr. Comput. Syst.* (Newport Beach, CA), June 1989, pp. 354–361.

[30] M. F. Kaashoek and A. S. Tanenbaum, "Group communication in the Amoeba distributed operating system," in *Proc. 11th Int. Conf. on Distrib. Comput. Syst.* (Arlington, TX), May 1991, pp. 222–230.

[31] R. M. Metcalfe and D. R. Boggs, "Ethernet: distributed packet switching for local computer networks," *Commun. ACM*, vol. 19, no. 7, pp. 395–404, July 1976.

[32] M. F. Kaashoek, A. S. Tanenbaum, S. Flynn Hummel, and H. E. Bal, "An efficient reliable broadcast protocol," *ACM Oper. Syst. Rev.*, vol. 23, no. 4, pp. 5–20, Oct. 1989.

[33] J.-F. Jenq and S. Sahni, "All pairs shortest paths on a hypercube multiprocessor," in *Proc. 1987 Int. Conf. on Parallel Process.* (St. Charles, IL), Aug. 1987, pp. 713–716.

[34] J. S. Chase, F. G. Amador, E. D. Lazowska, H. M. Levy, and R. J. Littlefield, "The Amber system: parallel programming on a network of multiprocessors," in *Proc. 12th ACM Symp. on Oper. Syst. Principles*, (Litchfield Park, AZ), Dec. 1989, pp. 147–158.

[35] P. Vishnubhotia, "Synchronization and scheduling in ALPS objects," in *Proc. 8th Int. Conf. on Distrib. Comput. Syst.* (San Jose, CA), June 1988, pp. 256–264.

[36] M. F. Kaashoek, H. E. Bal, and A. S. Tanenbaum, "Experience with the distributed data structure paradigm in Linda," in *Proc. Workshop on Experiences with Building Distributed and Multiprocessor Syst.* (Ft. Lauderdale, FL), Oct. 1989, pp. 175–191.

[37] R. G. Minnich and D. J. Farber, "Reducing host load, network load, and latency in a distributed shared memory," in *Proc. 10th Int. Conf. on Distrib. Comput. Syst.* (Paris), May 1990, pp. 468–475.

[38] P. W. Hutto and M. Ahamad, "Slow memory: weakening consistency to enhance concurrency in distributed shared memories," in *Proc. 10th Int. Conf. on Distrib. Comput. Syst.* (Paris), May 1990, pp. 302–309.

[39] J. K. Bennet, J. B. Carter, and W. Zwaenepoel, "Munin: distributed shared memory based on type-specific memory coherence," in *Proc. 2nd Symp. Principles and Practice of Parallel Program.* (Seattle, WA), (Mar. 1990).

[40] W. G. Levelt, M. F. Kaashoek, H. E. Bal, and A. S. Tanenbaum, "A comparison of two paradigms for distributed shared memory," Vrije Univ., Amsterdam, Rep. IR-221, Aug. 1990.

Henri E. Bal (S'86–A'89) received the M.Sc. degree in mathematics from the Delft University of Technology in 1982, and the Ph.D. degree in computer science from the Vrije Universiteit in Amsterdam in 1989.

From 1982 through 1985, he participated in the Amsterdam Compiler Kit project. He is the author of the ACK global optimizer. Since 1985 he has been working on Orca, a new programming language for implementing parallel applications on distributed systems. Orca has been implemented on top of the Amoeba distributed operating system and has been used for various applications. The language design, implementation, and usage are described in several published research papers and in his book, *Programming Distributed Systems*. He has been a Visiting Researcher at MIT, the University of Arizona, and Imperial College. At present he is a staff member of the Department of Computer Science at the Vrije Universiteit in Amsterdam, where his research interests include programming languages, parallel and distributed programming, and compilers.

M. Frans Kaashoek (S'89) is a Ph.D. degree student with Prof. A. Tanenbaum at the Vrije Universiteit, Amsterdam. His research interest includes communication protocols, distributed operating systems, parallel and distributed programming, and compiler construction.

Andrew S. Tanenbaum (M'75) received the S.B. degree from MIT and the Ph.D. degree from the University of California, Berkeley.

He is currently a Professor of Computer Science at the Vrije Universiteit, Amsterdam, where he teaches and does research in the areas of computer architecture, operating systems, networks, and distributed systems. He is the principal designer of three operating systems: TSS-11, MINIX, and Amoeba, and a system known as the Amsterdam Compiler Kit, which is used for producing portable compilers. In addition, he is the author of four books, most recently, *Modern Operating Systems* (Prentice-Hall, 1992), as well as more than 60 published papers on a variety of subjects. He has also lectured in a dozen countries.

Dr. Tanenbaum is a member of the ACM, the IEEE Computer Society, and Sigma Xi.

How to Write Parallel Programs: A Guide to the Perplexed

NICHOLAS CARRIERO AND DAVID GELERNTER

Department of Computer Science, Yale University, New Haven, Connecticut 06520

We present a framework for parallel programming, based on three conceptual classes for understanding parallelism and three programming paradigms for implementing parallel programs. The conceptual classes are result parallelism, which centers on parallel computation of all elements in a data structure; agenda parallelism, which specifies an agenda of tasks for parallel execution; and specialist parallelism, in which specialist agents solve problems cooperatively. The programming paradigms center on live data structures that transform themselves into result data structures; distributed data structures that are accessible to many processes simultaneously; and message passing, in which all data objects are encapsulated within explicitly communicating processes. There is a rough correspondence between the conceptual classes and the programming methods, as we discuss. We begin by outlining the basic conceptual classes and programming paradigms, and by sketching an example solution under each of the three paradigms. The final section develops a simple example in greater detail, presenting and explaining code and discussing its performance on two commercial parallel computers, an 18-node shared-memory multiprocessor, and a 64-node distributed-memory hypercube. The middle section bridges the gap between the abstract and the practical by giving an overview of how the basic paradigms are implemented.

We focus on the paradigms, not on machine architecture or programming languages: The programming methods we discuss are useful on many kinds of parallel machine, and each can be expressed in several different parallel programming languages. Our programming discussion and the examples use the parallel language C-Linda for several reasons: The main paradigms are all simple to express in Linda; efficient Linda implementations exist on a wide variety of parallel machines; and a wide variety of parallel programs have been written in Linda.

Categories and Subject Descriptors: D.1.3 [**Programming Techniques**]: Concurrent Programming; D.3.2 [**Programming Languages**]: Language Classifications—*parallel languages*; D.3.3 [**Programming Languages**]: Concurrent Programming Structures; E.1.m [**Data Structures**]: Miscellaneous—*distributed data structures; live data structures*

General Terms: Algorithms, Program Design, Languages

Additional Key Words and Phrases: Linda, parallel programming methodology, parallelism

INTRODUCTION

How do we build programs using parallel algorithms? On a spectrum of basic approaches, three primary points deserve special mention: We can use result parallelism, agenda parallelism, or specialist parallelism, terms we define. Corresponding to these basic approaches are three parallel *programming methods*—practical techniques for translating concepts into working programs; we can use message passing,

---

This working was supported by National Science Foundation SBIR Grant ISI-8704025 and by National Science Foundation Grants CCR-8601920, CCR-8657615, and ONR N00014-86-K-0310.

"How to Write Parallel Programs: A Guide to the Perplexed" by N. Carriero and D. Gelernter from *ACM Computing Surveys,* Vol. 21, No. 3, Sept. 1989, pp. 323-357. Copyright 1989, Association for Computing Machinery, Inc., reprinted with permission.

CONTENTS

---

distributed data structures, or live data structures.[1] Each programming method involves a different view of the role of processes and the distribution of data in a parallel program. The basic conceptual approaches and programming methods we have mentioned are not provably the only ones possible. But empirically they cover all examples we have encountered in the research literature and in our own programming experience.

Our goal here is to explain the conceptual classes, the programming methods, and the mapping between them. Section 1 explains the basic classes and methods, and sketches an example program under each of the three methods. Section 2 bridges the gap between the abstract and the practical by giving an overview of how these methods are implemented. Section 3 develops a simple example in greater detail, presenting and explaining code.

In presenting and explaining programming methods, we rely on the high-level parallel language C-Linda. Linda[2] is a language-independent set of operations that. when integrated into some base language, yields a high-level parallel dialect. C-Linda uses C; Fortran-Linda exists as well. Other groups are working on other languages[3] as Linda hosts. Our main topic is not Linda, any more than Pascal is the main topic in "Introductory Programming with Pascal" books. But we do need to present the basics of Linda programming. Linda is a good choice in this context for three reasons. (1) *Linda is flexible*: It supports all three programming methods in a straightforward fashion. This is important precisely because programming paradigms, *not* programming languages, are the topic here. The only way to factor language issues out of the discussion (at least partially) is to choose one language that will allow us to investigate all approaches. (2) *Efficient Linda implementations are available on commercial parallel machines.* We are discussing real (not theoretical) techniques, and for readers who want to investigate them, efficient Linda systems exist.[4] (3) *Linda has been used in a wide variety of programming experiments*—which give us a

---

[1] Although these methods are well-known, the latter two terms are not. Discussions of parallel programming methodology to date have been largely ad hoc, and as a result, the latter two categories have no generally accepted names. In fact, they are rarely recognized as categories at all.

[2] Linda is a trademark of Scientific Computing Associates. New Haven.

[3] Among them, Scheme, PostScript (see Leler [1989]), and C++; Borrman et al. [1988] describe a Modula-2 Linda, and Matsuoka and Kawai [1988] describe an object-oriented Linda variant.

[4] Linda has been implemented on shared-memory parallel computers like the Encore Multimax, Sequent Balance and Symmetry, and Alliant FX/8; on distributed memory computers like the Intel iPSC-2 hypercube; and on a VAX/VMS local-area network. Several independent commercial implementations now in progress—for example, at Cogent Research, Human Devices, and Topologix—will expand the range of supported architectures. Other groups have ports underway or planned to the Trollius operating system, to the BBN Butterfly running Mach, and to the NCUBE; Xu [1988] describes the design of a reliable Linda system based on Argus. A simulator that runs on Sun workstations also exists. The range of machines on which Linda is supported will be expanding significantly in coming months. Linda systems are distributed commercially by Scientific Computing Associates, New Haven.

basis in experience for discussing the strengths and weaknesses of various approaches. There are Linda applications for numerical problems like matrix multiplication, LU decomposition, sparse factorization [Ashcraft et al. 1989] and linear programming, and for parallel string comparison, database search, circuit simulation, ray tracing [Musgrave and Mandelbrot 1989], expert systems [Gelernter 1989], parameter sensitivity analysis, charged particle transport [Whiteside and Leichter 1988], traveling salesman, and others. We will refer to several of these programs in the following discussion.

1. CONCEPTS AND METHODS

How do we write parallel programs? For each conceptual class, there is a natural programming method; each method relates to the others in well-defined ways (i.e., programs using method x can be transformed into programs using method y by following well-defined steps). We will therefore develop the following approach to parallel programming:

To write a parallel program, (1) choose the concept class that is most natural for the problem; (2) write a program using the method that is most natural for that conceptual class; and (3) if the resulting program is not acceptably efficient, transform it methodically into a more efficient version by switching from a more-natural method to a more-efficient one.

First we explain the concepts—result, agenda, and specialist parallelism. Then we explain the methods: live data structures, distributed structures, and message passing. Finally, we discuss the relationship between concepts and methods, and give an example.

1.1 Conceptual Classes

We can envision parallelism in terms of a program's *result*, a program's *agenda of activities*, or an *ensemble of specialists* that collectively constitute the program. We begin with an analogy.

Suppose you want to build a house. Parallelism—using many people on the job—

is the obvious approach. But there are several different ways in which parallelism might enter.

First, we might envision parallelism by starting with the finished product, the *result*. The result can be divided into many separate components: front, rear and side walls, interior walls, foundation, roof, and so on. After breaking the result into components, we might proceed to build all components simultaneously, assembling them as they are completed; we assign one worker to the foundation, one to the front exterior wall, one to each side wall and so on. All workers start simultaneously. Separate workers set to work laying the foundation, framing each exterior wall and building a roof assembly. They all proceed in parallel, up to the point where work on one component can't proceed until another is finished. In sum, each worker is assigned to *produce one piece of the result*, and they all work in parallel up to the natural restrictions imposed by the problem. This is the *result-parallel* approach.

At the other end of the spectrum, we might envision parallelism by starting with the crew of workers who will do the building. We note that house building requires a collection of separate skills: We need surveyors, excavators, foundation builders, carpenters, roofers and so on. We assemble a construction crew in which each skill is represented by a separate specialist worker. They all start simultaneously, but initially most workers will have to wait around. Once the project is well underway, however, many skills (hence many workers) will be called into play simultaneously: The carpenter (building forms) and the foundation builders work together, and concurrently, the roofer can be shingling while the plumber is installing fixtures and the electrician is wiring, and so on. Although a single carpenter does all the woodwork, many other tasks will overlap and proceed simultaneously with the carpenter's. This approach is particularly suited to *pipelined* jobs—jobs that require the production or transformation of a series of identical objects. If we are building a group of houses, carpenters can work on one house while foundation builders work on a second and surveyors on a third. But this strategy will often yield parallelism even when the job is defined in terms of a single object, as it does in the case of the construction of a single house. In sum, each worker is assigned to *perform one specified kind of work*, and they all work in parallel up to the natural restrictions imposed by the problem. This is the *specialist-parallel* approach.

Finally, we might envision parallelism in terms of an agenda of activities that must be completed in order to build a house. We write out a sequential agenda and carry it out in order, but at each stage we assign many workers to the current activity. We need a foundation, then we need a frame, then we need a roof, then we need wallboard and perhaps plastering, and so on. We assemble a work team of generalists, each member capable of performing any construction step. First, everyone pitches in and builds the foundation; then, the same group sets to work on the framing; then they build the roof; then some of them work on plumbing while others (randomly chosen) do the wiring; and so on. In sum, each worker is assigned to *help out with the current item on the agenda*, and they all work in parallel up to the natural restrictions imposed by the problem. This is the *agenda-parallel* approach.

The boundaries between the three classes can sometimes be fuzzy, and we will often mix elements of several approaches in getting a particular job done. A specialist approach might make secondary use of agenda parallelism, for example, by assigning a team of workers to some specialty—the team of carpenters, for example, might execute the "carpentry agenda" in agenda-parallel style. It is nonetheless a subtle but essential point that *these three approaches represent three clearly separate ways of thinking about the problem*:

Result parallelism focuses on the shape of the finished product; specialist parallelism focuses on the makeup of the work crew; and agenda parallelism focuses on the list of tasks to be performed.

These three conceptual classes apply to software as well. In particular,

(1) we can plan a parallel application around the data structure yielded as

the ultimate result, and we get parallelism by computing all elements of the result simultaneously;

(2) we can plan an application around a particular agenda of activities and then assign many workers to each step; or

(3) we can plan an application around an ensemble of specialists connected into a logical network of some kind; parallelism results from all nodes of the logical network (all specialists) being active simultaneously.

How do we know what kind of parallelism, what conceptual class, to use? Consider the house-building analogy again. In effect, all three classes are (or have been) used in building houses. Factory-built housing is assembled at the site using prebuilt modules—walls, a roof assembly, staircases, and so on; all these components were assembled separately and (in theory) simultaneously back at the factory. This is a form of result parallelism in action. "Barn raisings" evidently consisted of a group of workers turning its attention to each of a list of tasks in turn, a form of agenda parallelism. But some form of specialist parallelism, usually with secondary agenda parallelism, seems like the most natural choice for house building: Each worker (or team) has a specialty, and parallelism arises in the first instance when many separate specialities operate simultaneously, secondarily when the many (in effect) identical workers on one team cooperate on the agenda.

In software as well, certain approaches tend to be more natural for certain problems. The choice depends on the problem to be solved. In some cases, one choice is immediate. In others, two or all three approaches might be equally natural. This multiplicity of choices might be regarded as confusing or off-putting; we would rather see it as symptomatic of the fact that parallelism is in many cases so abundant that the programmer can take his choice about how to harvest it.

In many cases, the easiest way to design a parallel program is to think of the resulting data structure—*result parallelism*. The programmer asks himself (1) is my program intended to produce some multiple-element data structure as its result (or can it be conceived in these terms)? If so, (2) can I specify exactly how each element of the resulting structure depends on the rest and on the input? If so, it's easy (given knowledge of the appropriate programming methods) to write a result-parallel program. Broadly speaking, such a program reads as follows: "Build a data structure in such-and-such a shape; attempt to determine the value of all elements of this structure simultaneously, where the value of each element is determined by such-and-such a computation. Terminate when all values are known." It may be that the elements of the result structure are completely independent—no element depends on any other. If so, all computations start simultaneously and proceed in parallel. It may also be that some elements can't be computed until certain other values are known. In this case, all element computations *start* simultaneously, but some immediately get stuck. They remain stuck until the values they rely on have been computed, and then proceed.

Consider a simple example: We have two n-element vectors, A and B, and need to compute their sum S. A result-parallel program reads as follows: "Construct an n-element vector S; to determine the ith element of S, add the ith element of A to the ith element of B." The elements of S are completely independent. No addition depends on any other addition. All additions accordingly start simultaneously and go forward in parallel.

More interesting cases involve computations in which there are dependencies among elements of the result data structure. We discuss an example in the next section.

Result parallelism is a good starting point for any problem whose goal is to produce a series of values with predictable organization and interdependencies, but not every problem meets this criterion. Consider a program that produces output whose shape and format depend on the input: a program to format text or translate code in parallel, for example, whose output may be a string of bytes and (perhaps) a set of tables, of unpredictable size and shape. Consider a program in which (conceptually) a *single* object is transformed repeatedly: an LU decomposition or linear programming problem, for example, in which a given matrix is repeatedly transformed in place. Consider a program that is executed not for value, but for effect: a real-time monitor-and-control program or an operating system, for example.

Agenda parallelism involves a transformation or series of transformations to be applied to all elements of some set in parallel. The most flexible embodiment of this type of parallelism is the master–worker paradigm. In a master–worker program, a master process initializes the computation and creates a collection of identical worker processes. Each worker process is capable of performing any step in the computation. Workers repeatedly seek a task to perform, perform the selected task, and repeat; when no tasks remain, the program (or this step) is finished. The program executes in the same way no matter how many workers there are, so long as there is at least one. The same program might be executed with 1, 10, and 1000 workers in three consecutive runs. If tasks are distributed on the fly, this structure is naturally load-balancing: While one worker is tied up with a time-consuming task, another might execute a dozen shorter task assignments.

For example, suppose we have a database of employee records and need to identify the employee with, say, the lowest ratio of salary to dependents. Given a record Q, the function $r(Q)$ computes this ratio. The agenda is simple: "Apply function r to all records in the database; return the identity of the record for which r is minimum." We can structure this application as a master-worker program in a natural way: The master fills a bag with data objects, each representing one employee record. Each worker repeatedly withdraws a record from the bag, computes r, and sends the result back to the master. The master keeps track of the minimum-so-far and, when all tasks are complete, reports the answer.

Specialist parallelism involves programs that are conceived in terms of a logical network. They arise when an algorithm or a system to be modeled is best understood as a network in which each node executes

56

a relatively autonomous computation and internode communication follows predictable paths. The network may reflect a physical model or the logical structure of an algorithm (e.g., as in a pipelined or systolic computation). Network-style solutions are particularly transparent and natural when there is a physical system to be modeled. Consider a circuit simulator, for example, modeled by a parallel program in which each circuit element is realized by a separate process. There are also problems that partition naturally into separate realms of responsibility, with clearly defined intercommunication channels; further on we discuss a "cooperating experts" type of heuristic monitor that uses this kind of organization. In the last section, we discuss a pipeline type of algorithm, an algorithm understood as a sequence of steps applied to a stream of input values, with each stage of the pipe transforming a datum and handing it forward.

For example, suppose a nationwide trucking company needs to produce a large number of estimates for travel time between two points, given current estimates for road conditions, weather, and traffic. We might design a specialist-parallel program as follows: We embody a map of the continental United States in a logical network; each state is represented by its own node in the network. The Wyoming node is responsible for staying up-to-date on travel conditions in and expected transit time through Wyoming, and so forth. To estimate travel time from New Hampshire to Arkansas, we plan out a route and include a representation of this route within a data object representing a truck. We hand the "truck" to New Hampshire, which estimates its travel time through New Hampshire and then hands the truck to the next state along its route. Eventually the "truck" reaches Arkansas, which prints out the final estimate for its transit time. Note that large numbers of trucks may be moving through the logical network at any one time.

We conclude this survey of conceptual classes by mentioning two special classes that we will not deal with further, *data parallelism* and *speculative parallelism*

(sometimes called *or-parallelism*). Data parallelism is a restricted kind of agenda parallelism: It involves a series of transformations each applied to all elements of a data structure simultaneously. If we start with an agenda of activities in which each item requires that a transformation be applied to a data structure, the agenda-parallel program we would derive would in effect be an example of data parallelism. Empirically, data parallelism is usually associated with synchronous machines (e.g., MPP [Goodyear Aerospace Co. 1979] and the Connection Machine [Hillis and Steele 1986]) and is accordingly tied to an implementation in which transformations are applied to all elements of some data structure not merely concurrently but *synchronously*: At each instant, each active worker is applying the same step of the same transformation to its own assigned piece of the structure. In this paper our focus is restricted to techniques that are used on general-purpose *asynchronous* parallel machines.[5] In "speculative parallelism," often associated with logic programming, but also significant in, for example, parallel algorithms for heuristic search (e.g., parallel alpha-beta search on game trees [Marsland and Campbell 1982]), a collection of parallel activities is undertaken with the understanding that some may ultimately prove to be unnecessary to the final result. Whenever a program's structure includes clauses like "try x, and if x fails, try y" (and so on through a list of other alternatives), we can get parallelism by working on x, y, and any other alternatives simultaneously. If and when x fails, y is already underway. We understand this under our schematization as another special form of agenda parallelism: Many workers are thrown simultaneously into the completion of a list of tasks, with the understanding that, ultimately, only one of the results produced will be incorporated in the finished product.

---

[5] This focus can be taken as arbitrary, but there is a reason for it. At present, synchronous or SIMD machines are rare and expensive; asynchronous machines can be built cheaply and are increasingly widespread. The imminent arrival of parallel workstations will add to the flood.

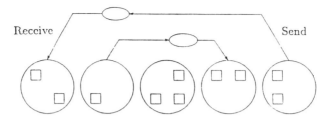

Figure 1. Message passing: The process structure—the number of processes and their relationships—determines the program structure. A collection of concurrent processes communicate by exchanging messages; every data object is locked inside some process. (Processes are round, data objects square, and messages oval.)

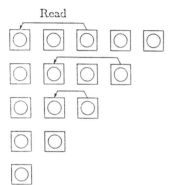

Figure 2. Live data structures: The result data structure—the number of its elements and their relationship—determines the program structure. Every concurrent process is locked inside a data object; it is responsible, in other words, for computing that element and only that element. Communication is no longer a matter of explicit "send message" and "receive message" operations; when a process needs to consult the value produced by some other process, it simply reads the data object within which the process is trapped.

1.2 The Programming Methods

In message passing, we create many concurrent processes and enclose every data structure within some process; processes communicate by exchanging messages. In message-passing methods, no data objects are shared among processes. Each process may access its own local set of private data objects only. In order to communicate, processes must send data objects from one local space to another; to accomplish this, the programmer must explicitly include send-data and receive-data operations in his code (Figure 1).

At the other extreme, we dispense with processes as conceptually independent entities and build a program in the shape of the data structure that will ultimately be yielded as the result. Each element of this data structure is implicitly a separate process, which will turn into a data object upon termination. To communicate, these implicit processes don't exchange messages;

they simply "refer" to each other as elements of some data structure. Thus, if process P has data for Q, it doesn't send a message to Q; it terminates, yielding a value, and Q reads this value directly. These are "live-data-structure" programs (Figure 2).

The message-passing and live-data-structure approaches are similar in the sense that, in each, all data objects are distributed among the concurrent processes; there are no global, shared structures. In message passing, though, processes are created by the programmer *explicitly*; they communicate *explicitly* and may send values *repeatedly* to other processes. In a live-data-structure program, processes are created *implicitly* in the course of building a data structure; they communicate *implicitly* by referring to the elements of a data structure, and each process produces only a *single* datum for use by the rest of the program. Details will become clear as we discuss examples.

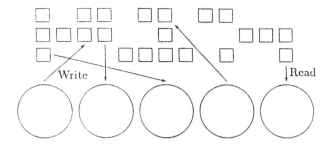

Figure 3. Distributed data structures: Concurrent processes *and* data objects figure as autonomous parts of the program structure. Processes communicate by reading and writing shared data objects.

Between the extremes of allowing all data to be absorbed into the process structure (message passing) or all processes to melt into data structures (live data structures), there is an intermediate strategy that maintains the distinction between a group of data objects and a group of processes. Because shared data objects exist, processes may communicate and coordinate by leaving data in shared objects. These are "distributed-data-structure" programs (Figure 3).

1.3 Where to Use Each

It's clear that result parallelism is naturally expressed in a live-data-structure program. For example, returning to the vector-sum program, the core of such an application is a live data structure. The live structure is an n-element vector called S; trapped inside each element of S is a process that computes $A[i] + B[i]$ for the appropriate i. When a process is complete, it vanishes, leaving behind only the value it was charged to compute.

Specialist parallelism is a good match to message passing: We can build such a program under message passing by creating one process for each network node and using messages to implement communication over edges. For example, returning to the travel-time program, we implement each node of the logical network by a process; trucks are represented by messages. To introduce a truck into the network at New Hampshire, we send New Hampshire a "new truck" message; the message includes a representation of the truck's route. New Hampshire computes an estimated transit time and sends another message, including both the route and the time-en-route-so-far to the next process along the route. Note that, with lots of trucks in the network, many messages may converge on a process simultaneously. Clearly, then, we need some method for queuing or buffering messages until a process can get around to dealing with them. Most message-passing systems have some kind of buffering mechanism built in.

Even when such a network model exists, though, message passing will sometimes be inconvenient in the absence of backup support from distributed data structures. If every node in the network needs to refer to a collection of global status variables, those globals can only be stored (absent distributed data structures) as some node's local variables, forcing all access to be channeled through a custodian process. Such an arrangement can be conceptually inept and can lead to bottlenecks.

Agenda parallelism maps naturally onto distributed-data-structure methods. Agenda parallelism requires that many workers set to work on what is, in effect, a single job. In general, any worker will be willing to pick up any subtask. Results developed by one worker will often be needed by others, but one worker usually won't know (and won't care) what the others are doing. Under the circumstances, it's far more convenient to leave results in a distributed data structure, where any worker who wants them can take them, than to worry about sending messages to particular recipients. Consider also the dynamics of a master–worker program, the kind of program that represents the most flexible embodiment of agenda parallelism. We have a collection of workers and need to distribute tasks, generally on the fly. Where do we keep the tasks? Again, a distributed data structure is the most natural solution. If the subtasks that make up an agenda item are strictly parallel, with no necessary ordering among them, the master process can store task descriptors in a distributed *bag* structure; workers repeatedly reach into the bag and grab a task. In some cases, tasks should be started in a certain order (even if many can be processed simultaneously); in this case, tasks will be stored in some form of distributed queue structure.

For example, we discussed a parallel database search carried out in terms of the master–worker model. The bag into which the master process drops employee records is naturally implemented as a distributed data structure—as a structure, in other words, that is directly accessible to the worker processes and the master.

1.4 An Example

Consider a naive *n*-body simulator: On each iteration of the simulation, we calculate the prevailing forces between each body and all the rest, and update each body's position accordingly.[6] We will consider this problem in the same way we considered house building. Once again, we can conceive of result-based, agenda-based, and specialist-based approaches to a parallel solution.

We can start with a result-based approach. It's easy to restate the problem description as follows: Suppose we are given n bodies and want to run q iterations of our simulation; compute a matrix M such that $M[i, j]$ is the position of the ith body after the jth iteration. The zeroth column of the matrix gives the starting position,

and the last column, the final position, of each body. We have now carried out step 1 in the design of a live data structure. The second step is to define each entry in terms of other entries. We can write a function $position(i, j)$ that computes the position of body i on iteration j; clearly $position(i, j)$ will depend on the positions of each body at the previous iteration—will depend, that is, on the entries in column $j - 1$ of the matrix. Given a suitable programming language, we're finished: We build a program in which $M[i, j]$ is defined to be the value yielded by $position(i, j)$. Each invocation of *position* constitutes an implicit process, and all such invocations are activated and begin execution simultaneously. Of course, computation of the second column can't proceed until values are available for the first column: We must assume that, if some invocation of *position* refers to $M[x, y]$ and $M[x, y]$ is still unknown, we wait for a value and then proceed. Thus, the zeroth column's values are given at initialization time, whereupon all values in the first column can be computed in parallel, then the second column, and so forth (Figure 4).

Note that, if the forces are symmetric, this program does more work than necessary, because the force between A and B is the same as the force between B and A. This is a minor problem that we could correct, but our goal here is to outline the simplest possible approach.

We can also approach this problem in terms of agenda parallelism. The task agenda states "repeatedly apply the transformation *compute next position* to all bodies in the set." To write the program, we might create a master process and have it generate n initial task descriptors, one for each body. On the first iteration, each worker in a group of identical worker processes repeatedly grabs a task descriptor and computes the next position of the corresponding body, until the pile of task descriptors is used up (and all bodies have advanced to their new positions); likewise for each subsequent iteration. A single worker will require time proportional to n^2 to complete each iteration; two workers together will finish each iteration in time proportional to $n^2/2$, and so on. We

---

[6] There is a better ($O(n)$) approach to solving the n-body problem, developed by Greengard and Rokhlin [1987] of Yale; the new algorithm can be parallelized, but to keep things simple, we use the old approach as a basis for this discussion.

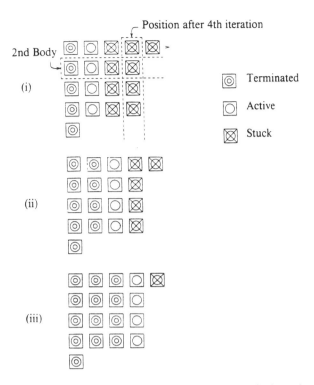

Figure 4. A live-data-structure approach to the n-body problem. To begin, we build an $n \times q$ matrix and install a process inside each element. The process trapped in element $M[i,j]$ will compute the position of the ith body after the jth iteration, by referring to the previous column, in which each body's last-known position will appear. The processes in column j are stuck until the processes in column $j-1$ terminate, at which point all of column j can be computed in parallel. Thus, each column computes in parallel until values are known for the entire matrix.

can store information about each body's position at the last iteration in a distributed table structure, where each worker can refer to it directly (Figure 5).

Finally, we might use a specialist-parallel approach: We create a series of processes, each one specializing in a single body—that is, each responsible for computing a single body's current position throughout the simulation. At the start of each iteration, each process informs each other process by message of the current position of its body. All processes are behaving in the same way; it follows that, at the start of each iteration, each process *sends data to* but also *receives data from* each other process. The data included in the incoming crop of messages are sufficient to allow each process to compute a new position for its body. It

does so, and the cycle repeats (Figure 6). (A similar but slightly cleaned up version of such a program is described by Seitz [1985].)

1.5 How Do the Three Techniques Relate?

The methodology we are developing requires (1) starting with a conceptual class that is natural to the problem, (2) writing a program using the programming method that is natural to the class, and then, (3) if necessary, transforming the initial program into a more efficient variant that uses some other method. If a natural approach also turns out to be an efficient approach, then obviously no transformation is necessary. If not, it's essential to understand the relationships between the techniques and

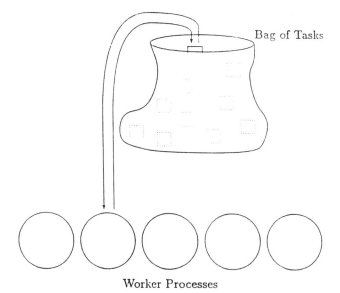

Bag of Tasks

Worker Processes

Figure 5. A distributed-data-structure version. At each iteration, workers repeatedly pull a task out of a distributed bag and compute the corresponding body's new position, referring to a distributed table for information on the previous position of each body. After each computation, a worker might update the table (without erasing information on previous positions, which may still be needed) or might send newly computed data to a master process, which updates the table in a single sweep at the end of each iteration.

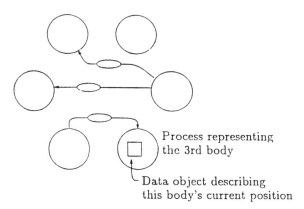

Process representing
the 3rd body

Data object describing
this body's current position

Figure 6. The message-passing version. Whereas the live-data-structure program creates nq processes (q was the number of iterations, and there are n bodies) and the distributed-data-structure program creates any number of workers it chooses, this message-passing program creates exactly n processes, one for each body. In each of the other two versions, processes refer to *global data structures* when they need information on the previous positions of each body. (In the live-data-structure version, this global data structure was the "live" structure in which the processes themselves were embedded.) But in the message-passing version, no process has access to any data object external to itself. Processes keep each other informed by sending messages back and forth.

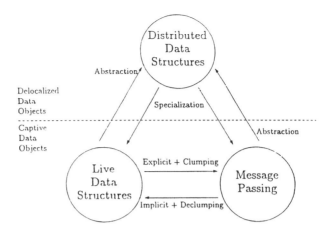

Figure 7. The game of parallelism.

the performance implications of each. After describing the relationships in general, we discuss one case of this transformation-for-efficiency in some detail.

1.5.1 The Relationships

The main relationships are shown in Figure 7. Both live data structures and message passing center on *captive data objects*: Every data object is permanently associated with some process. Distributed-data-structure techniques center on *delocalized* data objects, objects not associated with any one process, freely floating about on their own. We can transform a live-data-structure or a message-passing program into a distributed structure program by using *abstraction*: We cut the data objects free of their associated processes and put them in a distributed data structure instead. Processes are no longer required to fix their attention on a single object or group of objects; they can range freely. To move from a distributed structure to a live-data-structure or a message-passing program, we use *specialization*: We take each object and bind it to some process.

It is clear from the foregoing that live data structures and message passing are strongly related, but there are also some important differences. To move from the former to the latter, we need to make communication *explicit*, and we may optionally use *clumping*. A process in a live-data-structure program has no need to commu-

nicate information explicitly to any other process. It merely terminates, yielding a value. In a message-passing program, a process with data to convey must execute an explicit "send-message" operation. When a live-data-structure process requires a data value from some other process, it references a data structure; a message-passing process will be required to execute an explicit "receive-message" operation.

Why contemplate a move from live data structures to message passing, if the latter technique is merely a verbose version of the former? It isn't; message-passing techniques offer an added degree of freedom, which is available via "clumping." A process in a live-data-structure program develops a value and then dies. It can't live on to develop and publish another value. In message passing, a process can develop as many values as it chooses and disseminate them in messages whenever it likes. It can develop a whole series of values during a program's lifetime. Hence, clumping: We may be able to let a single message-passing process do the work of a whole collection of live-data-structure processes.

Table 1 summarizes the relationships in a different way. It presents an approximate and general characterization of the three classes. There are counterexamples in every category, but it's useful to summarize the spectrum of process and program types, from the large number of simple, tightly coordinated processes that usually occur in result parallelism, through

Table 1. Rough Characterization of the Three Classes

Complexity of processes

	Skills	Tasks	
Result	One	One	Simpler
Specialist	One	Many	
Agenda	Many	Many	More complex

Program structure

	Number of processes	Coordination
Result	High	Tight
Specialist	Moderate	Moderate
Agenda	Adjustable	Loose

the typically smaller collection of more complex, more loosely coupled processes in agenda parallelism.

1.5.2 Using Abstraction and Then Specialization to Transform a Live-Data-Structure Program

Having described some transformations in the abstract, what good are they? We can walk many paths through the simple network in Figure 7, and we can't describe them all in detail. We take up one significant case, describing the procedure in general and presenting an example; we close the section with a brief examination of another interesting case.

Suppose we have a problem that seems most naturally handled using result parallelism. We write the appropriate live-data-structure program, but it performs poorly, so we need to apply some transformations.

First, why discuss this particular case? When the problem is suitable, a live-data-structure program is likely to be rather easy to design and concise to express. It's likely to have a great deal of parallelism (with the precise degree depending, obviously, on the size of the result structure and the dependencies among elements). But it may also run poorly on most current-generation parallel machines, because the live-data-structure approach tends to produce *fine-grained* programs—programs that create a large number of processes each one of which does relatively little computing. Concretely, if our resulting data structure is, say, a ten-thousand-element matrix, this approach

will implicitly create ten thousand processes. There is no reason in theory why this kind of program·cannot be supported efficiently, but on most current parallel computers, there are substantial overheads associated with creating and coordinating large numbers of processes. This is particularly true on distributed-memory machines, but even on shared-memory machines that support lightweight processes, the potential gain from parallelism can be overwhelmed by huge numbers of processes, each performing a trivial computation.

If a live-data-structure program performs well, we're finished; if it does not, a more efficient program is easily produced by *abstracting* to a distributed data-structure version of the same algorithm. We replace the live data structure with a passive one and raise the processes one level in the conceptual scheme: Each process *fills in* many elements, rather than *becoming* a single element. We might create one hundred processes and have each process compute one hundred elements of the result. The resulting program is coarser grained then the original—the programmer decides how many processes to create and can choose a reasonable number. We avoid the overhead associated with huge numbers of processes.

This second version of the program may still not be efficient enough, however. It requires that each process read and write a single data structure, which must be stored in some form of logically shared memory. Accesses to a shared memory will be more expensive than access to local structures.

64

Ordinarily this isn't a problem; distributed data-structure programs can be supported efficiently even on distributed-memory (e.g., hypercube) machines. But, for some communication-intensive applications, and particularly on distributed-memory machines, we may need to go further in order to produce an efficient program. We might produce a maximally efficient third version of the program by using *specialization* to move from distributed data structures to message passing. We break the distributed data structure into chunks and hand each chunk to the process with greatest interest in that chunk. Instead of a shared distributed data structure, we now have a collection of local data structures, each encapsulated within and only accessible to a single process. When some process needs access to a "foreign chunk," a part of the data structure that it doesn't hold locally, it must send a message to the process that does hold the interesting chunk, asking that an update be performed or a data value returned. This is a nuisance and usually results in an ugly program, but it eliminates direct references to any shared data structures.

Under this scheme of things, we can see a neat and well-defined relationship among our three programming methods. We start with an elegant and easily discovered but potentially inefficient solution using live data structures, move on via abstraction to a more efficient distributed-data-structure solution, and finally end up via specialization at a low-overhead message-passing program. (We might alternatively have gone directly from live data structures to message passing via clumping.)

There is nothing inevitable about this procedure. In many cases, it's either inappropriate or unnecessary. It is inappropriate if live data structures are *not* a natural starting point. It is unnecessary if a live-data-structure program runs well from the start. It is partially unnecessary if abstraction leads to a distributed-data-structure program that runs well; in this case, there's nothing to be gained by performing the final transformation, and something to be lost (because the message-passing program will probably be sub-

stantially more complicated than the distributed-data-structure version). It's also true that message-passing programs are not always more efficient than distributed-data-structure versions; often they are, but there are cases in which distributed data structures are the optimal approach.

1.5.3 An Example

For example, returning to the n-body simulator, we discussed a live-data-structure version; we also developed distributed-data-structure and message-passing versions, independently. We could have used the live-data-structure version as a basis for abstraction and specialization as well.

Our live-data-structure program created $n \times q$ processes, each of which computed a single invocation of *position* and then terminated. We can create a distributed-data-structure program by *abstraction*. M is now a distributed data structure—a passive structure, directly accessible to all processes in the program. Its zeroth column holds the initial position of each body; the rest of the matrix is blank. We create k processes and put each in charge of filling in one band of the matrix. Each band is filled in column-by-column. In filling in the jth column, processes refer to the position values recorded in the $j-1$st column. We now have a program in which number of processes is under direct programmer control; we can run the program with two or three processes if this seems reasonable (as it might if we have only two or three processors available). We have achieved lower process-management overheads, but the new program was easy to develop from the original and will probably be only slightly less concise and comprehensible.

Finally, we can use *specialization* to produce a minimal-overhead message-passing program. Each process is given one band of M to store in its own local variable space; M no longer exists as a single structure. Since processes can no longer refer directly to the position values computed on the last iteration, these values must be disseminated in messages. At the end of each iteration, processes exchange messages; messages hold the positions computed by each process on the last iteration. We have now achieved low process-management overhead and also eliminated the overhead of referring to a shared distributed data structure. But the cost is considerable: The code for this last version will be substantially more complicated and messier than the previous one, because each process will need to conclude each iteration with a message-exchange operation in which messages are sent, other messages are received, and local tables are updated. We have also crossed an important conceptual threshold: Communication in the first two solutions was conceived in terms of *references to data structures*, a technique that is basic to all programming. But the last version relies on message passing for communication, thus substituting a new kind of operation that is conceptually in a different class from standard programming techniques.

1.5.4 When to Abstract and Specialize

How do we know whether we need to use abstraction or to move onward to a message-passing program? The decision is strictly pragmatic; it depends on the application, the programming system, and the parallel machine. Consider one concrete datum: Using C-Linda on current parallel machines, specialization leading to a message-passing program is rarely necessary. Most problems have distributed-data-structure solutions that perform well. In this context, though, abstraction to a distributed-data-structure program usually *is* necessary to get an efficient program.

1.5.5 Another Path through the Network: Abstraction from Message Passing

When live-data-structure solutions are natural, they may involve too many processes and too much overhead, so we use abstraction to get a distributed-data-structure program. It's also possible for a message-passing, network-style program to be natural, but to involve too many processes and too much interprocess communication, in which case we can use abstraction, again, to move from *message passing* to distributed data structures. Sup-

pose, for example, that we want to simulate a ten-thousand-element circuit. It is natural to envision one process for each circuit element, with processes exchanging messages to simulate the propagation of signals between circuit elements. But this might lead to a high-overhead program that runs poorly. Abstraction, again, allows us to create fewer processes and put each in charge of one segment of a distributed data structure that represents the network state as a whole.

In sum, there are many paths that a programmer might choose to walk though the state diagram shown in Figure 7. But the game itself is simple: Start at whatever point is most natural, write a program, understand its performance, and then, if necessary, follow the "efficiency" edges until you reach an acceptable stopping place.

1.6 Where Are the Basic Techniques Supported?

Although it is our intention in this article to survey programming techniques, not programming systems, a brief guide to the languages and systems in which the basic techniques occur may be helpful.

Message passing is by far the most widespread of the basic models; it occurs in many different guises and linguistic contexts. The best-known of message-passing languages is Hoare's influential fragment CSP [Hoare 1978], which inspired a complete language called Occam [May 1983]. CSP and Occam are based on a radically tight-knit kind of message passing: Both the sending and the receiving of a message are *synchronous* operations. In both languages, a process with a message to send blocks until the designated receiver has taken delivery. CSP and Occam are *static* languages as well: They do not allow new processes to be created dynamically as a program executes. CSP and Occam are for these reasons not expressive enough to support the full range of message-passing-type programs we discuss here.

Monitor and remote-procedure-call languages and systems are another subtype within the message-passing category (with a qualification we note below). In these systems, communication is modeled on procedure call: One process communicates with another by invoking a procedure defined within some other process or within a passive, globally accessible module. This kind of quasi-procedure call amounts to a specialized form of message passing: Arguments to the procedure are shipped out in one message, results duly returned in another. The qualification mentioned above is that, in certain cases, systems of this sort are used for quasi-distributed-data-structure programs. A global data object can be encapsulated in a module and then manipulated by remotely invoked procedures. (The same kind of thing is possible in any message-passing system, but is more convenient given a procedure-style communication interface.) Why *quasi*-distributed data structures? As we understand the term, a distributed data structure is directly accessible to many parallel processes *simultaneously*. (Clearly we may sometimes need to enforce sequential access to avoid corrupting data, but in general, many read operations may go forward simultaneously—and many write operations that affect separate and independent parts of the same structure may also proceed simultaneously, for example, many independent writes to separate elements of a single matrix.) Languages in this class support data objects that are global to many processes, but in general, they allow processes one-at-a-time access only. Nor do they support plain distributed data objects; a global object must be packaged with a set of access procedures.

Monitors were first described by Hoare [1974] and have been used as a basis for many concurrent programming languages, for example Concurrent Pascal [Brinch Hansen 1975], Mesa [Lampson and Redell 1980] and Modula [Wirth 1977]. (A *concurrent* language, unlike a parallel language, assumes that multiple processes inhabit the same address space.) Fairly recently they have been revived for use in parallel programming, in the form of parallel object-oriented programming languages (e.g., Emerald [Jul et al. 88]). A form of remote procedure call underlies Ada [U.S. Department of Defense 1982]; Birrell and Nelson's RPC kernel [Birrell

and Nelson 1984] is an efficient systems-level implementation.

Another variant of message passing centers on the use of *streams*: Senders (in effect) append messages to the end of a message stream, and receivers inspect the stream's head. This form of communication was first proposed by Kahn [1974] and forms the basis for communication in most concurrent logic languages (e.g., Concurrent Prolog [Shapiro 1987] and Parlog [Ringwood 1988]) and in functional language extended with constructs for explicit communication (e.g., [Henderson 1982]).

Message passing of one form or another appears as a communication method in many operating systems—for example, the V kernel [Cheriton and Zwaenpoel 1985], Mach [Young et al. 1987] and Amoeba [Mullender and Tanenbaum 1986].

Distributed data structures are less frequently encountered. The term was introduced in the context of Linda [Carriero et al. 1986]. Distributed data structures form the de facto basis of a number of specialized FORTRAN that revolve around parallel do-loops, for example, Jordan's Force system [Jordan 1986]. In this kind of system, parallelism is created mainly by specifying parallel loops—loops in which iterations are executed simultaneously instead of sequentially. Separate loop iterations communicate through distributed structures that are adaptations of standard FORTRAN structures. Distributed data structures are central in Dally's CST [Dally 1988] and Bal and Tanenbaum's Orca [Bal and Tanenbaum 1987], and are supported in MultiLISP [Halstead 1985] as well.

Live data structures are a central technique in several languages that support so-called nonstrict data structures—data structures that can be accessed before they are fully defined. Id Nouveau [Nikhil et al. 1986], MultiLISP [Halstead 1985], and Symmetric LISP [Gelernter et al. 1987] are examples. This same idea forms the implicit conceptual basis for the large class of functional languages intended for parallel programming (e.g., ParAlfl [Hudak 1986], Sisal [Lee et al. 1988] and Crystal [Chen 1986]). Programs in these languages consist of a series of equations specifying values to be bound to a series of names. One equation may depend on the values returned by other equations in the set; we can solve all equations simultaneously, subject to the operational restriction that an equation referring to a not-yet-computed value cannot proceed until this value is available. The equivalent program in live-data-structure terms would use each equation to specify the value of one element in a live data structure.

2. PROGRAMMING TECHNIQUES FOR PARALLELISM

We have discussed conceptual classes and general methods. We turn now to the practical question: How do we build working parallel programs? In this section we sketch implementations of the pieces out of which parallel programs are constructed.

We start with a systematic investigation of distributed data structures. We give an overview of the most important kinds of distributed structures, when each is used, and how each is implemented. This first part of the discussion should equip readers with a reasonable tool kit for building distributed-data-structure programs. Of course we intend to discuss all three programming methods, but the other two are easily derived from a knowledge of distributed data structures, as we discuss in the following sections. We arrive at message passing by restricting ourselves to a small and specialized class of distributed structures. We arrive at live data structures by building distributed structures out of processes instead of passive data objects.

2.1 Linda

Linda consists of a few simple operations that embody the "tuple-space" model of parallel programming. A base language with the addition of these tuple-space operations yields a parallel-programming dialect. To write parallel programs, programmers must be able to create and coordinate multiple execution threads. Linda is a model of process creation and coordination that is *orthogonal* to the base language in which it is embedded. The Linda model

doesn't care *how* the multiple execution threads in a Linda program compute what they compute; it deals only with how these execution threads (which it sees as so many black boxes) are created and how they can be organized into a coherent program. The following paragraphs give a basic introduction. Linda is discussed in greater detail and contrasted with a series of other approaches in Carriero and Gelernter [1989].

The Linda model is a *memory* model. Linda memory (called *tuple space* or *TS*) consists of a collection of logical tuples. There are two kinds of tuples: Process tuples are under active evaluation; data tuples are passive. The process tuples (which are all executing simultaneously) exchange data by generating, reading, and consuming data tuples. A process tuple that is finished executing turns into a data tuple, indistinguishable from other data tuples.

There are four basic TS operations, **out**, **in**, **rd**, and **eval**, and two variant forms, **inp** and **rdp**. **out**(t) causes tuple t to be added to TS; the executing process continues immediately. **in**(s) causes some tuple t that matches template s to be withdrawn from TS; the values of the actuals in t are assigned to the formals in s, and the executing process continues. If no matching t is available when **in**(s) executes, the executing process suspends until one is, then proceeds as before. If many matching t's are available, one is chosen arbitrarily. **rd**(s) is the same as **in**(s), with actuals assigned to formals as before, except that the matched tuple remains in TS. Predicate versions of **in** and **rd**, **inp** and **rdp**, attempt to locate a matching tuple and return 0 if they fail; otherwise, they return 1 and perform actual-to-formal assignment as described above. (If and only if it can be shown that, irrespective of relative process speeds, a matching tuple must have been added to TS before the execution of **inp** or **rdp** and cannot have been withdrawn by any other process until the **inp** or **rdp** is complete, the predicate operations are *guaranteed* to find a matching tuple.) **eval**(t) is the same as **out**(t), except that t is evaluated after rather than before it enters TS; **eval** implicitly forks a new process to perform the evaluation. When computation of t is complete, t becomes an ordinary passive tuple, which may be **in**ed or read like any other tuple.

A tuple exists independently of the process that created it, and in fact many tuples may exist independently of many creators and may collectively form a data structure in TS. It's convenient to build data structures out of tuples because tuples are referenced associatively, somewhat like the tuples in a relational database. A tuple is a series of typed fields, for example, (**"a string"**, **15.01**, **17**, **"another string"**) or (**0, 1**). Executing the **out** statements

out("a string", 15.01, 17, "another string")

and

out(0, 1)

causes these tuples to be generated and added to TS. (The process executing **out** continues immediately.) An **in** or **rd** statement specifies a template for matching: Any values included in the **in** or **rd** must be matched identically; formal parameters must be matched by values of the same type. (It is also possible for formals to appear in tuples, in which case a matching **in** or **rd** must have a type-consonant value in the corresponding position.) Consider the following statement:

in("a string", ? f, ? i, "another string")

Executing this statement causes a search of TS for tuples of four elements, first element **"a string"** and last element **"another string"**, middle two elements of the same types as variables f and i respectively. When a matching tuple is found, it is removed, the value of its second field is assigned to f and its third field to i. The read statement, for example,

rd("a string", ? f, ? i, "another string")

works in the same way, except that the matched tuple is not removed. The values of its middle two fields are assigned to f and i as before, but the tuple remains in TS.

A tuple created using **eval** resolves into an ordinary data tuple. Consider the following statement:

eval("e", 7, exp(7)).

It creates a three-element "live tuple" and continues immediately; the live tuple sets to work computing the values of the string "e", the integer 7, and the function call **exp(7)**. The first two computations are trivial (they yield "e" and 7); the third ultimately yields the value of e to the seventh power. Expressions that appear as arguments to **eval** inherit bindings from the environment of the **eval**-executing process for whatever names they cite explicitly and for read-only globals initialized at compile time. Thus, executing **eval("Q", f(x, y))** implicitly creates a new process and evaluates **"Q"** and **f(x, y)** in a context in which the names **f, y,** and **x** have the same values they had in the environment of the process that executed **eval**. The names of any variables that happen to be free in **f**, on the other hand, were *not* cited explicitly by the **eval** statement, and no bindings are inherited for them.[7] The statement

rd("e", 7, ? value))

might be used to read the tuple generated by this **eval**, once the live tuple has resolved to a passive data tuple—that is, once the necessary computing has been accomplished. (Executed before this point, it blocks until the active computation has resolved into a passive tuple.)

2.2 The Basic Distributed Data Structures

We can divide conventional "undistributed" data structures into three categories: (1) structures whose elements are identical or indistinguishable, (2) structures whose elements are distinguished by name, and (3) structures whose elements are distinguished by position. It's useful to subdivide the last category: (3a) structures whose elements are "random accessed" by position

---

[7] Future versions of the system may disallow the inheritance by eval-created processes of read-only globals. There are simple transformations from programs that rely on this feature to ones that do not.

and (3b) structures whose elements are accessed under some ordering.

In the world of sequential programming, category (1) is unimportant. A *set* of identical or indistinguishable elements qualifies for inclusion, but such objects are rare in sequential programming. Category (2) includes records, objects instantiated from class definitions, sets and multisets with distinguishable elements, associative memories, Prolog-style assertion collections, and other related objects. Category (3a) consists mainly of arrays and other structures stored in arrays, and category (3b) includes lists, trees, graphs, and so on. Obviously the groupings are not disjoint, and there are structures that can claim membership in several.

The distributed versions of these structures don't always play the same roles as their sequential analogs. Factors with no conventional analogs can furthermore play a major role in building distributed structures. *Synchronization* concerns arising from the fact that a distributed structure is accessible to many asynchronous processes simultaneously form the most important example. Notwithstanding, every conventional category has a distributed analog.

2.2.1 Structures with Identical or Indistinguishable Elements

The most basic of distributed data structures is a lock or semaphore. In Linda, a counting semaphore is precisely a collection of identical elements. To execute a V on a semaphore **"sem"**,

out("sem");

to execute a P,

in("sem").

To initialize the semaphore's value to n, execute **out("sem")** n times. Semaphores aren't used heavily in most parallel applications (as opposed to most concurrent systems), but they do arise occasionally; we elaborate in the next section.

A *bag* is a data structure that defines two operations: "add an element" and "withdraw an element." The elements in this case need not be identical, but are treated in a way that makes them indistinguishable. Bags are unimportant in sequential programming, but extremely important to parallel programming. The simplest kind of replicated-worker program depends on a bag of tasks. Tasks are added to the bag using

out("task", TaskDescription)

and withdrawn using

in("task", ? NewTask)

A simple example: consider a program that needs to apply some test to every element of a large file. (In one experiment we've done, the large file holds DNA sequences, and the test is "compare each sequence to a designated target sequence"; we need to discover which sequences in a database are "closest" under a string-matching-like algorithm to some designated sequence.) The program consists of a master and workers; the task is "compare the target sequence to sequence s." To withdraw a sequence from the bag, workers execute

in("sequence", ? seq)

The master reads sequences from the file and adds them to the bag (using a low-watermark algorithm to ensure that the bag doesn't overfill [Carriero and Gelernter 1988]); to add a sequence, it executes

out("sequence", seq)

Note that we can regard the set of all **("sequence", value)** tuples as a bag of indistinguishable 2-tuples; alternatively, we can say that "sequence" is the name of a bag of **values** and that **out("sequence", seq)** means "add **seq** to the bag called **"sequence"**."

Consider an example with some of the attributes of each of the two previous cases. Suppose we want to turn a conventional loop, for example

for (⟨loop control⟩)
    ⟨something⟩

into a parallel loop—all instances of *something* execute simultaneously. This construct is popular in parallel FORTRAN variants. One simple way to do the transformation has two steps: First we define a function **something( )** that executes one instance of the loop body and returns, say, 1. Then we rewrite as follows:

for (⟨loop control⟩)
  eval("this loop", something( ));
for (⟨loop control⟩)
  in("this loop", 1);

We have, first, created *n* processes; each is an active tuple that will resolve, when the function call **something( )** terminates, to a passive tuple of the form **("this loop", 1)**. Second, we collect the *n* passive result tuples. These *n* may be regarded as a bag or, equivalently, as a single counting semaphore that is V'ed implicitly by each process as it terminates. A trivial modification to this example would permit each iteration to "return" a result.

2.2.2 Name-Accessed Structures

Parallel applications often require access to a collection of related elements distinguished by name. Such a collection resembles a Pascal record or a C "struct." We can store each element in a tuple of the form

(name, value)

To read such a "record field," processes use **rd(name, ? val)**; to update it,

in(name, ? old);
out(name, new).

Consider, for example, a program that acts as a real-time expert monitor: Given a mass of incoming data, the system will post notices when significant state changes occur; it must also respond to user-initiated queries respecting any aspect of the current state. One software architecture for such systems is the so-called "process lattice": a hierarchical ensemble of concurrent processes, with processes at the bottom level wired directly to external sensors, and processes at higher levels responsible for increasingly more complex or abstract states. The model defines a simple internal information-flow protocol, with data flowing up and queries downward, and each node directly accessible at the user interface. Our prototype deals with hemodynamic monitoring in intensive care units [Carriero and Gelernter 1988]. Each process records its current state in a named tuple, whence it can be consulted directly by any interested party. The process that implements the "hypovolemia" decision procedure, for example, can update its state as follows:

in("hypovolemia", ? old)
out("hypovolemia", new).

Any process interested in hypovolemia can read the state directly. These state-describing tuples can thus be collectively regarded as a kind of distributed record, whose elements can be separately updated and consulted.

As always, the synchronization characteristics of distributed structures distinguish them from conventional counterparts. Any process attempting to read the hypovolemia field while this field is being updated will block until the update is complete and the tuple is reinstated. Processes occasionally need to wait until some event occurs; Linda's associative matching makes this convenient to program. For example, some parallel applications rely on "barrier synchronization": Each process within some group must wait at a barrier until all processes in the group have reached the barrier; then all can proceed. If the group contains *n* processes, we set up a barrier called **barrier-37** by executing

out("barrier-37", n)

Upon reaching the barrier point, each process in the group executes (under one simple implementation)

in("barrier-37", ? val);
out("barrier-37", val-1);
rd("barrier-37", 0).

That is, each process decrements the value of the field called **barrier-37** and then waits until its value becomes 0.

2.2.3 Position-Accessed Structures

Distributed arrays are central to parallel applications in many contexts. They can be programmed as tuples of the form (*Array name, index fields, value*). Thus, (**"V", 14, 123.5**) holds the 14th element of vector *V*, (**"A", 12, 18, 5, 123.5**) holds one element of the three-dimensional array *A*, and so forth. For example, one way to multiply matrices *A* and *B*, yielding *C*, is to store *A* and *B* as a collection of rectangular blocks, one block per tuple, and to define a task as the computation of one block of the product matrix. Thus, *A* is stored in TS as a series of tuples of the form

("A", 1, 1, ⟨first block of A⟩)
("A", 1, 2, ⟨second block of A⟩)

and *B* likewise. Worker processes repeatedly consult and update a *next-task* tuple, which steps though the product array pointing to the next block to be computed. If some worker's task at some point is to compute the *i, j*th block of the product, it reads all the blocks in *A*'s *i*th row band and *B*'s *j*th column band, using a statement like

for (next=0; next < ColBlocks;
   next++)
  rd("A", i, next, ? RowBand[next])

for *A* and similarly for *B*; then, using **RowBand** and **ColBand**, it computes the elements of *C*'s *i, j*th block and concludes the task step by executing the

out("C", i, j, Product)

Thus, **"C"** is a distributed array as well, constructed in parallel by the worker processes and stored as a series of tuples of the form

("C", 1, 1, ⟨first block of C⟩)
("C", 1, 2, ⟨second block of C⟩).

It's worth commenting at this point on the obvious fact that a programmer who builds this kind of matrix-multiplication program is dealing with two separate schemes for representing data: the standard array structures of the base language and a tuple-based array representation. It would be simple in theory to demote the tuple-based representation to the level of assembler language generated by the compiler: Let the compiler decide which arrays are accessed by concurrent processes and must therefore be stored in TS; then have the compiler generate the appropriate Linda statements. Not hard to do—but would this be desirable?

We tend to think not. First, there are distributed data structures with no conventional analogs, as we have noted; a semaphore is the simplest example. It follows that parallel programmers will not be able to rely exclusively on conventional forms and will need to master some new structures regardless of the compiler. But it's also the case that the dichotomy between *local memory* and *all other memory* is emerging as a fundamental attribute (arguably *the* fundamental attribute) of parallel computers. Evidence suggests that programmers cannot hope to get good performance on parallel machines without grasping this dichotomy and allowing their programs to reflect it. This is an obvious point when applied to parallel architectures without physically shared memory. Processors in such a machine have much faster access to data in their local memories than to data in another processor's local memory—nonlocal data are accessible only via the network and the communication software. But hierarchical memory is also a feature of shared-memory architectures. Thus, we note an observation like the following, which deals with the BBN Butterfly shared-memory multiprocessor:

Although the Uniform System [a BBN-supplied parallel programming environment] provides the illusion of shared memory, attempts to use it as such do not work well. Uniform System programs that have been optimized invariably block-copy their operands into local memory, do their computation locally, and block-copy out their results. . . . This being the case, it might be wise to optimize later-generation machines for very high bandwidth transfers of large blocks of data rather than single-word reads and writes as in the current Butterfly. We might end up with a computational model similar to that of LINDA . . . , with naming and locking subsumed by the operating system and the LINDA **in**, **read** and **out** primitives implemented by very high speed block transfer hardware. [Olson 1986]

Because the dichotomy between local and nonlocal storage appears to be fundamental to parallel programming, programmers should (we believe) have a high-level, language-based model for dealing with nonlocal memory. TS provides such a model.

Returning to position-accessed distributed data structures, synchronization properties can again be significant. Consider a program to compute all primes between 1 and n (we examine several versions of this program in detail in the last section). One approach requires the construction of a distributed table containing all primes known so far. The table can be stored in tuples of the following form:

("primes", 1, 2)
("primes", 2, 3)
("primes", 3, 5)
. . .

A worker process may need the values of all primes up to some maximum; it reads upward through the table, using **rd** statements, until it has the values it needs. It may be the case, though, that certain values are still missing. If all table entries through the kth are needed, but currently the table stops at j for $j < k$, the statement

rd("primes", j + 1, ? val)

blocks—there is still no j + 1st element in the table. Eventually the j + 1st element will be computed, the called-for tuple will be generated, and the blocked **rd** statement will be unblocked. Processes that read past the end of the table will simply pause, in other words, until the table is extended.

Ordered or linked structures make up the second class of position-accessed data structures. It's possible to build arbitrary structures of this sort in TS; instead of linking components by address, we link by logical name. If C, for example, is a *cons* cell linking A and B, we can represent it as

the tuple

("C", "cons", cell),

where **cell** is the two-element array **["A", "B"]**. If **"A"** is an atom, we might have

("A", "atom", value).

For example, consider a program that processes queries based on Boolean combinations of keywords over a large database. One way to process a complex query is to build a parse tree representing the keyword expression to be applied to the database; each node applies a subtransformation to a stream of database records produced by its inferiors—a node might and together two sorted streams, for example. All nodes run concurrently. A Linda program to accomplish this might involve workers executing a series of tasks that are in effect linked into a tree; the tuple that records each task includes "left," "right," and "parent" fields that act as pointers to other tasks [Narem 1988]. Graph structures in TS arise as well; for example, a simple shortest-path program [Gelernter et al. 1985] stores the graph to be examined one node per tuple. Each node-tuple has three fields: the name of the node, an array of neighbor nodes (Linda supports variable-sized arrays in tuples), and an array of neighbor edge-lengths.

These linked structures have been fairly peripheral in our programming experiments to date. But there *is* one class of ordered structure that is central to many of the methods we have explored, namely streams of various kinds. There are two major varieties, which we call in-streams and read-streams. In both cases, the stream is an ordered sequence of elements to which arbitrarily many processes may append. In the in-stream case, each one of arbitrarily many processes may, at any time, remove the stream's head element. If many processes try to remove an element simultaneously, access to the stream is serialized arbitrarily at run time. A process that tries to remove from an empty stream blocks until the stream becomes nonempty. In the read-stream case, arbitrarily many processes read the stream simultaneously: Each reading process reads the stream's first element, then its second element, and so on. Reading processes block, again, if the stream is empty.

In- and read-streams are easy to build in Linda. In both cases, the stream itself consists of a numbered series of tuples:

("strm", 1, val1)
("strm", 2, val2)
. . .

The index of the last element is kept in a tail tuple:

("strm", "tail", 14)

To append **NewElt** to **"strm"**, processes use the following:

in("strm", "tail", ? index);
  /* consult tail pointer */
out("strm", "tail", index+1);
out("strm", index, NewElt);
  /* add element */

An in-stream needs a head tuple also, to store the index of the head value (i.e., the next value to be removed); to remove from the in-stream **"strm"**, processes use

in("strm", "head", ? index);
  /* consult head pointer */
out("strm", "head", index+1);
in("strm", index, ? Elt);
  /* remove element */.

Note that, when the stream is empty, blocked processes will continue in the order in which they blocked. If the first process to block awaits the jth tuple, the next blocked process will be waiting for the $j + 1$st, and so on.

A read-stream dispenses with the head tuple. Each process reading a read-stream maintains its own local index; to read each element of the stream, we use

index = 1;
⟨loop⟩ {
    rd("strm", index++, ? Elt);
    . . .
  }

As a specialization, when an in-stream is consumed by only a single process, we can again dispense with the head tuple and allow the consumer to maintain a local index. Similarly, when a stream is appended-to by only a single process, we can dispense with the tail tuple, and the producer can maintain a local index.

In practice, various specializations of in- and read-streams seem to appear more often than the fully general versions.

Consider, for example, an in-stream with a single consumer and many producers. Such a stream occurs in one version of the prime-finding program we discuss: Worker processes generate a stream each of whose elements is a block of primes; a master process removes each element of the stream, filling in a primes table as it goes.

Consider an in-stream with one producer and many consumers. In a traveling-salesman program,[8] worker processes expand subtrees within the general search tree, but these tasks are to be performed not in random order but in a particular optimized sequence. A master process writes an in-stream of tasks; worker processes repeatedly remove and perform the head task. (This structure functions, in other words, as a distributed queue.)

Consider a read-stream with one producer and many consumers. In an LU-decomposition program [Bjornson et al. 1988], each worker on each iteration reduces some collection of columns against a pivot value. A master process writes a stream of pivot values; each worker reads the stream.

2.3 Message Passing and Live Data Structures

We can write a message-passing program by sharply restricting the distributed data structures we use: In general, a message-passing program makes use only of streams. The tightly synchronized message-passing protocols in CSP, Occam and related languages represent an even more drastic restriction: Programs in these languages use

---

[8] Written by Henri Bal of the Vrije Universiteit in Amsterdam.

no distributed structures; they rely only (in effect) on isolated tuples.

It's simple, then, to write a message-passing program. First, we use **eval** to create one process for each node in the logical network we intend to model. Often we know the structure of the network beforehand; the first thing the program does, then, is to create all the processes it requires. (Concretely, C-Linda programs have an **lmain** function that corresponds to **main** in a C program. When the program starts, **lmain** is invoked automatically. If we need to use **eval** to create n processes immediately, the **eval** statements appear in **lmain**.) In some cases the shape of a logical network changes while a program executes; we can use **eval** to create new processes as the program runs. Having created the processes we need, we allow processes to communicate by writing and reading message streams.

Live-data-structure programs are also easy to write given the passive distributed structures we've discussed. Any distributed data structure has a live as well as a passive version. To get the live version, we simply use **eval** instead of **out** in creating tuples. For example, we've discussed streams of various kinds. Suppose we need a stream of processes instead of passive data objects. If we execute a series of statement of the form

eval("live stream", i, f(i)),

we create a group of processes in TS:

("live stream", 1,
$\quad\quad\quad\quad\langle$**computation of f(1)**$\rangle$)
("live stream", 2,
$\quad\quad\quad\quad\langle$**computation of f(2)**$\rangle$)
("live stream", 3,
$\quad\quad\quad\quad\langle$**computation of f(3)**$\rangle$)
. . .

If **f** is, say, the function "factorial," then this group of processes resolves into the following stream of passive tuples:

("live stream", 1, 1)
("live stream", 2, 2)
("live stream", 3, 6)
. . .

To write a live-data-structure program, then, we use **eval** to create one process for each element in our live structure. (Again, **lmain** will execute the appropriate **evals**.) Each process executes a function whose value may be defined in terms of other elements in the live structure. We can use ordinary **rd** or **in** statements to refer to the elements of such a data structure. If **rd** or **in** tries to find a tuple that is still under active computation, it blocks until computation is complete. Thus, a process that executes

rd("live stream", 1, ? x)

blocks until computation of **f(1)** is complete, whereupon it finds the tuple it is looking for and continues.

3. PUTTING THE DETAILS TOGETHER

Finding all primes between 1 and n is a good example problem for two reasons: (1) It's not significant in itself, but there are significant problems that are similar; at the same time, primes finding is simple enough to allow us to investigate the entire program in a series of cases. (2) The problem can be approached naturally under several of our conceptual classes. This gives us an opportunity to consider what is natural and what isn't natural, and how different sorts of solution can be expressed.

3.1 Result Parallelism and Live Data Structures

One way to approach the problem is by using result parallelism. We can define the result as an n-element vector; j's entry is 1 if j is prime, and otherwise 0. It's easy to see how we can define entry j in terms of previous entries: j is prime if and only if there is no previous prime less than or equal to the square root of j that divides it.

To write a C-Linda program using this approach, we need to build a vector in TS; each element of the vector will be defined by the invocation of an **is_prime** function. The loop

for(i = 2; i < LIMIT; ++i) {
$\quad$**eval("primes", i, is_prime(i));**
}

creates such a vector. As discussed in Section 2.2.3, each tuple-element of the vector is labeled with its index. We can now read the jth element of the vector by using

rd("primes", j, ? ok).

The program is almost complete. The **is_prime(SomeIndex)** function will involve reading each element of the distributed vector through the square root of i and, if the corresponding element is prime and divides i, returning zero;[9] thus,

limit = sqrt((double) SomeIndex) + 1;

for (i = 2; i < limit; ++i) {
  rd("primes", i, ? ok);
  if (ok && (SomeIndex%i == 0))
    return 0;
}
return 1;

The only remaining problem is producing output. Suppose that the program is intended to print all primes **1** through **LIMIT**. Easily done: We simply read the distributed vector and print i if i's entry is **1**:

for(i = 2; i <= LIMIT; ++i) {
  rd("primes", i, ? ok);
  if (ok) printf("%d\n", i);
}

The complete program[10] is shown in Figure 8.

3.2 Using Abstraction to Get an Efficient Version

This program is concise and elegant, and was easy to develop. It derives parallelism from the fact that, once we know whether k is prime, we can determine the primality of all numbers from $k + 1$ through k^2. But it is potentially highly inefficient: It creates large numbers of processes and requires relatively little work of each. We can

---

[9] In practice, it might be cheaper for the ith process to compute all primes less than root of i itself, instead of reading them via **rd**. But we are not interested in efficiency at this stage.

[10] Users of earlier versions of C-Linda will note that, although formals used to be addresses, for example, "**? &ok**," C-Linda 2.0 assumes that formals will be variables, on analogy with the left side of assignment statements. The code examples use the new version.

```
lmain()
{
  int    i, ok;

  for(i = 2; i < LIMIT; ++i) {
    eval("primes", i, is_prime(i));
  }

  for(i = 2; i <= LIMIT; ++i) {
    rd("primes", i, ? ok);
    if (ok) printf("%d\n", i);
  }
}

is_prime(me)
    int        me;
{
  int        i, limit, ok;
  double     sqrt();

  limit = sqrt((double) me) + 1;

  for (i = 2; i < limit; ++i) {
    rd("primes", i, ? ok);
    if (ok && (me%i == 0)) return 0;
  }
  return 1;
}
```

Figure 8. Prime finder: Result parallelism.

use abstraction to produce a more efficient, agenda-parallel version. We reason as follows:

(1) Instead of building a live vector in TS, we can use a passive vector and create worker processes. Each worker chooses some block of vector elements and fills in the entire block. "Determine all primes from 2001 through 4000" is a typical task.

Tasks should be assigned in order: The lowest block is assigned first, then the next-lowest block, and so forth. If we have filled in the bottom block and the highest prime it contains is k, we can compute in parallel all blocks up to the block containing k^2.

How do we assign tasks in order? We could build a distributed queue of task assignments, but there is an easier way. All tasks are identical in kind; they differ only in starting point. So we can use a single tuple as a next-task pointer, as we discuss in the matrix-multiplication example in Section 2.2.3. Idle workers withdraw the next-task tuple, increment it, and then reinsert it, so the next idle worker will be assigned the next block of integers to examine. In outline, each worker will execute the following:

```
while(1) {
   in("next task", ? start);
   out("next task", start + GRAIN);

   〈find all primes from start to start +
      GRAIN〉

}
```

GRAIN is the size of each block. The value of **GRAIN**, which is a programmer-defined constant over each run, determines the granularity or task size of the computation. The actual code is more involved than this: Workers check for the termination condition and leave a marker value in the next-task tuple when they find it. (See the code in Figures 9 and 10 for details.)

(2) We have accomplished "abstraction," and we could stop here. But, since the goal is to produce an efficient program, there is another obvious optimization. Instead of storing a distributed bit vector with one entry for each number within the range to be searched, we could store a distributed *table* in which all primes are recorded. The *i*th entry of the table records the *i*th prime number. The table has many fewer entries than the bit vector and is therefore cheaper both in space and in access time. (To read all primes up to the square root of j will require a number of accesses proportional not to $\sqrt{j}$, but to the number of primes through $\sqrt{j}$.)

A worker examining some arbitrary block of integers doesn't know *a priori* how many primes have been found so far and therefore cannot construct table entries for new primes without additional information. We could keep a primes count in TS, but it's also reasonable to allow a master process to construct the table.

We will therefore have workers send their newly discovered batches of primes to the master process; the master process builds the table. Workers attach batches of primes to the end of an in-stream, which in turn is scanned by the master. Instead of numbering the stream using a sequence of integers, they can number stream elements using the starting integer of the interval they have just examined. Thus, the stream takes the following form:

```
("result", start, FirstBatch);
("result", start+GRAIN,
      SecondBatch);
("result", start+(2*GRAIN)
      ThirdBatch);
. . .
```

The master scans the stream by executing the following loop:

```
for (num = first_num; num < LIMIT;
      num += GRAIN) {
   in("result", num, ? new_primes);

   〈record the new batch for eventual
      output〉;

   〈construct the distributed primes
      table〉;

}.
```

This loop dismantles the stream in order, **in**ing the first element and assigning it to the variable **new_primes**, then the second element, and so on.

The master's job is now to record the results and to build the distributed primes table. The workers send prime numbers in batches; the master disassembles the batches and inserts each prime number into the distributed table. The table itself is a standard distributed array of the kind discussed previously. Each entry takes the form:

```
("primes", i, 〈ith prime〉,
                  〈ith prime squared〉).
```

We store the square of the *i*th prime along with the prime itself so that workers can simply read, rather than having to compute, each entry's square as they scan upward through the table. For details, see Figure 10.

(3) Again, we could have stopped at this point, but a final optimization suggests it-

```
#include "linda.h"

#define GRAIN 2000
#define LIMIT 1000000
#define NUM_INIT_PRIME  15

long primes[LIMIT/10+1] =
  {2,3, 5, 7, 11, 13, 17, 19, 23, 29, 31,  37,  41, 43,  47};
long p2[LIMIT/10+1] =
  {4,9,25,49,121,169,289,361,529,841,961,1369, 1681,1849,2209};

lmain(argc, argv)
     int argc;
     char *argv[];
{
  int eot, first_num, i, num, num_primes, num_workers;
  long new_primes[GRAIN], np2;

  num_workers = atoi(argv[1]);
  for (i = 0; i < num_workers; ++i)
    eval("worker", worker());

  num_primes = NUM_INIT_PRIME;
  first_num = primes[num_primes-1] + 2;

  out("next task", first_num);

  eot = 0;  /* becomes 1 at "end of table" -- i.e., table complete */
  for (num = first_num; num < LIMIT; num += GRAIN) {
    in("result", num, ? new_primes: size);

    for (i = 0; i < size; ++i, ++num_primes) {
      primes[num_primes] = new_primes[i];

      if (!eot) {
                np2 = new_primes[i]*new_primes[i];
                if (np2 > LIMIT) {
                        eot = 1;
                        np2 = -1;
                }
      out("primes", num_primes, new_primes[i], np2);
      }
    }
  }
  /*  " ? int" means  "match any int; throw out the value" */
  for (i = 0; i < num_workers; ++i) in("worker", ? int);

  printf("%d: %d\n", num_primes, primes[num_primes-1]);
}
```

Figure 9. Prime finder (master): Agenda parallelism.

```
worker()
{
  long count, eot, i, limit, num, num_primes, ok, start;
  long my_primes[GRAIN];

  num_primes = NUM_INIT_PRIME;

  eot = 0;
  while(1) {
    in("next task", ? num);
    if (num == -1) {
      out("next task", -1);
      return;
    }
    limit = num + GRAIN;
    out("next task", (limit > LIMIT) ? -1 : limit);
    if (limit > LIMIT) limit = LIMIT;

    start = num;
    for (count = 0; num < limit; num += 2) {
      while (!eot && num > p2[num_primes-1]) {
        rd("primes", num_primes, ? primes[num_primes], ? p2[num_primes]);
        if (p2[num_primes] < 0)
          eot = 1;
        else
          ++num_primes;
      }
      for (i = 1, ok = 1; i < num_primes; ++i) {
        if (!(num%primes[i])) {
          ok = 0;
          break;
        }
        if (num < p2[i]) break;
      }
      if (ok) {
        my_primes[count] = num;
        ++count;
      }
    }
    /* Send the control process any primes found. */
    out("result", start, my_primes: count);
  }
}
```

Figure 10. Prime finder (worker): Agenda parallelism.

self. Workers repeatedly grab task assignments and then set off to find all primes within their assigned interval. To test for the primality of k, they divide k by all primes through the square root of k; to find these primes, they refer to the distributed *primes* table. But they could save repeated references to the distributed global table by building local copies. Global references (references to objects in TS) are more expensive than local references.

Whenever a worker reads the global *primes* table, it will accordingly copy the data it finds into a local version of the table.

It now refers to the global table only when its local copy needs extending. This is an optimization similar in character to the *specialization* we described in Section 1: It saves global references by creating multiple local structures. It isn't "full specialization," though, because it doesn't eliminate the global data structure, merely economizes global references.

Workers store their local tables in two arrays of longs called **primes** and **p2** (the latter holds the square of each prime). Newly created workers inherit copies of these global arrays (declared above the master's code in Figure 9) when they are created. The notation **object: count** in a Linda operation means "the first **count** elements of the aggregate named **object**"; in an **in** or a **rd** statement, **? object: count** means that the size of the aggregate assigned to **object** should be returned in **count**.

3.3 Comments on the Agenda Version

This version of the program is substantially longer and more complicated than the original result-parallel version. On the other hand, it performs well in several widely different environments. On one processor of the shared-memory Sequent Symmetry, a sequential C program requires about 459 seconds to find all primes in the range of one to three million. Running with 12 workers and the master on 13 Symmetry processors, the C-Linda program in Figures 9 and 10 does the same job in about 43 seconds, for a speedup of about $10\frac{1}{2}$ relative to the sequential version, giving an efficiency of about 82 percent. One processor of an Intel iPSC-2 hypercube requires about 421 seconds to run the sequential C program; 1 master and 63 workers running on all 64 nodes of our machine require just under 8 seconds, for a speedup of about $52\frac{1}{2}$ and an efficiency of, again, roughly 82 percent.

If we take the same program and increase the interval to be searched in a task step by a factor of 10 (this requires a change to one line of code: We define **GRAIN** to be 20,000), the same code becomes a very coarse-grained program that can perform well on a local-area network. Running on eight Ethernet-connected IBM RTs under Unix,[11] we get roughly a 5.6-times speedup over sequential running time, for an efficiency of about 70 percent. Somewhat lower efficiencies on coarser-grained problems are still very satisfactory on local-area nets. Communication is far more expensive on a local-area net than in a parallel computer, and for this reason networks are problematic hosts for parallel programs. They are promising nonetheless because, under some circumstances, they can give us something for nothing: Many computing sites have compute-intensive problems, lack parallel computers, but have networks of occasionally underused or (on some shifts) idle workstations. Converting wasted workstation cycles into better performance on parallel programs is an attractive possibility.[12]

In comparing the agenda- to the result-parallel version, it's important to keep in mind that the more complicated and efficient program was produced by applying a series of simple transformations to the elegant original. So long as a programmer understands the basic facts in this domain—how to build live and passive distributed data structures, which operations are relatively expensive and which are cheap—the transformation process is conceptually uncomplicated and can stop at any point. In other words, programmers with the urge to polish and optimize (i.e., virtually all expert programmers) have the same kind of opportunities in parallel as in conventional programming.

Note that, for this problem, agenda parallelism is probably less natural than result parallelism. The point here is subtle, but is nonetheless worth making. The most natural agenda-parallel program for primes finding would probably have been conceived as follows: Apply T in parallel to all integers from 1 to *limit*, where T is simply "determine whether n is prime." If we understand these applications of T as completely independent, we have a program that will work and is highly parallel. It is

---

[11] Unix is a trademark of AT&T Bell Laboratories.

[12] The iPSC-2 system is largely the work of Robert Bjornson and the Unix LAN kernel of Mauricio Arango and Donald Berndt.

not an attractive solution, though, because it's blatantly wasteful: In determining whether j is prime, we can obviously make use of the fact that we know all previous primes through the square root of j.

The master–worker program we developed *on the basis of the result-parallel version* is more economical in approach, and we regard this version as a "made" rather than a "born" distributed-data-structure program.

3.4 Specialist Parallelism

Primes finding had a natural result-parallel solution, and we derived an agenda-parallel solution. There is a natural specialist-parallel solution as well.

The sieve of Eratosthenes is a simple prime-finding algorithm in which we imagine passing a stream of integers through a series of sieves: A 2-sieve removes multiples of 2, a 3-sieve likewise, then a 5-sieve, and so forth. An integer that has emerged successfully from the last sieve in the series is a new prime. It can be ensconced in its own sieve at the end of the line.

We can design a specialist-parallel program based on this algorithm. We imagine the program as a pipeline that lengthens as it executes. Each pipe segment implements one sieve (i.e., specializes in a single prime). The first pipe segment inputs a stream of integers and passes the residue (a stream of integers not divisible by 2) onto the next segment, which checks for multiples of 3 and so on. When the segment at the end of the pipeline finds a new prime, it extends the sieve by attaching a new segment to the end of the program.

One way to write this program is to start with a two-segment pipe. The first pipe segment generates a stream of integers; the last segment removes multiples of the last-known prime. When the last segment (the "sink") discovers a new greatest prime, it inserts a new pipe segment directly before itself in line. The newly inserted segment is given responsibility for sieving what had formerly been the greatest prime. The sink takes over responsibility for sieving the *new* greatest prime. Whenever a new prime is discovered, the process repeats.

First, how will integers be communicated between pipe segments? We can use a single-producer, single-consumer in-stream. Stream elements look like

("seg", ⟨destination⟩, ⟨stream index⟩, ⟨integer⟩).

Here, **destination** means "next pipe segment"; we can identify a pipe segment by the prime it is responsible for. Thus, a pipe segment that removes multiples of 3 expects a stream of the form

("seg", 3, ⟨stream index⟩, ⟨integer⟩).

How will we create new pipe segments? Clearly, the "sink" will use **eval**; when it creates a new segment, the sink detaches its own input stream and plugs this stream into the newly created segment. Output from the newly created segment becomes the sink's new input stream. The details are shown in Figure 11.

The code in Figure 11 produces as output merely a count of the primes discovered. It could easily have developed a table of primes and printed the table. There is a more interesting possibility as well. Each segment of the pipe is created using **eval**; hence, each segment turns into a passive tuple upon termination. Upon termination (which is signaled by sending a 0 through the pipe), we could have had each segment yield its prime. In other words, we could have had the program collapse upon termination into a data structure of the form:

("source", 1, 2)
("pipe seg", 2, 3)
("pipe seg", 3, 5)
("pipe seg", 4, 7)
. . .
("sink", MaxIndex, MaxPrime).

We could then have walked over and printed out this table.

This solution allows less parallelism than the previous one. To see why, consider the result-parallel algorithm: It allowed simultaneous checking of all primes between $k + 1$ and k^2 for each new prime k. Suppose there are p primes in this interval for some k. The previous algorithm allowed us to

```
lmain()
{
  eval("source", source());
  eval("sink", sink());
}
source()
{
  int   i, out_index = 0;

  for (i = 5; i < LIMIT; i += 2) out("seg", 3, out_index++, i);
  out("seg", 3, out_index, 0);
}
sink()
{
  int   in_index = 0, num, prime = 3, prime_count = 2;

  while(1) {
    in("seg", prime, in_index++, ? num);
    if (!num) break;
    if (num % prime) {
      ++prime_count;
      if (num*num < LIMIT) {
        eval("pipe seg", pipe_seg(prime, num, in_index));
        prime = num;
        in_index = 0;
      }
    }
  }
  printf("count: %d.\n", prime_count);
}
pipe_seg(prime, next, in_index)
    int        prime, next, in_index;
{
  int   num, out_index = 0;

  while(1) {
    in("seg", prime, in_index++, ? num);
    if (!num) {
      out("seg", next, out_index, num);
      return;
    }
    if (num % prime) out("seg", next, out_index++, num);
  }
}
```

Figure 11. Prime finder: Specialist parallelism.

discover all p simultaneously, but in this version they are discovered one at a time, the first prime after k causing the pipe to be extended by one stage, then the next prime, and so on. Because of the pipeline, "one at a time" means a rapid succession of discoveries; but the discoveries still occur sequentially.

The specialist-parallel solution is not quite as impractical as the result-parallel version, but it is impressively impractical nonetheless. Consider one data point: In searching the range from one to one thousand, the structure-parallel version is 30 times *slower* on an 18-processor Multimax than the sequential C program on a single processor. These results make an instructive demonstration of an important if largely *sub rosa* phenomenon in parallel programming. A parallel program is always costlier than a conventional, sequential version of the same algorithm: Creating and coordinating processes take time. Running an *efficient* parallel program on many processors allows us to recoup the overhead and come out ahead in absolute terms; thus, the master–worker primes-finding experiment demonstrates absolute speedup over a comparable sequential program. An *in*efficient parallel program may demonstrate impressive *relative* speedup—it may run faster on many processors than on one, which is true of the specialist-parallel program under discussion—without ever amortizing the "overhead of parallelization" and achieving *absolute* speedup. Readers should be alert to this point in assessing data on parallel programming experiments.

For this problem, our specialist-parallel approach is clearly impractical. Those are the breaks. But readers should keep in mind that exactly the same program structure *could* be practical if each process had more computing to do. In some related problem areas, this would be the case. Furthermore, the dynamic, fine-grained character of this program makes it an interesting but not altogether typical example of the message-passing *genre*. A static, coarse-grained message-passing program (e.g., of the sort we described in the context of the *n*-body problem) would be programmed using many of the same techniques, but would be far more efficient.

3.5 Simplicity

The prime-finding example raises a final interesting question. Our efficient parallel version is significantly more complicated than a conventional, sequential prime finder. Does parallelism mean that programming necessarily becomes a more complicated activity than it used to be?

It's clear that a "simple problem" in the sequential world is not necessarily still simple in the parallel world. But, to grasp the implications of this fact, we need to consider two others: Many problems that are "sequentially simple" are also simple in parallel, and some problems that are complex under sequential assumptions are *simpler* in parallel. Computing prime numbers efficiently is the kind of problem that, because of substantial interdependence among subtasks and the "sequential" nature of the underlying algorithm (larger primes are determined on the basis of smaller primes), is substantially trickier in parallel than it is sequentially.[13] Many of the most successful and widely used applications of parallelism, on the other hand, involve problems that are much simpler than this to parallelize, and in these cases the parallel codes are much closer to the sequential originals. These problems generally parallelize at a fairly coarse grain and require only limited intertask communication. They use exactly the same techniques we have developed here. They are less interesting as case studies, but often of great practical significance. A final category of application is simpler in parallel than it would be as a sequential program. The ICU monitor program discussed in Section 2.2.2 is a good example: It's most naturally expressed as an ensemble of concurrently active experts. This kind of application may sound esoteric, but it's our view that programs of this sort, programs involving large collections of heterogeneous experts communicating via a simple global protocol, will become increasingly widespread and significant.

What's the bottom line? It would be foolish to deny, when all is said and done, that parallelism *does* make programming a more complex skill to master. Expanding the range of choices makes any job harder; expanding the capabilities of a machine (whether a hardware or a software ma-

---

[13] As we discuss in [Carriero and Gelernter 1988], the problem was brought to our attention by a researcher who found it anything but simple to write an efficient parallel solution to a related primes-finding problem.

chine) often results in a more complicated design. (Compare a color to a black-and-white television, by way of analogy, or a modern workstation to a PDP-8.)

The parallel primes finder is a more complicated (software) machine than the sequential version, but it has acquired the new and valuable capacity to spread itself over a large collection of processors, where the sequential version can't cope with more than one. Good programmers will have no difficulty learning the new techniques involved, and once they do, they will have access to a new and powerful class of software machinery.

4. CONCLUSIONS

In the primes example, one approach is the obvious practical choice. But it is certainly *not* true that, having canvassed the field, we have picked the winner and identified the losers; that's not the point at all. The performance figures quoted above depend on the Linda system and the parallel machine we used. Most important, they depend on the character of the primes problem. We lack space to analyze more than one problem in this way. The fact is, though, that in almost every case that we have considered, an efficient parallel solution exists. Agenda-parallel algorithms programmed under the master–worker model are often but not always the best stopping point; all three methods can be important in developing a good program. Discovering a workable solution may require some work and diligence on the programmer's part, but no magic and nothing different in kind from the sketch-and-refine effort that is typical of all serious programming. All that is required is that the programmer understand the basic methods at his disposal and have a programming language that allows him to say what he wants.

We expect technology to move in a direction that makes finer-grained programming styles more efficient. This is a welcome direction for several reasons: Fine-grained solutions are often simpler and more elegant than coarser-grained approaches, as

we've discussed; larger parallel machines, with thousands of nodes and more, will in some cases require finer-grained programs if they are to keep all their processors busy. But the coarser-grained techniques are virtually guaranteed to remain significant as well. For one thing, they will be important when parallel applications run on loosely coupled nodes over local- or wide-area networks. (Whiteside and Leichter have recently shown that a Linda system running on 14 VAXes over a local-area network can, in one significant case at least, beat a Cray [Whiteside and Leichter 1988]. This Cray-beating Linda application is in production use at SANDIA.) Coarser-grained techniques will continue to be important on "conventional" parallel computers as well, so long as programmers are required or inclined to find maximally efficient versions of their programs.

Attempting an initial survey of a new, rapidly changing field is a difficult proposition. We don't claim that our categorization is definitive. We've left some issues out and swept others under the rug. We do think that this survey is a reasonable starting point, both for researchers intent on a better understanding of the field as a whole and for programmers with a parallel machine and some compute-intensive applications at hand. The evidence is clear: Parallelism can lead to major gains in performance; parallel programming is a technique that any good programmer can master. In short, as Portnoy's analyst so aptly put it [Roth 1985], *Now vee may perhaps to begin. Yes?*

ACKNOWLEDGMENTS

Thanks to the Linda group at Yale and particularly to its senior members—Robert Bjornson, Venkatesh Krishnaswamy, and Jerrold Leichter—for vital contributions to the research on which this paper is based. Thanks to the referees and to Professor Peter Wegner in particular for useful guidance. Thanks to Professor Martin Schultz for his indispensable support for our work and for the entire systems research effort at Yale. Thanks finally to the National Science Foundation and to the Office of Naval Research, who made the work possible, and above all to Dr. Richard Lau of ONR, a good example of the rarest and most valuable species in computer science, the funding visionary.

REFERENCES

ASHCRAFT, C., CARRIERO, N., AND GELERNTER, D. 1989. Is explicit parallelism natural? Hybrid DB search and sparse LDL^T factorization using Linda. Res. Rep. 744, Dept. of Computer Science, Yale Univ., New Haven, Conn., Jan.

BAL, H. E., AND TANENBAUM, A. S. 1987. Orca: A language for distributed object-based programming. Internal Rep. 140, Dept. Wiskunde en Informatica, Vrije Universiteit, Amsterdam, Dec.

BIRRELL, A. D., AND NELSON, B. J. 1984. Implementing remote procedure calls. *ACM Trans. Comput. Syst. 2*, 1 (Feb.), 39–59.

BJORNSON, R., CARRIERO, N., AND GELERNTER, D. 1989. The implementation and performance of hypercube Linda. Res. Rep. 690, Dept. of Computer Science, Yale Univ., New Haven, Conn., Mar.

BJORNSON, R., CARRIERO, N., GELERNTER, D., AND LEICHTER, J. 1988. Linda, the portable parallel. Res. Rep. 520, Dept. of Computer Science, Yale Univ., New Haven, Conn., Jan.

BORRMAN, L., HERDIECKERHOFF, M., AND KLEIN, A. 1988. Tuple space integrated into Modula-2, Implementation of the Linda concept on a hierarchical multiprocessor. In *Proceedings of CONPAR '88*, Jesshope and Reinartz, Eds. Cambridge Univ. Press, New York.

BRINCH HANSEN, P. 1975. The programming language Concurrent Pascal. *IEEE Trans. Softw. Eng. SE-1*, 2, 199–206.

CARRIERO, N., AND GELERNTER, D. 1988. Applications experience with Linda. In *Proceedings of the ACM Symposium on Parallel Programming* (New Haven, July). ACM, New York, pp. 173–187.

CARRIERO, N., AND GELERNTER, D. 1989. Linda in context. *Commun. ACM 32*, 4 (Apr.), 444–458.

CARRIERO, N., GELERNTER, D., AND LEICHTER, J. 1986. Distributed data structures in Linda. In *Proceedings of the ACM Symposium on Principles of Programming Languages* (St. Petersburg, Jan.). ACM, New York.

CHEN, M. C. 1986. A parallel language and its compilation to multiprocessor architectures or VLSI. In *Proceedings of the ACM Symposium on Principles of Programming Languages* (St. Petersburg, Jan.). ACM, New York.

CHERITON, D. R., AND ZWAENPOEL, W. 1985. Distributed process groups in the V Kernel. *ACM Trans. Comput. Syst. 3*, 2 (May), 77–107.

DALLY, W. J. 1988. Object-oriented concurrent programming in CST. In *Proceedings of the 3rd Conference on Hypercube Concurrent Computers and Applications*. (Pasadena, Jan, 1988) JPL/Caltech, p. 33.

DEPARTMENT OF DEFENSE, U.S. 1982. *Reference Manual for the Ada Programming Language.* ACM AdaTEC, July.

GELERNTER, D. 1989. Information management in Linda. In M. Reeve and S. E. Zenith, eds., *Parallel processing and artificial intelligence*, J. Wiley (1989):/23–34, *Proceedings of AI and Communicating Process Architectures* (London, July).

GELERNTER, D., JAGGANATHAN, S., AND LONDON, T. 1987. Environments as first class objects. In *Proceedings of the ACM Symposium on Principles of Programming Languages* (Munich, Jan.). ACM, New York.

GELERNTER, D., CARRIERO, N., CHANDRAN, S., AND CHANG, S. 1985. Parallel programming in Linda. In *Proceedings of the International Conference on Parallel Processing* (St. Charles, Ill., Aug.). IEEE, 255–263.

GILMORE, P. 1979. Massive Parallel Processor (MPP):/Phase One Final Report. Tech. Rep. GER-16684, Goodyear Aerospace Co., Akron.

GREENGARD, L., AND ROKHLIN, V. 1987. A fast algorithm for particle simulations. *J. Comput. Phys. 73*, 2 (Dec.), 325–348.

HALSTEAD, R. 1985. Multilisp: A language for concurrent symbolic computation. *ACM Trans. Program. Lang. Syst. 7*, 4 (Oct.), 501–538.

HENDERSON, P. 1982. Purely functional operating systems. In *Functional Programming and Its Applications*, J. Darlington, P. Henderson, and D. A. Turner, Eds. Cambridge Univ. Press, New York, pp. 177–192.

HILLIS, W. D., AND STEELE, G. L. 1986. Data parallel algorithms. *Commun. ACM 29*, 12 (Dec.), 1170–1183.

HOARE, C. A. R. 1974. Monitors: An operating system structuring concept. *Commun. ACM 17*, 10 (Oct.), 549–557.

HOARE, C. A. R. 1978. Communicating sequential processes. *Commun. ACM 21*, 11 (Aug.), 666–677.

HUDAK, P. 1986. Parafunctional programming. *Computer 19*, 8 (Aug.), 60–70

JORDAN, H. F. 1986. Structuring parallel algorithms in an MIMD, shared memory environment. *Parallel Comput. 3*, 93–110.

JUL, E., LEVY, H., HUTCHINSON, N., AND BLACK, A. 1988. Fine-grained mobility in the Emerald system. *ACM Trans. Comput. Syst. 6*, 1 (Feb.), 109–133.

KAHN, G. 1974. The semantics of a simple language for parallel processing. In *Proceedings of the IFIP Congress 74*. North Holland, 471.

LAMPSON, B. W., AND REDELL, D. D. 1980. Experience with processes and monitors in Mesa. *Commun. ACM 23*, 2 (Feb.), 105–117.

LEE, C. C., SKEDZIELEWSKI, S., AND FEO, J. 1988. On the implementation of applicative languages on shared-memory, MIMD multiprocessors. In *Proceedings of the ACM/SIGPLAN Symposium on Parallel Programming* (New Haven, Aug.). ACM, New York.

LELER, W. 1989. PIX, the latest NEWS. In *Proceedings of COMPCON Spring '89* (San Francisco, Feb.). IEEE.

MARSLAND, T. A., AND CAMPBELL, M. 1982. Parallel search of strongly ordered game trees. *ACM Comput. Surv. 14*, 4 (Dec.), 533–552.

MATSUOKA, S., AND KAWAI, S. 1988. Using tuple space communication in distributed object-oriented languages. In *Proceedings of OOPSLA '88* (San Diego, Sept. 25–30), 276–284.

MAY, M. D. 1983. Occam. *SIGPLAN Not.* (ACM) *18*, 4 (April), 69–79.

MULLENDER, S. J., AND TANENBAUM, A. S. 1986. The design of a capability-based distributed operating system. *Comput. J. 29*, 4 (Mar.), 289–300.

MUSGRAVE, F. K., AND MANDELBROT, B. B. 1989. Natura ex machina. *IEEE Comput. Graph. Appl. 9*, 1 (Jan.), 4–7.

NAREM, J. E. 1988. DB: A parallel news database in Linda. Tech. memo, Dept. of Computer Science, Yale Univ., New Haven, Conn., Aug.

NIKHIL, R., PINGALI, K., AND ARVIND. 1986. Id Nouveau. Memo 265, Computation Structures Group, MIT, Cambridge, Mass.

OLSON, T. J. 1986. Finding lines with the Hough Transform on the BBN Butterfly parallel processor. Butterfly Proj. Rep. 10, Dept. of Comput. Science, Univ. of Rochester, New York, Sept.

RINGWOOD, G. A. 1988. Parlog86 and the dining logicians. *Commun. ACM 31*, 1 (Jan.), 10–25.

ROTH, P. 1985. *Portnoy's Complaint*. Fawcett Crest, p. 309 (first published by Random House, New York 1967).

SEITZ, C. 1985. The cosmic cube. *Commun. ACM 28*, 1 (1985), 22–33.

SHAPIRO, E., ED. 1987. *Concurrent Prolog Collected Papers*. Vols. 1 and 2. MIT Press, New York.

WHITESIDE, R. A., AND LEICHTER, J. S. 1988. Using Linda for supercomputing on a local area network. In *Proceedings of Supercomputing*, (Orlando, Fla., Nov.), 192–199.

WIRTH, N. 1977. Modula: A language for modular multiprogramming. *Softw. Pract. Exp. 7*, 3–35.

XU, A. S. 1988. A fault-tolerant network kernel for Linda. Tech. Rep. MIT/LCS/TR-424, Laboratory for Computer Science, MIT, Cambridge, Mass., Aug.

YOUNG, M., ET AL. 1987. The duality of memory and communication in the implementation of a multiprocessor operating system. In *Proceedings of the 11th ACM Symposium on Operating Systems Principles* (Austin, Tex., Nov.). ACM, New York, pp. 63–76.

Received May 1988; final revision accepted April 1989.

Chapter 3:
Distributed-Memory Paradigms

A parallel program in a distributed-memory parallel computer (*multicomputer*) is composed of several processes that cooperate by message passing. The processes might be executed on different processing elements of the multicomputer. In such an environment, a high-level distributed concurrent programming language offers an abstraction level in which resources are defined like abstract data types encapsulated into cooperating processes. This abstraction reflects the model of distributed-memory architectures composed of a set of processors connected by a communication network.

This chapter discusses imperative languages for distributed programming. Other approaches, such as object-oriented languages, functional-programming languages, and concurrent logic languages, are discussed in the chapters that follow. Parallelism in imperative languages is generally expressed at the level of *processes* composed of a list of *statements*. A special case is the Occam language [MAY83], where each statement can be expressed as a process.

In the distributed-memory approach, a distributed concurrent program consists of a set of processes cooperating by message passing and located on one or many computers. In the implementation of typical distributed-programming techniques (for example, concurrent activities management, data and process replication, synchronization, and fault tolerance), a concurrent programming support isolates the techniques for distributed-software design from the underlying network architecture, communication protocols, and operating system.

The two major issues in designing distributed languages for parallel programming are related to process spawning and process cooperation.

1. *Process spawning.* In some languages, primitives are provided for explicit process creation during the parallel program execution (*dynamic creation*). In other languages, the total number of processes is defined at compile time (*static creation*).

   - *Dynamic creation.* For dynamic creation, constructs such as *fork/join*, *new*, and *create* have been defined. These constructs can be used to spawn an arbitrary number of concurrent processes.

   - *Static creation.* For static creation, constructs such as *parbegin*, *cobegin/coend*, and *par* have been defined. These constructs spawn a fixed number of processes. All processes are created at the program start and are activated as required during the program execution. This allows a strong check of the program to be performed at compile time but might limit the application areas of such languages.

Communicating Sequential Processes (CSP) and Occam are two examples of languages that do not allow dynamic creation of processes. On the other hand, Ada [MUN86], Concurrent C [GEH86], and Synchronizing Resources (SR) [AND88] provide constructs for dynamic process creation at any time during program execution.

1. *Process cooperation.* Several mechanisms have been designed to support the cooperation of concurrent processes that a parallel program comprises. These can be divided into three main classes: *explicit message passing*, *rendezvous communication*, and *remote procedure call (RPC)*.

   - *Explicit message passing.* Languages using explicit message-passing mechanisms define *send* and *receive* constructs for message exchanging. Some variants of explicit message passing have been designed. Message passing can be *synchronous* or *asynchronous*. In synchronous message passing, the sender process is blocked until the receiver has accepted the message. In asynchronous message passing; the sender continues its execution after sending the message. Also, explicit message passing can be *point-to-point* or *one-to-many*. In point-to-point communication, only two processes are involved. In one-to-many communication, many processes, or all the processes a parallel program comprises, can be involved. For example, Occam, the Network Implementation Language (NIL) [STR83], and Joyce [BRI87] are languages based on explicit message passing.

   - *Rendezvous communication.* In rendezvous communication, an interaction between two processes A and B takes place when A calls an *entry* of B and B executes an *accept* for that entry. An entry call is similar to a procedure call and an accept statement for the entry contains a list of statements to be executed when the entry is called. The best-known parallel-programming languages based on rendezvous cooperation are Ada [MUN86] and Concurrent C [GEH86].

   - *Remote procedure call (RPC).* The RPC mechanism is an extension of the traditional procedure call. An RPC is a procedure call between two different processes: the caller and the receiver. When a process calls a remote procedure on another process, the receiver executes the code of the procedure and passes the output parameters back to the caller. Like rendezvous, RPC is a synchronous cooperation form. During the execution of the procedure, the caller is blocked and is reactivated by the arrival of the output parameters. Full synchronization of RPC might limit the exploitation of a high degree of parallelism among the processes that a concurrent program comprises. In fact, when a process P calls a remote procedure r of a process T, the caller process P remains idle until the execution of r terminates, even if P could execute some other operation during the execution of r. To partially limit this effect, most new RPC-based systems use lightweight threads. Languages based on the RPC mechanism are Distributed Processes (DP) [BRI78], Cedar [SWI85], and Concurrent Cluster (Concurrent CLU) [COO88].

Another important issue in programming parallel computers is to ensure the correct *distributed termination* of processes that implement a concurrent program. If processes communicate with one another, stopping one could leave the others deadlocked rather than properly terminated. If processes do not communicate with one another, stopping one leaves the others still running. Notice that in a distributed system, processes communicate by exchanging messages, and there is no central controller to observe the state of all the processes and decide on global termination. Therefore, distributed termination must be implemented by the cooperation of all the processes that the concurrent program comprises. It must be decided whether a system of concurrent processes has already completed its execution. The detection of the termination of a distributed concurrent program is a nontrivial problem, and it is essential for program correctness. Some programming languages define statements for the explicit termination of processes and for the notification of termination of a process to that process' partners. If these statements are not available, a programmer of parallel applications must provide special code for the implementation of correct termination.

In the area of distributed-memory paradigms for parallel programming, the CSP model [HOA78] influenced the design of several other languages. According to this concurrent programming model, a program is regarded as a network of processes, each one with its local environment, that cooperate by means of explicit message passing. The main features of the CSP model are communication management by means of input and output commands and channels, the exploitation of parallelism by means of the parallel command, and nondeterminism management by means of guarded commands. Many variants of this language have been designed in the last decade. In particular, work by May [MAY83] produced the Occam language, a commercial parallel-programming language that is used to implement parallel programs in many application areas.

Many other distributed-memory-based languages have been defined. Several are new languages explicitly designed for parallel computing, while others are parallel extensions of sequential languages or toolkits that define a set of parallel constructs to be used on top of a sequential language. This chapter includes four papers that discuss four different approaches to the design of parallel languages based on the distributed-memory paradigm: Occam, High Performance Fortran (HPF), C*, and the Parallel Virtual Machine (PVM), respectively.

The first paper included in this chapter, "Communicating Process Architecture: Transputers and Occam," by May, Shepherd, and Keane, presents the Occam language. The Occam language is a message-passing concurrent language based on the CSP model. It has been under development at Inmos, Bristol, United Kingdom, since 1982. Occam programs are expressed in terms of concurrent processes, each one operating on its own variables and communicating through synchronous channels. Occam was designed for the Transputer in order to support the development of massively parallel programs. Even if Occam lacks some feature typical of modern languages, such as dynamic memory allocation, its simplicity leads to a simple and clean formal semantics that offers the possibility of a fully verified implementation. This paper discusses the language constructs and other important issues, such as compile time allocation, program development, and configuration. Finally, some programming examples, such as searching and systolic array algorithms, are sketched.

This chapter's second paper, "High Performance Fortran," by Loveman, discusses the High Performance Fortran (HPF) programming model. HPF is the result of an industry/academia/user effort to define a de facto consensus on language extensions of Fortran-90 for improving data locality, especially for distributed-memory parallel computers. HPF is a language for programming computationally intensive scientific applications. A programmer writes the program in HPF using the single-program, multiple-data (SPMD) style and provides information about desired data locality or distribution by annotating the code with data-mapping directives. The program is compiled by an architecture-specific compiler. The compiler generates the appropriate code, optimized for the selected architecture. This paper describes Fortran-90, its implications for parallel machines, and the HPF extensions in terms of parallel constructs and directives.

The third paper included in this chapter, "Data-Parallel Programming on Multicomputers," by Quinn and Hatcher, describes the C* data-parallel language. This language was designed by Thinking Machines Corporation, Cambridge, Massachusetts, to program the Connection Machine. However, it can be used to program several multicomputers using the data-parallel approach. C* is an extension of the C language that incorporates features of the single-instruction, multiple-data (SIMD) programming model. The language lets a programmer express algorithms as if data could be mapped onto an unbounded number of processors. The compiler automatically maps data onto processing elements. When data are mapped to their processing element, program constructs can be used to express parallel operations. This paper introduces the SIMD programming model and the language. Then, it presents an implementation of the C* language on an hypercube architecture and describes a compiler that translates C* programs into C programs. An example program in C* and its corresponding C code are listed and discussed.

The fourth paper included here is "Visualization and Debugging in a Heterogeneous Environment," by Beguelin et al. This paper describes the PVM environment and some experiences with visualization and debugging of PVM applications. The PVM system is gaining widespread acceptance as a methodology and toolkit for heterogeneous distributed computing. The PVM environment provides a set of primitives that can be incorporated into existing procedural languages in order to implement parallel programs. Problems of network delays and dynamically changing machine loads are important considerations in trying to debug or improve the performance of a PVM application. From a different perspective, certain types of monitoring information can aid in application debugging, particularly when appropriately transformed or augmented with code-specific information. This paper describes the Heterogeneous Network Computing Environment (HeNCE), a graphical interface that programs a heterogeneous network of computers built on PVM. The authors present several proposals for such visual displays, along with methods for debugging programs in a heterogeneous environment.

References cited

[AND88]   G.R. Andrews et al., "An Overview of the SR Language and Implementation," *ACM Trans. Programming Languages and Systems*, Vol. 10, No. 1, Jan. 1988, pp. 51–86.

[BRI78]   P. Brinch Hansen, "Distributed Processes: A Concurrent Programming Concept," *Comm. ACM*, Vol. 21, No. 11, Nov. 1978, pp. 934–941.

[BRI87]   P. Brinch Hansen, "Joyce—A Programming Language for Distributed Systems," *Software: Practice & Experience*, Vol. 17, No. 1, Jan. 1987, pp. 29–50.

[COO88]   R.C.B. Cooper and K.G. Hamilton, "Preserving Abstraction in Concurrent Programming," *IEEE Trans. Software Eng.*, Vol. 14, No. 2, Feb. 1988, pp. 258–263.

[GEH86]   H.H. Gehani and W.D. Roome, "Concurrent C," *Software: Practice & Experience*, Vol. 16, No. 9, Sept. 1986, pp. 821–844.

[HOA78]   C.A.R. Hoare, "Communicating Sequential Processes," *Comm. ACM*, Vol. 21, No. 8, Aug. 1978, pp. 666–677.

[MAY83]   D. May, "Occam," *ACM SIGPLAN Notices*, Vol. 18, No. 4, Apr. 1983, pp. 69–79.

[MUN86]   D.A. Mundie and D.A. Fisher, "Parallel Processing in Ada," *Computer*, Vol. 19, No. 8, Aug. 1986, pp. 20–25.

[STR83]   R. Strom et al., "NIL: An Integrated Language and System for Distributed Programming," *ACM SIGPLAN Notices, Proc. SIGPLAN '83 Symp. Programming Language Issues in Software Systems*, Vol. 18, No. 6, June 1983, pp. 73–82.

[SWI85]   D. Swinehart et al., "The Structure of Cedar," *ACM SIGPLAN Notices*, Vol. 20, No. 7, July 1985, pp. 230–244.

COMMUNICATING PROCESS ARCHITECTURE: TRANSPUTERS AND OCCAM

David May, Roger Shepherd, Catherine Keane
Inmos Limited

This chapter describes an approach to VLSI computer architecture based on communicating processes. Section one discusses the design of occam, a language intended for use in describing and programming concurrent systems. By careful choice of language primitives, occam allows a wide variety of implementation techniques including conventional sequential computers, networks of sequential computers, and dedicated concurrent hardware.

Section two explains how occam can be implemented efficiently by a programmable VLSI processing element known as the transputer. The transputer directly implements the concurrent processes of occam, using physical communication links to provide process communication between transputers, and using microcoded instructions to provide process scheduling and communication within a transputer. The transputer can be used as a building block for concurrent processing systems, with occam as the associated design formalism.

Section three discusses the construction of parallel computers from collections of transputers. A number of application-specific configurations used for compilers, computer graphics and animation, and statistical mechanics are described. Finally, the idea of a general purpose configuration is discussed.

Section four shows how communicating processes can be implemented directly on silicon. By use of a compiler which translates an occam program into a collection of dedicated processing elements, it is possible to design specialised VLSI systems rapidly. A system can be designed in occam, verified formally using the semantics of occam - or experimentally by execution on transputers - and finally compiled into correct silicon layout.

1   COMMUNICATING PROCESSES AND OCCAM

1.1   Introduction

The occam programming language [1.1] enables an application to be described as a collection of processes which operate concurrently and communicate through channels. In such a description, each occam process describes the behavior of one component of the implementation, and each channel describes a connection between components.

The design of occam allows the components and their connections to be implemented in many different ways. This allows the choice of implementation technique to be chosen to suit available technology, to optimise performance, or to minimise cost.

Occam has proved useful in many application areas. It can be efficiently implemented on almost any computer and is being used for many purposes - real time systems, compilers and editors, hardware specification and simulation.

1.2   Architecture

Many programming languages and algorithms depend on the existence of the uniformly accessible memory provided by a conventional computer. Within the computer, memory addressing is implemented by a global communications system, such as a bus. The major disadvantage of such an approach is that speed of operation is reduced as the system size increases. The reduction in speed arises both from the increased capacitance of the bus which slows down every bus cycle, and from bus contention.

The aim of occam is to remove this difficulty; to allow arbitrarily large systems to be expressed in terms of localised processing and communication. The effective use of concurrency requires new algorithms designed to exploit this locality.

The main design objective of occam was therefore to provide a language which could be directly implemented by a network of processing elements, and could directly express concurrent algorithms. In many respects, occam is intended as an assembly language for such systems; there is a one-one relationship between occam processes and processing elements, and between occam channels and links between processing elements.

1.3   Locality

Almost every operation performed by a process involves access to a variable, and so it is desirable to provide each processing element with local memory in the same VLSI device.

The speed of communication between electronic devices is optimised by the use of one directional signal wires, each connecting only two devices. This provides local communication between pairs of devices.

Occam can express the locality of processing, in that each process has local variables; it can express locality of communication in the each channel connects only two processes.

1.4   Simulated and Real concurrency

Many concurrent languages have been designed to provide simulated concurrency. This is not surprising, since until recently it has not been economically feasible to build systems with a lot of real concurrency.

Unfortunately, almost anything can be simulated by a sequential computer, and there is no guarantee that a language designed in this way will be relevant to the needs of systems with real concurrency. The choice of features in such languages has been motivated largely by the need to share one computer between many independant tasks. In contrast, the choice of features in occam has been motivated by the need to use many communicating computers to perform one single task.

An important objective in the design of occam was to use the same concurrrent programming techniques both for a single computer and for a network of computers. In practice, this meant that the choice of features in occam was partly determined by the need for an efficient distributed impementation. Once this had been achieved, only simple modifications were needed to ensure an efficient implementation of concurrency on a single sequential computer. This approach to the design of occam perhaps explains some of the differences between occam and other 'concurrent' languages.

1.5 The occam primitives

Occam programs are built from three primitive processes:

```
v := e    assign expression e to variable v
c ! e     output expression e to channel c
c ? v     input variable v from channel c
```

The primitive processes are combined to form constructs:

```
SEQ    sequence
IF     conditional

PAR    parallel
ALT    alternative
```

A construct is itself a process, and may be used as a component of another construct.

Conventional sequential programs can be expressed with variables and assignments, combined in sequential and conditional constructs. The order of expression evaluation is unimportant, as there are no side effects and operators always yield a value.

Conventional iterative programs can be written using a while loop. The absence of explicit transfers of control perhaps needs no justification in a modern programming language; in occam it also removes the need to prohibit, or define the effect of, transferring control out of a parallel component or procedure.

Concurrent programs make use of channels, inputs and outputs, combined using parallel and alternative constructs.

The definition and use of occam procedures follows ALGOL-like scope rules, with channel, variable and value parameters. The body of an occam procedure may be any process, sequential or parallel. To ensure that expression evaluation has no side effects and always terminates, occam does not include functions.

A very simple example of an occam program is the buffer process below.

```
WHILE TRUE
  VAR ch:
    SEQ
      in ? ch
      out ! ch
```

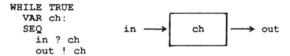

Indentation is used to indicate program structure. The buffer consists of an endless loop, first setting the variable **ch** to a value from the channel **in**, and then outputting the value of **ch** to the channel **out**. The variable ch is declared by **VAR ch**. The direct correspondance between the program text and the pictorial representation is important, as a picture of the processes (processors) and their connections is often a useful starting point in the design of an efficiently implementable concurrent algorithm.

1.6 The Parallel Construct

The components of a parallel construct may not share access to variables, and communicate only through channels. Each channel provides one way communication between two components; one component may only output to the channel and the other may only input from it. These rules are checked by the compiler.

The parallel construct specifies that the component processes are "executed together". This means that the primitive components may be interleaved in any order. More formally,

```
PAR              SEQ
  SEQ       =      x := e
    x := e         PAR
    P                P
  Q                  Q
```

so that the initial assignments of two concurrent processes may be executed in sequence until both processes start with an input or output. If one process starts with an input on channel **c**, and the other an output on the same channel **c**, communication takes place:

```
PAR                      SEQ
   SEQ          = \         x := e
      c ! e                 PAR
      P                        P
   SEQ                         Q
      c ? x
      Q
```

The above rule states that communication can be thought of as a distributed assignment.

Two examples of the parallel construct are shown below.

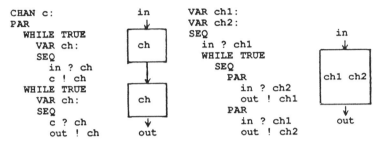

```
CHAN c:                  in          VAR ch1:
PAR                      ↓           VAR ch2:
   WHILE TRUE                        SEQ             in
      VAR ch:          ┌──────┐         in ? ch1     ↓
      SEQ             │  ch   │         WHILE TRUE
         in ? ch      └──────┘            SEQ      ┌──────┐
         c ! ch           │               PAR     │ ch1 ch2 │
   WHILE TRUE             ↓                  in ? ch2  └──────┘
      VAR ch:          ┌──────┐              out ! ch1    │
      SEQ             │  ch   │            PAR            ↓
         c ? ch        └──────┘              in ? ch1    out
         out ! ch         ↓                  out ! ch2
                         out
```

The first consists of two concurrent versions of the previous example, joined by a channel to form a "double buffer". The second is perhaps a more conventional version. As 'black boxes', each with an input and an output channel, the behavior of these two programs is identical; only their internals differ.

1.7   Synchronised communication

Synchronised, zero-buffered, communication greatly simplifies programming, and can be efficiently implemented. In fact, it corresponds directly to the conventions of self timed signalling[1.2]. Zero buffered communication eliminates the need for message buffers and queues. Synchronised communication prevents accidental loss of data arising from programming errors. In an unsynchronised scheme, failure to acknowledge data often results in a program which is sensitive to scheduling and timing effects.

Synchronised communication requires that a one process must wait for the other. However, a process which requires to continue processing whilst communicating can easily be written:

```
PAR
   c ! x
   P
```

1.8   The Alternative Construct

In occam programs, it is sometimes necessary for a process to input from any one of several other concurrent processes. This could have been provided this is by a channel 'test', which is true if the channel is ready, false otherwise. However, this is unsatisfactory because it requires a process to poll its inputs "busily"; in some (but by no means all) cases this is inefficient.

Consequently, occam includes an alternative construct similar to that of CSP [1.3]. As in CSP, each component of the alternative starts with a guard - an input, possibly accompanied by a boolean expression. From an implementation point of view, the alternative has the advantage that it can be implemented either "busily" by a channel test or by a "non-busy" scheme. The alternative enjoys a number of useful semantic properties more fully discussed in [1.4, 1.5]; in particular, the formal relationship between parallel and alternative is shown below:

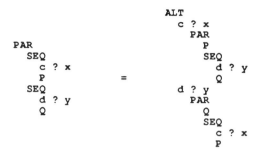

```
                                    ALT
                                      c  ?  x
                                      PAR
            PAR                         P
              SEQ                       SEQ
                c  ?  x                   d  ?  y
                P                         Q
              SEQ            =          d  ?  y
                d  ?  y                 PAR
                Q                         Q
                                        SEQ
                                          c  ?  x
                                          P
```

This equivalence states that if two concurrent processes are both ready to input (communicate) on different channels, then either input (communiation) may be performed first.

One feature of CSP omitted from occam is the automatic failure of a guard when the process connected to the other end of the channel terminates. Although this is a convenient programming feature, it complicates the channel communication protocol, introducing the need for further kinds of message. In addition, it can be argued that many programs are clearer if termination is expressed explicitly.

A simple example of the alternative is shown below; this is a 'stoppable' buffer program

```
WHILE going
  ALT
    in ? ch
      out ! ch
    stop ? ANY
      going := FALSE
```

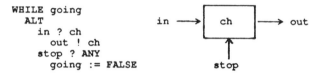

in which **stop ? ANY** inputs any value from the channel **stop**, and as a result causes the loop to terminate.

1.9   Output Guards

Output guards are a very convenient programming tool. In particular, they allow programs such as the following buffer process to be written in a natural way.

```
WHILE TRUE
  ALT
    count>0 & output ! buff [ outpointer ]
      SEQ
        outpointer := (outpointer + 1) REM max
        count := count - 1
    count<max & input ? buff [ inpointer ]
      SEQ
        inpointer := (inpointer + 1) REM max
        count := count + 1
```

It is very tempting to include output guards in a communicating process language, and attempts have been made to include output guards in occam. The major difficulty is in the distributed implementation; in a program such as

```
PAR
  ALT
    c ! x1
    d ? x2
  ALT
    c ? y1
    d ! y2
```

what is expected to happen in the event that two identical processors both enter their alternative at exactly the same time? Clearly some asymmetry must be introduced; the easiest way to do this is to give each processor in a system a unique number. Even so, the provision of output guards greatly complicates the communications protocol. For this reason, output guards are omitted from occam, and the above buffer must be written as shown below.

```
PAR
  WHILE TRUE
    ALT
      count>0 & req ? ANY
        SEQ
          reply ! buff [ outpointer ]
          outpointer := (outpointer + 1) REM max
          count := count - 1
      count<max & input ? buff [ inpointer ]
        SEQ
          inpointer := (inpointer + 1) REM max
          count := count + 1
  WHILE TRUE
    SEQ
      req ! ANY
      reply ? ch
      output ! ch
```

On the other hand, an occam implementation with only input guards can be used to write the communications kernel for a "higher level" version of occam with output guards. An example of an algorithm to implement output guards in CSP is given in [1.6]; and one for occam is given in [1.7].

1.10   Channels and hierarchical decomposition

An important feature of occam is the ability to successively decompose a process into concurrent component processes. This is the main reason for the use of named communication channels in occam. Once a named channel is established between two processes, neither process need have any knowledge of the internal details of the other. Indeed, the internal structure of each process can change during execution of the program.

The parallel construct, together with named channels provides for decomposition of an application into a hierarchy of communicating processes, enabling occam to be applied to large scale applications. This technique cannot be used in languages which use process (or 'entry') names, rather than channels, for communication.

In specifying the behavior of a process, it is important that a specification of the protocol used on the channel exists, and the best way to do this varies from program to program (or even from channel to channel!). For example, Backus-Naur Form is often suitable for describing the messages which pass between the individual processes of a linear pipeline of processes. On the other hand, for more complex interactions between processes, it is often useful to describe the interactions by an occam "program" in which all unnecessary features are omitted. This often enables the interactions between processes to be studied independently of the data values manipulated. For example:

```
SEQ
  request ?
  WHILE TRUE
    PAR
      reply !
      request ?
```

describes a process which inputs a request, and then endlessly inputs a new request and outputs a reply, in either order. Such a process would be compatible, in some sense, with any of the following processes:

```
WHILE TRUE          SEQ                 SEQ
  SEQ                 request !           request !
    request !         WHILE TRUE          WHILE TRUE
    reply ?             SEQ                 PAR
                          request !           request !
                          reply ?             reply ?
```

More design aids are needed to assist in the specification and checking of channel protocols.

1.11   Arrays and Replicators

The representation of arrays and 'for' loops in occam is unconventional. Although this has nothing to do with the concurrency features of occam, it seems to have significant advantages over alternative schemes.

To elimiate trivial programming errors, it is desirable that there is a simple relationship between an array declaration and a loop which performs some operation for every element of an array. This might lead a language designer to a choice of

ARRAY a [base TO limit] ...

FOR i IN [base TO limit] ...

It is also useful if the number of elements in an array, or the number of iterations of a loop, is easily visible. For this reason, a better choice might be

ARRAY a [base FOR count] ...

FOR i IN [base FOR count] ...

For the loop, this gives a further advantage: the 'empty' loop corresponds to **count=0** instead of limit<base. This removes the need for the unsatisfactory 'loop':

FOR i IN [0 TO -1]

Implementation can be simplified by insisting that all arrays start from 0. Finally, in occam the **FOR** loop is generalised, and its semantics simplified. An occam 'replicator' can be used with any of **SEQ**, **PAR**, **ALT** and **IF**; its meaning is defined by:

```
X n = b FOR c      =      X
  P (n)                     P (b)
                           P (b+1)
                           ...
                           P (b+c-1)
```

where **X** is one of **SEQ**, **PAR**, **ALT** and **IF**, **n** is a name and **b**, **c** expressions. This definition implicitly defines the 'control variable' **n**, and prevents it being changed by assignments within **P**.

The introduction of arrays of variables and channels does complicate the rules governing the correct use of channels and variables. Simple compile-time checks which are not too restrictive are:

> No array changed by assignment (to one of its components) in any of the components of a parallel may be used in any other component.

> No two components of a parallel may select channels from the same array using variable subscripts.

> A component of a parallel which uses an array for both input and output may not select channels from the array using variable subscripts.

where a variable subscript is a subscript which cannot be evaluated by the compiler.

1.12 Time

The treatment of time in occam directly matches the behavior of a conventional alarm clock.

Time itself is represented in occam by values which cycle through all possible integer values. Of course, it would have been possible to represent time by a value large enough (say 64 bits) to remove the cyclic behavior, but this requires the use of multiple length arithmetic to maintain the clock and is probably not justified.

Using an alarm clock, it is possible at any time to observe the current time, or to wait until the alarm goes off. Similary, a process must be able to read the clock at any time, or wait until a particular time. If it were possible only to read the clock, a program could only wait until a particular time "busily". Like the alternative construct, the "wait until a time" operation has the advantage that it can be implemented "busily" or "non-busily".

A timer is declared in the same way as a channel or variable. This gives rise to a relativistic concept of time, with different timers being used in different parts of a program. A localised timer is much easier to implement than a global timer.

A timer is read by a special 'input'

```
time ? v
```

which is always ready, and sets the variable **v** to the time. Similarly, the 'input'

```
time ? AFTER t
```

waits until time **t**.

The use of an absolute time in occam instead of a delay is to simplify the construction of programs such as

```
WHILE TRUE
  SEQ
    time ? AFTER t
    t := t + interval
    ouput ! bell
```

in which n rings of the bell will always take between **(n*interval)** and **n*(interval+1)** ticks. This would not be true of a program such as

```
WHILE TRUE
  SEQ
    DELAY interval
    ouput ! bell
```

because of the time taken to ring the bell.

It is not possible, in occam, for a process to implement a timer. This would require a 'timer output' such as

```
timer ! PLUS n
```

which advances the timer by **n** ticks. There is no obvious reason why this could not be included in occam. It would be particularly useful in constructing timers of different rates, or in writing a process to provide 'simulated time'.

1.13 Types and Data structures

The occam described so far makes few assumptions about data types. Any data type could be used - provided that values of that type can be assigned, input and output according to the rule

```
PAR
  c ! x      =      y := x
  c ? y
```

To preserve this rule, and keep the implementation of communication simple, it is best for assignment not to make type conversions.

The initial version of occam provides untyped variables and one dimensional arrays. No addressing operations are provided, as this would make it impossible for the compiler to check that variables are not shared between concurrent processes.

Occam has been extended to include data types. The simple variable is replaced with boolean, byte and integer types, and multi-dimensional arrays are provided. Communication and assignment operate on variables of any data type, allowing arrays to be communicated and assigned.

A detailed description can be found in [1.8].

1.14 Implementation of occam

The implementation of concurrent processes and process interaction in occam is straightforward. This results from the need to implement occam on the transputer using simple hardware and a small number of microcoded instructions. Conveniently, the transputer instructions used to implement occam can be used as definitions of the 'kernel primitives' in other implementations of occam. A discussion of the implementation of occam can be found in section 2. However, some measure of the efficiency of the occam primitives is provided by the performance of the Inmos transputer: about 1 microsecond/component of PAR, and 1.5 microseconds for a process communication.

Another interesting feature of occam is that the process interactions directly represent hardware mechanisms, which is one reason why occam is being used as a hardware description language.

1.15 Compile time allocation

For runtime efficiency, the advantages of allocating processors and memory at compile time are clear. To allow the compiler to allocate memory, some implementation restrictions are imposed. Firstly, the number of components of an array, and the number of concurrent processes created by a parallel replicator, must be known at compile time. Secondly, no recursive procedures are allowed. The effect of these restrictions is that the compiler can establish the amount of space needed for the execution of each component of a parallel construct, and this makes the run-time overhead of the parallel construct very small.

On the other hand, there is nothing in occam itself to prevent an implementation without these restrictions, and this would be fairly straightforward for a single computer with dynamic memory allocation.

A distributed implementation of 'recursive occam' might allow a tree of processors to be described by:

```
PROC tree (VALUE n, CHAN down, CHAN up)
  IF
    n=0
      leaf ( down, up )
    n>0
      CHAN left.down, left.up
      CHAN right.down, right.up
      PAR
        tree (n-1, left.down, left.up)
        tree (n-1, right.dowm, right.up)
        node ( down, up,
               left.down, left.up,
               right.down, right.up )
```

If the depth of the tree is known at compile time (as it normally would be if the program is to be executed on a fixed size processor array), the same effect can be achieved by a non-recursive program such as:

```
DEF p = TABLE [1, 2, 4, 8, 16, 32, 64, 128] :

-- depth of tree = n
CHAN down [n*(n-1)] :
CHAN up   [n*(n-1)] :

PAR
  PAR i = [0 FOR n - 1]
    PAR j = [0 FOR p[i]]
      branch ( down [p[i] + j], up [p[i] + j],
               down [p[i+1]+(j*2)], up [p[i+1]+(j*2)],
               down [p[i+1]+(j*2)+1], up [p[i+1]+(j*2)+1] )
  PAR i = [0 FOR p[n]]
    leaf ( down [p[n]+i], up [p[n]+i] )
```

Obviously, a pre-processor could be used to provide a correctness preserving transformation between these two programs.

If the depth of the tree above were not known, it is not clear how such a program could be mapped onto a processor array, either explicitly by the programmer or implicitly by the implementation. Fortunately, this problem can be left for the future; many applications require only simple compile time allocation of processors and memory space.

1.16   Program Development

The development of programs for multiple processor systems is not trivial. One problem is that the most effective configuration is not always clear until a substantial amount of work has been done. For this reason, it is very desirable that most of the design and programming can be completed before hardware construction is started.

This problem is greatly reduced by the property of occam mentioned above: the use of the same concurrent programming techniques for both a network and a single computer. A direct consequence of this is that a program ultimately intended for a network of computers can be compiled and executed efficiently by a single computer used for program development.

Another important property of occam in this context is that occam provides a clear notion of "logical behavior"; this relates to those aspects of a program not affected by real time effects. It is guaranteed that the logical behavior of a program is not altered by the way in which processes are mapped onto processors, or by the speed of processing and communication.

This notion of "logical behavior" results from the relatively abstract specification of parallel and alternative; it allows almost any scheduling system to be used to simulate concurrency. For the parallel construct, an implementation may choose the order in which the individual actions of the components are executed. If several components are ready (not waiting to communicate), the implementation may execute an arbitrary subset of them and temporarily ignore the rest. For the alternative, an implementation may select any ready component; there is no requirement to select the "earliest", or to select randomly.

1.17   Configuration

The configuration of a program to meet real time constraints is provided by annotations to the parallel and alternative constructs. For the parallel construct, the components may be placed on different processors, or may be prioritised. For the alternative construct, the components may be prioritised. A better version of the 'stoppable' buffer shown earlier would therefore be:

```
WHILE going
  PRI ALT
    stop ? ANY
      going := FALSE
    in ? ch
      out ! ch
```

101

A prioritised alternative can easily be used to provide either a prioritised or a 'fair' multiplexor:

```
WHILE TRUE -- prioritised
  PRI ALT i = 0 FOR 10
    in [i] ? ch
      out ! ch

WHILE TRUE -- 'fair'
  PRI ALT i = 0 FOR 10
    in [(i+last) REM 10] ? ch
      SEQ
        out ! ch
        last := (i+1) REM 10
```

In practice, only limited use is made of prioritisation. For most applications, the scheduling of concurrent processes and the method of selecting alternatives is unimportant. This is because, assuming that the system is executing one program, the processes which are consuming all of the processing resources must eventually stop, and wait for the other processes to do something. If this is not the case, the other processes are redundant, and can be removed from the program. An implementation should not, of course, allow a processor to idle if there is something for it to do. But this property is true of any programming language!

Scheduling is important where a system executes two disjoint processes, or has to meet some externally imposed constraint. Both of these occur, for example, in an operating system which deals with disjoint users, and needs to take data from a disk at an externally imposed rate.

1.18   Occam Programs

Despite being a fairly small language, occam supports a very wide variety of programming techniques. Most important, the programmer may choose between a concurrent algorithm or an equivalent sequential one. A final program often consists of a mixture of the two, in which the concurrent algorithm describes a network of transputers, each of which executes the sequential algorithm.

In practice, it is often best to write the concurrent algorithm first. The reason for this is that only the concurrent program provides freedom in the implemention. A pipeline of ten processes could be executed by a pipeline constructed from up to ten transputers; the number being chosen according to the performance required. It is very unlikely that a sequential program can easily be adapted to produce a concurrent program, never mind one suitable for execution by a network of transputers with no shared memory.

The following example is a concurrent searching algorithm. It uses the tree program shown earlier. The data to be searched is held in the leaf processors; the node processors are used to disperse the data to the leaves and collect the replies.

```
PROC leaf (CHAN down, up) =
  VAR data, enq:
  SEQ
    ... -- load data
    WHILE TRUE
      SEQ
        down ? enq
        up ! (enq = data)

PROC node (CHAN down, up,
           CHAN left.down, left.up,
           CHAN right.down, right.up) =
  WHILE TRUE
    VAR enq, left.found, right.found :
    SEQ
      down ? enq
      PAR
        left.down ! enq
        right.down ! enq
      PAR
        left.up ? left.found
        right.up ? right.found
      up ! left.found OR right.found
```

However, it is unlikely to be economic to store only one data item in each leaf. Although each leaf could itself execute the above algorithm using a tree of processes, this would not be very efficient. What is needed in each leaf is a conventional sequential searching algorithm operating on an array of data:

```
PROC leaf (CHAN down, up) =
  VAR enq, data [length], found:
  SEQ
    ... -- initialise data
    WHILE TRUE
      SEQ
        found := FALSE
        down ? enq
        SEQ i = [0 FOR length]
          found := (data [i] = enq ) OR found
        up ! found :
```

It now remains to choose the number of items held in each leaf so that the time taken to disperse the enquiry and collect the response is small relative to the time taken for the search at each leaf. For example, if the time taken for a single communication is 5 microseconds, and the tree is of depth 7 (128 leaves) only 70 microseconds is spent on communication, about one tenth of the time taken to search 1000 items.

1.19   Example - Systolic arrays

A very large number of concurrent algorithms require only the simplest concurrency mechanisms: the parallel construct and the communication channel. These include the 'systolic array' algorithms described by Kung [1.9]. In fact, occam enables a systolic algorithm to be written in one of two ways, illustrated by the following two versions of a simple pipeline, each element of which performs a 'compute' step. First, the traditional version:

```
VAR master [ n ]:
VAR slave [ n ] :
WHILE TRUE
  SEQ
    PAR i = 0 FOR n
      compute ( master [ i ], slave [ i ] )
    PAR
      input ? master [ 0 ]
      PAR i = 0 FOR n-1
        master [ i + 1 ] := slave [ i ]
      output ! slave [ n ]
```

This pipeline describes a conventional synchronous array processor. The compute operations are performed in parallel, each taking data from a master register and leaving its result in a slave register. The array processor is globally synchronised; in each iteration all compute operations start and terminate together, then the data is moved along the pipeline. The initialisation of the pipeline is omitted, so the first n outputs will be rubbish.

The main problem with the above program is the use of global synchronisation, which gives rise to the same implementation difficulties as global communication; it requires that the speed of operation must be reduced as the array size increases. A more natural program in occam would be

```
CHAN c [ n + 1 ] :
PAR i = 0 FOR n
  WHILE TRUE
    VAR d:
    VAR r:
    SEQ
      c [ n ] ? d
      compute ( d, r)
      c [ n + 1 ] ! r
```

In this program, c[0] is the input channel, c[n+1] the output channel. Once again, all of the compute operations are performed together. This time there is no need for initialisation, as no output can be produced until the first input has passed right through the pipeline. More important, the pipeline is self synchronising; adjacent elements synchronise only as needed to communicate data. It seems likely that many systolic array algorithms could usefully be re-expressed and implemented in this form.

103

1.20 Example - Occam compiler

The structure of the occam compiler is shown below. It demonstrates an important feature of the occam support system; the ability to 'fold' sections of program away, leaving only a comment visible. This enables a program, or part of a program, to be viewed at the appropriate level of detail.

```
-- occam compiler
CHAN lexed.program:
CHAN parsed.program:
CHAN scoped.program:
PAR
  -- lexer
  CHAN name.text:
  CHAN name.code:
  PAR
    -- scanner
    -- nametable

  -- parser
  CHAN parsed.lines :
  PAR
    -- line parser
    -- construct parser

  -- scoper

  -- generator
  CHAN generated.constructs :
  CHAN generated.program :
  PAR
    -- construct generator
    -- line generator
    -- space allocator
```

The compiler also illustrates an important programming technique. The nametable process contains data structures which are hidden from the rest of the program. These structures are modified only as a result of messages from the lexical analyser. They are initialised prior to receipt of the first message.

```
-- nametable
SEQ
  -- initialise
  WHILE going
    -- input text of name
    -- look up name
    -- output corresponding code
  -- terminate
```

From the outside, the compiler appears to be a single pass compiler. Internally, it is more like a multiple pass compiler; each process performs a simple transformation on the data which flows through it. The effect of decomposing the compiler in this way was that each component process was relatively easy to write, specify and test; this meant that the component processes could be written concurrently!

1.21 Conclusions

In many application areas, concurrency can be used to provide considerable gains in performance provided that programs are structured to exploit available technology. For many application areas (especially signal processing and scientific computation) suitable algorithms already exist, but many areas remain to be explored.

Writing programs in terms of communicating processes tends to produce programs with a large number of concurrent processes, ranging in size from 1 to 1000 lines. Consequently, it is particularly important that the concurrent processing features in the language are efficiently implementable. Occam demonstrates that this efficiency can be achieved for a widely applicable language.

In occam programs, the process/channel structure tends to be used as a major program structuring tool, procedures being used in the normal way within the larger concurrent processes. The process/channel structure seems to be effective for managing the construction of large programs, although more experience is needed in this area.

REFERENCES

1.1 Occam Programming Manual Prentice Hall International 1984.

1.2 C A Mead and L A Conway: Introduction to VLSI Systems. Addison Wesley 1980 Section 5.

1.3 Communicating Sequential Processes, C A R Hoare, Communications of the ACM Vol. 21, 8 (August 1978) p 666.

1.4 Denotational Semantics for Occam, A W Roscoe. Presented at NSF/SERC Seminar on Concurrency, Carnegie-Mellon University, July 1984. To be published.

1.5 The Laws of Occam Programming, A W Roscoe and C A R Hoare, Programming Research Group, Oxford University, 1986.

1.6 An Effective Implementation for the Generalised Input-Output Construct of CSP. G N Buckley and A Silberschatz, ACM Transactions on Programming Languages and Systems Vol. 5, 2 (April 1983) p. 224.

1.7 A Protocol for Generalised Occam, R Bornat, Department of Computer Science, Queen Mary College, London 1984.

1.8 Occam 2 Reference Manual, Inmos, 1986

1.9 Lets Design Algorithms for VLSI Systems, H T Kung, in: C A Mead and L A Conway: Introduction to VLSI Systems. Addison Wesley 1980 Section 8.3.

2.1 Occam Programming Manual, Prentice-Hall International, 1984

2.2 IMS T414 reference manual, Inmos Limited 1985.

3.1 Simulation of statistical mechanical systems on transputer arrays
C R Askew, D B Carpenter, J T Chalker, A J G Hey, D A Nicole and D S Pritchard
Physics Department, University of Southampton
To be published

3.2 Signal processing with transputer arrays
J G Harp, J B G Roberts and J S Ward
Royal Signals and Radar Establishment, Malvern, Worcestershire
Computer Physics Communications, 1985

4.1 Occam Programming Manual, Prentice-Hall International, 1984

4.2 The Laws of Occam Programming, A W Roscoe and C A R Hoare, Programming Research Group, Oxford University, 1986.

4.3 Formal Methods applied to a Floating Point Number System, G Barrett, Programming Research Group, Oxford University, 1986.

4.4 Compiling Communicating Processes into delay insensitive VLSI Circuits, Alain J Martin, Journal of distributed computing, 1986.

High Performance Fortran

David B. Loveman
Digital Equipment Corporation

After an intensive one-year effort, the High Performance Fortran Forum has written a language specification that improves the performance and usability of Fortran-90 for computationally intensive applications on a wide variety of machines.

Since its introduction more than three decades ago, Fortran has been the programming language of choice for difficult scientific and engineering problems on sequential computers. The recent Fortran-90 standard "modernized" Fortran-77, but exploiting the full capabilities of distributed-memory parallel computers still requires more information than either language can provide (such as how to allocate data among processors and where to place data in a single processor).

A coalition of computer vendors, government laboratories, and academic groups founded the High Performance Fortran Forum in 1992 to improve the performance and usability of Fortran-90 for computationally intensive applications on a wide variety of machines, including massively parallel SIMD and MIMD systems and vector processors. After an intensive one-year effort, the group has reached a consensus and written a language specification, and a number of vendors have announced plans for compilers supporting the language. The HPF language includes the full Fortran-90 standard plus HPF extensions; the specification also includes a minimum HPF subset and identifies work yet to be done.

This article presents Fortran-90, its basis in Fortran-77, its implications for parallel machines, and the HPF extensions. Sidebars describe SIMD and MIMD systems, previous attempts to develop languages for them, the genesis of the HPF Forum, how the group actually worked, and the HPF programming model.

Reprinted from *IEEE Parallel & Distributed Technology*, Vol. 1, No. 1, Feb. 1993, pp. 25-42. Copyright © 1993 by The Institute of Electrical and Electronics Engineers, Inc. All rights reserved.

Fortran-90

Fortran-90 is a new ISO and ANSI standard that includes as a subset all of Fortran-77 and MIL-STD-1753 for compatibility. (The Fortran standards committee uses "FORTRAN 77" to refer to the Fortran-77 standard language, "Fortran 90" to refer to the Fortran-90 standard language, and "Fortran" when a particular standard or product is not being referred to. The style of this magazine does not allow for the all-capital spelling, but my use of "Fortran-77" and "Fortran-90" throughout should alleviate any confusion.)

FORTRAN-77
Many of Fortran-77's language features have become well known to engineering and scientific programmers: array reference and arithmetic computation notation, iteration loops (Do), conditional statements (If ... Then ... Else If ... End If), subroutines and functions, global variables (Common), independent compilation of program units, complex numbers, character data type and operations, and formatted, unformatted, and direct-access file input and output.

Fortran-77 also provides direct visibility to a particular hardware architecture feature: a linear, one-dimensional, sequentially addressed memory. This feature is visible in Fortran-77 via

- Sequence association: the mapping of multidimensional arrays to a linear sequence ordering ("column-major order").
- Storage association: the mapping of Fortran data objects to underlying storage units.

Fortran-77 uses sequence and storage association in such language features as assumed size arrays, Common reshaping, Equivalence reshaping, and procedure argument reshaping. Whenever an architecture is directly visible in a programming language, we can expect good performance on that architecture and difficulty in porting applications to other computer architectures. Not surprisingly, Fortran-77 implementations tend to execute applications well on traditional CISC and RISC linear-memory architectures, but they are inadequate for distributed-memory architectures.

MIL-STD-1753
In 1978 the US Department of Defense published an addendum to the Fortran-77 standard with language features required by all compilers to be sold to the US government. Virtually every Fortran compiler supports these features: End Do statement, Do While statement, Include statement, Implicit None statement, an input/output semantic extension, 11 bit-manipulation procedures, and syntax for octal and hexadecimal constants.

Soon after the Fortran-77 standard was published, work began on a revision to "modernize Fortran, so that it may continue its long history as a scientific and engineering programming language."

FORTRAN-90
Soon after the Fortran-77 standard was published, work began on a revision with the working title of Fortran-8x. The objective was (in the words of the Fortran-90 standard) to "modernize Fortran, so that it may continue its long history as a scientific and engineering programming language." The Fortran-8x efforts were intended to provide modern language features that would let programmers stop using obsolescent and "politically incorrect" forms in Fortran-77, some of which are specifically identified in the standard as "decremental features": arithmetic If statements; real and double-precision Do loop control variables and expressions; shared Do termination and termination on a statement other than End Do or Continue; branching to an End If from outside the If statement; alternate return; Pause and Stop statements; Assign and assigned Go To statements; assigned Format specifiers; and cH edit descriptor.

Fortran-90 is a significantly larger language than Fortran-77, and in many ways it is a technically difficult language to implement. Features that improve on Fortran-77 include array operations, numerical computation facilities, parameterized intrinsic data types, user-defined data types, modularization of data and procedures, additional storage classes of objects, and additional intrinsic procedures.

Array operations
Fortran-90 contains new syntax to allow numeric oper-

Programming for distributed-memory parallel computers

Distributed-memory parallel computers include multiple-instruction, multiple-data (MIMD) machines such as Intel's Paragon XP/S; single-instruction, multiple-data (SIMD) machines such as the Thinking Machines CM-2, MasPar's MP-1 and MP-2, and Digital's DECmpp 12000/Sx; and farms of workstations such as Digital's Alpha AXP. Performance on all types of distributed-memory parallel computers can be boosted by keeping data local, which decreases costly interprocessor communication.

Distributed-memory MIMD systems must be programmed at quite a low level. Typically a developer must explicitly distribute data to the various processors, implement code that operates on local data on a per-processor basis, and provide for explicit message passing or other communication to access nonlocal data.

Programming for SIMD computers is at a somewhat higher level. The developer programs in a subset of Fortran-90, using Fortran-90 array operations to provide implicit parallelism. (The developer actually uses a subset of Fortran-8x, Fortran-90's precursor, which in addition to the array notation also included a statement that was eliminated as part of the Fortran-90 standardization process but added back by HPF.) Advanced compilers map the program to the underlying machine. For performance, the developer often must provide data locality information in the form of directives, which are vendor-specific although similar in style and intention.

In the early 1970s, the compiler developer Compass implemented language constructs for data placement and layout in its IVtran (pronounced "four-tran") compiler for the Illiac IV SIMD computer. In the 1980s, Compass and Thinking Machines developed static layout directives for a subset of Fortran-8x for the Connection Machine. Compass's technology was also used in Fortan compilers for MasPar and Digital Equipment Corporation.

Rice and Syracuse Universities have conducted research for several years on Fortran D, a language designed to support a data parallel programming style, providing linguistic support for data decomposition at two levels of parallelism: the problem mapping (the natural fine-grained parallelism defined by individual members of data arrays, independent of machine considerations) and the machine mapping (the coarse-grained parallelism defined by the physical parallel machine). They were specifically trying to define language constructs similar to those provided by SIMD vendors, but in a way that was neither vendor- nor SIMD-specific. Several other institutions have conducted research on data locality issues in Fortran, including the University of Vienna (Vienna Fortran), Syracuse University (Fortran-90 D), ICASE (Kali), and Yale University (the Yale extensions).

Early in 1991, Digital and Compass began a project to develop an industrywide Fortran dialect that could support an array-based, data-parallel programming style on both SIMD and MIMD massively parallel machines, as well as more conventional architectures. Digital felt that a standard language would make application development for parallel computers easier, thus increasing the size of the market to the benefit of all vendors, including Digital.

The major objectives of this project — called High Performance Fortran — included hardware architecture independence, comprehensive language features, support for language standards, pragmatic selection of language features, staged implementation possibilities, performance-tuning directives defined in the language, and industry and academic consensus on the primary language features.

The language was to be based on Fortran-90, Fortran D and SIMD Fortran experience (especially ForAll), except that the Fortran D data decomposition statements were replaced by directives in the form of structured comments. Project efforts included a preliminary language design, multiple one-on-one presentations to other vendors and major users, and a "birds of a feather" session at Supercomputing '91, where Digital agreed to cooperate with Rice University to set up the High Performance Fortran Forum.

---

ations on entire arrays without explicit Do loops: We can now say A = B + C to add two arrays together and store them in a third array. These features were introduced because many scientists find them a natural and readable way of expressing algorithms. They have also proven to have efficient implementations on a variety of computer architectures. Indeed, some of these facilities are already supported in product compilers. The introductory overview in the Fortran-90 standard states:

Operations for processing whole arrays and subarrays (array sections) are included in Fortran-90 for two principal reasons: (1) these features provide a more concise and higher level language that will allow programmers more quickly and reliably to develop and maintain scientific/engineering applications, and (2) these features can significantly facilitate optimization of array operations on many computer architectures.

Numerical computation facilities
Fortran-90 includes portability control over numeric precision specification, and provides intrinsic functions that let programmers determine the characteristics of numeric representation on a particular machine while a program is running.

Parameterized intrinsic data types
This feature lets vendors support additional data types, such as short integers, very large character sets (such as those used in China and Japan), more than two precisions for Real and Complex types, and packed logical.

User-defined data types
These let a developer define arbitrary data structures and the operations that act on them.

Modularization of data and procedures
Many developers consider this one of Fortran-90's best features. It is similar to Ada encapsulation. The basic idea is that related data declarations, derived type definitions, and procedures reside in one place — a Module program unit — the contents of which can be accessed by any program unit. This gives the Fortran developer an effective method for defining global data, global procedures, and encapsulated data abstractions. Modules are an improvement over Fortran-77's Entry statement because they provide an easy way to tie data and procedures together. Fortran-90's module facilities allow design implementation using data abstractions, and they support the specification of modules, including user-defined data types and structures, defined operators on those types, and generic procedures for implementing common algorithms to be used on a variety of data structures.

In addition to modules, interface blocks let a programmer explicitly specify interfaces to subprograms, which a high-quality compiler can use to provide better checking and optimization at the interface to other subprograms.

Additional storage classes of objects.
Fortran-90's new storage classes (such as allocatable, automatic, and assumed-shape objects) and pointer facility add significantly to those of Fortran-77 and should reduce the use of Fortran-77 constructs that depend on a linear memory model, such as Equivalenced array objects, Common definitions with nonidentical array definitions across subprograms, and actual-/dummy-

argument array shape transformations. The standards committee added pointers to Fortran-90, but it chose not to use the Cray pointer implementation that many Fortran vendors have adopted; Fortran-90 pointers have many of the same capabilities as Cray pointers, but with a different syntax and an architecture-independent semantics.

Additional intrinsic procedures
Fortran-90 defines a large number of new intrinsic procedures. Many of these support mathematical operations on arrays, including the construction and transformation of arrays. Also, there are numerical accuracy procedures to support numerical programming, and bit-manipulation procedures derived from MIL-STD-1753. Examples include Any, All, Bit_Size, Ceiling, Date_And_Time, Floor, Epsilon, Maxval, Minval, Range, and Sum.

Miscellaneous improvements
Fortran-90 also allows 31-character names, the use of "_" in names, end-of-line comments, a free source form, a larger character set including lowercase letters and operators such as "<," new control constructs such as the Case statement, and internal subprocedures.

> **Fortran-90's features for array calculation and dynamic storage allocation make it a natural base for HPF, which adds new directives and language constructs and imposes some restrictions.**

FORTRAN-90 ON PARALLEL MACHINES

Although the semantics of Fortran-90 is defined without reference to a particular underlying machine model, and can be viewed as providing a global name space and a single thread of control, efficient execution can be realized on parallel machines. Consider the context provided by these Fortran-90 declarations:

```
Real :: S   ! a scalar floating-point variable
Real, Dimension (N) :: A, B ! two N-element arrays
Integer :: I, J   ! two scalar integer variables
Integer, Dimension (N) :: P :: an integer index array
```

Fortran-90 provides for element-by-element operations on entire arrays, where the language does not specify the order of evaluation. The semantics of Fortran-90 allows these statements to be executed in parallel. The following array assignment statement multiplies each element of B by itself, adds that value to the square root

The High Performance Fortran Forum

More than 120 people attended the first HPF Forum meeting in January 1992 and developed the basic working procedures. The group considered extending Fortran in several areas: data distribution, parallel statements, extended intrinsic functions and standard library, extrinsic procedures, parallel I/O statements, and changes in sequence and storage association.

The members agreed that they could not solve all possible problems; instead, it was understood that the group was "trying to agree on what it agrees on," and trying to raise the level of commonality. Thus the group sought to develop a technical report of consensus, not a formal language standard. The HPF Forum determined to complete the document within a year, with meetings about every six weeks and extensive correspondence by electronic mail. The group also encouraged input from the high-performance computing community through widely distributed language drafts; the electronic-mailing list included more than 500 names.

The members agreed to deviate as little as possible from other standards, minimizing (and avoiding, if possible) direct conflicts with Fortran-77 and Fortran-90. The group also wanted to make sure that compilers could be developed quickly, so it decided to define

a HPF subset with the minimum essential Fortran-90 and HPF features. Taken as a whole, these goals were deemed quite aggressive when they were adopted in March 1992, and led to a number of compromises in the final language.

After the first meeting there were nine working-group meetings to specify the language. The group was led by Ken Kennedy of Rice University. There were never fewer than 30 participants, so to keep the process manageable, each major topic was addressed and debated at length by a subgroup, which reported its deliberations to the entire working group for review. After additional discussion, the subgroup would prepare one or more proposals for an initial formal vote. After a second formal vote a month later, the decision became part of HPF, subject to further review later in the process.

One person represented each organization, which agreed to support that person's attendance for the year. Representatives from Convex Computer, Cray Research, Digital Equipment Corporation, IBM, Rice University, Syracuse University, Thinking Machines, and the University of Vienna gave presentations at the first meeting, and many other organizations were represented at two or more meetings:

Alliant Computer Systems, Amoco Production Company, Applied Parallel Research, Archipel, Cornell Theory Center, DEC Massively Parallel Systems Group, Fujitsu America, Fujitsu Laboratories, GMD-I1.T, Sankt Augustin, Hewlett Packard, the Institute for Computer Applications in Science & Engineering, Intel Supercomputer Systems Division, Lahey Computer, Lawrence Livermore National Laboratory, Los Alamos National Laboratory, Louisiana State University, MasPar Computer, Meiko, nCube, Ohio State University, the Oregon Graduate Institute of Science and Technology, The Portland Group, the Research Institute for Advanced Computer Science, Schlumberger, Shell, State University of New York at Buffalo, SunPro and Sun Microsystems, TNO-TU Delft, United Technologies, the University of Stuttgart, and Yale University.

Readers can join the HPF process by sending an electronic mail message to hpff-request@cs.rice.edu with a subject line "add hpff." The current version of the HPF Language Specification is available electronically via anonymous FTP from the public/hpff directory at titan.cs.rice.edu, or from Theresa Chapman, CITI/CRPC, Box 1892, Rice University, Houston, TX 77251.

---

of the corresponding element of A, and replaces the corresponding element of A with the new value:

    A = Sqrt(A) + B**2

The following statement performs a masked array assignment in which each value of A is replaced by that value divided by the corresponding value of B except in those cases where the value of B is 0:

    Where (B /= 0) A = A/B

A number of Fortran-90 statements imply communication in a distributed-memory implementation, such as

* broadcast, when a scalar is assigned to an array:
    A = S/2

* permutation, when array section notation or index vectors are used:
    A(I:J) = B(J:I:-1)
    A(P) = B ! A(P(i)) = B(i), forall i = 1:N

* reduction, such as summing all of the elements of an array:
    S = Sum(B)

High Performance Fortran

Fortran-90's features for array calculation and dynamic storage allocation make it a natural base for HPF, which extends the language by adding new directives and language constructs and by imposing some restrictions.

The HPF directives are structured comments that

The HPF programming model

HPF helps developers write parallel programs for distributed-memory systems almost as easily as writing sequential programs. The developer writes the program in Fortran-90 in a single-program, multiple-data (SPMD), data parallel style, where conceptually the code has a single thread of control and a global address space. The developer provides information about desired data locality or distribution by annotating the code with HPF data-mapping directives, and then runs it through an architecture-specific compiler:

- For MIMD machines, the result is a multithreaded message passing implementation with local data and compiler-generated synchronization and send/receive code.
- For SIMD machines, the result is single-threaded parallel code with communication optimized by compiler placement of data.

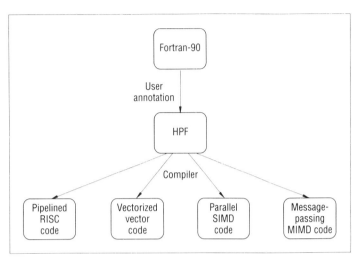

The HPF programming model.

- For vector machines, the result is vectorized code, optimized for the vector units.

- For RISC machines, the result is pipelined superscalar code with compiler-generated cache management

suggest implementation strategies or assert facts about a program to the compiler. They may affect the efficiency of the computation, but they do not change the value computed by the program; as long as the directives are used correctly, the program should generate the same results whether the directives are processed or not.

HPF directives are consistent with Fortran-90 syntax. If HPF were to be adopted as part of a future Fortran standard, the only change necessary to include a directive as a full statement would be to remove the HPF comment prefix: !HPF$.

A few new language features were made first-class constructs rather than comments because they can affect a program's interpretation (for example, by returning a value used in an expression). These are direct extensions to the Fortran-90 syntax and interpretation.

The new directives, language constructs, and restrictions give Fortran-90 new data-distribution features, statements allowing the explicit expression of parallel computation, extended intrinsic functions and standard library routines, extrinsic procedures, and changes in sequence and storage association.

DATA DISTRIBUTION
Parallel and sequential architectures attain their fastest speed when the data they access is local, but the se-

quential storage order defined in Fortran-77 and Fortran-90 often conflicts with this need.

HPF includes a distribution model and directives that let the user tell the compiler how to allocate data objects to processor memories. The compiler interprets these annotations to improve data storage allocation, minimizing communication while retaining parallelism (subject to the constraint that, semantically, every data object has only a single value at any point in the program).

The model is a two-level mapping of data objects to abstract processors (see Figure 1). Data objects, typically array elements, are first *aligned* relative to one another; a group of arrays is then *distributed* on a rectilinear arrangement of abstract processors. The implementation uses the same number of physical processors (or perhaps fewer) to implement these abstract processors. This mapping of abstract to physical processors is language processor-dependent.

The premise is that an operation on two or more data objects is likely to be carried out much faster if they all reside in the same processor, and that it might be possible to carry out many such operations concurrently if they can be performed on different processors.

A number of Fortran-90 features (such as array syntax) make it easier for a compiler to determine whether many operations can be carried out concurrently. The

HPF directives provide a way to tell the compiler to ensure that certain data objects reside in the same processor: If two data objects are mapped (via alignment and distribution) to the same abstract processor, that is a strong recommendation that they ought to reside in the same physical processor. The directives also provide a way to recommend that a data object be stored in multiple locations, which can make updating the object more complicated but makes it faster for multiple processors to read the object.

There is a clear separation between directives that serve as specification statements and those that serve as executable statements. Specification statements are carried out on entry to a program unit, pretty much as if all at once; only then are executable statements carried out. (While it is often convenient to think of specification statements as being handled at compile time, some of them may contain expressions that depend on runtime quantities. The values of these expressions may not be known until runtime when program control enters the scoping unit.)

Every array (indeed, every object) is created with some distribution onto some arrangement of processors. If the specification statements contain explicit directives specifying the alignment of array A with respect to array B, then the distribution of A will be dictated by the distribution of B; otherwise, the distribution of A itself may be specified explicitly. In either case, any such explicit declarative information is used when the array is created.

An allocatable object is created whenever it is allocated. Specification directives for allocatable objects (and allocated pointer targets) may appear in the declaration part of a program unit, but take effect each time the array is created, rather than on entry to the scoping unit. If object A is aligned (statically or dynamically) with object B, which in turn is already aligned with object C, this is regarded as a direct alignment of A with C, with B serving only as an intermediary at the time of specification. This matters when B is subsequently realigned; the result is that A remains aligned with C.

Every object is created as if according to some complete set of specification directives; if the program does not include complete specifications for mapping an object, the compiler provides defaults. By default, an object is not aligned with any other object. The default distribution is language processor-dependent, but must be expressible as explicit directives for that implementation. Identically declared objects need not be given identical default distribution specifications; the com-

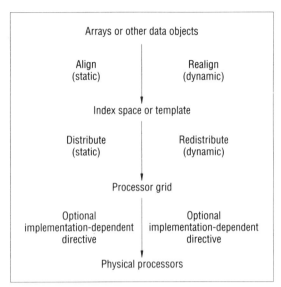

Figure 1. Distribution model.

piler may, for example, take into account the contexts in which objects are used in executable code. The programmer can force identically declared objects to have identical distributions by specifying such distributions explicitly. Identically declared processor arrangements are guaranteed to represent "the same processors arranged the same way."

An object can be realigned or redistributed. Redistributing an object causes all objects aligned with it also to be redistributed to maintain the alignment relationships.

Alignment is considered an attribute (in the Fortran-90 sense) of an array or scalar. Distribution is technically an attribute of the index space of the array. Sometimes we might speak loosely of the distribution of an array, but this really means the distribution of the index space of the array, or of another array to which it is aligned. The relationship of an array to a processor arrangement is properly called the mapping of the array.

Sometimes we want to consider a large index space with which several smaller arrays are to be aligned, but not to declare any array that spans the entire index space. HPF provides the notion of a Template, which is like an array whose elements have no content and therefore occupy no storage; it is merely an abstract index space that can be distributed and with which arrays may be aligned. (Guy Steele notes, "If an array is a cat, then a Template is a Cheshire cat, and the index space is the grin.")

HPF's Dynamic attribute is much like Fortran-90's Allocatable attribute: An array that has not been declared as Dynamic cannot be realigned, and an array or template that has not been declared as Dynamic cannot be redistributed.

The Processors directive and processor views

The Processors directive declares rectilinear processor arrangements, specifying their name, rank (number of dimensions), and size in each dimension. The intrinsic functions Number_Of_Processors and Processors_Shape inquire about the total number of actual physical processors used to execute the program. This information can be used to calculate sizes for the abstract processors arrangements. For example:

```
!HPF$ Processors P(N)
!HPF$ Processors Q(Number_Of_Processors( )), &
!HPF$ Processors R(8, Number_Of_Processors( )/8)
!HPF$ Processors ScalarProc
   ! a scalar-processors arrangement
```

A scalar-processors arrangement can be used to indicate that certain scalar data should be kept together but need not interact strongly with distributed data. Data distributed onto such a arrangement can reside in a single "control" or "host" processor (if the machine has one), in an arbitrarily chosen processor, or it can be replicated over all processors. For computers that have a set of computational processors and a separate scalar host computer, a natural implementation is to map every scalar-processors arrangement onto the host processor. For computers without a separate scalar host computer, data mapped to a scalar-processors arrangement might be mapped to some arbitrarily chosen computational processor or replicated onto all computational processors.

A specific HPF implementation can provide a way to specify at compile time the number of physical processors on which the program is to be executed. This might be either by a language processor-dependent directive or through a command-line argument. Such facilities are beyond the scope of HPF. It might also be desirable for the user to have a way to specify the precise mapping of the processor arrangement declared in a Processors statement to the physical processors of the executing hardware. Again, such facilities are beyond the scope of the HPF specification.

The View attribute provides a way to allow the same set of abstract processors to be viewed as having different rectilinear geometries, possibly of differing rank. This feature is sometimes loosely called "Equivalence for processors arrangements."

In the following example, the processor arrays P, Q, and R are equivalenced to designate the same set of 8,192 abstract processors. The first View specifies that P and Q are the same processor set, viewing P in column-major order. The second View specifies that P and R are the same processor set, viewing P in column-major order after permuting its dimensions.

```
!HPF$ Processors P(128,64), Q(8192), R(8192)
!HPF$ View of P :: Q
!HPF$ View of P(/2,1/) :: R
```

The Align directive

The Align directive specifies that certain data objects are to be distributed in the same way as certain other data objects. Operations between aligned data objects are likely to be more efficient than operations between data objects that are not known to be aligned, since two aligned objects will necessarily be mapped to the same abstract processor. The Align directive is designed to make it particularly easy to specify mappings for all the elements of an array at once.

The Align directive appears in the declaration part of a scoping unit and can specify alignment of an array with another array or with a template. HPF provides a variety of syntactic forms for specifying simple alignments, offsets, axis collapse, axis transposition, axis reversal, and replication:

```
!HPF$ Align X(:, :) with D2(:, :)    ! simple case
!HPF$ Align A(I) with B(I+2)    ! offset
!HPF$ Align X(:, *) with D1(:)  ! collapse second axis of X
!HPF$ Align X(J, K) with D2(K, J)    ! transpose two axes
!HPF$ Align X(J, K) with D2(M-J+1, N-K+1)
    ! reverse both axes
!HPF$ Align X(J, K) with D3(J, *, K)
    ! replicate X along second axis of D3
!HPF$ Align A(*) with D(:, *)
    ! align a copy of A with every column of D
```

Replication allows an optimizing compiler to arrange to read whichever copy is closest. (Of course, when an element of A is written, all copies must be updated, not just one. Replicated representations are useful for such tricks as small lookup tables, where it is much faster to have a copy in each physical processor but you don't want to be bothered giving it an extra dimension that is logically unnecessary to the algorithm.)

In the following, there are N processors and we want arrays of different sizes (3, 4, 43) within each. The numbers 3, 4, and 43 may be different, because those axes will be collapsed so that array elements with indices differing only along that axis will all reside in the same processor:

```
!HPF$ Template D1(N)
    Real A(3, N), B(4, N), C(43, N)
!HPF$ Align (*, :) with D1:: A, B, C
```

Alignment of dummy and actual arguments at a subprogram interface is particularly important. HPF provides a number of alternatives, including two extremes in which:

- the actual argument must be realigned to match the requirements of the dummy, and then realigned again on return, or
- the caller and callee agree on alignment and no action is required.

There is also an Inherit directive, specifying that a dummy inherits a copy of the index space of the actual argument.

The Distribute directive
The Distribute directive specifies a mapping of data objects to abstract processors in a processor arrangement. While Align directives let a programmer indicate logical relationships among the most closely associated array elements in a computation, Distribute directives let the programmer specify a distribution of data points onto the hardware to get a good tradeoff between load balance (which generally favors spreading neighboring data points across many processors) and communication costs (which might favor keeping neighboring data points on the same or neighboring processors). Distribute directives are thus more likely than Align directives to reflect the characteristics of the architecture on which the program is to be executed, and so are the most likely statements (along with Processors directives) to be changed when the program is ported to a new architecture. This is a principal reason for factoring the mapping process into separate alignment and distribution steps, instead of directly specifying the mapping of individual arrays. Nevertheless, the vocabulary used in the Distribute directive is quite architecture-neutral, so that no changes in Distribute directives are required when porting between architectures unless the tradeoffs between communication, computation, and synchronization costs on the new architecture are so different that they dictate a qualitatively different approach to the mapping of the computation.

HPF directives are consistent with Fortran-90 syntax. If HPF were to be adopted as part of a future Fortran standard, the only change necessary to include a directive as a full statement would be to remove the HPF comment prefix.

The Distribute directive

!HPF$ Distribute D1(Cyclic)

specifies that the machine's processors are to be considered a one-dimensional array (the implementation is encouraged to select that array so that communication between logically neighboring processors is inexpensive), and that points of the one-dimensional D1 are to be associated with processors in that array so that neighboring points of D1 are associated with logically neighboring processors in the array, "wrapping around" to the beginning of the processor array if D1 has more points than the machine has processors.

The Distribute directive

!HPF$ Distribute D2(Block, Block)

specifies that the processors are to be considered a two-dimensional array, and the points of the two-dimensional D2 are to be associated with processors in this array in a "blocked" fashion: Neighboring points of D2 are divided into blocks whose size along each dimension is the quotient of the size of that dimension of D2 divided by the size of that dimension of the logical processor array, and the neighboring points of D2 are associated with the same processor except at a block boundary, in which case neighboring points of D2 are allocated to logically neighboring processors along that dimension of the logical processor array.

Once the distributions of D1 and D2 have been specified, the mappings of any arrays aligned with D1 or D2 are determined, and the elements of these arrays are mapped to the processors to which the corresponding points of D1 or D2 are mapped.

HPF provides for "*" distribution, in which all points of the indicated dimension are mapped to a single processor; Block(n) distribution, in which blocks of the specified size are distributed; and explicit distribution to a processor arrangement specified in a Processors directive.

Dynamic, Realign, and Redistribute directives
If an array is mentioned in a Dynamic directive, it might be the object of an executable Realign or Redistribute directive:

```
!HPF$ Dynamic :: A, B, C
```

The Realign directive is similar to the Align directive but is executable; similarly, the Redistribute directive is similar to the Distribute directive but is executable. A Dynamic array or template can be realigned or redistributed at any time. Any other arrays currently aligned with an array or template when it is redistributed are also remapped to reflect the new distribution, in such a way as to preserve alignment relationships.

A Dynamic directive can be combined with other directives, with the attributes stated in any order, consistent with Fortran-90 attribute syntax. For example:

```
!HPF$ Align with Sneezy, Dynamic :: X, Y, Z
!HPF$ Distribute(Block, Block), Dynamic :: X, Y
```

Also, the three directives

```
!HPF$ Template A(64, 64),B(64, 64),C(64, 64)
!HPF$ Distribute(Block, Block) onto P :: A, B, C
!HPF$ Dynamic A, B, C
```

can be combined into the single directive:

```
!HPF$ Template, Dimension(64, 64), &
     !HPF$ Distribute(Block, Block) onto P, Dynamic :: A, B, C
```

Template directive

The Template directive declares templates, or abstract index spaces, specifying their name, rank (number of dimensions), and size of each dimension.

Templates are useful when several arrays must be aligned relative to one another but there is no need to declare a single array that spans the entire index space of interest. For example, we might want four $N \times N$ arrays aligned to the four corners of an index space of size $(N+1) \times (N+1)$:

```
!HPF$ Template, Distribute(Block, Block) :: Earth(N+1, N+1)
     Real, Dimension(N, N) :: NW, NE, SW, SE
!HPF$ Align NW(I, J) with Earth(I, J)
!HPF$ Align NE(I, J) with Earth(I, J+1)
!HPF$ Align SW(I, J) with Earth(I+1, J)
!HPF$ Align SE(I, J) with Earth(I+1, J+1)
```

As another example, consider the requirement to replicate a rank-two array across all processors:

```
!HPF$ Template, Distribute(Cyclic) :: &
!HPF$ T(Number_Of_Processors( ))
!HPF$ Align A(*, *) with T(*)
```

Templates are not passed through a subprogram argument interface; the template to which a dummy argument is aligned is always distinct from the template to which the actual argument is aligned. On exit from a subprogram, an actual argument is aligned to the same template to which it was aligned before the call.

Unlike arrays, templates cannot be in Common. Two templates declared in different scoping units will always be distinct, even if given the same name. The only way for two program units to refer to the same template is to declare the template in a module that is then used by the two program units. For example, suppose we need to map a dummy a in a subroutine, a global array b, and an array c in the main program so that their second dimensions are all within the same processor. An HPF solution using modules is:

```
Module Global_Subrs_And_Data
     !HPF$ Template, Dimension(10000), Distribute(Cyclic) :: d
     Real, Dimension(10000, 20) :: b
     !HPF$ Align b(i, j) with d(i)
Contains
     Subroutine sub1(a)
     Real, Dimension (:, :) :: a
     !HPF$ Align a(i, j) with d(i)
     b(:, 2) = b(:, 2) + a(:, 1)
     End
End Module Global_Subrs_And_Data

Program Caller
     Use Global_Subrs_And_Data
     Real, Dimension(10000, 10) :: c
     !HPF$ Align c(i, j) with d(i)
     c = 2; b = 1; Call sub1(c)
End
```

PARALLEL STATEMENTS

HPF provides a new statement and new directives to allow the explicit expression of parallel computation. The single- and multistatement ForAll constructs express assignments to sections of arrays; similar in many ways to array assignment, they allow more general sections to be specified. The Independent directive asserts that the statements in a particular section of code do not exhibit any sequentializing dependencies; when properly used, it does not change the semantics of the construct, but it can give the compiler more information to allow optimizations. Pure procedures are those that are sufficiently restricted (free of side effects) to be invoked within a ForAll.

The ForAll construct and related features

The ForAll construct can be viewed as an extension to the Fortran-90 array assignment and Where construct, but one that is intended to be more suggestive of local operations on each element of an array, and able to specify more general array sections than allowed by the basic array triplet notation.

The ForAll construct had its origins in the Fortran-8x definition; in the Fortran implementations of Compass, Digital, MasPar, and Thinking Machines; and in research at Rice, Syracuse, Vienna, and other universities. Precursors to the ForAll statement can be found as early as the Do For All statement in the Illiac IV IV-tran compiler.

ForAll specifies array assignments in terms of array elements or groups of array sections, optionally masked with a scalar logical expression. It is similar to array assignment statements, but more general array sections can be assigned in ForAll. The general form of a ForAll construct is an element array assignment:

    ForAll (triplet, ... , mask) assignment

or a block ForAll:

    ForAll (triplet, ... , mask)
        statement
        ...
    End ForAll

where triplet has the general form:

    subscript = lowerbound : upperbound : stride

and where stride is optional, where assignment is an arithmetic or pointer assignment statement, and where statement is an assignment, a Where statement, or another ForAll statement. Any procedure referenced in a ForAll construct must be a pure function, syntactically guaranteed not to have side effects.

An element array assignment ForAll executes in the following steps:

(1) Evaluation in any order of the lowerbound, upperbound, and stride expressions. The set of valid combinations of subscript values is then the Cartesian product of the sets defined by these triplets.
(2) Evaluation of the mask for all valid combinations of subscript values. The mask elements can be evaluated in any order. The set of active combinations of subscript values is the subset of the valid combinations for which the mask evaluates to true. If the scalar mask expression is omitted, it is as if it were present with the value true.

(3) Evaluation in any order of the expressions and subscripts contained in the assignment for all active combinations of subscript values.
(4) Assignment of these values to the corresponding elements of the array on the left-hand side. The assignments can be made in any order. An assignment in a ForAll construct must not cause more than one value to be assigned to any array element.

Since a function called from a ForAll construct must be pure, it is impossible for that function's evaluation to affect other expressions' evaluations, either for the same combination of subscript values or for different combinations.

A block ForAll is roughly the same as replicating the ForAll header in front of each statement in the block, except that any expressions in the ForAll header are evaluated only once, rather than being reevaluated before each statement in the body. The exceptions are for nested ForAll statements and Where statements.

We can think of a block ForAll as synchronizing twice per contained assignment statement: once after handling the right-hand side and other expressions, but before performing assignments; and once after all assignments have been performed but before commencing the next statement. In practice, appropriate dependence analysis will often permit the compiler to eliminate unnecessary synchronizations.

In many cases, compiler optimizations, such as copy propagation, can eliminate the requirement for temporaries for lowerbounds, upperbounds and strides. Similarly, dependence analysis can eliminate the requirement for array temporaries. Thus a ForAll statement such as

    ForAll (I=1:M, J=1:N:2) A(I, J) = I * B(J)

can be implemented on a scalar machine as

    Do I=1, M
      Do J=1, N, 2
        A(I, J) = I * B(J)
      End Do
    End Do

> **High Performance Fortran provides a new statement (ForAll) and a new directive (Independent) to allow the explicit expression of parallel computation.**

On a parallel SIMD or MIMD machine it can, of course, be implemented in parallel.

Examples

Examples of element array assignments with natural Fortran-90 equivalents include:

```
ForAll (I=1:N, J=1:N, A(I, J) .NE. 0.0) B(I, J) = 1.0 / A(I, J)
    ! is the same as
    Where (A /= 0.0) B = 1.0 / A
```

```
! the ForAll in effect gives a name to a section triplet
ForAll (I=1:L) R(I) = S(I)
    ! is the same as
    R(1:L) = S(1:L)
    ! is the same as
    R = S    ! since R and S are both of length L
```

```
ForAll (I=1:10:2, J=10:1:−1) A(I, J) = B(I, J) * C(I, J)
    ! is equivalent to
    A(1:10:2,10:1:−1) = B(1:10:2,10:1:−1)*C(1:10:2 10:1:−1)
```

```
! computational use of subscript values in one dimension
ForAll (I=1:100) R(I) = I
    ! is equivalent to the use of an array constructor
    R = (/ 1:100 /)
```

```
! certain cases of spreading
ForAll (I=1:10, J=1:20) A(I, J) = S(I)
    ! is equivalent to the implied spread
    A(1:10, 1:20) = Spread(S(1:10), Dim=2, NCopies=20)
```

```
! vector valued subscripts
ForAll (I=1:L) R(V(I)) = S(I)
    ! is equivalent to
    R(V(1:L)) = S(1:100)
    ! is equivalent to
    R(V) = S
```

```
! permutation of two axes, array transpose
ForAll (I=1:M, J=1:N) A(I, J) = B(J, I)
    ! is equivalent to
    A = Transpose(B)
```

```
ForAll (I=1:M, K=1:N) A(I, K) = Sum(A(I, :) * B(:, K))
    ! is equivalent to
    A = Matmul(A, B)
```

Examples of element array assignments without natural Fortran-90 equivalents include:

```
! skewed sections of arrays
ForAll (I=1:100) A(I, I) = B(I, I)! diagonal
ForAll (I=1:100) A(I, I) = B(I+1, I−1)
ForAll (I=1:M, J=1:N, K=1:10, I+J+K .EQ. 3*(N+1)/2) &
    A(I+J−K, J) = G(I, J, K)
```

```
! multidimensional array-valued subscripts
ForAll (I=1:100, J=1:100) R(IND(I, J)) = B(I, J)
```

```
! scatter addressing
ForAll (I=1:100) A(U(I), V(I)) = S(I)
ForAll (I=2:100) R(I) = R(I/2)
    ! array representing a binary tree
```

```
! parallel prefix operations
ForAll(I=1:100) R(I) = Sum(S(1:I))
    ! is equivalent to use of the HPF function
    R = Sum_Reduce(S)
```

```
! zeros the upper right triangle of C
ForAll (I=1:M, J=1:N, I<J) C(I, J) = 0
```

```
! assigns consecutive integers to all elements of array A
ForAll (I=1:M, J=1:N) A(I, J) = (I−1)*N + J − 1
```

```
! assign diagonal of A to R
ForAll (I=1:M) R(I) = A(I, I)
```

Examples of the ForAll construct include:

```
ForAll ( I = 2:N−1, J = 2:N−1 )
    A(I, J) = A(I, J−1) + A(I, J+1) + A(I−1, J) + A(I+1, J)
    B(I, J) = A(I, J)
End ForAll
```

```
ForAll ( I = 1:N−1 )
    ForAll ( J = I+1:N )
        A(I, J) = A(J, I)
    End ForAll
End ForAll
```

```
ForAll ( I = 1:N, J = 1:N )
    A(I, J) = Merge( A(I, J), A(I, J)**2, I.EQ.J )
    Where ( .Not. Done(I, J, 1:M) )
        B(I, J, 1:M) = B(I, J, 1:M)*X
    End Where
End ForAll
```

Pure procedures

A pure function obeys certain syntactic constraints that ensure it produces no side effects. The only effect of a pure function reference on the state of a program is to return a result — it does not modify the values, pointer associations or data mapping of any of its arguments or global data, and it performs no I/O. A pure subroutine produces no side effects except for modifying the values or pointer associations of certain arguments. A pure procedure (function or subroutine) can be used in any way that a normal procedure can. A procedure is required to be pure if it is used in a ForAll statement or construct, in the body of a pure procedure, or as an actual argument in a pure procedure reference.

This freedom from side effects ensures that a pure

function can be invoked concurrently in a ForAll statement without undesirable consequences such as nondeterminism. The compiler can also perform more extensive optimizations when all functions are pure.

A pure function can be invoked concurrently at each "element" of an array if it is referenced in a ForAll. In these cases, a limited form of MIMD parallelism can be obtained via branches in the pure procedure that depend on arguments associated with array elements or their subscripts (the latter especially in a ForAll context). For example:

```
Function f (x, i)
  !HPF$ Pure f
  Real x   ! associated with array element
  Integer i   ! associated with array subscript
  If (x > 0.0) Then
      ! content-based conditional
      x = x * 2
  Else If (i==1 .OR. i==n) Then
      ! subscript-based conditional
      x = 0.0
  EndIf
End Function


...
Real a(n)
Integer i
...
ForAll (i=1:n) a(i) = f( a(i), i)
```

This can sometimes provide an alternative to using sequences of masked ForAlls, with their potential synchronization overhead.

The Independent directive

The Independent directive asserts to the compiler that no data object is defined by one iteration of a Do loop and used (read or written) by another; it asserts similar information about the combinations of index values in a ForAll statement. In other words, the Independent directive asserts that the operations in a Do loop or ForAll statement or construct can be executed independently — in any order, or interleaved, or concurrently — without changing the program's semantics. A compiler can rely on this information to make optimizations, such as parallelization or reorganizing communication. If the assertion is true, the semantics of the program are not changed; if it is false, the program is not standard-conforming and has no defined meaning.

The following code asserts that array P does not have any repeated entries and that A and B are not storage associated:

```
!HPF$ Independent
Do I=1,100
  A(P(I)) = B(I)
End Do
```

In the next example, the inner loop is not independent because each element of A is assigned repeatedly. However, the three outer loops are independent because they access different elements of A. It is not relevant that the outer loops read the same elements from B and C, because those arrays are not assigned.

```
!HPF$ Independent (I1, I2, I3)
Do I1 = 1, N1
  Do I2 = 1, N2
      Do I3 = 1, N3
          Do I4 = 1, N4    ! The inner loop is not independent!
              A(I1,I2,I3) = A(I1,I2,I3) + B(I1,I2,I4)*C(I2,I3,I4)
          End Do
      End Do
  End Do
End Do
```

INTRINSIC FUNCTIONS AND LIBRARY ROUTINES

Fortran-90 anticipated some, but not all, of the basic operations that are valuable for parallel algorithm design. HPF adds several classes of parallel operations as intrinsic procedures: system inquiry intrinsics, new computational intrinsics and extensions of existing intrinsics, and distribution inquiry intrinsics. HPF also defines a standard library of computational functions.

System inquiry intrinsic functions

We can think of the processors in a multiprocessor system as being arranged in an implementation-dependent n-dimensional processor array. The system inquiry functions return values related to this underlying machine and processor configuration, including the size and shape of the array. Number_Of_Processors returns the total number of processors available to the program or the number of processors available to the program along a specified dimension of the array. Processors_Shape returns the shape of the array. Their values remain constant for (at least) the duration of one program execution, and can be used to specify, for example, array bounds. HPF programs can be compiled to run on machines whose configurations are not known at compile time. System inquiry functions query the physical machine, and have nothing to do with any Processors directive that may occur.

Let's consider two real computers. For a DECmpp 12000/Sx Model 200 with 8,192 processors:

```
Number_Of_Processors( ) == 8192
Number_Of_Processors(Dim=1) == 128
Number_Of_Processors(Dim=2) == 64
Processors_Shape( ) == (/ 128, 64 /)
```

while for a single processor DEC 3000 AXP workstation:

```
Number_Of_Processors( ) == 1
Number_Of_Processors(Dim=1) == 1
Processors_Shape( ) == (/ 1 /)
```

References to system inquiry functions can occur in HPF directives, as in:

```
!HPF$ Template T(100, 3*Number_Of_Processors( ))
```

System inquiry function calls can occur in, for example, lower or upper bounds of array declarations:

```
Integer, Dimension(Size(Processors_Shape( ))) :: PS
PS = Processors_Shape( )
! note that PS(2) == Number_Of_Processors(Dim=2)
```

The expression Size(Processors_Shape( )) returns the rank of the processor array.

Computational intrinsic functions

HPF extends Fortran-90's Maxloc and Minloc intrinsics to have an optional Dim argument that works in the same way as the Dim argument of Fortran-90's Maxval function. If such an argument is present, then the shape of the result equals the shape of the first argument with one dimension deleted (the one indicated by the Dim argument); it is as if a series of one-dimensional Maxloc or Minloc operations were performed.

Ilen is an elemental integer-length intrinsic. Its value when applied to a scalar is:

```
Ilen(x) = Ceiling(log2( If x < 0 Then –x Else x+1 ))
```

This value is the number of bits required to store a 2's-complement signed integer x. For example, $2**\text{Ilen}(N–1)$ rounds N up to a power of 2 (for $N > 0$), and $2**(\text{Ilen}(N)–1)$ rounds N down to a power of 2.

Mapping inquiry intrinsic subroutines

HPF provides a rich set of data-mapping directives. Users might need to know to what extent the compiler took their advice, especially when a user calls a non-HPF subroutine that needs to know the exact mapping. HPF includes inquiry intrinsic subroutines that describe how an array is actually mapped onto a machine. To keep the number of intrinsics small, the inquiry intrinsics are structured as intrinsic subroutines — HPF_Alignment, HPF_Template, and HPF_Distribution — with a number of optional arguments. Details of these functions are provided in the HPF specification.

Computational library functions

HPF also defines a library of computational functions to be provided as a Fortran-90 module (details are provided in the HPF specification):

- Reduction functions: AND, OR, EOR, and Parity.
- Combining scatter functions, one for each reduction function: Sum_Scatter, Count_Scatter, Product_ Scatter, All_Scatter, Any_Scatter, Maxval_ Scatter, Minval_Scatter, AND_Scatter, OR_Scatter, EOR_ Scatter, and Parity_Scatter.
- Parallel prefix functions, one for each reduction function: Sum_Prefix, Count_Prefix, Product_ Prefix, All_Prefix, Any_Prefix, Maxval_Prefix, Minval_ Prefix, AND_Prefix, OR_Prefix, EOR_ Prefix, and Parity_Prefix.
- Parallel suffix functions, one for each reduction function: Sum_Suffix, Count_Suffix, Product_Suffix, All_Suffix, Any_Suffix, Maxval_Suffix, Minval_ Suffix, AND_Suffix, OR_Suffix, EOR_Suffix, and Parity_Suffix.
- Sorting functions: Grade_Up, and Grade_Down.
- Bit manipulation: PopCnt, PopPar, and Leadz.

EXTRINSIC PROCEDURES

Some operations are difficult or impossible to express directly in a high-level, machine-independent language. For example, many applications benefit from finely-tuned systolic communications on certain machines; HPF's global address space does not express this well. To address such problems, HPF provides an extrinsic procedure interface as an escape mechanism for calling non-HPF code from an HPF program. Using it to call SPMD code, for example, lets the programmer descend to a lower level of abstraction to handle problems that are not efficiently addressed by HPF, and to hand-tune critical kernels or call optimized SPMD libraries. This interface can also be used to interface HPF to other languages, such as C.

A caller uses the same semantics to invoke an extrinsic HPF procedure as for a regular procedure, but the called procedure uses a different model. A call to an extrinsic procedure from "global" HPF code results in the transfer of control on each executing physical processor to a copy of a local procedure. All global arrays accessible to the extrinsic procedure (arrays passed as arguments) are logically carved into pieces; the copy of the local procedure executing on a particular physical processor sees an array containing just those elements of the global array that are mapped to that physical processor.

It is important not to confuse the extrinsic procedure called from the HPF program with the local procedures executed on each node: Invoking an extrinsic procedure results in a separate invocation of a local procedure on each processor. Executing an extrinsic procedure consists of concurrently executing a local procedure on each processor.

An extrinsic procedure can be defined as explicit SPMD code by specifying the local procedure code that is to execute on each processor. HPF provides a mechanism for defining local procedures in Fortran-90. Extrinsic procedures can also be defined in any other parallel language that maps to this basic SPMD execution model. The HPF compiler will compile the calling sequence for an extrinsic procedure when the local procedures are defined outside HPF and compiled separately.

With the exception of returning from a local procedure to the global caller that initiated local execution, there is no implicit synchronization of the locally executing processors. As a result, a local procedure can use any control structures whatsoever. Accessing data outside the processor requires either preparatory communication to copy data into the processor before running the local code, or communication between the separately executing copies of the local procedure. Individual implementations can provide implementation-dependent ways to communicate, such as through a message-passing library or a shared-memory mechanism. Such mechanisms are beyond the scope of HPF, but many useful portable algorithms that require only independence of control structure can take advantage of local routines, without requiring a communication facility.

The extrinsic procedure interface assumes only that array axes are mapped independently to axes of a rectangular processor grid, each array axis to at most one processor axis (no "skew" distributions) and no two array axes to the same processor axis. But the mapping of an array axis to a processor axis can be any mapping whatever. This restriction ensures that each physical processor contains a subset of array elements that can be locally arranged in a rectangular configuration. (Of course, computing the global indices of an element given its local indices, or vice versa, can be quite a tangle, but it will be possible.)

HPF specifies:

- the HPF interface to extrinsic routines, and the contract between the caller and the callee;
- a specific version of this interface for the case where extrinsic procedures are defined as explicit SPMD code, and local procedures are written in Fortran-90; and
- an extension of HPF that allows local (extended) Fortran-90 procedures to be included in an HPF program.

Fortran-90 anticipated some, but not all, of the basic operations that are valuable for parallel algorithm design.

For example:

```
! HPF Code
Interface
    Function F(X)
        Real, Dimension(:, :) ::X
        !HPF$ Distribute(Block, Cyclic) :: X
        !HPF$ Extrinsic
    End Function F
End Interface

... F(Y) ...

! Fortran-90 local implementation of F
Function F(X)
    Real, Dimension(:, :) ::X
    ! X is that part of the actual argument on this processor
    ...
```

SEQUENCE AND STORAGE ASSOCIATION

Fortran-77 and Fortran-90 constrain the location of data in two ways:

(1) Common and Equivalence statements constrain the alignment of different data items based on an underlying model of storage units and storage sequences: a single, linearly addressed memory.

(2) Sequence association specifies the order of array elements that Fortran requires when an array ex-

pression or array element is associated with a dummy array argument, a natural concept only in systems with a linearly addressed memory.

As an extension to Fortran-90, HPF allows codes that rely on sequence and storage association, although full support of these concepts is not compatible with HPF's goal of high performance through data distribution across multiple processors. HPF therefore provides directives to assert that full sequence and storage association for affected variables must be maintained. In the absence of these inhibiting features, reliance on the properties of association is not allowed. An optimizing compiler can then choose to distribute any variables across processor memories to improve performance. To protect program correctness, a given implementation should provide a mechanism to ensure that all such default optimization decisions are consistent across an entire program.

HPF defines the following relationship between HPF data mapping and Fortran sequence and storage association:

- Common blocks are nonsequential by default.
- Variables are nonsequential by default unless they have certain sequential properties.
- A Sequence directive allows explicit declaration that a variable or a Common block is to be sequential.

Although this approach is intuitively straightforward, the actual rules in the HPF specification are rather complex.

THE HPF SUBSET

Because full Fortran-90 compilers may not be available quickly on all platforms, and because some HPF extensions are more complex to implement than others, the HPF Forum defined an HPF subset. The group encouraged vendors to provide more rather than less in their first implementations and to move rapidly to full HPF implementations. However, HPF users who are concerned about multimachine portability may stay within this subset initially.

The subset includes those Fortran-90 features that are closely related to high performance on parallel machines:

- All of Fortran-77 (except sequence and storage association).
- The MIL-STD-1753 features: Do While statement; End Do statement; Implicit None statement; Include line; scalar bit-manipulation intrinsic procedures; binary, octal, and hexadecimal constants for use in Data statements.
- Arithmetic and logical array features: array sections (subscript triplet notation and vector-valued subscripts); array constructors limited to one level of implied Do; arithmetic and logical operations on whole arrays and array sections; array assignment; masked array assignment (Where statement and block Where . . . ElseWhere construct); array-valued external functions; Automatic arrays; Allocatable arrays and the Allocate and Deallocate statements; assumed-shape arrays
- Many intrinsic functions
- Declarations: type declaration statements (but no Kind, derived type, or Pointer), and attribute specification statements (Allocatable, Intent, Optional, Parameter, and Save)
- Procedure features: Interface blocks (but no generics or modules), optional arguments, and keyword argument passing.
- Syntax improvements: long (31-character) names, lowercase letters, use of "_" in names, and full-line and trailing "!" initiated comments

The subset also includes all HPF directives and language extensions except:

- The directives Realign, Redistribute, Dynamic, View, and Pure.
- The full ForAll construct (the subset does include the simple ForAll element array assignment).
- The HPF library.
- Values of the optional Dim arguments to the Fortran-90 Maxloc and Minloc intrinsic functions that are not initialization expressions.
- The Extrinsic directive, the Local directive, the definition of extrinsic procedures, and the Fortran-90 SPMD binding.

Future work

HPF considerably increases Fortran's expressive capabilities, but a number of simplifications were made to get agreement on the de facto standard within a year. In many cases, the HPF Forum agreed that a capability was needed without reaching consensus on how to provide it (without "agreeing on what to agree on"). For example, the group agreed on the need to specify both rectangular and nonrectangular arrangements of processors, but not on how to specify nonrectangular arrangements. Thus, even with the Processors directive, we can only specify rectangular arrangements.

Another example is parallel I/O. From the beginning there was a strong feeling against adding explicitly parallel I/O statements because:

- Fortran I/O is already highly expressive.
- I/O systems on different parallel computers are too architecturally different for there to be a useful abstraction on which to build a language model.
- An HPF compiler will know when it is performing I/O on distributed arrays, and can optimize the I/O to distributed files without any extensions to the source language.
- The management of distributed files (and their implementation) is a matter for the operating system, not the language.
- The current lack of extensions does not limit features that may be added by vendors.

By a narrow vote, the HPF Forum declined to extend Fortran I/O, but it included the topic in an appendix to the HPF specification — called the "Journal of Development" — that describes several features that were considered but not accepted into HPF. Many other features, including support for explicit MIMD computation, message-passing, and synchronization, were rejected or limited for lack of time or consensus rather than because of technical flaws. Other major "missing" capabilities include support for irregular and user-defined distributions, de facto extensions to Fortran such as the "*" notation for data typing, and support for MIMD computing paradigms other than data parallel. This last topic includes support "above" HPF (the ability to "tie together" multiple data parallel programs in a model we call "communicating data parallel programs") as well as support "below" HPF (in the form of extrinsic procedures).

Other topics covered in the "Journal of Development" are nested Where statements, Allocate in ForAll, generalized data references, ForAll with Independent directives, Execute-On-Home and Local-Access directives, and ForAll-ElseForAll construct.

HPF considerably increases Fortran's expressive capabilities, but a number of simplifications were made to get agreement on the de facto standard within a year.

At its December 1992 meeting, the HPF Forum discussed the possibility of holding an HPF workshop at the Supercomputing '93 conference this November in Portland, Oregon, followed by an HPF Forum II process beginning early in 1994.

So far, actual implementations related to Fortran-90 and HPF include SIMD implementations of Fortran-90 array operations, and a Fortran-90-to-C translator. There has also been university research on Fortran-D, Fortran-90 D, and Vienna Fortran, as well as SIMD experience with data locality directives defined in terms of the underlying machine.

HPF developers are confident they can build quality compilers, but as yet there is no real experience either with first compilers or with understanding the kind of code that users will actually write. Compilers under development are implementing the HPF subset, initially avoiding the harder HPF features and Fortran-90 features beyond the array features.

Following initial implementation of Fortran-90 and of HPF, there will be a necessary tuning phase in which the vendors discover how the features are actually used and optimize the compilers accordingly. Some constructs, such as ForAll, are not hard to implement correctly, but are rather difficult to implement in parallel efficiently. ▨

Acknowledgments

This article would not have been possible without the long hours put in by the members of the High Performance Fortran Forum. I specifically thank the other subgroup leaders, especially Bob Knighten, Chuck Koelbel, Rob Schreiber, Marc Snir, Guy Steele, and Mary Zosel, who wrote, integrated, and edited the chapters of the HPF Specification, from which I quoted and paraphrased liberally in this article without specific attribution. (The High Performance Fortran Language Specification is copyright 1992 by Rice University, Houston, Texas.) Thanks again to Chuck Koelbel for his extensive meeting notes, and to Ken Kennedy for his leadership in organizing and running the HPF Forum process. I also thank the members of the DEC Fortran-90 MPP and Alpha teams, especially Beth Benoit and Keith Kimball for input on the Fortran-90 sections of this article, and Bert Halstead for his leadership of Digital's original internal HPF project. The errors of omission and commission are, of course, my own.

Related works

ILLIAC IV FORTRAN

R.E. Millstein, "Control Structures in Illiac IV Fortran," *Comm. ACM,* Vol. 16, No. 10, Oct. 1973, pp. 621-627.

FORTRAN-77

American National Standard Programming Language Fortran, ANSI X3.9-1978, American National Standards Institute, 1978.

Parallel Extensions for Fortran-77, X3H5 Language Binding, X3H5 Technical Committee, July 1991.

MIL-STD 1753

Military Standard, MIL-STD-1753: Fortran, DoD Supplement to American National Standard X3.9-1978, US Department of Defense, Nov. 9, 1978.

FORTRAN-D

D. Callahan and K. Kennedy, "Compiling Programs for Distributed-Memory Multiprocessors," *J. Supercomputing,* Vol. 2, Oct. 1988, pp. 151-169.

G. Fox et al., "Fortran-D Language Specification," Tech. Report Comp TR90-141, Department of Computer Science, Rice University, Houston, Texas; and Tech. Report SCCS-42c, Syracuse Center for Computational Science, Syracuse University, Syracuse, New York; 1991.

FORTRAN-8x

E. Albert, J.D. Lukas, and G.L. Steele, Jr., "Data Parallel Computers and the ForAll Statement," *J. Parallel and Distributed Computing,* Vol. 13, No. 2, Oct. 1991, pp. 185-192.

American National Standard for Information Systems Programming Language Fortran, S8 (X3.9-198x) Revision of X3.9-1978, Draft S8, Version 104, American National Standards Institute, Apr. 1987.M. Metcalf and J. Reid, *Fortran-8x Explained,* Oxford University Press, Oxford, England, 1989.

FORTRAN-90

J.C. Adams et al., *Fortran-90 Handbook,* McGraw-Hill, New York, 1992.

W.S. Brainerd, C.H. Goldberg, and J.C. Adams, *Programmer's Guide to Fortran-90,* McGraw-Hill, New York, 1990.

M. Chen and J. Cowie, "Prototyping Fortran-90 Compilers for Massively Parallel Machines," *Proc. SIGPlan '92 Conf. on Programming Language Design and Implementation, ACM SIGPlan Notices,* 1992, pp. 94-105.

M. Chen and J. Wu, "Optimizing Fortran-90 Programs for Data Motion on Massively Parallel Systems," Tech. Report YaleU/DCS/TR-882, Yale University, 1991.

Fortran-90, ISO/IEC Standard 1539: 1991 (E), and ANSI Standard X3.198-1992.

M. Metcalf and J. Reid, *Fortran-90 Explained,* Oxford University Press, Oxford, England, 1990.

M.-Y. Wu and G. Fox, "Fortran-90 D Compiler for Distributed-Memory MIMD Parallel Computers," Tech. Report SCCS-88b, Syracuse Center for Computational Science, Syracuse University, Syracuse, New York, 1991.

VIENNA FORTRAN

B. Chapman, P. Mehrotra, and H. Zima, "Programming in Vienna Fortran," *Scientific Programming,* Vol. 1, No. 1, Aug. 1992, pp. 31-50.

KALI

C. Koelbel and P. Mehrota, "Programming Data-Parallel Algorithms on Distributed-Memory Machines Using Kali," *Proc. 1991 ACM Int'l Conf. Supercomputing,* ACM Press, New York, 1991.

P. Mehrotra and J. Van Rosendale, "Programming Distributed Memory Architectures Using Kali," in *Advances in Languages and Compilers for Parallel Processing,* A. Nicolau et al., eds., MIT Press, Cambridge, Mass., 1991, pp. 364-384.

HIGH PERFORMANCE FORTRAN

Draft High Performance Fortran Language Specification, Version 1.0 Draft, David Loveman, ed., January 1993, Tech. Report 92225, CRPC, Rice University, Houston, Texas, or by anonymous FTP from public/hpff/draft at titan.cs.rice.edu

C. Koelbel and P. Mehrota, "An Overview of High Performance Fortran," *Fortran Forum,* Vol. 11, No. 4, Dec. 1992, pp. 9-16.

D.B. Loveman, "Element Array Assignment: The ForAll Statement," *Third Workshop on Compilers for Parallel Computers,* Tech. Report ACPC/TR 92-8, Austrian Center for Parallel Computation, University of Vienna, Austria, 1992, pp. 109-120.

G.L. Steele, Jr., "High Performance Fortran: Status Report," *Workshop on Languages, Compilers, and Runtime Environments for Distributed-Memory Multiprocessors, ACM SIGPlan Notices,* Vol. 28, No. 1, Jan. 1993, pp. 1-4.

FORTRAN IMPLEMENTATIONS

CM Fortran Reference Manual, Thinking Machines Corp., Cambridge, Mass., 1991.

DEC Fortran Language Reference Manual, Digital Equipment Corporation, Maynard, Mass., Oct. 1992.

DECmpp 12000 Sx - DECmpp Sx Parallel Fortran Reference Manual, Digital Equipment Corporation, Maynard, Mass., July 1992.

MasPar Fortran Reference Manual, MasPar Computer Corp., Sunnyvale, Calif., 1991.

D.M. Pase, T. MacDonald, and A. Meltzer, "MPP Fortran Programming Model," tech. report, Cray Research, Eagan, Minn., 1992; available by electronic mail request to mppgrp@cray.com.

VAX Fortran Language Reference Manual, Digital Equipment Corporation, Maynard, Mass., June 1988.

David Loveman is a senior program manager at Digital Equipment Corporation. He is also Digital's representative to the High Performance Fortran Forum and editor of the HPF Language Specification. His technical interests include programming language strategies, compiler architectures, and parallel computing. Before joining Digital, Loveman was at Compass, Inc., where as president he planned and oversaw language design and compiler development for a number of massively parallel computers. He received an MS in applied mathematics from Harvard University and a BS in electrical engineering from Princeton University. He is a member of IEEE, the IEEE Computer Society, ACM, and SIGPlan. Readers can contact him at Digital Equipment Corporation, ML01-3/B11, 146 Main St., Maynard, MA 01754; Internet, loveman@rdvax.enet.dec.com

Data-Parallel Programming on Multicomputers

Michael J. Quinn, *Oregon State University*
Philip J. Hatcher, *University of New Hampshire*

Multicomputers are too hard to program with conventional parallel languages. The data-parallel approach offers both programmability and portability without sacrificing performance.

Since the introduction of the Sequent Balance in 1984 and the Intel iPSC in 1985, thousands of low-cost commercial multiprocessors and multicomputers have been sold. Given this large base of installed hardware, where is all the software?

The history of commercial parallel computers sheds some light on this question. Ever since the first Cray-1 was delivered without a compiler, manufacturers have developed and commercialized sophisticated hardware without developing equally sophisticated software. Instead, they have taken the simpler course of providing users a conventional programming language, enhanced with a few low-level constructs for creating and synchronizing parallel processes.

This approach lightens the compiler writer's load, but adding a set of parallel constructs to a sequential language does not support reasoning about a parallel program that embodies concurrent and distributed state changes among many processes. If programmers cannot reason about the behavior of their programs, how can they produce correct, maintainable code?

Data-parallel languages do not have this problem. Although the C* data-parallel language was developed by Thinking Machines Corp. for its Connection Machine processor array, C* also offers multicomputer programmers a more elegant and understandable model of parallel computation than conventional languages. We have designed a compiler that translates C* programs into C programs suitable for compilation and execution on a hypercube multicomputer. This compiler can translate C* programs into efficient C code.

Computation models

Michael Flynn's taxonomy of computer architectures provides a basis for programmer models of parallel computa-

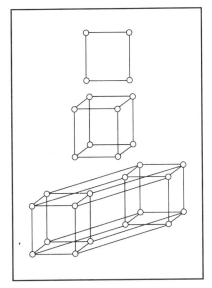

Figure 1. Two-, three-, and four-dimensional hypercubes.

tion.[1] In this taxonomy, you can view a single-instruction-stream/multiple-data-stream computer as a single control unit directing the activities of several arithmetic processing elements, each capable of fetching and manipulating its own local data. The SIMD programming model is called *synchronous* because all active processing elements execute the same operation simultaneously. The data-parallel programming model is based on the SIMD model with the following additional features:

• A global name space, which obviates the need for explicit message passing between processing elements,

• parallel objects, rather than merely parallel scalar types, and

• the ability to make the number of processing elements a function of the problem size, rather than a function of the target machine.

A multiple-instruction-stream/multiple-data-stream computer can execute multiple instruction streams concurrently; each MIMD processor manipulates its own data and can execute a unique program. Most people program MIMD computers in the same-code/multiple-data style — in the SCMD model, every processor node executes the same program. Both the MIMD and SCMD programming models are called *asynchronous*. Although processors may coordinate with each other at synchronization points, every processor executes instructions at its own pace between those points.

Conventional multicomputer languages

A multicomputer is a multiple-CPU computer designed for parallel processing but lacking a shared memory.[2] All multicomputer processors communicate and synchronize with each other by passing messages. A hypercube multicomputer organizes its processors into a binary *n*-cube, as Figure 1 shows.

Programmers must manage a lot of messages to program a hypercube in a conventional language that has been augmented by message-passing constructs. In a typical hypercube, like Intel's iPSC or N-Cube Corp.'s N-Cube 3200 (formerly known as the N-Cube 10), a host processor manages the I/O devices and the node processors, as Figure 2 shows. Implementing an application requires writing two programs: one for the host and one for the nodes.

The host program performs terminal I/O, allocates the hypercube, loads the node program, serves as an intermediary between the nodes and I/O devices (including the disk), reports results back to the user, and deallocates the hypercube.

Programs executing on the nodes implement the parallel algorithm. Every node processor must get its initial data from the host or other nodes; then it performs computations, communicates and synchronizes with other nodes by passing messages, and sends its portion of the final result back to the host.

Programming errors occur not so much in the parallel computation implementation within a node as in the interactions between processors. Managing these interactions through low-level asynchronous constructs is error-prone.

SCMD programming style. Asynchronous algorithms have much greater potential for time-related errors, like deadlocks and data incoherence, than synchronous algorithms. Thus, many programmers rely on the SCMD programming style for multicomputers. This style lets them distribute data over the memories of individual node processors and execute the same program on each processor.[3]

SCMD programs characteristically separate blocks of code by calls to message-passing routines. Processors execute the same block of code asynchronously, using data available in local memory. Then they exchange data with other processors; this communication point also serves a synchronization function.

Generic host program. The second major source of errors lies in the message-passing mechanism itself. Our experience confirms that novice programmers make

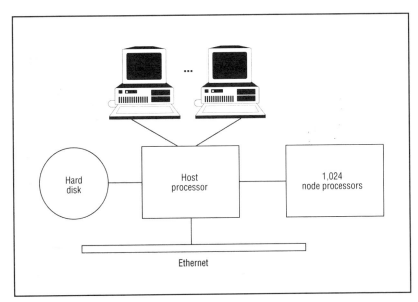

Figure 2. The architecture of the N-Cube 3200 hypercube multicomputer.

most of their mistakes with the message-passing protocols, and even experienced programmers can stumble over this awkward and error-prone method of communication and synchronization between processes.

One way to reduce the amount of message passing is to eliminate the host processor. Of course, you can't physically remove the host from current systems, since it is the only CPU connected to the I/O devices. However, you can simplify its role significantly by reducing its job to allocating and deallocating hypercubes and transferring data between nodes and I/O devices. In such a system, every node has access to routines in an I/O library, like open, read, and printf. You program the nodes as if they could perform the operations in the I/O library. In reality, the compiler translates each function call into code that sends a message to the generic host program to perform the required I/O and return the result.

Communication libraries. You can also simplify message passing between nodes by using libraries of standard communication routines. These libraries are available for relatively high-level functions, like broadcast, fan-in, and random-access read or write.

Combined advantages. These techniques — the SCMD programming style, generic host programs, and standard communication libraries — simplify multicomputer programming. Programs written within these restrictions have three valuable characteristics:

• They are easier to design, debug, and maintain.

• They can implement a wide variety of parallel algorithms. (In a study of 84 scientific problems addressed at the California Institute of Technology, Geoffrey Fox found that 83 percent of them were amenable to solutions based on synchronous or loosely synchronous algorithms,[4] which can be implemented as SCMD programs.)

• A compiler can generate such efficient SCMD object code automatically from a SIMD-based data-parallel source program.

The C* language

We believe a synchronous, massively

parallel model — in which all processes change state in a simple, predictable fashion — leads to understandable programs. The parallelism in this model comes from executing a single operation simultaneously across a large data set.

The data-parallel approach has several advantages. First, its control flow is simple. It is easy to determine the program state, because all processes are either active or inactive as a universal program counter works through the various control statements. Second, computation results are deterministic and independent of the number of physical processors. Third, building a debugger is straightforward; breakpoints make sense on a single-instruction-stream model. Fourth, data-parallel programs are portable. You can translate programs that run efficiently on

processor arrays into programs that run efficiently on multicomputers.

Data-parallel languages are not *the* solution to programming multicomputers; they are only *a* solution. You can use data-parallel programs to solve many problems, like low-level vision, protein mechanics, and most linear-algebra problems. However, a data-parallel language is inappropriate for implementing programs with multiple asynchronous processes, like database management systems and multiprogrammed operating systems. W. Daniel Hillis and Guy Steele have documented further insights into the data-parallel approach.[5]

C* is an extension of C that incorporates features of the data-parallel SIMD programming model. The language has been described in detail elsewhere.[6] The following highlights a few important features.

C* classifies all data into two kinds, scalar and parallel, referred to by the keywords mono and poly, respectively. C* lets you express algorithms as if data could be mapped onto an unbounded number of processors. Once you have mapped every piece of parallel data to its own processing element, you can use several simple program constructs to express parallel operations.

The most important of these constructs is an extension of the class type in C++. A class is an implementation of an abstract data type. You can use its member functions to manipulate the instances of a particular class type. In C*, member functions operate on several instances of a class in parallel. This parallel class type is called a domain.

C* programs map variables of a domain type to separate processing elements. All instances of a domain type may be acted upon in parallel by using that domain's member functions and the selection statement. In the parallel code, each sequential program statement is performed in parallel for all instances of the specified domain. The following code segment computes the maximum number of elements of two arrays:

```
domain vector { float a, b, max; } x[100];
intervening code
[domain vector].{
    if (a > b) max = a;
    else max = b;
}
```

The domain type vector defines a domain containing two real values, *a* and *b*. By declaring *x* to be a 100-element array of vector, the code creates 100 instances of the variable pair, one pair per processing element. The selection statement [domain vector] activates every processing element whose instance has domain type vector — that is, every element of *x*.

Every active processing element executes the statements within the selection statement. In this case, every processing element evaluates the expression $a > b$. The universal program counter enters the then clause, and those processing elements for which the expression is true perform the assignment statement max = *a*. Then the counter enters the max clause, and those processing elements for which the expression is false perform the assignment statement max = b.

C* programs have a single name space, and any expression can contain a reference to any variable in any domain. For example, in the following code segment, every active processing element sets its own value of temp to be the average of the temp values of its predecessor and successor processing elements:

```
#define N 100
domain rod { float temp; } x[N];
intervening code
[domain rod].{
    int index = this–x;   /* Meaning of the
        keyword "this" is the same as in C++ */
    intervening code
    if ((index > 0) && (index < N–1))
        temp = (x[index–1].temp +
            x[index+1].temp) / 2.0;
}
```

Each processing element's value of index gives its unique position in the domain — a value in the range of 0 to N–1. All active processing elements evaluate the right side of the assignment statement together. Then they all assign values together. Thus, an old value cannot be overwritten before an adjacent processing element has had the opportunity to read it.

In our experience programming hypercube multicomputers with conventional parallel languages, we have found that burying an entire class of messages — those between the host and the nodes — improves programmer productivity immensely. C* eliminates explicit message passing between processors, which should further improve productivity.

Translating C* to C

We designed our hypercube C* compiler primarily to minimize the penalty of using a data-parallel language. For a wide class of data-parallel algorithms, we hope to support C* programs that are nearly as efficient as the corresponding hypercube C programs that deal explicitly with message passing and synchronization.

Our basic compiler strategy is to use the input C* program — a SIMD specification — to extract an SCMD-style C program. The extracted program is similar to what a C programmer would have to produce by hand.

We faced four major design problems in implementing this strategy:
• How do we infer the message-passing

requirements of a C* program?
• How do we support the C* program's synchronization requirements efficiently when the target machine is MIMD?
• How do we emulate a massive number of processing elements efficiently on a machine that has no hardware support for virtual processors?
• Because message passing is expensive on our target machine, how do we minimize the message-passing costs of a particular C* program?

Message-passing requirements. If you spread C* processing elements around

---

The synchronization guarantees that the value each processor retrieves is the same as it would be under a fully synchronous implementation.

---

the hypercube nodes and add one special-purpose processing element to execute sequential code, you can trace the C* program's potential communication requirements to those points at which processing elements read or write values to or from each other.

A C* programmer uses expressions to refer to a variable located in a different processing element's memory. All C* variable declarations state, implicitly or explicitly, which processing element holds the variable. Therefore, you can reduce the location of potential communication points to a type-checking problem, where a compiler accesses declarations for identifiers to determine an expression's meaning.

(In this article, we talk in terms of *potential* communication because many situations require no physical communication. For example, a pointer may not point to a memory location until runtime, and then it may or may not point locally.)

Synchronization requirements. We ap-

proached the synchronization issue by asking how much we could loosen a language's synchronization requirements without affecting a program's behavior. If a set of processing elements was executing the same code block and each element accessed only its own local variables, it wouldn't matter if the processors were synchronized after every statement, after every other statement, or only at the end of the block.

However, if each processing element must read a value from its neighbor halfway through the code block, the processors must first be synchronized. The synchronization guarantees that the value each processor retrieves is the same as it would be under a fully synchronous implementation. Thus, synchronization points are those points where messages passing is potentially required. The compiler places message-passing primitives incorporating synchronization at those points.

Parallel-looping constructs may require additional synchronization, but only if the loop body requires message passing. If the processing elements executing the loop do not interact, it doesn't matter if they are executing different iterations of the loop concurrently. No synchronization is required because processors need only to synchronize just before they interact.

If the parallel loop body does require message passing, you must synchronize the processors every iteration before the message-passing step. No virtual processor can execute the statement after the loop until all virtual processors have exited the loop.

This constraint forces all virtual processors to communicate each iteration to compute a global logical Or of the virtual processors' Boolean loop-control values. A virtual processor can exit the loop only when the global logical Or is false. Because this global Or operation is required only when message passing occurs inside the loop, we bundled the global Or operation with the required message. This let us ensure that the points at which the messages are sent are exactly the points at which we synchronize the processors.

Of course, a virtual processor does not actually execute the loop body after its local loop-control value has become false. Instead, the physical processor on which it

```
while (condition) {
    statement_list₁;
    communication;
    statement_list₂;
}

(a)

temp = TRUE;
do {
    if (temp) {
        temp = condition;
    }
    if (temp) {
        statement_list₁;
    }
    communication;
    gtemp = global_or (temp);
    if (temp) {
        statement_list₂;
    }
} while (gtemp);

(b)
```

Figure 3. Translation of a C* while loop to rewrite its control structure: **(a)** the C* construct and **(b)** the translated C code.

```
if (condition) {
    statement_list₁;
    communication;
    statement_list₂;
}

(a)

temp = condition;
if (temp) {
    statement_list₁;
}
communication;
if (temp) {
    statement_list₂;
}

(b)
```

Figure 4. Translation of a simple if statement: **(a)** the C* construct and **(b)** the translated C code.

resides participates in the message passing and the global Or operation. This means that our C* compiler must rewrite the control structure of input programs. Figure 3 shows how to rewrite while loops.

To meet the requirement for all physical processors to actively participate in any message-passing operation through the hypercube, our compiler must rewrite all control statements that include message passing. It rewrites the statement to bring the message-passing operations to the surface of the control structure. Figure 4 shows how it handles an if statement. Communication steps buried inside nested control structures are pulled out of each enclosing structure until they reach the outermost level.

This technique will not handle arbitrary control-flow graphs, so we cannot implement the goto statement in our compiler. But it can handle the break and continue statements.

Emulating processing elements. Once the compiler completes these transformations, it is straightforward for it to emulate processing elements. The compiler puts for loops around the code blocks that have been delimited by message-passing/synchronization steps. Within the delimited blocks, no message passing occurs, so no interaction occurs between processing elements. Thus, it makes no difference in which order the virtual processors located on a particular physical processor execute their instructions.

Message-passing optimizations. Message passing is an expensive operation on a multicomputer, and minimizing the time spent on it is a primary compiler goal. You can eliminate one class of messages by keeping copies of the sequential code and data on each node. Every node executes the sequential code. This adds nothing to the program's execution time: If a single physical processor executed the code while the other physical processors sat idle, the execution time would be the same. When every physical processor has copies of the sequential variables, each processor can access sequential data by doing a local memory fetch. In other words, every processor can assign the value of a mono variable to a poly variable

without passing messages.

By putting a copy of the sequential code and data on each physical processor, we assumed that the processor retrieves mono values more often than it assigns them. With our design, mono retrieval is free — every physical processor has a local copy of the mono that a virtual processor can access without message passing. However, when a virtual processor stores to a mono variable, the value may have to be broadcast to update all physical processors' copies of the mono. The compiler can omit the subsequent broadcast if a control-flow analysis indicates that all virtual processors are active for the store to a mono and that the value being stored is the same on all virtual processors.

A simple analysis can track mono values to *sequentialize* loop constructs and avoid possible loop synchronizations. For example, if you initialize the loop-control variable to a mono value, if the loop-termination expression is essentially a mono expression, and if the loop-increment step is the same for all virtual processors, then the compiler knows in advance that all virtual processors will execute the loop the same number of times. It does not generate a global Or of the loop-termination expression value. Nor is a virtual processor emulation required for the control part of the loop structure. You can move the for loop that emulates virtual processors inside the C* loop.

You can also apply this type of analysis to expressions that require message passing. If the compiler determines that all virtual processors are requesting the same piece of nonlocal data, a physical processor can instead request the data once and share it among the resident virtual processors.

Message-passing expressions can be examined by a common subexpression-detection phase of the compiler. Since C* programmers refer to nonlocal values by writing an expression, equivalent expressions should cause the compiler to analyze the intervening code to see if it could affect the expression's value. If not, the processor can retrieve the distant value once with the expensive message-passing step. Then it can keep a local copy of the value for the second reference.

Viewing message passing as a possible vector operation offers another optimiza-

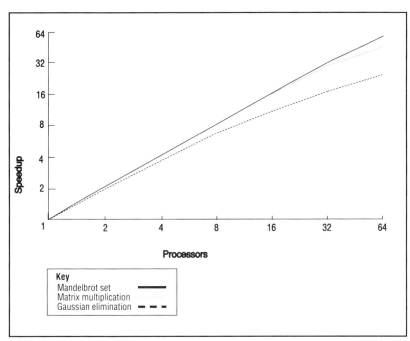

Figure 5. Speedup achieved by three hand-compiled C* programs executing on an N-Cube 3200 multicomputer. The Mandelbrot program computes the colors of a 128×128 image representing a square of the complex plane centered on the origin and having sides of length 4. The matrix multiplication program multiplies two 128 × 128 integer matrices. The Gaussian elimination program reduces a dense system of 256 linear equations with 256 unknowns.

tion. If the processor must send a block of data (like a matrix row) to another processor, it can send the whole block in one message, rather than as a series of shorter messages. This transfers essentially the same amount of data but drastically reduces the message-passing overhead. There are well-established techniques to perform this vectorization operation — techniques designed for use with machines that have vector instructions.[7]

You can perform a similar optimization on the code generated to support virtual processors. Instead of having each active virtual processor send an individual message, you can gather the message bodies of all active virtual processors on a single physical processor and ship them all at once. The reason once again is to reduce the number of communication steps.

The compiler tracks which virtual processors are assigned to which physical processors. If a message must pass between two virtual processors residing on the same node, there is no I/O between nodes. Instead, the processor makes a local memory transfer. Similarly, if two virtual processors reside on adjacent nodes, the compiler calls the library routine that exploits this fact to send a message between the two processors in constant time.

Because the compiler does not know the exact number of virtual and physical processors at compile time, it relies on hints from the programmer to know that two processors are in fact adjacent. The hints are in the form of function calls that compute references to domain instances. For example, RingSucc returns the processor identifier of the successor virtual processor, assuming processors are organized as a ring.

Our final optimization is another example of message-passing strength reduction (that is, replacing one message-passing operation with a less costly form of communication). If the compiler knows that all virtual processors will be active and the communication pattern is regular (for example, the RingSucc function is being invoked), the compiler can replace a read-message operation with a write-message operation. The read operation is more costly because the processor must send a message requesting a value and receive a subsequent reply message transferring the value. If all processors need to perform reads, each processor can write the proper value from its memory to the processor that needs the value. This cuts the message-passing cost in half.

We may need to extend these optimiza-tions as we gain more experience with data-parallel programs. For example, we could apply vectorization within expressions, not just for looping constructs. If a C* expression contains a mixture of poly and mono variables, it might be advantageous to reorder the expression, if possible, to gather the poly variables together. This would let the values be retrieved with a single message rather than with a sequence of messages. But we have not encountered this situation in the data-parallel programs we have examined to date.

Results

Figure 5 illustrates the efficiency of executing data-parallel programs on a hypercube multicomputer. It shows the speedup achieved by three hand-compiled C* programs executing on an N-Cube 3200 multicomputer. The first two programs — Mandelbrot set calculation and matrix multiplication — have a high degree of parallelism and a simple control structure. The C* compiler can generate relatively straightforward code with performance comparable to hand-written C code.

Figure 6 lists the C* program to perform Gaussian elimination with partial pivoting. (The code to initialize the system and print results is omitted.) The program overwrites a dense system of linear equations with its lower-upper factorization.

Each row has a virtual processor associated with it. The algorithm has N–1 iterations. During each iteration i, the column i value in every unmarked row is driven to 0 by taking a linear combination of the unmarked row and the pivot row. The pivot row is determined in lines 12-18.

The expression $(>?=ABS(a[i]))$ returns the maximum of the absolute value of each virtual processor's column i element; thus, the value assigned to picked at line 14 is the number of the virtual processor whose column i element has the greatest magnitude. The algorithm exits prematurely at line 19 if there is no nonzero element in column i (that is, if the system is singular). The unmarked rows are reduced in lines 20-25.

The algorithm for Gaussian elimination has a good measure of sequentiality to it, and virtual processors exchange data frequently (on lines 13, 19, 22, and 24). To produce efficient object code, a compiler must be able to perform numerous message-passing optimizations.

We have hand-translated this C* program into two C programs. Program 1 is a straightforward compilation, using the transformations described earlier for translating SIMD C* programs. Program 2 applies the message-passing optimizations, also described earlier, to program 1. We applied these optimizations to lines 21-25 in the C* program for Gaussian elimination.

Every virtual processor executes the for loops in lines 23-24 the same number of times, because the initial value of j (the bounding condition) and the increment are identical for every processor. Thus, the processors do not have to synchronize every iteration through the loop.

Lines 23-24 perform a vector operation. Rather than perform $N+1-i$ message-passing operations (one for each value of $a[j]$ that must be retrieved from virtual processor picked), all $N+1-i$ values can be fetched at one time, before entering the loop. Remember that every physical processor controls a set of virtual processors. Because every virtual processor needs the same $N+1-i$ elements from virtual processor picked, the physical processor has only to fetch these values once. Given a virtual-to-physical-processor ratio of V, these two optimizations reduce the number of messages sent on iteration i from $V(N+1-i)$ to 1.

You can eliminate another V communications by realizing that the nonlocal value needed in line 22 — $r[picked].a[i]$ — is the first vector element fetched for the for loop in lines 23-25. The message-passing step simply shifts to above line 22.

Figure 7 lists the C code produced from these optimizations. Figure 8 plots the time needed for the N-Cube 3200 to solve variously sized systems of linear equations using programs 1 and 2. In each example, the size of the system to be solved is identical to the number of physical processors (that is, the ratio of virtual processors to physical processors is one-to-one). The message-passing optimizations increase program efficiency by 288 percent at four processors to almost 691 percent at 64 processors. These optimizations are sufficient to translate the C* program into an

```
1.       #define N 256
2.       #define ABS(x) (((x) > 0) ? (x) : (−(x)))
3.       #define EPSILON 0.00001

4.       domain row {float a[N+1]; int pivot;} ;

5.       main() {
6.         int picked;
7.         domain row r[N];

8.         [domain row].{
9.           int i, j, temp;
10.          int marked = 0;

11.          for (i = 0; i < N − 1 ; i++) {
12.            /* Find pivot row */
13.            if (!marked && (ABS(a[i]) == (>?= ABS(a[i]))))
14.              picked = (this − r);          /* Virtual processor # */
15.            if ((this − r) == picked) {
16.              marked = 1;                   /* Mark pivot row */
17.              pivot = i;                    /* Remember permuted position */
18.            }

19.            if (fabs(r[picked].a[i]) < EPSILON) break;

20.                                            /* Reduce unmarked rows */
21.            if (!marked) {
22.              temp = a[i] / r[picked].a[i];
23.              for (j = i; j < N+1; j++)
24.                a[j] = a[j] − r[picked].a[j] * temp;
25.            }                               /* if */
26.          }                                 /* for */
27.        }                                   /* domain select */
28.      }
```

Figure 6. The C* program to perform Gaussian elimination with partial pivoting. The code to initialize the system and print results is not shown.

```
/* Physical processor controlling virtual processor 'picked' fills its broadcast vector. */
if (nodenum == picked/N)
  for (j = i; j < N+1; j++) t2[j] = a[picked%N][j];

/* Broadcast pivot row's value. */
broadcast (picked/N, &t2[i], (N+1−i)*sizeof(float));

/* Every physical processor reduces unmarked rows of its V virtual processors.
*/
for (vp = 0; vp < V; vp++) {
  if (!marked[vp]) {
    temp = a[vp][i] / t2[i];
    for (j = i; j < N+1; j++)
      a[vp][j] = a[vp][j] − t2[j] * temp;
  }
}
```

Figure 7. Segment of hand-compiled optimized C code translated from lines 21-25 of the C* program in Figure 6.

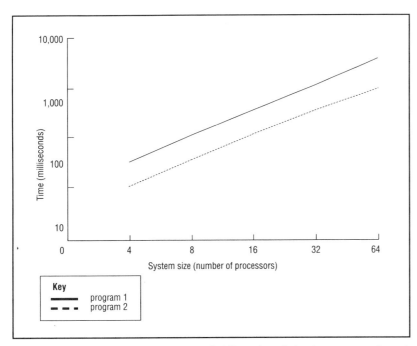

Figure 8. Execution time of two hand-compiled Gaussian-elimination programs. In each example, the size of the system to be solved is identical to the number of physical processors. The speedup of program 2 is identical to a hand-coded C program written in the SCMD style.

SCMD-style C program that equals the performance of a hand-coded, SCMD-style C program.

Inadequate programming languages are hindering the emergence of parallel applications on multicomputers. The typical commercial parallel language uses low-level constructs to manage parallel processes, making programs difficult to implement and debug.

By contrast, data-parallel languages like C* offer the programmer a high-level model of parallel computation incorporating synchronous execution, a global name space, parallel objects, and virtual processors. These high-level constructs make parallel programs easier to write.

With a mechanism like a compiler that can translate C* programs into C code comparable in speed to that written by programmers, users can enjoy portability and high performance, as well as programmability.

We do not see data-parallel programming as the only solution to the problem of programming multicomputers, but we do see a role for a language that is explicitly parallel yet very similar to existing sequential languages. An easy-to-learn data-parallel language like C* can help popularize parallel computing. ❖

Acknowledgments

We appreciate the work of the referees, whose helpful comments improved the quality of our presentation. This work was supported by National Science Foundation grants DCR-8514493 and CCR-8814662.

Part of this article appeared in different form in *Proceedings of the 1990 International Conference on Computer Languages* (CS Press).

Michael J. Quinn is an associate professor of computer science at Oregon State University. His research interests include the design, analysis, and implementation of parallel algorithms and parallel programming environments. He was at the University of New Hampshire when the work described here was conducted. He has also worked at Tektronix.

Quinn received a BS in mathematics from Gonzaga University, Spokane, Wash., an MS in computer science from University of Wisconsin at Madison, and a PhD in computer science from Washington State University. Quinn is a member of ACM and the IEEE Computer Society.

Philip J. Hatcher is an assistant professor of computer science at the University of New Hampshire. His primary research interest is designing and implementing programming languages.

Hatcher received a BS in mathematics and an MS in computer science from Purdue University and a PhD in computer science from the Illinois Institute of Technology. He is a member of ACM and the IEEE Computer Society.

Address questions about this article to Quinn at Computer Science Dept., Oregon State University, Corvallis, OR 97331; Internet quinn@ cs.orst.edu.

References

1. M.J. Flynn, "Very High-Speed Computing Systems," *Proc. IEEE*, Dec. 1966, pp. 1,901-1,909.

2. M.J. Quinn, *Designing Efficient Algorithms for Parallel Computers*, McGraw-Hill, New York, 1987.

3. M.T. Heath, "The Hypercube: A Tutorial Overview," *Hypercube Multicomputers 1987*, M.T. Heath, ed., SIAM Press, Philadelphia, 1987, pp. 7-10.

4. G.C. Fox, "What Have We Learnt from Using Real Parallel Machines to Solve Real Problems?" *Proc. Third Conf. Hypercube Concurrent Computers and Applications*, ACM, New York, 1988, pp. 897-955.

5. W.D. Hillis and G.L. Steele, Jr., "Data Parallel Algorithms," *Comm. ACM*, Dec. 1986, pp. 1,170-1,183.

6. J.R. Rose and G.L. Steele, Jr., "C*: An Extended C Language for Data Parallel Programming," Tech. Report PL 87-5, Thinking Machines Corp., Cambridge, Mass., 1986.

7. D.A. Padua and M.J. Wolfe, "Advanced Compiler Optimizations for Supercomputers," *Comm. ACM*, Dec. 1986, pp. 1,184-1,201.

Visualization and Debugging in a Heterogeneous Environment

Adam Beguelin, Carnegie Mellon University and Pittsburgh Supercomputing Center

Jack Dongarra, University of Tennessee and Oak Ridge National Laboratory

Al Geist, Oak Ridge National Laboratory

Vaidy Sunderam, Emory University

A monitoring tool and a graphical interface working on top of the PVM software can help programmers make better use of heterogeneous networks of computers.

The emergence of a wide variety of commercially available parallel computers has created a software dilemma. Will it be possible to design general-purpose software that is both efficient and portable across these new parallel computers? Moreover, will it be possible to provide programming environments sophisticated enough for explicit parallel programming to exploit the performance of these new machines? For many computational problems, the design, implementation, and understanding of efficient parallel algorithms can be a formidable challenge. Additional issues of synchronization and multiple-task coordination make efficient parallel programs more difficult to write and understand than efficient sequential programs. Parallel programs are often less portable than serial codes because their structure may depend critically on the hardware's specific architectural features (such as how it handles data sharing, memory access, synchronization, and process creation).

The computing requirements of many current and future applications, ranging from scientific computational problems in the material and physical sciences to simulation, engineering design, and circuit analysis, are best served by concurrent processing. Multiprocessors can frequently address the computational requirements of these high-performance applications, but other aspects of concurrent computing are not adequately addressed when conventional parallel processors are used.

For instance, software aspects, including program development methods, scalable programs, profiling tools, and support systems, require significant development. While hardware and architectural advances in parallelism have been rapid, the software infrastructure has not kept pace, resulting in unsystematic and ad hoc approaches to the implementation of concurrent applications. In recent years, several research groups have focused on various aspects of this shortcoming, producing significant developments in programming paradigms, data partitioning, algorithms, languages, and scheduling.

Heterogeneous networks of computers ranging from workstations to supercomputers are becoming commonplace in high-performance computing. Until recently, each computing resource on the network remained a separate unit, but now hundreds of institutions worldwide are using the Parallel Virtual Machine[1] soft-

Reprinted from *Computer*, Vol. 26, No. 6, June 1993, pp. 88-95. Copyright © 1993 by The Institute of Electrical and Electronics Engineers, Inc. All rights reserved.

PVM: Heterogeneous distributed computing

PVM (Parallel Virtual Machine) is a software package being developed by Oak Ridge National Laboratory, the University of Tennessee, and Emory University. It enables a heterogeneous collection of Unix computers linked by a network to function as a single large parallel computer. Thus, large computational problems can be solved by the aggregate power and memory of many computers.

PVM supplies the functions to start tasks and lets the computers communicate and synchronize with each other. It survives the failure of one or more connected computers and supplies functions for users to make their applications fault tolerant. Users can write applications in Fortran or C and parallelize them by calling simple PVM message-passing routines such as pvm_send() and pvm_recv(). By sending and receiving messages, application subtasks can cooperate to solve a problem in parallel.

PVM lets subtasks exploit the type of computer best suited for finding their solution. Thus some subtasks may run on a vector supercomputer and others on a parallel computer or powerful workstation. PVM applications can be run transparently across a wide variety of architectures; PVM automatically handles all message conversion required if linked computers use different data representations. Participating computers can be distributed anywhere in the world and linked by a variety of networks.

The PVM source code and user's guide are available by electronic mail. The software is easy to install. The source has been tested on Sun, DEC, IBM, HP, Silicon Graphics Iris, Data General, and Next workstations, as well as parallel computers by Sequent, Alliant, Intel, Thinking Machines, BBN, Cray, Convex, IBM, and KSR. In addition, Cray Research, Convex, IBM, Silicon Graphics, and DEC supply and support PVM software optimized for their systems.

PVM is an enabling technology. Hundreds of sites around the world already use PVM as a cost-effective way to solve important scientific, industrial, and medical problems. PVM users include petroleum, aerospace, chemical, pharmaceutical, computer, medical, automotive, and environmental cleanup companies. Department of Energy and NASA laboratories use PVM for research, and numerous universities around the US use it for both research and teaching.

The software described in this article is freely distributed to researchers and educators, allowing them to harness their distributed computation power into comprehensive virtual machines. PVM and Hence are available by sending electronic mail to netlib@ornl.gov containing the line "send index from pvm3" or "send index from hence." Instructions on how to receive the various parts of the PVM and Hence systems will be sent by return mail.

Xab is also available from netlib. The index from pvm explains how to obtain this software. PVM problems or questions can be sent to pvm@msr.epm.ornl.gov for a quick and friendly reply.

---

ware package to develop truly heterogeneous programs utilizing multiple computer systems to solve applications (see sidebar). We designed PVM with heterogeneity and portability as primary goals. It lets machines with different architectures and floating-point representations work together on a single computational task.

In the development of heterogeneous concurrent applications for heterogeneous target environments, coarse-grained subtask partitioning and processor allocation are critical. Additionally, program module construction, specification of interdependencies and synchronization, and management of multiple objects for different architectures are tedious, error-prone activities. To address these issues and to provide at least partial solutions, we developed Xab and Hence, two packages that work on top of PVM to aid in the use, programming, and analysis of parallel computers.

Xab (X Window Analysis and Debugging) is a tool for runtime monitoring of PVM programs. Using Xab, programmers can easily instrument and monitor PVM programs by simply relinking to the Xab libraries. Xab is itself a PVM program, so it is very portable. However, making it peacefully coincide with the programs it monitors is problematic.

Hence (Heterogeneous Network Computing Environment) is an environment for the development of high-level programming techniques for the type of concurrent virtual machines provided by PVM. Its goal is to simplify the task (and thus reduce the chance of error) of programming a heterogeneous network of computers, while still providing the programmer with access to the high performance available from such configurations. There are several systems with goals similar to those of Hence. The Code system[2] and Paralex[3] both allow graph-based high-level specifications of parallel programs. Code includes tools that can map the specification into several different parallel languages or libraries such as Ada or C with shared-memory extensions. Paralex directly maps its specifications into C with calls to the Isis library.[4]

PVM

With PVM, users can exploit the aggregate power of distributed workstations and supercomputers to solve the computational Grand Challenges.

Users view PVM as a loosely coupled distributed-memory computer programmed in C or Fortran with message-passing extensions. The hardware that constitutes a user's personal PVM may be any Unix-based network-accessible machine on which the user has a valid login.

We have tested the software with combinations of the following machines: Sun3, Sparcstation, MicroVAX, DEC-station, IBM RS/6000, HP-9000, Silicon Graphics Iris, Next, Sequent Symmetry, Alliant FX, IBM 3090, Intel iPSC/860, Thinking Machines CM-2 and CM-5, KSR-1, Convex, Cray Y-MP, Fujitsu VP-2000, DEC Alpha, Intel Paragon, and Cray C90. In addition, users can port PVM to new architectures by simply modifying a generic "makefile" supplied with the source and recompiling.

Using PVM, users can configure their own parallel virtual computers, which can overlap with other users' virtual computers. Configuring a personal parallel virtual computer involves simply listing the names of the machines in a file that is read when PVM is started. Several different physical networks can coexist inside a virtual machine. For example, a local Ethernet, a Hippi (High-Performance Parallel Interface), and a

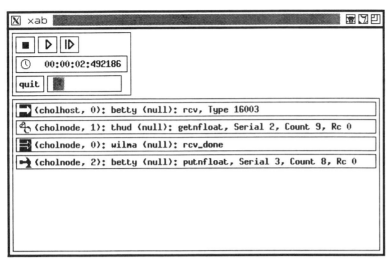

```
 X xab                                          ▦ ⊡ 回
  ┌─────────────────────┐
  │ ■  │ ▷  │ I▷ │
  ├─────────────────────┤
  │ ⊕  00:00:02:492186  │
  ├─────────────────────┤
  │ quit │ ▓            │
  └─────────────────────┘
  ┌──────────────────────────────────────────────┐
  │➡│ (cholhost, 0): betty (null): rcv, Type 16003│
  ├──────────────────────────────────────────────┤
  │⚷│ (cholnode, 1): thud (null): getnfloat, Serial 2, Count 9, Rc 0│
  ├──────────────────────────────────────────────┤
  │⮕│ (cholnode, 0): wilma (null): rcv_done       │
  ├──────────────────────────────────────────────┤
  │➡│ (cholnode, 2): betty (null): putnfloat, Serial 3, Count 8, Rc 0│
  └──────────────────────────────────────────────┘
```

Figure 1. Xab display while monitoring the PVM Cholesky demo.

fiber-optic network can all be part of a user's virtual machine. Each user can have only one virtual machine active at a time; however, since PVM is multitasking, several applications can run simultaneously on a parallel virtual machine.

The PVM package is small (approximately 1 Mbyte) and easy to install. It needs to be installed only once on each machine to be accessible to all users. Moreover, installation does not require special privileges on any machines, so any user can do it.

Application programs that use PVM are composed of subtasks at a moderately coarse level of granularity. The subtasks can be generic serial codes or specific to a particular machine. In PVM, the user may access computational resources at three different levels:

- the *transparent* mode, in which subtasks are automatically located at the most appropriate sites,
- the *architecture-dependent* mode, in which the user can indicate specific architectures on which particular subtasks are to execute, and
- the *machine-specific* mode, in which the user can specify a particular machine.

Such flexibility lets different subtasks of a heterogeneous application exploit particular strengths of individual machines on the network.

The PVM programming interface requires that programmers explicitly type all message data. PVM performs machine-independent data conversions when required, thus letting machines with different integer and floating-point representations pass data. Applications access PVM resources via a library of standard interface routines. These routines allow the initiation and termination of processes across the network, as well as communication and synchronization among processes.

Application programs under PVM can possess arbitrary control and dependency structures. In other words, at any point in the execution of a concurrent application, the existing processes can have arbitrary relationships with each other and, further, any process can communicate or synchronize with any other.

While PVM is a very popular system for programming heterogeneous networks of computers, it is not the only system of this type. The p4 system[5] from Argonne National Laboratory, Express[6] from Parasoft, and Linda[7] from Scientific Computing Associates provide functionality similar to that of PVM.

Monitoring, debugging, and performance tuning

Tools should help programmers write and debug applications and tune their performance. With small-scale changes based on analysis of execution profiles, communication patterns, and load imbalances, programmers can improve concurrent application performance by an order of magnitude. Previous research in visualization focused on homogeneous parallel processing for both shared- and distributed-memory machines.[8] Our work focuses on visualization and debugging for networks of heterogeneous computers. Xab and Hence provide tools to help users with the complex task of understanding a program's behavior for both correctness and performance.

Xab. While PVM provides a solid programming base, it does not give users many options for analyzing or debugging PVM programs. To help in the development of PVM programs, Xab, a runtime monitoring tool, gives users direct feedback about the PVM functions their programs are performing. Xab has three parts: an Xab library to which the user links applications, a PVM process called *abmon* that quietly receives tracing messages from the library routines, and a display process called *xab* that is a graphical X Window display of the trace events.

Real-time monitoring is particularly apropos in a heterogeneous multiprogramming environment where differences in computation and communication speeds result from both heterogeneity and external CPU and network loads. Monitoring gives the user insight into program behavior in such an environment.

Xab monitors a PVM program by instrumenting calls to the PVM library. The instrumented calls generate events displayed during program execution.

A Fortran program normally accesses the PVM user routines via the libfpvm library that comes with PVM. Fortran programs use Xab by simply linking to libxpvm in place of libfpvm. With C, the procedure is slightly more complicated. The programmer must add the include file xab.h to source files that call PVM routines and then recompile the modified source files. This include file contains macros that replace the normal PVM routines with calls to the Xab library. Both Fortran and C programs must be linked with the Xab library, called *libab*.

Event messages. The Xab libraries call the normal PVM functions for the user, but they also send PVM messages to a special monitoring process called *abmon*.

Xab event messages generally contain an event type, a time stamp (in microseconds), and event-specific information. The event type indicates which PVM call is being invoked. In some cases, a PVM call may generate two events. For instance, the PVM barrier function generates an event before and after the barrier call. This lets the user see when barriers are initiated and completed. The time stamp in the event message is the time of day on the machine executing the PVM call. The clocks on various machines involved in a computation may not be synchronized, so Xab does not rely on synchronized clocks. Events are simply displayed as they arrive.

Although future versions of Xab may use the time stamps, it is not always necessary to synchronize machine clocks. For instance, it may be informative to know how long processes wait at a particular program barrier. Xab could use the time stamps from barrier events to display this information, independent of relative machine clock synchronization. The event-specific information in an Xab message varies for different PVM routines. For the event generated at the start of a barrier, it is the name of the barrier and the number of processes that must reach the barrier before continuing. Other event messages contain similar event-specific information.

Besides the event messages, Xab also inserts one additional piece of information into user messages. Each message is given a serial number, prepended to the user's message buffer so that every message can be uniquely identified by its source process and serial number. Currently, we are exploring the usefulness of adding pseudo time stamps to Xab. Pseudo time stamps combine real clocks and logical clocks.

Monitoring processes. The abmon process receives event messages from the instrumented PVM calls and formats them into human-readable form. The abmon program must be running before the user's program starts, since it needs to receive event messages from the instrumented calls. The formatted event messages can be either written to a file or sent to the Xab display program. Just as an astronomer on Earth observes events that have traveled various distances, the abmon process observes events relative to its position in the virtual machine. When abmon formats events, it also adds its own perspective within the virtual machine by placing local time stamps into the event record. To discern its perspective, abmon may use the additional time stamps to ascertain how long it takes events to propagate from a user process to the monitor process.

The display process takes events formatted by abmon and displays them in a window, as shown in Figure 1. Xab supports two modes of event playback: continuous play or single step. When the user presses the play button, the events are displayed in real time. The slider controls the playback speed in continuous-play mode. Users can stop playback at any time by pressing the stop button. The single-step button will show only the next event.

The following command line executes Xab, displaying the events in real time and saving them in a file for later review:

% abmon | tee evfile | xab

The abmon program reads event messages and writes them to standard output. The Unix command tee copies the events to the file evfile and also passes them to xab via the pipe. The Xab program actually opens a window and displays the events.

Timeliness versus message traffic. Every user call to the PVM library uses the method for sending Xab monitor messages described in the previous section. This approach generates an inordinately large number of messages. There is a trade-off between the number of messages and the timeliness of the event display. If events are buffered and sent to the monitor after every n events, then the event display becomes more asynchronous as n grows. In fact,

when n reaches the number of events in the program, the monitor provides postmortem rather than real-time information. Since the display lags behind the program state, users cannot detect certain problems in program behavior. (We give an example in the next section.) Another factor that must be considered is the memory required to store events before sending them to the monitor. Xab immediately dispatches events. As a result, it adds little, in terms of memory requirements, to the PVM processes it monitors. We are exploring the possibility of allowing the user to dynamically alter the event flow. This extension requires the addition of bidirectional data exchanges to the one-way dataflow currently used for Xab's monitoring.

An example. An example program that comes with PVM 2.4 is a distributed-matrix decomposition program based on a Cholesky factorization of the matrix. The window in Figure 1 is the Xab display in progress for this program. The host process, (cholhost, 0), is blocked on a receive. Process (cholnode, 0) has just received a message. The node process (cholnode, 1) is extracting data from a message buffer, while (cholnode, 2) is placing eight floats into a message buffer.

As shown in Figure 2, an advantage of Xab's real-time display is its ability to

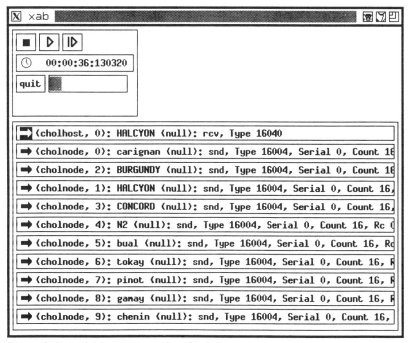

Figure 2. Xab displays an error in a Cholesky program.

135

detect errors in a dynamic environment. The same Cholesky example contains a deliberately introduced error. The host is waiting for a message of type 16040, while all the cholnode processes are sending messages of type 16004; thus the program has blocked indefinitely. In this case, postmortem monitoring would not work: The program would not complete and therefore would never flush the events for display.

Several research projects focus on displaying events generated by distributed-memory parallel programs, notably ParaGraph,[9] Pablo,[10] Upshot,[11] and Bee.[12] Currently, Xab events are stored in Xab's own ASCII-based format. Because of ParaGraph's wide availability, we provide a program that converts Xab event files to a ParaGraph-compatible format. The ParaGraph tool provides a rich set of displays for visualizing message-passing parallel programs. Figure 3 shows a ParaGraph visualization of the PVM Cholesky program with one host process and two slave processes.

There are several differences between the ParaGraph and the Xab displays. ParaGraph provides a variety of views but is limited to postmortem visualization. Xab currently has a limited display facility but can operate in real time. The ParaGraph trace events must be in temporal order. Xab simply displays events as they arrive. ParaGraph was developed originally for multicomputers that did not support multitasking.

Hence. In developing software, the programmer often designs the initial definitions and specifications graphically; flowcharts and dependency graphs are well-known examples. Designers can visualize the problem's overall structure far more easily from these graphical representations than from textual specifications. Such a representation enhances the quality of the resulting software. However, to be executed, these descriptions must be converted to program form, typically manifested as source code; that is, the graphical representations must be translated to operational programs. The graphical depiction of a concurrent application and strategies for its successful execution

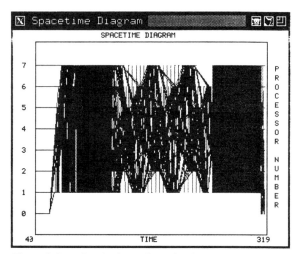

Figure 3. ParaGraph views of the Cholesky program.

on a heterogeneous network are the two fundamental inputs to the Hence environment.

With the Hence graphics interface implemented on a workstation, a user can develop a parallel program as a computational graph; the nodes in the graph represent the computations to be performed and the arcs represent the dependencies between the computations. From this graphical representation, Hence can generate a lower level portable program, which when executed will perform the computations specified by the graph in an order consistent with the dependencies specified. This programming environment allows for a high-level description of the parallel algorithm and, when the high-level description is translated into a common programming language, permits portable program execution. Thus the algorithm developer has an abstract model of computation that can bind effectively to a wide variety of parallel processors. We confined specific machine intrinsics to the tool's internal workings to provide a common user interface to various parallel processors.

Another problem facing the developers of algorithms and software for parallel computers is performance analysis of the resulting programs. Performance bugs are often far more difficult to detect and overcome than the synchronization and data-dependency bugs normally associated with parallel programs. We have developed a fairly sophisticated postprocessing performance-analysis tool for the Hence graphics programming interface. This tool is quite useful in understanding the execution flow and processor utilization in a parallel program.

Hence gives the programmer a higher level environment for using heterogeneous networks. The Hence philosophy of parallel programming is to have the programmer explicitly specify the parallelism of a computation and to automate, as much as possible, the tasks of writing, compiling, executing, debugging, and analyzing the parallel computation. Central to Hence is an X Window interface that the programmer uses to perform these functions (see Figure 4).

The Hence environment contains a compose tool that lets the user explicitly specify parallelism by drawing a graph of the parallel application. (If an X Window interface is not available, the user can input textual graph descriptions.)

Each node in a Hence graph represents a procedure written in either Fortran or C. The procedure can be a subroutine from an established library or a special-purpose subroutine supplied by the user. Arcs between nodes represent data dependency and control flow. A dependency arc from one node to another represents the fact that the arc's tail node must run before its head. Data is sent to a node from its ancestors in the graph (usually its parents).

In addition to simple nodes, four types of control constructs are available in the Hence graph language. The first represents looping, the second conditional dependency, the third a fan-out to a variable number of identical subgraphs, and the fourth pipelining. The graph can contain loops around subgraphs that execute a variable number of times on the basis of the expression in the loop construct. Using a conditional construct, Hence can execute or bypass a section of the graph on the basis of an expression evaluated at runtime. A variable fan-out (and subsequent fan-in) construct is available while composing the graph. The fan-out's width is specified as an expression evaluated at runtime. This construct is similar to a *parallel-do* construct found in several parallel Fortrans. In pipelined sections, when a node finishes with one set of input data, it reruns with the next piece of pipelined data.

Once users specify the dynamic graph,

they use a configuration tool in the Hence environment to specify the configuration of machines that will compose the parallel virtual machine. The configuration tool also helps users set up a cost matrix that determines which machine can perform which task and gives priority to certain machines. Hence uses this cost matrix at runtime to determine the most effective machine on which to execute a particular procedure in the graph.

The Hence environment also contains a build tool to perform three tasks. First, by analyzing the graph, Hence automatically generates the parallel program using PVM calls for all the communication and synchronization required by the application. Second, by knowing the desired PVM configuration, Hence automatically compiles the node procedures for the various heterogeneous architectures. Finally, the build tool installs the executable modules on the particular machines in the PVM configuration.

The execute tool in the Hence environment starts the requested virtual machine and begins application execution. During execution, Hence automatically maps procedures to machines in the heterogeneous network on the basis of the cost matrix and the Hence graph. Trace and scheduling information saved during execution can be displayed in real time or replayed later.

The Hence environment has a trace tool that enables visualization of the parallel run. The trace tool is X Window based and consists of three windows. One window shows a representation of the network and machines underlying PVM. This display illuminates icons of the active machines with different colors, depending on whether they are computing or communicating. Under each icon is a list of the node procedures mapped to this machine at any given instant. The second window displays the user's graph of the application, which changes dynamically to show the actual paths and parameters taken during a run. The nodes in the graph change colors to indicate the various activities in each procedure. The third window shows a histogram of processor utilization. Figure 5 on the next page shows a snapshot of the trace tool in action.

In addition to discovering mistakes in the graph specification, this representation helps expose more subtle aspects of the executing program, such as load balancing and network speeds. For example, the graph produced by Hence shows noticeable differences from the abstract user-specified graph. The Hence graph may expose inherent serial bottlenecks in the algorithm or a problem

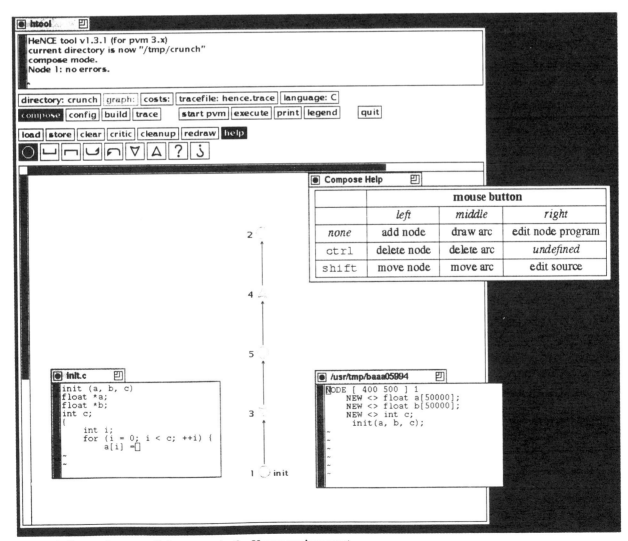

Figure 4. Composing a parallel program in the Hence environment.

with various networks used by the computation.

Our goals here are simple: to be able to schedule and trace the execution flow within an application and to understand where bottlenecks occur. In the past, users have monitored performance using a timing routine. This approach has a number of limitations in the parallel setting. We want an animation of runtime behavior that visualizes the parallel parts in execution as the application is running. We would like to know what performance issues arise during execution and what bottlenecks develop, and to see where programming errors cause

a parallel program to get into trouble.

A main advantage of sequential debuggers is that they show the point of failure. In fact, many programmers resort to debuggers only when they are mystified about the point of failure, for example, dividing by zero or dereferencing a null pointer. In a parallel program there may be multiple failures; or, perhaps more perplexing, one part of the program may crash while other parts continue executing for some time. An advantage of the Hence trace display is that its two-dimensional display can inform the programmer of such problems. If part of a Hence program fails and

other parts continue to execute, the trace tool displays the program node failure but continues to display the progress of other program nodes as they execute.

The trace animation is also important in performance tuning. Almost all the machines used with Hence are multitasking, and this leads to unpredictable execution-time profiles. The trace animation provided by Hence shows the programmer in real time how the program is progressing. From this animation, a programmer can analyze a program's behavior and tune it to better match the execution environment. For instance, a scientist using a network of

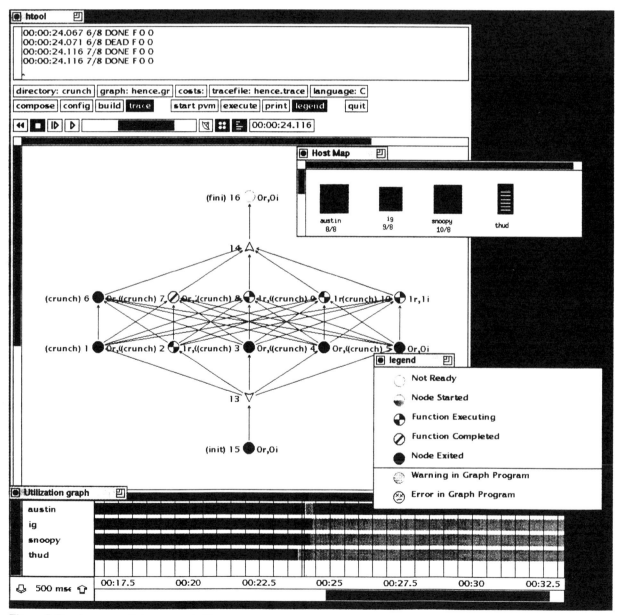

Figure 5. Tracing a parallel program in Hence.

workstations along with a Cray supercomputer may realize that during certain periods of the day it is more productive to map fewer processes to the Cray because it is heavily loaded. The Hence trace tools make this kind of information intuitively obvious. Moreover, Hence mapping is easily adjusted via the cost matrix. The user's program need not be recompiled during tuning.

The Hence tool evolved naturally as we programmed various parallel machines. We were motivated primarily by the lack of uniformity and the limited capabilities offered by vendors for explicit parallel programming. Our experience with Hence has been encouraging. We do not view it as a "solution" to the software problem we face in parallel programming. However, we think it will be useful in the short term, and perhaps it will have some influence on the development of a long-term solution.

T he focus of our work is to provide a paradigm and graphical support tools for programming a heterogeneous network of computers as a single resource. PVM and its auxiliary tools Xab and Hence help the user effectively use a heterogeneous computer network to solve scientific applications.

PVM, Xab, and Hence are active research projects and continue to evolve. Many of Hence's features will find their way into tools like Xab that eventually will fit directly into the PVM framework. We have already built prototype systems that are in use today.

There is a critical need for standards and tools for today's high-performance computer systems. By building prototype tools as outlined here and listening to users' feedback, we hope to provide an easy-to-use, portable system for heterogeneous computing. Many significant research issues about this approach to parallel programming remain. ∎

Acknowledgments

We thank Robert Manchek, Keith Moore, and James Plank for their contributions to PVM, Xab, and Hence. This work was supported in part by the Applied Mathematical Sciences subprogram of the Office of Energy Research, US Department of Energy, under contract DE-AC05-84OR21400, and in part by the National Science Foundation Science and Technology Center Cooperative Agreement No. CCR-8809615.

References

1. G.A. Geist and V.S. Sunderam, "Experiences with Network-Based Concurrent Computing on the PVM System," *Concurrency: Practice and Experience*, Vol. 4, No. 4, June 1992, pp. 293-311.

2. J.C. Browne, M. Azam, and S. Sobek, "CODE: A Unified Approach to Parallel Programming," *IEEE Software*, Vol. 6, No. 4, July 1989, pp. 10-18.

3. O. Babaoglu et al., "Paralex: An Environment for Parallel Programming in Distributed Systems," *Proc. 1992 Int'l Conf. Supercomputing*, ACM Press, New York, July 1992, pp. 178-187.

4. K.P. Birman and T.A. Joseph, "Reliable Communication in the Presence of Failures," *ACM Trans. Computer Systems*, Vol. 5, No. 1, Feb. 1987, pp. 47-76.

5. E. Lusk et al., *Portable Programs for Parallel Processors*, Holt, Rinehart, and Winston, New York, 1987.

6. J. Flower, A. Kolawa, and S. Bharadwaj, "The Express Way to Distributed Processing," *Supercomputing Review*, May 1991, pp. 54-55.

7. N. Carriero and D. Gelernter, "How to Write Parallel Programs: A Guide to the Perplexed," *ACM Computing Surveys*, Sept. 1989, pp. 323-357.

8. M. Simmons and R. Koskela, *Performance Instrumentation and Visualization*, ACM Press, New York, 1990.

9. M. Heath and J. Etheridge, "Visualizing the Performance of Parallel Programs," *IEEE Software*, Vol. 8, No. 5, Sept. 1991, pp. 29-39.

10. D.A. Reed et al., "Scalable Performance Environments for Parallel Systems," *Proc. Sixth Distributed-Memory Computing Conf.*, Q. Stout and M. Wolfe, eds., IEEE CS Press, Los Alamitos, Calif., Order No. 2290, 1991, pp. 562-569.

11. V. Herrarte and E. Lusk, "Studying Parallel Program Behavior with Upshot," Tech. Report ANL-91/15, Argonne Nat'l Laboratory, Mathematics and Computer Science Division, Aug. 1991.

12. B. Bruegge, "A Portable Platform for Distributed-Event Environments," *ACM SIGPlan Notices*, Vol. 26, No. 12, Dec. 1991, pp. 184-193.

Adam Beguelin holds a joint appointment at Carnegie Mellon University's school of computer science and the Pittsburgh Supercomputing Center. His primary interests are the design and development of programming tools and environments for high-performance parallel and distributed computing.

Beguelin received his PhD in computer science from the University of Colorado.

Jack Dongarra holds a joint appointment as professor of computer science at the University of Tennessee and as distinguished scientist in the Mathematical Sciences Section at Oak Ridge National Laboratory. He specializes in numerical algorithms in linear algebra, parallel computing, use of advanced computer architectures, programming methodology, and tools for parallel computers. He was involved in the design and implementation of the software packages Eispack, Linpack, Blas, Lapack, and PVM/Hence.

Al Geist leads the computer science group in the Mathematical Sciences Section at Oak Ridge National Laboratory. His research interests are parallel and distributed processing, scientific computing, and high-performance numerical software.

Vaidy Sunderam is a professor in the Department of Mathematics and Computer Science at Emory University. His research interests include parallel and distributed processing, particularly high-performance concurrent computing in heterogeneous networked environments.

Sunderam received a PhD in computer science from the University of Kent in Canterbury, England, in 1986.

Questions regarding this article can be directed to Al Geist at Oak Ridge National Laboratory, PO Box 2008, Oak Ridge, TN 37831-3153; Internet, pvm@msr.epm.ornl.gov.

Chapter 4:
Parallel Object-Oriented Programming

The parallel object-oriented paradigm is obtained by combining the parallelism concepts of *process activation* and *communication* with the object-oriented concepts of *modularity*, *data abstraction*, and *inheritance* [YON87]. An *object* is a unit that encapsulates private data and a set of associated operations, or *methods*, that manipulate the data and define the object behavior. The list of operations associated with an object is called its *class*. The data contained in an object are visible only within the object itself. An object interacts with the outside world exclusively through an interface defined by its operations. The only way an object can be used is by making a request, or an *operation invocation*, on one of the accessible operations. This permits the specification of object operations to be public (to the other objects) while at the same time keeping private the implementation of the operations and the object data.

Object-oriented languages are mainly intended for structuring programs in a simple and modular way that reflects the structure of the problem to be solved. The major properties that characterize object-oriented languages [MEY88] are

- *data abstraction*: an object is defined as implementation of an abstract data type;

- *modular structure*: a program can be designed as a set of modules;

- *classes*: every nonsimple type is a class;

- *automatic memory management*: unused objects are deallocated without programmer intervention; and

- *inheritance*: a class may be defined as an extension or restriction of another, previously defined class.

Languages that support objects but lack the inheritance property are usually said to be *object-based* languages, as opposed to *object-oriented* languages.

Sequential object-oriented languages are based on the concept of *passive objects*. At any time during the program execution, only one object is *active*. An object becomes active when it receives a request (or *message*) from another object. While the receiver is active, the sender is passive, waiting for the result. After returning the result, the receiver becomes passive again, and the sender continues. Examples of sequential object-oriented languages are Simula [KIR89], Smalltalk [ING78], C++ [STR86], and Eiffel [MEY92].

Objects and parallelism can be nicely integrated since object modularity makes objects natural units for parallel execution. The following are the two principle approaches that can be used to exploit parallelism in object-oriented languages:

- using the objects as the unit of parallelism, assigning one or more processes to each object, and

- defining processes as components of the language.

Parallel object-oriented languages use one of these two approaches to support parallel execution of object-oriented programs.

In the first approach, languages are based on *active objects*. Each process is bound to the particular object for which it was created. When one process is assigned to an object, *interobject parallelism* is exploited. If multiple processes execute concurrently within an object, *intraobject parallelism* is exploited also. When the object is destroyed, the associated processes terminate. Examples of languages that have adopted the first approach are An Object-Based Concurrent Language (ABCL/1), Actors, and Concurrent Smalltalk [YOK87], with the Actors model being the best-known example. Although the Actors model is not a pure object-oriented model, we include it here because it is tightly related to object-oriented languages. In the Actors model, an *actor* is similar to an active object that responds to a single message and terminates, thereby allowing the highest degree of concurrency. In this model, objects are arranged in dynamically changing hierarchies rather than in static classes.

In the second approach, two different kinds of entities are defined: *processes* and *objects*. A process is not bound to a single object but is used to perform all the operations required to satisfy an action. Therefore, a process can execute within many objects, changing its address space when an invocation to another object is made. Examples of systems that use this approach are Argus [LIS87], Presto [BER88], and Nexus [TRI87]. In these systems, languages provide mechanisms for creating and controlling multiple processes external to the object structure. Parallelism is implemented on top of the object organization and explicit constructs are defined to ensure object integrity.

An important aspect of object-oriented languages is the extension of object usability. *Inheritance* is a useful property that allows methods and data of a class to be reused in the definition of a new class. Subclasses become specialized versions of their parent class. Multiple inheritance is implemented when a subclass inherits from more than one class. Generally, object-oriented languages implement single inheritance. An example of a parallel object-oriented system that uses inheritance is Mentat [GRI93]. Another method of extending object usability is *delegation*. Delegation is based on the concept of *subcontracting a task* when an object cannot perform it. Delegation gives to another object the responsibility of handling a message of a particular name. Delegation can be used to incrementally define the behavior of an object from that of many other objects. The Actors model, Concurrent Aggregates (CA), and ABCL/1 use delegation.

Other important parallel object-oriented languages not already mentioned are the Parallel Object-Oriented Language (POOL-T) [PHI85], Emerald [BLA87], the Concurrent Object-Oriented Language (COOL) [CHA90],

Orient84/K [ISH86], Cantor [ATH88], and An Object-Based Concurrent Language with Reflection (ABCL/R) [WAT88].

This chapter includes four papers that describe four significant parallel object-oriented languages: Actors, ABCL/1, CA, and the Mentat Programming Language (MPL), respectively.

The first paper included here, "Abstraction and Modularity Mechanisms for Concurrent Computing," by Agha et al., describes the Actors model and some mechanisms, based on Actors, for developing modular and reusable components for parallel programs. The Actors model originally was proposed by Hewitt and then was developed by Agha at the Massachusetts Institute of Technology (MIT) [AGH86]. *Actors* are autonomous, distributed, parallel objects that can asynchronously send each other messages. When a message arrives, the actor executes a script that accepts the message if it recognizes it or delegates the rejected message to a proxy that can respond to the message. This paper gives an overview of the communication abstractions and object-oriented features of the model. It describes three mechanisms for developing modular software using Actors and presents some programming examples developed using these mechanisms.

The second paper included in this chapter, "Object-Oriented Concurrent Programming in ABCL/1," by Yonezawa, Briot, and Shibayama, presents the language ABCL/1. As the authors state, the primary design principles of ABCL/1 are practicality and clear semantics of message passing. In ABCL/1, independent objects can execute in parallel; however, within an object, messages are processed serially. This paper defines three modes of message passing: *past, now,* and *future:* The now mode operates synchronously, whereas the past and future modes operate asynchronously. In addition, the paper describes the computational model of the language and gives an overview of its basic mechanisms. Then, it discusses a simple scheme of distributed problem solving and a distributed algorithm for the same fringe problem in ABCL/1. Finally, the paper outlines the mechanism used to provide various delegation strategies.

This chapter's third paper, "Experience with Concurrent Aggregates (CA): Implementation and Programming," by Chien and Dally, describes the CA language and a programming experience using it. The language is well suited for exploiting parallelism on fine-grain parallel computers such as the J-Machine. An *aggregate* in CA is a homogeneous collection of objects that are grouped together and may be referenced by a single aggregate name. CA is an object-oriented language that allows users to construct unserialized hierarchies of abstractions by using aggregates. It incorporates many innovative features, including delegation, intra-aggregate addressing, first-class messages, and user continuations. This paper discusses the use of the language for the implementation of a wide range of application programs and gives simulation results for these programs.

In the fourth paper included in this chapter, "Easy-to-Use Object-Oriented Parallel Processing with Mentat," by Grimshaw, MPL and the Mentat runtime system are discussed. Mentat is a parallel object-oriented system designed to address the problems involved in developing architecture-independent parallel applications. The Mentat system integrates a data-driven computation model with the object-oriented paradigm. The data-driven model supports a high degree of parallelism, while the object-oriented paradigm hides much of the parallel environment from the user. MPL is an extension of C++ that supports both interobject and intraobject parallelism. The compiler and the runtime support of the language are designed to achieve high performance. This paper describes MPL, the Mentat virtual machine, and some performance results for two applications on different parallel architectures.

References cited

Those references marked with an asterisk are included in this book as reprinted papers.

[AGH86] G. Agha, *Actors: A Model of Concurrent Computation in Distributed Systems*, MIT Press, Cambridge, Mass., 1986.

[ATH88] W.C. Athas and C. Seitz, "Multicomputers: Message Passing Concurrent Computers," *Computer*, Vol. 21, No. 8, Aug. 1988, pp. 9–24.

[BER88] B.N. Bershad, E. Lazowska, and H. Levy, "Presto: A System for Object-Oriented Parallel Programming," *Software: Practice & Experience*, Vol. 18, No. 10, Aug. 1988.

[BLA87] A. Black et al., "Distribution and Abstract Types in Emerald," *IEEE Trans. Software Eng.*, Vol. SE-13, No. 1, Jan. 1987, pp. 65–76.

[CHA90] R. Chandra et al., "COOL: A Language for Parallel Programming," in *Languages and Compilers for Parallel Computing*, D. Gelernter et al., eds., MIT Press, Cambridge, Mass., 1990, pp. 126–148.

*[GRI93] A.S. Grimshaw, "Easy-to-Use Object-Oriented Parallel Processing with Mentat," *Computer*, Vol. 26, No. 5, May 1993, pp. 39–51.

[ING78] D.H. Ingalls, "The Smalltalk-76 Programming System Design and Implementation," *Proc. 5th Principles Programming Languages Conf. (POPL)*, ACM Press, New York, N.Y., 1978, pp. 9–16.

[ISH86] Y. Ishikawa and M. Tokoro, "A Concurrent Object-Oriented Knowledge Representation Language Orient84/K: Its Features and Implementation," *Proc. Object-Oriented Programming Systems, Languages and Applications Conf. (OOPSLA '86)*, ACM SIGPLAN Notices, Vol. 21, No. 11, Nov. 1986, pp. 232–241.

[KIR89] B. Kirkerud, *Object-Oriented Programming with SIMULA*, Addison-Wesley Pub. Co., Reading, Mass., 1989.

[LIS87] B. Liskov, "Implementation of Argus," *Proc. 11th Symp. Operating Systems Principles*, ACM Press, New York, N.Y., 1987, pp. 111–122.

[MEY88] B. Meyer, *Object-Oriented Software Construction*, Prentice-Hall, Inc., Englewood Cliffs, N.J., 1988.

[MEY92] B. Meyer, *Eiffel: The Language*, Prentice-Hall, Inc., Englewood Cliffs, N.J., 1992.

[PHI85] Philips Research Laboratories, "Definition of the Programming Language POOL-T," Esprit Project 415, Doc. 0091, Philips Research Laboratories, Eindhoven, The Netherlands, June 1985.

[STR86] B. Stroustrup, *The C++ Programming Language*, Addison-Wesley Pub. Co., Reading, Mass., 1986.

[TRI87] A. Tripathi, A. Ghonami, and T. Schmitz, "Object Management in the NEXUS Distributed Operating System," *Proc. Compcon Spring '87*, IEEE CS Press, Los Alamitos, Calif., 1987, pp. 50–53.

[WAT88] T. Watanabe et al., "Reflection in an Object-Oriented Concurrent Language," *ACM SIGPLAN Notices*, Vol. 23, No. 11, Nov. 1988, pp. 306–315.

[YOK87] Y. Yokote et al., "Concurrent Programming in Concurrent Smalltalk," in *Object-Oriented Concurrent Programming*, A. Yonezawa et al., eds., MIT Press, Cambridge, Mass., 1987, pp. 129–158.

[YON87] A. Yonezawa et al., eds., *Object-Oriented Concurrent Programming*, MIT Press, Cambridge, Mass., 1987.

Abstraction and Modularity Mechanisms for Concurrent Computing

Gul Agha, Svend Frølund, WooYoung Kim,
Rajendra Panwar, Anna Patterson, and Daniel Sturman
University of Illinois at Urbana-Champaign

/// Developers can become more productive through greater use of new abstractions and modularity mechanisms. The methods proposed here suggest ways to bring the power of parallel and distributed computing within reach of more developers.

In a parallel computation some actions overlap in time; by implication these events must be distributed in space. Such potentially parallel execution is called concurrency. In a concurrent computation, some parts of a program might execute sequentially, while others might be parallel. Concurrent programs specify a partial order of actions, giving us the flexibility to interleave the execution of commands or to run them in parallel. Therefore, a concurrent program leaves some of the details of the execution order unspecified. We can concentrate on conceptual issues without necessarily being concerned with the execution order that results from the quirks of a given system.

But this flexibility allows many potential execution paths, increasing the complexity of reasoning about concurrent programs. Furthermore, concurrent programs must explicitly address a number of design concerns, such as locality and synchronization, that are transparent in sequential environments. Concurrent abstractions must therefore be modular to simplify the construction of concurrent systems.

Specifically, the complexity of concurrent systems requires new abstraction methods that

- let us specify the complex organizational and coordination structures that are common in concurrent computing,
- provide genericity and reuse of coordination patterns, much as procedures do for sequential programming,
- simplify programming by separating design concerns, and
- allow efficient execution on concurrent architectures.

Reprinted from *IEEE Parallel & Distributed Technology,* Vol. 1, No. 2, May 1993, pp. 3-14. Copyright © 1993 by The Institute of Electrical and Electronics Engineers, Inc. All rights reserved.

To avoid incurring unnecessary costs, we optimize call/return communication using one of two concurrent versions of continuation-passing-style program transformations.[1]

First, if a sending actor's response to the next message does not depend on the results of a call/return communication, the program is transformed by changing the calls to asynchronous Sends and creating a *join continuation* actor, which performs the part of the sender's computations that depend on the results. Consider the following expression:

Send B (v, C.Request1(...), D.Request2(...))

When this asynchronous Send is executed, actors C and D receive messages Request1 and Request2, respectively. Actor B is then sent a message with results from C and D along with v. The accompanying figure shows the program's execution before and after the transformation.

Second, if the sending actor's response to the next message does depend partly on the results of a call/return communication, we separate out the continuation as a method within the original actor. There would be no point to creating a join continuation actor: The original sender cannot process other messages until it receives a result. The continuation method is triggered by the results of the remote actor invocations. To guarantee consistency between state changes, the transformation creates a synchronization constraint (explained later in the main text) for the continuation method. This new constraint prevents other messages from being processed until the continuation method has been invoked.

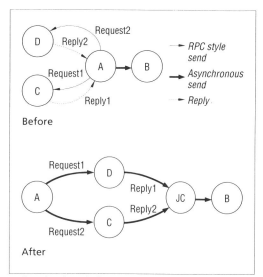

Before (top) and after the transformation creating a join continuation actor.

REFERENCE
1. W. Kim and G. Agha, "Compilation of a Highly Parallel Actor-Based Language," to appear in *Languages and Compilers for Parallel Computing*, Springer-Verlag, 1992.

There are a number of radical programming language concepts that support abstraction and provide modularity in concurrent systems. The Actor model, for example, provides basic building blocks for a wide variety of computational structures. Our proposed constructs build on the Actor model to allow abstract and modular specification of coordination patterns, temporal ordering, resource management, and dependability protocols. Specifications using these constructs are generic and reusable.

Actors

The universe we live in is inherently parallel and distributed, so the natural-language constructs we use to describe the world might also be useful for modeling computational systems. The most important concept we use to model the world is categorizing it in terms of objects. In fact, the first elements of natural language children learn are names of objects.

Computational objects encapsulate a state and an expected behavior, and they provide an interface defined in terms of the names of visible procedures. These procedures, called methods, manipulate the object's local state when invoked, which implies that we can transparently interchange representations that support the same functions. This is an important advantage of object-based programming, which has proved its usefulness in sequential software engineering.

But sequential languages allow only one object to be active at a time, confounding the natural autonomy and concurrency of objects. Such languages view an object's behavior as a sequence of actions, which is blocked by invoking a method in another object. This is a rather contrived view; it is more natural to view objects as (virtual) computational agents that can compute concurrently.

The Actor model unifies objects and concurrency. Actors are autonomous, distributed, concurrently executing objects that can send each other messages asynchronously. Asynchronous communication preserves the potential for parallel activity: An actor sending a message need not block its execution until the recipient is ready to receive or process a message. Requiring the sender to block execution, as in the sequential object-oriented approach, would reduce the potential concurrency.

In response to a message, an actor can

- Send a message asynchronously to a specified actor,
- Create an actor with the specified behavior, or
- "Become" a new actor, assuming a new behavior (local state) for responding to the next message.

The Send primitive is the asynchronous analog of procedure invocation. It is the basic communication primitive, causing a message to be put in an actor's mailbox (its mail queue). To send a message, the recipient's identity (its mail address) must be specified. Although the arrival order of messages is nondeterministic, every message sent to an actor is guaranteed to be delivered eventually.

The Become primitive gives actors the history-sensitive behavior necessary for shared, mutable data objects (in contrast to a purely functional programming model). The Create primitive is to concurrent programming what procedure abstraction is to sequential programming. Newly created actors are autonomous and have a unique mail address. Furthermore, Create dynamically extends computational space, encompassing the functionality of New in Pascal or Malloc in C. These Actor primitives form a simple but powerful set on which to build a wide range of higher level abstractions and concurrent programming paradigms.

COMMUNICATION ABSTRACTIONS

Although point-to-point asynchronous message sending is the most efficient form of communication in scalable distributed networks, concurrent languages must provide a number of communication abstractions to simplify programming. Developers need to understand the advantages and limitations of such basic abstractions as call/return communication, pattern-directed communication, and constrained reception.

Call/return communication

In call/return communication, an object invokes a number of other objects and waits for them to return a value before continuing. A standard mechanism for call/return communication in concurrent programming is the remote procedure call: A procedure calls another pro-

cedure at a remote node and waits for the result, which is returned to where the call was made. This model extends the sequential procedure call model, where procedure calls follow a stack discipline that can be implemented efficiently on sequential processors. In high-level actor languages, concurrent call/return communication allows a simple expression of functional parallelism. In actor languages, whether a message is sent to an actor on the same node or on a different node is transparent to the application code.

We generally do not want to block a sender in a call/return communication: If the actor invoked is on a different node, we could lose available concurrency unnecessarily. If the sender "holds" the processor while waiting for results, processor time is wasted; if not, extra context switching is needed to change the executing actor from the sender to another actor.

Whenever feasible, we allow the calling actor to continue computation as soon as it has sent a request. To support ease of programming without incurring an unnecessary performance penalty, we transform a program containing a call/return communication to a semantically equivalent one containing only asynchronous message Sends. The transformations preserve the maximal concurrency in a program (see the sidebar on call/return communication).

The universe we live in is inherently parallel and distributed, so the natural-language constructs we use to describe the world might also be useful for modeling computational systems.

Pattern-directed communication

Point-to-point asynchronous communication lets us express and optimize locality directly, but sometimes we only need to communicate with an arbitrary member of a group. If the recipient must name all potential receivers, the bookkeeping can become cumbersome, and a level of abstraction is lost. On the other hand, *pattern-directed* communication lets us abstractly specify a group of potential recipients so that the actual recipients can be transparently changed. None of the clients needs to know the exact identities of potential receivers or to poll them to determine if they satisfy some attributes.

The ActorSpace model uses a communication model based on destination patterns.[1] An actor space is a computationally passive container of actors that acts as a context for matching patterns; it can overlap or be wholly

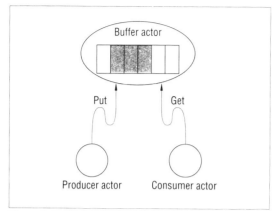

Figure 1. Producer and consumer actors communicating through a buffer actor.

contained in other actor spaces. Patterns are matched against listed attributes of actors and actor spaces that are visible in the actor space. Both visibility and attributes are dynamic. Messages can be sent to one or all members of a group defined by a pattern. An actor can send a message to a single arbitrary member of a group, or broadcast it to the entire group (to disseminate common protocols, for example).

The ActorSpace model is useful for many distributed applications. For example, if we define an actor space of servers, none of the clients need to know the exact identities of the potential servers or explicitly poll them to determine if particular ones are suitable. This provides an abstraction that allows replication of services, for example, to enhance reliability or increase performance.

Linda defines a communication abstraction similar to that in ActorSpace, but Linda's semantics require explicit read operations by recipients.[2] This results in at least two significant differences. First, race conditions can occur due to concurrent access by different processes to a common space. Second, communication cannot be made secure against arbitrary readers — for example, there is no way for a sender to specify that a process with certain attributes may not consume a message (called a tuple in Linda). By contrast, in ActorSpace, the sender determines the attributes of a message's potential recipient.

Synchronization constraints

Sequential programs have a single thread of control, and the programmer must explicitly fix a calling sequence for all objects — essentially by calling them one at a time and passing control to them. Generally a stack discipline is used, and control returns to the calling object once the called object has finished executing. In fact, this calling discipline corresponds quite poorly to the nature of many computations. Concurrent systems need more distributed forms of synchronization that support partial orders.

Consider producer and consumer actors that com-

municate through a buffer actor (see Figure 1). The producer deposits a data item in the buffer by invoking a Put method defined in the buffer; the consumer retrieves a data item by invoking a Get method. Since actors are autonomous and asynchronous, they do not know if a message they send can be meaningfully processed in the receiving actor's current state. In this case, the producer could send a Put request to a full buffer, or the consumer could send a Get request to an empty buffer. Thus, we have to specify when different computational objects may be invoked. Rather than reject messages that cannot be processed in the current state, we defer the request.

Constraints that limit invocation of a concurrent object — synchronization constraints — should be part of the actor's interface. Separating synchronization constraints from the actor itself lets programmers associate such constraints with each method and frees the developers from explicitly specifying code to manage messages when an actor is not in a state to process them. A message not satisfying the constraint is buffered until the actor's state satisfies it. Essentially, synchronization constraints provide an abstract representation of an actor's reactive behavior and let us reason about the effect of composing actors.

Actor programs, unlike iteration in sequential programming languages, do not use loops for sequencing actions. The usual semantics of such loops implies that an iteration should end before the next one starts. Instead, actors support message-driven programming in which synchronization constraints can ensure locally consistent sequencing of iterations. By not creating unnecessary data dependencies, message-driven programming maintains an algorithm's maximum concurrency (see the sidebar on overlapping communication and computation).

OBJECT-ORIENTED DESIGN

It is a natural progression to move from naming individual objects to naming categories or classes of objects. Object-oriented design provides a hierarchical framework that naturally models the world using classification, letting us build categories with shared attributes and functionality. By providing a tool for parsimony of representation, classification simplifies our ability to model the world.[3,4]

In more concrete terms, a class is a category of computational objects that can be specialized. For example, a Vehicle class has attributes such as position, velocity, occupants, and weight, and allows certain method invocations to change some of its attributes. We define a member of this class by specifying its initial attributes (its initial state). Some of these attributes might never change if the class does not contain operations to change them.

A subclass further specializes a class' operations. For example, a Car can have more specific attributes and functions than a Vehicle. By allowing a Car to inherit code from a Vehicle, object-oriented languages support incremental refinement and code reuse. Depending on the language, a method may be extended or redefined in a subclass.

Like any objects, actors can be organized into classes and include notions of inheritance. Delegation is one form of inheritance that lets us reuse the code of a prototype object. For example, it might not be meaningful to think of a stack as a kind of array, but a stack could be defined by using the representation and operations of an array. A stack could then delegate invocations of its methods to an array.

Because we specify synchronization constraints in a modular fashion, they can be inherited and incrementally modified; a synchronization constraint can be further strengthened, weakened, or overwritten in a subclass, whether or not the constrained methods are changed (see the sidebar on synchronization constraints).

Separating design concerns

We have developed three mechanisms for developing modular and reusable components for concurrent systems. These mechanisms allow:

- The use of abstractions to specify multiactor coordination patterns, including atomicity and temporal ordering.
- The separation of functionality and resource management strategies. For example, policies for actor placement can be specified in terms of an actor group abstraction, independent of the representation and invocations of a particular group satisfying that abstraction.
- The development of generic, application-independent code for protocols that increase dependability. We describe an architecture that allows the dynamic installation or removal of protocols to change the fault tolerance and security characteristics of a running system.

SYNCHRONIZERS
Synchronization constraints provide for the modular expression of constraints that a single actor must satisfy

before it can process a communication it has received. Although such constraints are often promoted as a way to describe the coordination of concurrent objects,[5,6] they are unsatisfactory for describing multiactor coordination; they depend only on the local state of a single actor.

In distributed computing, a group of object invocations often must satisfy temporal ordering or atomicity constraints. But conventional programming languages do not let us specify multiobject constraints in a modular and reusable manner. Considerable programming effort must be expended to express multiobject constraints in terms of low-level message passing. Moreover, expressing these constraints by explicit message passing "hard wires" both the constraints and their implementation into the application software. Thus, the same

Incremental modifications of synchronization constraints

Let's again consider the producer, consumer, and buffer actors in Figure 1 (in the main text). If the buffer is empty, it defers requests from the consumer. The code for such a buffer could be

```
CLASS Buffer
    VAR First, Count
    Restrict Get( ) With (Count > 0)
    INIT ( )
        Count := 0
        ...
    END
    METHOD Put(x)
    ...
    METHOD Get()
    ...
END
```

Now suppose we want to create a buffer that takes requests as long as the cumulative size of the pending

requests is smaller than its buffering capacity. If the buffer is a fast cache accessed by a number of printers, we could define it as an instance of the SizedBuffer class that extends the buffer class definitions:

```
CLASS SizedBuffer Inherits Buffer
    VAR UsedCapacity, TotalCapacity
    RESTRICT Put(x) WITH
        (x.Size + UsedCapacity <= TotalCapacity)
    INIT (BufferCapacity)
        UsedCapacity := 0
        TotalCapacity := BufferCapacity
    END
    METHOD Put(x)
        Super.Put(x);
        UsedCapacity := UsedCapacity + x.Size;
    END
    METHOD Get()
    ...
END
```

abstract multiobject constraints must be reprogrammed for use with different objects. Finally, the implementation of the multiobject constraints cannot be changed transparently. These difficulties suggest the need for new high-level coordination language constructs.

We have developed high-level language constructs that let us directly express two types of multiactor constraints: temporal orderings on, and atomicity of, invocations of shared distributed actors.[7] These constructs describe multiactor constraints in terms of conditions that must be satisfied for a group of method invocations to be accepted; if the conditions are not met, the invocations are delayed. Multiactor constraints thus coordinate concurrent objects by restricting their activation.

Many coordination schemes can be efficiently expressed using invocation constraints. Consider a group of cooperating resource administrators who must share a limited resource, and who must therefore adhere to a collective policy limiting the total number of resources allocated at a given time. We can express the enforcement of a collective policy as a multiactor constraint on invocations that request resources: An allocation request can only be serviced if there are resources available. Now consider a group of dining philosophers, organized so that each philosopher shares each of her two chopsticks with each philosopher on either side. The number of philosophers is equal to the number of chopsticks, and a philosopher needs both of the chopsticks next to her to eat. We can avoid deadlocks by enforcing a multiactor constraint that requires atomic invocation of the pick method in two chopstick actors by a single philosopher.

We can specify multiactor constraints in terms of an actor's interface, independent of its representation. Separating the code for coordination from that for the actor's functionality enables better description, reasoning, and modification of those constraints. This separation also lets us design systems with a larger potential for reuse: Actors can be reused independent of how they are coordinated; conversely, multiactor coordination patterns can be reused on different groups of actors. Moreover, we can abstract over coordination patterns and factor out generic coordination structures.

We describe multiactor constraints using *synchronizers*, a special kind of actor that observes and limits the invocations accepted by a group of actors. In Figure 2, the actors are the shaded circles, and the messages sent to those objects lie outside the two synchronizer boundaries. Synchronizers can disable certain patterns: The B messages are disabled (black), while the C message is enabled (white). The E message is unconstrained. Patterns can also be grouped into atomicity constraints (the boxed groups) to ensure that multiple invocations are scheduled as an atomic action: The A messages satisfy the atomicity constraint, while the D message is blocked waiting for another message.

Synchronizers are implemented via primitive actor communication, whether directly between the constrained actors, indirectly via a central "coordinator," or a combination. The message passing is transparent to the programmer, who specifies multiactor constraints abstractly at a high level. Thus, a high-level specification provides the flexibility to map the same multiactor constraint to different implementations.

A synchronizer can be defined and instantiated by a client actor when accessing shared servers; thus, clients can use constraints to enforce customized access schemes. A synchronizer can also be permanently associated with a group of servers when they are first put into operation, in which case the constraints can express the default interdependence between servers (see the sidebar on cooperating resource administrators).

The Kaleidoscope and Rapide systems use two other approaches to constraints. In Kaleidoscope, constraints capture relations between instance variables of multiple objects; they are formulated in terms of the representation of the constrained entities rather than their abstract interfaces.[5] The Rapide prototyping system does not express constraints on the invocations accepted by the involved actors; rather, the system provides pattern-based triggering of concurrent objects.[8]

MODULAR SPECIFICATION OF RESOURCE MANAGEMENT POLICIES

Expressing a parallel algorithm in terms of primitive actors provides a logical specification of the algorithm, or an *ideal algorithm*.[9] The time taken by an ideal algorithm — assuming unbounded resources and no communication costs — is determined by the sequential depth of the longest path in the partial order defined by the actor computation.

However, neither assumption is realistic. An algorithm's communication costs are a function of the architecture's latency (the time to send a message from one node to another) and bandwidth (the rate at which information can be transmitted between two halves of an architecture). If a sorting problem, for example, must move half the data on a distributed computer, then an algorithm's performance on the problem will be bound by the bandwidth. In any physically realizable architecture, the bandwidth may grow by at most $P^{2/3}$.

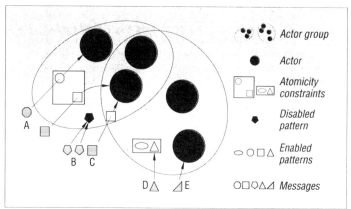

Figure 2. Overlapping groups of actors defined by two synchronizers.

Cooperating resource administrators

Consider two cooperating resource administrators (spoolers) that manage a common printer pool with n printers.[1] When an administrator receives a print request, it performs some bookkeeping and then sends it through a common bus so that one of the free printers can grab the request and start printing. The use of two spoolers allows greater concurrency and increases availability. We use a coordination constraint to ensure that requests are not relayed when there are no free printers. The constraint also ensures that the two spoolers cooperate to maintain the correct count of available printers.

A synchronizer outside the spoolers can maintain this common information and prevent the processing of a request when there is no free printer:

```
AllocationPolicy(Spooler1,Spooler2,NumPrinters) =
{ NumUsed := 0;
    NumUsed = NumPrinters DISABLES
        (Spooler1.Print + Spooler2.Print),
    (Spooler1.Print + Spooler2.Print) UPDATES
        Increment(NumUsed)
    (Spooler1.Done + Spooler2.Done) UPDATES
        Decrement(NumUsed)
}
```

A synchronizer has an encapsulated state that is updated through the Updates operator. In this case, the state is held by the variable NumUsed. The Disables operator delays invocation of the constrained actors; such delays are expressed as conditions over the synchronizer's state.

A synchronizer describes the interdependence of servers, independent of their representation. The resulting modularity lets us modify the coordination scheme without changing the servers, and to change servers without modifying the coordination scheme. In this case, we can dynamically add printers to the printer pool or administrators to the system without changing codes for existing printers or administrators; new synchronizers may simply be instantiated.

REFERENCE

1. S. Frølund and G. Agha, "A Language Framework for Multiobject Coordination," *Proc. Proc. European Conf. on Object-Oriented Programming '93*, Springer-Verlag, 1993.

Reuse of resource management strategies

Although we are developing better language support for resource management functions in terms of ActorSpace types, the same functionality could be mimicked in some cases using current tools. Consider a dense matrix Actor-Space type. We represent each matrix element by an actor in the space. The behavior of the actors is specified separately; for example, the actors might implement a Gaussian elimination or matrix multiplication. A simple set of functions can specify a placement of the actors. Changing the definitions of these functions changes the placement policy and can affect performance drastically.

Consider the problem of mapping a matrix M of size $n \times n$ to a $p \times p$ array of processors. We can divide M into submatrices of uniform size $k \times k$, where $k = n/p$, and place each submatrix on a separate processor. The placement is spec-ified using two functions: ElemToProc, which gives the processor coordinates for a given element, and LocalIndex, which specifies the coordinates within the submatrix.

The following C-like code specifies the block placement policy:

```
ElemToProc(i, j)  { Return(i/k, j/k)}
LocalIndex(i, j) { Return(i%k, j%k)}
```

These functions can be easily redefined to implement a different placement policy, such as the shuffle placement policy, without changing the code for an ideal algorithm:

```
ElemToProc(i, j)  { Return(i%p, j%p)}
LocalIndex(i, j) { Return(i/p, j/p)}
```

where P is the number of processors. (Space is three dimensional, so a given technology yields a constant bandwidth per unit area, and a bisecting plane may grow by at most $P^{2/3}$.) There is a similar theoretical bound on I/O, so for a sorting problem, the speed up is bound by $P^{2/3}$ in general (and by $\sqrt{P}$ on a two-dimensional network).[10]

Since an algorithm's performance depends on how many messages have to be sent and to which nodes, the execution efficiency depends in part on the placement and scheduling of objects. In general, the problem of finding an optimal placement policy is intractable. However, a developer might be able to determine the most efficient policy for a given algorithm.

Specifications of resource management policies, such as placement, introduce a new layer of complexity to programming concurrent computers. The same ideal

algorithm executed on the same architecture can yield different efficiencies under different resource management policies. The efficiency depends on a number of factors, including

- the problem or input size,
- the concurrent computer's characteristics (latency, bandwidth, size, processor speeds, and so on),
- the placement policy used to map objects to physical resources, and
- scheduling strategies used to manage concurrency.

Current programming methods for concurrent computers intermix the specification of resource management policies with the code specifying the ideal algorithm. The resulting conflation of design goals complicates the code and reduces its reusability.

We propose separating the ideal algorithm's specification from the strategies used to map it to a concurrent architecture. We describe a mapping policy in terms of an *actor space type*: a group of actors together with the abstract operations and the concurrent access constraints on them.

Consider an $n \times n$ array, which can be mapped onto a 2D mesh of $p \times p$ processors in several ways, including

- Block placement policy: The (i, j)th element is assigned to the $(i \text{ div } k, j \text{ div } k)$th processor, where $k = n/p$.
- Shuffle placement policy: The (i, j)th element is assigned to the $(i \text{ mod } p, j \text{ mod } p)$th processor.

Although the abstract operations and concurrent access constraints of an array are the same, different ideal algorithms can be executed more efficiently using different mapping policies. Techniques for solving linear equations, such as Gaussian elimination or Cholesky decomposition, are generally efficient when the matrix

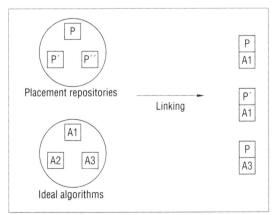

Figure 3. Combining an ideal algorithm with a placement policy to obtain architecture-specific code.

Applying reflection to a replicated server

To understand how Broadway's reflective architecture can support dependability protocols, consider the metalevel implementation of a protocol that replicates a server to resist crash failures.[1] The original system consists of server S1 and clients A and B. Broadway makes a clone of the server (S2) and installs metaactors at the servers and the clients. The metaactors manipulate generic messages, which in combination with the system's ability to clone actors lets us implement the protocol transparently of the base actors. Since the protocol is generic, it can also be reused with any application.

Each server has a customized dispatcher (Tagger) that tags all outgoing messages so that each client can use its own customized mail queue (Eliminator) to eliminate duplicate responses. Another mail queue (Broadcaster) handles messages from the clients, copying to server S2 all the messages sent to server S1. This repetition of messages keeps the state of the two servers consistent. A message sent to S1 invokes Broadcaster's Get method. When S1 requires a new message to process, it sends Broadcaster a Put message. The Get and Put methods manipulate entire messages without inspecting the contents, preserving the protocol's transparency.

The accompanying figure shows a sample message transaction. Client A sends a message to server S1. The message is routed through the mail queue Broadcaster, which passes a copy to S1 and S2. Both servers eventually reply, and their replies are tagged by the two Tagger dispatchers. The Eliminator mail queue then passes only one response to A. Additional dispatcher metaactors (not shown here) are required to handle messages sent by the client after the server has crashed, but before that crash is detected.

REFERENCE
1. G. Agha et al., "A Linguistic Framework for Dynamic Composition of Dependability Protocols," to appear in *Dependable Computing for Critical Application, III, IFIP Trans.*, Elsevier, 1993.

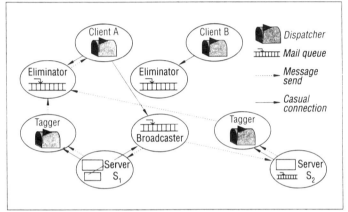

A message transaction in a replicated system.

is mapped using a shuffle placement policy. On the other hand, algorithms for low-level image-processing and for domain decomposition techniques for solving partial differential equations perform efficiently when their matrix representation is mapped using the block placement policy.

The correspondence between an algorithm and the optimal placement of its actor space type is not one-to-one. Different placement policies might be more efficient for the same ideal algorithm on different architectures, and sometimes for the same algorithm and architecture but for a different input size. Organizing a computation in terms of its actor space types provides modularity and promotes reuse. Programming can be simplified by composing and reusing modules from a repository of placement policies for a given actor space type (see the sidebar and Figure 3).

CUSTOMIZING FOR DEPENDABILITY
Currently, a protocol for dependability must be built into the system architecture or reimplemented for each application. Moreover, dependable software is expensive to develop: The increased complexity caused by mixing the code for a set of dependability protocols with that of the application code is itself a source of bugs.

We have developed a methodology that lets us specify the code for dependability protocols independently of application-specific code, thereby realizing a significant savings in software development and maintenance costs.[11] We have implemented the methodology in an experimental kernel called Broadway that allows *composition* of dependability protocols;[12] that is, we can specify and reason about a complex dependability scheme in terms of its constituents. This ability to separately describe a scheme's logically distinct aspects lets us implement dependability protocols as generic, composable components.

Our *reflective* approach lets an application access and manipulate a description of its own behavior and execution environment. The actors representing such a description are called metalevel actors. The metalevel contains a description sufficient to model the dependability characteristics of an executing application; reflection thus allows dynamic changes in the execution of an

Further reading

The Actor model was originally proposed by Carl Hewitt, who best describes its early conceptual foundation in "Viewing Control Structures as Patterns of Passing Messages," (*Journal of Artificial Intelligence*, Vol. 8, No. 3, 1977, pp. 323-364). Gul Agha describes a recent form of the model in *Actors: A Model of Concurrent Computation in Distributed Systems*, (MIT Press, 1986). Agha also develops a formal theory for reasoning about actor systems with Ian Mason, Scott Smith, and Carolyn Talcott in "Towards a Theory of Actor Computation," (*Proc. Third Int'l Conf. Concurrency Theory*, Springer-Verlag, 1992, pp. 565-579).

Multicomputer architectures use actors as a programming model. William Athas and Charles Seitz offer a good overview of multicomputers, including the use of actors for programming them, in "Multicomputers: Message-Passing Concurrent Computers" (*Computer*, Vol. 21, No. 8, Aug. 1988, pp. 9-23). William Dally describes an architecture directly realizing the functionality of actors in *A VLSI Architecture for Concurrent Data Structures* (Kluwer Academic Press, 1986).

A number of research efforts in concurrent object-oriented programming are described in *Object-Oriented Concurrent Programming*, edited by Akinori Yonezawa and Mario Tokoro (MIT Press, 1987). A more recent collection includes an excellent overview (by Satoshi Matsuoka and Yonezawa) of inheritance and synchronization constraints: *Research Directions in Concurrent Object-Oriented Programming*, edited by Agha, Peter Wegner, and Yonezawa (MIT Press, 1993).

In distributed data structures, Andrew Chien has recently described his important work extending the actor model to provide a representation for groups of actors in *Concurrent Aggregates: Supporting Modularity in Massively Parallel Programs* (MIT Press, 1993).

application with respect to dependability (see the sidebar on applying reflection to a replicated server).

The most general form of reflection leads to interpretation and is costly. Instead, we use a limited reflective model in which each actor has three metaactors: a dispatcher, a mail queue, and an acquaintance list. The acquaintance list represents the actor's current state (behavior). The dispatcher and mail queue implement the runtime system's communication primitives so that the interaction between actors can be modified to change the application's dependability characteristics.

Specifically, a dispatcher represents the implementation of an actor's transmission behavior. When customized, messages sent by the corresponding base actor are rerouted to the customized dispatcher. An actor's mail queue represents the mail buffer that holds the incoming messages. If a customized mail queue is installed, all messages to the base actor are rerouted through it. A customized mail queue can alter the order of messages to the base actor (to enforce local synchronization constraints, for example[6]).

Several protocols that increase system dependability can be expressed in terms of a customized mail queue, dispatcher and acquaintance list: two- and three-phase commit, primary back-up, full replication, checkpointing, and encryption. Our approach achieves composition of dependability protocols by transparently manipulating the metaactors of the metaactors. The resulting system allows not only the dynamic installation of generically specified protocols but also their dynamic removal. The limited form of reflection we use supports incremental compilation and increases execution time by only a very small constant.

The costs of learning new programming languages and rewriting old code have slowed the conversion to new programming approaches, leading some observers to downplay the importance of language research. But at the same time, the escalating cost of program maintenance has led to the perception of a software crisis. In fact, this "crisis" is exacerbated by the use of old languages and methodologies that are insufficiently expressive and provide little support for software maintenance.

But the parallel and distributed computing community is now more likely to accept new programming methods. For one thing, the cost of developing code in newer languages is often far lower than the cost of maintaining old code: Object-oriented technology, for example, provides design support and lets programmers incrementally modify their code, reducing development time and software maintenance costs. Furthermore, at least some code needs to be rewritten to take advantage of the increasing power and decreasing cost of concurrent computers.

The need for new programming approaches is by no means the dominant force in parallel or distributed computing research. For example, there has been a considerable effort to develop compilers that "parallelize" sequential code and map it to a concurrent architecture. While useful in the short term, this approach suffers from two limitations: Code based on sequential algorithms cannot be generally translated to the best parallel algorithms, and no general techniques can efficiently place and schedule arbitrary algorithms on a concurrent computer.

New programming methods should let developers write more complex programs with less effort and make the expression of potential parallelism simpler. However, these methods must not restrict expressiveness unrealistically; for example, although purely functional (stateless) programming has some nice concurrency properties, distributed computing requires a shared, mutable state.

Developers can become more productive through greater use of new abstractions and modularity mechanisms. Our methods for the modular construction of concurrent systems simplify programming, but that is only a small part of the gain. More importantly, application independence provides a basis for constructing software repositories consisting of constraint specifications and implementations, placement and scheduling policies, dependability protocols, and so on. The executable specifications could be dynamically linked with different application code without reimplementing them. The average application developer need not understand the details of the representation — rather she needs to know only the relevant properties of the abstraction (including properties such as the performance characteristics of certain access patterns).

The abstractions and modularity mechanisms we have proposed here are certainly not a complete set, but they do suggest ways to drastically reduce software development and maintenance costs, to scale up software systems, and to bring the power of parallel and distributed computing within reach of more developers. The successful application of these methods should further stimulate progress toward a new generation of realistic high-level programming languages. ▨

ACKNOWLEDGMENTS

This work is supported by the Office of Naval Research (ONR contract number N00014-90-J-1899), by the Digital Equipment Corporation, and by joint support from the Defense Advanced Research Projects Agency and the National Science Foundation (NSF CCR 90-07195). We thank the contributors to the Open Systems Laboratory, including Christian Callsen, Shingo Fukui, Chris Houck, Shakuntala Miriyala, Shangpin Ren, R.K. Shyamasundar, Nalini Venkatasubramanian, and Takuo Watanabe. This research has strongly benefited from Gul Agha's discussions with Carl Hewitt and Carolyn Talcott, among others.

REFERENCES

1. G. Agha and C.J. Callsen, "ActorSpace: An Open Distributed-Programming Paradigm," to be published in *Principles and Practice of Parallel Programming '93, ACM SIGPlan Notices*, May 1993.

2. N. Carriero and D. Gelernter, "How to Write Parallel Programs: A Guide to the Perplexed," *ACM Computing Surveys*, Vol. 21, No. 3, Sept. 1989, pp. 323-357.

3. B. Shriver and P. Wegner, eds., *Research Directions in Object-Oriented Programming*, MIT Press, Cambridge, Mass., 1987.

4. G. Agha, "Concurrent Object-Oriented Programming," *Comm. ACM*, Vol. 33, No. 9, Sept. 1990, pp. 125-141.

5. B.N. Freeman-Benson and A. Borning, "Integrating Constraints with an Object-Oriented Language," *Proc. European Conf. on Object-Oriented Programming '92*, Springer-Verlag, 1992, pp. 268-286.

6. C. Tomlinson and V. Singh, "Inheritance and Synchronization with Enabled Sets," *Proc. Conf. on Object-Oriented Programming Systems, Languages, and Applications (OOPSLA '89), ACM SIGPlan Notices*, Vol. 24, No. 10, Oct. 1989, pp. 103-112.

7. S. Frølund and G. Agha, "A Language Framework for Multiobject Coordination," *Proc. European Conf. on Object-Oriented Programming '93*, Springer-Verlag, 1993.

8. D.C. Luckham et al., "Partial Orderings of Event Sets and Their Application to Prototyping Concurrent Timed Systems," *Proc. 1992 DARPA Software Technology Conf.*, 1992, pp. 443-457.

9. L.H. Jamieson, "Characterizing Parallel Algorithms," in *The Characteristics of Parallel Algorithms*, R.J. Douglass, L.H. Jamieson, and D.B. Gannon, eds., MIT Press, Cambridge, Mass., 1987, pp. 65-100.

10. V. Singh et al., "Scalability of Parallel Sorting on Mesh Multicomputers," *Int'l J. Parallel Programming*, Vol. 20, No. 2, Apr. 1991, pp. 95-131.

11. G. Agha et al., "A Linguistic Framework for Dynamic Composition of Dependability Protocols," to appear in *Dependable Computing for Critical Application, III, IFIP Trans.*, Elsevier, 1993.

12. N. Venkatasubramanian and C. Talcott, "A Metaarchitecture for Distributed-Resource Management," *Proc. Hawaii Int'l Conf. System Sciences*, IEEE Computer Society Press, Los Alamitos, Calif., 1993, pp. 124-133.

Gul Agha is director of the Open Systems Laboratory at the University of Illinois at Urbana-Champaign and an assistant professor in the Department of Computer Science. He is also an ACM lecturer and a fellow at the university's Center for Advanced Study. His research interests include models, languages, and tools for parallel computing and open distributed systems. Agha received the Incentives for Excellence Award from Digital Equipment Corporation in 1989, and he was named a Naval Young Investigator by the US Office of Naval Research in 1990. He received an MS and PhD in computer and communication science, and an MA in psychology, all from the University of Michigan, Ann Arbor, and a BS in an interdisciplinary program from the California Institute of Technology.

Svend Frølund is a doctoral candidate and research assistant in the Open Systems Laboratory at the University of Illinois at Urbana-Champaign. His technical interests include infrastructures and languages for sharing and coordination in concurrent object-oriented systems. He received a research fellowship from the Natural Science Faculty of Århus University (Denmark) in 1990, from which he also received a Cand. Scient. (MS) degree in computer science.

WooYoung Kim is a doctoral candidate and research assistant in the Open Systems Laboratory at the University of Illinois at Urbana-Champaign. His research interests include the design of high-level actor-based languages, compilation and optimization techniques for distributed-memory machines, and runtime support for actor languages. He was awarded a fellowship by the Korean Ministry of Education in 1990. He received his BS magna cum laude in 1987 and his MS in 1989, both in computer engineering from Seoul National University, Korea.

Rajendra Panwar is a doctoral candidate and research assistant in the Open Systems Laboratory at the University of Illinois at Urbana-Champaign. His research interests include programming languages and environments for efficient parallel and distributed computation. He received an MS from the Department of Computer Science and Automation at the Indian Institute of Science in Bangalore, and a BS in electronics and communication engineering from Nagpur University, India.

Anna Patterson is a doctoral candidate and research assistant in the Open Systems Laboratory at the University of Illinois at Urbana-Champaign. Her research interests include formal methods, automated proof techniques, and model checking for open distributed computing. She received a BS in computer science and a BS in electrical engineering from Washington University in 1987, where she held a Langsdorf-Woodward Fellowship.

Daniel Sturman is a doctoral candidate and research assistant in the Open Systems Laboratory at the University of Illinois at Urbana-Champaign. His research interests include the development of fault-tolerant distributed systems and computer security. He received a BS with distinction from Cornell University in 1991.

All the authors can be reached at the Department of Computer Science, 1304 W. Springfield Avenue, University of Illinois at Urbana-Champaign, Urbana, IL 61801; Internet: agha, frolund, wooyoung, raju, annap, or sturman @cs.uiuc.edu

Object-Oriented Concurrent Programming in ABCL/1

Akinori Yonezawa Jean-Pierre Briot and Etsuya Shibayama

Department of Information Science
Tokyo Institute of Technology
Ookayama, Meguro-ku, Tokyo 152
(03)-726-1111 ext. 3209

Abstract

An object-oriented computation model is presented which is designed for modelling and describing a wide variety of concurrent systems. In this model, three types of message passing are incorporated. An overview of a programming language called ABCL/1, whose semantics faithfully reflects this computation model, is also presented. Using ABCL/1, a simple scheme of distributed problem solving is illustrated. Furthermore, we discuss the reply destination mechanism and its applications. A distributed "same fringe" algorithm is presented as an illustration of both the reply destination mechanism and the future type message passing which is one of the three message passing types in our computation model.

1. Introduction

Parallelism is ubiquitous in our problem domains. The behavior of computer systems, human information processing systems, corporative organizations, scientific societies, etc. is the result of highly concurrent (independent, cooperative, or contentious) activities of their components. We like to model such systems, and design AI and software systems by using various metaphors found in such systems [Smith 1985] [Special Issue 1981] [Yonezawa and Tokoro 1986] [Brodie et al. 1984]. Our approach is to represent the components of such a system as a collection of *objects* [Stefik and Bobrow 1986] and their interactions as *concurrent* message passing among such objects. The problem domains to which we apply our framework include distributed problem solving and planning in AI, modelling human cognitive processes, designing real-time systems and operating systems, and designing and constructing office information systems [Tschritzis 1985].

This paper first presents an object-based model for parallel computation and an overview of a programming language, called ABCL/1 [Yonezawa et al. 1986] [Shibayama and Yonezawa 1986a], which is based on the computation model.

Then, schemes of distributed problem solving are illustrated using ABCL/1. Though our computation model has evolved from the Actor model [Hewitt 77] [Hewitt and Baker 1977], the notion of *objects* in our model is different from that of *actors*.

2. Objects

Each *object* in our computation model has its own (autonomous) processing power and it may have its local persistent memory, the contents of which represent its *state*. An object is always in one of three modes: *dormant, active,* or *waiting*. An object is initially dormant. It becomes active when it receives a message that satisfies one of the specified patterns and constraints. Each object has a description called *script* (or a set of methods) which specifies its behavior: what messages it accepts and what actions it performs when it receives such messages.

When an active object completes the sequence of actions that are performed in response to an accepted message, if no subsequent messages have arrived, it becomes dormant again. An object in the active mode sometimes needs to stop its current activity in order to wait for a message with specified patterns to arrive. In such a case, an active object changes into the waiting mode. An object in the waiting mode becomes active again when it receives a required message. For instance, suppose a buffer object accepts two kinds of messages: a [:get] message from a consumer object requesting the delivery of one of the stored products, and a [:put <product>] message from a producer object requesting that a product (information) be stored in the buffer. When the buffer object receives a [:get] message from a consumer object and finds that its storage, namely the buffer, is empty, it must wait for a [:put <product>] message to arrive. In such a case the buffer object in the active mode changes into the waiting mode.

An active object can perform usual symbolic and numerical computations, make decisions, send messages to objects (including itself), create new objects and update the contents of its local memory. An object with local memory cannot be activated by more than one message at the same time. Thus, the activation of such an object takes place one at a time.

As mentioned above, each dormant object has a fixed set of patterns and constraints for messages that it can accept and by which it can be activated. To define the behavior of an object, we must specify what computations or actions the object performs for each message pattern and constraint. To

"Object-Oriented Concurrent Programming in ABCL/1" by A. Yonezawa, J.-P. Briot, and E. Shibayama from *Proc. Object-Oriented Programming Systems, Languages, and Applications Conference (OOPSLA '86), SIGPLAN Notices,* Vol. 21, No. 11, Nov. 1986, pp. 258-268. Copyright 1986, Association for Computing Machinery, Inc., reprinted with permission.

write a definition of an object in our language ABCL/1, we use the notation in Figure 1. Figure 2 shows a skeletal definition of an object.

```
[object object-name                        [object Buffer
  (state representation-of-local-memory )     (state ... )
  (script                                     (script
    (=> message-pattern where constraint          (=> [:put ... ]   ... )
        ...action... )


    (=> message-pattern where constraint          (=> [:get]  ... ) )]
        ...action... ) )]
```

Figure 1. Object Definition   Figure 2. Buffer

(state ...) declares the variables which represent the local persistent memory (we call such variables *state* variables) and specifies their initialization. *object-name* and the construct "where *constraint*" are optional. If a message sent to an object defined in the notation above satisfies more than one pattern-constraint pair, the first pair (from the top of the script) is chosen and the corresponding sequence of actions is performed.

An object changes into the waiting mode when it performs a special action. In ABCL/1, this action (i.e., the transition of an object from the active mode to the waiting mode) is expressed by a *select*-construct. A select construct also specifies the patterns and constraints of messages that are able to reactivate the object. We call this a *selective message receipt*.

```
(select
  (=> message-pattern where constraint    ... action ...)
       .
       .
       .
  (=> message-pattern where constraint    ... action ...))
```

Figure 3. Select Construct

As an example of the use of this construct, we give, in Figure 4, a skeleton of the definition of an object which behaves as a buffer of a bounded size.

```
[object Buffer
  (state declare-the-storage-for-buffer )
  (script
    (=> [:put aProduct]        ; aProduct is a pattern variable.
      (if the-storage-is-full
        then (select           ; then waits for a [:get] message.
              (=> [:get]
                  remove-a-product-from-the-storage-and-return-it )))
      store-aProduct  )

    (=> [:get]
      (if the-storage-is-empty
        then (select           ; then waits for a [:put ...] message.
              (=> [:put aProduct]
                  send-aProduct-to-the-object-which-sent-[:get]-message ))
        else remove-a-product-from-the-storage-and-return-it )) )]
```

Figure 4. An Example of the Use of Select Constructs

Suppose a [:put <product>] arrives at the object Buffer. When the storage in the object Buffer is found to be full, Buffer waits for a [:get] message to arrive. When a [:get] message arrives, Buffer accepts it and returns one of the stored products. If a [:put] message arrives in *this* waiting mode, it will not be accepted (and put into the *message queue* for Buffer, which

will be explained in §3). Then, Buffer continues to wait for a [:get] message to arrive. A more precise explanation will be given in the next section.

As the notation for a select construct suggests, more than one message pattern (and constraint) can be specified, but the ABCL/1 program for the buffer example in Figure 4 contains only one message pattern for each select construct.

3. Message Passing

An object can send a message to any object as long as it knows the name of the target object. The "knows" relation is dynamic: if the name of an object T comes to be known to an object O and as long as O remembers the name of T, O can send a message to T. If an object does not know or forgets the name of a target object, it cannot at least directly send a message to the target object. Thus message passing takes place in a point-to-point (object-to-object) fashion. No message can be broadcast.

All the message transmissions in our computation model are asynchronous in the sense that an object can send a message whenever it likes, irrespective of the current state or mode of the target object. Though message passing in a system of objects may take place concurrently, we assume message arrivals at an object be linearly ordered. No two messages can arrive at the same object simultaneously. Furthermore we make the following (standard) assumption on message arrival:

[Assumption for Preservation of Transmission Ordering]

> When two messages are sent to an object T by the same object O, the temporal ordering of the two message transmissions (according to O's clock) must be preserved in the temporal ordering of the two message arrivals (according to T's clock).

This assumption was not made in the Actor model of computation. Without this, however, it is difficult to model even simple things as objects. For example, a computer terminal or displaying device is difficult to model as an object without this assumption because the order of text lines which are sent by a terminal handling program (in an operating system) must be preserved when they are received. Furthermore, descriptions of distributed algorithms would become very complicated without this assumption.

In modelling various types of interactions and information exchange which take place among physical or conceptual components that comprise parallel or real-time systems, it is often necessary to have two distinct modes of message passing: *ordinary* and *express*. Correspondingly, for each object T, we assume two message queues: one for messages sent to T in the ordinary mode and the other for messages sent in the express mode. Messages are enqueued in arrival order.

[*Ordinary* Mode Message Passing]

> Suppose a message M sent in the ordinary mode arrives at an object T when the message queue associated with T is empty. If T is in the dormant mode, M is checked as to whether or not it is acceptable according to T's script. When M is acceptable, T becomes active and starts performing the actions specified for it. When M is not acceptable, it is discarded. If T is in the active mode, M is put at the end of the *ordinary* message queue associated with T.

If T is in the waiting mode, M is checked to see if it satisfies one of the pattern-and-constraint pairs that T accepts in *this* waiting mode. When M is acceptable, T is reactivated and starts performing the specified actions. When M is not acceptable, it is put at the end of the message queue.

In general, upon the completion of the specified actions of an object, if the ordinary message queue associated with the object is empty, the object becomes dormant. If the queue is not empty, then the first message in the queue is removed and checked as to whether or not it is acceptable to the object according to its script. When it is acceptable, the object stays in the active mode and starts performing the actions specified for the message. If it is not acceptable, the message is discarded and some appropriate default action is taken (for instance, the message is simply discarded, or a default failure message is sent to the sender of the message). Then if the queue is not empty, the new first message in the queue is removed and checked. This process is repeated until the queue becomes empty. When an object changes into the waiting mode, if the ordinary message queue is not empty, then it is searched from its head and the first message that matches one of the required pattern-and-constraint pairs is removed from the queue. Then the removed message reactivates the object. If no such message is found or the queue itself is empty, the object stays in the waiting mode and keeps waiting for such a message to arrive. Note that the waiting mode does not imply "busy wait".

[*Express* Mode Message Passing]

Suppose a message M sent in the *express* mode arrives at an object T. If T has been previously activated by a message which was also sent to T in the *express* mode, M is put at the end of the *express* message queue associated with T. Otherwise, M is checked to see if it satisfies one of the pattern-and-constraint pairs that T accepts. If M is acceptable, T starts performing the actions specified for M even if T has been previously activated by a message sent to T in the *ordinary* mode. The actions specified for the previous message are suspended until the actions specified for M are completed. If so specified, the suspended actions are aborted. But, in default, they are resumed.

An object cannot accept an *ordinary* mode message as long as it stays in the active mode. Thus, without the express mode message passing, no request would be responded to by an object in the active mode. For example, consider an object which models a problem solver working hard to solve a given problem (cf. §7). If the given problem is too hard and very little progress can be made, we would have no means to stop him or make him give up. Thus without the express mode, we cannot monitor the state of an object (process) which is continuously in operation and also cannot change the course of its operation. More discussion about the express mode will be found in §5.3, §10.2, and §10.3.

As was discussed above, objects are autonomous information processing agents and interact with other objects only through message passing. In modelling interactions among such autonomous objects, the convention of message passing should incorporate a *natural* model of synchronization among interacting objects. In our computation model, we distinguish

three types of message passing: *past, now,* and *future.* In what follows, we discuss each of them in turn. The following discussions are valid, irrespective of whether messages are sent in the ordinary or express mode.

[*Past* Type Message Passing] (send and no wait)

Suppose an object O has been activated and it sends a message M to an object T. Then O does not wait for M to be received by T. It just continues its computation after the transmission of M (if the transmission of M is not the last action of the current activity of O).

We call this type of message passing *past* type because sending a message finishes before it causes the intended effects to the message receiving object. Let us denote a past type message passing in the ordinary and the express modes by:

$$[T <\text{-} M] \quad \text{and} \quad [T <<\text{-} M],$$

respectively. The past type corresponds to a situation where one requests or commands someone to do some task and simultaneously he proceeds his own task without waiting for the requested task to be completed. This type of message passing substantially increases the concurrency of activities within a system.

[*Now* Type Message Passing] (send and wait)

When an object O sends a message M to an object T, O waits for not only M to be received by T, but also waits for T to send some information back to O.

This is similar to ordinary function/procedure calls, but it differs in that T's activation does not have to end with sending some information back to O. T may continue its computation after sending back some information to O. A now type message passing in the ordinary and express modes are denoted by:

$$[T <\text{-=} M] \quad \text{and} \quad [T <<\text{-=} M],$$

respectively. Returning information from T to O may serve as an acknowledgement of receiving the message (or request) as well as reporting the result of a requested task. Thus the message sending object O is able to know for certain that his message was received by the object T though he may waste time waiting. The returned information (certain values or signals) is denoted by the same notation as that of a now type message passing. That is, the above notation denotes not merely an action of sending M to T by a now type message passing, but also denotes the information returned by T. This convention is useful in expressing the assignment of the returned value to a variable. For example, $[x := [T <== M]]$.

Now type message passing provides a convenient means to synchronize concurrent activities performed by independent objects when it is used together with the parallel construct. This construct will not be discussed in this paper. It should be noted that recursive *now* type message passing causes a local deadlock.

[*Future* Type Message Passing] (reply to me later)

Suppose an object O sends a message M to an object T expecting a certain requested result to be returned from T. But O does not need the result immediately. ᵀ· this situation, after the transmission of M, O does not have to wait for T to return the result. It continues its computation immediately. Later on when O needs that result, it checks its special *private* object called *future object* that was specified at the time of the transmission of M. If the result has been stored in the future object, it can be used.

Of course, O can check whether or not the result is available before the result is actually used. A future type message passing in the ordinary and express modes are denoted by:

$$[T <= M \$ x] \quad \text{and} \quad [T <<= M \$ x],$$

respectively, where x stands for a special variable called *future variable* which binds a future object. We assume that a future object behaves like a queue. The contents of the queue can be checked or removed *solely* by the object O which performed the future type message passing. Using a special expression "(ready? x)", O can check to see if the queue is empty. O could access to the first element of the queue with a special expression "(next-value x)", or to all the elements with "(all-values x)". If the queue is empty in such cases, O has to wait. (Its precise behavior will be given in §6.2.).

A system's concurrency is increased by the use of future type message passing. If the now type is used instead of the future type, O has to waste time waiting for the currently unnecessary result to be produced. Message passing of a somewhat similar vein has been adopted in previous object-oriented programming languages. Act1, an actor-based language developed by H. Lieberman [1981] has a language feature called "future," but it is different from ours. The three types of message passing are illustrated in Figure 5.

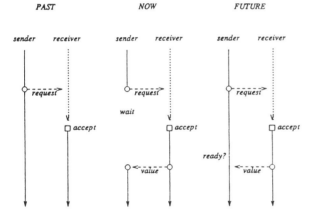

Figure 5. The Three Message Passing Types

Though our computation model for object-oriented concurrent programming is a descendant of the Actor computation model which has been proposed and studied by C. Hewitt and his group at MIT [Hewitt 1977] [Hewitt and Baker 1977] [Yonezawa and Hewitt 1979] [Lieberman 1981], it differs from the Actor computation model in many respects. For example, in our computation model, an object in the waiting mode can accept a message which is not at the head of the message queue, whereas, in the actor computation model, a (serialized) actor can only accept a message that is placed at the head of the message queue. Furthermore, now type and future type message passing are not allowed in the Actor computation model. Therefore, an actor A which sends a message to a target actor T and expects a response from T must terminate its current activity and receive the response as just one of any incoming messages. To discriminate T's response from other incoming

messages arriving at A, some provision must be made before the message is sent to T. Also the necessity of the termination of A's current activity to receive T's response causes unnatural breaking down of A's task into small pieces.

4. Messages

We will consider what information a message may contain. A message is composed of a singleton or a sequence of *tags*, *parameters*, and/or *names of objects*. Tags are used to distinguish message patterns. (In the buffer example mentioned in Figure 4, :get and :put are tags, and "aProduct" denotes a parameter in the [:put ...] message.) Object names contained in a message can be used for various purposes. For example, when an object O sends a message M to an object T requesting T to do some task, and O wishes T to send the result of the requested task to a specified object C1, O can include the name of C1 in the message M. Objects used in this way correspond to "continuation" (or customer) in the Actor computation model. Also, when O requests T to do some task in cooperation with a specified object C2, O must let T know the name of C2 by including it in the message M.

Besides the information contained in a message itself, we assume two other kinds of information can be transmitted in message passing. One is the *sender name* and the other is the *reply destination*. When a message sent from an object O is received by an object T, it is assumed that the name of the sender object O becomes known to the receiver object T. (We denote the sender name by "&sender" in ABCL/1.) This assumption considerably strengthens the expressive power of the model and it is easy to realize in the implementation of our computation model. A receiver object can decide whether it accepts or rejects an incoming message on the basis of who (or what object) sent the message.

When an object T receives a message sent in a now or future type message passing, T is required to reply to the message or return the result of the requested task (or just an acknowledgement). Since the destination to which the result should be returned is known at the time of the message transmission, we assume that such information about the destination is available to the receiver object T (and this information can be passed around among objects). We call such information the *reply destination*. To specify the object to which the result should be returned, the *reply destination* mechanism provides a more uniform way than simply including the name of the object in the request message. This mechanism is compatible with the three types of message passing, and enables us to use both explicit reply destinations in case of past type message as well as implicit ones in case of now or future type messages (cf. §6 and §9). Furthermore, the availability of the reply destination allows us to specify continuations and implement various *delegation* mechanisms [Lieberman 1986] uniformly. This will be discussed in the §8.

The fact that sender names and reply destinations can be known to message receiving objects not only makes the computation model powerful, but also makes it possible that the three different types of message passing: *past*, *now*, and *future*, be reduced to just one type of message passing, namely the *past* type message passing. In fact, a now type message passing in an object T can be expressed in terms of past type message passing together with the transition into the waiting mode in the execution of the script of the object T. And a future type message passing can be expressed in terms of past and now type message passing, which are in turn reduced to past type message passing. These reductions can be actually demonstrated, but to do so, we need a formal language. Since the programming language ABCL/1 to be introduced in the subsequent sections can also serve this purpose, we will give an actual demonstration after the explanation of ABCL/1 (cf. §6). The reply destination mechanism plays an important role in the demonstration.

5. An Overview of the Language ABCL/1

5.1. Design Principles

The primary design principles of our language, ABCL/1, are:

[1] [Clear Semantics of Message Passing] The semantics of message passing among objects should be transparent and faithful to the underlying computation model.

[2] [Practicality] Intentionally, we do not pursue the approach in which every single concept in computation should be represented purely in terms of objects and message passing. In describing the object's behavior, basic values, data structures (such as numbers, strings, lists), and invocations of operations manipulating them may be assumed to exist as they are, not necessarily as objects or message passing. Control structures (such as *if-then-else* and looping) used in the description of the behavior of an object are not necessarily based upon message passing (though they can of course be interpreted in terms of message passing).

Thus in ABCL/1, *inter*-object message passing is entirely based on the underlying object-oriented computation model, but the representation of the behavior (script) of an object may contain conventional *applicative* and *imperative* features, which we believe makes ABCL/1 programs easier to read and write from the viewpoint of *conventional* programmers. Since we are trying to grasp and exploit a complicated phenomenon, namely parallelism, a rather conservative approach is taken in describing the internal behavior of individual objects. Various applicative and imperative features in the current version of ABCL/1 are expressed in terms of Lisp-like parenthesized prefix notations, but that is not essential at all; such features may be written in other notations employed in various languages such as C or Fortran.

5.2. Creating Objects and Returning Messages

In our computation model, objects can be dynamically created. Usually, when an object A needs a new object B, A sends, in a now or future type message passing, some initial information to a certain object which *creates* B. Then B is returned as the value (or result) of the now/future type message passing. This way of creating an object is often described in ABCL/1 as follows:

```
[object CreateSomething
 (script
  (=> pattern-for-initial-info    ![object ... ] ) )]
```

where [object ....] is the definition of an object newly created by the object CreateSomething. The CreateAlarmClock object defined in Figure 6 creates and returns an alarm clock object when it receives a [:new ...] message containing the person (object) to wake. The time to ring is set by sending a [:wake-me-at ...] message to the alarm clock object. It is supposed to keep receiving [:tick ...] messages from a clock object (called the Ticker and which will be defined in the next subsection). When the time contained in a [:tick ...] message is equal to the time to ring, the alarm clock object sends a [:time-is-up] message to the person to wake in the express mode.

```
[object CreateAlarmClock
 (script
  (=> [:new Person-to-wake]

   ![object
     (state [time-to-ring := nil])
     (script
      (=> [:tick Time]
       (if (= Time time-to-ring)
        then [Person-to-wake <<= [:time-is-up]]))

      (=> [:wake-me-at T]
       [time-to-ring := T]) )] ) )]
```

Figure 6. Definition of CreateAlarmClock Object

Note that the "Person-to-wake" variable in the script of the alarm clock object to be created is a free variable (it is not a state variable nor a message parameter). It will be "closured" when creating this object, which implies that the scope rule of ABCL/1 is lexical. The notation using ! is often used in ABCL/1 to express an event of returning or sending back a value in response to a request which is sent in a now or future type message passing. In the following fragment of a script:

$$(=> pattern\text{-}for\text{-}request \quad ... \text{ !}expression ... \text{)},$$

where is the value of *expression* returned? In fact, this notation is an abbreviated form of a more explicit description which uses the reply destination. An equivalent and more explicit form is:

$$(=> pattern\text{-}for\text{-}request @ destination \quad ... [destination <= expression] ...)$$

where *destination* is a pattern variable which is bound to the reply destination for a message that matches *pattern-for-request*. When a message is sent in a past type message passing, if we need to specify the reply destination, it can be expressed as:

$$[T <= request @ reply\text{-}destination].$$

Note that *reply-destination* denotes an object. In the case of now or future type message passing, pattern variables for reply destination are matched with certain objects that the semantics of now/future type message passing defines. (See §6.) Thus the programmer is not allowed to explicitly specify reply destinations in now or future type message passing. So the following expressions [*target* <== *message* @ *reply-destination*], and [*target* <= *message* @ *reply-destination* $ x] are illegal.

There is another way to create an object. That is, an object can be obtained by copying some object. We can use the copy instantiation model [Briot 1984] after defining a prototype [Lieberman 1986], rather than defining a generator object (analog to a class). Each object can invoke a primitive function "self-copy" whose returning value is a copy of the object itself (Me), which will be exemplified in §9.

5.3. Ordinary Mode and Express Mode in Message Passing

The difference between the ordinary mode and express mode in message passing was explained in §3. The notational distinction between the two modes in message transmission is made by the number of "<", one for the ordinary mode and two for the express mode (namely <= and <==, vs. <<= and <<==). The same distinction should be made in message reception because a message sent in the ordinary mode should not be interpreted as one sent in the express mode. To make the distinction explicit, we use the following notation for expressing the reception of a message sent in the express mode.

$$(=>> \text{ message-pattern where } constraint \quad ... \text{ action } ...),$$

The reception of a message sent in the *ordinary* mode is expressed by the following notation as explained above:

$$(=> \text{ message-pattern where } constraint \quad ... \text{ action } ...)$$

This notational distinction protects an object from unwanted express mode messages because the object accepts only messages that satisfy the patterns and constraints declared after the notation "(=>>)". Express mode messages which do not satisfy such patterns and constraints are simply discarded.

Suppose a message sent in the express mode arrives at an object which has been currently activated by an ordinary mode message. If the script of the object contains the pattern and constraint that the message satisfies, the current actions are temporarily terminated (or suspended) and the actions requested by the express mode message are performed. If the object is accessing its local persistent memory when the express mode message arrives, the current actions will not be terminated until the current access to its local memory is completed. Also, if the object is performing the actions whose script is enclosed by "(atomic" and ")" in the following manner:

$$(\text{atomic} \quad ... \text{ action } ...),$$

they will not be terminated (or suspended) until they are completed. And if the actions specified by the express mode message are completed and no express mode messages have arrived yet at that time, the temporarily terminated actions are resumed by default. But, if the actions specified by the express mode message contains the "non-resume" command, denoted by:

$$(\text{non-resume}),$$

the temporarily terminated actions are aborted and will not be performed any more.

Note that, in the above explanation, the actions temporarily terminated by an express mode message are the ones that are activated (specified) by an ordinary mode message. When an object is currently performing the actions specified by an express mode message, no message (even in the express mode) can terminate (or suspend) the current actions.

To illustrate the use of express mode, we give the definition of the behavior of a clock object Ticker which sends [:tick ...] messages to all the alarm clocks he knows about (the value of its state variable "alarm-clocks-list"). The definition of the Ticker object is given in Figure 7. The two state variables of Ticker, "time" and "alarm-clocks-list", respectively contain the current time and a list of alarm clocks to be "ticked". When Ticker receives a [:start] message, it starts ticking and updating the contents of "time".

[alarm-clocks-list <= [:tick...]]

means sending [:tick ...] messages to each member of "alarm-clocks-list" simultaneously. We call this way of sending messages *multicast*. When Ticker receives a [:stop] message sent in the express mode, it stops ticking by the effect of (non-resume). This message must be sent in the express mode because Ticker always stays in the active mode to keep ticking (in the while loop). An [:add ...] message appends new alarm clock object to the "alarm-clocks-list" in Ticker. This message also should be sent in the express mode for the same reason.

```
[object Ticker
  (state [time := 0] [alarm-clocks-list := nil])
  (script
   (=> [:start]
     (while t do
       (if alarm-clocks-list
         then [alarm-clocks-list <= [:tick time]])
       [time := (1+ time)])))
   (=>> [:add AlarmClock]
     [alarm-clocks-list := (cons AlarmClock alarm-clocks-list)])
   (=>> [:stop] (non-resume)) )]
```

Figure 7. Definition of Ticker Object

The definition of the CreateAlarmObject (which appeared in Figure 6) should be slightly changed in order for a newly created alarm clock object to be known by Ticker. The description of an alarm clock object is the same as in Figure 6, but when created it will now be bound to a temporary variable "AlarmClock". Then, after the created object is sent to Ticker to be appended to Ticker's "alarm-clocks-list", it is returned to the sender of the [:new ...] message as in the case of Figure 6.

```
[object CreateAlarmClock
  (script
   (=> [:new Person-to-wake]
     (temporary
       [AlarmClock := [object  description of an alarm clock object ]])
     [Ticker <<= [:add AlarmClock]]
     !AlarmClock) )]
```

Figure 8. New Definition of CreateAlarmClock Object

6. A Minimal Computation Model

Below we will demonstrate that

[1] A now type message passing can be reduced to a combination of past type message passing and a selective message reception in the waiting mode, and

[2] A future type message passing can also be reduced to a combination of past type message passing and now type message passing.

Thus both kinds of message passing can be expressed in terms of past type message passing and selective message reception in the waiting mode, which means that now type message passing and future type message passing are derived concepts in our computation model. (The rest of this section could be skipped if one is not interested in the precise semantics of "now" and "future" types message passing.)

6.1. Reducing Now Type

Suppose the script of an object A contains a now type message passing in which a message M is sent to an object T. Let the object T accept the message M and return the response (i.e., send the response to the reply destination for M). This situation is described by the following definitions for A and T written in ABCL/1.

```
[object A
   ...
   (script
      ...
      (=> message-pattern          ... [T <== M] ...       ) ... )]

[object T
   ...
   (script
      ...
      (=> pattern-for-M @ R   ... [R <= expression ] ...    ) ... )]
```

** Note that the script of T can be abbreviated as:

```
         (=> pattern-for-M      ... !expression ...)
```

We introduce a new object "New-object" which just passes any received message to A, and also introduce a *select-construct* which receives only a message that is sent from "New-object". The behavior of the object A can be redefined without using now type message passing as follows:

```
[object A
   (script
      ...
      (=> message-pattern
         (temporary [New-object := [object (script (=> any   [A <= any]))] ])
         ...
         [T <= M @ New-object]
         (select
            (=> value where (= &sender New-object)
               ... value ... ))    ... ) ... )]
```

Note that the message M is sent by a past type message passing with the reply destination being the newly created "New-object." Immediately after this message transmission, the object A changes into the waiting mode and waits for a message that is passed by the "New-object". The constraint
                "where (= &sender New-object)"
in the select-construct means that the messages sent by New-Object can only be accepted. "New-object" serves as a unique identifier for the message transmission from A to T in past type: [T <= M @ New-object].

6.2. Reducing Future Type

Suppose the script of an object A contains a future type message passing as follows:

```
[object A
   (state ... )
   (future ... x ... )          ; declaration of a future variable x.
   (script
      ...
      (=> message-pattern
         ... [T <= M $ x] ...
         ... (ready? x) ... (next-value x) ... (all-values x) ... ) ... )]
```

Then we consider the future variable x in A to be a state variable binding a special object created by an object CreateFutureObject. (In general, such a object, namely a future object, is created for each future variable if more than one future variable is declared.) Also we rewrite the accesses to x by now type message passing to x as follows:

```
[object A
   (state ... [x := [CreateFutureObject <== [:new Me]]] ... )
   (script
      ...
      (=> message-pattern
         ... [T <= M @ x] ... [x <== [:ready?]] ...
         ... [x <== [:next-value]] ... [x <== [:all-values]] ... ) ... )]
```

Note that the future type message passing [T <= M $ x] is replaced by a past type message passing [T <= M @ x] with the reply destination being x. Thus, the future type message passing is eliminated. The behavior of the future object is defined in Figure 9. As mentioned before, it is essentially a queue object, but it only accepts message satisfying special pattern-and-constraint pairs. A queue object created by CreateQ accepts four kinds of messages: [:empty?], [:enqueue...], [:dequeue], and [:all-elements].

```
[object CreateFutureObject
   (script
      (=> [:new Creator]
         ![object
            (state [box := [CreateQ <== [:new]]])
            (script
               (=> [:ready?] where (= &sender Creator)        ; if [:ready?] is sent
                  !(not [box <== [:empty?]]))    ; by the Creator,
                                                 ; and if the box is non-empty, t is returned.
               (=> [:next-value] @ R where (= &sender Creator)
                  (if [box <== [:empty?]]
                     then (select  ; waits for a message to come, not sent by the
                        (=> message where (not (= &sender Creator))  ; Creator.
                           [R <= message]))              ; it is returned
                                                         ; to the reply destination for a [:next-value] message.
                     else ![box <= [:dequeue]]))
                  ; removes the first element in the queue and returns it.
               (=> [:all-values] @ R where (= &sender Creator)
                  (if [box <== [:empty?]]
                     then (select  ; waits for a message to come, not sent by the
                        (=> message where (not (= &sender Creator))  ; Creator.
                           [R <= [message]]))           ; sends a singleton list.
                     else ![box <= [:all-elements]]))
                  ; removes all the elements in the queue and returns the list of them.
               (=> returned-value
                  [box <= [:enqueue returned-value]]) )] ) )]
```

Figure 9. Definition of Future Object

Note the fact that the contents of the queue object stored in "box" can be checked or removed *solely* by the object which is bound to the pattern variable "Creator". Furthermore, if the queue is empty, the object which sends messages [:next-value] or [:all-values] has to wait for some value to arrive.

7. Project Team: A Scheme of Distributed Problem Solving

In this section, we present a simple scheme of distributed problem solving described in ABCL/1. In doing so, we would like to show the adequacy of ABCL/1 as a modelling and programming language in the concurrent object-oriented paradigm.

Suppose a manager is requested to create a project team to solve a certain problem by a certain deadline. He first creates a project team comprised of the project leader and multiple problem solvers, each having a different problem solving strategy. The project leader dispatches the same problem to each problem solver. For the sake of simplicity, the problem solvers are assumed to work independently in parallel. When a problem solver has solved the problem, it sends the solution to the project leader immediately. We assume the project leader also

164

tries to solve the problem himself by his own strategy. When either the project leader or some problem solvers, or both, have solved the problem, the project leader selects the best solution and sends the success report to the manager. Then he sends a *stop* message to all the problem solvers. If nobody has solved the problem by the deadline, the project leader asks the manager to extend the deadline. If no solution has been found by the extended deadline, the project leader sends the failure report to the manager and commits suicide. This problem solving scheme is easily modeled and described in ABCL/1 without any structural distortions. (See Figure 10.)

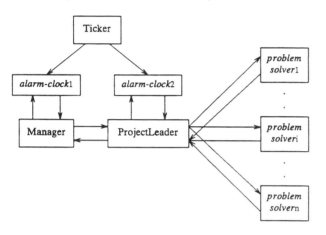

Figure 10. A Scheme for Distributed Problem Solving

The definition of the project leader object is given in Figure 11. Initially it creates an alarm clock object which will wake the project leader, and keeps it in a state variable "time-keeper". "Me" is a reserved symbol in ABCL/1 which denotes the innermost object whose definition contains the occurrence of "Me". We assume that the Ticker defined in Figure 7 is now ticking. When the project leader object receives a [:solve...] message from the manager object, it requests its alarm clock (time-keeper) to wake itself at certain time. Then, the project leader object *multicasts* to the project team members a message that contains the problem description. Note that dispatching the problem to each problem solver is expressed as a *multicast* of the problem specifications and also the message passing is of *future* type. If a problem solver finds a solution, it sends the solution to the future object bound to "Solutions" of the project leader object. While the project leader engages himself in the problem solving, he periodically checks the variable by executing "(ready? Solutions)" as to if it may contain solutions obtained by problem solvers. Note that there is a fair chance that more than one problem solver sends their solutions to the future object bound to "Solutions". As defined in the previous section, solutions sent by problem solvers are put in the queue representing the future object in the order of arrival. "(all-values Solutions)" evaluates to the list of all the elements in the queue. Note that the sequence of actions from selecting the best solutions to terminating the team members' tasks is enclosed by "(atomic" and ")" in Figure 11. Thus, the sequence of actions is not terminated (or suspended) by an express mode message.

```
[object ProjectLeader
  (state [team-members := nil] [bestSolution := nil]
    [time-keeper := [CreateAlarmClock <== [:new Me]]])
  (future Solutions)
  (script
    (=> [:add-a-team-member M]
      [team-members := (cons M team-members)])

    (=> [:solve SPEC :by TIME]
      (temporary [mySolution := nil]) ; temporary variable

      [time-keeper <= [:wake-me-at (- TIME 20)]]
      [team-members <= [:solve SPEC] $ Solutions]
                              ; multicast in future type
      (while (and (not (ready? Solutions)) (null mySolution))
        do  ... try to solve the problem by his own
                       strategy and store his solution in mySolution ...)
      (atomic
        [bestSolution := (choose-best mySolution (all-values Solutions))]
        [Manager <<= [:found bestSolution]]
        [team-members <<= [:stop-your-task]]))

    (=>> [:time-is-up] where (= &sender time-keeper)
      (temporary new-deadline)

      (if (null bestSolution)
        then
          [new-deadline := [Manager <<== [:can-extend-deadline?]]]
          (if (null new-deadline)
            then [team-members <<= [:stop-your-task]] (suicide)
            else [time-keeper <= [:wake-me-at new-deadline]])))

    (=>> [:you-are-too-late] where (= &sender Manager)
      (if (null bestSolution)
        then [team-members <<= [:stop-your-task]] (suicide))) )]
```

Figure 11. Definition of ProjectLeader Object

If no solution is found within the time limit the project leader himself has set, a [:time-is-up] message is sent by his time keeper (an alarm clock object) in the *express* mode. Then, the project leader asks the manager about the possibility of extending the deadline. If the manager answers "no" (i.e., answers "nil"), it sends a message to stop all the problem solvers and commits suicide.

Though the definition of the manager object (denoted by "Manager" in Figure 11) and problems solvers are easily written in ABCL/1, we omit them here.

8. Delegation

The *reply destination* mechanism explained in §4 and used in §6 is the basic tool to provide various delegation strategies [Lieberman 1986]. The explicit use of pattern variables for reply destinations enables us to write the script of an object which delegates the responsibility of returning a requested result to another object.

Below we define an object A, and an object B which will delegate all unknown messages to A. The pattern variable "any" will match any message not matched by the other patterns in the script of B (this is analog to the last clause with predicate t in a Lisp cond construct). The variable R will match the reply destination. So any kind of message, namely past type with or without reply destination, or now type, or future type message, will be matched and fully delegated to the object A, which could in turn, also delegate it to another object.

```
[object A                    [object B
  (state ... )                 (state ... )
  (script                      (script
    (=> patternA1                (=> patternB1
      ... )                        ... )
    ...                          ...
    (=> patternAn                (=> patternBp
      ... ) )]                     ... )
                               (=> any @ R   [A <= any @ R]) )]
```

This is illustrated by Figure 12, showing an answer is delivered directly to the asker without coming back through B.

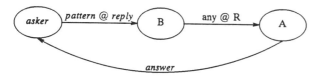

Figure 12. Illustration of Basic Delegation

9. A Distributed Algorithm for the Same Fringe Problem

The same fringe problem is to compare the fringes of two trees (Lisp lists). We will present a solution of the same fringe problem in ABCL/1, which will permit us to illustrate the use of both *future* type messages and *reply destinations*.

Our approach to the problem is similar to the one proposed by B. Serpette in [Serpette 1984]. Basically, there are three objects in this model:

- two tree extractors, extracting recursively the fringe of each tree,
- one comparator, comparing the successive elements of the two fringes.

These three objects will work in parallel. (See Figure 13.)

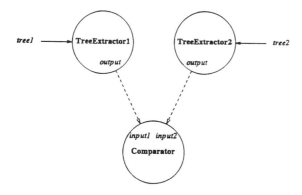

Figure 13. The Same Fringe: Tree Extractors and Comparator

The two tree extractors are linked to the comparator through two dashed arrows. Each one represents the data-flow of the successive elements of the fringe extracted by each tree extractor.

The Comparator object, defined in Figure 14, owns two state variables: "Extractor1" and "Extractor2" binding the two tree extractors, and two *future* variables "input1" and "input2"

which are used for receiving the fringes from these two extractors. "Extractor1" will be bound to the object TreeExtractor defined in Figure 15, the second extractor ("Extractor2") will be created by requesting TreeExtractor to copy itself. When the Comparator object receives the [tree1 :and tree2] message, it will send a future type message [:fringe tree] to each TreeExtractor in order to request it to compute the fringe of each of the trees. Comparator assumes that Extractor1 and Extractor2 will reply the successive elements of the fringes, which will be enqueued in the future objects bound to input1 and input2, respectively.

```
[object Comparator
  (state
    [Extractor1 := TreeExtractor]
    [Extractor2 := [TreeExtractor <== [:copy]]])
  (future  input1 input2)
  (script
    (=> [tree1 :and tree2]
      [Extractor1 <= [:fringe tree1] $ input1] ; future type message
      [Extractor2 <= [:fringe tree2] $ input2] ; future type message
      [Me <= [:eq (next-value input1) :with (next-value input2)]])

    (=> [:eq atom1 :with atom2]
      (if (eq atom1 atom2)
        then (if (eq atom1 'EOT)
               then (print "same fringe")
               else [Me <= [:eq (next-value input1)
                             :with (next-value input2)]])
        else (print "fringes differ"))) )]
```

Figure 14. The Same Fringe Comparator

When two values from the two extractors become available to Comparator through input1 and input2, Comparator sends an [:eq (next-value input1) :with (next-value input2)] message to itself. Note that if one of the two queues (i.e., the future objects bound to variables input1 and input2) is empty, Comparator has to wait until both queues become non-empty. (See the definition of a future object in §6.2.) If the two elements are equal, Comparator will compare next elements unless they were equal to the special atom EOT (as End Of Tree), which indicates the end of the extraction. If both are EOT, the two fringes are declared to be the same. On the other hand, if the two elements differ, Comparator will declare the two fringes to be different.

We could have defined a CreateTreeExtractor object, as generator of the tree extractors, but (to show a different way of creating objects) we will rather define the prototype object TreeExtractor, and later copy it to create the second tree extractor we need. The TreeExtractor object, defined in Figure 15, owns a single state variable "output" to remember the reply destination to which it has to send the successive elements of the fringe during the extraction.

The script [:copy] will return a copy of itself. This will be a *pure* (exact copy of the original object) copy of TreeExtractor. The [:fringe tree] script will bind the reply destination to the variable "Pipe". This reply destination is a future object which was bound to the future variable "input1" or "input2" of Comparator. It will be assigned to the state variable "output", thus connecting† its "output" with one "input" of the Comparator (like in the Figure 13). Then it will send to itself the message [:extract tree] with itself being the reply destination.

---

† like the communication pipes in the ObjPive model [Serpette 1984], inspired by the Un*x pipes. In contrast, these "pipes" are virtual (no assumption of shared memory).

```
[object TreeExtractor
 (state output)
 (script
  (=> [:copy]   !(self-copy))

  (=> [:fringe tree] @ Pipe
    [output := Pipe]
    [Me <= [:extract tree] @ Me])

  (=> [:extract tree] @ C
   (cond
    ((null tree)  [C <= [:continue]])
    ((atom tree)  [output <= tree] [C <= [:continue]])
    (t  [Me <= [:extract (car tree)]]
        @ [object
           (state [Extractor := Me])
           (script
            (=> [:continue]
                [Extractor <= [:extract (cdr tree)] @ C])] ]) ))

  (=> [:continue]  [output <= 'EOT]) )]
```

Figure 15. The Same Fringe TreeExtractor

To extract the fringe of a tree, the continuation-based programming style is adopted, which is in contrast to iterative or recursive ones. This model was initiated by Carl Hewitt [Hewitt et al. 1974], who gave a solution of the same fringe problem using continuations in a coroutine style. In contrast, our algorithm is fully parallel. The "[:extract tree] @ C" message script will bind the variable C to the reply destination, which represents the continuation, i.e., the object which will do the following:

- If the tree is null, the tree extractor just activates the continuation C, by sending it the message [:continue].
- If the tree is atomic, then this element is sent to the output, (so the corresponding "input1/2" of Comparator will receive a new element) and the continuation will be activated.
- The last case means that the tree is a node (a Lisp cons). We have to extract its left son (car), and then its right son (cdr). This second part to be performed later is specified in a dynamically created object (a new continuation), which will request the tree extractor to extract the cdr of the tree, when receiving the [:continue] message. The bindings of variables "tree" and "C" are memorized in the new continuation because of the lexical scoping of ABCL/1.

When the tree extractor receives the [:continue] message, that means the end of the extraction. So it will send EOT to the output, and stop there.

Note that in this algorithm if the two fringes are found to be different, the two extraction processes go on. Comparator could then send a *stop* message to either "freeze" or kill them. To deal with such a situation, we could devise various strategies which are related to the issues of objects' "capability" and garbage collection. This will be a subject for further study.

10. Concluding Remarks

10.1. Importance of the Waiting Mode

The computation model presented in this paper has evolved from the Actor computation model. One of the important differences is the introduction of the waiting mode in our computation model. As noted at the end of §3, without now type (and/or future type) message passing, module decomposition in terms of a collection of objects tends to become unnatural. Thus the now type message passing is essential in structuring solution programs. In our computation model, the now type message passing is derived from the waiting mode and the past type message passing in a simple manner as demonstrated in §6.1. In contrast, the realization of a now type message passing in the Actor computation model forces the unnatural decomposition of actors and requires rather cumbersome procedures for identifying a message that corresponds to the return (reply) value of now type message passing.

10.2. Express Mode Message Passing

We admit that the introduction of the express mode message passing in a high-level programming language is rather unusual. The main reason of introducing the express mode is to provide a language facility for *natural* modelling. Without this mode, the script of an object whose activity needs to be interrupted would become very complicated. When an object is continuously working or active, if no express mode message passing is allowed, there is no way of interrupting the object's activity or monitoring its state. One can only hope that the object terminates or suspends its activity itself and gives an interrupting message a chance to be accepted by the object. But this would make the structure of the script of the object unnatural and complicated. It should also be noted that the express mode message passing is useful for debugging because it can monitor the states of active objects.

10.3. Interrupt vs. Non-Interrupt

Our notion of *express* mode message passing is based on a very simple *interrupt* scheme. Even in this simple scheme, we must sometime protect the activity of an object from unwanted interruptions by using the "(atomic ...)" construct. (See the script of ProjectLeader in Figure 11.) Appropriate uses of this construct sometimes requires skills.

An alternative scheme might be what we call the *mail priority* model. In this model, objects are not interrupted during their activities. An express mode message sent to an object arrives at the express queue without interrupting the object. When the object is ready to check its message queues, it always first consult its express queue (with first priority), and consult its ordinary queue only when there is no (more) message in the express queue. Now there is no fear of *bad* interruptions that the programmer has to take care of. But, on the other hand, as noted in the previous subsection, the activity of an object cannot be stopped or monitored when it is in progress. To alleviate this situation, we can introduce a built-in primitive, say "(check-express)", with which an object can check to see whether an express mode message has arrived while the object is carrying out its actions. "(check-express)" can be placed in the script of an object and it is invoked as one of the actions performed by the object. When it is invoked, if a message is in the express queue and it satisfies one of the pattern-and-constraint pairs in the script, the execution of the actions specified for the message pattern intervenes.

Since both schemes have various advantages and disadvantages and they depend on the application areas of our language, we need more experiments to draw a firm conclusion.

10.4. Parallelism and Synchronization

Let us review the basic types of parallelism provided in ABCL/1:

[1] Concurrent activations of independent objects.

[2] Parallelism caused by past type and future type message passing.

[3] Parallelism caused by the *parallel* constructs [Yonezawa et al. 1986] (we did not explain in this paper) and *multicasting* (cf. §5.3 and §7).

Furthermore, ABCL/1 provides the following four basic mechanisms for synchronization:

[1] Object: the activation of an object takes place one at a time and a single first-come-first-served message queue for ordinary messages is associated with each object.

[2] Now type message passing: a message passing of the now type does not end until the result is returned.

[3] Select construct: when an object executes a select construct, it changes into the waiting mode and waits only for messages satisfying specified pattern-and-constraint pairs.

[4] Parallel construct: see [Yonezawa et al. 1986].

10.5. Relation to Other Work

Our present work is related to a number of previous research activities. To distinguish our work from them, we will give a brief summary of ABCL/1. Unlike CSP [Hoare 1978] or other languages, ABCL/1 has characteristics of *dynamic* nature: objects can be created dynamically, message transmission is asynchronous, and the "knows"-relation among objects (i.e., network topology) changes dynamically. An object in our computation model cannot be activated by more than one message at the same time. This "one-at-a-time" nature is similar to that of Monitors [Hoare 1974], but the basic mode of communication in programming with monitors is the call/return bilateral communication, whereas it is unilateral in ABCL/1.

10.6. Other Program Examples

A wide variety of example programs have been written in ABCL/1 and we are convinced that the essential part of ABCL/1 is robust enough to be used in the intended areas. The examples we have written include parallel discrete simulation [Yonezawa et al. 1984] [Shibayama and Yonezawa 1986], inventory control systems [Kerridge and Simpson 1984] [Shibayama et al. 1985] à la Jackson's example [Jackson 1983], robot arm control, mill speed control [Yonezawa and Matsumoto 1985], concurrent access to 2-3 trees and distributed quick sort [Shibayama and Yonezawa 1986].

Acknowledgements

We would like to thank Y. Honda and T. Takada for their implementation efforts on Vax/11s, Sun workstations, and a Symbolics.

References

[Briot 1984] Briot, J-P., *Instanciation et Héritage dans les Langages Objets,* (thèse de 3ème cycle), LITP Research Report, No 85-21, LITP - Université Paris-VI, Paris, 15 December 1984.

[Brodie et al. 1984] Brodie, M., J. Mylopoulos, J. Schmidt (Eds.), On Conceptual Modelling, Springer, 1984.

[Hewitt et al. 1974] Hewitt, C., et al., *Behavioral Semantics of Nonrecursive Control Structures,* Proc. Colloque sur la Programmation, Paris, April, 1974.

[Hewitt 1977] Hewitt, C., *Viewing Control Structures as Patterns of Passing Messages,* Journal of Artificial Intelligence, Vol. 8, No. 3 (1977), pp.323-364.

[Hewitt and Baker 1977] Hewitt, C., H. Baker, *Laws for Parallel Communicating Processes,* Proc. IFIP-77, Toronto, 1977.

[Hoare 1974] Hoare, C.A.R., *Monitors: An Operating System Structuring Concept,* Communications of the ACM, Vol. 17, No. 10 (1974), pp.549-558.

[Hoare 1978] Hoare, C.A.R., *Communicating Sequential Processes,* Communications of the ACM, Vol. 21 No. 8 (1978), pp.666-677.

[Jackson 1983] Jackson, M., System Development, Prentice Hall, 1983.

[Kerridge and Simpson 1984] Kerridge, J. M., D. Simpson, *Three Solutions for a Robot Arm Controller Using Pascal-Plus, Occam and Edison,* Software - Practice and Experience - Vol. 14, (1984), pp.3-15.

[Lieberman 1981] Lieberman, H., *A Preview of Act-1,* AI-Memo 625, Artificial Intelligence Laboratory, MIT, 1981.

[Lieberman 1986] Lieberman, H., *Delegation and Inheritance: Two Mechanisms for Sharing Knowledge in Object-Oriented Systems,* Proc. of 3rd Workshop on Object-Oriented Languages, Bigre+Globule, No. 48, Paris, January 1986.

[Serpette 1984] Serpette, B., *Contextes, Processus, Objets, Séquenceurs: FORMES,* (thèse de 3ème cycle), LITP Research Report, No. 85-5, LITP - Université Paris-VI, Paris, 30 October 1984.

[Shibayama et al. 1985] Shibayama, E., M. Matsuda, A. Yonezawa, *A Description of an Inventory Control System Based on an Object-Oriented Concurrent Programming Methodology,* Jouhou-Shori, Vol. 26, No. 5 (1985), pp.460-468. (in Japanese)

[Shibayama and Yonezawa 1986] Shibayama, E., A. Yonezawa, *Distributed Computing in ABCL/1,* in "Object-Oriented Concurrent Programming" edited by A. Yonezawa and M. Tokoro, MIT Press, 1986.

[Shibayama and Yonezawa 1986a] Shibayama, E., A. Yonezawa, *ABCL/1 User's Manual,* Internal Memo, 1986.

[Smith 1985] Smith, R. G., *Report on the 1984 Distributed Artificial Intelligence Workshop,* The AI Magazine Fall, 1985.

[Special Issue 1981] Special Issue on Distributed Problem Solving, IEEE Trans. on Systems, Man, and Cybernetics, Vol. SMC-11, No.1, 1981.

[Special Issue 1982] Special Issue on Rapid Prototyping, ACM SIG Software Engineering Notes Vol. 7, No. 5, December 1982.

[Stefik and Bobrow 1986] Stefik, M. K., D. G. Bobrow, *Object-Oriented Programming: Themes and Variation,* The AI Magazine, 1986

[Tschritzis 1985] Tschritzis, D. (Ed.), *Office Automation,* Springer, 1985.

[Yonezawa and Hewitt 1979] Yonezawa, A., C. Hewitt, *Modelling Distributed Systems,* Machine Intelligence, Vol. 9 (1979), pp.41-50.

[Yonezawa et al. 1984] Yonezawa, A., H. Matsuda, E. Shibayama, *Discrete Event Simulation Based on an Object-Oriented Parallel Computation Model,* Research Report C-64, Dept. of Information Science, Tokyo Institute of Technology, November 1984.

[Yonezawa et al. 1985] Yonezawa, A., Y. Matsumoto, *Object-Oriented Concurrent Programming and Industrial Software Production,* Lecture Notes in Computer Science, No.186, Springer-Verlag, 1985.

[Yonezawa et al. 1986] Yonezawa, A., E. Shibayama, T. Takada, Y. Honda, *Modelling and Programming in an Object-Oriented Concurrent Language ABCL/1,* in "Object-Oriented Concurrent Programming" edited by A. Yonezawa and M. Tokoro, MIT Press, 1986.

[Yonezawa and Tokoro 1986] Yonezawa, A., M. Tokoro (Eds.), Object-Oriented Concurrent Programming, MIT Press 1986 (in press).

Experience with Concurrent Aggregates (CA):[1] Implementation and Programming

Andrew A. Chien and William J. Dally
andrew@ai.mit.edu   billd@ai.mit.edu
Artificial Intelligence Laboratory
Massachusetts Institute of Technology
Cambridge, Massachusetts 02139

Abstract

To program massively concurrent MIMD machines, programmers need tools for managing complexity. One important tool that has been used in the sequential programming world is hierarchies of abstractions. Unfortunately, most concurrent object-oriented languages construct hierarchical abstractions from objects that serialize – serializing the abstractions. In machines with tens of thousands of processors, unnecessary serialization of this sort can cause significant loss of concurrency.

Concurrent Aggregates (CA) is an object-oriented language that allows programmers to build unserialized hierarchies of abstractions by using aggregates. An aggregate in CA is a homogeneous collection of objects (called representatives) that are grouped together and may be referenced by a single aggregate name. Aggregates are integrated into the object model, allowing them to be used wherever an object could be used. Concurrent Aggregates incorporates several other innovative language features (intra-aggregate addressing, delegation, first class messages and user continuations) to facilitate programming with aggregates.

We have implemented Concurrent Aggregates on a simulator for message passing machines. This implementation has been used to write a number of application programs. We describe our programming experience with the CA language. In addition, we present simulation results for our application programs. We find that aggregates are a useful tool for increasing the modularity of programs without reducing the concurrency.

---

[1] The research described in this paper was supported in part by the Defense Advanced Research Projects Agency and monitored by the Office of Naval Research under contracts N00014-88K-0738 and N00014-87K-0825, in part by an NSF Presidential Young Investigator Award with matching funds from GE Corporation and IBM Corporation, and in part by an Analog Devices Fellowship.

1 Introduction

Programming languages for massively parallel concurrent computers need multi-access data abstraction tools. Most concurrent object-oriented languages serialize hierarchical abstractions. Thus multiple levels of abstraction can result in greatly diminished concurrency, even if each level only causes a tiny amount of serialization. This leaves programmers with the choice of reduced concurrency or working without useful levels of abstraction. Going without these levels of abstraction makes programs more difficult to write, understand, and debug.

Concurrent Aggregates allows programmers to build hierarchical abstractions without serialization by providing *aggregates*, a multi-access abstraction tool. CA programmers can use aggregates to build hierarchies of abstraction. Each aggregate is multi-access and therefore can receive many messages simultaneously. By using appropriately sized aggregates in the upper levels of hierarchy, we can increase the message rate for lower levels in the hierarchy, allowing greater concurrency in the hierarchy. Concurrent Aggregates not only includes multi-access abstraction tools, but also integrates them into the ordinary data abstraction framework. Aggregate-based and object-based abstractions are used interchangeably.

1.1 Background

We are concerned with how to utilize the computing potential of large ensembles of processors. We focus on two major obstacles that stand between us and that goal. First, programming should be relatively easy. It must not be so difficult to write programs that a program takes years to construct and debug. As in large sequential programs, it must be possible to use abstraction (and hierarchies of abstractions) to relegate details to the appropriate level in a program. In fact, the importance of abstraction techniques is perhaps greater in parallel systems because the presence of nondeterministic behavior can complicate debugging. Second, the language must allow us to express sufficient concurrency to utilize the machine. In an ensemble of $10,000 - 100,000$ processors, unnecessary serialization may dramatically reduce the achievable performance.[2]

Most concurrent object-oriented languages serialize hierarchical abstractions. In languages such as ACORE [16], ABCL/1 [21], CANTOR [4] and POOL-T [3], hierarchical abstractions (abstractions built from other abstractions) are built from single objects. Their objects may accept only one message at a time, resulting in serialized abstractions.[3] Multiple levels of abstraction can result in greatly diminished concurrency, even if each level only causes a tiny amount of serialization. This leaves programmers with the choice of reduced concurrency or working without useful levels of abstraction. Going without these levels of abstraction makes programs more difficult to write, understand, and debug. Concurrent Aggregates allows programmers to build non-serializing hierarchies of abstraction.

Concurrent Aggregates has been developed in the Concurrent VLSI Architecture Group at MIT. For more information about CA, the interested reader can look in [9, 8]. CA is being developed in order to program fine-grain concurrent computers such as the J-machine [11, 10]. These machines are characterized by massive concurrency ($\approx 10^4$ nodes), fast communication networks [12] (latency of $\approx 2\mu s$ – roughly 20 instruction times), small local memories ($\approx 64K$ words), and support for fine-grain computation (hardware support for message passing, fast context switching, fast task creation and dispatch). Each of the nodes executes instructions from its own local memory (an MIMD machine). Although there is a global shared name space, there is no shared memory. Nodes communicate via asynchronous message passing. Machines such as the J-machine have tremendous performance potential if we can develop effective ways of programming them.

2   Aggregates and Naming

Concurrent Aggregates (CA) is an object-oriented language that allows programmers to build unserialized hierarchies of abstractions by using aggregates. An aggregate in CA is a homogeneous collection of objects (called representatives) that may be referenced by a single aggregate name. Each aggregate is multi-access and therefore can receive many messages simultaneously. By us-

---

[2] A simple argument based on Amdahl's law [2] confirms this.

[3] For example, in the Actor model, the serial message reception order is the actor's lifeline. This assumption is reflected in the notion that an actor's behavior can change at the reception of each message. In fact, any language that assumes each object resides on only one node makes that processing node a serialization point.

ing aggregates, programs can build arbitrary levels of hierarchy without introducing serialization. Aggregates are integrated with the object model, allowing them to be used wherever an object can be used.

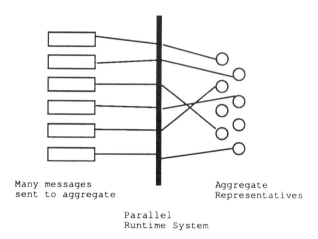

Many messages sent to aggregate

Aggregate Representatives

Parallel Runtime System

Figure 1: Aggregate to Sibling Translation

Messages sent to the aggregate are directed to arbitrary representatives as shown in Figure 1. Since this *one-to-one-of-many* direction is performed by the runtime system (which is itself multi-access), aggregates are multi-access and do not introduce serialization. Each representative can receive messages concurrently. Intra-aggregate addressing aids cooperation between parts of an aggregate. The representatives of an aggregate can communicate by sending messages to one another. The representatives can address one another. Representative's names are ordinary object names, allowing direct connection to aggregate representatives when performance is critical.

3   Support for Programming with Aggregates

Concurrent Aggregates incorporates several innovative language features that facilitate programming with aggregates. These innovations include intra-aggregate addressing, first class continuations, first class messages and delegation. We describe each of these features below.

Intra-aggregate addressing   In order to implement a coherent abstraction, representatives in an aggregate often need to send messages to each other. By transmitting data and synchronizing through message passing, the representatives can cooperate to implement an abstraction. Concurrent Aggregates allows representatives in an aggregate to compute each other's names.

Delegation Object and aggregate behavior can be defined by declaring handlers for messages. Behavior can also be specified via delegation. Delegations pass responsibility for handling a message of a particular name to another object or aggregate. Thus, delegations can be used to construct the behavior of an aggregate incrementally from that of several other aggregates.

First Class Messages First class messages allow programmers to write message manipulation abstractions. Such abstractions can be used to implement control structures that perform message reordering or implement data parallel[4] operations on aggregates. Such aggregate operations are an important source of concurrency in our programs. Messages are by-value parameters and their contents can be explicitly manipulated in a fashion similar to an array.

First Class and User Continuations The Concurrent Aggregates language allows programs to manipulate continuations as first class objects. Continuations may be stored, copied, and have messages sent to them. Programs can obtain references to continuations by explicitly manipulating a message or accessing the current continuation.

CA contains language constructs to perform some common operations on continuations. With one argument, the do form performs imperative sends. With two arguments, the second argument can be used to specify a continuation. This is especially useful in CA as programs can substitute ordinary objects and aggregates for continuations. Tail forwarding [13], the distributed machine analog of tail recursion optimization, can be done using the do form.

4 Implementation

We have implemented the CA language by building a compiler that transforms CA code into C++ functions. Each message handler is compiled into a C++ function.

The resulting code is compiled and linked with a runtime system – also written in C++. The runtime system supports the functionality required to implement the language as well as simulating parallel execution of Concurrent Aggregates programs[5]. The runtime interface is designed to be an operating system interface and could form the basis of a distributed memory computer implementation of Concurrent Aggregates.

Compiling to C++ has allowed us to build a reasonably efficient, portable implementation of CA. While the speed of our implementation does not approach bare C programs, we are able to execute 2400 message sends per second[6]. This level of performance has enabled us to run programs of several million messages. In fact, in simulating parallel machines, our primary limitation is due to main memory size (24MB) and excessive disk I/O in the simulating machine rather than computational limits.

5 Simulation Experience

We have used our implementation of Concurrent Aggregates to write and execute a wide variety of programs. These programs have ranged from application kernels to smaller toy programs. We present a brief description of our application programs and present some statistics from their execution.

Matrix Multiplication A concurrent matrix multiply made from n^2 dot products.

Multigrid Relaxation Solver An efficient partial differential equation solver. We used a three level grid, with various grid sizes.

N-body Simulation A simulation of the movement of bodies acting on each other with gravity. We used a simple algorithm that explicitly calculates all $\frac{n^2}{2}$ interactions each iteration.

Printed Circuit Board Router A program to route nets on a printed circuit board. Routes are found via a concurrent A* search.

Logic Simulator Discrete Event Simulation for logic testing and debugging. Concurrency within a time step (concurrent gate evaluations) and between time steps is exploited.

To evaluate these application programs in the context of a fine-grained message-passing machine, we imple-

---

[4]This differs from the usage of the term "Data Parallel" in the context of SIMD machines. We mean the parallelism arising from operations on large sets of data, be it heterogenous or homogeneous. No global synchronization is implied.

[5]The degree of flexibility afforded us by this framework allows us to model quite a large range of machines – the cost of computation, communication, context switching, task spawning, operating system calls, etc. can all be changed at will.

[6]Each message send is comparable to a function call in a block structured language.

Application	Data Size	% size	Crit. Path	# msgs	Peak Conc	Avg Conc
Matrix Mult	4096 elts	≈ 25%	5,922	1,880,055	3,595	2,098
N-body	64 bodies	<1%	71,134	2,130,878	747	117
PCB Router	8n 4096gp	<1%	136,796	1,283,174	63	30
Logic Sim.	3,584 gates	≈ 2%	265,416	1,056,782	122	14

Figure 2: Application Program Statistics

mented a message-passing machine simulator. The cost of various machine operations using this simulator is parameterizable. We describe the cost model we used for our simulations here.

5.1 Bounded-Resource Message-Passing Model

In the *Bounded Resource Model*, we model an message-passing machine with finite processing resources. It is quite difficult to accurately model the costs of a real machine. Not only is it computationally expensive, it is not yet clear exactly what operations a fine grain message-passing machines will ultimately cost. However, it is important to model contention for resources, as such contention can significantly change the behavior of a computation. Our solution to this problem is to use a very simple approximate model of future message-passing machines. Every local operation takes unit time. Local operations include primitive operations (+, *, -, etc.), context switches, function calls, method invocations, local object allocation, object location resolution, and aggregate to representative resolution. This overcharges for primitive arithmetic operations, but is quite a good approximation for the other local operations.

Communicating a message from one part of the machine to another takes a fixed latency of one time unit. This ratio of computation to communication cost roughly corresponds to the realities of our J-machine prototype[7]. This approximation is desirable as it reduces the complexity of the simulation, enabling us to simulate larger application problems. Our model assumes that the network is operating at a low-level of loading.

We present some simulation results for our application programs in Figure 2. The *Bounded Resource Model* simulations reflect a machine of 4096 nodes. This resource limit may reduce the average concurrency by truncating the peaks and smearing them out over time. All objects are randomly placed on nodes and do not migrate. We simulated these applications on modest size

---

[7]It overcharges for primitive local operations and reflects the assumption that the network is relatively lightly loaded.

data sets. For each program, we estimated the fraction of a real size data set to which this corresponds. The printed circuit board router was run on a 64 by 64 grid and routed 8 nets concurrently. For each application, we report the critical path length (time from initiation to total completion), the total number of messages, the peak concurrency and the average concurrency. These numbers show that we can construct MIMD programs with massive concurrency using Concurrent Aggregates.

5.2 An Example

To give the reader a flavor for how the programs have been modularized, we present a multigrid solver and give execution profiles from sample runs. Multigrid is an efficient algorithm for solving partial differential equations[17, 18]. It is an indirect method based on finite differences. The variable of interest is represented over a continuous space by a set of values at grid points. By performing successive relaxation operations (averaging local grid values), we solve for the variable over the space.

Multigrid is an improved relaxation-based solution technique. The crucial observation in multigrid is that relaxation techniques efficiently reduce the high frequency components of the error (the difference between the computed solution and true solution). By viewing the error on successively coarser grids, low frequencies in the error become high frequencies and hence can be reduced effectively by relaxation techniques. Thus, multigrid makes use of a hierarchy of grids. As we go up in the hierarchy, the the grids become smaller. Typically, the grid sizes get smaller exponentially, so only a few levels of grid are needed even for large problems.

The multigrid algorithm in Concurrent Aggregates consists of a number of abstractions. These abstractions are composed to produce a multigrid solver. The multigrid algorithm makes use of a hierarchy of grids. Each grid is implemented by an instance of the **grid** abstraction. The **grid** abstraction is a relaxation solver. It performs a fixed number of iterations. **grid** uses the **synch_relax** abstraction to enforce the necessary synchronization between successive iterations of the relax-

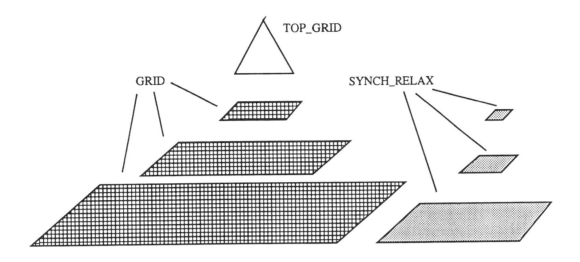

Figure 3: The Multigrid Algorithm in Concurrent Aggregates

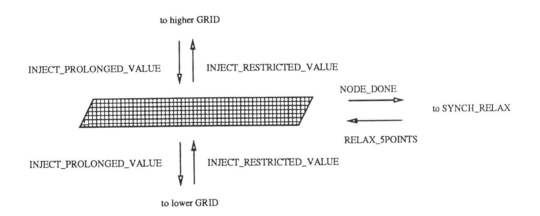

Figure 4: Interfaces for the Grid Abstraction

ation. If one node was too far ahead, some grid values
might be computed using values from the wrong iteration. The per grid point synchronization provided by
synch_relax allows different parts of the grid to get
out of synchrony but never too far – allowing the exploitation of inter-iteration and inter-grid concurrency.
After **a grid** has finished its relaxation steps, it injects
(interpolates) the grid values to its upper (lower) grid
neighbor. This operation is performed by a restriction
(prolongation) operator. At the top of the **grid** hierarchy, the **top_grid** abstraction performs a barrier synchronization and starts the algorithm back downward.
The structure of multigrid in CA is depicted in Figure
3.

CA language features are used in a number of places in
the multigrid program. Aggregates are used for **grid** –
the data grid, **synch_relax** – the fine-grained synchronization structure, **top_grid** – an interface between the
grid and a barrier and **barrier_tree** – a combining tree
used in the barrier synchronization. The aggregates
allow the grids to be connected by a single aggregate
pointer. The multiple access property of aggregates
also allows the use of a simple abstraction for synchronization – the **synch_relax** abstraction. **synch_relax**
supports fine-grain synchronization while maintaining
a simple interface. It could be replaced with a simple
structure that performed a coarser grain synchronization with no change to the multigrid relaxation code.
This abstraction would not be constructed in the absence of multi-access abstractions since the serialization
overhead would be too large.

In order to illustrate how Concurrent Aggregates allows the construction of clean interfaces for abstractions, we depict the **grid** aggregate with interfaces in
Figure 4. A **grid** has three ports: to the upper grid,
to the lower grid and to its cooperating **synch_relax**
aggregate. These interfaces are defined by handlers
and message sends used in the code shown in Figure
5. The interface to the **synch_relax** abstraction is very
clean. Each completing local relaxation operator ends
with a message **node_done** to the **synch_relax** abstraction, indicating its completion. When the **synch_relax**
abstraction determines that the next local relaxation
operator can be computed, it sends a **relax_5points**
message to the **grid**, beginning the next local grid point
computation.

In order to make all grids identical, we constrained the
top_grid abstraction to have an interface compatible
with the upward grid interface. Upward messages are
caught by **top_grid** and used to synchronize the computation globally. First class messages are used by the
top_grid to halt the upward phase of the computation,
synchronize and proceed to the downward phase. The

```
(aggregate grid value count synch_node
        scratch_value xsize
        restrict_prolong ;; 0 for up, 1 for down
        upgrid downgrid :no_reader_writer
        (parameters totalsize ixsize ival nr_iters)
        (initial totalsize ... ))
;;
;; Jacobi method indirect solution
;;      (also interface to synch_relax grid)
(handler grid relax_5points (local_x local_y)
... send relax_5points_step to neighbors ...)

(handler grid relax_5points_step (xval yval val)
    ...
    (if (= (count self) 4)    ;; local operator done
        (do (node_done (synch_node self)))
    ...))                 ;; tell synch_grid we're done
;;
;; upward and downward interfaces
;;
(handler grid inject_restricted_value (val x y)
... put it in the right place
    and start relaxation step ... )
(handler grid inject_prolonged_value (val x y)
... put it in the right place
    and start relaxation step ... )
```

Figure 5: The code for a Grid Abstraction

```
(aggregate top_grid downgrid msg_list barrier_tree
        ...)

;; 1) Catches the messages
;; 2) Modifies the selector,
;;      receiver and two arguments
;; 3) Saves the message
;; Counting is for global barrier synchronization
;;
(handler top_grid inject_restricted_value (val x y)
  (seq (msg_atput msg inject_prolonged_value 0)
       (msg_atput msg (downgrid self) 2)
       (msg_atput msg (* 2 x) 4)
       (msg_atput msg (* 2 y) 5)
       (set_msg_list self
            (new msg_pair msg (msg_list self)))
       (do (barrier_synch (barrier_tree self) 1)))))
```

Figure 6: The code for a Top_Grid Abstraction

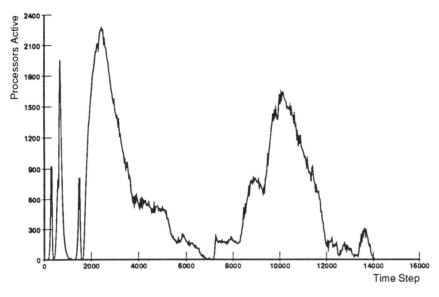

Processor Concurrency Profile

Figure 7: Multigrid Trace Concurrency Profile

	Bounded Resource Model		
Grid Size (finest)	256	1024	4096
Critical Path	10130	10050	14066
Number of Messages	123984	481021	1805808
Avg Concurrency	57	225	612
Ideal Concurrency	112	448	1792

Figure 8: Bounded Resource Model Simulation Results for Multigrid

top_grid catches, modifies and resends the messages as shown in Figure 6.

In Figure 7, we present a concurrency profile for the multigrid application. The largest grid (most points) had 4096 points, and the smallest grid had 256 points. Some initialization occurs from time 0 to num. The progress of the computation up and down the grid are clearly shown in the concurrency profile. The average concurrency and critical path length are presented in Figure 8.

The maximum achievable concurrency for this algorithm is shown as the Ideal Concurrency in Figure 8. The ideal numbers are not achieved due to grid creation and initialization overhead as well as communication latency and imperfect load balancing.

6 Programming Experience

Based on the application programs we have written, we evaluate the language and its features. We first discuss the use of multi-access data abstraction tools in CA programs, then evaluate language features designed to facilitate programming with aggregates.

6.1 Non-serializing Data Abstractions

The multi-access abstraction tools provided in Concurrent Aggregates were used to construct a variety of non-serializing abstractions. These abstractions allowed hierarchical structuring and complexity hiding in the application programs without causing serialization. The power of these tools stems from giving the programmer explicit control over distribution, consistency and update of state. Such control allows programmers to build efficient implementations of traditional abstractions as well as some novel abstractions. In this section, we describe a number of these different paradigms for using multi-access abstractions.

Replicated State Each representative in an aggregate can be used to hold a replica of the abstraction state. Read requests (non-mutating) can be handled locally by any representative. Write requests must lock all representatives, perform the write, and then propagate the new state to each representative before unlock-

175

ing it[8]. If writes do not occur frequently, the replication will increase the effective bandwidth of the abstraction. For read-only (immutable) objects, aggregates can effectively increase an abstraction's bandwidth. No mutations are ever performed, so there is no locking overhead. If there are many more reads than writes, replication can be used to increase the effective bandwidth of mutable state. One example of replicated mutable state is a replicated, coherent memory.

Loosely-Consistent Replicated State As in the previous case, each representative in an aggregate is used to hold a replica of the abstraction state. However, these copies are not kept completely consistent. Updates are propagated gradually. Use of loosely consistent replication can provide many of the benefits of replication – higher availability and throughput – with lower cost updates. Some read requests may get stale data, so it is only useful when a consistent view of the state is not required. One scheme for loosely-consistent replicated state is multi-version memories [20]. In a multi-version memory, a request may be a read, write, or a read_newest. Reads may get stale data, read_newest and write requests are serialized by a single copy of the data. We used multi-version memories to implement a B-tree. Based on a scheme developed in [15, 14], multi-version memories can be used for internal tree nodes because 1) using the most recent information was not essential for most operations and 2) high bandwidth is essential for internal nodes to allow many B-tree requests to proceed concurrently. In a B-tree multi-version memories may work better than replicated memories because the overhead for updating internal nodes may be less if the query-to-update ratio is appropriate.

Partitioned State Aggregates can be used to implement abstractions with partitioned, non-interacting state. Many program abstractions consist of collections of non-interacting state – the elements in an array, for instance. While requests to the abstraction need only access the data at a single representative – the state is non-interacting, the abstraction still forms a useful program structuring. This structuring improves program modularity. Consistency amongst the parts of the abstraction is not an issue as the state of each representative corresponds to a different part of the abstraction state. Typically, partitioned state abstractions divide the abstraction state evenly over the collection of representatives in an aggregate. Each representative is responsible for operations on its part of the state. If a representative receives a request to operate on part of the state, it handles the request. If the request requires operation on another representative's state, it forwards the message to the appropriate representative. Examples of partitioned state abstractions include: hash tables, arrays, grids, and collections of abstractions such as an abstraction for all bodies in an N-body simulation.

Structured Cooperation A more complex use of aggregates involves structured cooperation. An aggregate is organized into a network with a particular interconnection pattern. When requests are received, the interconnection pattern shapes the resulting computation. One example of this is a dynamic combining tree. In each of these cases, the representatives are initially structured into a tree. Using this interconnection structure, requests are combined and propagated up the tree. Another example of structured cooperation is a grid. Representatives of an aggregate can be linked into a 2-dimensional grid and thereafter refer to their neighbors by their north, south, east or west direction. This cooperation result in simpler code, allowing singularities and boundary conditions to be handled uniformly.

Using aggregates for structured cooperation is interesting because different representatives are not consistent. Representatives are linked together, each forming a different part of the overall abstraction. They are specialized by the interconnection. The behavior of the abstraction emerges from the interconnection of representatives.

6.2 Program Modularity

Aggregates allow programmers to implement an abstraction barrier without reducing concurrency. Programmers can structure their programs without fear of reducing concurrency. This ability improves the modularity of Concurrent Aggregates programs.

All of the abstractions described in Section 5.2 would have been impractical to implement in an Actor language [1] because they would reduce concurrency dramatically[9]. One example of this is the grid abstraction in our multigrid solver which processed thousands of message simultaneously. Implementing it as a serializing abstraction would be unacceptable[10]. In fact, data

---

[8]This use of aggregates is very similar to caching of data in a shared memory machine [19, 7]. Object caching schemes with similar functionality have been used in distributed systems [6, 5].

[9]In fairness to the Actor model, it was developed for programming in distributed systems, not tightly-coupled, fine-grain message-passing machines.

[10]One way of reducing serialization due to an abstraction is to use caching or replication schemes. However, they are unlikely to help in this case as the grid points are written quite often (making coherence expensive) and the number of copies required to supports the thousands of simultaneous accesses would be quite

parallelism over the grid points was the primary source of concurrency in multigrid. If all of our abstraction tools were serializing, we would be forced to avoid using them in many cases. In a grid abstraction, a few instructions of serialization would cause many thousands of cycles of serialization, drastically reducing concurrency.

The grid abstraction in the multigrid application not only has well-defined interfaces to its upward grid and downward grid, it has a well defined interface to a synchronization abstraction, synch_relax. We have even modularized the synchronization structure of our program. The synch_relax abstraction could be replaced by any other appropriate synchronization abstraction, such as a barrier, that had a compatible interface. The grid abstraction would not need to be modified.

6.3 Language Support for Aggregates

Concurrent Aggregates contains a variety of features which facilitate the construction and use of aggregates in programs. In this section, we use our programming experience to evaluate these features.

Intra-Aggregate Addressing An aggregate is a cooperating collection of objects. In order to cooperate, it is often convenient to be able to access the names of the other parts of the aggregate. The intra-aggregate addressing facility was used extensively. The representative indices were used to compute state partitionings and object interconnection. For example, the representative indices were used to determine which representative handled which part of the state in the synchronizing array abstraction. In combining tree abstractions, the indices determine the intra-aggregate interconnection to form the tree structure. The efficient implementation of aggregate name operations is essential because it is used pervasively in CA programs.

First Class Continuations and User Continuations Continuations were used in many of our application programs. The ability to explicitly manipulate continuations made it possible to construct synchronizing structures such as futures, a synchronizing array and a barrier synchronization within the CA language. Without this ability, more restrictive control synchronization would probably have to be applied in these programs. User constructed continuations found use in fewer places – a barrier synchronization, fanning out replies in a combining tree, and a race construct (speculative concurrency). While allowing the user to man-

_____

large.

age continuations explicitly was convenient at times, the use-once characteristic of system continuations caused quite a number of subtle bugs in programs. Two or more replies to a system continuation cause unpredictable behavior due to the reuse of activation frames. Debugging programs with double replies is difficult because the extra reply may have come from any activation that handled the continuation, not only the one called locally.

First Class Messages Allowing programmers to manipulate messages as first class objects turned out to be a useful feature. First class messages were used as partial applications, factoring the details of a partial application from the code that manipulates the application. For example, we constructed several varieties of fan out trees that implemented do-all operations on each representative of an aggregate. We also used first class messages to construct message reordering abstractions. For instance, we built a message queue abstraction and used it to defer the processing of messages. A variant of this message queue was used in the top_grid abstraction from the multigrid application. First class message manipulation in Concurrent Aggregates can also be used to explicitly change the order in which messages are processed. It could even be used to construct a message-ordering system, implementing point-to-point order-preserving message transmission.

Delegation Our CA programs did not make much use of delegation. We had hoped that delegation would allow us to compose behaviors incrementally, piecing together the desired behavior and message interface for an abstraction. However, we did not use it often because for most of our abstractions, the subparts needed to cooperate quite closely. Abstractions not designed as a subpart, in general did include the appropriate code for cooperation. This experience may be due to the type of program we examined, our limited experience, or perhaps the way we chose to integrate delegation into the Concurrent Aggregates language. It may be the case that delegation will become more important as we construct larger and larger programs.

7 Summary

Our experience with Concurrent Aggregates has been quite positive. We have found that the multi-access abstraction tools in CA make it possible to build modular programs without sacrificing concurrency. We have used our implementation of Concurrent Aggregates to write a significant number of application programs. These application programs have provided ample opportunity to explore the usefulness of programming with aggregates. In the process, we have discovered that aggregates can be used in a number of interesting ways to implement abstractions. These include familiar paradigms such as replication and partition of state as well as more novel schemes of loose consistency and structured cooperation.

With a suite of application programs, we were able to perform meaningful simulations of CA programs. These simulations show that CA programs are likely to have large amounts of fine-grain concurrency. Such concurrency is well suited for fine-grain concurrent computers such as the J-machine. We are optimistic that further refinement of the approach embodied on Concurrent Aggregates will provide a means of writing programs for massively parallel MIMD machines.

References

[1] Gul Agha. *Actors: A Model of Concurrent Computation in Distributed Systems.* MIT Press, Cambridge, MA, 1986.

[2] G. M. Amdahl. Validity of the Single Processor Approach to Achieving Large Scale Computing Capabilities. In *AFIPS Conference Proceedings*, pages 483–5. AFIPS, 1967.

[3] P. America. Inheritance and Subtyping in a Parallel Object-Oriented Language. In *Proceedings of ECOOP*, pages 234–42. Springer-Verlag, June 1987.

[4] William C. Athas. *Fine Grain Concurrent Computations.* PhD thesis, California Institute of Technology, 1987. 5242:TR:87.

[5] Henri E. Bal. *The Shared Data-Object Model as a Paradigm for Programming Distributed Systems.* PhD thesis, Vrije Universiteit Te Amsterdam, Amsterdam, 1989.

[6] J. Bennett, J. B. Carter, and Willy Zwaenepoel. Munin: Distributed Shared Memory Based on Type-Specific Memory Coherence. Technical Report Rice COMP TR89-98, Rice University, 1989.

[7] David Chaiken, Craig Fields, Kiyoshi Kurihara, and Anant Agarwal. Cache and Interconnect Architectures in Multiprocessors. *IEEE Computer*, June 1990.

[8] Andrew A. Chien. *Concurrent Aggregates: an Approach to Programming Fine-Grained Concurrent Computers.* PhD thesis, Massachusetts Institute of Technology, 1990. Expected June 1990.

[9] Andrew A. Chien and William J. Dally. Concurrent Aggregates (CA). In *Proceedings of Second Symposium on Principles and Practice of Parallel Programming.* ACM, March 1990.

[10] William J. Dally and et. al. Architecture of a Message-Driven Processor. In *Proceedings of the 14th ACM/IEEE Symposium on Computer Architecture*, pages 189–196. IEEE, June 1987.

[11] William J. Dally and et.al. The J-Machine: A Fine-Grain Concurrent Computer. In *Proceedings of the IFIPS Conference*, 1989.

[12] William J. Dally and Paul Song. Design of a Self-Timed VLSI Multicomputer Communication Controller. In *Proceedings of the International Conference on Computer Design*, pages 230–4. IEEE Computer Society, 1987.

[13] W. Horwat, A. Chien, and W. Dally. Experience with CST: Programming and Implementation. In *Proceedings of the SIGPLAN Conference on Programming Language Design and Implementation*, pages 101–9. ACM SIGPLAN, ACM Press, 1989.

[14] V. Lanin and D. Shasha. A Symmetric Concurrent B-tree Algorithm. In *Proceedings of the Fall Joint Computer Conference*, pages 380–6, November 1986.

[15] P. L. Lehman and S. B. Yao. Efficient Locking for Concurrent Operations on B-trees. *ACM Transactions on Database Systems*, 6(4):650–70, December 1981.

[16] Carl R. Manning. ACORE: The Design of a Core Actor Language and its Compiler. Master's thesis, Massachusetts Institute of Technology, August 1987.

[17] W. J. A. Mol. On the Choice of Suitable Operators and Parameters in Multigrid Methods. Technical Report NW 107/81, Department of Numerical Mathematics, stichting mathematisch centrum, June 1981.

[18] V. Faber Olaf M. Lubeck. Modeling the Performance of Hypercubes: A Case Study Using the Particle-in-Cell Application. Technical Report LA-UR-87-15222, Los Alamos National Laboratory, Los Alamos, New Mexico 87545, 1987.

[19] A. J. Smith. Cache Memories. *ACM Computing Surveys*, 14(3):473–530, September 1982.

[20] William E. Weihl and Paul Wang. Multi-Version Memory: Software Cache Management for Concurrent B-trees. In *Proceeding of Principles of Distributed Computing*, 1990. Submitted for Publication.

[21] A. Yonezawa, E. Shibayama, T. Takada, and Y. Honda. Object-Oriented Concurrent Programming – Modelling and Programming in an Object-Oriented Concurrent Language ABCL/1. In Aki Yonezawa and Mario Tokoro, editors, *Object-Oriented Concurrent Programming*, pages 55–89. MIT Press, 1987.

Easy-to-Use Object-Oriented Parallel Processing with Mentat

Andrew S. Grimshaw, University of Virginia

Two problems plague programming for parallel multiple-instruction, multiple-data (MIMD) architectures. First, writing parallel programs by hand is very difficult. The programmer must manage communication, synchronization, and scheduling of tens to thousands of independent processes. Correctly managing the environment requires considerable time and energy and often overwhelms the programmer. Second, code implemented on a particular architecture is seldom usable on other MIMD architectures, since the tools, techniques, and library facilities to parallelize the application are platform specific. Thus, porting the application to a new architecture requires considerable effort. Given the plethora of new architectures and the rapid obsolescence of existing architectures, this represents a continuing time investment.

Mentat, an object-oriented parallel processing system that I developed with my students at the University of Virginia, directly addresses the difficulty of programming MIMD architectures and the portability of applications. Its three primary design objectives are to provide (1) easy-to-use parallelism, (2) high performance via parallel execution, and (3) application portability across a wide range of platforms. The underlying premise is that writing programs for parallel machines does not have to be difficult. Instead, it's the lack of appropriate abstractions that has made parallel architectures difficult to program and kept them inaccessible to mainstream production-system programmers.

The Mentat philosophy on parallel computing is guided by two observations. The first is that the programmer understands the application domain and can make better data and computation partitioning decisions than the compiler. The truth of this is evidenced by the fact that most successful production parallel applications have been hand-coded using low-level primitives. In these applications the programmer has decomposed and distributed both the data and the computation.

The second observation is that management of tens to thousands of asynchronous tasks, where timing-dependent errors are easy to make, is beyond the capacity of most programmers. Compilers, on the other hand, are very good at ensuring that events happen in the right order and can more readily and correctly manage communication and synchronization, particularly in highly asynchronous, non-SPMD (single program, multiple data) environments.

Lack of appropriate abstractions makes programming for parallel architectures more difficult than writing sequential software. Mentat addresses this problem by extending C++ to include parallelism encapsulation.

Reprinted from *Computer,* Vol. 26, No. 5, May 1993, pp. 39-51. Copyright © 1993 by The Institute of Electrical and Electronics Engineers, Inc. All rights reserved.

These two observations lead to our underlying philosophy of exploiting the comparative advantages of both humans and compilers. Therefore, in Mentat, the programmer tells the compiler, using a few key words, what computations are worth doing in parallel and what data are associated with the computations. The compiler then takes over and does what it does best, manage parallelism.

What makes Mentat different from the dozens of other concurrent and distributed object-oriented systems is its emphasis on parallelism and high performance. Mentat is not yet-another-RPC-based system. Unlike RPC (remote procedure call) systems, it uses parallel-processing compiler and run-time support technology in conjunction with the object-oriented paradigm to produce an easy-to-use high-performance system that facilitates hierarchies of parallelism.

Mentat accomplishes these objectives through two primary components. The Mentat programming language,[1] an object-oriented programming language based on C++, masks the complexity of the parallel environment from the programmer. The underlying Mentat runtime system[2] provides a virtual machine abstraction for easy portability to new architectures. The language and runtime system are introduced below, followed by performance figures for two applications on different platforms, a network of Sun workstations and the Intel iPSC/2. (For more detailed performance figures, see our companion article in the May 1993 issue of *IEEE Parallel & Distributed Technology*.)

Mentat programming language

The Mentat programming language (MPL) is a C++ extension designed to simplify the writing of high-performance parallel applications by supporting both intra- and interobject parallelism encapsulation. This high-level ease-of-use objective is realized via four specific design features.

First, MPL is object-oriented. The object-oriented paradigm is ideal for parallel and distributed systems because users of an object interact with the object via the object's interface. The ob-

Emphasis on parallelism and high performance distinguishes Mentat from many of other object-oriented systems.

ject's data hiding, or encapsulation, properties prevent direct access of private object data. This simplifies concurrency control on object data structures, since objects can be treated as monitors. MPL extends the notions of data and method encapsulation to include parallelism encapsulation (see sidebar on encapsulation).

Second, MPL extends an existing language, C++, with minimal changes. The syntax and semantics of the extensions follow the pattern set by the base language, maintaining its basic structure and philosophy whenever possible.

Third, the language constructs have a natural mapping to the macro dataflow model, the computation model underlying Mentat. It is a medium-grain data-driven model in which programs are directed graphs. The vertices of the program graphs are computation elements (called actors) that perform some function. The edges model data dependencies between the actors.

Fourth, since the extensions are based on concepts applicable to a broad class of languages, the Mentat approach is easily used in other contexts.

These goals have been met in MPL by extending C++ in three ways: the specification of Mentat classes, the *rtf()* value return mechanism, and the select/accept statement. The basic idea is to let the programmer specify which C++ classes are of sufficient computational complexity to warrant parallel execution and let the compiler manage communication and synchronization between instances of these classes.

Instances of Mentat classes are called Mentat objects. The programmer uses Mentat objects just as any other C++ object. The compiler generates code to construct and execute data dependency graphs in which the nodes are Mentat-object member-function invocations and the arcs are the data dependencies found in the program. Thus, interobject parallelism encapsulation is largely transpar-

ent to the programmer. To obtain intraobject parallelism encapsulation, a graph node (member function) can be transparently implemented by a subgraph; the caller sees only the member function invocation.

(The examples that follow assume familiarity with C++ terms. See the sidebar on p. 42 for a short primer on C++.)

Mentat class definition. C++ objects are defined by their class. Each class has an interface section that defines member variables and functions. Not all objects should be Mentat objects. In particular, objects not having a sufficiently high computation ratio (that is, whose object operations are not sufficiently computationally complex) should not be Mentat objects. The required complexity depends on the architecture, but in general, the minimum size is several hundred instructions. At smaller sizes, the communication and runtime overhead takes longer than the member function, resulting in a slowdown rather than a speedup.

Mentat's object model distinguishes between two types of objects: contained objects and independent objects — a not unusual distinction driven by efficiency considerations. Contained objects are objects contained in another object's address space, including instances of C++ classes, integers, structs, and so on. Independent objects possess a distinct address space, a systemwide unique name, and a thread of control. Communication between independent objects is accomplished via member function invocation. Independent objects are analogous to Unix processes. Mentat objects are independent objects.

Because Mentat objects are address-space disjoint, member function calls are by value. Results of member functions are also returned by value. Pointers to objects, particularly variable-size objects, can be used as both parameters and return types. To provide programmer control of the degree of parallelism, Mentat allows both standard C++ classes and Mentat classes. By default, a standard C++ class definition defines a standard C++ object.

The programmer defines a Mentat class by using the keyword "mentat" in the class definition. The programmer can further specify whether the class is persistent or regular. The syntax for Mentat class definitions is

```
new_class_def ::
    mentat_definition class_definition |
    class_definition
mentat_definition ::
    persistent mentat |
    regular mentat |
class_definition ::
    class class_name {class_interface};
```

Persistent objects maintain state infor-mation between member function invo-cations, while regular objects do not. Thus, regular-object member functions are pure functions, which frees the system to instantiate new instances of regular classes at will. Regular classes can have local variables, much as procedures do, and can maintain state information for the duration of a function invocation.

A class should be a Mentat class when its member functions are computationally expensive, when its member functions exhibit high latency (for example, I/O), or when it holds state information that needs to be shared by many other objects (for example, shared queues, databases, physical devices). Classes whose member functions have a high computation cost or high latency should

Intraobject and interobject parallelism encapsulation

A key feature of Mentat is the transparent encapsulation of parallelism within and between Mentat-object member-function invocations. Consider for example an instance *matrix_op* of a *matrix_operators* Mentat class with the member function *mpy()* that multiplies two matrices together and returns a matrix. As a user, when I invoke *mpy()* in *x = matrix_op.mpy(B,C);*, it is irrelevant whether *mpy()* is implemented sequentially or in parallel; all I care about is whether the correct answer is computed. We call the hiding of whether a member function implementation is sequential or parallel "intraobject parallelism encapsulation."

Similarly, we make the exploitation of parallelism opportunities between Mentat-object member-function invocations transparent to the programmer. We call this "interobject parallelism encapsulation." It is the responsibility of the compiler to ensure that data dependencies between invocations are satisfied, and that communication and synchronization are handled correctly.

Intraobject parallelism encapsulation and interobject parallelism encapsulation can be combined. Indeed, interobject parallelism encapsulation within a member function implementation is intraobject parallelism encapsulation as far as the caller of that member function is concerned. Thus, multiple levels of parallelism encapsulation are possible, each level hidden from the level above.

To illustrate parallelism encapsulation, suppose X, A, B, C, D, and E are matrix pointers. Consider the sequence of statements

```
X = matrix_op.mpy(B,C);
A = matrix_op.mpy(X,matrix_op.mpy(D,E));
```

On a sequential machine, the matrices *B* and *C* are multiplied first, with the result stored in *X*, followed by the multiplication of *D* and *E*. The final step is to multiply *X* by the result of *D*∗*E*. If we assume that each multiplication takes one time unit, then three time units are required to complete the computation.

In Mentat, the compiler and runtime system detect that the first two multiplies, *B*∗*C* and *D*∗*E*, are not data dependent on one another and can be safely executed in parallel. The two matrix multiplications will be executed in parallel, with the result automatically forwarded to the final multiplication. That result will be forwarded to the caller, and associated with *A*. The execution graph is shown at the left in the figure.

The difference between the programmer's sequential model, and the parallel execution of the two multiplies afforded by Mentat, is an example of interobject parallelism encapsulation. In the absence of other parallelism, or overhead, the speedup for this example is a modest 1.5.

$$\text{Speedup} = \frac{T_{\text{Sequential}}}{T_{\text{Parallel}}} = \frac{3}{2} = 1.5$$

However, that is not the end of the story. Additional, intraobject, parallelism can be realized within the matrix multiply. Suppose the matrix multiplies are themselves executed in parallel (with the parallelism detected in a manner similar to the above). Further, suppose that each multiply is executed in eight pieces (shown on the right-hand side in the figure). Then, assuming zero overhead, the total execution time is 0.125 + 0.125 = 0.25 time units, resulting in a speedup of 3/0.25 = 12. As matrix multiply is implemented using more pieces, even larger speedups result. The key point is that the programmer need not be concerned with data dependence detection, communication, synchronization, or scheduling; the compiler does it.

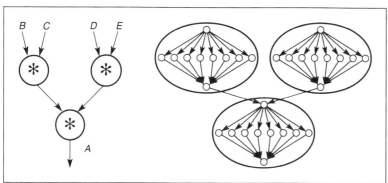

Parallel execution of matrix multiply operations: (left) interobject parallelism encapsulation; (right) intraobject parallelism encapsulation where the multiples have been transparently expanded into parallel subgraphs.

be Mentat classes to permit overlapping with other computations and latencies, that is, executing them in parallel with other functions. Shared state objects should be Mentat classes for two reasons. First, since there is no shared memory in the model, shared state can be realized only by using a Mentat object with which other objects can communicate. Second, because Mentat objects service a single member function at a time, they provide a monitor-like synchronization, providing synchronized access to their state.

> ## All Mentat objects have a separate address space, a thread of control, and a systemwide unique name.

To illustrate the difference between regular and persistent Mentat classes,

suppose we wish to perform matrix operations in parallel, for example, a matrix-matrix multiply. Recall that a matrix-matrix multiply forms a new matrix. Each element in the result is found by performing a dot product on the appropriate rows and columns of the input matrices (Figure 1a). Because matrix-matrix multiply is a pure function, we could define a regular Mentat class *matrix_operators* (Figure 1b). In this case, every invocation of an *mpy()* creates a new Mentat object to perform the multiplication, and the arguments are

---

Introduction to C++

C++, an object-oriented extension of C developed by Bjarne Stroustrup of AT&T Bell Labs, avoids the performance penalty usually associated with object-oriented languages. C++ supports object-oriented concepts such as objects, classes, encapsulation, inheritance, polymorphism, and function and operator overloading. The most important extensions revolve around classes. Classes are structurally similar to C structs.

Classes support the concept of encapsulation via the provision of private and protected member variables and member functions. Private members (for example, *top*) can be accessed only by member functions of the class (for example, *push()*). Protected members can be accessed only by members of the class and by members of derived classes. Nonaccessible members can still be indirectly manipulated via public member functions. By limiting access to members, the language supports encapsulation.

Inheritance means that classes can be defined in terms of other classes, inheriting their behavior (public, private, and protected members). When a class can have at most one super (parent) class, we say a language supports single inheritance, and a tree-like class structure results. When there can be multiple super classes, we say the language supports multiple inheritance. C++ supports multiple inheritance.

A limited form of polymorphism is supported in C++ via virtual functions. Multiple classes, all derived from the same base class, may all define different implementations of a virtual function. When the function is invoked on a pointer or reference to an instance of the base class, the appropriate function is bound and called. The function binding is done at runtime and depends on the class of the object to which the pointer points. This can be contrasted with compile-time binding where the compiler decides at compile-time which function to use. The canonical example is a base class *shape* and a virtual function *draw()*. The classes *square* and *triangle* are derived from *shape*. Suppose *x* is defined as *shape *x;*. At runtime, *x* may point to a *shape*, a *square*, or a *triangle*. When *x->draw()* is executed, the correct draw (*square* or *triangle*) will be bound and invoked.

Function and operator overloading permits the programmer to redefine, or overload, the meaning of both the standard binary and unary operators, as well as user-defined functions. The compiler determines which function to use, based on the number and type of the arguments.

Classes in C++ are defined in a manner similar to structs in C. The class *int_stack*

```
class int_stack {
protected:
    int max_elems, top;
    int *data;
public:
    int_stack(int size = 50);
    void push(int);
    int pop();
};
```

has three protected member variables defined: *max_elems*, *top*, and *data*. They cannot be directly manipulated by users of instances of *int_stack*, but they can be used by derived classes. The constructor for *int_stack*, *int_stack(int size)*, is called whenever a new instance is created. Constructors usually initialize private data structures and allocate space. Instances are created when a variable comes into scope (for example, *{int_stack x(40);}*) or when instances are allocated on the heap (for example, *int_stack *x = new int_stack(30);*). The member functions *push(int)* and *int pop()* operate on the stack and are the sole mechanism to manipulate private data.

To illustrate member function invocation, suppose that *x* is an instance of *int_stack*. Member functions are invoked using either the dot notation, *x.push(5);*, or if *x* is a pointer, the arrow notation, *x->push(5);*.

References

1. B. Stroustrup, "What is Object-Oriented Programming?" *IEEE Software*, Vol. 5, No. 3, May 1988, pp. 10-20.

2. B. Stroustrup, *C++ Programming Language*, 2nd ed., Addison-Wesley, Reading, Mass., 1991.

---

transported to the new instance. Successive calls create new objects and transport the arguments to them.

Alternatively, we could define a persistent Mentat class *p_matrix* (Figure 1c). To use a *p_matrix*, an instance must first be created and initialized with a *matrix**. Matrix-matrix multiplication can then be accomplished by calling *mpy()*. When *mpy()* is used, the argument matrix is transported to the existing object. On successive calls, argument matrices are transported to the same object. In both the persistent and the regular case, the implementation of the class may hierarchically decompose the object into subobjects and operations into parallel suboperations.

Mentat object instantiation and destruction. An instance of a Mentat class is a Mentat object. All Mentat objects have a separate address space, a thread of control, and a systemwide unique name. Instantiation of Mentat objects differs slightly from standard C++ object instantiation semantics. First, consider the C++ fragment

```
{// A new scope
   int x;
   p_matrix mat1;
   matrix_operators m_ops;
} // end of scope
```

In C++, when the scope in which *x* is declared is entered, a new integer is created on the stack. In MPL, because *p_matrix* is a Mentat class, *mat1* is a name of a Mentat object of type *p_matrix*. It is not the instance itself. Thus, *mat1* is analogous to a pointer.

Names (for example, *mat1*) can be in one of two states, bound or unbound. An unbound name refers to any instance of the appropriate Mentat class. A bound name refers to a specific instance with a unique name. When an instance of a Mentat class (a Mentat variable) comes into scope or is allocated on the heap, it is initially an unbound name; it does not refer to any particular instance of the class. Thus, a new *p_matrix* is not instantiated when *mat1* comes into scope. When unbound names are used for regular Mentat classes (for example, *m_ops*), the underlying system logically creates a new instance for each invocation of a member function. This can lead to high levels of parallelism, as we'll see later.

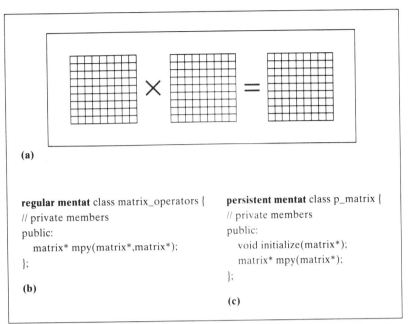

```
regular mentat class matrix_operators {
// private members
public:
    matrix* mpy(matrix*,matrix*);
};
```
(b)

```
persistent mentat class p_matrix {
// private members
public:
    void initialize(matrix*);
    matrix* mpy(matrix*);
};
```
(c)

Figure 1. Matrix-matrix multiplication (a) performed by regular (b) and persistent (c) Mentat class definitions.

Binding and instantiation. A Mentat variable (for example, *mat1*) can become bound in one of three ways: It can be explicitly created using *create()*, it can be bound by the system to an existing instance using *bind()*, or the name can be assigned to a bound name by an assignment.

The *create()* call tells the system to instantiate a new instance of the appropriate class. There are five flavors of *create()*, as shown below (assuming the definition *p_matrix mat1;*):

(a) mat1.create();
(b) mat1.create(COLOCATE another_object);
(c) mat1.create(DISJOINT object1, object2);
(d) mat1.create(HIGH_COMPU-TATION_RATIO);
(e) mat1.create(int on_host);
(f) mat1 = expression;
(g) mat1.bind(THIS_HOST);

When *create()* is used as in (a), the system chooses the processor to instantiate the object.[2] The programmer can also use location hints, as in (b), (c), (d), and (e), to specify where he or she wants the new object to be instantiated. In (b), the programmer specified placing the new Mentat object on the same processor as the object *another_object*. In (c), the programmer specified that the new object should not be placed on the same processor as any of the listed Mentat objects. In (d), the programmer specified that the new object will have a high computation-to-communication ratio and can be placed on a processor with high communication expense. In (e), the programmer specified placing the new object on a specific processor. Names can also be bound as the result of assignment to an expression, as in (f).

Mentat variables can also be bound to an existing instance, using the *bind(scope)* member function, as shown in (g). The parameter scope can take any one of three values, BIND_LOCAL, BIND_CLUSTER, and BIND_GLO-BAL, to restrict the search for an instance to the local host (the host can be a multiprocessor), to the cluster (subnet), and to the entire system, respectively.

Mentat-object member-function invocation. Member-function invocation on Mentat objects is syntactically the same as for C++ objects. Semantically, there are two important differences. Mentat member functions are always call-by-value, and Mentat member-function invocation is nonblocking. The nonblocking nature of Mentat-object member functions provides for the parallel execution of member functions whenever data dependencies permit. This is

```
class string {
public:
   int size-of ();
};

int string::size_of() {return(strlen(this)+1);}
persistent mentat class m_file {
public:
   int open(string* name, int mode);
   data_block* read(int offset, int num_bytes);
   void write(int offset, data_block* data);}
{
   // A code fragment using m_file
   m_file f;
   f.create(); // No location hints.
   int x = f.open((string*) "my_file",1);
   if (x < 0) {/* error code */}
}
```

Figure 2. Class m_file declaration and use. Note that execution does not block on the open() call until the result *x* is used.

```
regular mentat class data_processor {
public:
   data_block* filter_one(data_block*);
   data_block* filter_two(data_block*);
};

m_file in_file,out_file;
data_processor dp;
in_file.create();
out_file.create();
int i,x;
x = in_file.open((string*)"input_file",1);
x = out_file.open((string*)"output_file",3);
data_block *res;
for (i=0;i<MAX_BLOCKS,i++) {
   res = in_file.read_block(i);
   res = dp.filter_one(res);
   res = dp.filter_two(res);
   out_file.write_block((i*BLK_SIZE,res);
}
```

Figure 3. A pipelined data processor. The main loop reads MAX_BLOCKS data_blocks, passes them through filter_one() and filter_two(), and then writes them to the output file. The loop is unrolled at runtime and a pipeline (Figure 4) is formed.

transparent to the user and is called interobject parallelism encapsulation.

Because Mentat objects are address-space disjoint, Mentat-class member functions always use call-by-value semantics. When pointers are used as arguments, the designated object (or structure) is sent to the callee. If the object size is variable, the class of the object must provide a member function *int size_of()* that returns the size of the object in bytes. If a structure or class has contained pointers, they are not "chased." Call-by-value semantics is common in systems that provide an RPC-like service. The alternative is to allow pointer passing between address spaces.

Example 1. Consider the code fragment shown in Figure 2. The member function *open()* takes two parameters and returns an integer. The first parameter is of type *string*. Because strings are of variable length, we provided the function *int size_of()*. *Size_of* is called

at runtime to determine the size of the first parameter, and *size_of()* bytes will be sent to the Mentat object *f*. The second argument is an integer. Fixed-size arguments such as integers and structs do not require a *size_of()* function. The compiler ensures that the correct amount of data is transferred.

The example in Figure 2 illustrates the creation of a persistent object and a simple RPC to a member function of that object. The difference between Mentat and a traditional RPC is what happens when an RPC call is encountered. In traditional RPC, the arguments are marshalled (packaged into a message), sent to the callee, and the caller blocks waiting for the result. The callee accepts the call, performs the desired service, and returns the results to the caller. The caller then unblocks and proceeds.

In Mentat, when a Mentat-object member function is encountered, the arguments are marshalled and sent to the callee, but the caller does not block

waiting for the result (*x* in Figure 2). Instead, the runtime system monitors (with compiler-provided code) where *x* is used. If *x* is later used as an argument to a second or third Mentat object invocation, then arrangements are made to send *x* directly to the second and third member-function invocations. If *x* is used locally in a strict operation, for example, *y* = *x* + 1, or *if (x<0)*, then the runtime system will automatically block the caller and wait for the value of *x* to be computed and returned. This is the case in Example 1. Note, though, that if *x* is not used locally (except as an argument to a Mentat-object member function), then the caller never blocks and waits for *x*. Indeed, *x* might never be sent to the caller, it might only be sent to the Mentat-object member functions for which it is a parameter. This is illustrated in the next example.

Example 2. This example illustrates construction of a simple pipeline process. We define the regular Mentat class *data_processor*. The member functions *filter_one()* and *filter_two()* are filters that process blocks of data. Consider the code fragment in Figure 3. After some initialization, creating and opening input and output files, the loop in the code fragment sequentially reads MAX_BLOCKS data blocks from

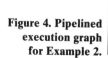

Figure 4. Pipelined execution graph for Example 2.

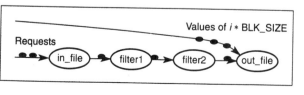

184

input_file, processes them through filters one and two, and writes them to *output_file*. Note that the variable *res* is used as a temporary variable and as a conduit for passing information between the filters. This fragment is written in a manner that is natural to C programmers.

In a traditional RPC system, this fragment would execute sequentially. Suppose each member-function execution takes 10 time units and each communication takes 5 time units. Then the time required to execute an iteration of the loop in a sequential RPC system is the sum of four times the member-function execution time, plus seven times the communication time (because all parameters and results must be communicated from/to the caller). Thus, the total time required is 75 time units.

The average time per iteration for the Mentat version is considerably less, just over 10 time units. First, observe that the time for a single iteration is four times the communication time, 20 time units, plus four times the execution time, 40 time units, for a total of 60 time units. There are only four communications because intermediate results are not returned to the caller; rather, they are passed directly where needed. Next, consider that the reads, the two filter operations, and the writes can be executed in a pipelined fashion with each operation executing on a separate processor (see Figure 4).

Under these circumstances, each of the four member-function invocations, and all of the communication, can be performed concurrently. The communication for the *i*th iteration can be overlapped with the computation of the *i*th + 1 iteration. (We assume that communication is asynchronous and that sufficient computation and communication resources exist.)

Using a standard pipe equation

T_{All} = time for all iterations
T_{Stage} = time for longest stage
= 10 time units
T_1 = time for first iteration
= 60 time units
T_{Avg} = average time per iteration
T_{All} = $T_1 + T_{Stage}$ * (MAX_BLOCKS − 1)
T_{All} = 60 + 10*(MAX_BLOCKS − 1)
T_{Avg} = $\dfrac{(60 + 10*(\text{MAX\_BLOCKS}-1))}{\text{MAX\_BLOCKS}}$

When MAX_BLOCKS is one, the time to complete is 60 time units, with

an average of 60 time units. This is marginally faster than a pure RPC (75 time units) because intermediate results are not sent to the caller. When MAX_BLOCKS is greater than one, the time required for the first iteration is 60 time units, and successive results are available every 10 time units. Thus, as MAX_BLOCKS increases, the average time per iteration drops and approaches 10 time units.

Now consider the effect of quadrupling the time to execute *filter_one()* from 10 to 40 time units. The time to execute the traditional RPC version goes from 75 to 105 time units. Using the standard pipe equation, the first result is available at time 90, and successive values every 24 time units. The standard pipe equation assumes that there is just one functional unit for each stage. This assumption is invalid in Mentat in this example, and the time per iteration for the Mentat version remains unchanged at 10 time units, if there are sufficient computation resources. To see why, consider that the *data_processor* class is a regular Mentat class. This means that the system can instantiate new instances at will to meet demand. A new instance of *data_processor* to service *filter_one()* requests is created whenever a result is generated by the read. There would be five instances of the *data_processor* class active at a time, four performing *filter_one()* and one performing *filter_two()*.

There are four items to note from this example. First, the main loop may have executed to completion (all MAX_BLOCKS iterations) before the first write has completed. Second, suppose our "caller" (the main loop) was itself a server servicing requests for clients. Once the main loop is complete, the caller can begin servicing other requests while the first request is still being completed. Third, the order of execution of the different stages of the

different iterations can vary from a straight sequential ordering (for example, the last iteration may "complete" before earlier iterations). This can happen, for example, if the different iterations require different amounts of filter processing. This additional asynchrony is possible because the runtime system guarantees that all parameters for all invocations are correctly matched and that member functions receive the correct arguments. The additional asynchrony permits additional concurrency in those cases where execution in strict order would prevent later iterations from executing even when all of their synchronization and data criteria have been met. Finally, in addition to the automatic detection of interobject parallelism opportunities, we may also have intraobject parallelism encapsulation, where each of the invoked member functions may be internally parallel. Thus, we obtain even more parallelism.

Return-to-future mechanism. The return-to-future function, *rtf()*, is Mentat's analog to C's *return*. It allows Mentat member functions to return a value to the successor nodes in the macro dataflow graph in which the member function appears. Mentat member functions use *rtf()* as the mechanism for returning values. The returned value is forwarded to all member functions that are data dependent on the result and to the caller if necessary. In general, copies can be sent to several recipients.

While there are many similarities, *rtf()* differs from *return* in three significant ways. First, in C, before a function can return a value, the value must be available. This is not the case with *rtf()*. Recall that when a Mentat-object member function is invoked, the caller does not block, and results are forwarded wherever they are needed. Thus, a member function may *rtf()* a "value" that is the result of another Mentat-object member function that has not completed, or perhaps even begun, execution. Indeed, the result can be computed by a parallel subgraph obtained by detecting interobject parallelism.

Second, a C *return* signifies the end of the computation in a function, while an *rtf()* does not. An *rtf()* indicates only that the result is available. Since each Mentat object has its own thread of control, additional computation can be performed after the *rtf()*, for example, to update state information or to communicate with other objects. By making the result available as soon as possible, we permit data-dependent computations to proceed concurrently with the local computation that follows the *rtf()*.

Third, a *return* returns data to the caller. *Rtf()* may or may not return data to the caller, depending on the program's data dependencies. If the caller does not use the result locally, then the caller does not receive a copy. This saves on communication overhead. The next two examples illustrate these features.

Example 3. Consider a *persistent class sblock* used in Gaussian elimination with partial pivoting. In this problem, illustrated in Figure 5a, we are trying to solve for *x* in *Ax = b*. The *sblocks* contain portions of the total system to be solved. The *sblock* member function

vector* sblock ::
reduce(vector*);

performs row reduction operations on a submatrix and returns a candidate row. Pseudocode for the reduce operation is given in Figure 5b. The return value can be quickly computed and returned via *rtf()*. The remaining updates to the *sblock* can then occur in parallel with the communication of the result (Figure 5c). In general, best performance is realized when the *rtf()* is used as soon as possible.

Example 4. Consider a transaction manager (TM) that receives requests

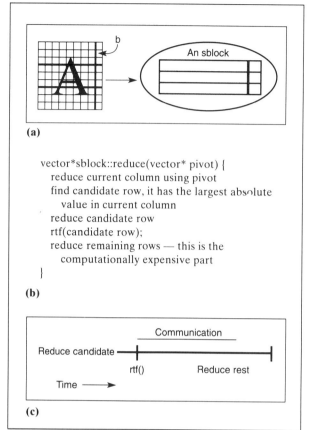

(a)

```
vector*sblock::reduce(vector* pivot) {
    reduce current column using pivot
    find candidate row, it has the largest absolute
        value in current column
    reduce candidate row
    rtf(candidate row);
    reduce remaining rows — this is the
        computationally expensive part
}
```

(b)

(c)

Figure 5. Gaussian elimination with partial pivoting illustrating the use of rtf() to overlap communication and computation: (a) decomposition into sblocks; (b) sblock::reduce() pseudocode; (c) overlap of communication and computation with rtf().

for reads and writes, and checks to see if the operation is permitted. If it is, the TM performs the operation via the data manager (DM) and returns the result. Figure 6a illustrates how the read operation might be implemented. In an RPC system, the record *read* would first be returned to the TM and then to the user. In MPL, the result is returned directly to the user, bypassing the TM (Figure

6b). Further, the TM can immediately begin servicing the next request instead of waiting for the result. This can be viewed as a form of distributed tail recursion or simple continuation passing.

MPL compiler. The MPL compiler (MPLC) is responsible for mapping MPL programs to the macro dataflow model. It accomplishes this by translating MPL programs to C++ programs with embedded calls to the Mentat runtime system. These C++ programs are, in turn, compiled by the host C++ compiler (see Figure 7). This approach is similar to that used by the AT&T C++ compiler, which translates C++ programs into a portable assembly language, C.

Runtime system

The Mentat runtime system[2] supports Mentat programs via a portable virtual macro-dataflow machine (Figure 8). The virtual machine provides support routines that perform runtime data dependence detection, program graph construction, program graph execution, token matching, scheduling, communication, and synchronization. The compiler generates code that communicates with the runtime system to correctly manage program execution.

The Mentat runtime system is not an operating system. Instead, the runtime system is layered on top of an existing host operating system, using the host operating system's processes, memory,

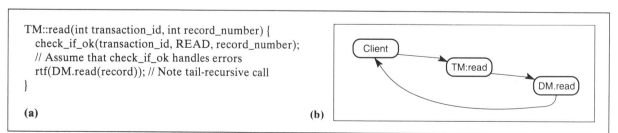

```
TM::read(int transaction_id, int record_number) {
    check_if_ok(transaction_id, READ, record_number);
    // Assume that check_if_ok handles errors
    rtf(DM.read(record)); // Note tail-recursive call
}
```

(a)

(b)

Figure 6. Tail recursion in MPL: (a) code fragment for transaction manager read; (b) call graph illustrating communication TM:read() with arcs representing message traffic.

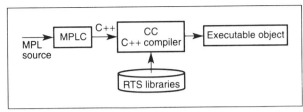

Figure 7. Compilation steps for the Mentat programming language.

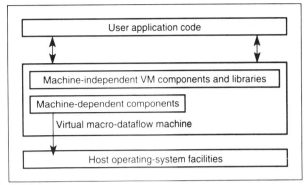

Figure 8. Mentat virtual-machine model.

C library, and interprocess communication services.

The virtual machine model permits the rapid transfer of Mentat to new architectural platforms. Only the machine-specific components need to be modified. Because the compiler uses a virtual machine model, porting applications to a new architecture does not require any user source-level changes.* Once the virtual machine has been ported, user applications are recompiled and can execute immediately.

The Mentat virtual macro-dataflow machine is implemented by the Mentat runtime system (RTS). The RTS is in two sections, runtime libraries that are linked into Mentat objects and runtime objects that provide runtime services such as scheduling, naming, and binding. The runtime libraries are responsible for program graph construction, select/accept execution, and reliable communication.

The logical structure of a Mentat system is that of a collection of hosts communicating through an interconnection network (see Figure 9a). Each host can communicate with any other host via the interconnection network, although not necessarily at uniform cost.

The logical interconnection network is provided by the lowest layer of the runtime system, the modular message-passing system. MMPS provides an extensible point-to-point message service that reliably delivers messages of arbitrary size from one process to another.

Each host has a complete copy of the runtime system server objects (Figure

9b). These include the instantiation manager i_m and the token matching unit (TMU). The instantiation manager is responsible for high-level Mentat-object scheduling (deciding on which host to locate an object) and for instantiating new instances. The high-level scheduling algorithm is distributed, adaptive, and stable. The TMU is responsible for matching tokens for regular objects and instantiating new instances (via the i_m) when needed.

Dynamic data dependence detection and program graph construction are accomplished by the MPLC in conjunction with the runtime system (Figure 9c). The MPLC generates library calls that tell the RTS when certain variables, called potential result variables (PRVs), are used on either the lefthand or righthand side of expressions (for example, X in $X = matrix\_op.mpy(B,C)$; in the sidebar on encapsulation). By carefully observing where PRVs are used at runtime, the RTS can construct data-dependency program graphs and man-

age communication and synchronization.

One final note on the runtime system: Because we use a layered approach and mask differences in the underlying operating system and interprocess communication, applications are completely source-code portable between supported architectures. We routinely develop and debug software on Sun workstations and use the sources unchanged on the Intel iPSC/2. In this day of incompatible parallel computers, this is quite useful. The fact that the sources are identical allows us to compare architectures using the same code and to measure the effect of known architectural differences on algorithm performance (for example, to measure algorithm sensitivity to communication latency).

The only real difficulty when porting applications is grain size selection. Each platform has a different optimum grain size. To date, we have overcome this problem either by decomposing the

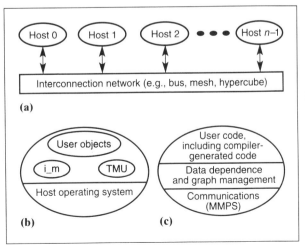

(a)

(b) **(c)**

Figure 9. Mentat runtime system structure: (a) logical system structure, a collection of hosts; (b) logical host structure, user objects and system objects; (c) Mentat object structure.

---

*Application code may benefit from changes but does not require them. For example, on the Sun 3/60, loop unrolling provides no benefit; on the Sparcstation it may.

problem with the largest grain size needed for any platform, or by parameterizing the Mentat class to indicate the number of pieces into which the problem should be decomposed. We are currently examining ways to automate this process based on information provided by the programmer.

Performance

Ease of use and programming models aside, the bottom line for parallel processing systems is performance. As of this writing, we have implemented the Mentat runtime system and run benchmarks on a network of Sun 3 and 4 workstations, the Silicon Graphics Iris,

the Intel iPSC/2, and the Intel iPSC/860. Speedups for two benchmarks on the Sun 3 and the iPSC/2 are given below.

In each case the speedup shown is relative to an equivalent C program,

> **Ease of use and programming models aside, the bottom line for parallel processing systems is performance.**

not relative to the Mentat implementation running on one processor. We have been very careful to use the same level of inner-loop hand optimization and compiler optimization for both the C and MPL versions. In both cases the inner loops were optimized in C using standard loop-optimization techniques; no assembly language was used.

The two benchmarks are matrix multiply and Gaussian elimination. Each benchmark was executed for several matrix dimensions (for example, 100×100, 200×200). Single-precision 32-bit values were used. Matrix multiply and Gaussian elimination were chosen because they are de facto parallel processing benchmarks. Execution times were measured from just after the main pro-

Related work

Mentat does not exist in a vacuum. There are many other systems and projects that are similar in some respects to Mentat, and that share many of the same goals. Mentat has much in common with both distributed object-oriented systems and with parallel processing systems. Mentat inherits features from both, ease of use from the object-oriented paradigm, and models and compiler techniques from the parallel processing domain.

What distinguishes Mentat from other distributed object-oriented systems is the combination of its objectives: easy-to-use high performance via parallelism and reliance on compiler and runtime techniques to transparently exploit parallelism. Many other systems[1,2] have fault tolerance (for example, transaction support), the use of functional specialization (for example, file servers), and the support of inherently distributed applications (for example, e-mail), as their primary objectives. For most of these systems, high-performance is simply not an issue, leading the implementations to rely on blocking RPC-like mechanisms, as opposed to the nonblocking invocations of Mentat. Alternatively, many systems permit parallelism but require the programmer to exploit and manage it.

In the object-oriented parallel processing domain, Mentat differs from systems such as Presto[3] and other shared-memory C++ systems[4] in its ability to easily support both shared-memory MIMD and distributed-memory MIMD architectures, as well as hybrids. PC++,[5] on the other hand, is a data-parallel C++. Mentat accommodates both functional and data parallelism, often within the same program. ESP[6] is perhaps the most similar of the parallel object-oriented systems. It too is a high-performance extension to C++ that supports both functional and data parallelism. What distinguishes Mentat is our compiler support. In ESP, remote invocations either return values or futures. If a value is returned, then a blocking RPC is performed. If a

future is returned, it must be treated differently. Futures may not be passed to other remote invocations, limiting the amount of parallelism. Finally, ESP supports only fixed-size arguments (except strings). This makes the construction of general-purpose library classes (for example, matrix operators) difficult.

The parallel processing (as opposed to distributed) domain has many languages for writing parallel applications, from fully explicit manual approaches to implicit compiler-based approaches. In fully explicit approaches, a traditional language such as C or Fortran is extended with communication and synchronization primitives such as send and receive or shared memory and semaphores. The advantages of this approach are that it (1) is relatively easy to implement, (2) reflects the underlying hardware model, and (3) lets the programmer use application domain knowledge to partition and schedule the problem. However, the programmer must also correctly manage communication and synchronization. This can be an overwhelming task, particularly in the presence of Heisenbugs.* Low-level primitives such as send and receive are the assembly language of parallelism. Anything can be done with them, but at the cost of increased burden on the programmer. Therefore, much as high-level languages and compilers were developed to simplify sequential programming, compilers have been built for parallel systems.

In fully automatic compiler-based approaches the compiler is responsible for performing dependence analysis and finding and exploiting opportunities for parallelism.[7] Compiler-based approaches are usually applied to Fortran. Ideally, application of this approach would permit the automatic parallelization of "dusty deck" Fortran programs. The advantage of compiler-based techniques is that the compiler can be trusted to get communication and synchronization right. The problem is that compilers are gram had been loaded and arguments parsed to just before the program exited. All overhead costs, including loading Mentat object executables, I/O, and data distribution, have been included in the execution times.

Execution environment. The network of Suns consists of eight Sun 3/60s serviced by a Sun 3/280 file server running NFS connected by thin Ethernet. All of the workstations have eight megabytes of memory and an MC68881 floating-point coprocessor.

The Intel iPSC/2 is configured with 32 nodes. Each node has four megabytes of physical memory and an 80387 math coprocessor. The nodes are not equipped with either the VX vector processor or the SX scalar processor. The NX/2 operating system provided with the iPSC/2 does not support virtual memory. The lack of virtual memory, coupled with the amount of memory consumed by the operating system, limited the problem sizes we could run on the iPSC/2.

Matrix multiply. The implementation tested is for the regular Mentat class *matrix_operators*. The Mentat times include the time to copy the arguments. The speedups for matrix multiply are shown in Figures 10a and 10b. The algorithm (and application source) is the same for both systems. Suppose the matrices A and B are to be multiplied. If k pieces are to be used, the B matrix is split into sqrt(k) vertical slices, and the A matrix into k/sqrt(k) horizontal slices. Each of the sqrt(k)*(k/sqrt(k)) workers gets an appropriate piece of A and of B to multiply. The results of the invocations are merged together and sent to

> **Overhead, including loading Mentat object executables, I/O, and data distribution, is included in the execution times.**

---

best at finding fine-grain and loop-level parallelism, and not good at detecting large-grain parallelism. This is because they lack knowledge of the application, forcing them to "reason" about the program using a fine-grain dependence graph. Message-passing MIMD architectures require medium- to coarse-grain parallelism to operate efficiently. Thus, purely compiler-based approaches are inappropriate for this class of machines because of the mismatch of granularity. Recently, there have been attempts to exploit programmer knowledge to improve data distribution.[8] This approach is best suited to data parallel problems.

Mentat strikes a balance that captures the best aspects of both explicit and compiler-based approaches. The user makes granularity and partitioning decisions using high-level Mentat class definitions, while the compiler and runtime system manage communication, synchronization, and scheduling. We believe that such hybrid approaches offer the best ease-of-use/performance trade-off available today. In the long term, we expect compiler technology to improve, and the need for programmer intervention to decrease.

Several recently introduced mechanisms provide application portability across platforms. Examples include PVM[9] and Linda.[10] They, like Mentat, achieve portability by providing a virtual machine interface to the programmer. The virtual machine can then be ported to new architectures, and if the applications programmer is limited to that interface, the application will port.**

The key difference between Mentat and these systems is the level at which applications must be written. Other systems are low-level, explicit parallel systems, suffering all of the disadvantages, and gaining all of the advantages, of fully explicit systems. Mentat provides a high-level language, eliminating many of the disadvantages.

References

1. H. Bal, J. Steiner, and A. Tanenbaum, "Programming Languages for Distributed Computing Systems," *ACM Computing Surveys*, Vol. 21, Vol. 3, Sept. 1989, pp. 261-322.

2. R. Chin and S. Chanson, "Distributed Object-Based Programming Systems," *ACM Computing Surveys*, Vol. 23, No. 1, Mar. 1991, pp. 91-127.

3. B.N. Bershad, E.D. Lazowska, and H.M. Levy, "Presto: A System for Object-Oriented Parallel Programming," *Software Practice and Experience*, Vol. 18, No. 8, 1988, pp. 713-732.

4. B. Beck, "Shared Memory Parallel Programming in C++," *IEEE Software*, Vol. 7, No. 4, July 1990, pp. 38-48.

5. J.K. Lee and D. Gannon, "Object-Oriented Parallel Programming Experiments and Results," *Proc. Supercomputing 91*, IEEE CS Press, Los Alamitos, Calif., Order No. 2159-02, pp. 273-282.

6. S.K. Smith et al., "Experimental Systems Project at MCC," MCC Tech. Report ACA-ESP-089-89, Austin, Tex., Mar. 1989.

7. C. Polychronopoulos, *Parallel Programming and Compilers*, Kluwer Academic Publishers, 1988.

8. D. Callahan and K. Kennedy, "Compiling Programs for Distributed-Memory Multiprocessors," *J. of Supercomputing*, Kluwer Academic Publishers, No. 2, 1988, pp. 151-169.

9. V.S. Sunderam, "PVM: A Framework for Parallel Distributed Computing," *Concurrency: Practice and Experience*, Vol. 2, No. 4, Dec. 1990, pp. 315-339.

10. N. Carriero and D. Gelernter, "Linda in Context," *Comm. ACM*, Apr. 1989, pp. 444-458.

---

*Heisenbugs are timing-dependent bugs that go away when debugging, or tracing, is turned on. They are among the most frustrating bugs to find.

**Virtual machine abstractions are not new. The concept was carried to its logical extreme in the 1970s in the University of California at San Diego's p-machine. There were p-machine implementations for every major microprocessor of the day. Programs were object-code compatible between supported architectures. Only one executable was ever needed.

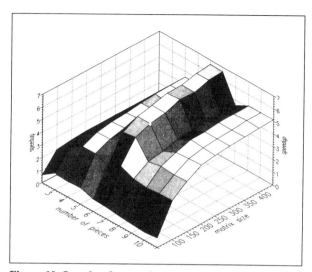
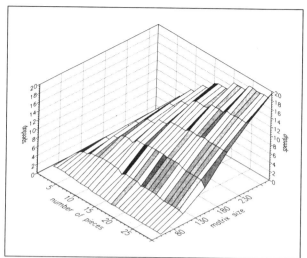

Figure 10. Speedup for matrix multiply: (a) eight-processor Sun 3/60 network; (b) 32-processor Intel iPSC/2.

computations that are dependent on the result of the *A*B* operation. The effect of the partitioning can be clearly seen in Figure 10a. The speedup for four pieces is the same as five pieces, and the speedup for six pieces is the same as for seven pieces. This is because the underlying object will not split the work into five or seven pieces. The falloff in Figure 10a at eight pieces is due to the fact that there are only eight processors, as a result of which the scheduler must place two objects on one processor.

Gaussian elimination. In our algorithm, the controlling object partitions the matrix into *n* strips and places each

strip into an instance of an *sblock*, a Mentat class. Then, for each row, the reduce operator is called for each sblock using the partial pivot calculated at the end of the last iteration. The reduce operation of the *sblock* reduces the *sblock* by the vector, selects a new candidate partial pivot, and forwards the candidate row to the controlling object for use in the next iteration. This algorithm results in frequent communication and synchronization. The effect of frequent synchronization can be clearly seen when the speed-up results for Gaussian elimination in Figures 11a and 11b are compared to the results for matrix multiply.

Writing software for parallel and distributed systems that effectively uses available CPU resources has proven more difficult than writing software for sequential machines. This is true even though most of the work has been done by programmers who have a good understanding of the machines on which they're working.

Given the current software crisis for sequential machines, it is unlikely that parallel architectures will be widely used until software tools are available that hide the complexity of the parallel environment from the programmer. Mentat is one such tool. With Mentat, we have

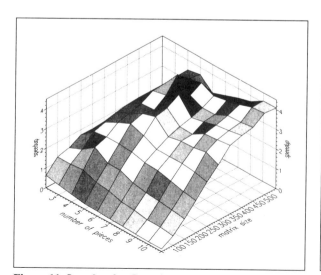
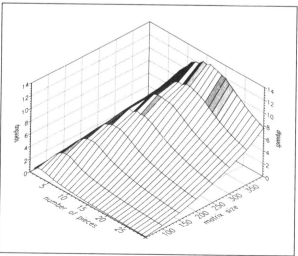

Figure 11. Speedup for Gaussian elimination: (a) eight-processor Sun 3/60 network; (b) 32-processor Intel iPSC/2.

demonstrated that writing object-oriented, high-performance parallel software is possible.

It is possible, indeed probable, that a good programmer could write more efficient concurrent programs using raw send and receive. We believe, though, that send and receive (and semaphores) are the assembly language of parallelism. Just as early high-level language compilers could be beaten by a good programmer writing in assembly language, MPL performance can be beaten by a hand-coded application using send and receive. Extending the analogy, just as high-level languages now have good optimizing compilers that do as well as most programmers, and better than many, we expect MPL compiler technology to improve. Indeed, several optimizations are already planned.

The question that must be answered, for both high-level languages versus assembly languages and for MPL versus raw send and receive, is whether the simplicity and ease of use are worth the performance penalty. We believe they are. ∎

Acknowledgment

This work was partially supported by NSF Grants ASC-9201822 and CDA-8922545 and by NASA Grant NAG-1-1181.

References

1. A.S. Grimshaw, E. Loyot Jr., and J. Weissman, "Mentat Programming Language (MPL) Reference Manual," Univ. of Virginia, Computer Science TR 91-32, 1991.

2. A.S. Grimshaw, "The Mentat Runtime System: Support for Medium-Grain Parallel Computation," *Proc. Fifth Distributed Memory Computing Conf.*, IEEE CS Press, Los Alamitos, Calif., Order No. 2113, Vol. II, 1990, pp. 1,064-1,073.

Andrew S. Grimshaw is an assistant professor of computer science at the University of Virginia. His research interests include high-performance parallel processing, compilers for parallel systems, operating systems, and high-performance parallel I/O. He is the chief designer and architect for Mentat.

Grimshaw received his MS and PhD degrees from the University of Illinois at Urbana-Champaign in 1986 and 1988. He is a member of Phi Kappa Phi, Tau Beta Pi, the IEEE Computer Society, and ACM.

Readers may contact Grimshaw at the Department of Computer Science, University of Virginia, Charlottesville, VA, 22903. His e-mail address is grimshaw@virginia.edu. For more information on Mentat, write mentat@virginia.edu.

Chapter 5:
Parallel Functional Programming

Parallelism is often regarded as one of the automatic benefits of functional programming, with its emphasis on asking "What?" rather than "How?" In fact, implementing a functional language in a way that generates useful parallelism is surprisingly difficult: Either there isn't enough parallelism or there's far too much. The three main issues in extracting parallelism in a functional setting are discussed below.

1. *Normal-order evaluation.* Normal-order evaluation does not generate very much parallelism because it is very conservative, computing nothing until it is certain to be needed. This introduces long, dependent chains of decisions about which parts of a computation are needed. Computing the strict argument's built-in functions provides the only opportunity for parallelism in a naively implemented, normal-order, reductive implementation of a functional program. Doing a strictness analysis at compile time and implementing data structures (for example, I-structures) so that they have "random-access" properties can quite dramatically improve upon this opportunity.

2. *The order of functions that are allowed in the programming language.* At one extreme is higher order functional programming, exemplified by Haskell [FAS92], in which functions of all orders are permitted. At the other extreme is dataflow, in which all functions are first-order. Higher order functional programming can be a very powerful and compact style, but it is unquestionably hard to implement: Implementations whose performance approaches that of imperative languages are just becoming available after 15 years of research. Dataflow is less powerful than higher order functional programming, but fast dataflow implementations have been in existence for some years, and the best of these outperform conventional imperative programs. There is some feeling that the "right" style of functional programming might be based on limited-order functions—perhaps second- or third-order. We return to this point in Chapter 7, which covers more innovative approaches.

3. *The trade-off between letting compilers discover parallelism and having programmers specify parallelism (or at least the potential for it) via annotations.* Putting the responsibility on compilers increases the abstraction level of the programming language and helps with portability. Clearly, a large group of people feel that the performance that this produces is unacceptable and that some extra information should be provided with which the compiler

can work. Providing such extra information creates problems such as the following:

- The annotation part of each program may have to be recast when the program is moved to another machine or architecture.

- The programmer must understand enough about the target architecture to make the annotations helpful.

Both of these problems have occurred in sequential programming.

The four papers included in this chapter cover the range of proposed solutions to the above issues.

The first paper included here, "Parallel Symbolic Computing," by Halstead, describes the language Multilisp, an extension of Lisp in which opportunities for parallelism are created using *futures*. A future applied to an expression creates a task to evaluate that expression (this evaluation begins immediately—that is, eagerly). An attempt to use the result of a future suspends until the value of the future has been computed. Futures are first-class objects that can be passed around regardless of their internal status. Futures allow an eager, controlled evaluation that fits between the fine-grain eagerness of dataflow evaluation and the laziness of higher order functional languages.

This chapter's second paper, "A Report on the Sisal Language Project," by Feo, Cann, and Oldehoeft, describes the Sisal language. Sisal began as an abstract dataflow language. Its syntax is a lot like that of conventional imperative languages, but the meaning of most statements is different in Sisal in important ways, including those discussed below.

1. Sisal is a single-assignment language, so that only a single value can be assigned to each named variable in each scope. Thus, in effect, all statements are expressions.

2. Structures for arrays, records, and streams exist, but they all have I-structure semantics; that is, their elements have the same semantics as that of ordinary variables, and the structure names are syntactic only. Most of the parallelism in Sisal programs comes from parallel loops whose bounds are defined by range generators that only incidentally impose an ordering on loop bodies.

3. A powerful Sisal compiler for shared-memory machines exists, and many Sisal scientific programs have better speedup than that of equivalent Fortran programs. Much of this gain comes from better compilation, thanks to simpler language semantics.

The third paper included in this chapter, "Para-Functional Programming," by Hudak, describes Paralfl. This language is an extension of a conventional functional-programming language in which programmers may annotate expressions with the processor identifier on which they are to be evaluated. A number of researchers [KEL89], [ROE91] have followed up on this idea, and many different styles of annotation have been suggested. However, little agreement exists concerning the best approach and the success of the annotation idea. Although higher order functional programming has more or less agreed on Haskell as a common language, very little has yet been done to build parallel Haskell implementations.

The fourth paper included here, "High-Performance Parallel Graph Reduction," by Peyton Jones, Clack, and Salkild, describes the issues involved in implementing higher order functional programming using graph reduction. This paper describes GRIP, a project now coming to maturity that will presumably make a parallel Haskell implementation possible within a few years. The authors give a clear exposition of the design choices involved.

References cited

[FAS92]   J.H. Fasel and P. Hudak, eds., *ACM SIGPLAN Notices*, Vol. 27, No. 5, May 1992 (Haskell special issue).

[KEL89]   P. Kelly, *Functional Programming for Loosely-Coupled Multiprocessors*, Pitman, London, United Kingdom, 1989.

[ROE91]   P. Roe, *Parallel Programming Using Functional Languages*, doctoral thesis, Dept. of Computer Sci., Univ. of Glasgow, Glasgow, United Kingdom, Feb. 1991.

Parallel Symbolic Computing

Robert H. Halstead, Jr.

Massachusetts Institute of Technology

Futures find parallelism in symbolic programs by allowing the manipulation of partially computed data.

Programs differ from one another in many dimensions. In one such dimension, programs can be laid out along a spectrum with predominantly symbolic programs at one end and predominantly numerical programs at the other. The differences between numerical and symbolic programs suggest different approaches to parallel processing. This article explores the problems and opportunities of parallel symbolic computing and describes the language Multilisp, used at M.I.T. for experiments in parallel symbolic programming.

Numerical versus symbolic computation

Much of the attention focused on parallel processing has concerned numerical applications. High-performance numerical computers have been designed using varying degrees of concurrency. Programming tools for these computers range from compilers that automatically identify concurrency in Fortran programs to languages featuring explicit parallelism following a communicating-sequential-processes[1] model. Numerical computation emphasizes arithmetic. The principal function of a numerical program may be described as delivering numbers to an arithmetic unit to calculate a result. Numerical programs generally have a relatively data-independent flow of control. Within broad limits, the same sequence of calculations will be performed no matter what the operand values are. Inner loops of numerical programs may contain conditionals, and overall control of a program generally includes tests of convergence criteria and such, but most numerical programs have a relatively predictable control sequence when compared with the majority of symbolic programs. Matrices and vectors are common data structures in numerical programs, a fact exploited by single-instruction stream, multiple data stream (SIMD) techniques in many numerically-oriented supercomputers.

In contrast, symbolic computation emphasizes rearrangement of data. Partly because of this, heavily symbolic programs are more likely to be written in a language such as Lisp[2] or Smalltalk than in Fortran. The principal function of a symbolic program may be broadly stated as the reorganization of a set of data so that the relevant information in it is more useful or easier to extract. Examples of primarily symbolic algorithms include sorting, compiling, database management, symbolic algebra, expert systems, and other artificial intelligence applications. The sequence of operations in symbolic programs is often highly data dependent and less amenable to compile-time analysis than in numerical computation. Moreover, there does not appear to be any simple operation style, comparable to vector operations in numerical programs, that can easily be exploited to increase performance with a SIMD type of architecture. Some operations, such as procedure calling, pointer following, and even tree search, occur frequently in symbolic programs, but it is not obvious how SIMD parallelism can help efficiently with these.

The structure of symbolic computations generally seems to lend itself less well to analysis of loops (the major focus in

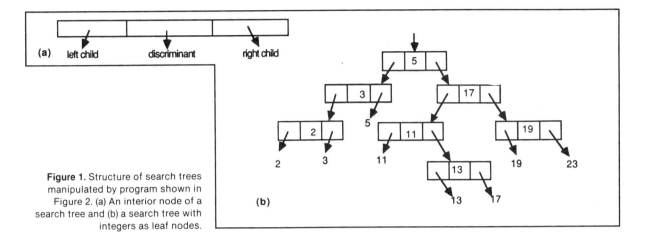

Figure 1. Structure of search trees manipulated by program shown in Figure 2. (a) An interior node of a search tree and (b) a search tree with integers as leaf nodes.

parallelizing numerical computation), favoring recursions on composite data structures such as trees, lists, and sets as the major source of concurrency. Programming languages such as QLisp[3] and Multilisp[4,5] include constructs to take advantage of these sources of concurrency.

Overview of Multilisp

Multilisp is a version of the Lisp-like programming language Scheme[2] extended to allow the programmer to specify concurrent execution. Multilisp shares with Scheme two properties that distinguish them from the more common members of the Lisp family. The first is exclusive reliance on lexical scoping, which promotes modularity. The second is "first-class citizenship" for procedures: Procedures in Scheme and Multilisp may be passed freely as arguments, returned as values of other procedures, stored in data structures, and treated in the same way as any other kind of value.

Multilisp includes the usual Lisp side-effect primitives for altering data structures and changing the values of variables. Therefore, control sequencing beyond that imposed by explicit data dependencies may be required in order to assure determinate execution. In this respect, Multilisp parts company with many concurrent Lisp languages,[6,7] which include only a side-effect-free subset of Lisp.

The default in Multilisp is sequential execution. This allows Lisp programs or subprograms written without attention to parallelism to run, albeit without using the potential concurrency of the target machine. Concurrency can be introduced into a Multilisp program by means of the **future** construct. The form (**future** X) immediately returns a **future**[8] for the value of X and creates a task to concurrently evaluate X, allowing concurrency between the computation of a value and the use of that value. When the evaluation of X yields a value, that value replaces the future. We say that the future *resolves* to the value. Any task that needs to know a future's value will be suspended until the future is resolved.

A task T examines, or *touches,* a future when it performs an operation that causes T to be suspended if the future is not yet resolved. Most operations, such as arithmetic, comparison, and type checking, touch their operands. (Any operation that is *strict* in an operand touches that operand.) However, simple transmission of a value from one place to another, such as by assignment, passing as a parameter to a procedure, returning as a result from a procedure, or building the value into a data structure, does not touch the value. Thus, many things can be done with a future without waiting for its value.

In Multilisp, **future** is the only primitive for creating a task. There is a one-to-one correspondence between tasks and the futures whose values they were created to compute. Every task ends by resolving its associated future to some value.

future is related to the idea of *lazy evaluation,* often used in designs for graph-reduction architectures.[7,9] In lazy evaluation, an expression is not evaluated until its value is demanded by some other part of a computation. When an expression is encountered in a program, it is not evaluated immediately. Instead, a *suspension* is created and returned, and evaluation of the expression is delayed until the suspension is touched (in the Multilisp sense). A suspension is much like a future; the only difference between **future** and lazy evaluation is that **future** does not wait for the suspension to be touched before beginning evaluation of the expression. Multilisp has a **delay** primitive that implements lazy evaluation exactly (it returns a future and does not begin evaluation of the expression until the future is touched), but **delay** by itself does not express any concurrency.

Although **future** induces some patterns reminiscent of those found in graph-reduction architectures, in other ways **future** creates a style of computation much like that found in data flow architectures.[10] Every task suspended waiting for a future to resolve is like a data flow operator waiting for an operand to arrive. As in the case of data flow, each such task becomes eligible to proceed as soon as all its operands become available. When a task proceeds, it will eventually resolve another future, reactivating other suspended tasks in a pattern very reminiscent of the flow of data tokens in a data flow graph. Futures thus offer access to an interesting mixture of styles of parallel computation.

An example program in Multilisp

To get an idea of what programming with futures is like, consider an example

Multilisp program that manipulates sets represented as binary trees. The precise nature of the elements of these sets is not important—they could be integers, ordered pairs, character strings, or whatever—but assume that they are totally ordered by the Lisp predicate **elt<**, so **(elt< *A B*)** returns true if and only if the element *A* precedes the element *B* in the total order. The existence of the total order allows us to arrange the *N* elements of a set for lookup in $O(\log N)$ time by any of a variety of well known techniques. Possible uses of such a set are to collect integers or character strings with certain properties in common, or to record pairs of values from the domain and range of some function.

Our example program uses binary trees built out of *nodes* as suggested by Figure 1. Each leaf node of a tree is an actual set element; each interior node is a triple, as shown in Figure 1a. A Lisp function **leaf?** distinguishes between the two types of nodes: **(leaf?** *X*) returns true if *X* is a leaf node and false if *X* is an interior node. Each interior node has left and right children that are other nodes, plus a discriminant equal to the largest element stored in the left subtree of that node, as shown in Figure 1b. A Lisp function **(make-node** *L D R*) makes and returns a new interior node whose left child is *L*, whose discriminant is *D,* and whose right child is *R.* Given an interior node *N,* **(left-child** *N*), **(discriminant** *N*), and **(right-child** *N*) return, respectively, the left child, discriminant, and right child of *N.*

A Multilisp procedure to insert an element **elt** into a tree **tree** is shown in Figure 2. This is a *nondestructive* insert; it copies the tree nodes to be modified and returns a new tree rather than performing side effects on existing nodes. Except for its two uses of **future,** Figure 2 is the straightforward Lisp procedure for insertion into this kind of tree. The case of inserting into an initially empty tree needs special treatment. In this case, **insert** just returns **elt** (a single leaf node) as the resulting tree. If **tree** is not empty, then it may be a leaf or an interior node. If it is a leaf, **insert** returns an interior node with **elt** and **tree** as children in the proper order. If **tree** is an interior node, **insert** determines whether **elt** belongs in the left or right subtree of **tree** and returns a new interior node with the same discriminant and suitable left and right children.

```
(defun insert (elt tree)
  (if (empty-tree? tree)
    elt
    (if (leaf? tree)
      (if (elt < tree elt)
        (make-node tree tree elt)
        (make-node elt elt tree))
      (if (elt < (discriminant tree) elt)
        (make-node (left-child tree)
          (discriminant tree)
          (future (insert elt (right-child tree))))
        (make-node (future (insert elt (left-child tree)))
          (discriminant tree)
          (right-child tree))))))
```

Figure 2. Insert routine for search trees, using **future.** In addition to the procedures discussed in the text, this program uses two standard Lisp special forms. **(defun** *f*(v$_1$ v$_2$ . . .) *body*) defines a procedure *f* whose formal parameters are v$_1$, v$_2$, . . . , and whose value is the value of the expression *body*. **(if** *X Y Z*) returns the value of *Y* if *X* evaluates to true; otherwise the value of *Z* is returned.

The use of **future** in Figure 2 allows **insert** to return even before the insertion has completed. If **future** were not used, then an **insert** applied to an interior node would not return until its recursive call to **insert** had returned. Thus the new tree would be constructed in a bottom-up order and no result would be returned until the new tree had been completely constructed. Using **future,** however, **insert** can construct a new node and return it without waiting for completion of recursive calls to **insert.** If **tree** is an interior node, **insert** makes a new node that points to a future that will resolve to the value of the recursive call to **insert.** Consequently, the result of an insertion develops in more of a top-down fashion, as shown in Figure 3.

In order to insert three new elements *A, B,* and *C* into some tree *T,* we could write

(insert *C* (insert *B* (insert *A T*)))

A naive analysis might conclude that no concurrency is available in this expression, due to data dependencies (the insertion of *B* requires the result of inserting *A,* and so on). Yet with futures we find that some concurrency is available. For example, if *T* were the tree of Figure 1b and *A, B,* and *C* were 7, 4, and 29, respectively, then the insert of *B* could begin as soon as the insert of *A* returns, and the insert of *C* need only await the return of the insert of *B* and the determination of the first future created during *A*'s insertion. The remaining work for the three insertions can then proceed in parallel.

The fallacy in the naive analysis is in treating structured values such as binary trees as indivisible units. In fact, many (if not most) operations on structured values require only partial information about their operands. Futures give us a way to represent partially computed values, so they can be released for use while they are still being computed. As illustrated by the example, this can expose concurrency not easily accessible using conventional **fork-join** control structures. This is especially significant in symbolic computing, where operations on structured data are the norm, and where opportunities to use the well-known loop and flow analysis techniques are often much more limited than in the case of numerical computing.

It is of course possible to select values for *A, B,* and *C* above such that futures will yield relatively little concurrency (such as *A* = 7, *B* = 9, and *C* = 10). In this case the lack of concurrency results from real data dependencies: all three insertions are operating in the same region of the tree. Even in this case there will be some concurrency as the insertions of *A, B,* and *C* follow each other down the tree, but each insertion will be prevented from completely finishing until the previous one has finished most of its work. **future** cannot remove actual data dependencies, but can remove apparent dependencies by allowing structured values to be computed piecemeal.

This example illustrates the character of futures in a relatively simple setting, rather than illustrating the best in parallel tree management schemes. At the superficial level, we can certainly extend the program in Figure 2 to cope with insertion of an item already in the tree. We can also add the **delete** and **lookup** routines desired in many applications.

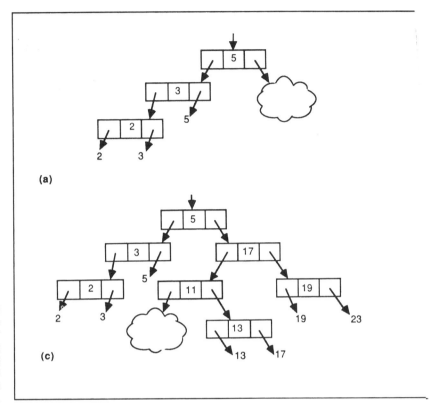

Figure 3. Top-down behavior of **insert** using **future.** (a) through (d) depict successive stages resulting from inserting 7 into the tree shown in Figure 1b. (a) shows the initial value returned, while (d) shows the final value after all futures have been resolved. The cloud-like shapes represent unresolved futures.

More serious for some applications than the lack of these features is the fact that the program does not necessarily produce balanced search trees. If insertions are performed in some unfortunate order (such as strictly increasing), the result of inserting K items can be a tree of depth K that takes $O(K^2)$ time to build.

Various schemes exist for building balanced search trees, such as 2-3 trees and AVL trees.[11] These schemes can be adapted using **future** to yield parallelism, but the results can be disappointing. The reasons are instructive. Balanced tree schemes generally try to maintain rough equality at each node N between the number of nodes in the subtrees headed by the children of N. The common sequential algorithms for insertion into balanced trees first find the place where the new leaf node will be added, then work back up the tree toward the root, rearranging the structure as needed to ensure the proper balance. Thus, the final shape of the tree, even near the root, may be determined only after the location of the new leaf node has been determined.

Unfortunately, the concurrency in the program in Figure 2 comes from releasing information about the structure of the resulting tree even before an insertion has progressed all the way to a leaf node. Every recursive invocation of **insert** ends by specifying the left and right children of some newly created node. One of the children may be specified as a future, so its value may not be known, but its identity is known. In the case of both 2-3 trees and AVL trees, at certain points it can be seen that any tree reorganization resulting from an insertion cannot propagate above that point. But at other points, the identities of the child nodes cannot be fixed without additional information generated as the insertion progresses. At such points, construction of a new node must be delayed until it becomes clear what its children should be. This delays the top-down evolution suggested by Figure 3 and therefore reduces the opportunities for parallelism. Balanced-tree schemes are not necessarily unsuitable for parallel execution, but we need different algorithms that operate in a more top-down manner, perhaps by accepting a more relaxed standard of balance for search trees.

Parallel programming in the large

Although our tree-insertion program is a simple example, it shows how futures can be used to expose concurrency in dealing with composite data structures by providing a representation for partially computed data. It also shows the importance of algorithms able to release partial information about their results as soon as possible. However, applications for parallel computing are generally large programs, not 20-line programs such as Quicksort or tree insertion. Therefore, a useful system for applying parallel computation to real problems must support powerful ways of combining pieces together into large programs, not just techniques for making small subprograms use concurrency. Constructs such as **future**, which help us easily glue programs together in concurrent ways, are only part of what we need. We also need adequate control over the allocation of resources (notably processors) to the execution of various parts of a program. In effect, we need control over the

199

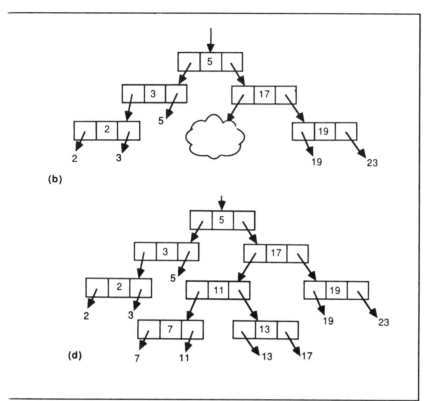

(b)

(d)

focus of attention of a parallel computer as it executes a program.

Other aids for the development and structuring of large programs include support for debugging, exception handling, data abstractions, and atomic modification of mutable data objects. Except for the last item, all of these are also important in sequential programming, but parallel programming brings new dimensions to them.

Scheduling. Algorithms may have opportunities for concurrency at any of several levels of granularity, ranging from short sequences of primitive operations to large program modules. These opportunities are multiplicative. If the application of medium- or fine-grain parallelism within a module is sufficient to occupy m processors and n of these modules can be executed in parallel, then mn processors can be used efficiently to execute the program as a whole (unless contention for shared resources imposes a smaller limit). Thus, we should exploit opportunities for concurrency at all levels if we desire execution on a highly parallel machine.

Concurrency, however, arises from a variety of program structures. One way to write a concurrent program is to start with a suitably chosen sequential program and then relax some of the precedence constraints in that program to produce opportunities for executing some operations concurrently. This *mandatory work* style of parallel programming is supported by **future**, as well as by the **fork-join** constructs of other languages. A concurrent program written in the mandatory work style executes precisely the same set of operations as its sequential counterpart; only the scheduling of operations is different. Language constructs, such as **future** and **fork-join**, may differ in their effectiveness at relaxing precedence constraints and may therefore be more or less useful in support of the mandatory work style, but the basic equivalence between the sets of operations performed by sequential and mandatory work parallel programs remains.

The mandatory work style contrasts with the *speculative* approach, where parallelism is obtained by eagerly spawning tasks before it is certain that their values

will be needed. A characteristic particularly prevalent in artificial intelligence programs, but also found elsewhere, is the existence of multiple techniques to solve a class of problems. For any particular problem, some of the techniques may work very quickly, while others may fail altogether. We therefore desire the ability to start using several techniques in parallel and to terminate execution of the others when one of the techniques produces an answer.

There are many opportunities for speculative parallelism outside the domain of artificial intelligence, especially in searching problems. An example is the use of branch-and-bound techniques for problems such as the traveling salesman problem. A simple example of speculative parallelism from yet another domain is the Fermat test to see if a number is prime. The Fermat test is based on the observation that, if p is prime, then a^{p-1} mod p = 1 whenever $0 < a < p$. Furthermore, if p is not prime, then a^{p-1} mod p has a certain probability of not being 1 when a is chosen randomly from $0 < a < p$. The primality of a number p can be tested by randomly selecting several values a from $0 < a < p$ and evaluating a^{p-1} mod p for each a. If all evaluations yield 1, then with high probability p is prime. Otherwise, p is certainly not prime. (This test has a high probability of being fooled for certain pathological non-prime numbers p. Other, more sophisticated tests on a and p yield more reliable results, but the overall organization, and probabilistic nature, of the algorithm remain the same.)

A sequential program for the Fermat test would select one a after another until either a sufficient number of a's have been tested or a^{p-1} mod $p \neq 1$ for one of the choices of a. One strategy for using parallelism in the Fermat test would be to test several different a's concurrently. In the case where p is prime, this would make the test go much faster, but if p is not prime, it might be that a^{p-1} mod $p \neq 1$ for the very first a. Then the work done on the other a's would be wasted and any remaining work associated with testing the primality of p should be cancelled. Therefore, if there is other mandatory work to do, the successive a's should be tested sequentially, but if processing capacity would otherwise go idle, then the a's might as well be tested in parallel.

> To exploit concurrency at all levels and from all sources, both mandatory work and speculative parallelism should be used.

Compared to speculative parallelism, mandatory work parallelism is especially nice because scheduling is less critical and, except for process management overhead, no extra operations are performed during parallel execution. Assuming the original sequential algorithm is efficient, the mandatory work approach represents a kind of lower bound. It may be possible to increase concurrency beyond that available in a mandatory work program by adding speculative operations, but these operations represent an overhead justified only if the increase in parallelism outweighs the extra work done.

Scheduling of mandatory operations is not very critical because all mandatory operations must be done eventually, so any mandatory operation ready to be performed may be executed with assurance that it will not be wasted work. In fact, the Multilisp implementation uses an unfair scheduler, which is perfectly legal in the case of mandatory work and helps solve some resource allocation problems[4] very hard to solve using a fair scheduler. (For utmost efficiency, mandatory operations on the critical path of a computation should be treated as more mandatory than others and always included in the set that gets scheduled. In practice, the precedence graphs of most parallel programs seem to have a "bushy" enough structure that this is not a major concern.)

Scheduling is much more critical in the presence of speculative parallelism. Usually, some speculative tasks have a higher potential payoff than others. Low-payoff speculative tasks should not be executed in preference to high-payoff speculative tasks or mandatory tasks. The only time to execute speculative tasks is when process-

ing resources would otherwise go idle; they should not take resources away from more important tasks.

To exploit concurrency at all levels and from all sources, both mandatory work and speculative parallelism should be used. Therefore, both need to be supported by parallel programming languages. However, tools for expressing speculative parallelism cannot replace good constructs for mandatory work parallelism. The latter is higher quality parallelism and should always be exploited as fully as possible before resorting to speculative parallelism.

Multilisp's **future** construct is a fairly effective tool for exposing mandatory work parallelism, but **future** does not give the information needed to properly schedule speculative tasks. One idea on how to do this is to associate a *sponsor*[12] with each task. The sponsor answers questions from the scheduler regarding the importance of its task relative to others. Although sponsors are a mechanism that can be used for scheduling speculative tasks, the policy implemented by the sponsors remains an issue. In some cases, the scheduling of tasks could be dictated by associating numerical priorities with the tasks, but the general question of what tools to give the programmer for use in specifying the scheduling of speculative tasks remains an interesting question for research.

Data abstractions and mutable objects. An important characteristic of a language for parallel computing is whether or not it allows the writing of nondeterminate programs, programs that may produce different results for different (legal) orders of execution. Multilisp and QLisp, by including side effects, allow nondeterminism, while functional languages forbid side effects and assure determinate execution. Issues relating to determinacy are discussed elsewhere.[2,4] A capsule summary of the debate is that potentially nondeterminate programs can be very hard to debug and verify, but that the language restrictions needed to assure determinacy are substantial and rule out many familiar and useful program structures. Multilisp allows side effects and hence permits these program structures. To help control the resulting software engineering problems, Multilisp supports side-effect-free expression of many computations and, through the first-class

citizenship of Multilisp procedures, supports the construction of data abstractions within which side effects can be compartmentalized. This reduces their contribution to program complexity.

Correct implementation of first-class citizenship for procedures, in combination with lexical scoping, requires the use of garbage-collected heap storage for procedural environments. Once this expense is incurred, however, procedures can be used as data abstractions. The nonlocal variables of a procedure, found in the lexically enclosing environment, can be considered the underlying state variables of a data abstraction implemented by the procedure. Operations on this data abstraction can be performed by calls to the procedure. As with other implementations of abstract data types, the underlying state variables can be protected from access except through the channels provided by the abstraction.[2]

Although it does include side effects, Lisp is superior to most common programming languages in that it includes a side-effect-free subset with substantial expressive power. This subset is part of Multilisp; thus it is possible to write significant bodies of Multilisp code in a completely side-effect-free way. Furthermore, where side effects are used, as in maintaining a changing database, they can be encapsulated within a data abstraction that synchronizes concurrent operations on the data. The data abstraction can ensure that the data are only accessed according to the proper protocol.

Multilisp thus supports a programming syle in which most code is written without side effects and data abstractions are used to encapsulate data on which side effects may be performed, to present a reasonable interface to the exterior. A programmer's aim in using this style should be to produce a program whose side effects are compartmentalized carefully enough that any module may safely be invoked in parallel with any other. If this style is followed, the difficulties caused by the presence of side effects will be isolated to small regions of the program and should therefore be reduced to manageable proportions.

Debugging and exception handling. Debugging and exception handling are closely related topics. The need for debugging is often revealed by the occurrence of some runtime exception not anticipated by the programmer. At times, however, a programmer may anticipate the possible occurrence of an exception such as an end-of-file on read or an attempt to divide by zero. In such cases, the ability to flexibly specify a handler for an exception can be an important program structuring tool.

The occurrence of exceptions in a parallel environment presents an interesting problem. If a task has been created to calculate the value of some future and is unable to complete due to the occurrence of an exception, what value should be given to the future? Before the occurrence of the exception, the procedure that created the future may have returned and the future itself may have been distributed to many other tasks, some of which may already have become suspended waiting for the future's value. If the occurrence of an exception causes the future never to receive a value, then these tasks will never resume execution and nontermination of the program containing them is a likely result. On the other hand, what meaningful value do we give a future created by an expression such as **(future (/ 3 0))**, which has been asked to perform a division by zero? Multilisp's solution to this problem involves *error values*.[5] If the evaluation of an expression X in **(future X)** cannot complete normally, the future can resolve to an error value. An exception will be raised in any task that touches an error value. In this way, the consequences of an exception that occurs while calculating a value propagate back through all users of the value. This propagation mirrors the popping of stack frames that occurs when unwinding a sequential computation after an exception.

Program debugging also takes on new dimensions in a parallel environment. Broadly speaking, debugging is concerned with two properties of programs: correctness and performance. Correctness rightly takes first place. A fast program is of little use if it produces incorrect results. Nevertheless, the reason for using parallel processing in the first place is to improve performance, so it is important for a programmer to be able to find and remove any obstacles to maximum performance (such as unnecessary data dependencies). To do this, programmers need good tools for visualizing the operation of concurrent programs. The factors affecting the performance of a program in a parallel environment are more complex and subtle than in the sequential case; thus debugging for performance should be taken less for granted in parallel programming.

Experience with Multilisp

A complete Multilisp implementation including a parallel, incremental garbage collector[4] exists on Concert,[13] an experimental multiprocessor under construction in the author's laboratory. The Concert multiprocessor, when fully built, will comprise 32 MC68000 processors and a total of about 20M bytes of memory. It can be described most concisely as a shared-memory multiprocessor, although its organization includes various local paths from processors to nearby memory modules. Concert thus provides a higher overall bandwidth between processors and memory if most memory accesses are local.

As of this writing, the largest part of Concert on which it has been possible to test Multilisp is a 24-processor section of the eventual Concert machine. Multilisp has also been implemented on a 128-processor Butterfly machine,[14] but a suitably tuned version of Butterfly Multilisp has not been available in time to include meaningful Butterfly measurements here.

The Concert Multilisp implementation uses a layer of interpretation, so it is not fast in absolute terms. Understanding Concert Multilisp performance measurements is also complicated by several other factors, such as garbage collector performance, discussed elsewhere.[4] Despite these complications, the measured performance of Multilisp programs on Concert does offer some indication of the concurrency made available by the use of futures. To gauge the impact of using futures in the program of Figure 2, the program was tested on Concert by successively inserting long lists of random numbers into an initially empty tree. The test was essentially to evaluate the expression

```
(insert v_n
    (future (insert v_{n-1} ...
        (future (insert v_1 empty-tree)) ... )))
```

and then walk the resulting tree to wait for all futures to be resolved. $v_1, v_2,...,v_n$

represent the n numbers inserted into the tree. The running times on Concert, using varying numbers of processors, are plotted in Figure 4a for lists of length 128, 256, and 512. In each case, the performance of the parallel program with futures is plotted along with that of a sequential program just like the parallel program except that all instances of the **future** operator have been removed. For comparison, Figure 4b shows the performance on Concert of a Quicksort routine using futures,[4] along with figures for the corresponding sequential Quicksort.

Unfortunately, futures are quite expensive in the current Multilisp implementation, causing **insert** with futures to take about twice as long as **insert** without futures. **future** has been measured as taking about four times as long as a procedure call. Some ideas that promise to make **future** considerably cheaper are currently under investigation at M.I.T.

Even though each data point in Figure 4 is the average of many trials, the curves are somewhat uneven and have several peculiar features. Some of the variations are due to the garbage collector and also to the fact that some sequences of random numbers yield more nearly balanced trees than others. Other features are caused by lack of parallelism in the programs being measured, while yet others may be due to bus contention or other effects rooted in the implementation. Unfortunately, the data are quire recent and it is not yet clear what causes all of the features in these graphs. Furthermore, space limitations preclude a full explanation here of even those features of the graphs whose causes are understood.

It is clearly too early to judge the ultimate success of the programming language ideas embodied in Multilisp. Nevertheless, it is clear both that a substantial amount of concurrency can be exploited and that the speedup due to concurrency, for these examples, is limited. Although Figure 4 leaves many questions unanswered, at least it shows that, for small numbers of processors, the promise of futures can be fulfilled. The challenge ahead is to remove the bottlenecks apparent in Figure 4, show good speed-ups on larger numbers of processors, and increase the Multilisp performance of the individual processors to more competitive levels.

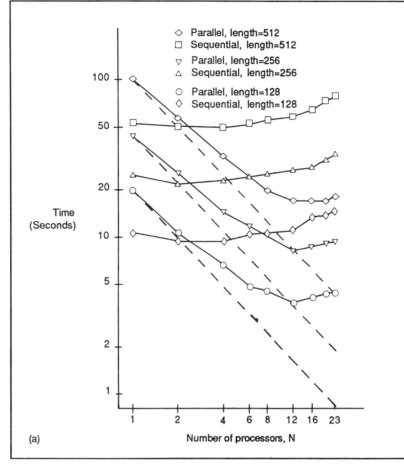

Figure 4. Performance measurements for Concert Multilisp. The performance of the tree insertion procedure is shown in (a) and that of the Quicksort procedure in (b). The dashed lines are the curves of linear speedup.

Directions for research in parallel symbolic computing

The critical research questions in parallel symbolic computing may be grouped into three areas:

(1) programming languages and programming environments,

(2) algorithm and application development, and

(3) implementation and architecture.

The first area encompasses most of the questions addressed in this article. A programming language for parallel symbolic computing must support both the mandatory work and speculative flavors of parallelism. Its associated programming environment must include debugging tools to help in finding both correctness and performance bugs. Furthermore, the language must support the construction of reasonably modular programs and the constructs for obtaining concurrency must fit neatly within the modular structure of programs. A final major decision point in language design concerns the degree of nondeterminacy that can exist in program behavior.

The development of programming languages and environments should always be guided by the needs of application programs. Since there are not many parallel symbolic application programs in existence, research in programming languages for parallel machines must be complemented by the development of parallel application programs. Some of these programs should be of substantial size. Although "toy" programs such as the **insert** example of the program in Figure 2 promote insight into parallel language constructs, the ultimate application of parallel computers will be to much more complex programs, and it is well known that the engineering of large programs is qualitatively different from that of small programs. Language research and application development can reinforce each other. Language ideas can suggest new application programming strategies, and the requirements of application programs can suggest areas where language design decisions should be re-examined.

Both language design and application program requirements should influence the architecture of systems for parallel computing. Language constructs may require clever implementation algorithms and/or special hardware support for efficient execution. Application programs provide the invaluable service of helping focus the design of implementations and architectures by indicating how much effect the efficient implementation of each language feature has on bottom-line performance. Thus, application programs are not just useful for calibrating language design decisions, they also serve an important role as benchmarks to help evaluate proposed architectures.

Of course, all these aspects of design interact. The art of the desirable in language design must be balanced against the art of the possible. Also, as we learn more about parallel computing, old decisions will be seen in new lights and sometimes modified. Nevertheless, we must make substantial progress on language definition and application development before we can have any very solid objective grounds for evaluating proposed architectures for parallel symbolic computing. Developing the grounds for such evaluation is the principal research goal of the Multilisp project. □

Acknowledgments

This research could not have progressed as far as it has without the Concert

203

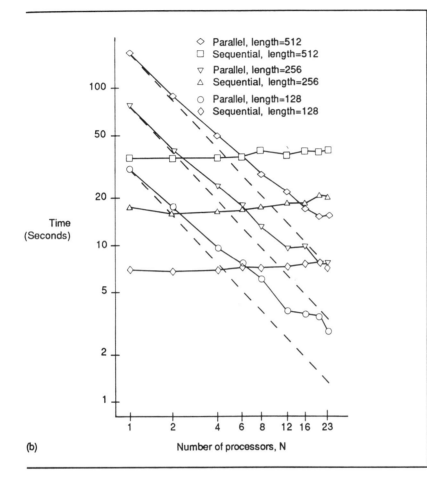

Legend:
◇ Parallel, length=512
□ Sequential, length=512
▽ Parallel, length=256
△ Sequential, length=256
○ Parallel, length=128
◇ Sequential, length=128

Time (Seconds)

100
50
20
10
5
2
1

1 2 4 6 8 12 16 23

(b)

Number of processors, N

multiprocessor,[13] which served as the implementation vehicle for Multilisp. Many people have contributed to making Concert a reality. Particularly noteworthy contributions were made by Tom Anderson, Jeff Arnold, Sharon Gray, Dan Nussbaum, Peter Nuth, Randy Osborne, Peter Osler, Doug Robinow, Tom Sterling, and Gautam Thaker. The collaboration of the Advanced Technology Department of Harris Corporation's Government Systems Sector has also been vital. The Multilisp implementation itself exists only as a result of the outstanding efforts of Juan Loaiza.

This research was supported in part by the Defense Advanced Research Projects Agency and was monitored by the Office of Naval Research under contract number N00014-83-K-0125.

References

1. C. A. R. Hoare, "Communicating Sequential Processes," *CACM*, Aug. 1978.

2. H. Abelson and G. Sussman, *Structure and Interpretation of Computer Programs*, M.I.T. Press, Cambridge, Mass., 1984.

3. R. P. Gabriel and J. McCarthy, "Queue-based Multiprocessing Lisp," *ACM Symp. on Lisp and Functional Programming*, Austin, Tex., Aug. 1984.

4. R. Halstead, "Multilisp: A Language for Concurrent Symbolic Computation," *ACM Trans. on Programming Languages and Systems*, Oct. 1985.

5. R. Halstead and J. Loaiza, "Exception Handling in Multilisp," *1985 Int'l Conf. on Parallel Processing*, St. Charles, Ill., Aug. 1985.

6. D. Friedman and D. Wise, "Aspects of Applicative Programming for Parallel Processing," *IEEE Trans. Comp.*, Vol. C-27, No. 4, April 1978, pp. 289-296.

7. R. Keller and F. Lin, "Simulated Performance of a Reduction-Based Multiprocessor," *Computer*, Vol. 17, No. 7, July 1984, pp. 70-82.

8. H. Baker and C. Hewitt, "The Incremental Garbage Collection of Processes," M.I.T. Artificial Intelligence Laboratory Memo 454, Cambridge, Mass., Dec. 1977.

9. P. Henderson and J. H. Morris, "A Lazy Evaluator," *Proc. 3rd ACM Symp. on Principles of Programming Languages*, 1976, pp. 95-103.

10. J. B. Dennis, "Data Flow Supercomputers," *Computer*, Vol. 13, No. 11, Nov. 1980, pp. 48-56.

11. A. V. Aho, J. E. Hopcroft, and J. D. Ullman, *The Design and Analysis of Computer Algorithms*, Addison-Wesley, Reading, Mass., 1974, pp. 145-169.

12. D. Theriault, *Issues in the Design and Implementation of Act2*, M.I.T. Artificial Intelligence Laboratory tech. report AI-TR 728, Cambridge, Mass., June 1983.

13. R. Halstead, T. Anderson, R. Osborne, and T. Sterling, "Concept: Design of a Multiprocessor Development System," *13th Int'l Symp. on Computer Architecture*, Tokyo, June 1986, pp. 40-48.

14. W. Crowther et al., "Performance Measurements on a 128-Node Butterfly Parallel Processor," *1985 Int'l Conf. on Parallel Processing*, St. Charles, Ill., Aug. 1985, pp. 531-540.

Robert H. Halstead, Jr., is an associate professor in the Department of Electrical Engineering and Computer Science at the Massachusetts Institute of Technology. His research interests include languages, algorithms, and architectures for general-purpose parallel processing, with an emphasis on symbolic computing. He has taught in the areas of programming languages, computer architecture, compilers, and operating systems.

Halstead received the SB, SM, and PhD degrees from the Massachusetts Institute of Technology, graduating with the PhD in 1979. He is on the editorial board of the *International Journal of Parallel Programming*.

Readers may write to the author at M.I.T. Laboratory for Computer Science, 545 Technology Square, Cambridge, MA 02139.

A Report on the Sisal Language Project*

John T. Feo and David C. Cann

Computer Research Group (L-306), Lawrence Livermore National Laboratory, P.O. Box 808, Livermore, California 94550

AND

Rodney R. Oldehoeft

Department of Computer Science, Colorado State University, Fort Collins, Colorado 80523

Sisal (Streams and Iterations in Single Assignment Language) is a general-purpose applicative language intended for use on both conventional and novel multiprocessor systems. In this report we discuss the project's objectives, philosophy, and accomplishments and state our future plans. Four significant results of the Sisal project are compilation techniques for high-performance parallel applicative computation, a microtasking environment that supports dataflow on conventional shared-memory architectures, execution times comparable to those of Fortran, and cost-effective speedup on shared-memory multiprocessors. © 1990 Academic Press, Inc.

1. INTRODUCTION

Sisal (Streams and Iterations in a Single Assignment Language) is a general-purpose applicative language intended for use on both conventional and novel multiprocessor systems. The project began as a collaborative effort by Lawrence Livermore National Laboratory, Colorado State University, University of Manchester, and Digital Equipment Corp.

Sisal, a derivative of Val [4], was defined in 1983 [28] and revised in 1985 [29]. Since then the language definition has not changed, providing a stable testbed for implementors, programming language researchers, and users. The project's objectives are:

1. define a general-purpose applicative language,

2. define a language-independent intermediate form for dataflow graphs,

3. develop optimization techniques for high-performance parallel applicative computing,

4. develop a microtasking environment that supports dataflow on conventional computer systems,

5. achieve execution performance comparable to that of Fortran, and

6. validate the applicative style of programming for large-scale scientific applications.

These goals address issues in programming languages, compilers, operating systems, performance, and software engineering. The first three are typical of dataflow projects. The last three set the Sisal effort apart—they reflect the computing environment at Lawrence Livermore National Laboratory and other government facilities. In particular, the focus on conventional systems is in sharp contrast to that of other dataflow language projects that assume hardware support. Our intention is to define a language and an intermediate form independent of architecture and then to develop code generators and run time systems for specific target machines. This approach has paid off handsomely, as Sisal is running today on uniprocessors, conventional shared-memory multiprocessors [26, 37], the Cray X/MP [27], the Warp [19], the Connection Machine [15], the Mac II [32], and a variety of dataflow machines [2, 20].

Why the interest in applicative languages at the national laboratories? Scientists there, and elsewhere, realize that the next generation of single-processor systems will not deliver the magnitude of increase in computing power that they require. They understand that they must parallelize their codes and move to multiprocessor systems. However, despite the availability of such systems, the number of scientific parallel applications in use today remains virtually zero. The reason: conventional parallel programming languages thwart programmer productivity and hinder analysis. They fail to separate problem specification and implementation, fail to emphasize modular design, and inherently hide data depen-

* This report was prepared as an account of work sponsored by the U.S. Government. Neither the United States nor the U.S. Department of Energy, nor any of their employees, nor any of their contractors, subcontractors, or their employees, makes any warranty, express or implied, or assumes any legal liability or responsibility for the accuracy, completeness, or usefulness of any information, apparatus, product, or process disclosed, or represents that its use would not infringe privately owned rights. Reference to a company or product name does not imply approval or recommendation of the product by the University of California or the U.S. Department of Energy to the exclusion of others that may be suitable. The views, opinions, and/or findings contained in this report are those of the authors and should not be construed as an official Department of the Army position, policy, or decision, unless so designated by other documents.

dencies. Compilers that automatically parallelize programs written in sequential languages are a solution [38, 39], but we believe that these languages restrict the formulation of parallel algorithms and will always deter the automatic exploitation of parallel architectures [48].

Applicative languages provide an easy-to-use and clean parallel programming model that facilitates algorithm development and simplifies compilation. In an applicative program the value of any expression depends only on the values of its subexpressions and not on their order of evaluation. Applicative semantics only allow programmers to define data dependencies among operations. The scheduling of operations, the communication of data values, and the synchronization of concurrent operations are the responsibility of the run time system. The user does not (in fact cannot) manage these system operations. Relieved of the most onerous chores of parallel programming, the user is free to concentrate on algorithm design and application development.

Although ease of programming is important, at the national laboratories performance is the bottom line. If applicative languages are to gain adherents in the scientific community they must achieve execution speeds comparable to that of Fortran on state-of-the-art supercomputers. Since current dataflow machines are not capable of supercomputer performance, we have defined Sisal and IF1 [43] (our intermediate form) independent of architecture and have developed a run time system that supports dataflow on conventional shared-memory computer systems typical of today's supercomputers.

In Section 2, we discuss Sisal's characteristics and features. In Section 3, we describe the Sisal compiler and its optimization techniques for high-performance parallel applicative computing. In Section 4, we describe a microtasking environment that supports dataflow on conventional shared-memory computer systems. In Section 5, we show that Sisal programs can execute as fast as Fortran programs on conventional single-processor systems, plus automatically exploit conventional shared-memory multiprocessor systems. In Section 6, we discuss our future plans.

2. SISAL LANGUAGE SUMMARY

Sisal is a strongly typed, general-purpose applicative language that supports data types and operations for scientific computation and has a Pascal-like syntax for minimizing learning time and enhancing readability. Sisal has several important semantic properties. First, all functions are mathematically sound—there are no side effects. Second, Sisal programs are referentially transparent. Since names are bound to values and not memory locations, there is no aliasing. Third, the language is single assignment—a name is assigned a value only once. In general, a Sisal program defines a set of mathematical expressions where names stand

TABLE I
Array Create Operations

Operations	Comments
`returns array of x`	Gather array
`array [1: 1, 2, 3]`	Create array
`array_fill(1, N, 0)`	Create array of 0's
`A[1: 0]`	Replace A[1] with 0
`A || B`	Catenate A and B

for specific values, and computations progress without state. These properties make the transformation from source code to dataflow graph trivial.

A Sisal program is a collection of separately compiled files called compilation units. Each compilation unit includes a list of declared function names visible outside the unit, a list of corresponding function definitions, and possibly the definitions of additional functions. A function can take zero or more arguments and must return one or more values. The type of each argument and result value is declared in the function's definition header. A function has access only to its arguments and there are no side effects. Each function invocation is independent; functions cannot retain state between invocations.

Sisal handles exceptions by producing special error values.[1] Although an efficient implementation may require special hardware, error values have three advantages:

(1) their presence alerts the user to an exception,
(2) they permit the computation to continue, and
(3) correct data are preserved to the extent possible.

The value **error** is a proper element of every Sisal type. Conditions that produce errors include underflow, overflow, divide by zero, subscript out of bounds, and conditional expressions whose test clauses are in error. The semantics of the language defines rules for propagating error values. Every effort is made to preserve data not in error. For example, an array is **error** if it includes error values, but the elements of the array are still accessible.

Sisal includes the standard scalar data types: boolean, character, integer, real, and double precision. It also includes the aggregate types: array, record, union, and stream. All arrays are one-dimensional. Multidimensional arrays are defined as arrays of arrays. The type, size, and lower bound of an array are a function of execution. The components of a multidimensional array may have different lengths and lower bounds, resulting in jagged arrays. Arrays are created by gathering component elements, "modifying" existing arrays, or catenation. Table I gives examples of each. The ex-

---

[1] Errors are supported in the interpreter and the native code compiler being developed at Lawrence Livermore National Laboratory; they are not supported in Osc, the native code compiler developed at Colorado State University and discussed in this paper.

TABLE II

Stream Operations

Operations	Comments
stream_append(A, B)	Append B to A
stream_first (A)	First element of A
stream_rest (A)	Tail of A
stream_empty (A)	Empty stream?
A || B	Catenate A and B

plicit, concise form of these operations greatly simplifies memory preallocation and update-in-place analysis.

A stream is a sequence of values of uniform type. In Sisal, stream elements are accessible in order only; there is no random access to elements. Table II lists the stream operations in Sisal. A stream can have only one producer, but any number of consumers. By definition, Sisal streams are nonstrict—each element is available as soon as it is produced. Run time systems must support the concurrent execution of a stream's producer and consumers. As such, streams can express pipelined parallelism and are a natural medium for program input and output.

Sisal supports both sequential and parallel loops. The **for initial** expression, illustrated in Fig. 1, resembles sequential iteration in conventional languages, but retains single-assignment semantics. It comprises four segments: initialization, loop body, termination test, and result clause. The initialization segment defines all loop constants and assigns initial values to all loop-carried names. It is the first iteration of the loop. The loop body computes new values for the loop names, possibly on the basis of their previous values. The rebinding of loop names to values is implicit and occurs between iterations. Loop names prefixed with **old** refer to previous values. The termination test may appear either before or after the body. If it appears before, the body might not execute; if it appears after, the body will execute at least once. The returns clause defines the results and arity of the expression. Each result is either the final value of some loop name or a reduction of the values assigned to a loop name during loop execution. Sisal supports seven intrinsic reductions: **array of, stream of, catenate, sum, product, least,** and **greatest.** The order of reduction is determinate.

The **for** expression, illustrated in Fig. 2, provides a means for specifying independent iterations. The semantics of the expression does not allow references to values defined in other iterations. The **for** expression comprises three parts: a range generator, a loop body, and a returns clause. The range generator is a dot or cross product of a set of sequences or scatters (see Table III). An instance of the loop body is executed for each index, value, or n-tuple. The returns clause defines the results and arity of the expression. Each result is a reduction of values defined in the loop body (**array of, stream of, catenate, sum, product, least,** or **greatest**). The range generator specifies the order of reduction and defines the size and structure of aggregate objects. For example, the expression

```
for i in 1,n cross j in 1,m
returns array of (i + j)
end for
```

returns a two-dimensional array of n rows and m columns. At first, many Sisal programmers fail to understand the subtleties of this syntax. A common mistake is to write the transpose of an $(n \times m)$ matrix as

```
for i in 1,n cross j in 1,m
returns array of X[j, i]
end for
```

The correct expression is

```
for i in 1,Om cross j in 1,n
returns array of X[j, i]
end for
```

To allow for mutually recursive functions and to encourage modular design Sisal includes **global** and **forward** function definitions. Although Sisal permits recursive function definitions, it does not permit recursive definitions of value names. The compiler enforces a strict *definition before use* policy on all value names. One consequence of this policy is that users must specify the order in which elements of recursive aggregates are computed. Consider the array definition

$$X(i, j)$$

$$= \begin{bmatrix} 1, & i = 1, \\ 1, & j = 1, \\ X(i, j - 1) + X(i - 1, j), & 2 \leqslant i \leqslant n, \quad 2 \leqslant j \leqslant n. \end{bmatrix}$$

$$(1)$$

```
for  initial
    i := 1;
    x := Y[1]
while i < n repeat
    i := old i + 1;
    x := old x + Y[i]
returns  array  of  x
end  for
```

FIG. 1. The **for initial** expression.

```
for i in 1, N
    x := A[i] * B[i]
returns value of sum x
end for
```

FIG. 2. The for expression.

The Sisal expression

```
X := for i in 1, n cross j in 1, n
  returns array of
      if (i = 1) | (j = 1) then
      1
      else
        X[i, j − 1] + X[i − 1, j]
      end if
      end for
```

is illegal. A legal Sisal expression for Eq. (1) is

```
X := for initial
    i   := 1;
    row := array_fill (1, n, 1);
  while i < n repeat
    i   := old i + 1;
    row := for initial
        j := 1;
        x := 1
      while j < n repeat
        j := old j + 1;
        x := old x + old row[j]
      returns array of x
      ends for
  returns array of row
  end for
```

Note that the order of computation is explicit. In a functional language that permits recursive definitions, such as Id [31], the equivalent expression is

```
X = makearray (1, n)
  { if (i == 1) or (j == 1) then
    1
    else
      X[i, j − 1] + X[i − 1, j]
  }
```

Here the order of computation is implicit, resolved at run time by the availability of results.

Although it obscures parallelism at the source level, excluding recursive definitions simplifies language implementation. First, we do not need special hardware such as full-and-empty bits to delay reads at run time. Second, we do

not need sophisticated analysis routines or special hardware to detect recursive definitions that deadlock. Third, the system can bound parallelism without restriction because deadlock is impossible. On the matter of clarity, consider Eq. (1). If we maximize parallelism, the computation sweeps across the matrix from the top left-hand corner to the bottom right-hand corner in a diagonal wave—the computations along a diagonal are data independent and can execute in parallel. But the parallel nature of the expression is not apparent from the Sisal code. However, if the Sisal run time system schedules all the loop bodies simultaneously and has each wait for its inputs, we will realize the parallelism hidden in the source code.

Strict adherence to applicative semantics may introduce substantial execution costs, possibly negating the effects of parallelism. Consider the Sisal expression

```
X := Y[1: 3]
```

Strict adherence to single-assignment semantics requires construction of a new array identical to Y except at index location 1. If the expression is the last consumer of Y, the copy is unnecessary. Worse yet consider the Sisal expression

```
for initial
    i := 1;
    n := 50000;
    A := array[1: 1]
  while i < n repeat
    i := old i + 1;
    A := array_addh (old A, i + old i)
  returns value of A
  end for
```

A strict applicative implementation of the *array_addh* operation requires construction of a new array each iteration, resulting in the copy of $O(n^2)$ values. On the Sequent Balance 21000, for $n = 50,000$, the Sisal expression executes in about 1 h, while the equivalent Fortran code

```
integer A(50000)
do 5 i = 1, 50000
5     A(i) = i
```

executes in less than half a second. Since there is only one

TABLE III

Range Generators

Operations	Comments
for x in A	A scatter
for i in 1, n	A sequence
for x in A dot y in B	A dot product of two scatters
for i in 1, n cross j in 1, m	The cross product of two sequences

208

consumer of A, the *array_addh* operation on the next iteration, the copying is superfluous. In the next section we present analysis procedures that identify these and other instances where copy operations are not needed to maintain referential transparency.

In the last example, even if we build the array in place, the run time system may still have to copy the array every iteration to find room for the new elements. Again, in the worst case, we will copy $O(n^2)$ values. We can eliminate the copying by calculating the size of the final array and preallocating memory. **For** expressions can also generate extraneous copying when constructing aggregates. Since the loop bodies are data independent, they may be executed by independent processors. On completion of the expression, the run time system will have to gather (copy) the partial results. In the next section we describe compile time techniques that insert operations into the code to compute the size of most aggregates and preallocate memory.

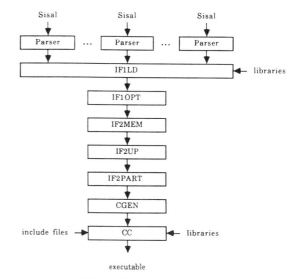

FIG. 3. Sisal language processing.

3. THE COMPILER

In this section we present an overview of our current Sisal compiler (called Osc) and provide a brief enumeration and illustration of its optimization subphases. Osc successfully eliminates unnecessary copying and greatly reduces storage management overhead for most Sisal programs. In this discussion, we assume that the reader has a working knowledge of reference counting and its use in storage management [12] and dataflow graphs and their use in compilation [18, 25]. We also assume that the reader has an understanding of conventional optimization techniques [5], including interprocedural analysis [6].

Osc, an extensive rework of a prototype developed for the Hep multiprocessor [35], is a state-of-the-art optimizing compiler. Figure 3 diagrams its phases and subphases of operation. The front end compiles Sisal source into IF1 [43], an intermediate form defining dataflow graphs adhering to applicative semantics. An IF1 program consists of one or more acyclic graphs made up of simple nodes, compound nodes, graph nodes, edges, and types. Nodes denote operations, edges transmit data between nodes, and types describe the transmitted data. Simple nodes represent operations such as addition, division, and array and stream manipulation. Compound nodes encapsulate one or more subgraphs to define structured expressions such as conditionals and **for initial** and **for** expressions.

Because the production of quality code requires complete information, the second phase of compilation (IF1LD) forms a monolithic IF1 program. The monolith is then read by a machine-independent optimizer (IF1OPT) that applies conventional optimizations such as function expansion, invariant code removal, common subexpression elimination, constant folding, loop fusion, and dead code removal. Except when presented with recursive calls or user directives, all functions, by default, are in-lined to form a single dataflow graph. The common subexpression eliminator looks outside branches of conditional statements in an attempt to find more common subexpressions. See [45] and [10] for further discussion of these optimizations.

After the machine-independent optimizations, a *build-in-place* analyzer (IF2MEM) preallocates array storage where compile time analysis or run time expressions can calculate their sizes [41]. The result of this analysis is a semantically equivalent program graph in IF2 [47]. IF2 is a superset of IF1, but is not applicative because it supports operations that directly reference and manipulate "abstract" memory (called **AT-nodes**). The next phase of compilation (IF2UP) does *update-in-place* analysis [10]. The analyzer restructures some graphs, while preserving program correctness, to help identify (at compile time) operations that can execute in place and to improve chances for in-place operation at run time when analysis fails. The analysis routines are based on work done at Yale University [21]. We discuss these two phases in detail in the next two subsections.

After update-in-place analysis, we invoke a parallellizer called IF2PART to define the desired granularity of parallelism. The analysis is based on estimates of execution time and other parameters. The user can change these parameters at compile time to have some control over the parallelization. Currently, IF2PART selects only **for** expressions and stream producers and consumers for parallel execution. Only **for** expressions with estimated costs greater than a threshold and nested no deeper than a defined parallel nesting level (the default being all levels) are selected. We do not exploit function-level parallelism because our experience has shown that most nonparallel functions are too small to justify the overhead of task creation and synchronization. Note that a function's parallel subtasks (namely, the included **for** expressions and stream producers and consumers) will be selected for parallel execution. IF2PART is a simplification of work by Sarkar [42]. Many experiments and possible elaborations await future work, especially as we target more unusual architectures.

In the last phase, CGEN translates the optimized IF2 graphs into C code, which is then compiled using the local C compiler to produce an executable program. Preprocessor directives provide the definition of target-dependent operations and values. Library software, linked during this phase of compilation, provides support for parallel execution, storage management, and interaction with the user. We chose C as an intermediate form to shorten development time, increase system portability, and allow experimentation with future optimizations by manual editing. However, the quality of the available C compiler can limit overall performance; hence, for the Sequent Balance we wrote a simple machine-dependent optimizer, which works at the assembly language level, to improve register utilization and reduce code size.

3.1. Build-in-Place Analysis

This optimization, IF2MEM, attacks the incremental construction problem introduced in the previous section. The algorithm is two-pass in nature. Pass 1 visits nodes in dataflow order and builds, where possible, expressions to calculate array sizes at run time. These expressions are IF1 code fragments; they are inserted in the graphs before the nodes producing the arrays whose sizes they define. We call these nodes **potential AT-nodes**. Their definition is a function of the semantics of the array constructor and the size expressions of its inputs. Determining the size of an array built during loop execution requires an expression to calculate the number of loop iterations before the loop executes. Deriving this expression is not possible for all loops. The final function of pass 1 is to push, in the order of encounter, the **potential AT-nodes** onto an **AT-node** conversion stack. This stack drives the second pass of the algorithm.

Pass 2, considering only **potential AT-nodes**, inserts nodes for memory preallocation and manipulation, converts the **potential AT-nodes** to **AT-nodes**, and appropriately wires memory references among them (inserting edges transmitting pointers to memory). If the node under consideration is the parent of an already converted node, it can build its result directly into the memory allocated to its child, thus eliminating the intermediate array. If the node is not the parent of an already converted node, it must build its result in a "new" memory location. Note that the ordering of nodes in the **AT-node** stack guarantees processing of children before parents. As a final responsibility, pass 2 must add **P** mark pragmas (edge annotations) to those edges carrying arrays built in place. These annotations specify that arguments to array constructors were built in place.

Consider the Sisal expression

```
A || array_fill (1,N,0)
```

and its unoptimized IF1 graph

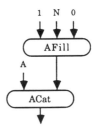

Figure 4 is the result of applying IF2MEM to the expression (assuming $N \geqslant 1$). In pass 1, the **AFill** node and then the **ACat** node are assigned size expressions and pushed onto the **AT-node** conversion stack. The two size expressions are N and $array\_size(A) + N$, respectively. In pass 2, the nodes are considered in reverse order. Because it is not the parent of an **AT-node**, the **ACat** node requires new memory. IF2MEM builds a graph fragment to allocate this memory (using **ACat**'s size expression), changes the **ACat** node into an **ACatAT** node, and builds an edge from the graph fragment to the node. Next, the **AFill** is popped from the **AT-node** conversion stack. Since it is now the parent of an **AT-node** child (the **ACatAT** node), IF2MEM does not build a fragment to allocate storage for its result, but instead builds a code fragment to derive the location of its result in the storage already allocated to its child. The fragment shifts the base address of the storage by the size expression associated with the first input to the **ACatAT** node: $array\_size(A)$.

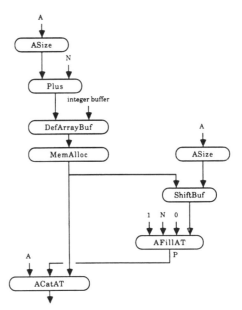

FIG. 4. Optimized IF2 graph for memory preallocation.

Pass 2 completes by converting **AFill** to **AFillAT**, wiring a reference from the shifted address to the node, and placing a **P** mark on the edge linking the converted nodes (communicating that the **AFillAT** node built its result in-place).

3.2. Update-in-Place Analysis

This optimization, IF2UP, attacks the aggregate update problem introduced in the previous section. Also, it serves to enhance the build-in-place analysis described above. That is, IF2UP treats an array as two separately reference counted objects: a dope vector defining the array's logical extent and the physical space containing its constituents. IF2MEM only produces IF2 computations to preallocate physical space and direct the placement of constituents; it does not preallocate dope vectors or optimize their access. As subcomputations place constituents in the preallocated memory, dope vectors cycle between dependent nodes to communicate the current status of the regions under construction. As a result, multiple dope vectors may reference the same or different regions of the physical space and the individual participants in the construction will produce new dope vectors to communicate the current status of the regions to their predecessors. Without update-in-place optimization, each stage in construction will copy a dope vector.

As an additional benefit, IF2UP eliminates most reference count operations. Reference counting can be a source of wasted computer time and parallel bottlenecks [37]. A prototype reference count eliminator developed at LLNL on the average elminated 67% of reference count operations in Sisal programs while opting, as a priority, to preserve parallelism among operations [46]. In contrast, IF2UP eliminates up to 98% of explicit reference counting in larger programs, ordering nodes using artificial dependence edges without regard for lost parallelism [8]. In practice this loss in parallelism potential has been small and of no effect in current implementations [10]. As a result, the inefficiencies of reference counting largely disappear, but the mechanism is preserved. Moreover, the few remaining occurrences do not merit special hardware support.

IF2UP also recognizes single-consumer streams to allow generation of support code with fewer critical sections. This is important because, in the most general instance, a stream may be the result of catenating many streams, each with its own producer, and there may be many consumers of the entire stream or substreams. The run time support for such an object is extensive. Elements are in linked lists attached to stream control blocks that are themselves linked because of catenation operations, and each stream element needs a reference count since there are multiple consumers. However, programmers usually do not use concatenation to form streams, and most streams have only one consumer. Here a simple circular buffer with minimal synchronization between the producer and the consumer suffices.

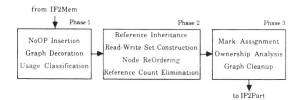

FIG. 5. The internal operation of IF2Up.

Figure 5 diagrams the internal operation of IF2UP. It takes as input an IF2 program and produces a semantically equivalent IF2 program. Phase 1 (subphases 1, 2, and 3) prepares each graph in the program for analysis. Phase 2 (subphases 4, 5, 6, and 7) eliminates unnecessary reference count operations. Phase 3 (subphases 8, 9, and 10) eliminates unnecessary copy operations and identifies single-consumer streams. The subphases operate as follows:

1. **NoOp** *insertion.* Here we simply insert **NoOp** nodes (data duplicators) to decouple copy logic from all nodes modifying aggregates. This isolates copying to a single node type to simplify later analysis. After this subphase, all modifiers work in place and the inserted **NoOps** unconditionally copy the consumed aggregates. The goal of the remaining subphases is to identify the unnecessary **NoOp** nodes.

2. *Graph decoration.* This subphase annotates edges transmitting aggregates with pragmas that explicitly express a program's worst-case reference count behavior. The assignments naively assume that all nodes will execute in parallel, which requires that all consumers reference count their inputs. The three reference count pragmas of interest are **sr** for setting counts, **pm** for incrementing counts, and **cm** for decrementing counts.

3. *Usage classification.* Here we classify each edge transmitting aggregates as either write or read depending on destination node semantics and port of entry. A write-classified edge, in contrast to a read-classified edge, transmits aggregates destined for in-place modification (provided conditions guarantee correctness) or placement within other aggregates. This subphase assigns **W** marks to write-classified edges and leaves read-classified edges unmarked. To classify usage across graph boundaries, we examine functions in topological order and traverse graphs bottom up. This allows classification of actual arguments based on formal argument classifications and classification of compound node inputs based on subgraph usages.

Consider the Sisal function

```
type TwoDim = array[array[integer]];
function Main (i,j: integer; A: TwoDim
              returns TwoDim, integer)
  A[i,j: 0.0], A[j,i]
end function
```

211

and its unoptimized IF1 graph

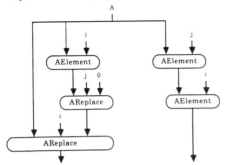

Without optimization, both replace operations might require copying. Figure 6 shows the program graph after the first three subphases. Subphase 1 inserted two **NoOp** nodes and

marked the replace operations to execute in place, as indicated by the **RO** marks. Subphase 2 annotated the graph with the **pm, cm**, and **sr** pragmas. Subphase 3 marked the edges carrying aggregates to write operations with the **W** marks.

4. *Reference inheritance.* This subphase eliminates implicit reference counting[2] where safe, to improve run time opportunities for copy avoidance when modifying inner dimensions of nested arrays. In unoptimized form, a replacement operation implicitly decrements the reference count of the constituent it replaces (assuming the constituent is an aggregate). However, preserving this constituent until the

---

[2] Implicit reference count operations are implicit in the management of nested aggregates and are not explicitly represented in the program graph.

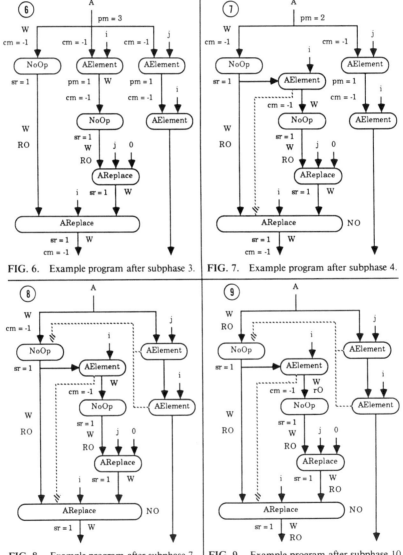

FIG. 6. Example program after subphase 3.

FIG. 7. Example program after subphase 4.

FIG. 8. Example program after subphase 7.

FIG. 9. Example program after subphase 10.

time of replacement can sometimes cause copying. During reference inheritance we restructure some replacement operations to give the implicit references to operations working on the replaced constituents.

5. *Read–write set construction.* Here to simplify the remaining subphases in phase 2, we build sets summarizing the usage of aggregates and their constituents. For each aggregate output of a node we build a local read and write set pair. The former identifies the read-classified edges attached to the output and the latter identifies the write-classified edges attached to the output. Then for each aggregate output that is either not the result of a dereference node or part of a reference inheritance transformation, we build a global read and write set pair. A global read set identifies both the output's immediate read-classified references and those of its constituents. Similarly, a global write set identifies both the output's write-classified references and those of its constituents.

6. *Node reordering.* This subphase defines a new partial ordering that maximizes opportunities for reference count and copy elimination without violating the original data dependencies. Where possible, we insert artificial dependence edges, without concern for lost parallelism, to force readers of an aggregate and its constituents to execute before modifiers of the aggregate and its constituents. The previously allocated global read and write sets drive this subphase of analysis.

7. *Reference count elimination.* This subphase proceeds in two independent steps. The first, called *phantom elimination,* eliminates reference counting that unnecessarily preserves aggregates across graph boundaries—we need only preserve aggregates imported to two or more graphs. The second, called *edge neutralization,* eliminates reference count pragmas on inputs to some read operations on the basis of the execution order derived during node reordering. As in the previous subphase, this step is a function of the usage sets. Consider node **R** that reads aggregate **A** transmitted by edge **E**. The analyzer removes the **cm** pragma annotating **E** if an artificial dependence edge occurs between **R** and a member of **A**'s local write set. It also erases the pragma if an artificial dependence edge occurs between **R** and all members of **A**'s global write set. If **A**'s global write set is empty, then **A** is, or is part of, a read only aggregate and does not require reference counting. In removing **E**'s **cm** pragma, the analyzer decrements the value associated with its antagonistic **pm** or **sr** pragma.

To continue the example begun above, Figs. 7 and 8 show the program graph after reference inheritance and the remaining subphases of phase 2, respectively. The dashed arrows represent artificial dependence edges. The **NO** pragma on the outermost **AReplace** node instructs it not to decrement the reference count of the replaced row. Analysis gave this reference to the **AElement** node dereferencing the *i*th

row to improve the chances for in-place modification of the row at run time.

8. *Mark assignment.* Here we assign mark pragmas defining data access rights and drive them across graph boundaries and through function graphs and subgraphs of compound nodes. Intuitively, this subphase partially interprets a reference count optimized program, not to realize execution, but to derive information about aggregate mutability and appropriately record it in the graphs. We use **R** marks to annotate edges known to transmit *mutable* aggregates and **r** marks to annotate edges known to transmit *potentially mutable* aggregates. In the case of arrays and streams, the **R** and **r** marks apply only to dope vectors. We use **O** marks to annotate edges known to transmit arrays with mutable physical space and streams with a single consumer. We use **unknown** marks to annotate edges known to transmit *immutable* data; this is equivalent to unmarked edges.

This phase of the optimization begins at the program entry point and visits all nodes in dataflow order. All call paths are followed except those that form a cycle. The assigned marks are a function of an edge's reference count pragmas, source node semantics, and source node input marks. With regard to functions, if two or more call sites propagate different marks to the same formal argument, we label the callee *unstable.* After examining all call paths to an unstable function entry point, we remark the arguments causing the instability with **r** marks. The analyzer handles **for initial** expressions similarly; it remarks with an **r** any loop-carried value whose initial mark is different from the mark assigned by the redefinition of the value in the body. We assume that arguments to the main function from the outside world are mutable. Note that for simplicity, this subphase of analysis assumes that physical space of an array or stream dereferenced from another aggregate is immutable.

9. *Ownership analysis.* This subphase attempts to compensate for the previous phases' inability to assign **O** marks to edges transmitting extracted arrays or streams. Further, this subphase identifies streams with single consumers. In the current implementation, however, the analysis is conservative. This subphase only assigns an **O** mark to an array if it can assign it to all arrays in the program. Similarly, it only identifies a stream as having a single consumer if it can identify that all streams in the program have single consumers. To assign **O** marks to all arrays in a program, the analyzer attempts to verify that during execution the reference count of each array's physical space will remain at one. Because this is a function of dope vector copying, which is the only means of incrementing physical space reference counts, the analyzer need only analyze the marks assigned to **NoOp** nodes. If those that copy only dope vectors have input edges with **R** marks, then all arrays in the program will have mutable physical space at run time. Similar analysis identifies single-consumer streams.

10. *Graph cleanup.* This subphase simply removes **cm** pragmas annotating the inputs of unnecessary **NoOp** nodes.

Completing our example, Fig. 9 shows the final program graph. Because the outermost **NoOp** is now the final consumer of **A**, it is marked to execute in place (the **RO** pragma). On the other hand, because of the possibility of row sharing, subphases 8 and 9 marked the innermost **NoOp** for run time copy avoidance (the **rO** mark).

3.3. Code Generation

CGEN translates optimized IF2 graphs into C code. With two exceptions, each IF2 function graph is directly mapped into an equivalent C function. The first exception concerns the **for** expressions selected for parallel execution by IF2PART. Here CGEN removes each selected expression from its enclosing computation, leaving in its place a run time system call to instantiate its parallel execution. The body of each expression is then compiled into a generic function, which takes iteration bounds as arguments. The second exception concerns expressions that produce and consume streams. CGEN also removes these expression from their enclosing computations, leaving run time system calls to instantiate their parallel execution. The compiler then packages them as separate functions. In both of the above cases, synchronization primitives are added to coordinate parallel execution.

It is the responsibility of CGEN to recognize the pragmas inserted during IF2 optimization and generate the appropriate code. Reference count operations, where required, are compiled directly into the resulting C code. Memory preallocation operations are compiled into dynamic storage allocation requests and pointer manipulations.

4. THE RUN TIME SYSTEM

The run time software supports the parallel execution of Sisal programs, provides general-purpose dynamic storage allocation, implements operations on major data structures, and interfaces with the operating system for input/output and command line processing. The system was first described in [33] and considerable evolution has since occurred.

Sisal run time support makes modest demands of the host operating system. Support for parallel execution is in the form of threads or lightweight processes (similar to those provided by the Mach operating system [3]). The run time system maintains two queues of executable tasks: the *Ready List* and the *For Pool*. Execution begins at the function *Main*. At program initiation, run time options and the formal parameters of *Main* are read from the command line. For nonstream values, inputs are read at initiation and results are written at termination in Fibre format [44], a text form that describes scalar and structured Sisal values. For stream parameters and results, associations are made with files, and special stream producing (input) and consuming (output)

threads are added to the *Ready List* for processing during execution. The run time system allocates stacks for threads on demand, but every effort is made to reuse previously allocated stacks and thus reduce allocation and deallocation overhead. Stack overflow is not monitored, however, and can result in program termination. The programmer can use a run time option to adjust stack size when anticipating overflow. The weakness of Sisal input/output is in the construction of simple interactive Sisal programs; solutions are under investigation.

4.1. Threads

At program initiation a command line option specifies the number of operating system processes to be instantiated for the duration of the program. These processes, called workers, are constant in number and look for work to do in the form of threads, whose number varies over the program's execution. While general-purpose thread support is available from other sources (see [7], for example), our thread management subsystem is optimized for Sisal and does not rely on vendor-supplied software.

Figures 10, 11, and 12 show the various activities a worker may engage in as it seeks work provided by Sisal execution and identify the major data structures needed to support parallel execution. A worker persists in one of three modes of operation, depending on whether it has recently handled *For* work, *Ready List* work, or is idle because neither kind of work is available.

4.1.1. *For Pool Threads*

A worker examines the *For Pool* for a piece of a **for** expression to execute. A "**for** slice" (one or more consecutive **for** bodies) is obtained and the thread stack already held by the worker is used to execute the code for the slice. Now one of three events can occur:

1. The slice may terminate normally. If the slices of this **for** expression are depleted, the worker places the thread in which the **for** expression occurs on the *Ready List* and returns to the *For Pool*; otherwise, the worker returns to the *For Pool* for another slice of the expression. By persisting in executing **for** slices, a worker avoids deallocating and allocating stacks in which to execute.

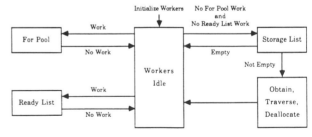

FIG. 10. Worker's state diagram.

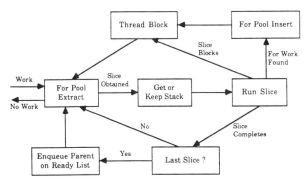

FIG. 11.   For pool state diagram.

2. More work (a nested **for** expression) may be encountered. A new entry is made in the *For Pool,* containing these values:

    a. the address of the loop,
    b. the initial lower bound,
    c. the upper bound,
    d. the size of the **for** slice, and
    e. the address of the descriptor for the thread in which the **for** expression occurs.

Depending on a compile time option, the size of the **for** slice is either constant or specified by "guided self-scheduling" [40]. The original **for** expression becomes a blocked thread to be reactivated when the new **for** expression completes.

3. The slice may block because dynamic storage is unavailable, in which case the slice becomes a blocked thread and the worker returns to the *For Pool* for more work.

4.1.2. *Ready List Threads*

Threads appear on the *Ready List* as a result of being made executable by other events. A **for** expression may complete, enabling the thread in which it appears to become runnable, or storage may become available, enabling a thread that blocked due to lack of storage to run. At program initiation, a single thread for the main function is placed on the *Ready List.* All *Ready List* entries have allocated thread stacks attached, so a worker in this mode of processing does not need its own stack. Upon obtaining a thread, execution begins. Once again, three events are possible:

1. If the thread terminates normally, the worker checks the parent context thread to see if it is waiting only for this thread to complete. If it is, the worker places the parent thread on the *Ready List,* deallocates the obsolete stack, and returns to the *Ready List* for more work; otherwise, it deallocates the obsolete stack and returns to the *Ready List.*

2. A **for** expression may be encountered. The worker handles it in a fashion similar to that of *For Pool* processing. Note that the worker must return to the *Ready List* for more work since it has no stack of its own.

3. The thread may block, in which case the worker returns to the *Ready List* for more work.

4.1.3. *Overlapped Storage Deallocation*

If a worker in either of the preceding modes finds no work to do, it returns to the central state shown in Fig. 10. If neither *For Pool* nor *Ready List* threads are available, the worker examines the *Storage Deallocation List* for deferred storage deallocation work. This list has entries for hierarchically structured aggregates, such as multidimensional arrays, which are no longer in use. If these structures were deallocated as soon as they were not needed, we could potentially introduce sequential code sections in parallel constructs, degrading parallelism. See [9] for an example of this phenomenon. Moreover, by deferring the traversal and deallocation of hierarchically structured aggregates, a program may complete without doing it at all. If unavailable storage idles enough threads, at least one worker will eventually idle and deallocate the needed space. Currently, overlapped storage deallocation is not implemented.

4.2.   Storage Management

Sisal relies on dynamic storage allocation for many data values, such as arrays and streams, and for internal objects, such as thread descriptors and execution stacks. To support this, we needed a mechanism that was fast, efficient, and parallelizable. A two-level method that has proven satisfactory evolved.

4.2.1.   *Parallel Boundary Tag Method*

The standard boundary tag scheme [22] was augmented with multiple entry points to a circular list of free blocks. We have an array of pointers, each addressing a zero-size free block on the list. A worker selects a pointer on the basis of its own integer identifier, thereby spreading list entry contention across the array. The free list search was parallelized, even though blocks are sometimes completely removed from

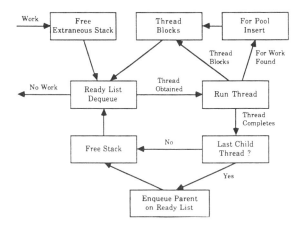

FIG. 12.   Ready list state diagram.

the list. Likewise, deallocation involves coalescing physically adjacent but logically distant blocks in parallel.

4.2.2. *Exact Fit Caching Using Working Sets*

To increase the speed of allocation and deallocation, an exact fit caching mechanism was interposed before the boundary tag scheme for most storage operations [34]. It uses a working set of different sizes of recently freed blocks (blocks of the same size are chained in a sublist). As in the working set method for virtual memory management [14], a "clock" which ticks at each allocation is compared with a time stamp stored when each size is allocated or deallocated. This occurs as an allocation request looks for an exact fit and finds a mismatch. If a size is too "old" (the definition of "old" is a run time option), all blocks in the sublist are recycled to the boundary tag pool. If an exact fit is found, that block is unlinked, and the time stamp is updated in the new first sublist block. If this was the only block of this size, the list of differently sized blocks reduces in size by one. If no exact fit is found, an allocation occurs from the boundary tag pool. Our first implementation used a single, shared exact-fit cache for all workers. To eliminate synchronization overhead, each worker now has its own cache. This results in faster execution, but can cause exact-fit misses if the size desired is in another worker's cache.

4.2.3. Storage Deadlock

Contention among threads for dynamically allocated storage is the only source of possible deadlock in Sisal. A thread that cannot obtain needed storage becomes blocked and is reactivated when later deallocations occur. The last worker to become idle because there is no work to do checks for the presence of threads blocked for storage. It empties all the exact-fit caches to maximize boundary tag coalescing and seeks one or more threads to place on the *Ready List*. If this fails, the program stops with a deadlock message. A run time option specifies the total amount of storage to manage, and a larger value usually solves the problem.

4.3. Run Time Support for Arrays

Arrays in Sisal are one-dimensional data values of elements of the same type. Our implementation places elements in contiguous, dynamically allocated storage, sometimes followed by space for dynamic growth. Arrays are strict in this implementation; a thread containing a **for** expression that produces an array blocks until that expression has been pro-

cessed. Since arrays are dynamic in size, bookkeeping information is kept in a *dope vector:*

# of elements	Pointer to physical space	Pointer to first element	Reference Count

Multidimensional arrays are arrays of dope vectors pointing to other such arrays; the last dimension is a one-dimensional array of base type. The layout of the physical space is

# of bytes	Reference Count	Expansion Count	Size of free space	Array elements	Free space

Both the dope vector and the physical space require reference counts because more than one thread may have access to the dope vector and more than one dope vector may point to the physical space (subarrays of the original). In Section 2 we explained that arrays can grow during execution. Although build-in-place analysis can compute the final size of most arrays and preallocate storage, in those cases where it cannot, we reduce copying by allocating *free space*. The size of the extra storage is the product of a run time option value and the number of times the array has been copied owing to expansion.

4.4. Run Time Support for Streams

In Sisal streams must be nonstrict. Typically an iteration produces values, and another iteration consumes them. As already mentioned, to implement parallelism, stream producing and consuming iterations are packaged by the Sisal compiler as sequential loops in separate threads. They are instantiated with stacks and placed on the *Ready List* for processing by workers. If a consumer thread attempts to use a value not yet produced, it blocks. Likewise, to prevent excessive consumption of memory, a producer thread blocks if it gets some number of elements ahead of the slowest consumer. To prevent continuous blocking and unblocking, producers and consumers awake only after some number of values have been consumed or produced, respectively; these numbers are run time options with defaults.

In the most general case, a stream value may be a concatenation of many constituent streams, each with its own producer thread and one or more consumer threads operating at different points in the overall value. The implementation is complex. A stream has a descriptor with an attached list of extant values. Descriptor components are

Pointer to producer thread	# of living consumer threads	Pointers to first and last blocked consumer threads	
Pointers to first and last extant elements	# extant elements	EOS Signal	Link to next descriptor in concatenation

The attached elements each require a reference count since all consumers must see all elements. The cells for all stream elements in a Sisal program come from a special pool, not from general-purpose dynamic storage. All element types can be accommodated because nonscalar values are pointers to dynamic storage throughout the implementation.

IF2UP analyzes a program using streams to decide if a stream has a single consumer and is not a concatenation of substreams. Under these conditions (which are almost always true) we use a much simpler structure—a fixed-size circular buffer. No reference counts are needed, and synchronization is simple and minimal. As expected, this organization yields performance superior to that of the general version.

5. PERFORMANCE RESULTS

To evaluate the current status of Sisal, we compared the execution performance of equivalent Sisal and Fortran versions of the Livermore Loops and four large scientific programs on a Sequent Balance 21000. The four scientific programs were Gauss–Jordan elimination with full pivoting, RICARD, SIMPLE, and an instance of parallel simulated annealing. Four of the five Sisal codes ran as fast as the equivalent Fortran codes on one processor, and all five Sisal codes achieved good speedup. Note that we did not have to rewrite or recompile the Sisal codes to run on multiple processors; we simply increased the number of participating workers at run time. IF2MEM preallocated all arrays and built all but five in place. IF2UP eliminated all absolute copy operations, marked 29 copy operations for run time check, and eliminated approximately 97% of the reference count operations.

Table IV shows the performance results for the 24 Livermore Loops. Column 2 indicates whether the Sisal loop was parallel or sequential, and columns 3–5 give the execution performance in KFlops for the Fortran loops on one processor and the Sisal loops on one and five processors. Table V lists the execution times of the other four applications. Table VI gives compilation statistics for each program. Columns 2–4 give the number of static arrays built, preallocated, and built in-place; columns 5 and 6 list the number of copy and reference count operations before optimization; and columns 7–10 list the number of copy, conditional copy, and reference count operations after optimization and the number of artificial dependency edges introduced by IF2UP.

5.1. The Livermore Loops

The Livermore Loops [30] are a set of 24 scientific kernels from production codes run at Lawrence Livermore National Laboratory. For many years scientists have used the Loops to benchmark high-performance computers. The speed of a parallel computer is a function of the system's hardware, communication topology, operating system, compilers, and the computational nature of the test suite. The Livermore

TABLE IV
Execution Performance of the Livermore Loops (in kflops)

Loop	P/S	Fortran	Sisal (1)	Sisal (5)	Speedup
1	P	70	77	331	4.3
2	S	58	59		
3	P	54	70	279	4.0
4	P	42	41		Too little parallel work
5	S	49	50		
6	P	50	69		Too little parallel work
7	P	88	83	393	4.7
8	P	36	55	194	3.5
9	P	85	74	255	3.4
10	P	45	25	73	2.9
11	S	37	45		
12	P	37	34	131	3.8
13	S	12	15		
14	P	28	37	94	2.5
15	P	59	54	244	4.5
16	P	75	30	89	3.0
17	S	53	46		
18	P	77	60	241	4.0
19	S	45	51		
20	S	86	90		
21	P	56	55	240	4.3
22	P	46	44	173	3.8
23	S	74	66		
24	P	50	28	101	3.6

Loops encompass a variety of computational structures, including independent parallel processes, recurrent processes, wavefronts, and pipelines [17]. As such, the Loops are an appropriate benchmark suite for parallel computers.

We ran the Fortran Loops without change, but we wrote the Sisal to reflect the computational nature of each loop (see [16] for an early version of the Sisal Loops). We wrote parallel algorithms unless input size was too small to justify parallel execution, or the parallel algorithm increased the number of computations to an extent not warranted by the input size or the hardware parameters of the Sequent Balance. We converted operations from column order to row order to compensate for the lack of true rectangular arrays in Sisal. For accurate measurement of both the Sisal and the Fortran codes, we executed each loop 300 times, except for Loop 4, which was so thin that we executed it 4000 times. On one processor, the harmonic mean of the Fortran and Sisal versions of the Loops were 45 and 44 KFlops, respectively.

5.1.1. *The Sequential Loops*

Discrepancies in the execution times of the Sisal and Fortran version of the sequential loops were due primarily to common subexpression removal, loop invariant removal, register allocation, paging, and the storage of multidimensional arrays in Sisal as arrays of arrays. The latter prevents fast column access and increases the cost of array allocation and deallocation.

For Loops 4 and 6 we wrote Sisal routines that were maximally parallel, but still, IF2PART instructed the code generator not to slice the **for** expressions—the overhead of loop slicing could not be recovered by the parallel execution of the loop bodies. Loops 2 and 23 are recursive array definitions. As we explained before, Sisal does not permit such expressions. Although it is possible to write Sisal versions of both loops that do demonstrate some parallelism (see [16]), we did not do so for three reasons. First, the parallel algorithms are not natural. Second, the amount of parallel work is small—in Loop 23 the maximum number of concurrent operations is seven. Third, given a nonstrict implementation, both the parallel and the sequential versions would realize maximum parallelism.

We wrote two versions of Loops 5, 11, and 19: a sequential version and a version based on the method of recursive doubling [23, 24]. Although the latter introduces some parallelism, it increases the number of computations from $O(n)$ to $O(n \log n)$. In trial runs, the recursive doubling codes ran much slower than the sequential codes, regardless of the number of participating processors. However, they did achieve good speedup. Sisal's implementation of recursive doubling requires array concatenations and subarray selections. The compiler was able to preallocate memory for the former, but was not able to build all sections of the arrays in place (thus introducing copying). We are not sure whether the degradation in execution times resulted from the copying or the extra computations; however, it is our general impression that recursive doubling on medium-grain and coarse-grain shared-memory multiprocessors is not an appropriate technique.

5.1.2. *The Parallel Loops*

Despite incurring the overhead of parallel constructs, the Sisal implementations of the parallel loops (with the exception of Loops 10, 16, and 24) produced kiloflop rates equivalent to or better than Fortran on one processor. The discrepancies in performance were primarily the result of common subexpression elimination, loop invariant removal, register allocation, and paging. Loop 10 is an extreme example of the effects of register allocation on performance.

TABLE V

Execution Times for Four Large Scientific Programs

Program	Fortran	Sisal (1)	Sisal (processors)	Speedup
GJ	54.0 s	54.5 s	8.8 s (10)	6.2
RICARD	30.63 h	31.00 h	3.45 h (10)	9.0
SIMPLE	3081.3 s	3099.3 s	422.0 s (10)	7.3
PSA	476.6 s	956.2 s	267.8 s (5)	3.6

On a single processor, the Sisal version of Loop 16 executed 60% slower than that of Fortran. This Loop searches for a particle in a two-dimensional grid of zones subdivided into groups. The Fortran code sequentially searches each group, one at a time, and quits as soon as it finds the particle. The Sisal version examines all the groups in parallel. Since Sisal does not support asynchronous broadcasts, the processor that finds the particle cannot broadcast the discovery and stop the other processors. Consequently, the Sisal code searches the entire space. The lack of asynchronous broadcasts is a characteristic of determinate languages. Another reason for the poor performance is that the Fortran code includes a large number of *arithmetic ifs*. Each **if** statement compiles to a single comparison and a jump on a condition bit. The equivalent Sisal expression

```
if ... elseif ... else ... end if
```

compiles to two comparisons and two jump instructions.

On one processor, the Sisal implementation of Loop 24 executed 44% slower than that of Fortran. This Loop returns the first location of the minimum value in an array. The Fortran and Sisal codes are, respectively,

```
loc := 1
do 24 k = 2, n
24    if ( X ( k ) .lt. X ( loc ) ) loc = k
```

and

```
let
  min := for i in 1, n
           returns value of least X[i]
         end for;
in for i in 1, n
     returns value of least i when X[i] = min
   end for
end for
```

The Fortran code executes only $(n - 1)$ comparisons, but the Sisal algorithm executes $3n$ comparisons. Sisal's limited repertoire of reduction operations and lack of user-defined reductions prevented use of a single expression.

Eight of the sixteen parallel loops achieved speedups of 3.8 or better. Loops 9, 10, 16, and 24 achieved smaller speedups because of insufficient parallel work. Loop 14 comprises two loops, one parallel and one sequential. The parallel loop showed good speedup, but the sequential loop amortized the gains. Despite considerable parallel work Loop 8 achieved a speedup of only 3.5. We observed that the loop spent considerable time building and recycling arrays, which idled processors. Loop 8 manipulates three-dimensional arrays which are built and recycled one dimension at a time. Although the memory subsystem can handle simultaneous

TABLE VI

Compilation Statistics

Programs	Arrays			Before Opt		After Opt			
	Built	PreA	In	Copy	RefC	Copy	Copy	RefC	ADE
Loops	76	76	76	39	1565	0	0	43	114
GJ	7	7	7	5	118	0	0	1	9
RICARD	29	29	28	17	207	0	6	7	5
SIMPLE	261	261	261	214	2066	0	19	61	347
PSA	46	46	42	18	696	0	4	41	168

requests, some sections require atomic access to shared data limiting the loop's potential parallelism. We saw the same effect, but to a smaller degree, in Loops 15 and 18, which manipulate two-dimensional arrays.

5.2. The Other Applications

5.2.1. Gauss–Jordan Elimination

Gauss–Jordan elimination with full pivoting solves a set of linear equations of the form

$$Ax = B,$$

where A is an $n \times n$ matrix and x and B are $n \times 1$ column vectors. The algorithm comprises n iterative steps. At each step, the largest element in a previously unselected row is found and moved onto the major diagonal. Say the element is found at position (i, j); then the element is moved onto the diagonal by interchanging rows i and j. In the new matrix, row j is the pivot row and $A(j, j)$ is the pivot element. After the interchange, A and B are reduced by the pivot row. The reduction is a parallel operation of $O(n^2)$.

IF2MEM preallocated and built all arrays in place. IF2UP eliminated all copy operations and all but one reference count operation. For $n = 100$, the execution times of the Sisal and Fortran versions on one processor were equivalent. On 10 processors, the Sisal code achieved a speedup of 6.2. Although both phases of a step (finding the pivot element and reducing the matrix) are parallel, neither phase is computationally intensive. In our implementation sequential work accounted for 6% of the execution time, which is enough to limit speedup on 10 processors to at most 6.4.

5.2.2. RICARD

RICARD [11] simulates experimentally observed elution patterns of proteins and ligands in a column of gel by numerical solution of a set of simultaneous second-order partial differential continuity equations. As the system evolves over time, the protein concentrations at the bottom of the column are sampled to construct the elution patterns. At each time step, the program calculates the change in protein concen-

trations at each level of the column due to, first, chromatography and, then, chemical reaction. The new values serve as the initial conditions for the next time step. The computations during the chromatography step are data independent, whereas the computations of the chemical reaction phase are independent across levels and dependent across proteins. Since the independent tasks are computationally intensive, the program should achieve near linear speedup on medium- and course-grain machines.

Osc preallocated memory for all the arrays, and built all but one of the arrays in place. The one array not built in place was constructed during program initialization, thus the copying was inconsequential. IF2UP eliminated all absolute copy operations, marked six copy operations for run time check, and eliminated 97% of the reference count operations. The six conditional copy operations were introduced because of *row sharing*. In the current Sisal implementation, arrays may share common rows. When the shared rows are updated, they have to be copied, but once copied, the rows are unique and can be updated in place. In RICARD, the conditional copies executed only once each. For a 1315-level, five-protein problem, the execution times of the Sisal and Fortran programs on 1 processor differed by less than 2%. On 10 processors, the Sisal program achieved a speedup of 9.0.

5.2.3. SIMPLE

SIMPLE [13] is a two-dimensional Lagrangian hydrodynamics code developed at Lawrence Livermore National Laboratory that simulates the behavior of a fluid in a sphere. The hydrodynamic and heat conduction equations are solved by finite difference methods. A tabular ideal gas equation for determining the relation between state variables is provided. The implementation of SIMPLE in Sisal 1.2 is straightforward and exposes considerable parallel work.

IF2MEM preallocated and built all arrays in place (261 of them). IF2UP eliminated all absolute copy operations, marked 19 copy operations for run time check, and eliminated 2005 out of 2066 reference count operations. The 19 conditional copy operations were introduced because of row sharing. They executed only once each. For 62 iterations of a 100 × 100 grid problem, the Sisal and Fortran version of SIMPLE on 1 processor executed in 3099.3 and 3081.3 s, respectively. On 10 processors, the Sisal code realized a speedup of 7.3. Although the speedup of the Sisal code is good, it could be better. We are losing at least an equivalent of 1.5 processors in the allocation and deallocation of two-dimensional arrays. We noted the same phenomenon in some of the Livermore Loops that handled two- and three-dimensional arrays.

5.2.4. *Parallel Simulated Annealing*

Simulated annealing is a generic Monte Carlo optimization technique that has proven effective at solving many difficult combinatorial problems. In this study, we employed the method to solve the school timetable problem [1]. The objective is to assign a set of tuples to a fixed set of time slots (periods) such that no critical resource is scheduled more than once in any period. Each tuple is a record of four fields: class, room, subject, and teacher. Classes, rooms, and teachers are critical resources and subjects are not. At each step of the procedure, a tuple is chosen at random and moved to another period. If the new schedule has equivalent or lower cost, the move is accepted. If the new schedule has higher cost, the move is accepted with probability,

$$e^{(-\Delta C/T)},$$

where ΔC is the change in cost and T is a control parameter. If the move is not accepted, the tuple is returned to its original period. We parallelized the procedure by simultaneously choosing one tuple from each nonempty period and applying the move criterion to each. We then carried out the accepted moves one at a time. Note that more than one move may involve the same period.

IF2MEM preallocated memory for all the arrays and built all but 4 of the arrays in place. IF2UP removed all absolute copy operations, marked 4 copy operations for run time check, and removed all but 41 reference count operations. The 4 conditional copy operations were introduced because of the possibility of row sharing. In fact, there was no row sharing and no copying. The 4 arrays not built in place result from the expressions that add a tuple to a period. Since the old period is created on the previous iteration, the new period cannot be built in place. Although the compiler did not mark the new periods for build in place, the periods were rarely copied. This is because the Sisal run time system decouples the physical and logical sizes of arrays. If an element is removed from the high end of an array, the array's logical size shrinks by one (assuming the array can be shrunk in place), but its physical size remains constant; that is, the physical space is not released. When an element is added to the high end of an array, the run time system checks to see if there is space. If there is space, the element is added; if there is not space, the run time system allocates a new, larger space

and copies the array. Whenever the run time system allocates new space, it always allocates a few extra bytes to accommodate future growth. In the school timetable problem, the periods are continually growing and shrinking as tuples are removed and added. Our implementation of arrays saved over 15,000 copies at the cost of a few hundred bytes of storage.

For a problem size of (30 periods, 300 tuples, 10 classes, 10 rooms, 10 teachers), the Sisal program ran twice as slow as the Fortran program (956.2 s versus 476.6 s). The difference is due to the allocation and deallocation of data structures in the Sisal program on every iteration. However, it is a simple optimization (loop invariant removal) to save the structures and pass them to the next iteration. We expect that once this optimization is implemented, the Sisal and Fortran execution times will be comparable. The Sisal version did achieve a speedup of 3.6 on five processors. This is quite good given the fact that the update of the schedule is sequential.

6. FUTURE PLANS

In the next few years, we plan to

1. define and implement Sisal 2.0,
2. design SisalCity, a comprehensive programming environment, and
3. develop run time systems for conventional, distributed-memory multiprocessors.

Early in 1990 we expect to release Sisal 2.0, the first revision of the language since 1985. Over the past 5 years, we have gained much experience in implementing and using Sisal 1.2. In workshop after workshop, the applicative programming model has been proven effective. After a week students with little or no knowledge of applicative languages and with no knowledge of Sisal have designed, written, debugged, and run programs of more than 100 lines. However, we can still make Sisal easier to use, more expressive, and faster without compromising our objectives. Currently, the language lacks features found in other functional programming languages and has constructs that are clumsy or severely impact performance.

New features will include higher-order functions, user-defined reductions, parameterized data types, foreign language modules, and rectangular arrays. Higher-order functions and user-defined reductions will allow users to create functions and reduction operations tailored to their exact needs. In Loop 24, we saw the effects of not having user-defined reductions. We believe we can implement a flexible, but robust, interface to modules written in foreign languages [36]. This will give us access to existing mathematics and graphics libraries, an important advance in supporting scientific computations. Sisal 2.0 will support true multidimensional arrays stored in contiguous space. Implementing multidimensional arrays as arrays of arrays was our greatest single mistake. While we have found occasional use for "ragged" arrays (for example, as aggregates of dynamic sets), their disadvantages greatly outweigh their advantages: they prevent vectorization (constant stride exists between elements only in the last dimension), and deallocation requires complete traversal to decrement reference counts and recycle each component separately. Sisal 2.0 will include more extensive array operations such as vector operations, nonrectangular subarray selection, and a general array constructor that allows a set of expressions to contribute in parallel to parts of an array value. The physical space of a multidimensional array will contain only elements, so more efficient storage management will be possible.

Currently, we are designing a comprehensive programming environment for Sisal 2.0 based on X11 windows, called SisalCity. We will include tools to design, debug, and interpret Sisal 2.0 programs. An advantage of determinate functional programs is that if they run correctly on a uniprocessor, they are guaranteed to run correctly on any system regardless of resources or configuration. The environment will support a robust simulation package capable of simulating the logical performance of Sisal 2.0 programs on a variety of parallel architectures. In order to study the mapping problems, we will include different scheduling and partitioning heuristics. We will also design tools to collect and analyze actual performance data for certain target machines.

The run time system developed for Sisal 1.2 showed that conventional, shared-memory multiprocessors can support dataflow languages effectively. We plan to extend the run time system for conventional, distributed-memory machines with both local and global address spaces. We expect such machines to play an increasingly important role at the national laboratories. Note that our present system should port easily to the latter, providing us an important benchmark. Critical to our efforts will be efficient heuristics that map dataflow graphs (both tasks and data) to the resources of distributed machines.

ACKNOWLEDGMENTS

In a project of this size it is not possible to thank everyone; our apologizes to anyone we overlook. We acknowledge our collaborators, in particular, the groups at University of Manchester, Royal Melbourne Institute of Technology, Adelaide University, University of Southern California, Carnegie Mellon University, ETH Zurich, McGill University, and Syracuse University. Without their support and independent research, Sisal would not enjoy the large, worldwide user community it does today. Special thanks to Steve Skedzielewski, who led the Sisal research effort at Lawrence Livermore National Laboratory, Jim McGraw and Jon Ranelletti for their research contributions and support, and Don Austin of the Office of Energy Research (U.S. Department of Energy). We thank members of the Sisal research staff at Lawrence Livermore National Laboratory (Rea Simpson, Kim Yates, C. C. Lee, Patrick Miller, and David Zimmerman) and at Colorado State University (Tom Hanson, Tam Richert, and Seetharaman Harikrishnan).

This project was supported (in part) by the Office of Energy Research (U.S. Department of Energy) under Contract W-7405-Eng-48 to Lawrence Livermore National Laboratory and by the U.S. Army Research Office under Contract DAAL03-86-K-0101 to Colorado State University.

REFERENCES

1. Abramson, D. Using simulated annealing to solve school timetables: Serial and parallel algorithms. RMIT Tech. Rep. TR-112-069R, Royal Melbourne Institute of Technology, Melbourne, Australia, 1988.

2. Abramson, D., and Egan, G. K. An overview of the RMIT/CSIRO parallel system architecture project. *Austral. Comput. J.* **20**, 3 (Aug. 1988).

3. Accetta, M., *et al.* Mach: A new kernel foundation of Unix development. *Proc. USENIX 1986 Summer Conference.* USENIX, Atlanta, GA, 1986, pp. 93–112.

4. Ackerman, W. B., and Dennis, J. B. VAL—A value-oriented algorithmic language. MIT Tech. Rep. LCS/TR-218, MIT, Cambridge, MA, June 1979.

5. Aho, A. V., Sethi, R., and Ullman, J. D. *Compilers: Principles, Techniques, and Tools.* Addison–Wesley, Reading, MA, 1986.

6. Barth, J. M. An interprocedural dataflow analysis program. *Proc. 4th ACM Symposium of the Principles of Programming Languages,* ACM, 1978, pp. 119–131.

7. Bershad, E. D., and Levy, H. M. PRESTO: A system for object-oriented parallel programming. University of Washington Tech. Rep. 87-09-01, University of Washington, Seattle, WA, Jan. 1987.

8. Cann, D. C., and Oldehoeft, R. R. Reference count and copy elimination for parallel applicative computing. Colorado State University Tech. Rep. CS-88-129, Colorado State University, Fort Collins, CO, Nov. 1988.

9. Cann, D. C., and Oldehoeft, R. R. High performance parallel applicative computing. Colorado State University Tech. Rep. CS-89-104, Colorado State University, Fort Collins, CO, Feb. 1989.

10. Cann, D. C. Compilation techniques for high performance applicative computation. Ph.D. thesis, Department of Computer Science, Colorado State University, 1989.

11. Cann, J. R., *et al.* Small zone gel chromotography of interacting systems: Theoretical and experimental evaluation of elution profiles for kinetically controlled macromolecule–ligand reactions. *Anal. Biochem.* **175**, 2 (Dec. 1988), 462–473.

12. Cohen, J. Garbage collection of linked data structures. *ACM Comput. Surveys* **13**, 3 (Sept. 1981), 341–367.

13. Crowley, W. P., Hendrickson, C. P., and Rudy, T. E. The SIMPLE code. Lawrence Livermore National Laboratory Tech. Rep. UCID-17715, Lawrence Livermore National Laboratory, Livermore, CA, Feb. 1978.

14. Denning, P. J. The working set model for program behavior. *Comm. Appl. Math. Comput.* **11**, 5 (May 1968), 323–333.

15. Dennis, J. B. Mapping programs for data parallel execution on the Connection Machine, in preparation.

16. Feo, J. T. The Livermore Loops in Sisal. Lawrence Livermore National Laboratory Tech. Rep. UCID-21159, Lawrence Livermore National Laboratory, Livermore, CA, Aug. 1987.

17. Feo, J. T. An analysis of the computational and parallel complexity of the Livermore Loops. *Parallel Comput.* **8**, 7 (July 1988), 163–185.

18. Ferrante, J., Ottenstein, K. J., and Warren, J. D. The program dependence graph and its use in optimization. Michigan Technological University Tech. Rep. CS-TR-86-8, Michigan Technological University, Houghton, MI, Aug. 1986.

19. Gross, T., and Sussman, A. Mapping a single-assignment language onto the Warp systolic array. In Kahn, G. (Ed.). *Proc. Functional Programming Languages and Computer Architecture.* Springer-Verlag, Portland, OR, 1987, pp. 347–363.

20. Gurd, J. R., Kirkham, C. C., and Watson, I. The Manchester prototype dataflow computer. *Comm. Appl. Math. Comput.* **28**, 1 (Jan. 1985), 34–52.

21. Hudak, P., and Bloss, A. The aggregate update problem in functional programming systems. *Proc. 12th ACM Symposium on the Principles of Programming Languages.* ACM, New Orleans. LA, Jan. 1985, pp. 300–313.

22. Knuth, D. *The Art of Computer Programming: Fundamental Algorithms.* Addison–Wesley, Reading, MA, 1973, Vol. 1.

23. Kogge, H. S., and Stone, P. M. A parallel algorithm for the efficient solution of a general class of recurrence equations. *IEEE Trans. Comput.* C-22, 8 (Aug. 1973), 786–793.

24. Kogge, H. S. Parallel solution of recurrence problems. *IBM. J. Res. Develop.* **19**, 2 (Mar. 1975), 138–148.

25. Kuck, D. J., et al. Dependence graphs and compiler optimizations. *Proc. 8th ACM Symposium on the Principles of Programming Languages.* ACM, Williamsburg, VA, Jan. 1981, pp. 207–218.

26. Lee, C-C., Skedzielewski, S. K., and Feo, J. T. On the implementation of applicative languages on shared-memory, MIMD multiprocessors. *Proc. Parallel Programming: Environments, Applications, Language, and Systems Conference.* IEEE Computer Society, New Haven, CT, July 1988, pp. 188–197.

27. Lee, C-C. Experience of implementing applicative parallelism on Cray X/MP. *Proc. CONPAR '88.* British Computer Society, Manchester, England, Sept. 1988, pp. 19–25.

28. McGraw, J. R., et al. Sisal: Streams and iterations in a single-assignment language. In *Language Reference Manual, Version 1.1, Lawrence Livermore National Laboratory Manual M-146.* Lawrence Livermore National Laboratory, Livermore, CA, June 1983.

29. McGraw, J. R., et al. Sisal: Streams and iterations in a single-assignment language. *Language Reference Manual, Version 1.2. Lawrence Livermore National Laboratory Manual M-146 (Rev. 1).* Lawrence Livermore National Laboratory, Livermore, CA, Mar. 1985.

30. McMahon, F. H. Livermore fortran kernels: A computer test of the numerical performance range. Lawrence Livermore National Laboratory Tech. Rep. UCRL-53745, Lawrence Livermore National Laboratory, Livermore, CA, Dec. 1986.

31. Nikhil, R. S. *ID Reference Manual, Version 88.1.* Computation Structures Group Memo 284, Laboratory for Computer Science, MIT, Cambridge, MA, Aug. 1988.

32. Mitrovic, S. Personal communications.

33. Oldehoeft, R. R., and Allen, S. J. Execution support for HEP Sisal. In Kowalik, J. (Ed.). *Parallel MIMD Computation: The HEP Supercomputer and Its Applications.* MIT Press, Cambridge, MA, 1985, pp. 151–180.

34. Oldehoeft, R. R., and Allen, S. J. Adaptive exact-fit storage management. *Comm. Appl. Math. Comput.* **28**, 5 (May 1985), 506–511.

35. Oldehoeft, R. R., Cann, D. C., and Allen, S. J. Sisal: Initial MIMD performance results. *Proc. 1986 Conference on Algorithms and Hardware for Parallel Processing.* Aachen, Federal Republic of Germany, Sept. 1986, pp. 120–127.

36. Oldehoeft, R. R., and McGraw, J. R. Mixed applicative and imperative programs. Lawrence Livermore National Laboratory Tech. Rep. UCRL-96244, Lawrence Livermore National Laboratory, Livermore, CA, Feb. 1987.

37. Oldehoeft, R. R., and Cann, D. C. Applicative parallelism on a shared-memory multiprocessor. *IEEE Software* **5**, 1 (Jan. 1988), 62–70.

38. Padua, D., Kuck, D., and Lawrie, D. High-speed multiprocessors and compilation techniques. *IEEE Trans. Comput.* C-29, 9 (Sept. 1980), 763–776.

39. Padua, D., and Wolfe, M. Advanced compiler optimizations for supercomputers. *Comm. Appl. Math. Comput.* **29**, 12 (Dec. 1986), 1184–1201.

40. Polychronopoulos, C. D., and Kuck, D. J. Guided self-scheduling: A practical scheduling scheme for parallel supercomputers. *IEEE Trans. Comput.* C-36, 12 (Dec. 1987), 1425–1439.

41. Ranelletti, J. E. Graph transformation algorithms for array memory optimization in applicative languages. Ph.D. thesis, Department of Computer Science, University of California at Davis/Livermore, 1987.

42. Sarkar, V., and Hennessey, J. Compile-time partitioning and scheduling of parallel programs. *Proc. SIGPLAN 1986 Symposium on Compiler Construction.* ACM, Palo Alto, CA, June 1986, pp. 17–26.

43. Skedzielewski, S. K., and Glauert, J. *IF1—An Intermediate Form for Applicative Languages, Lawrence Livermore National Laboratory Manual M-170.* Lawrence Livermore National Laboratory, Livermore, CA, July 1985.

44. Skedzielewski, S. K., and Yates, R. K. *Fibre: An External Format for Sisal and IF1 Data Objects, Version 1.0, Lawrence Livermore National Laboratory Manual M-154.* Lawrence Livermore National Laboratory, Livermore, CA, Jan. 1985.

45. Skedzielewski, S. K., and Welcome, M. L. Dataflow graph optimization in IF1. In Jouannaud, J. P. (Ed.). *Functional Programming Languages and Computer Architectures.* Springer-Verlag, New York, 1985, pp. 17–34.

46. Skedzielewski, S. K., and Simpson, R. J. A simple method to remove reference counting in applicative programs. *Proc. ACM SIGPLAN '89 Conference on Programming Language Design and Implementation,* Portland, OR, June 1989.

47. Welcome, M. L., et al. IF2: An Applicative Language Intermediate Form with Explicit Memory Management. *Lawrence Livermore National Laboratory Manual M-195.* Lawrence Livermore National Laboratory, Livermore, CA, November 1986.

48. Wolfe, M. Automatic parallelism detection: What went wrong? *Proc. SRC Parallelism Packaging Workshop.* Supercomputing Research Center, Leesburg, VA, Apr. 1988.

JOHN T. FEO earned a B.A. in mathematics, physics, and astronomy at the University of Pennsylvania. He received an M.A. in astronomy and a Ph.D. in computer science at The University of Texas at Austin. He is currently the Acting Group Leader of the Computer Research Group at Lawrence Livermore National Laboratory. His research interests include parallel processing, applicative and functional programming, algorithms, and performance. Dr. Feo is a lecturer at the University of California, Davis/Livermore, and a member of the UCD Computer Science Executive Committee.

DAVID C. CANN earned a B.S. in general biology and an M.S. and a Ph.D. in computer science at Colorado State University. He is currently a member of the Computing Research Group at Lawrence Livermore National Laboratory. His research interests include parallel processing, applicative and functional programming, compilers, and operating systems. Dr. Cann is a member of the ACM and the Computer Society of the IEEE.

RODNEY R. OLDEHOEFT earned a B.S. in mathematics at Southern Illinois University and an M.S. and a Ph.D. in computer science at Purdue. He is now a professor of computer science and the department chair at Colorado State University. His research interests include parallel processing software and systems, applicative and functional programming, operating systems, and performance evaluation. Dr. Oldehoeft is a cofounder of the Sisal Project and has contributed primarily to language design, run time parallelism management, and performance optimizations. He is on the editorial board for the Wiley Series on Parallel Computing and is an accreditation visitor for the ACM/IEEE Computer Science Accreditation Board.

Received December 1. 1989: revised May 30. 1990: accepted July 31, 1990

Para-Functional Programming

Paul Hudak

Yale University

This methodology treats a multiprocessor as a single autonomous computer onto which a program is mapped, rather than as a group of independent processors.

The importance of parallel computing hardly needs emphasis. Many physical problems and abstract models are seriously compute-bound, since sequential computer technology now faces seemingly insurmountable physical limitations. It is widely believed that the only feasible path toward higher performance is to consider radically different computer organizations, in particular ones exploiting parallelism. This argument is indeed rather old now, and considerable progress has been made in the construction of highly parallel computers.

One of the simplest and most promising types of parallel machines is the well-known *multiprocessor architecture,* a collection of autonomous processors with either shared or distributed memory that are interconnected by a homogeneous communications network and usually communicate by sending messages. The interest in machines of this type is not surprising, since not only do they avoid the classic "von Neumann bottleneck" by being effectively decentralized, but they are also extensible and in general quite easy to build. Indeed, more than a dozen commercial multiprocessors either are now or will soon be available.

Although designing and building multiprocessors has proceeded at a dramatic pace, the development of effective ways to program them has generally not. This is an unfortunate state of affairs, since experience with sequential machines tells us that software development, not hardware development, is the most critical element in a system's design. The immense complexity of parallel computation can only increase our dependence on software. Clearly we need effective ways to program the new generation of parallel machines.

In this article I introduce *para-functional programming,* a methodology for programming multiprocessor computing systems. It is based on a functional programming model augmented with features that allow programs to be mapped to specific multiprocessor topologies. The most significant aspect of the methodology is that it treats the multiprocessor as a single autonomous computer onto which a program is mapped, rather than as a group of independent processors that carry out complex communication and require complex synchronization. In more conventional approaches to parallel programming, the latter method of treatment is often manifested as processes that cooperate by message-passing. However, such notions are absent in para-functional programming; indeed, a single language and evaluation model can be used from problem inception, to prototypes targeted for uniprocessors, and ultimately to realizations on a parallel machine.

Functional programming and parallel computing

The future of parallel computing depends on the creation of simple but effective parallel-programming models (reflected in appropriate language designs) that make the details of the underlying architecture transparent to the user. Many researchers feel that conventional imperative languages are inadequate for such models, since these languages are intrinsically tied to the "word-at-a-time" von Neumann machine model.[1] Extending such a sequential model to the parallel world is like putting on a shoe that doesn't fit. It makes more sense to use a language with a nonsequential semantic base.

One of the better candidates for parallel computing is the class of *functional languages* (also known as *applicative* or *dataflow* languages). In a functional language, no side effects (such as those caused by an assignment statement) are permitted. The lack of side effects accounts at least partially for the well-known *Church-Rosser Property,* which essentially states that no matter what order of computation is chosen in executing a program, the program is guaranteed to give the same result (assuming termination). This marvelous determinacy property is invaluable in parallel systems. It means that programs can be written and debugged in a functional language on a sequential machine, and then the *same* programs can be executed on a parallel machine for improved performance. The key point is that in functional languages the parallelism is implicit and supported by their underlying semantics. There is generally no need for special message-passing constructs or other communications primitives, no need for synchronization primitives, and no need for special "parallel" constructs such as "parbegin...parend."

On the other hand, doing without assignment statements seems rather radical. Yet clearly the assignment statement is an artifact of the von Neumann computer model and is not essential to the most abstract form of computation. In fact, a major goal of high-level language design has been the introduction of *expressions,* which transfer the burden of generating sequential code involving assignments from programmer to compiler. Functional languages simply carry this goal to the extreme: *Everything* is an expression. The advantages of the resulting programming style have been well-argued elsewhere,[1-2] and will not be repeated here. However, I wish to emphasize the following point: Although most experienced programmers recognize the importance of minimizing side effects, the importance of doing so in a parallel system is intensified significantly, due to the careful synchronization required to ensure correct behavior when side effects are present. Without side effects, there is no way for concurrent portions of a program to affect one another adversely—this is simply another way of stating the Church-Rosser Property.

The use of functional languages for parallel programming is really nothing new. Such use has its roots in early work on dataflow and reduction machines, in the course of which many functional languages were developed simultaneously with the design of new parallel architectures. Consider, for example, J. B. Dennis's dataflow machine and the language VAL, Arvind's U-interpreter and the language ID, A. L. Davis's dataflow machine DDM1 and the language DDN, and R. M. Keller's reduction machine AMPS and the language FGL. Such work on automatically decomposing a functional program for parallel execution continues today, and includes Rediflow[3] and my own work on serial combinators.[4]

The aforementioned systems automatically extract parallelism from a program and dynamically allocate the resultant tasks for parallel execution. But what about a somewhat different scenario— one in which the programmer knows the optimal mapping of his or her program onto a particular multiprocessor? One cannot expect an automated system to determine this optimal mapping for all program-processor combinations, so it is desirable to provide the user with the ability to express the mapping *explicitly.* (The need for this ability often arises, for example, in scientific computing, where many classic algorithms have been redesigned for optimal performance on particular

> ParAlfl provides a mechanism for mapping a program onto an arbitrary multiprocessor.

machines.) As it stands, almost no languages provide this capability.

ParAlfl is a functional language that provides a simple yet powerful mechanism for mapping a program onto an arbitrary multiprocessor. The mapping is accomplished by *annotating subexpressions* so as to show the processor on which they will be executed. With annotations, the mapping can be done in such a way that the program's functional behavior is not altered; that is, the program itself remains unchanged. The resulting methodology is referred to as *para-functional programming,* since it provides not only a much-needed tool for expressing parallel computation, but also an operational semantics that is truly "extra," or "beyond" the functional semantics of the program. It is quite powerful, for several reasons:

• It is very flexible. Not only is para-functional programming easily adapted to any functional language, but also any network topology can be captured by the notation, since no a priori assumptions are made about the structure of the physical system. All the benefits of conventional scoping disciplines are available to create modular programs that conform to the topology of a given machine.

• The annotations are natural and concise. There are no special control constructs, no message-passing constructs, and in general no forms of "excess baggage" to express the rather simple notion of where and when to compute things.

• With some minor constraints, if a para-functional program is stripped of its annotations, it is still a perfectly valid functional program. This means that it can be written and debugged on a uniprocessor that ignores the annotations, and

> ## An important semantic feature of ParAlfl is lazy evaluation.

then executed on a parallel processor for increased performance. Portability is enhanced, since only the annotations need to change when one moves from one parallel topology to another (unless the algorithm itself changes). The ability to debug a program independently of the parallel machinery is invaluable.

ParAlfl: a simple para-functional programming language

ParAlfl forms the testbed of Yale's para-functional programming research. It was derived from a functional language called ALFL,[5] which is similar in style to several modern functional languages, including SASL (and its successors KRC and Miranda),[6] FEL,[7] and Lazy ML.[8]

The base language. To make ParAlfl accessible to a broader audience, the base language, as shown here, was changed somewhat; for example, the arguments in function calls are "tupled" rather than "curried." The interested reader is referred to Henderson[2] and to Darlington, Henderson, and Turner[9] for a more thorough treatment of the functional programming paradigm. The salient features of the base language are

• Block-structuring is used, and takes the form of an *equation group* with the following configuration:

$$\{ f_1(x_1,...,x_{k_1}) = = exp_1;$$
$$f_2(x_1,...,x_{k_2}) = = exp_2;$$
$$...$$
$$result\ exp;$$
$$...$$
$$f_n(x_1,...,x_{k_n}) = = exp_n \}$$

An equation group is simply a collection of mutually recursive equations (each defining a local identifier) together with a single *result clause* that expresses the value to which the equation group will evaluate (*result* is a reserved word). Equation groups are just expressions, and can thus be nested to an arbitrary depth.

• A double equal-sign (" = = ") is used to distinguish equations from Boolean expressions of the form *exp1 = exp2*. The argument list is optional, allowing definitions of simple values, such as *x = = exp*. Since the equations are mutually recursive, and since ParAlfl is a lazy functional language, the order of the equations is irrelevant. All values are essentially evaluated "on demand."

• As in Lisp, the *list* is a fundamental data structure in ParAlfl. The operators ^ , ^^ , *hd*, and *tl* are like *cons, append, car,* and *cdr*, respectively, in Lisp. ^ and ^^ build lists: *a^l* is the list whose first element is *a* and the rest is just the list *l*, and *l1^^l2* is the list resulting from appending the lists *l1* and *l2* together. *Hd* and *tl* decompose lists: *hd(a^l)* returns *a*, and *tl(a^l)* returns *l*. A *proper list* (one ending in "nil") can be constructed with square brackets, as in [*a,b,c*], which is equivalent to *a^b^c^[]* (^ is right associative). Lists are constructed lazily.

• ParAlfl has functional arrays. The equation *v = = mka(d,f)* (*mka* is short for "make array") defines a vector *v* of *d* values, indexed from 1 to *d*, such that the *i*th element *v[i]* is the same as *f(i)*. Generally, the equation *a = = mka(d1,d2, ...,dn,f)* defines an *n*-dimensional array *a* such that *a[i1,...,in] = f(i1,...,in)*. Arrays are constructed lazily, although the elements are computed in parallel. (See the section entitled "Eager Expressions," below.) In an earlier article on para-functional programming[10] arrays were defined as being non-lazy, or *strict*. In reality, both kinds of array construction are provided in ParAlfl.

An important semantic feature of ParAlfl is *lazy evaluation.** That is, expressions are evaluated on demand instead of according to some syntactic rule, such

---

*Lazy evaluation is closely related to the *call-by-name* semantics of Algol, but is different in that once an expression is computed, its value is retained. In function calls, lazy evaluation is sometimes referred to as *call-by-need evaluation.*

---

as the order of identifier bindings. For example, one can write

$$\{ a = = b*b;$$
$$b = = 2;$$
$$result\ f(a,b);$$
$$f(x,y) = = if\ p\ then\ y\ else\ x + y \}$$

Note that *a* depends on *b*, yet is defined *before b*. Indeed, the order of these equations and the result clause is totally irrelevant. Note further that the function *f* does not use its first argument if *p* is true. Thus, in the call *f(a,b)*, the argument *a* is never evaluated (that is, the multiplication *b*b* never happens) if *p* is true.

An often highlighted feature of lazy evaluation is its ability to express unbounded data structures, or *infinite lists*. For example, an infinite list of the squares of the natural numbers can be defined by

$$\{ result\ squares(0);$$
$$squares(n) = = n*n\ ^\ squares(n + 1) \}$$

However, an important but often overlooked advantage of lazy evaluation is simply that it frees the programmer from extraneous concerns about the order of evaluation of expressions. Being freed from such concerns is very liberating for programming in general, but is especially important in parallel programming because over-specifying the order of evaluation can limit the potential parallelism.

Mapped expressions. A program can be mapped onto a particular multiprocessor architecture through the use of *mapped expressions*. These form one of the two classes of extensions (annotations) to the base language. (The other class is made up of *eager expressions,* which are described below.) Mapped expressions have the simple form

exp $on proc

which declares that *exp* is to be computed on the processor identified by *proc* (*on proc* is prefixed with $ to emphasize that $*on proc* is an annotation). The expression *exp* is the *body* of the mapped expression, which is to say, it represents the value to which the overall expression will evaluate (and thus can be any valid ParAlfl expression, including another mapped expression). The expression *proc* must evaluate to a processor ID. Without loss of generality, we will assume in all examples below that processor IDs, or *pids,* are integers and that there is some predefined mapping from those integers to the physical processors they denote. For example, a tree of

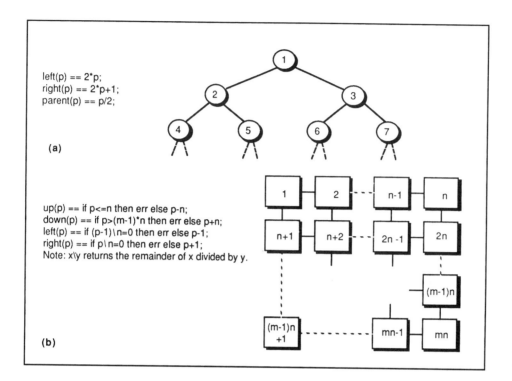

left(p) == 2*p;
right(p) == 2*p+1;
parent(p) == p/2;

(a)

up(p) == if p<=n then err else p-n;
down(p) == if p>(m-1)*n then err else p+n;
left(p) == if (p-1)\n=0 then err else p-1;
right(p) == if p\n=0 then err else p+1;
Note: x\y returns the remainder of x divided by y.

(b)

Figure 1. Two possible network topologies: infinite binary tree (a), and finite mesh of size $m \times n$ (b). Listed with each topology are functions that map pids to neighboring pids.

processors might be numbered as shown in Figure 1(a) and a mesh as shown in Figure 1(b). The advantage of using integers is that the user can manipulate them with conventional arithmetic primitives; for example, Figure 1 also defines functions that map pids to neighboring pids. However, a safer discipline might be to define a pid as a unique data-type, and to provide primitives that enable the user to manipulate values having that type.

Simple examples of mapped expressions. Consider the program fragment

f(x) + g(y)

The strict semantics of the + operator allows the two subexpressions to be evaluated in parallel. If we wish to express precisely where the subexpressions are to be evaluated, we can do so by annotating them, as in

(f(x) $on 0) + (g(y) $on 1)

where *0* and *1* are processor IDs.

Of course, this static mapping is not very interesting. It would be nice, for example, if we were able to refer to a processor with respect to the currently executing one. ParAlfl provides this ability through the reserved identifier $*self*, which when evaluated returns the pid of the currently executing processor. Using

$*self* we can be more creative. For example, suppose we have a mesh or tree of processors as shown in Figure 1; we can then write

(f(x) $on left($self)) +
(g(y) $on right($self))

to denote the computation of the two subexpressions in parallel on neighboring processors, with the sum being computed on $*self*.

We can describe the behavior of $*self* more precisely as follows: $*self* is bound implicitly by mapped expressions; thus, in

exp $on pid

$*self* has the value *pid* in *exp*, unless it is further modified by a nested mapped expression. Although $*self* is a reserved word that cannot be redefined, this implicit binding can be best explained with the following analogy:

exp $on pid

is like

{ $self == pid; result exp }

However, the most important aspect of $*self* is that it is *dynamically bound* in function calls. Thus, in

{ result (f(a) $on pid₁) + (f(b) $on pid₂);
    f(x) == x * x } $on pid₃

$a * a$ is computed on processor pid_1, $b * b$ on processor pid_2, and the sum on pro-

cessor pid_3. As before, an analogy is useful in describing this behavior:

f(x,y,z,) = = exp;
... f(a,b,c) ...

is like

f(x,y,z,$self) = = exp;
... f(a,b,c,$self) ...

In other words, all functions implicitly take an extra *formal parameter*, $*self,* and all function calls use the current value of $*self* as the value for the new *actual parameter.*

Although very powerful, $*self* is not always needed. Particular cases illustrating this are those in which mappings can be made from composite objects, such as vectors and arrays, to specific multiprocessor configurations. For example, if *f* is defined by $f(i) = = i * * 2$ $on i, then the call $mka(n,f)$ will produce a vector of squares, one on each of *n* processors, such that the *i*th processor contains the *i*th element (namely i^2). Further, suppose we have two vectors *v* and *w* and we wish to create a third that is the sum of the other two, but distributed over the *n* processors. This can be done very simply by

mka(n,g);
g(i) = = (v[i] + w[i]) $on i

If *v* and *w* were already distributed in the same way, this would express the pointwise

226

> ## The value of an "eager expression" is that of the expression without the annotation.

parallel summation of two vectors on n processors.

A note on lexical scoping and data movement. Consider the following typical situation: A shared value v is to be computed for use in two independent subexpressions, *e1* and *e2*; the values of these subexpressions are then to be combined into a single result. In a conventional language one might express this as something like

```
begin v := code-for-v;
      e1 := code-for-e1;
           (Comment: uses v)
      e2 := code-for-e2;
           (Comment: uses v)
      result := combine(e1,e2);
end;
```

and in ParAlfl one might write

```
{ v = = code-for-v;
  e1 = = code-for-e1; (Comment: uses v)
  e2 = = code-for-e2; (Comment: uses v)
  result combine(e1,e2) }
```

Both of these programs are very clear and concise.

But now suppose that this same computation is to begin and end on processor p, and the subexpressions *e1* and *e2* are to be executed in parallel on processors q and r, respectively. In a conventional language augmented with explicit process-creation and message-passing constructs, one might write the following program:

```
process P0;
    v := code-for-v;
    send(v,P1);
    send(v,P2);
    e1 := receive(P1);
    e2 := receive(P2);
    result := combine(e1,e2)
end-process;
```

```
process P1;
    v := receive(P0);
    e1 := code-for-e1; (Comment: uses v)
    send(e1,P0);
end-process;
```

```
process P2;
    v := receive(P0);
    e2 := code-for-e2; (Comment: uses v)
    send(e2,P0);
end-process;
```

which is then actually run by executing something like

```
invoke P0 on processor p;
invoke P1 on processor q;
invoke P2 on processor r;
```

Note that the structure of the original program has been completely destroyed. Explicit processes and communications between them have been introduced to coordinate the parallel computation. The semantics of both the process-creation and communications constructs need to be carefully defined before the run-time behavior can be understood. This program is no longer as clear nor as concise as the original one.

On the other hand, a ParAlfl program for this same task is simply

```
{ v = = code-for-v;
  e1 = = code-for-e1 $on q;
          (Comment: uses v)
  e2 = = code-for-e2 $on r;
          (Comment: uses v)
  result combine(e1,e2) } $on p
```

Note that if the three annotations are removed, the program is identical to the ParAlfl program given earlier! No communications primitives or special synchronization constructs are needed to send the value of v to processors q and r; standard lexical scoping mechanisms accomplish the data movement naturally and concisely. The values of *e1* and *e2* are sent back to processor p in the same way.

Eager expressions. The second form of annotation, the *eager expression,* arises out of the occasional need for the programmer to override the lazy-evaluation strategy of ParAlfl, since normally ParAlfl does not evaluate an expression until absolutely necessary. (This second type of annotation is not needed in a functional language with non-lazy semantics, such as pure Lisp, but as mentioned earlier, we prefer the expressiveness afforded by lazy semantics.) An eager expression has the simple form

$$\#exp$$

which forces the evaluation of *exp* in parallel with its immediately surrounding syntactic form, as defined below:

If #*exp* appears as

- an argument to a function (for example, $f(x,\#y,z)$), then it executes in parallel with the function call.
- an arm of a conditional (for example, *if p then #x else y*), then it executes in parallel with the conditional.
- an operand of an infix operator (for example, $x \hat{} \#y$; another example is x *and* #y), then it executes in parallel with the whole operation.
- an element of a list (for example, $[x,\#y,z]$), then it executes in parallel with the construction of the list.

Thus, for example, in the expression *if p then $f(\#x,y)$ else z*, the evaluation of x begins as soon as p has been determined to be true, and simultaneously the function f is invoked on its two arguments. Note that the evaluation of *some* subexpression begins when *any* expression is evaluated, and thus to evaluate that subexpression "eagerly" accomplishes nothing. For example, note the following equivalences:

```
if #p then x else y ≡ if p then x else y
#x and y ≡ x and y
#x + #y ≡ x + y
```

A special case of eager computation occurs in the construction of arrays, which are almost always used in a context where the elements are computed in parallel. Because of this, the evaluations of the elements of an array are defined to occur eagerly (and in parallel, of course, if appropriately mapped).

Eager expressions are commonly used within lists. Consider, for example, the expression $[x,\#y]$; normally lists are constructed lazily in ParAlfl, so the values of x and y are not evaluated until selected. But with the annotation shown, y would be evaluated as soon as the list was demanded. As with arrays, however, the expression does not wait for the value of y to return a fully computed value. Instead, it returns a partially constructed list just as it would with lazy evaluation.

The above discussion leads us to an important point about eager expressions: The *value* of an eager expression is that of the expression without the annotation. As with mapped expressions, the annotation only adds an operational semantics, and thus the user can invoke a nonterminating subcomputation, yet have the overall program terminate. Indeed, in the above example, even should y not terminate, if only the first element of the list is selected for later use, the overall program may still terminate properly. The "runaway process" that computes y is often called an *irrelevant task*, and there exist strategies for finding and deleting such tasks at run time. Such considerations are beyond the scope of this article, although it should be pointed out that given an automatic task-collection mechanism there are real situations in which one may wish to invoke a nonterminating computation (an example of this is given in Hudak and Smith[10]).

A note on determinacy. All ParAlfl programs possess the following determinacy property:

> A ParAlfl program in which (1) the identifier $self$ appears only in pid expressions, and (2) all pid expressions terminate without error, is functionally equivalent to the same program with all of the annotations removed. That is, both programs return the same value.

(A formal statement and proof of this property depends on a formal denotational semantics for ParAlfl, which is beyond the scope of this article, but such semantics can be found in Hudak and Smith.[10])

The reason for the first constraint is that if the mapping annotations are removed, all remaining occurrences of $self$ have the same value, namely the pid of the root processor. Thus, removing the annotations may change the value of the program. The purpose of the second constraint should be obvious: If the system diverges or errs when determining the processor on which to execute the body of a mapped expression, then it will never get around to computing the value of that expression.

Although neither determinacy constraint is severe, there are practical reasons for wanting to violate the first one (that is, for wanting to use the value of $self$ in other than a pid expression). The most typical situation where this arises is in a nonisotropic topology where certain processors form a boundary for the network (for example, the leaf processors in a tree, or the edge processors in a mesh). There are many distributed algorithms whose behavior at such boundaries is different from their behavior at internal nodes. To express this, one needs to know when execution is occurring at the boundary of the network, which can be conveniently determined by analyzing the value of $self$.

Sample application programs

In this section two simple examples are presented that highlight the key aspects of para-functional programming. Space limitations preclude the inclusion of examples that are more complex, but some can be found in Hudak and Smith[10] and Hudak.[11]

Parallel factorial. Figure 2 shows a simple parallel factorial program annotated for execution on a finite binary tree of $n = 2^d - 1$ processors. Although computing factorial, even in parallel, is a rather simple task, the example demonstrates several important ideas, and most other divide-and-conquer algorithms could easily fit into the same framework.

The algorithm is based on splitting the computation into two parts at each iteration and mapping the two subtasks onto the "children" of the current processor. Note that through the normal lexical scoping rules, *mid* will be computed on the current processor and passed to the child processors as needed (recall the discussion in the section on "Mapped expressions," above). The functions *left* and *right* describe the network mapping necessary

```
{ result pfac(1,k) $on root;

  pfac(lo,hi) = = if lo = hi then lo
                 else if lo = (hi - 1) then lo*hi
                      else { result (pfac(lo,mid) $on left($self)) *
                                    (pfac(mid + 1,hi) $on right($self));
                             mid = = (lo + hi)/2 };

  left(pe) = = if 2*pe > n then pe else 2*pe;
  right(pe) = = if 2 *pe > n then pe else 2*pe + 1;
  root = = 1;
}
```

Figure 2. Divide-and-conquer factorial on finite tree.

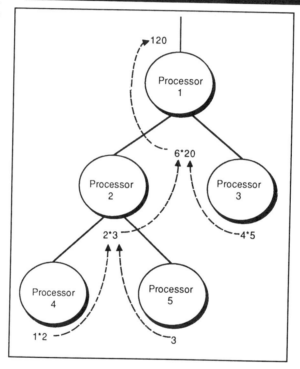

Figure 3. Dataflow for parallel factorial.

Figure 4. Parallel factorial, with unique behavior at leaves.

```
{ result pfac(1,k) $on root;

  pfac(lo,hi) = =if lo =hi then lo
                else if lo =(hi − 1) then lo*hi
                     else { result if leaf?($self) then sfac(lo,hi,1)
                                   else (pfac(lo,mid) $on left($self)) *
                                        (pfac(mid + 1,hi) $on right($self));
                            mid = =(lo +hi)/2 } ;

  sfac(lo,hi,acc) = =if lo =hi then lo*acc
                    else sfac(lo + 1,hi,lo*acc);

  leaf?(pe) = =pe  > = 2**(d − 1);
  left(pe) = =2*pe;
  right(pe) = =2*pe + 1;
  root = =1;
}
```

Figure 5. ParAlfl program to solve $Ux = b$.

```
{ result xvect;
  xvect = =mka(n,x);
  x(i) = = { result (b[i] −sum(n,0)) / U[i,i];
             sum(j,acc) = =if j <i + 1 then acc
                          else sum(j − 1,acc +xvect[j]*U[i,j]) }
}
```

for this topology, and Figure 3 shows the process-mapping and flow of data between processes when $k = 5$.

Note that the program in Figure 2 obeys the constraints required for determinacy, and thus the program returns the same value regardless of the annotations. Note further that with the mapping used, when processing reaches a leaf node all further calls to *pfac* are executed on the leaf processor. Routing functions of greater complexity could be devised that, for example, would reflect the computation upward once a leaf processor is reached. Alternatively, it might be desirable to use a more efficient factorial algorithm at the leaf nodes. An example of this is given in Figure 4, where the tail-recursive function *sfac* is invoked at the leaves. Determining that execution has reached a leaf processor requires inspection of $self, and thus the determinacy constraints are violated, yet the program still returns the same value regardless of the annotations. This constancy of values is, of course, often the case, but it cannot be guaranteed in general without the previously discussed constraints.

Solution to upper triangular block matrix. The next example is typical of problems encountered in scientific computing: The problem is to solve for the vector x in the matrix equation $Ux = b$, where U is an *upper triangular block matrix* (that is, a matrix whose elements are themselves matrices, and whose elements below the main diagonal contain all zeros). Algorithms using block matrices are especially suited to multiprocessors with nontrivial communications costs, since typically the subcomputations involving the submatrices can be done in parallel with little communication between the processors.

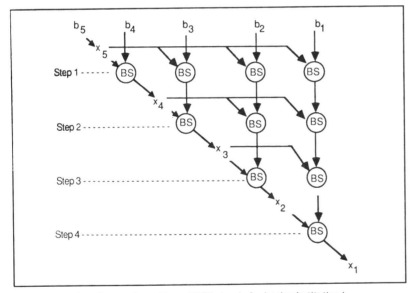

Figure 6. Dataflow for matrix problem. ("BS" stands for backsubstitution.)

```
Processor 5  Compute x5
                ⇓
Processor 4  Back-substitute x5  ⇒ Compute x4
                ↓                     ⇓
Processor 3  Back-substitute x5  ⇒ Back-substitute x4  ⇒ Compute x3
                ↓                     ↓                     ⇓
Processor 2  Back-substitute x5  ⇒ Back-substitute x4  ⇒ Back-substitute x3  ⇒ Compute x2
                ↓                     ↓                     ↓                     ⇓
Processor 1  Back-substitute x5  ⇒ Back-substitute x4  ⇒ Back-substitute x3  ⇒ Back-substitute x2  ⇒ Compute x1
```

Key:
⇒ ≡ Data (and temporal) dependency
— ≡ Temporal dependency imposed by pipelining

Figure 7. Pipelining data for matrix problem.

If we ignore parallelism at the moment and concentrate instead on a functional specification of this problem, it is easy to see from basic linear algebra that each element x_i in the solution vector x (of length n) can be given by the following equation:

$$x_i = (b_i - \sum_{j=n}^{i+1} x_j U_{i,j}) / U_{i,i}$$

where we assume for convenience that the submatrices are of unit size (and are thus represented simply as scalar quantities). Given this equation for each element, it is easy to construct the solution vector in ParAlfl, as shown in Figure 5.

This problem, as it is, has plenty of parallelism. To see this, look at Figure 6, a dataflow graph showing the data dependencies when $n=5$. Clearly, once an element of the solution is computed, all of the backsubstitutions of it can be done in parallel; that is, each of the horizontal "steps" in Figure 6 can be executed. This parallelism derives solely from the data dependencies inherent in the problem, and is mirrored faithfully in the ParAlfl code. Indeed, if we have n processors sharing a common memory, we can annotate the program in Figure 5 very simply:

```
{ result xvect;
    xvect = = mka(n,x);
    x(i) = = { ... } $on i
}
```

where "..." denotes the same expression used in Figure 5 for $x(i)$. (Recall that the elements of an array are computed in parallel, and thus do not require eager annotations.)

But let us consider topologies that are more interesting. Consider, for example, a *ring* of n processors. Although the topology of a ring is simple, its limited capacity for interprocessor communication makes it difficult to use effectively, and it is thus a challenge for algorithm designers. We will assume that the processors are labeled consecutively around the ring from "1" to "n," and that the ith row of U and ith element of b are on processor i. We wish the solution vector x to be distributed in the same way.

We should first note that the annotated program two paragraphs above would run perfectly well on such a topology, especially with the given distribution of data. The only data movement, in fact, would be that of each submatrix x_i for use on each processor j, $j > i$. This data movement

```
{ result xvect;
    xvect = = mka(n,x);
    x(i) = = { result (b[i] − sum(n,0)) / U[i,i];
               sum(j,acc) = = if j < i + 1 then acc
                             else sum(j − 1,acc + xpipe[i][n − j + 1]*U[i,j])
             } $on i;
    xpipe = = mka(n,xfn);
    xfn(i) = = { result mka(n − i + 1,xlocal);
               xlocal(j) = = if j = n − i + 1 then xvect[i]
                            else xpipe[i + 1][j] } $on i
}
```

Figure 8. A program for pipelining x_i around a ring of processors.

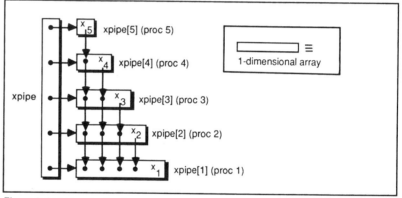

Figure 9. A vector pipeline for x.

would be done transparently by the underlying operating system, and in this case the program would probably perform adequately.

Yet in our dual role of programmer and algorithm designer we may have a particular routing strategy that is provably good and that we wish to express explicitly in the program. For example, one efficient strategy is to "pipeline" the x_i around the ring as they are generated. That is, the element x_i is passed to processor i-1, used there, passed to processor i-2, used there, and so on, as shown graphically in Figure 7. There are several ways to accomplish this effect in the program, and we shall explore two of them.

The first requires the least change to the existing program, and is based on shifting the data by creating a partial copy of the solution vector on each processor, as shown in Figure 8. Note that the first four lines of this program are essentially the same as those given earlier. Figure 9 shows the construction of *xpipe*—note the cor-

respondence between this diagram and the one in Figure 7.

The second way to express the pipelining of data is to interpret the algorithm from the outset as a network of dynamic processes rather than as a static set of vectors and arrays. In particular, we can conjure up the following description of a process running on processor i:

"Process i takes as input a stream of values x_n, x_{n-1}, ..., x_{i+1}. It passes this stream of values to process i-1 while back-substituting each value into b_i. When the end of the stream is reached, it computes x_i and adds this to the end of the stream being passed to process i-1."

Assuming the same distribution of U and b used earlier, we can represent this process description in ParAlfl as shown in Figure 10. Note that xi is annotated for eager evaluation, to override the lazy evaluation of lists. Also note the correspondence between this program and the last. The main

```
{ result process(n,[]);          (Comment: begin on processor n with empty stream)
  process(i,xstr) = =
    { xi = = (b[i] − sum(xstr,n,0))/U[i,i];
      result if i = 1 then addtostr(xstr,#xi)
                  else process(i − 1,addtostr(xstr,#xi));
      addtostr(old,x) = = old ˆˆ [x];
      sum(str,j,acc) = = if str = [] then acc
                    else sum(tl(str),j − 1,acc + hd(str) ∗ U[i,j])
    } $on i
}
```

Figure 10. Program for $Ux = b$ simulating network of processes.

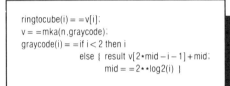

```
ringtocube(i) = = v[i];
v = = mka(n,graycode);
graycode(i) = = if i < 2 then i
            else { result v[2∗mid − i − 1] + mid;
                   mid = = 2∗∗log2(i) }
```

Figure 11. Program to embed ring in hypercube.

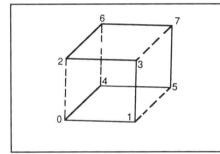

Figure 12. Embedding of ring of size 8 into 3-cube.

difference is in the choice of data structure for x—a list is used here, resulting in a recursive structuring of the program, whereas a vector was used previously, resulting in a "flat" program structure. Choices of this kind are in fact typical of any suitably rich programming language, and are equally important in parallel and sequential programming. Different data structures can, of course, be mapped in different ways to machines, but in this example the annotations are essentially the same in both programs.

To carry this example one step further, let us now consider running any of the above ParAlfl programs on a multiprocessor with a hypercube interconnection topology rather than a ring. One way to accomplish this is to simulate a ring in a hypercube by some suitable embedding. Probably the simplest such embedding is the *reflected gray-code*, captured by the ParAlfl functions shown in Figure 11. In

that figure, *log2* (i) returns the base-2 logarithm of i, rounded down to the nearest integer (the vector v is used to "cache" values of *graycode* (i)). For example, Figure 12 shows the embedding of a ring of size 8 into a 3-cube.

If we then replace the previous annotations "... $on i" with "... $on ringtocube($i$)," we arrive at the desired embedding. Note that the code for the algorithm itself did not change at all, just the annotations. Of course, a more efficient algorithm for the hypercube might exist or the initial data distribution might be different, and both cases would naturally require recoding of the main functions.

When viewed in the broad scope of software development methodologies, the use of para-functional programming suggests the following scenario:

1. One first conceives of an algorithm and expresses it cleanly in a functional programming language. This high-level program is likely to be much closer to the problem specifications than conventional language realizations, thus aiding reasoning about the program and facilitating the debugging process.

2. Once the program has been written, it is debugged and tested on either a sequential or parallel computer system. In the latter case, the compiler extracts as much parallelism as it can from the program, but with no intervention or awareness on the part of the user.

3. If the performance achieved in step two does not meet one's needs, the program is refined by affixing *annotations* that provide more subtle control over the evaluation process. These annotations can be added without affecting the program's functional behavior.

There are two aspects of this methodology that I think significantly facilitate program development: First, the functional aspects of a program are effectively separated from most of the operational aspects. Second, the multiprocessor is viewed as a single autonomous computer onto which a program is mapped, rather than as a group of independent processors that carry out complex communication and require complex synchronization. Together with the clean, high-level programming style afforded by functional languages, these two aspects promise to yield a simple and effective programming methodology for multiprocessor computing systems.

Extensions and implementation issues. In this article I have presented only the fundamental ideas behind para-functional programming. Work continues on several advanced features and alternative annotations that provide even more expressive power. These include: (1) annotations that reference other operational aspects of a processor, such as processing load; (2) mappings to operating system resources, such as disks and I/O devices; (3) introduction of nondeterministic primitives where needed; and (4) annotations to control memory usage. The latter two features are especially important, since they allow one to overcome two traditional objections to programming in the functional style: the inability to deal with the nondeterminism that is prevalent, for example, in an operating system, and inefficiency in handling large data structures. Space limitations preclude me from delving into such issues, but the reader can find additional details in Hudak and Smith[10] and Hudak.[11]

In addition, by concentrating in this article on how to *express* parallel computation, I have left unanswered many questions about how one can *implement* a para-functional programming language. In recent years great advances have been made in implementing functional languages for both sequential and parallel machines, and much of that work is applicable here. In particular, *graph reduction* provides a very natural way to coordinate the parallel evaluation of subexpressions, and solves problems such as how to migrate the values of lexically bound variables from one processor to another. At Yale a virtual parallel graph reducer called *Alfalfa* is currently being implemented on two commercial hypercube architectures: an Intel iPSC and an NCube hypercube. This graph-reduction engine will be able to support both implicit (dynamic) and explicit (annotated) task allocation. The only difficult language feature to support efficiently in para-functional programming is a mechanism for referencing elements in a distributed array; in most cases this is quite easy, but in certain cases it can be difficult. Although good progress has been made in this area, the work is too premature to report here.

Related work. The work that is most similar in spirit to that presented in this article is E. Shapiro's systolic programming in Concurrent Prolog[12]; the mapping semantics of systolic programming was derived from earlier work on "turtle programs" in Logo. Other related efforts include those of R. M. Keller and G. Lindstrom,[13] who, independent of our research at Yale and in the context of functional databases, suggest the use of annotations similar to mapped expressions; and F. W. Burton's[14] annotations to the lambda calculus to provide control over lazy, eager, and parallel execution. A more recent effort is that of N. S. Sridharan,[15] who suggests a "semi-applicative" programming style to control evaluation order. All in all, these efforts contribute to

what I think is a powerful programming paradigm in which operational and functional behavior can coexist with little adverse interaction. □

Acknowledgments

I am especially indebted to Lauren Smith (now at Los Alamos National Laboratory), to whom most of these ideas were first presented for critical review. Her efforts at applying the ideas to real problems were especially useful. A special thanks is extended to Yale's Research Center for Scientific Computation (under the direction of Martin Schultz), which provided the motivation for much of this work. The research also benefited from useful discussions with Jonathan Young and Adrienne Bloss at Yale, Bob Keller at the University of Utah, and Joe Fasel and Elizabeth Williams at Los Alamos National Laboratory. Finally, I wish to thank the three anonymous reviewers for *Computer* magazine who worked with my article, as well as Assistant Editor Louise Anderson; their comments helped improve the presentation.

This research was supported in part by NSF Grants DCR-8403304 and DCR-8451415, and a Faculty Development Award from IBM.

References

1. J. Backus, "Can Programming Be Liberated from the von Neumann Style? A Functional Style and Its Algebra of Programs," *CACM,* Vol. 21, No. 8, Aug. 1978, pp. 613-641.

2. P. Henderson, *Functional Programming: Application and Implementation,* Prentice-Hall, Englewood Cliffs, N. J., 1980.

3. R. M. Keller and F. C. H. Lin, "Simulated Performance of a Reduction-based Multiprocessor," *Computer,* Vol. 17, No. 7, July 1984, pp. 70-82.

4. P. Hudak and B. Goldberg, "Distributed Execution of Functional Programs Using Serial Combinators," *Proc. 1985 Int'l Conf. on Parallel Processing,* Aug. 1985, pp. 831-839; also appeared in *IEEE Trans. Computers,* Vol. C-34, No. 10, Oct. 1985, pp. 881-891.

5. P. Hudak, "ALFL Reference Manual and Programmer's Guide," research report YALEU/DCS/RR-322, 2nd ed., Oct. 1984, Yale University, Dept. of Computer Science, Box 2158 Yale Station, New Haven, CT 06520.

6. D. A. Turner, "Miranda: A Non-strict Functional Language with Polymorphic Types," *Functional Programming Languages and Computer Architecture,* Sept. 1985, Springer-Verlag, New York, pp. 1-16.

7. R. M. Keller, tech. report, "FEL Programmer's Guide," No. 7, Mar. 1982, University of Utah, Dept. of Computer Science, Merrill Engineering Bldg., Salt Lake City, UT 84112.

8. L. Augustsonn, "A Compiler for Lazy ML," *ACM Symp. on LISP and Functional Programming,* Aug. 1984, pp. 218-227.

9. J. Darlington, P. Henderson, and D. A. Turner, *Functional Programming and Its Applications,* Cambridge University Press, Cambridge, UK, 1982.

10. P. Hudak and L. Smith, "Para-Functional Programming: A Paradigm for Programming Multiprocessor Systems," *12th ACM Symp. on Principles of Programming Languages,* Jan. 1986, pp. 243-254.

11. P. Hudak, "Exploring Para-Functional Programming," research report YALEU/DCS/RR-467, Apr. 1986, Yale University, Dept. of Computer Science, Box 2158 Yale Station, New Haven, CT 06520.

12. E. Shapiro, "Systolic Programming: A Paradigm of Parallel Processing," tech. report CS84-21, Aug. 1984, The Weizmann Institute of Science, Dept. of Applied Mathematics; appeared in *Proc. Int'l Conf. on Fifth-Generation Computer Systems,* Nov. 6-9, 1984, pp. 458-470.

13. R. M. Keller and G. Lindstrom, "Approaching Distributed Database Implementations Through Functional Programming Concepts," *Int'l Conf. on Distributed Systems,* May 1985.

14. F. W. Burton, "Annotations to Control Parallelism and Reduction Order in the Distributed Evaluation of Functional Programs," *ACM Trans. on Programming Languages and Systems,* Vol. 6, No. 2, Apr. 1984.

15. N. S. Sridharan, tech. report, "Semi-applicative Programming: An Example," Nov. 1985, BBN Laboratories, Cambridge, Mass.

Paul Hudak received his BS degree in electrical engineering from Vanderbilt University, Nashville, Tenn., in 1973; his MS degree in computer science from the Massachusetts Institute of Technology, Cambridge, Mass., in 1974; and his PhD degree in computer science from the University of Utah, Salt Lake City, Utah, in 1982. From 1974 to 1979 he was a member of the technical staff at Watkins-Johnson Co., Gaithersburg, Md.

Hudak is currently an associate professor in the Programming Languages and Systems Group in the Dept. of Computer Science at Yale University, New Haven, Conn., a position he has held since 1982. His primary research interests are functional and logic programming, parallel computing, and semantic program analysis.

He is a recipient of an IBM Faculty Development Award (1984-85), and an NSF Presidential Young Investigator Award (1985).

Readers may write to Paul Hudak at Yale University, Dept. of Computer Science, Box 2158 Yale Station, New Haven, CT 06520.

High-performance parallel graph reduction

Simon L Peyton Jones, Chris Clack and Jon Salkild
Department of Computer Science, University College London
Gower Street, London WC1E 6BT, United Kingdom
email: clack@uk.ac.ucl.cs, simonpj@uk.ac.ucl.cs

Abstract

Parallel graph reduction is an attractive implementation for functional programming languages because of its simplicity and inherently distributed nature. This paper outlines some of the issues raised by parallel compiled graph reduction, and presents the approach we have adopted for our parallel machine, GRIP.

We concentrate on two main areas:

- Static and dynamic techniques to control the growth of parallelism, so as to provide enough parallelism of an appropriate granularity to keep the machine busy without swamping it.

- Dynamic techniques to exploit the memory hierarchy, so that frequently-referenced data is held near to the processor that references it.

1. Introduction

Graph reduction is an attractively simple foundation for the execution of functional programs on parallel hardware[Peyt87a]. In this paper we raise some of the key issues involved in the implementation of a parallel graph reduction machine, with particular emphasis on performance. Based on our experience with the GRIP project, we also describe our current design decisions.

There are substantial communication and administration overheads to be paid for parallel execution. The main problems are

- The overheads of creating a new task. This involves not only the creation of a task descriptor, but also the insidious cost of packaging the work so that it can be communicated to an independent agent.

- The synchronisation costs involved when tasks communicate with each other.

- The danger of memory overflow due to the unrestricted growth of partly-completed tasks.

- Most serious of all, the loss of locality caused when one processor executes a task whose data is local to a different processor.

These issues raise two broad design questions, which are echoed by all parallel graph reduction systems of which we are aware:

- When should a new task be created? Enough parallelism is required to keep the machine busy, but excessive parallelism only increases the overheads without providing any new opportunities for increased performance.

- How can locality be achieved? We want to make effective use of the memory hierachy provided by the underlying architecture, which invariably provides a latency/size spectrum in which fast memory is provides only limited storage, and bulk storage is slow.

The paper comprises three parts. We begin with an overview of the GRIP systems architecture, to provide a concrete basis for the rest of the paper. This is followed by two main sections which address the design questions raised above.

The ideas we discuss represent the current state of our thinking, but we have not yet completed the compiler and system software based on these ideas. As a result, we make many conjectures, but are unable to support them with hard performance measurements, something which will be corrected in future papers.

2. Parallel compiled graph reduction on GRIP

In this section we present the mechanisms that enable parallel compiled graph reduction to be performed on GRIP. We discuss both hardware and software system architecture and then introduce the key features of the virtual machine. Further details can be found elsewhere[Peyt87b, Peyt88a]. In order to provide a specific context within which to discuss the issues of parallel graph reduction, we begin with a brief overview of the system architecture of our parallel graph reduction machine, GRIP.

2.1 Overview of GRIP system architecture

2.1.1 Hardware architecture

The GRIP hardware consists of:

- up to eighty M68020 Processing Elements (PEs), each with one megabyte of private memory.

- up to twenty microprogrammable Intelligent Memory Units (IMUs), each with 5 megabytes of globally-addressable memory (upgradable to 20 megabytes when 4Mbit RAMS are available);

- a high-bandwidth packet-switched bus which interconnects the components.

GRIP provides a **shared-memory architecture** in which the globally-addressable heap is held in the IMUs. The IMUs support a range of memory operations which manipulate heap-structured data, thus localising all the low-level synchronisation and heap-management operations. They may alternatively be re-programmed, for example to support the memory operations required for a parallel logic language[Reyn88a]. This shared-memory approach allows us to concentrate initially on the challenges of parallel graph reduction, whereas a distributed-memory architecture would force us first to solve the problem of achieving a high degree of locality.

The following range of operations is supported by our current IMU microcode:

- Variable-sized graph nodes may be allocated and initialised.

- Garbage collection is performed autonomously by the IMUs in parallel with graph reduction, using a variant of Baker's real-time collector[Bake78a].

- Each IMU maintains a pool of executable tasks. Idle processors poll the IMUs in search of these tasks.

- Synchronised access to graph nodes is supported. A lock bit is associated with each unevaluated node, which is set when the node is first fetched. Any subsequent attempt to fetch it is refused, and a task descriptor is automatically attached to the node.

  When the node is overwritten with its evaluated form (using another IMU operation), any task descriptors attached to the node are automatically put in the task pool by the IMU.

2.1.2 System software

GRIP spends most of its resources performing graph reduction, but there are also several administrative activities such as program loading, input and output and garbage collection. In particular, there is exactly one **system manager** (which can reside on any PE) which is responsible for global resource-management policy decisions.

We could assign a separate PE to each of these activities, but many of them have rather a low duty-cycle so that the PE would be idle much of the time. This would be particularly serious in a small GRIP with only a few PEs. Each processor therefore runs a small special-purpose multi-tasking operating system called GLOS, which allows a single processor to be multiplexed between graph reduction and administrative activities.

2.2 Compiled graph reduction

Our first model for parallel reduction was an *interpretive* one called the **four-stroke reduction engine**[Clac86a], and we now have a running parallel implementation of this machine.

In the last few years, much progress has been made on *compiled* graph-reduction techniques for sequential processors, so that the functional program is compiled to native machine code, with substantial performance improvements over interpretive methods[Peyt87a]. Generally speaking, these efforts have been reported in the form of the design of an abstract machine for executing functional programs; examples include the G-machine[John87a], Tim[Fair87a], the Oregon G-machine chip[Kieb87a], the Spineless G-machine[Burn88a], and the Spineless Tagless G-machine[Peyt89a]. The best of these implementations produce programs which run at speeds broadly competitive with compiled imperative languages[2].

The time is now ripe to extend this compiler technology to parallel machines. We are currently in the midst of extending the Spineless Tagless G-machine in this way, and the ideas in this paper have grown out of this work. The details of this abstract machine are beyond the scope of this paper, but for our present purposes the following are the key features:

- The functional program is lambda-lifted as usual, and then compiled to native machine code.

- Evaluation takes place with the aid of a stack to hold intermediate results.

2.3 Tasks and concurrency - a model for parallel graph reduction

The functional program is held as a graph in the heap. Execution proceeds by **reductions**, which transform the graph to a simpler form. Each reduction physically updates the graph node representing the reducible expression (or **redex**) with the result of the reduction. Reductions may take place concurrently at different sites in the graph, and this is the source of parallelism in GRIP.

A **task** is a sequential computation which executes a series of reductions whose purpose is to reduce some sub-graph to (weak head) normal form. Tasks are the finest schedulable unit of concurrency in GRIP, and the set of executable tasks is called the **task pool**. Each IMU holds part of the task pool, and idle PEs poll the IMUs to

---

1. Of course, graph reduction is not the only possible implementation technique for functional languages; others models include the Imperial FPM system FP field and the Categorical Abstract Machine[Cous85a]. Graph reduction lends itself particularly easily to parallel implementations.

2. We argue elsewhere that it is unreasonable to expect functional-language programs to run as fast as their imperative programs, but that this will become increasingly unimportant, provided that the performance loss is sufficiently small[Peyt89b].

request an executable task from the pool.

During its execution, a task may encounter a sub-graph whose value will be required in the future. If so, the task creates a child task, by placing a pointer to the sub-graph in the task pool: this is called **sparking a child**. For example, if a task is evaluating the expression ($E_1 + E_2$) where E_1 and E_2 are arbitrary expressions, it may choose to evaluate E_1 itself, and to spark a child to evaluate E_2 (whose value will certainly be required in the future).

Subsequently the parent task will require the value of the sub-graph it sparked; in our example, after completing the evaluation of E_1 the parent will require the value of E_2. In GRIP *the parent simply tries to evaluate E_2 just as if it had never sparked the child*. There are then three possibilities:

(i)   The child task has not started execution, because no PEs were free. In this case the parent evaluates E_2 itself, and the child task becomes an **orphan**.

(ii) The child task has completed evaluation of E_2, and overwritten the root node of E_2 with its value. The parent will therefore find that evaluating E_2 is rather easy, because it is already in normal form! The parent's attempt to evaluate E_2 then degenerates to a fetch of the evaluated result.

(iii) The child task has begun to evaluate E_2, but has not completed. In this case the parent is **suspended** until the child does complete its evaluation. Then the parent is **resumed**, and the situation is just like that of case (ii).

The suspension mechanism in case (iii) above also guarantees mutual exclusion between any two concurrent tasks which share a common subexpression. The second task to reach the subexpression will be suspended until the first has completed its evaluation: the second task is then resumed.

3. The efficient generation and control of parallelism

We are bound to pay some overhead penalty in exchange for parallel execution. We believe, however, that an unacceptable performance penalty will be paid if every opportunity for parallel execution is taken, irrespective of whether there is spare processing capacity to exploit it. In other words, we believe that the key to high performance is *to pay the overheads of parallel execution only when there is spare capacity available to exploit it, and otherwise to execute the program sequentially using all the short-cuts and optimisations that thereby become available.*

One way to achieve this goal is to require the programmer to take very close control over the way in which his or her program is partitioned into parallel activities. This is what is required by an array processor, for example. Unfortunately, for complex programs, with irregular structure, figuring out how best to partition the program can become extremely hard, and we believe that one of the prime merits of parallel functional programming is exactly that it frees the programmer from being forced to specify this level of detail.

Accordingly, we are interested in developing compile-time and run-time strategies for partitioning and scheduling the program. We do not expect these strategies to outperform a program explicitly scheduled by a programmer, except perhaps for very complex programs. Instead, our goal is to do a sufficiently good job for practical purposes. This section discusses some possible strategies.

3.1 Speculative and conservative parallelism

The first thing to consider is whether or not the result of a child task will actually be required. In our present implementation of GRIP we make the simplifying assumption that *a task is only sparked if it is certain that its result will be required*. This is called **conservative** parallelism, in contrast to **speculative** parallelism, where a task may be sparked if it is **likely** that its result will be required. Speculative parallelism is a sort of job-creation scheme to usefully exploit idle processors. For example, consider the expression if E_1 then E_2 else E_3

While E_1 is being evaluated, we could imagine speculatively starting parallel evaluation of E_2 and E_3, so that some progress had already been made by the time the evaluation of E_1 was complete.

It is well known that speculative parallelism raises many problems, which we summarise briefly as follows[Huda83a]:

- Speculative tasks compete for resources with vital tasks. In the example, there is danger that the machine will spend all its resources evaluating E_2 and E_3, and never make progress with E_1. Hence, some sort of priority scheme is required.

- Speculative tasks may become vital. For example, if E_1 evaluates to True, the evaluation of E_2 becomes vital, and should have its priority upgraded (and so should its children, and their children...).

- Speculative tasks may become useless. If E_1 evaluates to True, the evaluation of E_3 is positively pernicious, since it is consuming machine resources to compute a result which is now known not to be required. Hence the task evaluating E_3 must be killed (and its children, and their children...).

- The situation becomes more murky still when we realise that speculative and vital tasks may share sub-expressions.

The unrestrained use of speculation therefore risks causing a lot of extra administration in return for modest increases in parallelism, so GRIP only initiates conservative parallelism at present. For the future, there are situations where speculation seems inevitable[Burt85a]:

- Indeterministic choice, where the programmer simply wants to select the result of whichever of two or more computations completes first. Some of the computations may not terminate at all, so considerations of fairness are involved here as well.

- Program aborts, where the programmer wants to abort a computation using "Control-C", without halting the entire machine.

3.2 Achieving dynamic granularity

Once we realise the costs imposed by parallelism, it becomes clear that we should strive to generate only enough parallel activities to keep the machine busy, which will be some (small) constant multiple of the number of processors in the machine. Our goal is to generate parallel tasks until the machine becomes "sufficiently" heavily loaded, and then to run each task sequentially in the local memory of its processor, communicating with the rest of the world only when necessary. When the load drops, new tasks should be generated again. Thus, as the machine becomes loaded, each task runs longer sequential threads of execution, thereby dynamically increasing the grain size.

The parent-child synchronisation mechanism in GRIP makes this particularly easy to achieve. Recall that a child task *does not notify the parent of its completion*. This is in contrast to ALICE, FLAGSHIP, and Alfalfa, all of which require the parent task to wait for notification from every child. This property has a number of important consequences:

- **The length of threads of execution are maximised.** The parent is only suspended if the child has begun evaluation but not completed. In all other cases, the parent continues uninterrupted. In other words, *the costs of synchronisation are only paid if a collision actually takes place.* In effect, the grain of execution is increased dynamically.

- **A task should never spark an expression it is about to evaluate.** In the expression ($E_1 + E_2$), it would be possible for the parent to spark two children, for E_1 and E_2. However, the next action of the parent is to evaluate E_1 itself anyhow! Hence it is better for the parent to spark E_2 and to evaluate E_1 itself.

- **Orphan tasks can be discarded.** A task in the task pool is held in the IMU that contains the root node of the task. When an IMU fetches a newly-sparked task from the task pool, in response to a request from an idle PE, it may first check to see if the graph specified by the task is already being, or has been, evaluated. If so, the task is an orphan, and can simply be discarded.

- **The system is free to discard sparks at will.** This is possible because of the absence of explicit notification. It may be desirable if the machine is heavily loaded. We think of sparks as advisory messages to the system, giving advance warning that a sub-graph will later be evaluated, and thus giving the opportunity to evaluate it in parallel. Discarding sparks has two beneficial effects for a heavily-loaded system:

  (i)   locality cannot be lost by the task migrating to another processor;
  (ii) a parent-child collision cannot take place, thereby reducing synchronisation overheads.

We regard this policy, of discarding sparks when the machine is sufficiently loaded, as extremely important. It allows us to run dynamically-sized tasks with efficiency approaching that of high-quality compiled sequential implementations.

Of course the notion of "sufficiently loaded" is hard to quantify, but fortunately great precision is not required. In the GRIP system, the System Manager computes a slowly-varying load average and distributes it regularly to each processor. (In a more distributed system, the load average could be computed using only local information.) Each processor then decides whether or not to spark new tasks, by comparing this load average with some threshold value. The value of this threshold, and the frequency of load average collection and distribution, is a matter for experiment.

There is a risk of losing concurrency by this method. Consider a function which sparks several large arguments, and then evaluates them sequentially, and suppose that these sparks were discarded because the machine was busy at the time. Now, if machine becomes un-loaded midway through the execution of the function, it would be committed to sequential evaluation of the remaining arguments, despite the abundance of idle processors!

We believe that the risk of loss of concurrency is far outweighed by the benefits of dynamic granularity, and but this remains to be demonstrated.

3.3 The effect of scheduling policy

The scheduling policy governs which processor executes which executable task. There are two main considerations: *when* a task should be scheduled, which affects memory usage; and *where* it should be executed, which affects locality. We discuss the former immediately, and postpone discussion of the latter until a later section.

In a conservative parallel regime, the order in which tasks are scheduled is immaterial, since all tasks are doing useful work. Nevertheless, scheduling policy can have a substantial effect on the rate of growth of parallelism and storage usage, as the Manchester dataflow group have discovered[Rugg87a]. Far from lacking parallelism, they encountered serious problems because their machine's memory rapidly filled up with partly-executed tasks. This led them to suggest two possible policies for scheduling sparked tasks: LIFO (last-sparked-first-scheduled) and FIFO (first-sparked-first-scheduled). This decision has a dramatic effect on the rate of growth of parallelism in divide-and-conquer algorithms, and hence on the storage used to hold partly-executed tasks.

In effect, LIFO scheduling explores the process tree in a depth-first manner, and FIFO scheduling in a breadth-first manner. The former minimises storage usage while the latter maximises parallelism. Switching dynamically between LIFO and FIFO scheduling allows this tradeoff to be adjusted at run time.

Similar effects have been observed in the Concert Multilisp system[Hals86a] in which depth-first execution is pursued by each individual processor, with breadth-first execution arising when processors steal tasks from each other's task stacks.

The IMUs can easily implement such scheduling policies, provided the System Manager informs them regularly of which policy to pursue. We also have the additional freedom to schedule resumed tasks before or after sparked tasks, which should have a similar effect.

If we omit considerations of the amount of intermediate storage used, how much effect can scheduling policy have on the overall speedup? At first it might appear that poor scheduling policies may give very bad processor utilisation and seriously limit speedup. However, Eager, Zahorjan and Lazowska [Eage86a] show that for any work-conserving[3] scheduling policy the speedup for N processors must be larger than $NA/(N+A+1)$, where A is the average level of parallelism which would be attained by executing the same program with an unbounded number of processors. If $A >> N$, then this lower bound approaches N, which as good as we can hope for. This reassures us that scheduling policy is comparatively unimportant to overall speedup for highly-parallel problems, a result which is strongly supported by Goldberg's experiments[Gold88a].

3.4 Sequential and parallel versions

The loss of the efficiency of sequential code, coupled with the overhead of building closures, represents another source of inefficiency. Suppose we have to compile code for the function g, where

$$g \; x_1 \dots x_m = f \; E_1$$

and E_1 is some arbitrary expression. A sequential G-machine would build a closure (or graph) for E_1 and pass this to f (this is call-by-need). Now suppose that f is known to evaluate its argument; one of the most important optimisations of the G-machine is now to evaluate E_1 in-line before calling f (this is call-by-value, which is substantially more efficient). In the G-machine jargon, we can use the E compilation scheme for E_1, instead of the C scheme, because f is strict[4].

To generate maximum parallelism in a *parallel* machine the code for g should build a closure for E_1 in the heap, spark it, and then enter the code for f (eager evaluation). However, if the machine is busy then call-by-value would have been better, because the opportunity for parallel evaluation of E_1 cannot be exploited.

In general, the opportunities for in-line evaluation are *exactly those* where parallelism demands eager evaluation (namely, where the function is known to evaluate its argument). The tension between these two evaluation mechanisms is vitally important to the performance of the machine - by building closures we risk losing the benefits of one of the most important G-machine optimisations, and yet in-line evaluation may lose opportunities for parallelism.

This hidden cost, of building closures rather than evaluating them in-line, suggests that there should be two versions of g, one of which has in-line evaluation of E_1, and one of which generates a closure for E_1 and sparks it (the sequential version and parallel version respectively). The version of g which is used at run-time can be chosen dynamically, depending as before on the load on the machine. While there are idle processors, we choose

---

3. A work-conserving scheduling discipline is one that never leaves idle a task that is eligible for execution when there is a processor available.

4. This approach to parallelism differs from our earlier work[Clac86a], in which the application of g to its arguments was rewritten to the graph of (f E_1), where the application node had a special run-time annotation to indicate a strict application. Then, evaluation of (f E_1) was begun, and the evaluation mechanism (the four-stroke engine) sparked E_1 when it found the annotation on the application node.

If a closure must be built and sparked, it is far better for the code for g to do this sparking in-line. In effect, the annotation is now embedded in the code for g.

function versions which generate lots of parallelism; then when all the processors are "busy enough", we switch to the (more efficient) sequential versions of the functions.

Generating multiple versions of the code for a function clearly involves a significant expansion in the size of the code for the program. How much of a problem this will be depends very much on the particular architecture, but we observe that the size of the heaps required to run typical functional programs substantially exceeds the size of the code so, to first order, code size is not a problem.

4. How to achieve locality

The memory of any scalable parallel machine is arranged in a hierarchy in which increasing size carries the cost of increasing latency. For high performance it is essential that a large fraction of memory references are to local memory; that is, a high degree of locality is essential.

There are two main techniques that can be used to increase locality in a graph-reduction machine, where the graph is spread through the machine's memory:

- Wherever possible, ensure that a processor is working on local data.

- Use caching techniques to keep local copies of remote graph nodes.

There is one trivial way to ensure that each processor is always working on local data, namely to run the whole program sequentially on a single processor; this observation shows up the fundamental tension between parallelism and locality. It follows that the granularity-increasing techniques of the previous section, which suppress unnecessary parallelism, will have the effect of increasing locality of reference as well; indeed, this is the main motivation for increasing granularity. The section begins with a brief discussion of scheduling techniques to improve locality.

The rest of the section focuses on the second technique for increasing locality, namely caching. We discuss a number of ideas we are implementing in the GRIP machine, which have quite general applicability.

4.1 The effect of scheduling policy on locality

In a parallel machine with distributed memory, the question of where a task is executed is of crucial importance to locality[5].

There are some simple scheduling expedients which may increase locality. For example:

- We can ensure that tasks allocate new graph in their local memory, and flush it to their local IMU, so a task's locus of activity should gradually become more and more local.

- We can attempt to resume a blocked task on the same PE which was executing it before it became blocked, because that PE probably has much of the task's data in its cache (see the discussion below on caches).

In a more general setting, experiments by Goldberg[Gold88a] and Eager et al[Eage86b] provide a good starting point for further study. Happily, both conclude that simple scheduling policies work nearly as well as more complex ones.

---

5. It is not as important on GRIP because of the bus-based architecture. We deliberately chose this organisation precisely because it allowed us to achieve good performance without solving this difficult problem!

All these ideas concern run-time scheduling heuristics. Unfortunately, efficient algorithms for distributed-memory multiprocessors often rely on distributing the *key data structures* for the problem across the memory of the machine, which gives rise to a natural distribution of the *tasks*. This requires compile-time pre-planning of data allocation policies, which is certainly a hard problem.

Currently, we make no attempt to perform this sort of planning. Instead, we rely on the caching strategies outlined below to migrate the relevant data into the processor(s) which are accessing it, regardless of where the data was first allocated. It would be interesting to study whether the benefits of more sophisticated compile-time planning justify the costs of performing it.

4.2 Caching in a graph-reduction machine

Caching is a well-known technique for increasing locality by keeping copies of recently-referenced data, so that the copy is rapidly available if the same data is referenced again. In a multiprocessor system with multiple caches, it is essential to maintain *coherence* between the caches, so that all caches contain up-to-date copies of their data, which is awkward if unrestricted writes are allowed. This problem has been effectively solved for bus-based multiprocessors, using "bus-watching" techniques, but appears much more intractable for non-bus-based multiprocessors.

However, it turns out that *cache coherence is not a problem in a graph-reduction system*, because arbitrary writes are not permitted. The natural unit of caching is a single graph node, which may or may not be in normal form:

- When a graph node is not in normal form, only one task will be allowed to access it, so the processor running that task can cache it freely. Other tasks attempting to access the node will be blocked until it has been updated with its normal form.

- When a graph node is in normal form, it can never change any further, so it can be freely cached by any processor that wishes to do so.

In other words, the same mechanism that deals with synchronisation between tasks also ensures that all accessible nodes are cacheable with no loss of coherence. This is a significant benefit: to our knowledge, no viable automatic cache-coherence scheme for an arbitrary multiprocessor has even been proposed, let alone implemented.

Functional languages are often praised for their clean semantics, deriving from the absence of side effects. It is rather pleasant to discover the same property leading to a significant architectural benefit, with important consequences for performance.

4.3 Exploiting a two-level store

The GRIP hardware provides a two-level address space: the fast, private memory in the PEs (the local address space) providing a simple read/write interface and the slower, larger, shared memory in the IMUs (the global address space) providing a more sophisticated interface. The former is an order of magnitude faster than the latter, and the two are addressed in different ways. This is unlike the flat address-space provided by commercially-available bus-based multiprocessors, and by the FLAGSHIP machine. In these machines, each PE's local memory forms a part of a single global address space.

The IMU address space also has two levels. Each GRIP board contains four PEs and one IMU, so that access to the on-board IMU has a somewhat lower latency than access to an off-board IMU, though the protocol is identical.

A flat address space is certainly an easier model to use from a programming point of view, but we believe that a two-level address space has important advantages which make it worth careful consideration. We make some preliminary observations.

- There is a clear analogy with the registers of a conventional CPU, which form a separate address space from the main memory, and whose effective exploitation is crucial to high performance. Indeed, the recent trend is to increase the size of the register set, rather than to eliminate it in favour of a flat address space.

- The use of a flat one-level address space requires an effective caching system *implemented in hardware*, since every memory access is made to this address space. Unfortunately, the usual cache-management hardware structures are probably inappropriate, because of the lack of spatial locality, the need to set lock bits when fetching non-local graph nodes, and the variable size of graph nodes. It is particularly inappropriate for the GRIP system, because of our use of intelligent memories: conventional cache technology depends on a simple read/write interaction of the processor with memory, whereas we use a more sophisticated processor-memory interaction protocol.

- Graph nodes in the PE's private address space need less administrative information attached to them, because they cannot be accessed by other tasks concurrently. Hence, manipulation of local data is likely to be faster than manipulation global data, even discounting the effects of latency.

- As we discuss below, it is possible for a PE to garbage-collect its local store independently of the rest of the system. This is an important benefit which is not easily available in a flat address space.

Just as compilers strive to use the registers effectively in a CPU, so we use the local PE memory as a large, explicitly-managed cache. Local memory is used, of course, for system software residing in the processor, and we devote all the remaining local memory to implement a **local heap**, which acts as a cache for the global heap.

A task running on a particular processor allocates new graph nodes in the processor's local heap. The new nodes are not immediately written out to the global heap. Indeed, they may never be written out, because each local heap has the important property that *it can be garbage-collected independently of the rest of the system*. Thus a node may be allocated, used, and garbage-collected locally without ever migrating into the global heap. (This can be thought of as a sophisticated form of write-back cache: data is not written back into main memory if it is known to be garbage.)

When a task needs to access a non-local graph node, it fetches it and creates a local copy in its heap, including with the local copy a pointer back to the original non-local node.

Whenever a task updates a local node with its normal form, it must also check whether it is a local copy of a global node; if so, it must also write the normal form out to the global node, in case there are tasks blocked on it. Of course, if the local node has no global counterpart, no further action need be taken.

When the local heap becomes too full, local copies of global nodes can be discarded freely; they will be reloaded again if they are required. (This corresponds to flushing a datum out of a cache.) If it is still too full, local nodes without global counterparts can be flushed out of the cache by allocating them as new nodes in the global heap.

All of this results in rather a fine grain of non-local access. For example, if a task is iterating down a non-local list, each list node would be fetched individually. This problem affects all caches, and the standard solution is to fetch rather more data than is actually required, in the hope that the extra data will subsequently prove useful. Conventional caches normally prefetch data which is *physically adjacent* to the data actually required, but in our situation it would clearly be better to prefetch data *pointed to* by the required node. In this way, larger units of data can be fetched from non-local memory. (How much extra data should be prefetched will certainly be specific to the particular architecture.)

There is an important complication: it is dangerous to prefetch unevaluated objects. When a node is fetched into a processor's local memory, the global copy must be locked to prevent other tasks from attempting to evauate it. The danger is that if the node is prefetched, it will thereby be locked even though the prefetching processor may never evaluate it. Other tasks may then block indefinitely on the node.

243

4.4 Local heap management

In order for the local heap to be independently garbage-collectable, it is essential for the processor to have knowledge of all the pointers into the local heap. This raises an interesting design issue: should it be possible for pointers into a particular processor's local heap to exist elsewhere in the system? For example, should it be possible for a global node in an IMU to point to a local node in some processor's local heap?

If this is allowed, then the processor has to maintain an "entry table", which contains an entry for each such inbound pointer. Then these entries can be used as starting-points for garbage collection, and the indirection they provide allows the garbage collector to move nodes around within the local heap. Furthermore, the processor has to be prepared to service remote requests from other processors, and to implement the complete task synchronisation mechanism on local nodes.

We have elected to take the alternative view: *no pointers can exist from outside a processor into its local heap*. This obviates the need for an entry table, and allows the processor to concentrate on graph reduction without concern about being unavailable to service remote fetch requests. Furthermore, a local node can be accessed without fear that a remote fetch is simultaneously accessing it. Nevertheless, our approach carries its own costs.

For example, a task sparks a child task by placing a pointer to the subgraph representing the child in the task pool held in an IMU. If there are to be no pointers into the processor's local memory, the entire subgraph representing the task must be flushed into global memory. (Here is another strong reason to avoid unnecessary sparks!)

4.5 Global heap management

The IMUs support an instruction set which includes allocation of variable-sized graph nodes, and synchronised access to these (cf Section 2.1.1). Garbage collection is performed using a variant of Baker's copying collector. There are three phases:

- First there is a global synchronisation, in which all PEs and IMUs agree to start garbage collection.

- All the processors perform a local garbage collection and tell the IMUs about each pointer into the global heap which they hold. The IMUs move the indicated node from From-space into To-space, and respond with new location of the node. This corresponds to "copying the roots" in a normal Baker collector.

- Now the processors can revert to graph reduction, while the IMUs concurrently scavenge To-space in the usual manner, communicating directly with each other when they encounter inter-IMU references. The usual Baker real-time method can be used to ensure that processors only have To-space pointers.

Thus, the vast bulk of global garbage collection is performed autonomously by the IMUs, which are highly optimised for just this kind of pointer-manipulation.

4.6 Stacks, blocking and resumption

Two sorts of graph node deserve special attention, namely stack segments, and function code blocks, which we discuss in this section and the next.

As mentioned earlier, each task uses an evaluation stack in a similar way to conventional compiled programs. When a task becomes blocked, this stack forms part of its state which must be preserved so that it can be resumed later.

We implement the stack by allocating a fixed-size local graph node, called a **stack segment**, to use as stack space for the task. If the stack overflows this node, we allocate a new stack segment, copy up the top section of the old stack into the new one, and place a link in the new stack segment back to the old one. When the stack shrinks again, we discard the new segment and revert to the old one.

Stacks are thereby regarded as perfectly ordinary graph nodes, and can be flushed out into global memory like any other node. (Of course, we don't actually flush the unused words in a stack segment.) When a task is blocked, its stack is tidied up, flushed into global memory, and a pointer to the topmost segment is attached to the blocking node. When the blocking node is finally updated with its final value, the IMU places the pointer to the stack object into the task pool, where any processor may pick it up, load in the stack, and resume the task.

We implement the following optimisation to this scheme. When a task is blocked, a pointer to its current *processor* is attached to the blocking node. Meanwhile, the processor maintains a task table containing pointers to the suspended tasks which it is holding. When the node is updated, the IMU sends notification of this fact to the processor concerned, which can then resume the task when it next has an opportunity. In this way, the task's stack never gets flushed. On the other hand, if the processor needs to clear some local heap space, it may flush the suspended stack, and inform the IMU of its (now global) location.

4.7 Function code blocks

Each closure in the heap contains a code-pointer and some arguments. But to what does the code-pointer point?

One method is to place the code for the closure in another graph node, and point to that. When a PE needs to execute the code, it dynamically loads the graph node in the usual way from the IMU which holds it, unless it already has a copy of that node. Since the PE's local heap will normally be significantly larger than the code for the program being executed, the local heap will eventually contain all the code for the currently-executing program.

Regarding code as graph nodes is elegant, because it provides a uniform way to garbage-collect code that is no longer in use, which in turn allows "eternal" programs to be written, such as operating systems.

Unfortunately, it also prevents the code being executed as efficiently as a sequential machine. For example, a return address pushed on the stack now has to be a pointer to a proper graph node, rather than a simple code address, because by the time it is activated the code to which it points may have been flushed or moved. In general, *a layer of address translation is added to almost every control transfer in the implementation.*

A better alternative is to use a conventional paging system in each processor to handle executable code. Code exhibits substantial spatial locality (in contrast to arbitrary graph nodes), so the communication system would be used more efficiently by moving pages at a time rather than individual function code segments. Paged-out pages can be represented in the global address space as graph nodes, but when they are paged in they become part of the processors local address space, with conventional hardware address-translation support.

We regard this as the right way to go, but GRIP does not support paged virtual memory, so for the present we load each processor with the code for the whole program.

5. Related work

A number of groups are working on parallel graph reduction machines, but so far only a few designs have been implemented.

The ALICE multiprocessor[Darl81a], built at Imperial College, is probably the first genuine parallel graph reduction machine. The graph is held (only) in a global memory connected to the processors by a switching network, and scheduling is on the basis of individual reduction steps. The processors and memory units are built from transputers running Occam, which imposes a layer of interpretation on many operations. As a result of these factors the machine is quite slow, but quite a lot has been learned from it[Harr86a].

The Alfalfa and Buckwheat systems, built by Ben Goldberg[Gold88a], are impressive implementations of compiled parallel graph reduction on an Intel Hypercube multicomputer and an Encore Multimax bus-based multiprocessor respectively. His systems are broadly similar to ours, but differ in many important details (for example, children use explicit notification to reawaken their parents; and tasks do not use an evaluation stack). Each graph node carries quite large amounts of administration information, so it seems likely that his systems pay a fairly heavy overhead for parallelism whether or not the machine has capacity to exploit it.

The Flagship project[Wats87a, Wats87b] is far more wide-ranging than ours, but part of it concerns the architecture and organisation of the parallel graph reduction machine itself, and a prototype has been built. The architecture provides a flat address space, and this is the main source of differences between their approach and ours. They are clearly targetted at a scalable architecture, and so the issues of scheduling and locality are of crucial importance to them. One aspect of this is that Flagship has a rather sophisticated (perhaps oversophisticated?) mechanism for distributing work thorough the machine.

Other projects with well-advanced designs include the Dutch Parallel Reduction Machine project[Brus87a], the Mars project[Cast86a] and the PAM project[Loog88a].

6. Summary

Our overall goal is to execute functional programs on a parallel machine, where each processor runs with efficiency broadly comparable with a sequential implementation, except when communication and synchronisation are unavoidable. We believe this goal is achievable, and expect to have a working implementation of the ideas we have discussed by the middle of 1989.

References.

Bake78a. Henry Baker, "List processing in real time on a serial computer", *CACM* 21(4) pp. 280-294 (Apr 1978).

Brus87a. TH Brus, MCJD van Eckelen, MO van Leer, and MJ Plasmeijer, "Clean - a language for functional graph rewriting", pp. 364-384 in *Functional programming languages and computer architecture, Portland*, ed. G Kahn, LNCS 274, Springer Verlag (Sept 1987).

Burn88a. Geoff Burn, Simon L Peyton Jones, and John Robson, "The Spineless G-machine", pp. 244-258 in *Proc ACM Conference on Lisp and Functional Programming. Snowbird* (July 1988).

Burt85a. F Warren Burton, "Speculative computation, parallelism and functional programming", *IEEE Trans Computers* C-34(12) pp. 1190-1193 (Dec 1985).

Cast86a. M Castan and et al, "MARS - a multiprocessor machine for parallel graph reduction", in *Proc 19th Hawaii Intl Conf on System Sciences* (1986).

Clac86a. Chris Clack and Simon L Peyton Jones, "The four-stroke reduction engine", *Proc ACM Conference on Lisp and Functional Programming*, pp. 220-232 (Aug 1986).

Cous85a. G Cousineau, PL Curien, and M Mauny, "The Categorical Abstract Machine", pp. 50-64 in *Functional Programming Languages and Computer Architecture, Nancy*, ed. JP Jouannaud, LNCS 201, Springer Verlag (Sept 1985).

Darl81a. John Darlington and Mike Reeve, "ALICE - a multiprocessor reduction machine for the parallel evaluation of applicative languages", pp. 66-76 in *Proc Conference on Functional Programming Languages and Computer Architecture, Portsmouth, New Hampshire*, ACM (Oct 1981).

Eage86a. DL Eager, J Zahorjan, and ED Lazowska, "Speedup versus efficiency in parallel systems", Tech Report 86-08-01, University of Sasketchewan (Aug 1986).

Eage86b. DL Eager, ED Lazowska, and J Zahorjan, "Adaptive load sharing in homogeneous distributed systems", *IEEE Trans Software Engineering* SE-12(5) pp. 662-675 (May 1986).

Fair87a. Jon Fairbairn and Stuart Wray, "TIM - a simple lazy abstract machine to execute supercombinators", pp. 34-45 in *Proc IFIP conference on Functional Programming Languages and Computer Architecture, Portland*, ed. G Kahn, Springer Verlag LNCS 274 (Sept 1987).

Gold88a. Benjamin F Goldberg, "Multiprocessor execution of functional programs", YALEU/DCS/RR-618, Dept of Computer Science, Yale University (April 1988).

Hals86a. RH Halstead, "An assessment of Multilisp - lessons from experience", *International Journal of Parallel Programming* 15(6) (Dec 1986).

Harr86a. PG Harrison and M Reeve, "The parallel graph reduction machine ALICE", pp. 181-202 in *Graph reduction: proceedings of a workshop, Santa Fe,* ed. RM Keller, LNCS 279, Springer Verlag (Oct 1986).

Huda83a. Paul Hudak, "Distributed task and memory management", pp. 277-289 in *Symposium on Principles of Distributed Computing,* ed. NA Lynch et al, ACM (Aug 1983).

John87a. Thomas Johnsson, "Compiling lazy functional languages", PhD thesis, PMG, Chalmers University, Goteborg, Sweden (1987).

Kieb87a. RB Kieburtz, "A RISC architecture for symbolic computation", in *Proc ASPLOS II* (Oct 1987).

Loog88a. R Loogen, H Kuchen, K Indermark, and W Damm, "Distributed implementation of programmed graph reduction", in *Proc workshop on implementation of lazy functional languages, Aspenas* (Sept 1988).

Peyt89b. SL Peyton Jones, "Parallel implementations of functional programming languages", *Computer Journal,* (April 1989).

Peyt87a. Simon L Peyton Jones, *The implementation of functional programming languages,* Prentice Hall (1987).

Peyt87b. Simon L Peyton Jones, Chris Clack, Jon Salkild, and Mark Hardie., "GRIP - a high-performance architecture for parallel graph reduction", pp. 98-112 in *Proc IFIP conference on Functional Programming Languages and Computer Architecture, Portland,* ed. G Kahn, Springer Verlag LNCS 274 (Sept 1987).

Peyt88a. Simon L Peyton Jones, Chris Clack , Jon Salkild , and Mark Hardie, "Functional programming on the GRIP multiprocessor", in *Proc IEE Seminar on Digital Parallel Processors, Lisbon, Portugal,* IEE (1988).

Peyt89a. Simon L Peyton Jones and Jon Salkild, "The Spineless Tagless G-machine", RN/89/21, Dept of Computer Science, University College London (March 1989).

Reyn88a. TJ Reynolds, SA Delgado-Rannauro, ASK Cheng, and AJ Beaumont, "BRAVE on GRIP", Department of Computer Science, University of Essex (1988).

Rugg87a. Carlos A Ruggiero and John Sargeant, "Control of parallelism in the Manchester dataflow machine", pp. 1-15 in *Proc IFIP conference on Functional Programming Languages and Computer Architecture, Portland,* ed. G Kahn, Springer Verlag LNCS 274 (Sept 1987).

Wats87b. I Watson, J Sargeant, P Watson, and V Woods, "Flagship computational models and machine architecture", *ICL Technical Journal* 5(3) pp. 555-574 (May 1987).

Wats87a. Paul Watson and Ian Watson, "Evaluating functional programs on the FLAGSHIP machine", pp. 80-97 in *Proc IFIP conference on Functional Programming Languages and Computer Architecture, Portland,* ed. G Kahn, Springer Verlag LNCS 274 (Sept 1987).

Chapter 6:
Parallel Logic Programming

Parallel logic programming is born from the integration of logic programming and concurrent programming. Logic-programming languages, such as Prolog [STE86], are founded on the procedural interpretation of Horn clauses proposed by Kowalski [KOW74], [KOW79]. According to this interpretation, a Horn clause

$$H \leftarrow B_1, \ldots, B_n \ (n \geq 0)$$

is regarded as a procedure definition, where H is the procedure name and $B_1, \ldots, B_n$ is the set of procedure calls that constitute the procedure body. According to this interpretation, the proof procedure for sequential logic programs solves subgoals in a sequential way. In particular, Prolog solves literals in a conjunction from left to right and solves clauses in a program in textual order, using the backtracking mechanism for handling nondeterminism. Nondeterminism results from a given program and activating goal statement admitting more than a single legitimate computation. In fact, if the unification of a goal with a clause fails, Prolog chooses the next clause with the same head and tries to unify the goal with it. This proof procedure is not the only possible proof strategy for Horn clauses. In particular, a parallel strategy may be a valid alternative to this one. In fact, the resolution process of a logic query contains many activities with embedded parallelism; thus, these activities can be performed in parallel.

For the implementation of logic-programming systems on parallel computers, many abstract models have been proposed that exploit the parallelism of logic programs. These models can be divided into *explicit-parallelism models* and *implicit-parallelism models*, depending on the kind of parallelism they exploit and how they exploit it.

1. In explicit parallelism, the parallelism is specified in a logic program by the programmer. Models of explicit parallelism are called *concurrent logic-programming languages*. Example of these are Parlog, P-Prolog, Delta-Prolog, and Concurrent Prolog. Using these languages, the programmer must specify, by means of annotations, which clauses can be solved in parallel.

2. In implicit parallelism, the parallelism is extracted by the language support both during static analysis and at runtime. Parallel logic models based on implicit parallelism are the Parallel Prolog Processor (PPP) [FAG90], the And/Or Process model [CON87], the Reduce/Or model [KAL91], Opera [BRI91], and the Parallel Logic Machine (PALM) [CAN91]. These models provide an automatic decomposition of the execution tree of a

logic program into a network of parallel processes by the language support. No explicit annotations must be added to the logic program.

We are interested in discussing concurrent logic-programming languages. These languages are designed to execute on parallel machines using explicit parallelism [TAL93]. Thus, a user must specify, by means of annotations, which clauses can be solved in parallel. To offer this computational model, languages embody some relevant concepts coming from concurrent programming models, such as the Communicating Sequential Processes (CSP) model. The aim of concurrent logic languages [SHA89], [TAK86] is the exploitation of the parallelism that is inside logic programs by means of a parallel proof strategy. Such languages can be used to design and implement concurrent applications.

There are two major types of parallelism: *Or parallelism* and *And parallelism*. These are described below.

1. Or parallelism is the parallel evaluation of several clauses, with the head of each clause unifying with the subgoal. For instance, if we have the subgoal ?– $p(X)$ and the clauses

    $$p(X) :- q(X).$$

    $$p(X) :- r(X).$$

    $$p(X) :- s(X).$$

then Or parallelism is exploited by unifying the subgoal with the head of each of the three clauses in parallel.

1. And parallelism consists of the parallel evaluation of each subgoal that the current goal comprises. For instance, if the goal to be solved is

    $$?– p(X), q(Y).$$

then using And parallelism, subgoals $p(X)$ and $q(Y)$ are solved in parallel.

Concurrent logic languages can be viewed as a new interpretation of Horn clauses: the process interpretation. According to this interpretation, an atomic goal $\leftarrow C$ can be viewed as a process, a conjunctive goal $\leftarrow C_1, ..., C_n$ can be viewed as a process network, and a logic variable shared between two subgoals can be viewed as a communication channel between two processes.

The exploitation of parallelism is achieved through the enrichment of a logic language like Prolog with a set of mechanisms for the annotation of programs. One of these mechanisms, for instance, is the annotation of shared logical variables in order to ensure that they are instantiated by only one subgoal. The goal of the logic variable annotation is to avoid conflicts between subgoals that are solved in parallel (And parallelism) since they could bind different values to the same variable.

A program in a concurrent logic language is a finite set of guarded clauses, as follows:

$$H \leftarrow G_1, G_2, ..., G_n \mid B_1, B_2, ..., B_m \qquad (n, m \geq 0)$$

where H is the clause head, $\{G_i\}$ is the guard, and $\{B_i\}$ is the body of the clause. Operationally, the guard is a test that must have been evaluated successfully with the head unification so that the clause could be selected. "$\mid$" is called a *commit operator*, and it is used as a conjunction between the guard and the clause body. If the guard is empty ($n = 0$), then the commit operator is omitted. The declarative reading of a guarded clause is the following: H is true if both $\{G_i\}$ and $\{B_i\}$ are true. According to the process interpretation, in order to solve H, the guard $\{G_i\}$ must be solved, and if its resolution is successful, then $B_1, B_2, ..., B_m$ are solved in parallel.

During the search for a candidate clause by which to solve a goal, a guard evaluation must not be allowed to bind any variables in the goal. If this were to be allowed, a guard might bind a variable in the goal even if the guard were to subsequently fail. Partial results that are obtained from head unification and solving the guard will become available to other subgoals. Nondeterminism incorporated into the computation model of these languages is called *committed-choice nondeterminism*, or *don't-care nondeterminism* to distinguish it from the *don't-know nondeterminism* that is typical of Prolog. According to don't-know nondeterminism, Prolog implements backtracking when an alternative fails. That is, if a resolution step fails, Prolog backtracks to the last choice point, selects the next clause in the procedure, and proceeds with this new clause. According to don't-care nondeterminism, when a choice is made during the execution of a concurrent logic program, then the evaluation commits to that choice, and no backtracking is performed; thus, variable bindings are never retracted. To ensure a correct choice, guards and input matching (that is, the unification of the input arguments) are utilized.

Concurrent logic languages implement *stream-And parallelism*. Using this type of parallelism, many subgoals can be executed concurrently. The subgoals communicate incrementally through the values bounded to their shared variables. From the semantics point of view, concurrent logic languages such as Parlog and Concurrent Prolog are not complete, because they are single-assignment languages. In fact, because of don't-care nondeterminism, these languages compute only one solution among those that a program logically defines. This kind of incompleteness (that is, that of Parlog and Concurrent Prolog) requires a different style of programming as regards Prolog, but it is not a real problem in the implementation of system-level applications.

IC-Prolog, proposed by Clark and McCabe [CLA79], can be considered to be the ancestor of the concurrent logic language family. IC-Prolog is an experimental language that implements stream-And parallelism and embodies concepts like the *pseudoparallel evaluation of calls in a conjunction* and a *dataflow-like execution mechanism*. The immediate successor of IC-Prolog is the Relational Language, proposed by Clark and Gregory [CLA81]. This language incorporates the main features of today's concurrent logic languages. Since the development of the Relational Language, several concurrent logic languages have been proposed. Among the most significant of these are Concurrent Prolog [SHA83a], Parlog [CLA86], Guarded Horn Clauses (GHC) [UED85], P-Prolog [YAN86], Delta-Prolog [PER84], concurrent constraint (cc) [SAR89], and Strand [FOS90].

Although concurrent logic languages extend the application areas of logic programming from expert systems, natural languages, and databases to system-level applications, program annotation requires a different style of programming in Prolog. In some cases, this may jeopardize the declarative feature typical of logic programming. Another problem of concurrent logic languages is the lack of abstraction mechanisms; this lack may limit the application areas of these languages. However, it has been shown that object-oriented mechanisms can be implemented using concurrent logic languages [SHA83b].

Included in this chapter are three papers that discuss Parlog, GHC, and cc, respectively.

The first paper included here, "PARLOG and Its Applications," by Clark, introduces the basic concepts of Parlog and discusses the major application areas of the language. The Parlog language (a parallel logic-programming language) can be considered to be the immediate descendant of the Relational Language. Parlog uses *mode* declaration of predicate arguments to establish access restriction to variables. This paper describes how applications in the areas of system programming, object-oriented programming, and discrete event simulation can be developed using Parlog. Some comparisons are made between Parlog, Concurrent Prolog, and GHC.

The second paper included in this chapter, "Guarded Horn Clauses," by Ueda, discusses GHC, selected as the language of the Future Generation Computer Systems (FGCS) project of ICOT, Tokyo, Japan. This language inherits the basic concepts of Parlog and Concurrent Prolog, but it is simpler than both of these languages and allows a more efficient implementation. The most characteristic feature of GHC is that the *guard* is the only syntactic construct added to Horn clauses, because synchronization is realized by the semantic rules of guards. After providing an overview of the language, this paper presents a collection of example programs developed using GHC. Then, it discusses the main features of GHC and compares it with other parallel and sequential languages.

This chapter's third paper, "Semantic Foundations of Concurrent Constraint Programming," by Saraswat, Rinard, and Panangaden, describes a concurrent constraint (cc) logic-programming framework. Constraint logic programming is an important generalization of logic programming aimed at replacing the pattern-matching mechanism of unification by a more general operation called *constraint satisfaction*. In this environment, a *constraint* is a subset of the space of all possible values that a variable of interest can take. This paper gives the semantic foundations of a framework of constraint logic programming in which a computation progresses by processes that communicate by placing constraints in a global store and synchronize by checking that a constraint is entailed by the store. This approach offers a framework for dealing with domains other than those of Herbrand terms such as *integers* and *Booleans*. The authors formalize the basic notions of a constraint system and present operational and denotational semantics for cc languages.

References cited

[BRI91]   J. Briat et al., "Scheduling of OR-parallel Prolog on a Scalable Reconfigurable Distributed Memory Multiprocessor," *Lecture Notes in Computer Sci.—Proc. Parallel Architectures and Languages Europe (PARLE '91)*, Vol. 506, Springer-Verlag, New York, N.Y., 1991, pp. 385–402.

[CAN91]   M. Cannataro, G. Spezzano, and D. Talia, "A Parallel Logic System on a Multicomputer Architecture," *Future Generation Computer Systems*, Vol. 6, No. 4, Sept. 1991, pp. 317–331.

[CLA79]   K.L. Clark and F.G. McCabe, "The Control Facilities of IC-PROLOG," in *Expert Systems in the Micro-Electronic Age*, Edinburgh Univ. Press, Edinburgh, United Kingdom, 1979, pp. 122–149.

[CLA81]   K.L. Clark and S. Gregory, "A Relational Language for Parallel Programming," *Proc. Conf. Functional Programming Languages and Computer Architecture*, 1981, pp. 171–178.

[CLA86]   K.L. Clark and S. Gregory, "PARLOG: Parallel Programming in Logic," *ACM Trans. Programming Languages and Systems*, Vol. 8, No. 1, Jan. 1986, pp. 1–49.

[CON87]   J.S. Conery, *Parallel Execution of Logic Programs*, Kluwer Academic Pub., Norwell, Mass., 1987.

[FAG90]   B.S. Fagin and A.M. Despain, "The Performance of Parallel Prolog Programs," *IEEE Trans. Computers*, Vol. 39, No. 12, Dec. 1990, pp. 1434–1445.

[FOS90]   I. Foster and S. Taylor, *Strand : New Concepts in Parallel Programming*, Prentice-Hall, Inc., Englewood Cliffs, N.J., 1990.

[KAL91]   L.V. Kale, "The REDUCE-OR Process Model for Parallel Execution of Logic Programs," *J. Logic Programming*, No. 11, July 1991, pp. 55–84.

[KOW74]   R. Kowalski, "Predicate Logic as a Programming Language," *Proc. IFIP Congress '74*, North Holland Pub., Amsterdam, The Netherlands, 1974, pp. 569–574.

[KOW79]   R. Kowalski, "Algorithm = Logic + Control," *Comm. ACM*, Vol. 22, No. 7, July 1979, pp. 424–436.

[PER84]   L.M. Pereira and R. Nasr, "Delta-Prolog: A Distributed Logic Programming Language," *Proc. Int'l Conf. 5th Generation Computer Systems 1984*, North-Holland, Amsterdam, The Netherlands, 1984, pp. 283–291.

[SAR89]   V.A. Saraswat, *Concurrent Constraint Programming Languages*, doctoral thesis, Carnegie Mellon Univ., Pittsburgh, Pa., Jan. 1989 (also published as Tech. Report CMU-CS-89-108, Carnegie Mellon Univ., Pittsburgh, Pa., Jan. 1989).

[SHA83a] E. Shapiro, "A Subset of Concurrent Prolog and Its Interpreter," Tech. Report Vol. TR-003, ICOT, Tokyo, Japan, 1983.

[SHA83b] E. Shapiro and A. Takeuchi, "Object Oriented Programming in Concurrent Prolog," *New Generation Computing,* Vol. 1, No. 1, 1983, pp. 25–48.

[SHA89] E. Shapiro, "The Family of Concurrent Logic Programming Languages," *ACM Computing Surveys,* Vol. 21, No. 3, Sept. 1989, pp. 412–510.

[STE86] L. Sterling and E. Shapiro, *The Art of Prolog,* MIT Press, Cambridge, Mass., 1986.

[TAK86] A. Takeuchi and K. Furakawa, "Parallel Logic Programming Languages," *Lecture Notes in Computer Sci.—Proc. 3rd Int'l Logic Programming Conf.,* Vol. 225, Springer-Verlag, New York, N.Y., 1986, pp. 242–254.

[TAL93] D. Talia, "A Survey of PARLOG and Concurrent Prolog: The Integration of Logic and Parallelism," *Computer Languages,* Vol. 18, No. 3, 1993, pp. 185–196.

[UED85] K. Ueda, "Guarded Horn Clauses," Tech. Report Vol. TR-103, ICOT, Tokyo, Japan, 1985.

[YAN86] R. Yang and H. Aiso, "P-Prolog: A Parallel Logic Language Based on Exclusive Relation," *Lecture Notes in Computer Sci.—Proc. 3rd Int'l Logic Programming Conf.,* Vol. 225, Springer-Verlag, New York, N.Y., 1986, pp. 255–269.

PARLOG and Its Applications

KEITH L. CLARK

Abstract—The key concepts of the parallel logic programming language PARLOG are introduced by comparing the language with Prolog. Some familiarity with Prolog and with the concepts of logic programming is assumed. Two major application areas of PARLOG, systems programming and object oriented programming are illustrated. Other applications are briefly surveyed. This paper is a revision of [3].

Index Terms—Communicating processes, logic programming applications, logic programming languages, object oriented programming, parallel programming languages.

I. PARLOG VERSUS PROLOG

PARLOG is one of a family of parallel logic programming languages characterized by the use of the concept of guards and committed choice nondeterminism as in Dijkstra's language of guarded commands [15]. The family comprises three main languages: Concurrent Prolog [39], GHC [45], and PARLOG [6]. All three can be viewed as descendants of the Relational Language [5], which was the first parallel logic programming language to incorporate the concept of committed choice. The languages are surveyed in [43]. Following Ringwood [38], the key concepts of PARLOG will be introduced by comparing it with Prolog.

Single Solution Language

The use of committed choice makes programming in PARLOG and its sister languages very different from programming in Prolog. Given a conjunction of conditions

a(X),b(X,Y),c(Y)

only one solution to the conjunction can be found because PARLOG will commit to using just one clause to solve each condition/call in the conjunction. If the clause that is selected to solve the **a(X)** call ultimately fails, or if the use of the clause generates a binding for **X** for which there is no solution to the **b(X,Y)** call, then the whole conjunction fails. There will be *no* backtracking on the choice of the clause.

Shallow Backtracking as Search for a Candidate Clause

At first sight this may seem to be overly restrictive and to be throwing away much of the power of Prolog. However, there are many applications of Prolog which only

Manuscript received April 5, 1987; revised December 15, 1987. This work was supported by the SERC via three Alvey contracts. The author was also supported by the SERC through its Senior Fellowship Scheme.

The author is with the Department of Computing, Imperial College, London SW7 2B2, England.

IEEE Log Number 8824632.

make use of very shallow backtracking to search for a clause which unifies with the call, or to search for a unifying clause for which some initial sequence of test calls in the body of the clause succeeds. A cut after the sequences of test calls is then used to prevent backtracking—to *commit* to the use of this clause. For these programs the deep search capability of Prolog is not needed.

An example of this type of program is the following Prolog program for partitioning a list into two sublists comprising respectively all the elements greater than and all the elements less than or equal to some partition element **PE**. The program is written in Edinburgh syntax. Names beginning with an uppercase letter are variables.

> **partition(PE,[],[],[]).**
> **partition(PE,[H|T],[H|G],L) :- PE < H,!, partition(PE,T,G,L).**
> **partition(PE,[H|U],G,[H|L]) :- partition(PE, T,G,L).**

Given some call **partition(2,[1,4,−1,−7,9],Gr,Ls)** the Prolog backtracking search will first try to unify the call with the head of the first clause **partition(PE,[],[],[])**. This will fail. Prolog will backtrack to try to unify with the head of the second clause **partition(PE,[H|T],[H|G],L)**. This unification will succeed with **H** bound to **1** and **Gr** bound to **[1|G]**. The evaluation will continue with the test condition **2 < 1**, which will fail. A shallow backtrack will cause Prolog to undo the bindings to **H** and **Gr** and to try the last clause. This will bind **H** to **1** and **Ls** to **[1|L]**.

Parallel Search for Candidate Clause

In PARLOG, the search for a *candidate* clause, a clause to which the evaluation can commit to in the attempt to solve some call, can either be done sequentially, as in Prolog, or in parallel. That is, all the clauses for the relation of a call can be tried in parallel to find a matching clause for which some initial sequence of test calls succeeds. Following Dijkstra [15], the unification with the head of the clause and the evaluation of the test calls is called the *guard* computation of the clause, and the test calls are called the *guard* calls. Successful completion of the guard computation of a clause makes the clause a candidate clause. When a candidate clause is found the evaluation commits to the use of that clause. It will commit to the first candidate clause to be found.

The PARLOG program for partition is:

> **partition(PE,[],[],[]).**

partition (PE,[H|T],[H|G],L) < − PE < H : partition(PE,T,G,L).
partition (PE,[H|T],G,[H|L] < − H = < PE : partition(PE,T,G,L).

where the : separates the *guard* calls from the *body* calls. Given the call **partition(2,[1,4, − 1, − 7,9],Gr,Ls)** PARLOG will try the three clauses in parallel. The second and third clauses will unify with the call, but only the third clause will have a succeeding guard call. This is the only candidate clause. Notice that because of the parallel search we need to have an explicit **H = < PE** test in the last clause. In Prolog, because of the sequential search, we can "cheat" and drop the test because it is the complement of the test **PE < H** of the second clause which must have failed if Prolog ever tries the last clause. PARLOG's parallel search for a candidate clause forces a more declarative style.

Delaying the Binding of Call Variables Until Commitment

In Prolog, during the sequential search for a candidate clause for a call **G**, provisional bindings may be made to variables in **G**—the *call variables*—as a clause **C** is being tried. These provisional bindings to the call variables are then undone it is found that the head of **C** does not fully unify with **G** or if one of the guard calls of **C** fails. This happens with the **partition(2,[1,4 − 1, − 7,9],Gr,Ls)** call when the second clause is being tested. The provisional bindings **H=1, Gr=[1|G]** to the call variable **H** and **G1** are undone when the test **P < H** fails and Prolog backtracks to try the third clause.

In PARLOG, because clauses may be tried in parallel, no clause is allowed to bind variables in the call until the evaluation commits to the use of some candidate clause. This is achieved by associating with each relation **R** a mode of use, a specification of which argument positions are *input* and which *output*. During the unification between a call and clause head to select a candidate clause only the terms in the input argument positions are unified (in parallel) and this unification is constrained so that only variables in the clause may be bound. The unification between call and clause head in an input argument position will *suspend* if it can only proceed by binding a call variable. The unification on each input argument is therefore just an input match which suspends if the call argument is not sufficiently instantiated to determine whether the match should succeed or fail.

Unification between the call and clause head terms in the output argument positions of a clause is attempted (again in parallel) only after the commitment to use the clause. This is full unification in which both call and clause head variables may be bound. Note that holding back of the unification of the output argument terms until after commitment means that the output argument terms given in the call *cannot* effect which clause is selected. Failure of any output argument unification for the selected clause will result in failure of the call. There will be no backtracking to try another candidate clause which might unify with the call in the output argument positions. This forces a style of programming in which call outputs arguments are either unbound variables or terms that we know will unify with the output arguments terms of any candidate clause for the call.

The mode declaration for the **partition** program is

mode partition(PE?,L?,Gr^,LS^).

The ? signals an input argument position, the ^ an output argument position. Because the third argument and fourth arguments are specified as output arguments, the variables **Gr** and **Ls** of the call **partition(2,[1,4, − 1, − 7,9],Gr,Ls)** will not be unified with the head arguments while the three **partition** clauses are being tested. For example, during the guard evaluation of the third clause, only the first two arguments **PE** and **[H|T]** of the clause will be matched with the first two arguments of the call generating input bindings **PE=2,H=1,T=[4, − 1,7,9]** for variables of the clause. The unification for the third and fourth arguments will be delayed pending the result of the test **1 = < 2**. Only when this guard test has succeeded, and the evaluation has committed to the use of this clause, will the unification of the third and fourth arguments be attempted, resulting in the bindings **Ls=[1|L], G=Gr**.

Communication on Commitment

This delaying of the binding of any call variable until after commitment has a double benefit.

First, it allows efficient implementation of the or-parallel search for a candidate clause. The implementation does not need to allow for competing and incompatible bindings being generated for the same call variable by the parallel testing of alternative clauses. As with Prolog, the PARLOG implementation can represent variables as addresses of a single memory location.

Second, it allows efficient implementation of the and-parallel evaluation of a conjunction of calls *with shared variables*.

Suppose that we have two calls **G** and **G'** being evaluated in parallel with a shared variable **X** that will be bound by **G**. By delaying the binding of **X** until the evaluation of **G** commits to the use of some clause, we are also delaying the communication of the binding to the concurrent call **G'** until **G** *commits*. Commitment to some clause for **G** means that the programmer *guarantees* the communicated binding. This is a very significant property of the language. It means that the implementation does not need to be able to handle messages to undo the binding of a variable and to roll back the evaluation of a parallel call to the point where the binding was received. This key idea, that communication between parallel indeterminate processes be delayed until the communicating process commits to an evaluation path, is derived from CSP [28]. Unlike Prolog, in PARLOG a variable is bound once only and the binding is never undone. PARLOG does not need to keep a trial of the variables bound by a call.

Consider the parallel conjunction:

partition(2,[1,4,−1,−7,9],Gr,Ls),process(Gr,Ls,SI)

The binding **[1|G]** for **Gr** made by the **partition** call will be communicated to the **process** call only when the **partition** call commits to the use of the third clause.

Data Flow Versus Control Flow

In Prolog, because of the sequential evaluation, the first call in which a shared variable **X** appears usually generates the first partial binding, say binding **X** to a list pattern term of the form **[A|X1]**. This first call will also usually generate the complete and final binding for **X** by subsequently generating a list structure binding for the variable **X1** and some term binding for the variable **A**. (Of course, it is not essential that the first Prolog call generates the complete binding for a variable. A very useful Prolog programming feature has the first call generate only a partial binding that is completed by later calls. We shall see that the generalization of this, where the calls are evaluating concurrently, is an exeedingly powerful feature of PARLOG.)

In PARLOG, because the calls are evaluated in parallel, the textual order of the calls does not tell us which call will first bind some shared variable. Instead, the mode declarations for the calls determine a data flow network. Because of the mode declarations, usually only one call of a parallel conjunction is able to generate the first binding for some shared variable.

Remember that during the matching between the input arguments of the call and the clause head no variable in the call can be bound and that the attempt to bind a call variable **V** during the matching on a particular input argument leads to a suspension of that input match. The input match will remain suspended until the evaluation of some other call generates a binding for **V**. At that point the input matched is resumed.

Suspension of input matching until a variable is bound is the process synchronization mechanism of PARLOG. Shared variables are communication channels between processes, a process being the evaluation of some call of a parallel conjunction.

Suppose that **partition** is invoked within a parallel conjunction:

feeder(List),partition(0,List,X,Y),c1(X),c2(Y)

Because of the mode declaration for **partition** the input matching against the variable **List** of each of the three **partition** clauses will immediately suspend until the variable is bound to a nonvariable term. The input matching of the first clause will suspend because it is trying to match **List** against **[]**, and the input matching of each of the other two clauses will suspend because it is an attempt to match the variable with the term **[H|T]**. Because the input matching of all three clauses is suspended, the evaluation of the **partition** call is suspended. Let us also assume that because of their mode declarations both **c1** and **c2** suspend during input matching on each of their clauses waiting respectively for nonvariable bindings for **X** and **Y**.

The **partition** call will remain suspended until the evaluation of the only other call in which **List** appears generates a nonvariable binding for the call. So, the **feeder** call cannot similarly suspend on input matching against **List**. If it does, there is deadlock.

Let us suppose that some output unification of **feeder** binds **List** to the term **[E|L1]** where **E** and **L1** are still unbound variables. Immediately the input matching of each of the three partition clauses is resumed. That of the first clause fails, but that of the second and third clause will succeed with **H** and **T** bound respectively to **E** and **L1**. The input match on the first argument has already bound **PE** to 0.

The guard calls **0 < E** and **E = < 0** of the respective clauses are now attempted but will immediately suspend waiting for the value of **E** to be generated by **feeder**. Remember that no clause is allowed to generate a binding for a call variable until after successful termination of all the input matching and all the guard calls. So guard calls must also suspend if they need the value of a call variable. In this case, the guards are calls to primitives that will automatically suspend until both arguments are nonvariable. Where a guard call is a call to a program defined relation, the programmer must ensure that any call variable **V** to which it might get access via the input matching will suspend if it needs the value **V**. The call will automatically suspend if it attempts to match **V** against a nonvariable term during some input match. But it will not suspend it the binding is attempted during some output unification. There is a PARLOG primitive, **data(X)**, which can be used to suspend a computation until its argument variable **X** is bound to a nonvariable. Suspending primitives such as **>** and **= <** are implemented using **data**. Guard calls that cannot generate bindings for call variables are called *safe* guard calls. We shall return to the topic of safe guards later.

Let us suppose that **feeder** eventually binds **E** to 2. The competing guard calls of the two suspended **partition** clauses are resumed. The guard calls are now the tests **0 < 2, 2 = < 0**. Only the **0 < 2** call will succeed. The evaluation of the **partition** call will commit to the second clause and the output unifications of the clause will bind **X** to **[2|G]**. At this point the suspended **c1** call is resumed. The **c2** call will remain suspended until the **partition** process is passed an element on its input list that is less than or equal to 0. The **partition** process, which has now been reduced to the recursive call **partition(0,L1,G,Y)** will again suspend if the **feeder** process has not yet generated a binding for the variable **L1**.

Two Way Communication

In the above example, the interprocess communication was one way. Only one process, the process that generated the first partial binding for each shared variable, had a hand in generating the complete and final binding. Thus, **feeder**, which generated the first partial binding **[2|L1]** for shared variable **List**, also had to incrementally generate the complete list structure binding for **List** by further incremental binding of the variable **L1**. This was because the program for partition recursed to another call which suspended on any unbound variables in its list structure input.

The strict one way communication is not essential. The **partition** process could have reduced to a nonrecursive call in which **L1** was passed in an output argument position. (Of course, it would no longer be a program for partitioning lists.) Correspondingly, the **feeder** process could reduce to a call in which **L1** was passed in an input argument position and the process suspended on an input match against the variable. The communication between the processes would then be two way, the two processes would cooperate in the construction of the complete binding for **List**.

Back Communication

The alternating generation of the next term on some list structure is not the normal form of two way communication used in PARLOG programs. More usually, one process generates the entire sequence of terms on the list structure but the terms are incomplete; they contain variables that are bound by some other process. In this style of program, the incrementally constructed list of terms is a stream of incomplete messages generated by one process and communicated to one or more other processes. Suppose that after generating each incomplete message the generator reduces to a conjunction of calls one of which suspends waiting for a variable in the incomplete message to be bound by one of the processes that received the message. The binding of the message variable has the role of a *back communication* from the receiving process to the generating process.

For example, suppose that a call **G(X)** generates a partial binding of the form **[t(A)|X1]** for some shared variable **X** where **t(A)** is some term containing variable **A**. Suppose that **G(X)** now reduces to two calls **C(A),G(X1)** and that **C(A)** suspends until **A** is bound to a nonvariable. The binding of **A** will be a back communication from some process that receives the message **t(A)**.

Back communication is an exceedingly powerful programming technique of PARLOG and the other concurrent logic programming languages Concurrent Prolog and GHC. Its potential and power was first recognized by Shapiro [39]. It is much used in the applications of these languages to operating systems and to object oriented programming. Although the concurrent languages are essentially eager evaluation languages—processes generate output bindings as fast as they can and are constrained only by availability of input—one can also use the technique of incomplete messages to emulate demand driven lazy evaluation.

In demand driven evaluation, a process is constrained by the need for its output. To convert an eager generator **G** of a list of terms into a demand driven generator we essentially reprogram **G** so that it becomes a consumer of

an input list of incomplete messages which are just unbound variables. Each unbound variable is a request for a value to be generated by the generator. On receipt of each unbound variable, the process binds the variable to the next value it would have generated and it then suspends waiting for the next message variable. The consumer of the values that **G** generates is the generator of the sequence of request variables sent to **G**.

Demand Driven Generator

```
mode integers(?,^).
integers(N,[N|L) < −
    N1 is N+1,
    integers(N1,L).
```

is an eager generator of an infinite list of integers. The call **integers(0,List)** will result in **List** being incrementally bound to the infinite list **[1,2,3,. . .]**. Once started, there is no constraint on the evaluation of the call.

The lazy version of the program is:

```
mode integers(?,?).
integers(N,[N1|L) < −
    N1 is N+1,
    integers(N1,L).
integers(N,[]).
```

Now the second argument is input and so the call **integers(0,List)** is suspended until some other call generates a partial binding for **List**. This other call is the "consumer" of sequence of intergers that will be generated by **integers** on request. When the other call binds **List** a term of the form **[X|L1]**, the **X** is the first request variable and the **L1** is the yet to be generated sequence of further request variables. N1 is bound to **X** during the input matching, so the **is** call of the **integers** process binds **X** to **1**. The process reduces to **integers(1,L1)** which suspends waiting for the next request variable to be sent on **L1**. If the "consumer" does not need any more integers it simple binds **L1** to [] at which point the **integers** process will terminate (using the second clause).

This emulation of lazy evaluation, and its generalization which allows the implementation of bounded communication buffers between processes, was first described by Takeuchi and Furakawa [42] using Concurrent Prolog. The PARLOG emulation of bounded buffers and lazy evaluation, and techniques for converting eager programs into lazy programs, are further discussed in [6] and [25].

II. The PARLOG Language

A PARLOG program for a relation **r** comprises a *mode* declaration and a sequence of clauses separated by . or ;.

The mode declaration is of the form $r(m_1,m_2,. . .,m_k)$ where each m_i is an optional argument identifier followed by ? or ^. A ? specifies an input argument position and a ^ an output argument position. Following the example of GHC, we shall also adopt the convention (first proposed for use with PARLOG by Ringwood [38]) that in the absence of a mode declaration all the argument positions of a relation are implicitly declared as input positions.

The **.** and **;** clause separators determine the control used to search for a candidate clause. Each group of **.** separated clauses is tried in parallel. The clauses following a **;** are only tried if all the clauses that precede the **;** have been found to be noncandidate clauses.

For example, suppose that a relation is defined by a sequence of clauses:

C1. C2; C3.

The clauses **C1** and **C2** will be tested for candidacy in parallel but the clause **C3** will be tested only if both **C1** and **C2** are found to be noncandidate clauses. If **C1** and **C2** were separated by a **;** instead of a **.** then the search for a candidate clause would be entirely sequential, as in Prolog.

Each PARLOG clause is of the form

$r(t_1, t_2, \ldots, t_n) < -$ <guard calls> : <body calls>

where the **:** separates the <guard calls> from the <body calls>.

The clause is a *candidate* clause for a call $r(t'_1, t'_2, \ldots, t'_n)$ if and only if for each input argument position j of the mode declaration for **r** the call argument t'_j input matches t_j (that is it unifies with t_j *without* generating a nonvariable binding for any variable in the call) and each call in <guard calls> succeeds *without* generating a nonvariable binding for any variable in the call. The input matching for each input argument position and the evaluation of <guard calls> proceed in parallel. Together, they constitute the *guard computation* of the clause.

The clause is a *noncandidate* if and only if one of the input matches fails or one of the <guard calls> fails.

An input match or a guard call may suspend waiting for a nonvariable binding of a call variable to be generated by some concurrently evaluating call.

The evaluation of a call can commit to any clause found to be a candidate clause for the call.

On commitment to some clause, the output unification is performed and in parallel the evaluation of the <body calls> is started. There is no backtracking on the choice of the clause. Output unification is the full unification of the call argument t'_k with the corresponding head argument term t_k (possibly further instantiated as a result of the input matching and the evaluation of the <guard calls>) for each k that is an output argument position of the mode declaration for **r**.

<guard calls> and <body calls> are either empty or a single call or a conjunction of calls. The single call to the primitive **true**, which always succeeds, is equivalent to the empty call. When <guard calls> is empty the separating **:** is dropped.

There are two types of conjunction: the parallel conjunction **G1,G2** and the sequential conjunction **G1 & G2**. **G1** and **G2** are themselves single calls or conjunctions of calls. **&** is assumed to be more binding than **,**. Brackets are used to override this precedence. In a parallel conjunction **G1,G2** the component calls **G1** and **G2** are evaluated in parallel. In a sequential conjunction **G1 & G2**

the evaluation of **G2** is only started when the evaluation of **G1** successfully terminates, as in Prolog.

Example Program—A Queue as a Process

```
queue(M) < - empty_queue(Q),aux_queue(M,Q).

aux_queue([],Q).
aux_queue([insert(E)|MoreM],Q) < -
   insert_at_back(E,Q,NewQ),
   aux_queue(MoreM,NewQ).
aux_queue([remove(V)|MoreM],Q) < -
   remove_from_front(V,Q,newQ),
   aux_queue(MoreM,NewQ).
```

This is a PARLOG program which represents a queue as a process that receives messages to insert and delete elements from the queue. The sequence of **remove** and **insert** messages must be generated by some other call because, in the absence of an explicit mode declaration, the first argument of **aux_queue** is implicitly declared an input argument.

In the intended use of the program, the incoming messages are of the form **insert(t)**, where **t** is some given element to insert, or of the form **remove(A)**, where **A** is a variable. The **remove** messages are incomplete messages that are completed by the **aux_queue** process. The input matching between the incoming **remove(A)** message and the **remove(V)** term in the head of the second clause will bind **V** to **A**. The variable **A** is then bound by the call to **remove_from_front**. The binding of the message variable **A** will be a back communication to the sender of the incomplete **remove** message.

The second argument of the **aux_queue** process is some data structure recording the current state of the queue. As in Prolog, the most efficient representation of a queue is as a *difference list*. A difference list is a term of the form $L - T$.

If **L** is $[t_1, t_2, \ldots, t_k | T]$, we have a difference list $[t_1, t_2, \ldots, t_k | T] - T$ which represents a positive queue of length k with $t_1, t_2, \ldots, t_k$ the elements on the queue. t_1 is the head of the queue and t_k is the last element to have been inserted.

If **T** is **L**, we have a difference list of the form $L - L$ which is the empty queue.

Finally, if **T** is $[t_1, t_2, \ldots, t_k | L]$ we have a difference list $L - [t_1, t_2, \ldots, t_k | L]$ which represents a negative queue, a queue from which $t_1, t_2, \ldots, t_k$ have already been removed. It is a queue to which only $t_1, t_2, \ldots, t_k$ can be inserted, and in that order. When they have all been inserted we shall end up with the empty queue.

Assuming a difference list representation of queues, the following clauses define **empty_queue**, **remove_from_front**, and **insert_at_back**.

```
mode empty_queue(^).
empty_queue(L-L).

remove_from_front(V,Q,NewQ) < -
   Q=[V|L]-T,
   NewQ=L-T.
```

```
insert_at_back(E,Q,NewQ) < -
    Q = L - [E|T],
    NewQ = L - T.
```

The definition of **remove_from_front** tells us that if the old queue **Q** is a difference list of the form [**V**|**L**] – **T** then **V** is the head of the queue and the difference list **L** – **T** is therefore the queue **Q** with **V** removed from the front.

The definition of **insert_at_back** tells us that if the old queue **Q** is of the form **L**–[**E**|**T**] then it must be of the form [t1,t2,...,tk,E | T] – [E | T] representing a queue comprising [t1,t2,...,tk. Consequently, the difference list [t1,t2,...,E|T] –T will represent the new queue [t1,t2,...,tk,E which has **E** as a new last element.

queue([insert(7),remove(A),. . .])

The call immediately reduces to

empty_queue(Q),
aux_queue([insert(7),remove(A),. . .],Q)

The **empty_queue** call immediately binds **Q** to the difference list **L** – **L** where **L** is a variable. This is the most general representation of the empty queue. We are left with the call

aux_queue([insert(7),remove(A),. . .],L–L)

The second clause for **aux_queue** is the only candidate clause. The call input matches with the head of this clause

aux_queue([insert(E)|MoreM],Q)

and reduces to the parallel conjunction

insert_at_back(7,L–L,NewQ),
aux_queue([remove(A)],NewQ)

The **insert_at_back** call will now reduce to the pair of unifications

L–L = L1–[7|T1],   (1)
NewQ = L1–T1

where **L1** and **T1** are new variables of the invoked clause. Providing **NewQ** has not yet been bound by the recursive **aux_queue** call these two unifications result in **NewQ** being bound to [7|T1]–T1 representing the queue with 7 as its only element. By this time the **aux_queue** call will have reduced to

remove_from_front(A,NewQ,NewQ1),
aux_queue([. . .],NewQ1)

and the **remove_from_front** call immediately reduces to the pair of unifications

NewQ = [A|L2]–T2,   (2)
NewQ1 = L2–T2

Both pairs of unifications (1) and (2) are able to generate a binding for the shared variable **NewQ**. If it is the first pair, this corresponds to the processing of the **insert(7)** message before the **remove(A)** message. The unifications

(1) result in **NewQ** being bound to [7|T1]–T1. In that event the unification pair (2) will bind **A** to 7 and **NewQ1** to L1–L1 which is a new representation of the empty queue which results after the processing of the **insert(7)**, **remove(A)** messages. If pair (2) are the first to bind **NewQ**, it will be given the binding [A|L2]–T2 which must have the removed **A** as its head. The pair of unifications (1) will now bind **A** to 7 and make **NewQ1** either T2–T2 or T1–T1 or L1–L1 depending on the variable/ variable bindings that are generated by the unifications.

As an exercise, we leave the reader to examine in detail what will happen if the first two messages are reversed, i.e., if the sequence is [**remove(A)**,**insert(7)**,. . .]. You will discover that the program can handle this reverse order just as well. If the **remove(A)** message is processed first, **NewQ** will be bound to a negative queue of the form L1–[A|L1] and the message variable **A** will only be bound when the **insert(7)** message is processed.

The above PARLOG program is based on a Concurrent Prolog program given in [39]. It is a very flexible represenation of a queue because it can handle **remove** and **insert** messages received in any order. If it receives a **remove(A)** message when the queue is empty it simply stores the **A** as a negative queue element to be bound when an **insert** message arrives. It can process any number of **remove** message before the first **insert message** arrives. The variables of the messages are simply inserted as negative queue elements to be bound in order by **insert** messages when they arrive.

Safe Guards

To ensure that the input matching component of the guard computation of a clause cannot bind call variables, nonvariable terms in input argument positions in the head of a clause are compiled into matching code that automatically suspends if there is an attempt to bind a call variable. Full details are given in [25]. Use is made of the suspension primitive **data(X)** to suspend an input match if call variable **X** must be matched against a nonvariable term.

As an example, a clause of the form

P(f(Z),a) < - G : B.

where both arguments are input mode, will be compiled into code corresponding to the clause

```
P(X,Y) < -
    data(X) & functor(X,f,1) & arg(1,X,Z),
    data(Y) & functor(Y,a,0),
    G :
    B.
```

Notice that the matching for the two input argument terms is performed in parallel so failure of either match can fail the guard even if the other match is suspended.

Primitives for use in guards, such as the > and = < of the **partition** program, are test only primitives which suspend if their arguments are unbound.

Since the output unification for a clause head is only executed after the guard, only a call to a program defined relation in the guard carries the risk of a variable in the call being accidentally bound during the guard evaluation.

As an example of an unsafe guard consider the program with the form:

$$r([g(U,V)|X]) < - \; test1(U,V):r(X).$$
$$r([g(U,V)|X]) < - \; test2(U,V):r(X).$$
$$test1(S,T) \; < - \; S > = 0 \; , \; T' \; is \; -S.$$

When called by $r([g(2,A),...]$ the guard of the first clause will bind the variable **A** of the call. (**V** will be bound to **A** during the input matching for **r** and then **T** will be bound to **A** during the input matching for the call **test1(U,V)**. **A** is then bound by the **is** call of the body of the **test1** clause.)

Testing for Safe Guards

As with the above program, it is usually fairly obvious when a program defined relation called in a guard is likely to bind a variable of the call that invoked the guard computation. The chief role of guards is to test given components of incoming messages and to suspend if they are not yet computed. As a discipline of PARLOG programming, one should only call program defined relations in guards that cannot in any way instantiate there arguments. For example, if **test1** was defined by the clause

$$test1(U,V) \; < - \; U > = 0, \; V \; =:= \; -U.$$

in which the **is** call is replaced by a suspending arithmetic equality tester the guard of the first clause will suspend when given the call $r([g(2,A),...]$.

Compile Time Safety Check

Details are given in [25] of a algorithm that can be used as the basis of a compile time test for guard safety of PARLOG programs. The algorithm is not ideal in that it certifies as unsafe some guards that are actually safe. However, no unsafe guard is certified as safe.

Runtime Safety Test

An alternative to a compile time certification of safety is a runtime test. At runtime the attempt by a program defined relation in a guard to bind a variable in the call that invoked the guard is trapped and signaled as an error. The major drawback of such a run time test is the implementation overhead. The implementation must be able to distinguish between call variables and variables in terms constructed during the guard evaluation, because the latter variables can be bound by calls in the guard. It requires some scheme of dynamic scoping of variables. Because of this complexity, current implementations of PARLOG do not perform such a runtime test. Indeed, a major advantage of PARLOG is that a compile time analysis rather than a runtime test can be used to guarantee guard safety. This is the major difference between PARLOG and GHC [45].

GHC is very like PARLOG without explicit mode declarations. All nonvariable terms in the head of the clause are assumed to be input matching terms. All output

matching must be done using explicit = calls in the body of the clause. The major difference between PARLOG and GHC is that in GHC an attempt to bind a call variable *at any point during the guard computation* gives rise to suspension. So GHC must have the equivalent to a runtime safety test. In GHC, the above program for **r** with the unsafe guard would suspend on the attempt to bind the call variable **A** by the **is** call.

Flat PARLOG

If guard calls are restricted to test only primitives the language is *flat*. It is called flat because the implementation does not need to support nested or-parallel invocations of program defined relations (required for the evaluation of competing guards which call user defined relations). In Flat PARLOG, which is in all essential respects the same as Flat GHC (FGHC), guards are automatically safe. Flat Concurrent Prolog (FCP) was the first proposed flat variant of a concurrent logic language [36].

Time Dependent Behavior

Consider the program

mode merge(In1?,In2?Out^).
merge([],In2,In2).
merge(In1,[],In1).
merge([X|MIn1],In2,[X|MOut]) < −
    merge(MIn1,In2,MOut).
merge(In1,[Y|MIn2],[Y|MOut]) < −
    merge(In1,MIn2,MOut).

Suppose that it is called from a parallel conjunction

gen1(L1),gen2(L2),merge(L1,L2,L).

The merging of the two lists **L1**, **L2** that will be generated on **L** will partly depend upon the rate at which **gen1** and **gen2** generate their output lists. This is because the merge call will invoke a parallel attempt to find a candidate clause from amongst its four clauses. They will all be suspended until **L1** or **L2** is given a nonvariable value by one of the other processes. Suppose **L1** is the first to be bound, to the partial list value **[2|MoreL1]** by **gen1**. Then the third clause for **merge** will immediately become a candidate clause and the **merge** evaluation will commit to using the clause, binding **L** to a partial list **[2|MOut]** and reducing the **merge** call to the recursive call **merge(MoreL1,L2,MOut)**. If **gen2** now binds **L2** to a partial list before **gen1** binds **MoreL1** then the fourth clause will be the one used to reduce the recursive **merge** call. Only when both **gen1** and **gen2** have generated output at the same time will the **merge** evaluation have more than one candidate clause from which to select the clause to which it commits. Which clause is then selected is not determined by the program.

Time dependent merging of message streams from one or more sources is what one wants for many applications. It is exactly what one wants for an operating system where a communal resource is shared and accessed by sending messages. The messages from the different clients can be merged and passed through to the resource as and when they arrive.

The above **merge** program is not a fair merge because, when messages are always waiting on both input streams, the program may repeatedly select the third clause. However, fair and efficient merge programs can be written in PARLOG. We refer the reader to [6] and [40] for details.

Example Use of Merge

Consider the parallel conjunction:

printer(RemoveReqs),user1(InsertReqs1),
user2(InsertReqs2),merge3(RemoveReqs,
InsertReqs1,InsertReqs2,AllReqs),
queue(Allreqs)

in which **printer** generates a stream of **remove(A)** requests, with **A** a variable, and **user1** and **user2** each generate a sequence of **insert(*text*)** requests, with *text* some ASCII text to be printed. The data flow is depicted in Fig. 1. The four argument **merge3** is the obvious generalization of the three argument **merge** to allow merging of three streams.

The **merge3** and **queue** processes together implement a spooler for a printer control process. **user1** and **user2** send print requests as **insert** messages. These are merged in the order that they arrive and placed on the queue. The **printer** controller sends **remove** requests when it is ready to print. If there is no item in the queue when a **remove** request is received the back communication of the text to be printed, via the message variable, is delayed until either **user1** or **user2** sends an **insert** request.

III. THE META CALL AND SYSTEMS PROGRAMMING

Prolog has a meta call facility which enables a term to be evaluated as a call. This is done using a Prolog primitive **call(G)**. Among other uses, the Prolog meta call can be used to write a user supervisor entirely in Prolog (see, for example [34]).

PARLOG also has such a meta call facility, but the PARLOG meta call (first introduced in [7] and later generalized by Ringwood [37] and Foster [18]) is much more powerful than its Prolog cousin. In addition to the term to be evaluated as a call, the PARLOG meta call has two extra arguments that respectively carry control and status messages. It has the form:

call(G?,Status^,Control?)

The **Control** argument is an input stream of messages that can be used by a supervisor or monitoring program to control the evaluation of the goal **G**. The meta call accepts the control messages **stop, suspend,** and **continue**.

The **Status** argument, which must be a variable at the time of the call, will be instantiated to a stream of messages reporting key states of the evaluation of the call. For example, on termination, the last message call sent will be **failed, succeeded,** or **stopped** indicating the form of termination. **stopped** indicates a premature termination due to an input control message **stop** sent on the **Control**

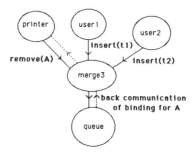

Fig. 1.

stream. Before termination, messages **suspend, continue** may be echoed on the **Status** stream when the same messages are received on the control stream. Finally, **exception** messages may also be output on the status stream, signaling program exceptions such as deadlock, overflow or a call to an undefined relation. A monitoring program can then handle the exceptions. For the call to an undefined relation, the exception message is of the form

exception(undefined,UndefCall,NewCall)

where **UndefCall** is the call to the undefined relation and **NewCall** is an unbound variable. In the meta call evaluation, the call to **UndefCall** is replaced by a call to **NewCall**. The evaluation of **NewCall** is of course suspended waiting for the monitoring program to bind the variable to a call term. The monitoring program must substitute some other call for the undefined call by binding **NewCall**. Binding **NewCall** to **true** will make the undefined call succeed, binding it to **false** will make it fail. More usefully, especially in program development, the monitoring program can inform and even query the programmer about the undefined call allowing him to either provide solution bindings for the variables in the **UndefCall**, or to edit it to produce the substitute call. Some implementations of Prolog offer this facility [34].

The meta call plays a crucial role in the implementation of the PPS, a PARLOG programming system implemented in PARLOG [17]. For details of how the PPS uses this powerful meta call primitive we refer the reader to [4]. Here we give the flavour of its use in the PPS by showing how it can be used to implement a Unix style shell that accepts a stream of user commands to execute user programs. The shell program is a slight modification of one given in [7]. The user programs are to be executed as either background commands (a command term of the **bg(Call)**) or foreground commands (**fg(Call)**). Whenever a foreground command arrives, the shell suspends all the current background processes until the foreground command terminates. So priority is given to foreground processes. The second argument of the **prishell** program is a control message stream into each of the meta calls running a background process. When first called, this will be an unbound variable.

mode pri-shell(?,^).
pri-shell([],BControl).

262

```
pri-shell([bg(Call)|Commands],BControl) < −
    call(Call,Status,BControl),
    pri-shell(Commands,BControl).
pri-shell([fg(Call)|Commands],
        [suspend|BControl]) < −
    call(Call,Status,FControl) &
    (BControl = [continue|NBControl]) ,
    pri-shell(Commands,NBControl) ).
```

Notice the essential use of the sequential conjunction in the last clause. This delays the sending of the **continue** message to the suspended background calls, and the concurrent accepting of more commands, until the foreground evaluation terminates.

A more elaborate version of the shell would have a monitor process which communicated with the meta call via the status and control streams. The monitor process can then handle exceptions, and prematurely terminate a user process when given a kill command for that process. Elaborations of the above program to allow the killing of processes are given in [7] and both the killing of processes and exception handling is described in [4].

IV. OBJECT ORIENTED PROGRAMMING

The parallel logic programming languages lead themselves naturally to the object oriented style of programming in which data and the procedures for manipulating and accessing the data are encapsulated in an *object*. The data can only be accessed or updated by sending a message to the object. A computation is a network of communicating objects.

An object can be represented in PARLOG as a tail recursive process which accepts an input stream of messages sent by other objects. The data stored in the object is recorded by the values of unshared arguments of the process which will be updated for the recursive call when an update message is received. Communicating objects are other processes that access and update the state of the object by putting messages on the message stream. Messages with variables are used to retrieve information about the state of the object by back communication.

This way of representing objects in a parallel logic language was first explored in [41]. It has been further developed in [31] and [12].

The program given above for **queue** is an example of an object represented as a process. For a more complex example, let us consider the representation of an object which is, in Smalltalk terms, a counter class object which can spawn and kill counter objects. Counter class can accept messages to create a new counter object with some initial value, and messages to retrieve or check the number of counter objects that are currently active. When a counter object **C** is created, as a result of a message sent by some other object **O**, **O** is given the identity of **C** and subsequently can send messages directly to **C**. The *identity* of **C** is a variable that is the input message stream to **C**.

Let us assume that a counter object **C** can accept messages to:

1) increase or decrease its count value—with messages **up** and **down**

2) to retrieve the current value—with a message of the form **retrieve(Count)** whre **Count** is a variable for the back communication of the current value of the counter,

3) to disply the value—with a **display** message,

4) to kill itself—with a **kill** message.

The **kill** message, which will be the last message, must be relayed up to the counter class object for it has to know that a counter has been killed in order to decrement its recorded value of the number of current counter objects. We shall also assume that the **display** message has to be handled by counter class, so it must also be relayed to counter class by any counter object that receives the message. Because of the need to relay messages to counter class, each counter object must "know" the identity of the counter class that created it, in our terms, it must have access to the counter class input message stream.

We can implement a counter object as a PARLOG program with the mode

counter(Inmessages?,Value?,Outmessages^)

Inmessages is its input message stream. Any other object that can place messages on this message stream, knows about the counter object. **Value** is the unshared local argument that is the current value of the counter. **Outmessages** is the message stream that will link the counter to the counter class object that created it. Any message **Mess** that the counter object cannot handle for itself, such as the **display** message, is relayed to counter class on this message stream as a message **handle_for_me(Mess,Me)** where **Me** is the "identity" of the counter object, i.e., it is an unbound variable which can be used by the counter class to send a message back to the counter object that has passed up the **handle_for_me** message.

The program for **counter** is:

```
mode counter(Inmessages?,Value?,Outmessages^).
counter([up|Inmess,Value,Outmess) < −  % up
                                        % message
    NValue in Value+1, % causes Value to be
                       % incremented
    counter(Inmess,NValue,Outmess).
counter([down|Inmess],Value,Outmess) < −
                       %down message
    NValue is Value−1, % causes Value to be
                       % decremented
    counter(Inmess,NValue,Outmess).
counter([retrieve(Count)|Inmess],Value,Outmess)
    < −
    Count = Value, % Back communication of current
                   % value
    counter(Inmess,Value,Outmess).
counter([kill],Value,[kill]); % counter is termined
    % and kill message is relayed to counter class
```

```
counter([Other|In],V,
        [handle_for_me(Other,Me)|Out) < -
merge(Me,In,NewIn),

counter(NewIn,V,Out).
```

The last clause deals with all the messages that **counter** cannot handle for itself. It puts these out on its output stream linking it to counter class. **Me** is a communication channel through which the counter class can send back a message to the counter object. Note that this message stream is merged with the regular input message stream.

The program for **counter_class** is given below. The **counter_class** object will be invoked with a call of the form

```
counter_class(Inmess,0,Outmess)
```

where **Inmess** will be a shared variable link to other objects that need to create counters and **Outmess** will be a link to some object that can handle the messages that **counter_class** cannot handle. These will include messages, other than the **display** message, that cannot be handled by **counter**. It can be the message stream link to some higher object in an object hierarchy, or just a link to a monitor process that outputs error messages.

In the **new(Value,Counter)** message handled by the first clause **Value** will be the initial count value of the created counter and **Counter** will be a variable down which subsequent messages will be sent to the created counter. It becomes the first argument of the call

```
counter(Counter,Value,Back)
```

that sets up the counter. **Back** is a variable that will be used by the created counter to send messages back to **counter_class**. This message stream is therefore merged with the rest of the messages coming into **counter_class** to produce the new incoming message stream.

```
mode counter_class(Messages?,Number?,
        Outmess^).
counter_class([new(Value,Counter)|Inmess],
        N,Out) < -
    counter(Counter,Value,Back), %create new
                                  % counter
    merge(Back,Inmess,Allmess), % merge in its Back
                                % stream
    NewN is N+1, % increment record of number of
                 % counters
    counter_class(Allmess,NewN,Out).
counter_class([how_many(Num)|More],N,Out) < -
    Num = N, % retrieve current number of counters
    counter_class(More,N,Out).
counter_class([kill|More],N,Out) < - % a kill mes-
             % sage passed up by some killed counter
    NewN is N-1 &
    counter_class(More,NewN,Out);
counter_class([handle_for_me(display,Me)|More],
        N,Out) < -
```

```
    Me = [retrieve(V)], % ask Me for its value
    (data(V) & % wait until value is returned then
        display_somehow(V)), % display somehow
    counter_class(More,N,Out);
counter_class([Other|More],N,[Other|MoreOut])
        < - % default clause
    counter_class(More,N,MoreOut).
```

Syntactic Sugar

The above representation of object classes and objects is a style of PARLOG programming that can easily be supported by a front end that accepts syntactic sugar for the program in which the message streams and recursive calls are implicit. This is similar to the implicit difference lists of the Definite Clause Grammar notation supported as a front end to Prolog.

Using italic for reserved words, a possible syntactic sugar for the **counter_class** and **counter** programs is:

```
class counter.
class_arguments Number?.
object_arguments Value?.
class_messages:
    new(Value,Counter) - >
        create Counter state Value,
            Number becomes Number + 1.
    how_many(Num) - > Number=Num.
    kill - > Number becomes Number - 1.
    handle_for_me(display,Me) - >
        send Me retrieve(V),
            (data(V) &
                display_somehow(V)).
object_messages:
    up - > Value becomes Value + 1.
    down - > Value becomes Value - 1.
    retrieve(Count) - > Count=Value.
    kill - > terminate_object,send_class kill.
```

The sugar suppresses the message stream aspects of the PARLOG representation and the explicit recursive calls. Ken Kahn and colleagues [31] at Xerox Parc and Andrew Davison [12] at Imperial College are producing front ends to accept such sugared input for the process representation of objects in parallel logic languages. Andrew Davison is building such an interface to PARLOG as one component of a PARLOG based knowledge representation system.

V. OTHER APPLICATIONS

Simulation

Broda and Gregory [1] show how PARLOG can be used for discrete event simulation and in that paper present a graphical notation for PARLOG. Buckle [2] is another investigation of the use of PARLOG for process modelling. A taxi scheduler is implemented in PARLOG and coupled with a graphic display of the activities of the taxis. This is also another study of the use of PARLOG for object oriented programming, since taxis are represented as processes (objects) that receive and respond to messages.

Specification of Concurrent Systerms

As a high level language incorporating concurrency and communication, PARLOG is a natural candidate for the specification of communicating systems. Reference [27] reports on its use for the specification and simulation of communication protocols. An extension of PARLOG, incorporating the concept of a real time clock, has been used for specifying the behavior of a telecommunications switching system [16]. PARLOG has also been used to implement a subset of LOTOS, a specification language for communicating systems, enabling a LOTOS specification to be executed [23], [24].

Expert Systems

PARAMEDICL [11] is a medical diagnosis expert system engineered as a collection of 10 communicating knowledge bases each represented as a PARLOG process which was itself a collection of communicating processes. The main feature of the system was its degree of parallelism. To quote from the paper:

A single message representing a patient symptom and received by a knowledge-base-manager typically triggered around 20 concurrent processes. Each kbm acted concurrently with all the other kbms; thus a parallelism of around 200 was not unusual. In addition, sets of messages could themselves be processed concurrently and these sets were typically of size 20. Despite the possibility of parallelism of around 4000 we feel that PARAMEDICL is a small system and that future systems could exhibit far greater parallelism.

Other work [13] is investigating the use of PARLOG to implement blackboard based expert systems.

Language Parsing

Matsumoto [35] describes a parallel bottom up parser implemented in PARLOG. Trehan and Wilk [44] also describe a PARLOG implemented parallel parser.

VI. CURRENT IMPLEMENTATIONS

On Uniprocessors

A C implementation running on Sun workstations [21] is the main system currently used by the PARLOG research group at Imperial College. This has an interface to the Sun windows system and is based on an abstract PARLOG machine called the SPM [26]. The parallelism is emulated using a process queue and time slicing. Tapes of this implementation, for Sun 3 or VAX under UNIX, are available from the PARLOG Research Group for a small licence fee.

Reference [22] describes another implementation of PARLOG using the SPM design but on a microprogrammable symbolic processor.

We also have an Prolog based implementation—a compiler from PARLOG to Prolog. This is available from Steve Gregory (same address as author). as a stand alone compiled LPA Prolog application for IBM PCs and compatibles and Apple Macintosh computers.

On the Sun 3 we have developed in PARLOG a programming environment, the PPS [17] which uses windows and mouse to allow the user to interact with and control multiple evaluations. Under the PPS a PARLOG program is a collection of databases, or modules, with local name spaces. Programs in one database can call relations defined in another database. The linking is handled by the PPS. It also has an integrated editor which automatically archives old versions of programs. We are constructing other program development tools, such as debuggers and partial evaluators [29], [30], to be integrated into the environment.

On Multiprocessors

We are developing a parallel implementation on a six processor shared memory machine, the Sequent Balance [10]. Like the Sum implementation, this is an implementation of full PARLOG which allows user defined programs to be called in guards—*deep guards*. The implementation supports both and-parallel and or-parallel evaluation.

One alternative approach to implementation is to first precompile a PARLOG program with deep guards into a flat PARLOG program. The PARLOG meta call is used to convert the or-parallel evaluation of alternative deep guards into an and-parallel evaluation as illustrated in [8]. The flat PARLOG program is then further compiled into abstract instructions for a flat PARLOG machine with a meta call implementation. A flat PARLOG machine is simpler to implement as it only needs to support and-parallel evaluation. This is the approach being pursued [32] to implement PARLOG on a sixteen agent prototype ALICE machine [14], and to implement PARLOG on DACTL [33]. DACTL is a compiler target language for parallel declarative languages being implemented on several multiprocessor machines under the U.K. Alvey program.

Forster [19], [20] reports preliminary work on the design of a distributed implementation of flat PARLOG and its meta call.

VII. PARLOG + PROLOG

As specified in [6], PARLOG contains two set constructor primitives for interfacing with Prolog or some other multisolution relational system such as a relational database. One is an eager constructor of the list of all solutions to a conjunctive Prolog query, the other is a lazy constructor which generates the next solution to the query only when sent a new request variable.

More recently, inspired by P-Prolog [46], we have been investigating ways in which PARLOG and Prolog might be more tightly integrated allowing PARLOG and Prolog to access and bind each others variables. Possible applications for such an integration are:

1) a multiprocessing programming environment for Prolog.

2) distributed expert systems comprising communicating concurrent experts implemented as PARLOG processes accessing and updating Prolog knowledge bases.

Different degrees of integration, and some applications for each degree of integration, are discusses in [9].

ACKNOWLEDGMENT

I much appreciate the careful reading and helpful comments on earlier versions of this paper by R. Bahgat, I. Foster, D. Gilbert, and G. Ringwood.

REFERENCES

[1] K. Broda and S. Gregory, "PARLOG for discrete event simulation," in Proc. 2nd Int. Conf. Logic Programming, S.-A. Tarnlund, Ed., Uppsala, July 1984, pp. 301–312.

[2] M. Buckle, "Process modelling in PARLOG," M.Sc. thesis, Dep. Artificial Intell., Univ. Edinburgh, 1987.

[3] K. L. Clark, "PARLOG: The language and its applications," in Proc. PARLE Conf., Eindoven, The Netherlands. Berlin: Springer-Verlag, 1987, pp. 212–242.

[4] K. L. Clark, and I. T. Foster, "A declarative environment for concurrent logic programming," in Proc. Tapsoft 87 Conf., Pisa, Italy. Berlin: Springer-Verlag, 1987.

[5] K. L. Clark and S. Gregory, "A relational language for parallel programming," in Proc. ACM Conf. Functional Languages and Computer Architecture, Portsmouth, NH, Arvind and J. Dennis, Eds., 1981, pp. 171–178.

[6] —, "PARLOG: Parallel programming in logic," Dep. Comput., Imperial College, London, Res. Rep. DOC 84/4, 1984; also in ACM Trans. Program. Lang. Syst., vol. 8, no. 1, pp. 1–49, 1986.

[7] —, "Notes on systems programming in PARLOG," in Proc. Int. Conf. Fifth Generation Computer Systems, Tokyo, H. Aiso, Ed. Amsterdam, The Netherlands: Elsevier/North-Hollland, 1984, pp. 299–306.

[8] —, "Notes on the implementation of PARLOG," J. Logic Programming, vol. 2, no. 1, pp. 17–42, 1985.

[9] —, "PARLOG and Prolog united," in Proc. 4th Int. Logic Programming Conf., Melbourne. Cambridge, MA: MIT Press, 1987, pp. 927–961.

[10] J. Crammond, "Implementation of committed choice languages on shared memory multiprocessors," PARLOG Group, Dep. Comput., Imperial College, London, Res. Rep. (in preparation), 1988.

[11] M. G. Cutcher and M. J. Rigg, "PARAMEDICL: A computer aided medical diagnosis system for parallel architectures," ICL Tech. J., vol. 5, no. 3, pp. 376–384, 1987.

[12] A. Davison, "POLKA, a PARLOG object oriented language," PARLOG Res. Group, Dep. Comput., Imperial College, London, Res. Rep., 1987.

[13] —, "Representing blackboards in PARLOG," PARLOG Res. Group, Dep. Comput., Imperial College, London, Res. Rep., 1987.

[14] J. Darlington, and M. J. Reeve, "ALICE: A multiprocessor reduction machine," in Proc. ACM Conf. Functional Languages and Computer Architecture, Portsmouth, NH, Arvind and J. Dennis, Eds., ACM publication, 1981.

[15] E. W. Dijkstra, A Discipline of Programming. Englewood Cliffs, NJ: Prentice-Hall, 1976.

[16] N. A. Elshiewy, "Logic programming of real time control of telecommunication systems," Comput. Sci. Lab., Ericsson Telecom, Sweden, Res. Rep., 1987.

[17] I. T. Foster, "The PARLOG programming system: Reference manual," PARLOG Res. Group, Dep. Comput., Imperial College, London, 1986.

[18] —, "Logic operating systems: Design issues," in Proc. 4th Int. Logic Programming Conf., Melbourne. Cambridge, MA: MIT Press, 1987, pp. 910–926.

[19] —, "Parallel implementation of PARLOG," PARLOG Res. Group, Dep. Comput., Imperial College, London, Res. Rep., 1987.

[20] —, "Efficient metacontrol in parallel logic programming languages,

" PARLOG Res. Group, Dep. Comput., Imperial College, London, Res. Rep., 1987.

[21] I. T. Foster, S. Gregory, G. A. Ringwood, and K. Satoh, "A sequential implementation of PARLOG," in Proc. 3rd Int. Logic Programming Conf., London. Berlin: Springer-Verlag, 1986, pp. 149–156.

[22] J. Garcia, M. Jourdan, and A. Rizk, "An implementation of PARLOG using high level tools," in Proc. ESPRIT 87: Achievements and Impact. Amsterdam, The Netherlands: North-Holland, 1987, pp. 1265–1275.

[23] D. Gilbert, "Implementing LOTOS in PARLOG," M.Sc. thesis, Dep. Comput., Imperial College, London, 1987.

[24] —, "Executable LOTOS: Using PARLOG to implement an FDT," in Proc. Protocol Specification, Testing and Verification VII, Zurich, 1987.

[25] S. Gregory, Parallel Logic Programming in PARLOG. Reading, MA: Addison-Wesley, 1987.

[26] S. Gregory, I. Foster, A. D. Burt, and G. A. Ringwood, "An abstract machine for the implementation of PARLOG on uniprocessors," PARLOG Res. Group, Dep. Comput., Imperial College, London, Res. Rep., 1987.

[27] S. Gregory, R. Neely, and G. A. Ringwood, "PARLOG for specification, verification and simulation," in Proc. 7th Int. Symp. Computer Hardware Description Languages and their Applications, Tokyo, C. J. Koomen and T. Moto-oka, Eds. Amsterdam, The Netherlands: Elsevier/North-Holland, 1985, pp. 139–148.

[28] C. A. R. Hoare, "Communicating sequential processes," Commun. ACM, vol. 17, no. 10, 1978, pp. 666–677.

[29] M. H. Huntbach, "Algorithmic PARLOG debugging," in Proc. 1987 Symp. Logic Programming, San Francisco, CA, IEEE Comput. Soc. Press, 1987, pp. 288–297.

[30] —, "The partial evaluation of PARLOG programs," PARLOG Res. Group, Dep. Comput., Imperial College, London, Res. Rep., 1987.

[31] K. Kahn, E. D. Tribble, M. S. Miller, D. G. Bobrow, "Objects in concurrent logic languages," in Proc. OOPSLA '86, Portland, OR, ACM, 1986.

[32] M. Lam and G. Gregory, "PARLOG and ALICE: A marriage of convenience," in Proc. 4th Int. Logic Programming Conf., Melbourne. Cambridge, MA: MIT Press, 1987, pp. 294–310.

[33] —, "Implementation of PARLOG on DACTL," PARLOG Res. Group, Dep. Comput., Imperial College, London, Draft Paper, 1987.

[34] F. G McCabe, K. L. Clark, and B. D. Steel, micro-PARLOG 3.1 Programmers Reference Manual, Logic Programming Associates Ltd., London, 1984.

[35] Y. Matsumoto, "A parallel parsing system for natural language analysis," in Proc. 3rd Int. Logic Programming Conf., London. Berlin: Springer-Verlag, 1986, pp. 396–409.

[36] C. Mierkowsky, S. Taylor, E. Shapiro, J. Levy, and M. Safra, "The design and Implementation of Flat Concurrent Prolog," Dep. Appl. Math., Weizmann Inst., Tech. Rep. CS85-09, 1985.

[37] G. A. Ringwood, "The dining logicians," M.Sc. thesis, Dep. Comput., Imperial College, London, 1984.

[38] —, "PARLOG86 and the dining logicians," PARLOG Res. Group, Dep. Comput., Imperial College, London, 1987; to appear in Commun. ACM, 1988.

[39] E. Y. Shapiro, "A subset of Concurrent Prolog and its interpreter," ICOT, Tech. Rep. TR-003, Tokyo, 1983.

[40] E. Y. Shapiro and C. Mierowsky, "Fair, biased, and self balancing merge operators," in Proc. IEEE Symp. Logic Programming, Atlantic City, NJ, IEEE Comput. Soc. Press, 1984, pp. 83–90.

[41] E. Y. Shapiro and A. Takeuchi, "Object oriented programming in Concurrent Prolog," New Generation Comput., vol. 1, pp. 25–48, 1983.

[42] A. Takeuchi and K. Furakawa, "Bounded buffer communication in Concurrent Prolog," New Generation Comput., vol. 3, no. 2, pp. 145–155, 1985.

[43] —, "Parallel logic programming languages," in Proc. 3rd Int. Logic Programming Conf., London. Berlin: Springer-Verlag, 1986, pp. 242–254.

[44] R. Trehan and P. Wilk, "A parallel shift-reduce parser for committed choice non-deterministic logic languages," Artificial Intell. Applicat. Inst., Edinburgh Univ., Tech. Rep. AIA1-TR-26, 1987.

[45] K. Ueda, "Guarded horn clauses," ICOT, Tokyo, Tech. Rep. TR-103, 1985.

[46] R. Yang and H. Aiso, in "P-Prolog: A parallel logic language based on exclusive relation," in Proc. 3rd Int. Logic Programming Conf., London. Berlin: Springer-Verlag, 1986, pp. 259–269.

Keith L. Clark was born in England. He received the B.A. degree in mathematics from Durham University, the M.A. degree in philosophy from Cambridge University, and the Ph.D. degree in computing from London University.

He is currently Professor of Computational Logic at Imperial College, London. He has spent sabatical terms at Syracuse University and UC Santa Cruz. Since 1975, his research area has been logic programming, being one of the pioneers of this research area. He has been involved in the design of two logic programming languages, IC-Prolog, and PARLOG, and has published papers on both the theory and methodology of logic programming. He is coauthor of two introductory books one on automata theory, the other on Prolog. He is also the co-editor of an influential collection of research papers on logic programming.

Currently Dr. Clark is the President of the Association of Logic Programming and the Editor of the Addison-Wesley Series on Logic Programming.

Chapter 4

Guarded Horn Clauses

Kazunori Ueda

NEC Corporation

Abstract

A set of Horn clauses augmented with a *guard* mechanism is shown to be a simple and yet powerful parallel logic programming language.

4.1 Introduction

Kowalski (1974) showed that a Horn clause is amenable to procedural interpretation. Prolog was developed as a sequential programming language based on the procedural interpretation of Horn clauses (Roussel, 1975). and it has proved to be a simple, powerful, and efficient sequential programming language (Warren et al., 1977).

As Kowalski (1974) points out, a Horn clause program allows parallel or concurrent execution as well as sequential execution. However. although a set of Horn clauses may be useful for uncontrolled search as it is. it is inadequate for a parallel programming language capable of describing important concepts such as communication and synchronization. We need some additional mechanism to express these concepts, and this paper shows that this can be effected with only one construct. the *guard*.

We introduce guarded Horn clauses in the following sections. Guarded Horn Clauses (GHC) will be used as the name of our language. We compare GHC with other logic/parallel programming languages. GHC is intended to be the machine-independent core of the Kernel Language for ICOT's Parallel Inference Machine.

4.2 Design Goals and Overview

Our goal is to obtain a logic programming language that allows parallel execution. It is expected to fulfill the following requirements:

(1) It must be a parallel programming language 'by nature'. It must not be a sequential language augmented with primitives for parallelism. That is, the language must assume as little sequentiality among primitive operations as possible in order to preserve parallelism inherent in a Horn-clause program. This would lead to a clearer formal semantics, as well as to an efficient implementation on a novel architecture in the future.

(2) It must be an expressive, general-purpose parallel programming language. In particular, it must be able to express important concepts in parallel programming — processes, communication, and synchronization.

(3) It must be a simple parallel programming language. We do not have much experience with either theoretical or pragmatic aspects of parallel programming. Therefore, we must first establish the foundations of parallel programming with a simple language.

(4) It must be an efficient parallel programming language. We have a lot of simple, typical problems to be described in the language as well as complex ones. It is very important that such programs run as efficiently as comparable programs written in existing parallel programming languages.

Concurrent Prolog (Shapiro, Chapter 2) and PARLOG (Clark and Gregory, Chapter 3) seem to lie near the solution. Both realize processes by goals and communication by streams implemented as lists. Synchronization is realized by read-only variables in Concurrent Prolog and by one-way unification in PARLOG.

GHC inherits the *guard* construct and the programming paradigm established by these languages. The most characteristic feature of GHC is that the guard is the only syntactic construct added to Horn clauses. Synchronization in GHC is realized by the semantic rules of guards.

GHC is expected to fulfill all the above requirements. We have succeeded in rewriting most of our Concurrent Prolog programs. Miyazaki and Ueda have independently written GHC-to-Prolog compilers in Prolog by modifying different versions of Concurrent Prolog compilers on top of Prolog (Ueda and Chikayama, 1985).

4.3 Syntax and Semantics

4.3.1 Syntax

A GHC program is a finite set of guarded Horn clauses of the following form:

$$H \leftarrow G_1, \ldots, G_m \mid B_1, \ldots, B_n. \qquad m \geq 0, n \geq 0.$$

where H, G_i's, and B_i's are atomic formulas that are defined as usual. H is called a clause head, G_i's are called guard goals , and B_i's are called body goals. The operator '|' is called a commitment operator. The part of a clause before '|' is called the guard, and the part after '|' is called the body. Note that *the clause head is included in the guard*. The set of all clauses whose heads have the same predicate symbol with the same arity is called a procedure. Declaratively, the above guarded Horn clause is read as "H is implied by $G_1, \ldots,$ and G_m and $B_1, \ldots,$ and B_n".

A goal clause has the following form:

$$\leftarrow B_1, \ldots, B_n. \qquad n \geq 0.$$

This can be regarded as a guarded Horn clause with an empty guard. A goal clause is called an empty clause when n is equal to 0. The nullary predicate *true* is used for denoting an empty set of guard or body goals.

4.3.2 Semantics

The semantics of GHC is quite simple. Informally, to execute a program is to reduce a given goal clause to an empty clause by means of input resolution using the clauses constituting the program. This can be done in a fully parallel manner under the following rules of suspension:

Rules of Suspension:

(a) Any piece of unification invoked directly or indirectly in the guard of a clause cannot bind a variable appearing in the caller of that clause with

  (i) a non-variable term or

  (ii) another variable appearing in the caller.

(b) Any piece of unification invoked directly or indirectly in the body of a clause cannot bind a variable appearing in the guard of that clause with

  (i) a non-variable term or

  (ii) another variable appearing in the guard

  until that clause is selected for commitment (see below).

A piece of unification which can succeed only by making such bindings is suspended until it can succeed without making such bindings. ∎

Note that a set of variables whose instantiation is inhibited by the above rules can vary as computation proceeds. When a variable X in the set S is bound to a non-variable term T (in a way not disallowed above), we include all the variables in T in S and remove X itself from S.

Another rule we have to add is the *commitment* rule. When some clause succeeds in solving (see below) its guard for a given goal, that clause tries to be selected exclusively for subsequent execution of the goal. To be selected, it must first confirm that no other clauses belonging to the same procedure have been selected for the same goal. If confirmed, that clause is selected indivisibly; we say that the goal is committed to that clause and also that that clause is selected for commitment.

We say that a set of goals *succeeds* (or is *solved*) if it is reduced to an empty set of goals by using a selected clause for each initial or intermediate goal: We are interested in a reduction path in which only selected clauses are involved. The notion of failure is not introduced here, but it will be discussed in Section 4.6.1.

It must be stressed that under the rules stated above, anything can be done in parallel: Conjunctive goals can be executed in parallel; candidate clauses for a goal can be tested in parallel; head unification involved in resolution can be done in parallel; head unification and the execution of guard goals can be done in parallel. However, what is even more important is that we can also execute a set of tasks in a predetermined order as long as this does not change the meaning of the program.

The rules of suspension could be more informally restated as follows:

(a) The guard of a clause cannot export any bindings to (or, make any bindings observable from) the caller of that clause, and

(b) the body of a clause cannot export any bindings to (or, make any bindings observable from) the guard of that clause before commitment.

Rule (a) is used for synchronization, so it could be called the rule of synchronization. Rule (b) is rather tricky; it states that we can solve the body of a clause not yet selected for commitment. However, the above restrictions guarantee that this never affects the selection of candidate clauses nor the other goals running in parallel with the caller of the clause. So Rule (b) is effectively the rule of sequencing.

In Concurrent Prolog, the result of unification performed in a guard (including a head) and which would export bindings is recorded locally. In GHC, such unification simply suspends. Suspension of unification due to some guard may be released when some goal running in parallel with the goal for which the guard is being executed has instantiated the variable that caused suspension.

An example may be helpful in understanding the rules of suspension. Let us consider the following program:

$$\begin{array}{lll} \text{Goal:} & \leftarrow p(X), q(X). & \text{(i)} \\ \text{Clauses:} \ p(ok) & \leftarrow \text{true} \mid \dots . & \text{(ii)} \\ q(Z) & \leftarrow \text{true} \mid Z=ok. & \text{(iii)} \end{array}$$

The predicate '=' is a predefined predicate which unifies its two arguments. This predicate must be considered as predefined, because it cannot be defined in the language.

Clause (ii) cannot instantiate the argument X of its caller to the constant ok, since this unification is executed in the guard. This clause has to wait until X is instantiated to ok by some other goal. On the other hand, Clause (iii) can instantiate X to ok after it is selected for commitment, and this clause can be selected almost immediately. Therefore, no matter which of the two goals of Clause (i) starts first, the head unification of Clause (ii) can succeed only after the $Z=ok$ goal in Clause (iii) is executed.

The semantics of the following program should be more carefully understood:

$$\begin{array}{lll} \text{Goal:} & \leftarrow p(X), q(X). & \text{(i)} \\ \text{Clauses:} \ p(Y) & \leftarrow q(Y) \mid \dots . & \text{(ii')} \\ q(Z) & \leftarrow \text{true} \mid Z=ok. & \text{(iii)} \end{array}$$

To solve the guard of Clause (ii'), we have to do two things in parallel: unify X and Y (i.e., parameter passing), and solve $q(Y)$. Let us assume that parameter passing occurs first. Then the goal $q(Y)$ tries to unify Y (now identical to X) with ok. However, this unification cannot instantiate X because it is indirectly invoked by the guard of Clause (ii'). Let us then consider the other case where the goal $q(Y)$ is executed prior to parameter passing. The variable Y is bound to *ok* because this itself does not export a binding to the caller of Clause (ii′), namely $p(X)$. However, this binding causes the subsequent parameter passing to suspend because it would export a binding. Hence, no matter which case actually arises, Clause (ii′) behaves exactly like Clause (ii) with respect to bindings given to the variable X.

Some important consequences of the above rules follow:

(1) Any unification intended to export bindings to the caller of a clause through its head arguments must be specified in the body. Such unification must be specified using the predefined predicate '='.

(2) The unification of the head arguments of a clause may, but need not, be executed in parallel. It can be executed sequentially in any predetermined order.

(3) The unification of head arguments and the execution of guard goals can be executed in parallel. That is, the execution of guard goals can start before the unification of head arguments has completed. However, the usual execution method that solves guard goals only after head unification is also allowed: it does not change the meaning of a program.

(4) The execution of the body of a clause may, but need not, start before that clause is selected. Bindings made by the body are unobservable from the guard before commitment, so the meaning of the program is independent of whether the body starts before or only after commitment.

(5) We need not implement a multiple environment mechanism, i.e., a mechanism for binding a variable with more than one value. This mechanism is in general necessary when more than one candidate clause for a goal is tried in parallel. In GHC, however, at most one clause, a selected clause, can export bindings, thus eliminating the need of a multiple environment mechanism.

Unfortunately, properties (2) and (3) do not hold if we introduce the concept of failure. For example, the following goal

$$\text{Goal:} \qquad\qquad \leftarrow \text{and(X, false)}.$$
$$\text{Clause: and(true, true)} \leftarrow \text{true} \mid \text{true}.$$

fails if the arguments are unified in parallel, but suspends if they are unified from left to right (Gregory, private communication).

4.4 Program Examples

4.4.1 Binary merge

```
merge([A|Xs], Ys, Zs) ← true | Zs=[A|Zs1], merge(Xs, Ys, Zs1).
merge(Xs, [A|Ys], Zs) ← true | Zs=[A|Zs1], merge(Xs, Ys, Zs1).
merge([ ], Ys, Zs)    ← true | Zs=Ys.
merge(Xs, [ ], Zs)    ← true | Zs=Xs.
```

The goal *merge(Xs, Ys, Zs)* merges two streams *Xs* and *Ys* (implemented as lists) into one stream *Zs*. This is an example of a nondeterministic program. The language rules of GHC do not state that the selection of clauses should be fair. In a good implementation, however, the elements of *Xs* and *Ys* are expected to appear on *Zs* almost in the order of arrival.

Note that no bindings can be exported from the guards; bindings to *Zs* must be made within the bodies. This programming style, however, serves to clarify causality. In most cases, bi- (or multi-) directionality of a logic program is only an illusion; it seems far better to specify the data flow which we have in mind and to enable us to read it from a given program.

Note that the declarative reading of the above program gives the usual, logical specification of the nondeterministic merge: arbitrary interleaving of the two input streams makes the output stream.

4.4.2 Generating primes

primes(Max, Ps) ← true | gen(2, Max, Ns), sift(Ns, Ps).

gen(N, Max, Ns) ←
    N ≤ Max | Ns=[N|Ns1], N1 := N+1, gen(N1, Max, Ns1).
gen(N, Max, Ns) ←
    N > Max | Ns=[ ].

sift([P|Xs], Zs) ← true | Zs=[P|Zs1], filter(P, Xs, Ys), sift(Ys, Zs1).
sift([ ],   Zs) ← true | Zs=[ ].

filter(P, [X|Xs], Ys) ← X mod P=:=0 | filter(P, Xs, Ys).
filter(P, [X|Xs], Ys) ← X mod P≠0 | Ys=[X|Ys1], filter(P, Xs, Ys1).
filter(P, [ ],   Ys) ← true | Ys=[ ].

The call *primes(Max, Ps)* returns through *Ps* a stream of primes up to *Max*. The stream of primes is generated from the stream of integers by filtering out the multiples of primes. For each prime *P*, a filter goal *filter(P, Xs, Ys)* is generated which filters out the multiples of *P* from the stream *Xs*, yielding *Ys*.

The binary predicate ':=' evaluates its right-hand side operand as an integer expression and unifies the result with the left-hand side operand. The binary predicate '=:=' evaluates its two operands as integer expressions and succeeds iff the results are the same. These predicates cannot be replaced by the '=' predicate because '=' never evaluates its arguments. The predicate '≠' is the negation of '=:='.

Readers may wish to improve the above program by eliminating unnecessary filtering.

4.4.3 Bounded buffer stream communication

test(N) ← true | buffer(N, Hs, Ts), ints(0, 100, Hs), consume(Hs, Ts).

buffer(N, Hs, Ts) ← N > 0 | Hs=[_|Hs1], N1:=N−1, buffer(N1, Hs1, Ts).
buffer(N, Hs, Ts) ← N=:=0 | Ts=Hs.

ints(M, Max, [H|Hs]) ←
    M < Max | H=M, M1:=M+1, ints(M1, Max, Hs).
ints(M, Max, [H|_]) ←
    M ≥ Max | H='EOS'.

consume([H|Hs], Ts) ← H\='EOS' | Ts=[_|Ts1], consume(Hs, Ts1).
consume([H|Hs], Ts) ← H ='EOS' | Ts=[ ].

This program illustrates the general statement that demand-driven computation can be implemented by means of data-driven computation. It uses the bounded-buffer concept first introduced by Takeuchi and Furukawa (Chapter 18) in a logic programming framework. The predicate *ints* returns a stream of integers through the third argument in a lazy manner. It never generates a new box by itself; it only fills a given box created elsewhere with a new value. In the above program, the goal *consume* creates a new box by the goal $Ts=[_|Ts1]$ every time it has confirmed the top element H of the stream. The top and the tail of the stream are initially related by the goal *buffer*(N, Hs, Ts).

The binary predicate '\=' is the negation of the predicate '='. It succeeds when its two arguments are proved to be ununifiable; it suspends until then.

4.4.4 Meta-interpreter of GHC

call(true)   ← true | true.
call((A, B)) ← true | call(A), call(B).
call(A = B) ← true | A = B.
call(A)   ← A \= true, A \= (_, _), A \= (_ = _) |
     clauses(A, Clauses), resolve(A, Clauses, Body), call(Body).

resolve(A, [C|Cs], B) ← melt_new(C, (A ← G|B2)), call(G) | B = B2.
resolve(A, [C|Cs], B) ← resolve(A, Cs, B2) | B = B2.

This program is basically a GHC version of the Concurrent Prolog meta-interpreter by Shapiro (Chapter 19). The predicate *clauses* is a system predicate which returns in a *frozen* form (Nakashima et al., 1984) a list of all clauses whose heads are potentially unifiable with the given goal. Each frozen clause is a ground term in which original variables are indicated by special constant symbols, and it is *melted* in the guard of the first clause of *resolve* by *melt_new*. The goal *melt_new*(C, (A ← $G|B2$)) creates a new term (say T) from a frozen term C by giving a new variable for each frozen variable in C and tries to unify T with (A ← $G|B2$).

The predicate *resolve* tests the candidate clauses and returns the body of an arbitrary clause whose guard has been successfully solved. This many-to-one arbitration is realized by the combination of binary clause selection performed in the predicate *resolve*.

It is essential that each candidate clause is melted after it has been brought into the guard of the first clause of *resolve*. If it were melted before passed into the guard, all variables in it would be protected against instantiation from the guard.

4.5 Important Features of GHC

4.5.1 Simplicity

GHC has only a small number of primitive operations all of which are considered small:

(1) calling a predicate leaving all its arguments unspecified, i.e., after making sure only that they are new distinct variables,

(2) unifying a variable with another variable or with a non-variable term whose arguments are all new distinct variables, and

(3) commitment.

Operation (1) is effectively resolution without unification. From the viewpoint of parallel execution, resolution in the original sense (Robinson, 1965) need not be considered as an indivisible operation. Resolution can be decomposed into goal rewriting and unification, and the latter can be executed in parallel with the newly created goals, as stated in Section 4.3.2.

Operation (2) shows that the unification of a variable and a non-variable term is not necessarily a primitive operation. For example, the unification $X=f(a)$ can be decomposed into the two operations $X=f(Y)$ and $Y=a$, where Y is a new variable. This was also suggested by Hagiya (1983).

Furthermore. the semantics of guard and commitment is powerful enough to express the following notions:

(1) conditional branching,

(2) nondeterministic choice, and

(3) synchronization.

This feature is much like CSP (Hoare, 1978), but CSP provides additional constructs '?' (input command) and '!' (output command) for synchronization. The Relational Language (Clark and Gregory, Chapter 1) was the first to introduce the guard concept to logic programming for reasons similar to ours[*]. However, GHC has removed the restrictions on the guard of the Relational Language together with mode declarations and annotations.

4.5.2 Descriptive power

We have succeeded in rewriting most of the Concurrent Prolog programs we have. In particular, we have written a GHC program which performs bounded buffer communication (Section 4.4.3), and a meta-interpreter of GHC itself (Section 4.4.4).

4.5.3 Efficiency

It cannot be immediately concluded that GHC can be efficiently implemented on parallel computers. The efficiency of GHC will depend very much on future research on the language itself and its implementation. However. GHC is more amenable than Concurrent Prolog to efficient implementation: It needs no mechanism for multiple environments; and it provides more information on synchronization statically. We made a compiler of a subset of GHC which compiles a GHC program into Prolog (Ueda and Chikayama , 1985), and an *append* program ran at more than 12KLIPS on DEC2065. The current restriction is that user-defined goals are not allowed in guards. Another GHC-to-Prolog compiler was made by Miyazaki (unpublished). Although less efficient than ours, his compiler is capable of handling nested guards.

For applications in which efficiency is the primary issue but little flexibility is needed, we could design a restricted version of GHC which allows only a subclass

---

[*] IC-Prolog (Clark et al., 1982) was the first to introduce the guard concept to logic programming. but for rather different purposes.

of GHC and/or introduces declarations which help optimization. Such a variant should have the properties that additional constructs such as declarations are used only for efficiency purposes and that a program in that variant is readable as a GHC program once the additional constructs are removed from the source text.

4.6 Possible Extensions

This section suggests some possible extensions, which are currently not part of GHC. Issues such as their necessity, implementability, and compatibility with other language features should be examined carefully before they are actually introduced.

4.6.1 Finite failure and the predicate *otherwise*

The semantics of GHC as described in Section 4.3.2 does not include the concept of failure. However, failure of unification can be readily introduced into the language. We can say that a set of goals fails if it contains or derives some unification goal and its two arguments are instantiated to different principal functors. Then, in general, a suspended unification may turn out later either to fail or to succeed.

Another kind of failure is caused by a goal for which there proves to be no selectable clauses. Calling a non-existent predicate also falls under this category. This kind of failure must be detected as failure only under the *closed world assumption*; otherwise, that goal would have to suspend until somebody adds a selectable clause to the program.

The predicate *otherwise* proposed by Shapiro and Takeuchi (1983) can be introduced to express 'negation as failure'. The predicate *otherwise* can appear only as a guard goal. A goal *otherwise* succeeds when the guards of all the other candidate clauses for a given goal have failed; until then it suspends. This predicate could be conveniently used for describing a *default* clause.

4.6.2 Metacall facilities

We sometimes want to see whether a given goal succeeds or fails without making the test itself fail. Consider, for example, a monitor program. A monitor program may create several processes, some of which are user programs and others service programs. In this case, the user programs must be executed in a fail-safe manner, because if one of them should fail, so does the whole system. Furthermore, a monitor program must have some means to abort its subordinate user programs.

Let us consider a program tracer next. A program tracer must execute a given program, generating trace information every moment. Even if the program fails, the tracer should generate appropriate diagnostic information without failing. The tracer may even have to trace the execution of guards, which is really an impure feature since information should be extracted from the place from where no bindings must otherwise be exported.

A partial evaluator is another example. A partial evaluator rewrites a program clause by executing the goals in the clause. For example, the first clause in the program

$$p(Y) \leftarrow q(Y) \mid \ldots .$$
$$q(Z) \leftarrow true \mid Z=ok.$$

in Section 4.3.2 can be partially evaluated to the following clause:

$$p(ok) \leftarrow true \mid \ldots .$$

To do such rewriting, it must be possible to execute a given goal to obtain a finite set of substitutions and, in the case of suspension, a finite set of remaining (suspended) goals. In this case, the initial goal and the result must be represented in a frozen form. For if ordinary variables were used, the solver of the initial goal could not know when that goal had been fully instantiated, nor could we know when all bindings had been made. The binding delay is not guaranteed to be bounded.

We are considering language facilities which support all of these applications. However, we have not reached a satisfactory solution yet. The metacall facility proposed by Clark and Gregory (1984) was a candidate solution, but it proved to have some semantical problems. Their two-argument metacall *call(Goal, Result)* tries to solve *Goal* possibly generating output bindings, and it unifies *Result* with *succeeded* upon success and with *failed* upon failure. However, consider the following example (Sato and Sakurai, 1984):

$$\leftarrow call(X=0, \_), X=1.$$

If the first goal is executed first, X becomes 0. Then the unification $X=1$ fails and so does the whole clause. If the second goal is executed first, X becomes 1. But since the first goal never fails, the whole clause succeeds. This is a new kind of nondeterminism resulting from the order of unification: without this facility, all nondeterminism would result from the arbitrary choice of selectable clauses.

Let us consider another example:

$$\leftarrow call(X=0, \_), call(X=1, \_).$$

The semantics of a GHC variable is intended to allow the above goal to be rewritten as follows (Ueda, 1985),

$$\leftarrow call(X=0, \_), X = Y, call(Y=1, \_).$$

because they are logically equivalent. However, this rewriting shows that the failure of unification cannot be confined in either *call*. The failure can creep out and topple the whole goal. This means that the metacall facilities as proposed by Clark and Gregory cannot protect a system program from unpredictable behavior by a user program. Further investigation is necessary to find a better solution.

4.7 Implementation Outline

The purpose of this section is to demonstrate that the suspension mechanism of GHC can be implemented. We will first show an easy-to-understand but possibly inefficient method: pointer coloring. Here we do not consider the suspension of bodies. The body of a clause is assumed to start after the clause has been selected.

When a term in a goal and a variable in the guard of a clause are unified, we color the pointer which indicates the binding. A term dereferenced using one or more colored pointers cannot be instantiated. When the clause is selected, colored pointers created in its guard are uncolored. For this purpose, the guard of a clause must record all pointers colored for that guard. Uncoloring can be done in parallel with the other operations in the body.

Care must be taken when the term in a goal to be unified with the variable in the guard is itself dereferenced using colored pointers. Consider the following example:

$$\begin{aligned}&\leftarrow \text{p(f(A))}. &&\text{(i)}\\ \text{p(X)} &\leftarrow \text{q(X)} \mid \dots. &&\text{(ii)}\\ \text{q(Y)} &\leftarrow \text{true} \mid \text{Y=f(b)}. &&\text{(iii)}\end{aligned}$$

If the variable Y should directly point to the term $f(A)$ by a colored pointer and uncolor it upon selection of Clause (iii), the variable A would be erroneously instantiated to the constant b. There are a couple of possible remedies:

(1) Disallow a pointer which goes directly out of nested guards and use a chain of pointers instead.

(2) Let each pointer know how many levels of guards it goes through.

(3) Allow a pointer to go directly through nested guards. However, let each colored pointer know for what guard it is colored. When directly pointing a term dereferenced using colored pointers, that new pointer must be recorded in the guard which records the last colored pointer in the dereferencing chain (Miyazaki, unpublished).

The pointer-coloring method explained above is general. In many cases, however, we can analyze suspension statically. The simplest case is the following clause:

$$\text{p(true)} \leftarrow \dots \mid \dots.$$

The head argument claims that the corresponding goal argument must have been instantiated to *true* for this clause to be selected. We can statically generate the code for this check and need not use colored pointers in this case.

In general, if a guard calls only system predicates for simple checking (e.g., integer comparison), compile-time analysis is easy because no consideration is needed on other clauses. On the other hand, if it calls a user-defined predicate, global analysis is necessary to determine which unification may suspend and which unification cannot. There will be no general method for static analysis, but in many useful cases, static analysis like PARLOG's compile-time mode analysis (Clark and Gregory, 1985) will be effective.

4.8 Comparison with Other Languages

4.8.1 Comparison with Concurrent Prolog and PARLOG

GHC is like Concurrent Prolog and PARLOG in that it is a parallel logic programming language which supports committed-choice nondeterminism and stream communication. However, GHC is simpler than both Concurrent Prolog and PARLOG.

Firstly, unlike Concurrent Prolog, GHC has no read-only annotations. In GHC, the semantics of guards enables process synchronization.

Secondly, Concurrent Prolog needs a multiple environment mechanism while GHC and PARLOG do not. In Concurrent Prolog, bindings generated in each guard are recorded locally until commitment and are exported into the global environment upon commitment. However, this mechanism contains semantical problems whose solution would require an additional set of language rules, as Ueda (1985) pointed out. More importantly, we have not obtained any evidence that we need multiple environments in stream-And-parallel programming.

Thirdly, unlike PARLOG, we require no mode declaration for each predicate. PARLOG's mode declaration is nothing but a guide for translating PARLOG program into Kernel PARLOG (Clark and Gregory, 1984), so we can do without modes. In fact, GHC is closer to Kernel PARLOG than to PARLOG. However, unlike Kernel PARLOG, we have only one kind of unification. Although each unification operation occurring in a GHC program might be compiled into one of several specialized unification procedures, GHC itself needs (and has) only one.

Another difference from (Kernel) PARLOG is that a (Kernel) PARLOG program requires compile-time analysis in order to guarantee that it is legal, i.e., it contains no unsafe guard which may bind variables in the caller of the guard (Clark and Gregory, 1984). On the other hand, a GHC program is legal if and only if it is syntactically legal; it can be executed without any semantic analysis.

4.8.2 Comparison with Qute

Qute (Sato and Sakurai, 1984) is a functional language based on unification. Qute allows parallel evaluation which corresponds to And-parallelism in logic programming languages, but the result of evaluation is guaranteed to be the same irrespective of the particular order of evaluation. That is, there is no observable nondeterminism.

Although Qute and GHC were developed independently and may look different, their suspension mechanisms are essentially the same. The Qute counterpart of GHC's guard is the condition part of the *if-then-else* construct, from which no bindings can be exported.

The major difference between Qute and GHC is that Qute has no committed-choice nondeterminism while GHC has one. Qute does not have committed-choice nondeterminism (though Sato and Sakurai, 1984, suggest it could), because it pursues the Church-Rosser property of the evaluation algorithm. GHC has one because our applications include a system which interfaces with the real world (e.g., peripheral devices).

Another difference is that Qute has sequential And while GHC does not. We deliberately excluded sequential And, because our programming experience with Concurrent Prolog has never called for this construct. One may think that sequential And could be used for the specification of scheduling and for synchronization. However, the primitives for scheduling should be introduced at a different level from that of GHC, and sequential And as a synchronization primitive is of no use in the intended computation model of GHC which allows delay for communication by shared variables.

4.8.3 Comparison with CSP

GHC is similar to CSP (Communicating Sequential Processes) (Hoare, 1978) in the following points:

(1) Both encourage programming based on the concept of communicating processes.

(2) The guard mechanism plays an important role for conditional branching, nondeterminism and synchronization.

(3) Both pursue simplicity.

The major difference is that CSP tries to rule out any dynamic constructs — dynamic process creation, dynamic memory allocation, recursive call, etc. — while GHC does not. Another major difference is that CSP has a concept of sequential processes while GHC does not. CSP is at a level nearer to the current computer architecture. GHC is more abstract and has a smaller set of primitives: it uses unification instead of input, output, and assignment commands, and it uses a recursive call instead of a repetitive command.

4.8.4 Comparison with (sequential) Prolog

Comparison with sequential Prolog must be made from the viewpoint of logic programming languages, not of parallel programming languages.

First of all, GHC has no concepts of the order of clauses or the order of goals in a clause. GHC is undoubtedly nearer Horn clause logic on this point. The semantics of Prolog must explain its sequentiality: without it, we cannot discuss some properties of a program such as termination.

GHC deviates from first-order logic in that it introduces the guard construct. It will be hard to give a semantics to the guard within the framework of first-order logic. However, Prolog also suffers from the same problem because of the notorious, but useful, cut operator. The commitment operator corresponds to the cut operator. However, since the commitment operator of GHC has been introduced in a more controlled way, it should be easier to give a formal semantics to it.

One problem with Prolog is that the use of *read* and *write* predicates prevents declarative reading of a program. In GHC, we no longer need imperative predicates because the concept of streams can well well be adapted to input and output. Large data structures such as mutable arrays and databases can also be logically and efficiently handled using transaction streams as the interface (Ueda and Chikayama, 1984).

4.8.5 Comparison with Delta Prolog

Delta-Prolog (Pereira and Nasr, 1984) is an extension of Prolog which allows multiple processes. Communication and synchronization are realized using the notion of an *event*. The underlying logic which explains the meaning of events is called Distributed Logic.

One of the differences between Delta-Prolog and GHC is that Delta-Prolog retains the sequentiality concept and the cut operator of Prolog. Both seem to be peculiarities of Prolog, so GHC avoided them. A parallel program in Delta-Prolog may look quite different from comparable sequential programs in Delta-Prolog itself and in Prolog. On the other hand, a class of GHC programs which have only unidirectional information flow (like pipelining) is easily rewritable to Prolog by replacing commitment operators by cuts, and a class of Prolog programs which use no deep backtracking and each of whose predicates has only one intended input/output mode is also easily rewritable to GHC.

4.9   Conclusions

We have described the parallel logic programming language Guarded Horn Clauses. Its syntax, informal semantics, programming examples, important features, possible extensions, implementation technique of synchronization mechanism, and comparison with other languages were outlined and discussed. ,

We hope the simplicity of GHC will make it suitable for a parallel computation model as well as a programming language. The flexibility of GHC makes its efficient implementation difficult compared with CSP-like languages. However, a flexible language could be appropriately restricted in order to make simple programs run efficiently. On the other hand, it would be very difficult to extend a fast but inflexible language naturally.

Acknowledgments

The author would like to thank Akikazu Takeuchi, Toshihiko Miyazaki, Jiro Tanaka, Koichi Furukawa, Rikio Onai and other ICOT members, as well as the ICOT Working Groups, for useful discussions on GHC and its implementation. Thanks are also due to Ehud Shapiro, Steve Gregory, Anthony Kusalik and Vijay Saraswat for their comments on the earlier versions of this paper. Katsuya Hakozaki, Masahiro Yamamoto, and Kazuhiro Fuchi provided very stimulating research environments.

This research was done as part of the R&D activities of the Fifth Generation Computer Systems Project of Japan.

Yosee Feldman assisted in editing this paper.

References

Clark, K.L., and Gregory, S., "A Relational Language for Parallel Programming," in *Concurrent Prolog: Collected Papers*, Vol. 1, pp. 9-26, MIT Press, 1987.

Clark, K.L., McCabe, F.G., and Gregory, S., "IC-PROLOG—Language Features," in Clark, K.L., and Tarnlund, S.-A. (eds.), *Logic Programming*, pp. 253-266, Academic Press, London, 1982.

Clark, K.L., and Gregory, S., "Notes on Systems Programming in PARLOG," *Proc. Int'l Conf. on Fifth Generation Computer Systems*, pp. 299-306, Tokyo, 1984.

Clark, K.L., and Gregory, S., "PARLOG: Parallel Programming in Logic," in *Concurrent Prolog: Collected Papers*, Vol. 1, pp. 140-156, MIT Press, 1987.

Hagiya, M., "On Lazy Unification and Infinite Trees," *Proc. Logic Programming Conference '83*, ICOT, Tokyo, 1983 (in Japanese).

Hoare, C.A.R., "Communicating Sequential Processes," *Comm. ACM*, Vol. 21, No. 8, pp. 666-677, 1978.

Kowalski, R.A., "Predicate Logic as Programming Language," *Proc. of IFIP Congress 74*, pp. 569-574, North-Holland, Stockholm, 1974.

Nakashima, H., Tomura, S., and Ueda, K., "What is a Variable in Prolog," *Proc. Int'l Conf. on Fifth Generation Computer Systems*, pp. 327-332, Tokyo, 1984.

Pereira, L.M., and Nasr, R., Delta-Prolog: "A Distributed Logic Programming Language," *Proc. Int'l Conf. on Fifth Generation Computer Systems*, pp. 283-291, Tokyo, 1984.

Roussel, P., *Prolog: Manual de Reference et d'Utilisation*, Groupe d'Intelligence Artificielle, Marseille-Luminy, 1975.

Sato, M., and Sakurai, T., "Qute: A Functional Language Based on Unification," *Proc. Int'l Conf. on Fifth Generation Computer Systems*, pp. 157-165, Tokyo, 1984.

Shapiro, E., "A Subset of Concurrent Prolog and its Interpreter," in *Concurrent Prolog: Collected Papers*, Vol. 1, pp. 84-139, MIT Press, 1987.

Shapiro, E., "System Programming in Concurrent Prolog," in *Concurrent Prolog: Collected Papers*, Vol. 2, pp. 2-27, MIT Press, 1987.

Shapiro, E., and Takeuchi, A., "Object-Oriented Programming in Concurrent Prolog," *New Generation Computing*, Vol. 1, No. 1, pp. 25-49, 1983.

Takeuchi. A., and Furukawa, K., "Bounded Buffer Communication in Concurrent Prolog," in *Concurrent Prolog: Collected Papers*, Vol. 1, pp. 464-475, MIT Press, 1987.

Ueda, K., and Chikayama, T., "Concurrent Prolog Compiler on Top of Prolog," *Proc. IEEE Symp. on Logic Programming*, pp. 119-126, 1985.

Ueda, K., "Concurrent Prolog Re-examined," ICOT Tech. Report TR-102, ICOT, 1985.

Ueda, K., and Chikayama, T., "Efficient Stream/Array Processing in Logic Programming Languages," *Proc. Int'l Conf. on Fifth Generation Computer Systems*, pp. 317-326, Tokyo, 1984.

Warren, D.H.D., Pereira, L.M., and Pereira, F.C.N., "PROLOG—The Language and its Implementation Compared with Lisp," *SIGPLAN Notices*, Vol. 12, No. 8, pp. 109-115, 1977.

Semantic foundations of concurrent constraint programming

Vijay A. Saraswat, Xerox PARC

Martin Rinard, Stanford University

Prakash Panangaden, McGill University

(Preliminary Report)

Abstract

Concurrent constraint programming [Sar89,SR90] is a simple and powerful model of concurrent computation based on the notions of *store-as-constraint* and *process as information transducer*. The *store-as-valuation* conception of von Neumann computing is replaced by the notion that the store is a constraint (a finite representation of a possibly infinite set of valuations) which provides partial information about the possible values that variables can take. Instead of "reading" and "writing" the values of variables, processes may now *ask* (check if a constraint is entailed by the store) and *tell* (augment the store with a new constraint). This is a very general paradigm which subsumes (among others) nondeterminate data-flow and the (concurrent)(constraint) logic programming languages.

This paper develops the basic ideas involved in giving a coherent semantic account of these languages. Our first contribution is to give a simple and general formulation of the notion that a constraint system is a system of partial information (*a la* the information systems of Scott). Parameter passing and hiding is handled by borrowing ideas from the cylindric algebras of Henkin, Monk and Tarski to introduce diagonal elements and "cylindrification" operations (which mimic the projection of information induced by existential quantifiers).

The second contribution is to introduce the notion of determinate concurrent constraint programming languages. The combinators treated are ask, tell, parallel composition, hiding and recursion. We present a simple model for this language based on the specification-oriented methodology of [OH86]. The crucial insight is to focus on observing the *resting points* of a process—those stores in which the process quiesces without producing more information. It turns out that for the determinate language, the set of resting points of a process completely characterizes its behavior on all inputs, since each process can be identified with a closure operator over the underlying constraint system. Very natural definitions of parallel composition, communication and hiding are given. For example, the parallel composition of two agents can be characterized by just the intersection of the sets of constraints associated with them. We also give a complete axiomatization of equality in this model, present

a simple operational semantics (which dispenses with the explicit notions of renaming that plague logic programming semantics), and show that the model is fully abstract with respect to this semantics.

The third contribution of this paper is to extend these modelling ideas to the nondeterminate language (that is, the language including bounded, dependent choice). In this context it is no longer sufficient to record only the set of resting points of a process—we must also record the path taken by the process (that is, the sequence of ask/tell interactions with the environment) to reach each resting point. Because of the nature of constraint-based communication, it turns out to be very convenient to model such paths as certain kinds of closure operators, namely, bounded trace operators. We extend the operational semantics to the nondeterminate case and show that the operational semantics is fully consistent with the model, in that two programs denote the same object in the model iff there is no context which distinguishes them operationally.

This is the first simple model for the cc languages (and *ipso facto*, concurrent logic programming languages) which handles recursion, is compositional with respect to all the combinators in the language, can be used for proving liveness properties of programs, and is fully abstract with respect to the obvious notion of observation.

1 Introduction

The aim of our enterprise is simple—to develop the semantic foundations of a new paradigm for concurrent computing [Sar89,SR90].

The basic paradigm. The crucial concept underlying this paradigm is to replace the notion of *store-as-valuation* behind imperative programming languages with the notion of *store-as-constraint*. By a constraint we mean a (possibly infinite) subset of the space of all possible valuations in the variables of interest. For the store to be a constraint rather than a valuation means that at any stage of the computation one may have only partial information about the possible values that the variables can take. We take as fundamental the possibility that the state of the computation may only be able to provide partial information about the variables of interest.

This paradigm shift renders the usual notions of of (imperative) "write" and "read" incoherent. For example, there may be no single, finitely-describable value left to return as the result of a "read" operation on a variable. Similarly,

"Semantic Foundations of Concurrent Constraint Programming" by V.A. Saraswat, M. Rinard, and P. Panangaden from *Proc. Principles of Programming Languages Conf. (POPL '91)*, pp. 333-352. Copyright 1991, Association for Computing Machinery, Inc., reprinted with permission.

an assign operation is only capable of prescribing a fully formed, concrete value for a variable and the new value may have nothing to do with the previous value. This runs into difficulties with the notion that the store specifies some constraints that must always be obeyed by the given variables.

Instead, [Sar89] proposes the replacement of read with the notion of *ask* and write with the notion of *tell*. An ask operation takes a constraint (say, c) and uses it to probe the structure of the store. It succeeds if the store contains enough information to entail c. Tell takes a constraint and conjoins it to the constraints already in place in the store. That is, the set of valuations describing the resultant store is the intersection of the set of valuations describing the original store and those describing the additional constraint. Thus, as computation progresses, more and more information is accumulated in the store—a basic step does not *change* the value of a variable but rules out certain values that were possible before; the store is *monotonically refined*.

The idea of monotonic update is central to the theoretical treatment of I-structures in Id Nouveau [JPP89]. I-structures were introduced in order to have some of the benefits of in-place update without introducing the problems of interference. It is interesting that the concurrent constraint paradigm can be seen as arising as a purification of logic programming [Sar89], an enhancement to functional programming and as a generalization of imperative programming. From the viewpoint of dataflow programming, the concurrent constraint paradigm is also a generalization in that the flow of information between two processes is *bidirectional*. It might relate to the goal of a more symmetrical theory of computation advocated by Girard [Gir87,Gir89].

Central to our notion of constraint system is a theory of partial information and entailment between partial information. Such a theory exists in the form of Scott's treatment of information systems [Sco82]. In our case it is natural to imagine two concurrent processes imposing inconsistent constraints on the store. Thus, we need to represent the possibility of inconsistent information.

The approach of this paper makes the possibilities for concurrency quite apparent. Instead of a single agent interacting with the store via ask and tell operations, any number of agents can simultaneously interact with the store in such a fashion. Synchronization is achieved via a blocking ask—an agent blocks if the store is not strong enough to entail the constraint it wishes to check; it remains blocked until such time as (if ever) some other concurrently executing agents add enough information to the store for it to be strong enough to entail the query. Note, in particular, that even though the paradigm is based on the notion of a shared store, ideas such as "read/write locks" do not have to be introduced for synchronization. The basic reason is that only a benign form of "change"—accumulation of information—is allowed in the system.[1] If desired, indeterminacy can be introduced by allowing an agent to block on multiple distinct constraints simultaneously, and specify distinct actions which must be invoked if the corresponding ask condition is satisfied by the store.

Thus, in this view, an agent ("computing station") is thought of as an *information transducer*. An agent can either add a constraint to the store (tell), suspend until there is enough information in the store to entail a given constraint, or decompose into a number of other agents running in parallel, possibly with hidden interconnections, and communicating and synchronizing via the store. Of course, as is standard, computations of unbounded length can be achieved by using recursion.

Compuational significance of the paradigm. While these ideas are extremely simple, they conceal a powerful programming paradigm which derives its strength from the versatility of its communication mechanism. It is not possible in a short introduction to describe the many interesting communication schemes possible here. We shall just attempt to indicate the basic ideas and refer the reader to more detailed treatments such as [Sar89].

The essential idea is that variables serve as communication channels between multiple concurrently executing agents. The computational framework does not insist that there be an *a priori* partitioning of the agents into "producers" and "consumers" of information on the variables (as happens, for example, in function application, where information flows from an argument to the function body, or in CSP/CCS-style or actor-style languages). In fact, the *same* agent may simultaneously add or check constraints on the same variables.

Also, the computational framework allows for the underlying "network transport protocol" to perform (potentially arbitrarily sophisticated) inferences on the "messages" entrusted to them—these, of course, are the deductions sanctioned by the entailment relation of the constraint system. This allows each agent to state the constraints as it sees them and frees up the programmer from having to put in agents for explicitly collecting these messages and drawing the appropriate inferences ("reformatting the data"). This allows for very "high-level" languages in which a lot of computation can be expressed merely by posting constraints.

Even in a constraint system (Herbrand) over a domain as mundane as that of finite trees, such a communication scheme leads to many interesting idioms such as incomplete messages, short-circuits, difference-lists, "messages to the future" etc. [Sar89]—the techniques that have colloquially been referred to as stemming from "the power of the logical variable".[2] For instance, it is possible to embed a communication channel (variable) in a message as a "first-class" object, in exactly the same way as data. This makes for an elegant form of dynamic reconfigurability, of a kind which is difficult to achieve in a simple way within frameworks such as those of CCS and CSP. The practicality of this framework is attested to by the fact that several implemented cc languages are now available, including at least one commercial implementation [FT89].

This paper focusses on the use of constraints for communication and control in concurrent constraint programming languages. It is worth pointing out that the concurrent constraint programming framework is, however, concerned with

---

[1] Which of course, is not to say that systems with changable state are not describable in the cc paradigm. State change can be represented without compromising the basic paradigm by adapting standard techniques from logic and functional programming. Namely, "assignable variables" are embedded in the local state of a recursive agent—the agent "changes" the value of the variable by merely recurring with a new value for one of its arguments. In some languages in the cc framework (e.g., Janus[SKL90]) there is considerable hope that such mechanisms for representing state change can be competitive in performance with traditional assignment-based techniques.

[2] The kind of constraint-based communiation schemes we are describing here are the essence of computation in the logic programming style. Indeed, the origins of the cc framework are in concurrent logic programming and in the notion of constraint logic programing introduced by [JL87,Mah87]. See [Sar89] for further details.

much more than just concurrency—it takes the first step towards a general architecture for computing with constraints that is dependent only on the form of constraint systems, not on their particular details (following [JL87]). As such, it provides one coherent attempt to articulate the vision of *constraint programming* manifest in the work of Sutherland, Sussman, Steele, Borning and others. In particular, the cc framework is also concerned with many other combinators for introducing and controlling logic-programming style "search nondeterminism".[3]

One of the goals of our research is defining a general class of *constraint systems* to which the concurrent constraint paradigm applies. A beginning has been made in the present paper. The presence of constraint systems in computational and engineering problems is very widespread. For example, several applications to AI are usefully viewed in terms of constraints. A general enough definition would allow one to define constraint systems as over data types as diverse as finite trees, streams, intervals of rational numbers, various types of functions spaces and data types derived from knowledge rerpesentation applications. Indeed the design of constraint systems of use in computational systems is limited only by our imaginations. It is not difficult to consider any data-structure of interest in computer science — enumerate types, records, bags, arrays, hash-tables, graphs, binary search trees — and devise constraint systems of interest over them which can usefully and interestingly be embedded within a cc language.

Generality. The cc framework is parametrized by an arbitrary constraint system. This schematic treatment brings with it all the usual advantages: results need to be proven only once and are immediately applicable to all members of the class. In particular the models we develop in this paper are in fact a class of models, for a large class of programming languages.

We place very few restrictions on the nature of a constraint system: we demand only that there be some system of partial information, some notion of what it means for various pieces of partial information to be true about the same objects (the notion of *consistency*), and what it means for certain pieces of information to always hold, given that some other pieces of information must also hold (the notion of entailment).

Relationship to other theories of concurrency. Recently there have been radical new ideas about concurrency. Two of particular note are the so called Chemical Abstract Machine [BB90], due to Boudol and Berry, and mobile processes, due to Milner and his co-workers [MPW89]. In both of these approaches the key new ingredient is that processes can alter their interactions and are, in efffect, mobile. In our approach the interactions between processes is dynamic too in the sense that there is no predetermined set of agents that a given agent is limited to interact with. The relationships need, however, to be understood carefully. It would be particularly interesting to understand how a lambda abstraction mechanism could be incorporated into the concurrent constraint paradigm. Understanding the relationships with

the work on mobile processes or Boudol's gamma calculus would be very helpful, as it is known that the latter can encode the lazy lambda calculus [Mil90,JP90].

1.1 Contributions of this paper

The central task of this paper is to develop the semantic foundations of the programming paradigm discussed above. Towards this end, we formalize the basic notion of a constraint system, and present operational and denotational semantics for the determinate and nondeterminate cc languages. The next several paragraphs discuss each of these contributions in detail.

Constraint systems. We formalize the notion of constraint system, generalizing and simplifying previous treatments in [Sar89,JL87,SR90]. The basic insight is to treat constraint systems as systems of partial information, in the style of Dana Scott's development of information systems, together with operators to express hiding of information. From a programming point of view such operations allow the introduction of parameter-passing in constraint programming languages, and the introduction of "local variables" within procedures.

Philosophy of modeling. The models developed in this paper are based on the philosophy of modeling discussed in [OH86,Hoa90]. In the next few paragraphs we summarize the basic ideas and ontological commitments made in this style.

Crucial to this philosophy is the identification of the notion of *observation* of a process. A process is then equated with the set of observations that can be made of it. The set of processes is identified by presenting a collection of naturally motivated closure conditions on sets of observations.

It is important that the observations of a process include all ways in which the process can "go wrong", that is, fail to meet obligations imposed on it by the environment. Once a process "goes wrong", further detailed modeling of the process is irrelevant, since the emphasis of this approach is on guaranteeing that as long as the environment honors its obligations to the process, the process cannot "go wrong" This ontological commitment is usually captured in the slogan "divergence is catastrophic", or, "anything can happen" once the process goes wrong.

One way in which the process can go wrong is by engaging in "internal chatter", that is, in an infinite sequence of internal actions (possibly continually producing output in the meantime), without asking the environment for some input (and thereby giving the environment the ability to control its execution by denying it that input). Within the cc framework, another way in which a process can "go wrong" is if it causes the shared store to become inconsistent — for in such a state the process is again completely uncontrollable from the environment. No action that the environment can take can then influence the course of execution of the process, since the inconsistent store can answer *any* ask request. Hence the process is free to follow any branch that it could potentially follow, without more input from the environment. In particular, if the process recursively calls another process, then it can engage in an infinite execution sequence because every ask operation guarding a recursive procedure call will be answered successfully.

---

[3]Throughout this paper when we talk of the "cc languages" we shall mean the cc languages with Ask and Tell as the only primitive constraint-related operations. Other coherent and very useful primitives can be (and have been, in [Sar89]) defined, but they are outside the scope of this paper.

This suggests that in the semantic model the process that can produce **false** should not be distinguished form the process that can engage in an infinite execution sequence; both such processes should be treated as "catastrophic". This is indeed the approach followed in the main body of the paper. However, other alternative treatments of failure and divergence are possible, and in Section 3 we shall indicate some of the possibilities and how they can be treated.

Determinate constraint programming. Sixteen years ago, Kahn gave a theory of determinate data-flow [Kah74]. Today this theory (with some extensions, e.g. to concrete data structures) remains the dominant theory of determinate concurrent computation. While simple, elegant and widely applicable, the theory's emphasis on computing with directional point-to-point communication channels imposes some expressibility restrictions: channels carry only fully formed values from the underlying data domain; networks are not dynamically reconfigurable in that connections cannot themselves be passed as data on communication channels; and each channel has only one reader and one writer. Because of these restrictions, Kahn's theory cannot model such useful programming idioms as incomplete messages, difference lists, recursive doubling, multiple readers/writers of a communication channel, dynamic reconfiguration, etc. Although these techniques were originally developed in the context of nondeterminate concurrent logic programming, they are all both inherently determinate and usefully expressible in determinate contexts.

This paper presents a simple theory of determinate computation which can model all of the above idioms and more: our theory preserves the essential features of Kahn's theory while substantially extending its domain of applicability. From the constraint programming point of view it is useful and interesting to focus on the determinate subset because a mathematically much simpler treatment can be given, without sacrificing any essential novelty—the major semantic and computational ideas underlying the cc paradigm can already be illustrated in the determinate case.

We present a simple algebraic syntax for determinate concurrent constraint programs. We also present an operational semantics based on a labelled transition system in which a configuration is just an agent and a label is a pair of constraints (the store in which the transition is initiated and the store in which it terminates). The transition system is able to completely avoid using substitutions and "variable-renamings", thereby considerably simplifying the treatment. Past theoretical treatments of (constraint) logic programming have had to use various *ad hoc* techniques for dealing with this problem.

The denotation of a process is taken to be a set of constraints (the "resting points" of the process) satisfying certain properties. Various combinators are defined on such processes, corresponding to ask and tell operations, to running two agents in parallel, and to creating a new "local" communication channel. We show that the denotational semantics is fully abstract with respect to he operational semantics. We also give a sound and complete axiomatization of equality for finite programs, so that finite program equivalence can be established purely by equational reasoning. We also develop a slightly different model in which limits of (fair) infinite execution sequences are observed.

Models for nondeterminate cc languages. The denotation of a nondeterminate process is somewhat more complex than in the determinate case: rather than storing just the resting points of a process, we must also associate with each resting point the "path" followed by the process in reaching that point. Such a path is also called a *failure*. The denotation of a process is the set of all its failures. The set of all processes is identified by presenting some naturally motivated closure conditions on sets of failures, following [Jos90]. (For example, one of the major conditions ensures that processes are finitely nondeterminate.) The resulting notion of a process is intuitive and easy to understand. Combinators corresponding to ask, tell, nondeterminate (dependent) choice, parallel composition and hiding are defined. A simple operational semantics is given, and a full correspondence with the denotational semantics is established. In particular, we believe that this treatment gives a completely satisfactory account of the semantics of concurrent logic programming languages.

A central issue in our semantic treatment is the representation of a failure. A failure could be represented as a sequence of ask/tell annotated constraints. Such a strategy is followed in earlier work on related languages, for example in [Sar85,Lev88,GL90], [GCLS88], [GMS89] etc. However, ask-tell sequences are far too concrete in this setting. They store too much information which must then be abstracted from (usually via complex closure conditions) since they encode the precise path followed by a process to arrive at a resting point. Furthermore, the definition of various combinators becomes rather cumbersome because of the need to "propagate" information down the trace. Instead, we chose to represent observations via various kinds of closure operators. To capture various operational notions of interest, we introduce the concept of *trace operators*, and *bounded closure operators*, and present some portions of their theory relevant to this paper.

We also establish a very simple relationship between the nondeterminate and determinate semantics, showing that the two semantics are essentially identical for determinate programs over finitary constraint systems.

In summary, we present a simple model for the cc languages that is fully able to account for nondeterminism and divergence, thus permitting the use of this model in reasoning about liveness properties of programs. The model is also shown to be fully consistent with the intuitive operational semantics of cc programs.

1.2 Related work

The basic concepts of concurrent constraint programming were introduced in [Sar88,Sar89]. Subseqently, we developed an operational semantics and a bisimulation semantics in [SR90]. This line of research extends and subsumes (for all intents and purposes) earlier work on the semantics of concurrent logic programming languages.[4]

The power of the "logical variable" has been amply recognized in recent years, and numerous authors—too numerous for us to survey their work in this extended abstract—have investigated the combination of functional and logic

---

[4]The semantics presented in this paper does not account for the language Concurrent Prolog studied in [GCLS88]; we do not, however, view this as a defect in our approach/ Indeed, researchers working with Concurrent Prolog have moved to the Ask-and-Tell cc framework [KYSK88,GMS89].

programming languages [Lin85,DL86,ANP89,JPP89]. However, no account of the basic paradigm comparable with Kahn's original account in simplicity and generality has been forthcoming.

Perhaps the most noteworthy in this context is the work of [JPP89], which discusses a subset of the functional programming language *Id Noveau* with "logical" arrays [ANP89]. Their semantic treatment also identifies a program as a closure operator. However, their treatment is specialized to the particular kinds of arrays they were dealing with; our work is parametrized by a very general notion of constraint system. Further, they do not explicitly discuss the hiding and the Ask operations; though their "Tell" operation does implicit asks. We also present an axiomatization for the model. Their operational model includes an explicit discussion of how the constraints are resolved and represented, we achieve considerable simplicity by abstracting away the details of the constraint resolution process.

The characterization of concurrency via intersection of sets of fixed points has also been elaborated by Hoare in a recent paper [Hoa89], in a setting related to Unity [CM88]. Our paper develops that viewpoint, and presents a characterization of other combinators as well, in the same style. We believe that the concurrent constraint programming languages are the natural setting for the development of a theory of computing with closure operators.

The semantics of nondeterminate concurrent constraint programming languages is becoming an active area [SR90, GMS89,GL90,dBP90a]. However none of this work explores the very simple characterizations possible for the determinate languages, dealing instead with the representation of processes as various sorts of trees or sets of i/o annotated sequences of constraints. The notion of determinacy was studied in the set-up of logic programming languages in [Mah87], but no characterizations of the kind we provide here were given.

[GMS89] does not consider most of the combinators we treat here, besides having a complicated treatment of ask/tell sequences. Neither does it treat recursion.

In work to appear, deBoer and Palamidessi [dBP90a, dBP90b] propose a model which is similar to ours in many respects. In particular, they have also recognized that it is sufficient to take sequences of ask/tell actions in order to get a model for the cc languages. However, their treatment ignores recursion. Much of the sophistication of the present model lies in the way finite nondeterminate axioms need to be introduced in order to correctly model divergence. Their model in [dBP90b] is not compositional with respect to the choice operator.

Our development follows closely Mark Josephs' treatment of receptive processes in [Jos90]. A receptive process can always accept any input from the environment, but may produce different (or no) output depending on the input. Josephs gives a set of axioms for reactive processes that turn out to be more or less what is needed in order to develop a model for the cc languages as well. The primary differences lie in the nature of communication, and in the combinators treated. Josephs' theory treats communication in the usual CCS/CSP style as the exchange of uninterpreted tokens with the environment. The constraint-based nature of the cc languages imposes additional structure which must be considered. However, as this paper demonstrates, it is possible to adapt his basic model to the cc setup without major reworking, which should confirm the essential robustness of his conceptualization of asynchronous systems.

2 Constraint Systems

Our presentation here is simplified and generalized from the presentation in [SR90]. More details may be found in [SPRng].

What do we have when we have a constraint system? First, of course, there must be a *vocabulary* of assertions that can be made about how things can be — each assertion will be a syntactically denotable object in the programming language. Postulate then a set D of *tokens*, each giving us partial information about certain states of affairs. At any finite state of the computation, the program will have deposited some finite set u of such tokens with the embedded constraint-solver and may demand to know whether some other token is *entailed* by u. Postulate then a *compact entailment relation* $\vdash \subseteq pD \times D$ (pD is the set of finite subsets of D), which records the inter-dependencies between tokens. The intention is to have a set of tokens v entail a token P just in case for every state of affairs for which we can assert every token in v, we can also assert P. This leads us to:[5]

Definition 2.1 A *simple constraint system* is a structure $\langle D, \vdash \rangle$, where D is a non-empty (countable) set of *tokens* or *(primitive) constraints* and $\vdash \subseteq pD \times D$ is an *entailment relation* satisfying (where pD is the set of *finite* subsets of D:

C1 $u \vdash P$ whenever $P \in u$, and,

C2 $u \vdash Q$ whenever $u \vdash P$ for all $P \in v$, and $v \vdash Q$.

Extend $\vdash$ to be a relation on $pD \times pD$ by: $u \vdash v$ iff $u \vdash P$ for every $P \in v$. Define $u \approx v$ if $u \vdash v$ and $v \vdash u$. □

Of course, in any implementable language, $\vdash$ must be decidable—and as efficient as the intended class of users of the language demand. Compactness of the entailment relation ensures that one has a semi-decidable entailment relation. If a token is entailed, it is entailed by a finite set and hence if entailment holds it can be checked in finite time. If the store does not entail the constraint it may not be possible for the constraint solver to say this at any finite stage of the computation.

Such a treatment of systems of partial information is, of course, well-known, and underlies Dana Scott's information systems approach to domain theory [Sco82]. A simple constraint system is just an information system with the consistency structure removed, since it is natural in our setting to conceive of the possibility that the execution of a program can give rise to an inconsistent state of affairs.

Following standard lines, states of affairs (at least those representable in the system) can be identified with the set of all those tokens that hold in them.

Definition 2.2 The *elements* of a constraint system $\langle D, \vdash \rangle$ are those subsets c of D such that $P \in c$ whenever $u \subseteq_f c$ (i.e. u is a finite subset of c) and $u \vdash P$. The set of all such elements is denoted by $|D|$. For every $u \subseteq_f D$ define $\bar{u} \in |D|$ to be the set $\{P \in D \mid u \vdash P\}$. □

---

[5]In reality, the systems underlying most concrete concurrent constraint programming languages have slightly more structure to them, namely they are ask-and-tell constraint systems [Sar89]. The additional structure arises because it is possible to state at the level of a constraint system that the imposition of certain constraints can be delayed until such time as some associated constraint is entailed by the store ("implicit Ask-restriction"). However, this additional structure is not crucial, and can be easily handled by extending the techniques presented in this paper.

As is well known, $(|D|, \subseteq)$ is a complete algebraic lattice, the compactness of $\vdash$ gives us algebraicity of $|D|$, with least element $\mathtt{true} = \{P \mid \emptyset \vdash P\}$, greatest element D (which we will mnemonically denote $\mathtt{false}$), glbs (denoted by $\sqcap$) given by intersection and lubs (denoted by $\sqcup$) given by the closure of the union. The lub of chains is, however, just the union of the members in the chain. The finite elements of $|D|$ are just the elements generated by finite subsets of D; the set of such elements will be denoted $|D|_0$. We use a, b, c, d and e to stand for elements of $|D|$; $c \geq d$ means $c \vdash d$. Two common notations that we use when referring to the elements of $|D|$ are $\uparrow c = \{d \mid c \leq d\}$ and $\downarrow c = \{d \mid d \leq c\}$.

The alert reader will have noticed that the constraint system need not generate a *finitary*[6] algebraic lattice since, in general, Scott information systems do not generate finitary domains. Indeed many common constraint systems are not finitary even when the data type that they are defined over is finitary. For the interpretation of determinate concurrent constraint programs we do not need the constraint system to be finitary but we do for the nondeterminate case. If we drop the requirement that the entailment relation is compact we will generate, in general, lattices that are not algebraic. We always need the entailment relation to be compact since we do not know, as yet, whether these ideas can be extended to nonalgebraic constraint systems.

In what follows, by a *finite constraint* we shall mean a finite set of tokens. We also take the liberty of confusing a finite constraint u with $\bar{u} \in |D|_0$.

Example 2.1 Generating constraint systems.
For any first-order vocabulary $\mathcal{L}$, and countably infinite set of variables $\mathtt{Var}$, take D to be an arbitrary subset of open $(\mathcal{L}, \mathtt{Var})$-formulas, and $\vdash$ to be the entailment relation with respect to some class Δ of $\mathcal{L}$-structures. That is, $\{P_1, \ldots, P_n\} \vdash Q$ iff for every structure $\mathcal{M} \in \Delta$, an $\mathcal{M}$-valuation realizes Q whenever it realizes each of $P_1, \ldots, P_n$. Such a $\langle D, \vdash \rangle$ is a simple constraint system. □

Example 2.2 The Kahn constraint system.
More concretely, let us define the Kahn constraint system $\mathcal{D}(\mathcal{B}) = \langle D, \vdash_\mathcal{D} \rangle$ underlying data-flow languages [Kah74], for $\mathcal{B} = \langle B, \vdash_B \rangle$ so some underlying constraint system on a domain of data elements, E. Let $\mathcal{L}$ be the vocabulary consisting of the predicate symbols $=/2, c/1$ and the function symbols $f/1, r/1, a/2, \Lambda/0$. Postulate an infinite set $(X, Y \in)\mathtt{Var}$ of variables. Let the set of tokens D consist of *atomic* $(\mathcal{L}, \mathtt{Var})$ formulas. Let Δ consist of the single structure with domain of interepretation B^ω the set of (possibly infinite) sequences over B, (including the empty sequence Λ) and interpretations for the symbols in $\mathcal{L}$ given by:

- $=$ is the equality predicate,

- c is the predicate that is true of all sequences except Λ.

- f is the function which maps Λ to Λ, and every other sequence s to the unit length sequence whose first element is the first element of s,

- r is the function which maps Λ to Λ, and every other sequence s to the sequence obtained from s by dropping its first element,

---
[6]This means that a finite element dominates only finitely many elements.

- a is the function which returns its second argument if its first argument is Λ; otherwise it returns the sequence consisting of the first element of its first argument followed by the elements of the second argument.

Now, we can define $\vdash_\mathcal{D}$ by:

$$\{c_1, \ldots, c_n\} \vdash_\mathcal{D} c \iff \Delta \vdash_\mathcal{D} (c_1 \wedge \ldots c_n \Rightarrow c)$$

thus completing the definition of the constraint system $\mathcal{D} = \langle D, \vdash_\mathcal{D} \rangle$.

Note that in this constraint system the set of elements are not finitary. The constraint $X = Y$, which is finite, entails infinitely many constraints of the form $f(r^n(X)) = f(r^n(Y))$. Since the constraint system has a compact entailment relation we will have algebraicity. In the lattice generated by the entailment closed sets of tokens the set consisting of the entailment closure of $\{X = Y\}$ will contain all the tokens of the form $f(r^n(X)) = f(r^n(Y))$; the set consisting of all the latter, however, will not contain $X = Y$. It is possible to define a variant system that is finitary. The data type of streams is, of course, finitary. □

Example 2.3 The Herbrand constraint system.
We describe this example quickly. There is an ordinary first-order language L with equality. The tokens of the constraint system are the atomic propositions. Entailment can vary depending on the intended use of the predicate symbols but it must include the usual entailment relations that one expects from equality. Thus, for example, $f(X, Y) = f(A, g(B, C))$ must entail $X = A$ and $Y = g(B, C)$. If equality is the only predicate symbol then the constraint system is finitary. With other predicates present the finitariness of the lattice will depend on the entailment relation. □

Example 2.4 [Rational intervals.
The underlying tokens are of the form $X \in [x, y]$ where x and y are rational numbers and the notation $[x, y]$ means the closed interval between x and y. We assume that every such membership assertion is a primitive token.

The entailment relation is the one derived from the obvious interpretation of the tokens. Thus, $X \in [x_1, y_1] \vdash X \in [x_2, y_2]$ if and only if $[x_1, y_1] \subseteq [x_2, y_2]$. Whether this yields a compact entailment relation is a slightly delicate issue. If we assume the usual definition of intersection and unions of infinite families of intervals, we will definitely not have a compact entailment relation. For example, since $\bigcap_{n>0}[0, 1 + 1/n] = [0, 1]$, we would have $\{X \in [0, 1 + 1/n] \mid n > 0\} \vdash (X \in [0, 1])$ but no finite subset of $\{X \in [0, 1 + 1/n] \mid n > 0\}$ would entail $X \in [0, 1]$. We may take the definition $u \vdash X \in [x, y]$ to mean that u must be a finite collection of intervals. In this case the entailment relation is, by definition, compact and the lattice generated is algebraic. It will, however, appear slightly peculiar with respect to one's normal expectations about intervals. The join of a family of assertions involving membership of X in a nested family of intervals will not yield an assertion about membership in the intersection of the family. Instead there will be a new element of $|D|$ that sits below the intersection. Thus, for example, the join $\bigsqcup_{n>0} X \in [0, 1 + 1/n]$ will not be $X \in [0, 1]$ but rather a new element that sits below $X \in [0, 1]$. Clearly the lattice is not finitary but the entailment relation is compact and the lattice is indeed algebraic. It is worth noting that this example shows that we can model determinate computations over domains that are not *incremental*[7]. In fact we have an *order-dense subset*[8] We can work with such a lattice when we model the determinate language but, as yet, we cannot model the nondeterminate languages over such constraint systems. It is known that the closure operators over a lattice with an order-dense subset cannot form an algebraic complete partial order[9]. Thus, the extension of these ideas to higher-order programming will be challenging. □

Hiding in constraint systems. Any reasonable programming language supports modularity by providing a notion of hiding the internal structure of an agent from its context. We support this hiding with a family of hiding operators on the underlying constraint system; these operators capture the notion of projecting away information. In this we use the axiomatization of cylindric algebra[HMT71]. In future research we plan to give a more principled account of hiding and of the choice of axioms using notions from categorical logic.

Definition 2.3 A *cylindric constraint system* is a structure $\langle D, \vdash, \mathsf{Var}, \{\exists_X \mid X \in \mathsf{Var}\}\rangle$ such that:

- $\langle D, \vdash\rangle$ is a simple constraint system,

- Var is an infinite set of *indeterminates* or *variables*,

- For each variable $X \in \mathsf{Var}$, $\exists_X : pD \to pD$ is an operation satisfying:

  E1 $u \vdash \exists_X u$

  E2 $u \vdash v$ implies $\exists_X u \vdash \exists_X v$

  E3 $\exists_X(u \cup \exists_X v) \approx \exists_X u \cup \exists_X v$,

  E4 $\exists_X \exists_Y u \approx \exists_Y \exists_X u$

□

For every variable X, $\exists_X$ is extended to be a continuous function from $|D| \to |D|$ in the obvious way:

$$\exists_X c = \{P \mid \exists_X u \vdash P, \text{ for some } u \subseteq_f c\}$$

Example 2.5 Let the token set consist of some subclass of $(\mathcal{L}, \mathsf{Var})$ formulas closed under existential quantification of finite conjunctions. Each operator $\exists_X$ is then interpreted by the function which maps each finite set $\{P_1, \ldots, P_n\}$ of tokens to the set of tokens $\{\exists X. P_1 \wedge \ldots \wedge P_n\}$. It is easy to see that the four conditions above will be satisfied. □

Diagonal elements. For all useful programming languages in this framework, it is necessary to consider procedures with parameter passing. In usual logic programming languages, parameter passing is supported by using substitutions. We use a trick due to Tarski and his colleagues. For the class of constraint systems discussed above, this trick can be illustrated by providing, as tokens, the "diagonal" formulas $X = Y$, for $X, Y \in \mathsf{Var}$. Now, the formula $\phi[Y/X]$ is nothing else but the formula $\exists X.(X = Y) \wedge \phi$. More generally, for an arbitrary constraint system, we can axiomatize the required properties of the diagonal elements, following [HMT71]. We demand that the token set D contain, for every pair of variables $X, Y \in \mathsf{Var}$, the token d_{XY} satisfying the properties:

D1. $\emptyset \vdash d_{XX}$

D2. if $X \neq Y$, $\{d_{XY}\} \approx \exists_Z\{d_{XY}, d_{YZ}\}$

D3. $\{d_{XY}\} \cup \exists_X(u \cup \{d_{XY}\}) \vdash u$

The defect of this axiomatization is that it "appears out of thin air". In particular, categorical logic, as expounded by Lambek and Scott [LS86] has a thorough analysis of variables and also of variable-free calculi and the relationship between them. If we cast the notion of constraint system in categorical terms, we would be able to use the vast body of results about categorical logic [LS86] in the course of our development of the concept of constraint system. The axioms for hiding would emerge from fundamental principles. Investigations into catgorical logic suggest that the logic implicit in our treatment is a form of coherent logic [MR97][10].

3 The determinate language

... the most important observations are those which can be made only indirectly by a more or less elaborate experiment ... a successful choice of the right kind of indirect observation can provide a remarkably coherent and general explanation of a wide range of diverse phenomena.

— C.A.R. Hoare (1990)

Our basic semantic insight is that the crucial observation to make of a process is the set of its *resting points*. A process is an information processing device that interacts with its environment via a shared constraint representing the known common information. A resting point of a process is a constraint c such that if the process is initiated in c, it will eventually halt without producing any more information.[11]

While the basic idea is the same, the semantics for the nondeterminate language is significantly more complex than the semantics for the determinate language. The reason is simple. For the determinate language, it turns out to be *sufficient* to store with a process just the set of its resting points, as we now discuss.

To be determinate, the process must always produce the same output constraint when given the same input constraint. We can therefore identify a process with a function:

$$f : |D|_0 \to |D|_0$$

This function maps each input c to false if the process when initiated in c engages in an infinite execution sequence, and to d if the process ultimately quiesces having upgraded the store to d. [12] It turns out that *there is sufficient information*

---

[7] A prime interval is a pair of finite elements such that there is no finite element properly between them. An incremental domain is one in which between every two related finite elements there is a finite sequence of prime intervals that interpolates between them.

[8] This means that between any two elements there is a another distinct element.

[9] We are indebted to Michael Huth for pointing this out.

[10] We are indebted to Robert Seely and Phil Scott for this observation.

[11] Strictly speaking, this is not true. In the continuous closure operator semantics we consider later in this section, a resting point of a process is a constraint c such that if the process were to be initiated in c, it would not be able to ouput any new information without receiving some more information from the outside. The point is that the process may engage in an infinite execution sequence in c, as long as it produces no new information.

[12] Thus we shall confuse the process that on input c produces false and halts with the process that on input c engages in an infinite execution sequence. Recall from the introduction that this is in tune with the specification-oriented approach to semantics.

in the resting points of the process to uniquely determine its associated function. This property highlights the semantic simplicity of the Ask-and-Tell communication and synchronization mechanism.

Let f be the operator on $|D|_0$ corresponding to a given process. Now, the only way in which this process can affect the store is by adding more information to it. Therefore, f must be *extensive*:

$$\forall c. c \leq f(c) \tag{1}$$

Second, the store is accessible to the process as well as its environment: therefore if on input c a process produces output d and halts, it must be the case that d is a resting point, that is, on input d the process cannot progress further (because if it could, then it wouldn't have stopped in d). That is, f must be idempotent:

$$\forall c. f(f(c)) = f(c) \tag{2}$$

Finally, consider what happens to the output of such a function when the information content of the input is increased. If the invocation of the function corresponds to the imposition of a constraint, then as information in the input is increased, information in the output should not decrease. Such a function is called *monotone*:

$$\forall c, d. c \leq d \Rightarrow f(c) \leq f(d) \tag{3}$$

An operator over a partial order that is extensive, idempotent and monotone is called a *closure operator* (or, more classicaly, a *consequence* operator, [Tar56]). Closure operators are extensively studied in [GKK$^+$80] and enjoy several beautiful properties which we shall exploit in the following. Within computer science, continuous closure operators have been used in [Sco76] to characterize data-types.

We list here some basic properties. The most fundamental property of a closure operator f over a lattice E is that it can be represented by its range $f(E)$ (which is the same as its set of fixed points). f can be recovered from $f(E)$ by mapping each input to the least element in $f(E)$ above it. This is easy to see: by extensiveness, $f(c)$ is above c; by idempotence, $f(c)$ is a fixed-point of f, and by monotonicity, it is the least such fixed-point. This representation is so convenient that in the following, we shall often confuse a closure operator with its range, writing $c \in f$ to mean $f(c) = c$. In fact, a subset of E is the range of a closure operator on E iff it is closed under glbs of arbitrary subsets (whenever such glbs exist in the lattice). Thus, the range of every closure operator is non-empty, since it must contain $\mathtt{false} = \sqcap\emptyset$.

Partial order. For a closure operator f over $|D|_0$, let df be the *divergences* of f, that is, those inputs in which the process diverges. As discussed above, the divergences are exactly those constraints which are mapped to $\mathtt{false}$ by f, that is, $f^{-1}(\mathtt{false})$. The partial order on determinate processes of interest to us will be based partly on the processes' divergences. The intention is that a process f can be improved to a process g iff the divergences of g are contained in those of f and at every point in the convergences of f, f and g take on identical values. In terms of fixed points, this yields:

Definition 3.1 The divergence order on closure operators over $|D|_0$ is given by:

$$f \leq g \iff f \subseteq g \subseteq f \cup df$$

□

The bottom element of this partial order is $\{\mathtt{false}\}$ which diverges everywhere. It is not hard to see that this order is complete, with limits of chains given by unions of the set of fixed-points.

3.1 Process Algebra

In this section we develop a simple language, the determinate cc language, for expressing the behavior of concurrent determinate constraint processes. We consider agents constructed from tells of finite constraints, asks of finite constraints, hiding operators, parallel composition and procedure calls. Throughout this section we shall assume some fixed cylindrical constraint system (with diagonal elements) D. As usual, $|D|$ denotes this constraint system's set of elements, while $|D|_0$ denotes its set of finite elements.

We also define a quartic *transition* relation

$$\longrightarrow \subseteq Env \times (|D|_0 \times |D|_0) \times A \times A$$

which will be used to define the operational semantics of the programming language. (Here Env is the set of all partial functions from procedure names to (syntactic) agents.) Rather than write $\langle \rho, (c, d), A, B \rangle \in \longrightarrow$ we shall write $\rho \vdash A \xrightarrow{(c,d)} B$ (omitting the "$\rho \vdash$" if it is not relevant) and take that to mean that when initiated in store c, agent A can, in one uninterruptible step, upgrade the store to d, and subsequently behave like B. In the usual SOS style, this relation will be described by specifying a set of axioms, and taking the relation to be the smallest relation satisfying those axioms.

The syntax and semantics of the determinate language are given in Table 1. We discuss these semantic definitions in this section. For purposes of exposition we assume that procedures take exactly one variable as a parameter and that no program calls an undefined procedure. We also systematically confuse the syntactic object consisting of a finite set of tokens from D with the semantic object consisting of this set's closure under $\vdash$.

Tells. The process c augments its input with the finite constraint c. Thus it behaves as the operator $\lambda x. c \sqcup x$, which in terms of fixed points, is just:

$$c = \{d \in |D|_0 \mid d \geq c\}$$

The operational behavior of c is described by the transition axiom:

$$c \xrightarrow{(d, c \sqcup d)} \mathtt{true} \quad (c \neq \mathtt{true}) \tag{4}$$

corresponding to adding the information in c to the shared constraint in a single step.[13]

Asks. Let c be a constraint, and f a process. The process $c \rightarrow f$ waits until the store contains at least as much information as c. It then behaves like f. Such a process can be described by the function $\lambda x. if\ x \geq c\ then f(x)\ else\ c$. In terms of its range:

$$c \rightarrow f = \{d \in |D|_0 \mid d \geq c \Rightarrow d \in f\}$$

---

[13] Throughout the rest of this paper, depending on context, we shall let c stand for either a syntactic object consisting of a finite set of tokens, the constraint obtained by taking the closure of that set under $\vdash$, the (semantic) process that imposes that constraint on the store, or the (syntactic) agent that imposes that constraint on the store

Syntax.

$$P ::= D.A$$
$$D ::= \epsilon \mid p(X) :: A \mid D.D$$
$$A ::= c \mid c \rightarrow A \mid A \wedge A \mid \exists X A \mid p(X)$$

Semantic Equations.

$$\mathcal{A}(c)e = \{d \in |D|_0 \mid d \geq c\}$$
$$\mathcal{A}(c \rightarrow A)e = \{d \in |D|_0 \mid d \geq c \Rightarrow d \in \mathcal{A}(A)e\}$$
$$\mathcal{A}(A \wedge B)e = \{d \in |D|_0 \mid d \in \mathcal{A}(A)e \wedge d \in \mathcal{A}(B)e\}$$
$$\mathcal{A}(\exists X A)e = \{d \in |D|_0 \mid \exists c \in \mathcal{A}(A)e. \exists_X d = \exists_X c\}$$
$$\mathcal{A}(p(X))e = \exists_\alpha (d_{\alpha X} \sqcup e(p))$$
$$\mathcal{D}(\epsilon)e = e$$
$$\mathcal{D}(p(X) :: A.D) = \mathcal{D}(D)e[p \mapsto \exists_X (d_{\alpha X} \sqcup \mathcal{A}(A)e)]$$
$$\mathcal{P}(D.A) = \mathcal{A}(A)(\underline{\texttt{fix}}\ \mathcal{D}(D))$$

Above, c ranges over basic constraints, that is, finite sets of tokens. P is the syntactic class of programs, D is the syntactic class of sequences of procedure declarations, and A is the syntactic class of agents. α is some variable in the underlying constraint system which is not allowed to occur in user programs. (It is used as a dummy variable during parameter passing.) e maps procedure names to processes, providing an environment for interpreting procedure calls. We use the notation $c \sqcup f$ to stand for $\{c \sqcup d \mid d \in f\}$.

Table 1: Denotational semantics for the Ask-and-Tell Determinate cc languages

The ask operation is monotone and continuous in its process argument. It satisfies the laws:

$$(L1) \quad c \rightarrow d = c \rightarrow (c \wedge d)$$
$$(L2) \quad c \rightarrow \text{true} = \text{true}$$
$$(L3) \quad c \rightarrow d \rightarrow A = (c \sqcup d) \rightarrow A$$
$$(L4) \quad \text{true} \rightarrow A = A$$

The rule for $c \rightarrow A$ is:

$$c \rightarrow A \xrightarrow{(d,d)} A \quad \text{if} \quad d \geq c \tag{5}$$

Parallel composition. Consider the parallel composition of two processes f and g. Suppose on input c, f runs first, producing $f(c)$. Because it is idempotent, f will be unable to produce any further information. However, g may now run, producing some more information, and enabling additional information production from f. The system will quiesce exactly when *both* f and g quiesce. Therefore, the set of fixed points of $f \wedge g$ is exactly the intersection of the set of fixed points of f with the set of fixed points of g:

$$f \wedge g = f \cap g$$

It is straightforward to verify that this operation is well-defined, and monotone and continuous in both its arguments.

While the argument given above is quite simple and elegant,[14] it hides issues of substantial complexity. The basic property being exploited here is the *restartability* of a determinate process. Suppose an agent A is initiated in a

---

[14] And should be contrasted with most definitions of concurrency for other computational models which have to fall back on some sort of interleaving of basic actions.

store c, and produces a constraint d before quiescing, leaving a "residual agent" B to be executed. To find out its subsequent behavior (e.g., to find out what output it would produce on a store $e \geq d$), it is *not* necessary to maintain any explicit representation of B in the denotation of A. Rather, the effect of B on input $e \geq d$ can be obtained simply by running the *original* program A on e! Indeed this is the basic reason why it is possible to model a determinate process accurately by just the set of its resting points.

As we shall see in the next section, this restartability property is not true for nondeterminate processes. Indeed, we cannot take the denotation of a process to be a function (nor even a relation) from finite stores to finite stores; rather it becomes necessary to also preserve information about the *path* (that is, the sequence of ask/tell interactions with the environment) followed by the process in reaching a resting point.

From this definition, several laws follow immediately. Parallel composition is commutative, associative, and has an identity element.

$$(L5) \quad A \wedge B = B \wedge A$$
$$(L6) \quad A \wedge (B \wedge C) = (A \wedge B) \wedge C$$
$$(L7) \quad A \wedge \text{true} = A$$

Telling two constraints in parallel is equivalent to telling the conjunction. Prefixing distributes through parallel composition.

$$(L8) \quad c \wedge d = (c \sqcup d)$$
$$(L9) \quad c \rightarrow (A \wedge B) = (c \rightarrow A) \wedge (c \rightarrow B)$$
$$(L10) \quad (a \rightarrow b) \wedge (c \rightarrow d) = (a \rightarrow b)$$
$$\qquad \text{if } c \geq a, b \geq d$$
$$(L11) \quad (a \rightarrow b) \wedge (c \rightarrow d) = (a \rightarrow b) \wedge (c \sqcup b \rightarrow d)$$
$$\qquad \text{if } c \geq a$$
$$(L12) \quad (a \rightarrow b) \wedge (c \rightarrow d) = (a \rightarrow b) \wedge (c \rightarrow d \sqcup b)$$
$$\qquad \text{if } d \geq a$$

The transition rule for $A \wedge B$ reflects the fact that A and B never communicate synchronously in $A \wedge B$. Instead, all communication takes place asynchronously with information added by one agent stored in the shared constraint for the other agent to use.

$$\frac{A \xrightarrow{(c,d)} A'}{\begin{array}{l} A \wedge B \xrightarrow{(c,d)} A' \wedge B \\ B \wedge A \xrightarrow{(c,d)} B \wedge A' \end{array}} \tag{6}$$

Projection. Suppose given a process f. We wish to define the behavior of $\exists X f$, which, intuitively, must hide all interactions on X from its environment. Consider the behavior of $\exists X f$ on input c. c may constrain X; however this X is the "external" X which the process f must not see. Hence, to obtain the behavior of $\exists X f$ on c, we should observe the behavior of f on $\exists_X c$. However, $f(\exists_X c)$ may constrain X, and this X is the "internal" X. Therefore, the result seen by the environment must be $c \sqcup \exists_X f(\exists_X c)$. This leads us to define:

$$\exists X f = \{c \in |D|_0 \mid \exists d \in f. \exists_X c = \exists_X d\}$$

These hiding operators enjoy several interesting properties. For example, we can show that they are "dual" closure operators (i.e., kernel operators), and also cylindrification operators on the class of denotations of determinate programs.

In order to define the transition relation for $\exists X A$, we extend the transition relation to agents of the form $\exists X(d, A)$, where d is an internal store holding information about X which is hidden outside $\exists X(d, A)$. The transition axiom for $\exists X A$ yields an agent with an internal store:

$$\frac{A \xrightarrow{(\exists_X c, d)} B}{\exists X A \xrightarrow{(c, c \sqcup \exists_X d)} \exists X(d, B)} \tag{7}$$

This axiom reflects the fact that all information about X in c is hidden from $\exists X A$, and all information about X that A produces is hidden from the environment. Note that B may need the produced information about X to progress; this information is stored with B in the constraint d.

The axiom for agents with an internal store is straightforward. The information from the external store is combined with information in the internal store, and any new constraint generated in the transition is retained in the internal store:

$$\frac{A \xrightarrow{(d \sqcup \exists_X c, d')} B}{\exists X(d, A) \xrightarrow{(c, c \sqcup \exists_X d')} \exists X(d', B)} \tag{8}$$

In order to canonicalize agents with this operator, we need the following law:

$$(Ex1) \quad \exists X c = \exists_X c$$

In order to get a complete equational axiomatization for finite agents containing subagents of the form $\exists X B$, we need the constraint system to be expressive enough. Specifically, we require:

(C1) For all $c \in |D|_0$ and $X \in Var$, there exists $d \in |D|_0$ (written $\forall_X c$) such that for all $d' \in |D|_0$, $d' \geq d$ iff $\exists_X d' \geq c$.

(C2) For all $c, c' \in |D|_0$ and $X \in Var$, there exists a $d \in |D|_0$ (written $\Rightarrow_X (c, c')$) such that for all $d' \in |D|$, $c \cup \exists_X d' \geq c'$ iff $\exists_X c \cup \exists_X d' \geq d$.

Now we can state the remaining laws needed to obtain a complete axiomatization.

$$\begin{aligned}
(Ex2) \quad & \exists X(c \to A) = \forall_X(c) \to \exists X.A \\
(Ex3) \quad & \exists X \wedge_{i \in I} c_i \to d_i = \\
& \wedge_{i \in I} \exists X(c_i \to (d_i \wedge_{j \in I, j \neq i} c_j \to d_j)) \\
(Ex4) \quad & \exists X(c \wedge_{i \in I} c_i \to d_i) = \\
& \exists X c \wedge \exists X \wedge_{i \in I} \Rightarrow_X (c, c_i) \to d_i
\end{aligned}$$

Recursion. Recursion is handled in the usual way, by taking limits of the denotations of all syntactic approximants, since the underlying domain is a cpo and all the combinators are continuous in their process arguments.

Operationally, procedure calls are handled by looking up the procedure in the environment ρ. The corresponding axiom is:

$$\rho \vdash p(X) \xrightarrow{(d, d)} \exists \alpha(d_\alpha X, \rho(p)) \tag{9}$$

Example 3.1 (Append) To illustrate these combinators, consider the append procedure in the determinate cc language, using the Kahn constraint system:

```
append(In1, In2, Out) ::
    In1 = Λ → Out = In2
    ∧ c(In1) → ∃X (Out = a(f(In1), X) ∧ append(r(In1), In2, X)).
```

This procedure waits until the environment either equates X to Λ or puts at least one data item onto the communication channel X. It then executes the appropriate branch of the body. Note that because the ask conditions in the two branches are mutually exclusive, no call will ever execute the entire body of the procedure. This procedure therefore uses the $\wedge$ operator (which ostensibly represents parallel execution) as a determinate choice operator. This is a common idiom in determinate concurrent constraint programs. □

Completeness of axiomatization. Completeness of axiomatization is proven via the following "normal form".

Definition 3.2 An agent A is in normal form iff $A = \text{true}$ or $A = \wedge_{i \in I} c_i \to d_i$ and A satisfies the following properties:

$$\begin{aligned}
(P1) \quad & c_i < d_i \\
(P2) \quad & i \neq j \text{ implies } c_i \neq c_j \\
(P3) \quad & c_i < c_j \text{ implies } d_i < c_j \\
(P4) \quad & c_i \leq d_j \text{ implies } d_i \leq d_j
\end{aligned}$$

□

Lemma 3.1 *Any agent A containing no constructs of the form $\exists X B$ can be converted to normal form using equations $(L1) - (L12)$.*

Lemma 3.2 *For any agent $A = \wedge_{i \in I} c_i \to d_i$ in normal form, $\mathcal{P}(\epsilon.A)(c_i) = d_i$.*

We use this lemma when proving the following completeness theorem:

Theorem 3.3 *$\mathcal{P}(\epsilon.A) = \mathcal{P}(\epsilon.B)$ iff A and B have the same normal form.*

Thus the laws $(L1) \ldots (L12)$ are both sound and complete for finite agents built using tells, asks and parallel composition.

In addition, we also have:

Theorem 3.4 *Laws $(L1) - (L12)$ and $(Ex1)-(Ex4)$ are sound and complete for all finite agents.*

Operational semantics. In order to extract an environment from $D.A$ in which to run A, we define:

$$\begin{aligned}
\mathcal{R}(\epsilon)\rho &= \rho \\
\mathcal{R}(p(X) :: A.D)\rho &= \mathcal{R}(D)\rho[p \mapsto (\exists X d_\alpha X \wedge A)]
\end{aligned}$$

A computation in this transition system is a sequence of transitions in which the environment is constrained to produce nothing. Hence the final constraint of each transition should match the initial constraint of the succeding transition. The following definition formalizes the notion of a computation starting from a finite constraint c:

Definition 3.3 A c-transition sequence s for a program $D.A$ is a possibly infinite sequence $\langle c_i, A_i \rangle_i$ of pairs of agents and stores such that $c_0 = c$ and $A_0 = A$ and for all i, $\mathcal{R}(D)\rho_0 \vdash A_i \xrightarrow{(c_i, c_{i+1})} A_{i+1}$. Here ρ_0 is the partial map from procedure names to (syntactic) agents whose domain is empty. Such a transition sequence is said to be *terminal* if it is finite, of length $n \geq 1$ and A_{n-1} is *stuck* in c_{n-1} (that is, there is no constraint d and agent B such that $\mathcal{R}(D)\rho_0 \vdash A_{n-1} \xrightarrow{(c_{n-1}, d)} B$). In such a case, c_{n-1} is also called the *final* store. □

One can prove a number of operational results in a fairly straightforward way.

Lemma 3.5 (Operational monotonicity.) *If* $A_1 \xrightarrow{(c,d)} A_2$ *is a possible transition and* $c \leq c'$ *then* $A_1 \xrightarrow{(c', d \sqcup c')} A_2$.

This is essentially an operational *monotonicity* property.

Definition 3.4 Suppose that an agent A in a store c has two transitions enabled, i.e. it could do either one of $A \xrightarrow{(c, c_1)} A_1$ and $A \xrightarrow{(c, c_2)} A_2$. We say that these transitions commute if $A_1 \xrightarrow{(c_1, c_1 \sqcup c_2)} A_3$ and $A_2 \xrightarrow{(c_2, c_1 \sqcup c_2)} A_3$ are both possible. □

The following lemma is almost immediate and characterizes a key property of determinate agents.

Lemma 3.6 *If an agent has more than one transition possible in a given store they will commute.*

The following theorem can be proved by appealing to commutativity.

Theorem 3.7 (Confluence) *For any constraint c and determinate program $D.A$, if $D.A$ has a terminal c-transition sequence with final store d, then $D.A$ has no infinite c-transition sequence. Further, all terminal c-transition sequences have the same final store.*

This theorem allows us to define an observation function on programs mapping $|D|_0$ to $|D|_0$ by: $\mathcal{O}(P)(c) = d$ if P has a terminal c-transition sequence with final store d, and $\mathcal{O}(P)(c) = \mathtt{false}$ otherwise.

Theorem 3.8 *The function $\mathcal{O}(P)$ is a closure operator.*

The only nontrivial part of this proof is showing idempotence; it is done by induction on the length of reduction sequences and use of Lemma 3.5.

We can now connect the operational semantics with the denotational semantics.

Theorem 3.9 (Strong adequacy) $\mathcal{O}(P) = \mathcal{P}(P)$

Therefore, two programs P and Q are observationally equal ($\mathcal{O}(P) = \mathcal{O}(Q)$) iff their denotations are equal ($\mathcal{P}(P) = \mathcal{P}(Q)$). Thus the denotations of programs contain enough information to distinguish programs that are operationally different. **Proof sketch**: One can show that a single reduction step preserves the denotational semantics. Then we show that the sets of fixed points of the two closure operators are the same. In order to do this we use a structural induction and a fixed-point induction for the recursive case. The proofs are not trivial but they are not particularly novel either. The full paper will contain a more thorough discussion.

It remains to show that the denotations of two programs are identified if, from the viewpoint of the operational semantics, they behave identically in all *contexts*.

Definition 3.5 A context $\mathcal{C}[\bullet]$ is a program $D.A[\bullet]$ whose agent A contains a "placeholder" (denoted by $\bullet$). We put a program $D'.A'$ into this context by taking the union of the definitions (renaming procedures where necessary to avoid name clashes) and replacing the placeholder $\bullet$ in A with A', yielding $\mathcal{C}[D'.A'] = D \cup D'.A[A']$. □

Theorem 3.10 (Full abstraction) $\mathcal{P}(P) = \mathcal{P}(Q)$ *iff for all contexts* $\mathcal{C}[\bullet]$, $Obs(\mathcal{C}[P]) = Obs(\mathcal{C}[Q])$.

The theorem is easy to prove given that we have strong adequacy and a compositional definition of the denotational semantics.

3.2 Alternate semantic treatments

The first semantics is based on the notion that it is appropriate to confuse the process that takes some input c to $\mathtt{false}$ and halts, with the process that diverges on input c. However, several other coherent alternative notions for handling divergence can be modelled with minor variations on the above theme. In this section we show briefly how to generate a model which distinguishes between $\mathtt{false}$ and $\mathtt{div}$, and also how to generate a model which associates with each input the limit of fair execution sequences of the program on that input. In each case we sketch the major idea and leave a full development as an exercise for the reader.

Distinguishing div from false. Suppose for each input to a process we observe whether or not the process diverges, and if it does not, we observe the resultant store. Thus, the denotation f of an agent A will be a *partial* function from $|D|_0$ to $|D|_0$. What sort of function? Observe that if a determinate cc process engages in an infinite execution sequence in c, then it must also engage in an infinite execution sequence in a store $d \geq c$. Therefore the domain of f will be downward-closed. However, as before, on this domain f will be a closure operator. This motivates the definition:

Definition 3.6 A *partial closure operator* on a lattice E is a closure operator on a downward-closed subset of E. □

As before, the range of a partial closure operator contains enough information to recover the function. In particular, the domain of the function is just the downward closure of the range of the function. In fact, the set of fixed points of a partial closure operator can be characterized quite simply as follows: For any lattice E, a set $S \subseteq E$ is the set of fixed points of a partial closure operator on E iff S is closed under glbs of arbitrary *non-empty* subsets. Thus, the added generality arises merely from the fact that $\mathtt{false}$ is not required to be a fixed point of a partial closure operator!

Note that the (range of the) partial closure operator corresponding to $\mathtt{div}$, the program that diverges on every input, is just $\emptyset$, since the domain of the function is the empty set. On the other hand, the (range of the) partial closure operator corresponding to $\mathtt{false}$ is $\{\mathtt{false}\}$. Thus this semantics distinguishes between these two programs.

As before, partial closure operators can be partially ordered by the divergence ordering:

$$f \leq g \iff f \subseteq g \subseteq f \cup df$$

where df, the set of inputs on which f is undefined is just the complement in $|D|_0$ of the domain of f (i.e., $|D|_0 \setminus \downarrow f$).

Rather surprisingly, the definition of the combinators remains *unchanged*, even though the "meaning" (operational interpretation) of the denotation has changed:

$$c\star = \{d \in |D|_0 \mid d \geq c\}$$
$$c \rightarrow A = \{d \in |D|_0 \mid d \geq c \Rightarrow d \in A\}$$
$$A_1 \wedge A_2 = \{d \in |D|_0 \mid d \in A_1 \wedge d \in A_2\}$$
$$\exists X A = \{d \in |D|_0 \mid \exists c \in A. \exists_X c = \exists_X d\}$$

Each of these definitions yields a partial closure operator when its process arguments are partial closure operators. Each defines a function that is monotone and continuous in its process arguments.

Connections with the operational semantics can be established in a manner analogous to the connections established above.

A semantics based on observing limits. The above semantics treats a divergent computation as catastrophic—it is treated as the computation that causes the store to become inconsistent. As discussed earlier, it is possible to develop a different semantics, one in which limits of fair execution sequences are observed. For example, such a semantics would associate the cc/Kahn process:

ones(X) :: ∃Y X = a(1.A, Y) ∧ ones(Y).

with the closure operator that maps true to the (limit) constraint that forces X to be the infinite sequence of 1s, whereas the previous semantics would associate this program with the partial closure operator that diverges in true.

First we need to define the notion of fair execution sequence. At any stage of the computation there may be several enabled transitions, each of which reduces one of the agent's subagents. Note that if a subagent can be reduced at a given stage of the computation, it can be reduced at every successive stage of the computation until a transition is taken that actually carries out the reduction. We say that a c-transition sequence s is *fair* if it eventually reduces every subagent that can be reduced at some stage of s. This is a common notion that one needs in defining the operational semantics of concurrent systems.

In such a semantics, the denotation of a process associates with each input the limit of the sequence of store on any fair execution sequence of the process. Hence, the denotation is taken to be an operator over $|D|$ (instead of over $|D|_0$). As above, the denotation must be a closure operator—but in addition, it seems reasonable to demand that no process can decide to produce some output after it has examined an infinite amount of input. That is, we demand that f be *continuous*: for every directed $S \subseteq D$:

$$f(\sqcup S) = \sqcup f(S) \tag{10}$$

In terms of fixed points, it is not hard to see that if S is the set of fixed points of a closure operator f, then f is continuous iff S is closed under lubs of directed subsets.

The partial order on processes is now the extensional one: $f \sqsubseteq g$ iff $f \supseteq g$. The bottom element in the partial order is Id (that is, $|D|$) (thus limits of chains are given by interesection) and the top element is $\{\texttt{false}\}$, the operator which maps every element to $\texttt{false}$.

Even more surprisingly, the definition of combinators remains unchanged from the previous section, modulo the fact

that fixed points must now be taken from $|D|$ instead of just $|D|_0$:

$$c\star = \{d \in |D| \mid d \geq c\}$$
$$c \rightarrow A = \{d \in |D| \mid d \geq c \Rightarrow d \in A\}$$
$$A_1 \wedge A_2 = \{d \in |D| \mid d \in A_1 \wedge d \in A_2\}$$
$$\exists X A = \{d \in |D| \mid \exists c \in A. \exists_X c = \exists_X d\}$$

Each of these combinators is seen to be well-defined (they yield continuous closure operators when their process arguments are continuous closure operators), and monotone and continuous in their process arguments.

The following result follows from the commutativity properties of transitions.

Theorem 3.11 *If s_1 and s_2 are both fair c-transition sequences for A, then $\sqcup Cons(s_1) = \sqcup Cons(s_2)$, where $Cons(s)$ yields the set of constraints from s.*

This theorem allows us to define an observation function on programs mapping $|D|_0$ to $|D|$ by:

$$Obs(P)(c) = \sqcup Cons(s)$$

for s any fair c-transition sequence for P.

Relationship with the denotational semantics. This discussion is quite brief as it is quite similar to the previous discussion. The new issues one must to deal with are that transition sequences have to be fair and the semantic domain has an entirely different order. Also, the operational semantic function is defined on the entire domain generated by the constraint system rather than just the finite elements.

The relevant theorems are as follows.

Theorem 3.12 $\mathcal{O}(P)$, *the continuous extension of $Obs(P)$ is a closure operator on $|D|$.*

Theorem 3.13 $\mathcal{O}(P) = \mathcal{P}(P)$.

Theorem 3.14 (Full abstraction) $\mathcal{P}(P) = \mathcal{P}(Q)$ *iff for all contexts $C[\bullet]$, $Obs(C[P]) = Obs(C[Q])$.*

4 The nondeterminate language

Let us now consider the determinate cc language in the previous section, together with (bounded) nondeterminate choice. Syntactically, admit as an agent expressions of the form

$$c_1 \rightarrow A_1 \square c_2 \rightarrow A_2 \square \ldots \square c_n \rightarrow A_n$$

for finite constraints c_i and agents A_i, $n \geq 1$. Intuitively, in any store d, such an agent can in one uninterruptible step reduce to A_i, without affecting the store provided that the ith branch is "open", that is, $d \geq c_i$. If no branch is open, the agent remains stuck, and if more than one branch is open, then any one can be chosen. Thus the axiom for dependent choice satisfied by the $\longrightarrow$ relation is:

$$\square_{j \in J}(c_j \rightarrow A_j) \xrightarrow{(d,d)} A_j \quad \text{if } d \geq c_j, \text{ for some } j \in J \tag{11}$$

With this construct admitted into the language, the denotation of an agent can no longer be a function from $|D|_0$ to $|D|_0$. Neither can it be just a relation in $|D|_0 \times |D|_0$, since parallel composition will not be definable. Instead we model a process as a set of *failures*, which record the interactions that a process engages in with the environment before reaching a state ("resting point") in which it cannot progress without intervention by the environment. This simple idea turns out to be adequate to give us a denotational semantics which is fully abstract with respect to a notion of observation that includes observation of divergence and the final (quiescent) stores of an execution sequence.

The rest of this section is devoted to giving an exposition of this model. Because of the nature of constraint-based communication, it turns out to be very convenient to model failures as certain kinds of closure operators, namely, bounded trace operators. In the next subsection we treat some of the basic ideas underlying bounded trace operators, before turning to a presentation of the model.

4.1 The basic model

Trace operators. In general (provided that that the underlying constraint system is expressive enough, see Section 3), a finite closure operator can be represented as the parallel composition of a finite set of finite sequences of asks and tells, where a sequence $a_1!b_1 \star \ldots a_n!b_n \star$ (called a *trace*) is thought of as representing the closure operator $a_1 \rightarrow (b_1 \wedge (a_2 \rightarrow b_2 \ldots (a_n \rightarrow b_n) \ldots))$.[15]

A *trace operator* over a finitary lattice E is, intuitively, a closure operator that can be represented by a *single* (possibly infinite) ask/tell sequence. The characterizing property of a trace operator f is that if $S \subseteq E$ is a set of elements none of which are fixed points of f, then neither is $\sqcap S$ (provided that it exists):

Definition 4.1 A trace operator over a finitary lattice E is a closure operator f over E such that for any $S \subseteq E$, if S is disjoint from f, then $\sqcap S \not\subseteq f$ (whenever $\sqcap S$ is defined). Let $\mathcal{T}(E)$ be the set of all trace operators over E. □

Intuitively this definition can be justified as follows. Let d be an arbitrary element in S, and suppose that t is a trace. Then, if d is not a fixed point of t, it should be possible for t to execute some prefix of its actions, including at least one tell action involving a constraint stronger than d, before quiescing. Similarly for any other $e \in S$. Let s be the smallest prefix executed by t in e or d. $d \sqcap e$ will be $\geq$ all the asks in s, so t will be able to execute all of s, including a tell involving a constraint stronger than $d \sqcap e$.

The characteristic condition of a trace operator can be stated much more elegantly as follows. For f a closure operator over a lattice E, define f^{-1}, the *inverse* of f to be the set of elements $(E \setminus f) \cup \{\top_E\}$.

Lemma 4.1 A closure operator $f : E \rightarrow E$ is a trace operator iff f^{-1} is a closure operator. If f is a trace operator, then so is f^{-1}.

f^{-1} is said to be the inverse of f because it is the weakest g satisfying $f \wedge g = f \sqcap g = \{\top_E\}$. Intuitively, f^{-1} is exactly the sequence of asks and tells that "unzips" f: it asks exactly what f tells and tells exactly what f asks. Consequently, on any input to $f \wedge f^{-1}$, both the sequences can be traversed completely, yielding the final answer $\top_E$. Thus trace operators can be thought of as *invertible* closure operators.

Conversely, it is possible to show that each trace operator can be represented canonically as a sequence of ask/tell actions:

Lemma 4.2 *Every trace operator $f : E \rightarrow E$ can be represented by an alternating, strictly increasing sequence of ask/tell actions.*

The basic idea behind the construction of the canonical sequence is quite simple. Let f be a trace operator and $g = f^{-1}$. Then the canonical trace corresponding to f is just:

$$f(\text{true}) \star g(f(\text{true}))!f(g(f(\text{true}))) \star \ldots$$

The following lemma is not difficult to show:

Lemma 4.3 *Let $\mathcal{D} = \langle D, \vdash, \text{Var}, \{\exists_X | X \in \text{Var}\} \rangle$ be a cylindric constraint system. For every $c \in |D|_0$, $Y \in \text{Var}$ and $f \in \mathcal{T}(|D|_0)$, $c, c \rightarrow f, c \wedge f, \exists_Y f \in \mathcal{T}(|D|_0)$, where c is the closure operator $\{d \in |D|_0 \mid d \geq c\}$.*

Thus trace operators are closed under almost all the operations of interest to us—except, naturally enough, arbitrary parallel composition.

Bounded trace operators. The failures of a process record a "resting point" of the process, together with information about how to get there. So it would seem as if a failure should be represented as a pair (f, c) where $c \in f$ is the resting point, and f is a trace operator describing the set of ask/tell interactions needed to reach c. Note however, that the only information of interest in f is its behavior on $\downarrow c$. But if $c \in f$, then $f \cap \downarrow c$ is also a trace operator—but on the sub-lattice $\downarrow c$.

Therefore, a *bounded* trace operator (or bto, for short) on a finitary lattice E is defined to be a trace operator on $\downarrow c$, for some $c \in E$. This makes bounded trace operators a special kind of partial trace operators—specifically, those whose range contains a maximal element. (Partial trace operators are just the partial closure operators of Section 3 that are in addition traces.) Let $b\mathcal{T}(E) = \cup_{c \in E} \mathcal{T}(\downarrow c)$ denote the set of all such operators.

Just like any other (partial) trace operator, a bto f is also representable by its range, and its domain of definition is just $\downarrow \tilde{f}$, where $\tilde{f}$ (read "max f") is the greatest fixed point of f. Various operations defined on closure operators are applicable to btos, with obvious adjustments. Thus, for any constraint c, we shall take the bto corresponding to the imposition of c to be just the bto (whose set of fixed points are) $\{c\}$. Similarly, for a constraint c and trace operator f, with $\tilde{f} \geq c$, the bto $c \rightarrow f$ is just the bto $\{d \leq \tilde{f} \mid d \geq c \Rightarrow d \in f\}$.

However, some additional operations are also of interest over btos. We next discuss operations that reflect the operational notion of extending a sequence of ask/tell interactions with more ask/tell actions.

Let f be a (finite) bto, with canonical sequence of ask/tell actions s, and let $c \geq \tilde{f}$ be any constraint. Define $f.c\star$ (read: "f output extended by c") to be the bto corresponding to the sequence of actions $s.c\star$. It is not hard to find a direct representation of $f.c\star$ in terms of f and c: [16]

$$f.c\star = \{d \leq c \mid d \sqcap \tilde{f} \in f, d \not\geq \tilde{f}\} \cup \{c\}$$

In the following, we shall assume that the expression $f.c\star$ is well-defined even if $c \not\geq \tilde{f}$, and take it to stand for f in such cases. Note that $f.c \star .d\star = f.d\star$, if $c \leq d$.

---

[15] Recall that for $c \in E$ and f a closure operator on e, $c \rightarrow f$ is the closure operator on E with fixed points $\{d \in E \mid d \geq c \Rightarrow d \in f\}$.

[16] The expression $d \sqcap \tilde{f} \in f$ should be taken to stand for "$d \sqcap \tilde{f}$ is contained in f, provided that it exists".

Similarly, we can define the notion of input extending a bto f with a constraint c by:

$$f.c! = \begin{cases} \{d \leq c \mid d \sqcap \tilde{f} \in f\} & \text{if } \tilde{f} \leq c \\ f & \text{o.w.} \end{cases}$$

As above, note that $f.c!.d! = f.d!$, if $c \leq d$.

Given the definitions of input- and output-extensions, it is not hard to see that for any sequence of ask/tell actions $s = e_1 e_2 \ldots e_n$, the corresponding closure operator is just $(\ldots((\{true\}.e_1).e_2)\ldots).e_n$ (where we have abused notation by writing $f.e$ for the expression $f.c!$ in case $e \equiv c!$ and for the expression $f.c\star$ in case $e \equiv c\star$).

Let us write $f \sqsubseteq g$ for the case in which f can be thought of as a "prefix" of g, that is, g can be thought of as extending the sequence of interactions with the environment engaged in by f. How can this partial order be expressed directly in terms of (the set of fixed-points of) f and g? Clearly, none of the additional interactions in g can cause g to take on a different value from f at all points in f's domain ($\downarrow \tilde{f}$), except possibly at $\tilde{f}$.[17] Therefore, we can define:

$$f \sqsubseteq g \iff \tilde{f} \leq \tilde{g} \text{ and } f = (g \cap \downarrow \tilde{f}) \cup \{\tilde{f}\}$$

As can be verified from the definition, $\sqsubseteq$ is a partial order.

Finally, one more partial order will be of interest in what follows. We say that f asks more than g (and write $f \leq g$) if the resting point of both f and g are identical, but f records more contributions from the environment than g. This happens just in case $\tilde{g} = \tilde{f}$ and $\forall x \in \downarrow \tilde{g}.f(x) \leq g(x)$, that is, just in case $\tilde{g} = \tilde{f}$ and $f \supseteq g$.

4.2 The model

Let the set of all observations, $Obs(|D|_0)$, be the set of finite, bounded trace operators on $|D|_0$. A process will be a subset of Obs satisfying certain conditions which we now motivate, following [Jos90] closely.

At any stage of the computation, a process will have engaged in some ask/tell interactions with the store. Subsequently, it may produce some output and then quiesce (perhaps to be activated on more input at a subsequent stage) or it may engage in an infinite sequence of actions, without requiring any input from the environment to progress (perhaps producing more and more output as it progresses). We will model a process as divergent if it can quiesce in infinitely many ways (or output forever) or if it causes the store to become inconsistent.[18] (Thus we are requiring that processes be finitely nondetermininate.) If F is the set of failures of such a process, its divergences can then be defined as:

$$dF = \{f \mid \{c \mid f.c\star \in F\} \text{ is infinite}\} \cup \{f \mid f.false\star \in F\}$$

Each of these situations is considered undesirable, and we are not concerned about detailed modelling of the process

---

[17] For an example of a closure operator g which extends f but takes on a different value at $\tilde{f}$ than f, consider the closure operators obtained from the sequences $a!b\star$ and $a!b \star c\star$, for $a \leq b < c$.

[18] As discussed in the introduction, it is quite reasonable in this set-up to regard the process that produces the inconsistent store as divergent. It is possible to give a minor variation of the current treatment which distinguishes the process that diverges from the process that tells false, but this is outside the scope of this paper.

once it has become divergent. Thus such a process is treated as "chaotic", as being able to exhibit any behavior whatsoever. Further, we require that the set of possible behaviors of a process contain *all* its possible behaviors, especially its diverging ones. Thus the first condition we impose on a process F is:

$$edF \subseteq F \tag{12}$$

where for any $S \subseteq Obs$, eS is the set $\{s \sqsupseteq t \mid t \in S\}$ of extensions of S.

Note that $f.c\star \in dF$ implies $f \in dF$. Thus the last action in a sequence of ask/tell interactions constituting a minimal divergence must be an ask action. In other words, a divergence characterizes those inputs from the environment that are *undesirable*, that can cause the process to break.

From the definition, it should be clear that d distributes through finite unions and arbitrary intersections of arbitrary sets of observations. Also, the divergences of a process can be characterized rather nicely:

Lemma 4.4

$$f \in dF \iff \forall g \sqsupseteq f.g \in F \iff f.false\star \in F$$

The next few conditions are best motivated by considering the *traces* of a process. A trace of a process is just a sequence of ask/tell interactions that the process many engage in (without necessarily reaching a quiescent state). But the traces of a process can be recovered in a simple way from its failures: they are just the observations which can be output-extended to obtain a failure:

$$tF = \{f \mid \exists c.f.c\star \in F\}$$

Clearly, $F \subseteq tF$ and t distributes through arbitrary unions of sets of observations.

We require that if a process exhibits a trace, then it should be possible for it to exhibit a prefix of the trace as well—this is inherent in the very idea of a trace:

$$g \sqsubseteq f \in tF \Rightarrow g \in tF \tag{13}$$

We also require that every process should have *some* behaviors, hence a non-empty set of failures. Given Condition 13, this is equivalent to stating that the "empty" bto $true! = true\star = \{true\}$ be a trace of every process:

$$\{true\} \in F \tag{14}$$

Since cc processes are asynchronous, the environment can never be prevented from adding constraints to the store. Therefore, it should be possible to extend every sequence of interactions that a process may have with its environment with an input action: (the *receptiveness* condition):

$$f \in tF \Rightarrow f.c! \in tF \tag{15}$$

It is not hard to show that for any chain of processes $F_1 \supseteq F_2 \ldots$, $t \cap_{i \geq 1} F_i = \cap_{i \geq 1} tF_i$.

We require one final condition on processes. If a process can engage in a sequence of actions recorded by a bto f before quiescing, then it can engage in the same sequence of actions even if at some or all stages the environment were to supply more input than the minimum required by the process to engage in f. Thus we require that the failures of a process be closed under the "ask more" relationship:

$$g \leq f \in F \Rightarrow g \in F \tag{16}$$

296

In essence, this condition represents the monotonic nature of the basic ask and tell actions.

Now we are ready to define:

Definition 4.2 A (nondeterminate) process is a subset of $Obs(|D|_0)$ satisfying Conditions 12–16. Let NProc be the set of all such subsets. □

The following lemma establishes that the convergences of a process already contain enough information to generate its divergences. (The converse is not true.) For F a process, define iF, the input extensions of F to be the set $\{f.c! \mid f \in F\}$, and cF, the *convergences* of F to be the set $F \setminus dF$.

Lemma 4.5 $dF = e((icF \cup \{\{\text{true}\}\}) \setminus tcF)$

Essentially, any input extension of a convergent trace of a process must have an output extension that is a failure of the process (Condition 15); if this output extension is not a convergence, it must be a divergence and so must its extensions. Conversely, a divergence of a process must have a prefix which input-extends a convergence and is not itself a convergent trace; otherwise the process is chaotic, and every bto is a divergence.

Partial order on processes. Usually, processes in specification-oriented semantics are ordered by the so-called *nondeterminism* ordering:

$$F \sqsubseteq G \stackrel{d}{=} F \supseteq G$$

which corresponds to the intuition that a process is "better" than another if it is more deterministic. The completely undefined process is the chaotic process, which can exhibit all possible behaviors: as more and more information about a process is generated, more and more behaviors get ruled out.

However, in many senses, this ordering is more liberal than desired, as discussed by Roscoe in [Ros88]. For example, one way in which a process G can improve a process F is by dropping some *convergent* behavior of F. This sort of capability is not manifested by any cc combinator (or, indeed, any CSP combinator), and we find it more convenient to adopt instead the *divergence* ordering proposed by Roscoe. In this ordering G is "better" than F iff it diverges at fewer places than F, and the convergent behaviors of F are preserved in G. More precisely, the partial order is:

$$F \leq G \iff cF \subseteq cG \subseteq F$$

It is easy to see from the definition that $F \leq G$ implies $F \sqsubseteq G$. Furthermore, the least element in the partial order is Obs, and limits of increasing chains are given by intersection. In fact, if $F_1 \leq F_2 \leq \ldots$ is an increasing chain with lub $F = \cap_{i \geq 1} F_i$, we have $cF = \cup_{i \geq 1} cF_i$ and $dF = \cap_{i \geq 1} dF_i$.

Theorem 4.6 $\langle \text{NProc}, \leq \rangle$ *is a complete partial order.*

Syntax.

$$P ::= D.A$$
$$D ::= \epsilon \mid p(X) :: A \mid D.D$$
$$A ::= c \mid A \wedge A \mid \exists X A \mid p(X) \mid c_1 \rightarrow A_1 \square \ldots \square c_j \rightarrow A_j$$

Auxiliary Definitions.

$$dF = \{f \mid \{c \mid f.c\star \in F\} \text{ is infinite}\}$$
$$\cup \{f \mid f.\mathbf{false}\star \in F\}$$
$$tF = \{f \mid \exists c.f.c\star \in F\}$$
$$F\|G = \{f \cap g \in Obs \mid \bar{f} = \bar{g}, f \in F, g \in G\}$$
$$X^{\hat{}}F =$$
$$\{g \in Obs \mid g \leq \downarrow d \cap (\exists X(f.\mathbf{false}!)), \exists_X d = \exists_X \bar{f}, f \in F\}$$
$$\exists_X(d_{XY} \sqcup F) = \{\{\exists_X(d_{XY} \sqcup c) \mid c \in f\} \mid f \in F\}$$

Semantic Equations.

$$\mathcal{A}(c)e = \{f \mid \bar{f} \cap \uparrow c \subseteq f, c \leq \bar{f}\}$$
$$\cup \{g \sqsupseteq f \mid \bar{f} \cap \uparrow c \subseteq f, c \sqcup \bar{f} = \mathbf{false}\}$$
$$\mathcal{A}(\square_{j \in J}(c_j \rightarrow A_j))e =$$
$$\{f \in \mathcal{A}(A_j)e \mid f = c_j \rightarrow f, \bar{f} \geq c_j, j \in J\}$$
$$\cup \{\downarrow d \mid \forall j \in J.d \not\geq c_j\}$$
$$\mathcal{A}(A \wedge B)e = \mathcal{A}(A)e\|\mathcal{A}(B)e \cup ed(t\mathcal{A}(A)e\|t\mathcal{A}(B)e)$$
$$\mathcal{A}(\exists X A)e = (X^{\hat{}}\mathcal{A}(A)e) \cup \{g \leq f \mid f \in ed(X^{\hat{}}\mathcal{A}(A)e)\}$$
$$\mathcal{A}(p(X))e = \exists_\alpha(d_{\alpha X} \sqcup e(p))$$
$$\mathcal{E}(\epsilon)e = e$$
$$\mathcal{E}(p(X) :: A.D) = \mathcal{E}(D)e[p \mapsto \exists_X(d_{\alpha X} \sqcup \mathcal{A}(A)e)]$$
$$\mathcal{P}(D.A) = \mathcal{A}(A)(\underline{\mathbf{fix}}\ \mathcal{E}(D))$$

Above, c ranges over basic constraints, that is, finite sets of tokens. P is the syntactic class of programs, D is the syntactic class of sequences of procedure declarations, and A is the syntactic class of agents. α is some variable in the underlying constraint system which is not allowed to occur in user programs. (It is used as a dummy variable during parameter passing.) e maps procedure names to processes, providing an environment for interpreting procedure calls. We use the notation $c \sqcup f$ to stand for $\{c \sqcup d \mid d \in f\}$.

Table 2: Denotational semantics for the Ask-and-Tell non-determinate cc languages

4.3 Process algebra

In this section, we define various processes in and combinators on NProc, including div, the process that immediately diverges, the tell (of finite constraints), parallel composition, nondeterminate choice and hiding combinators. The syntax of the programming language is given in Table 2, where the semantic definitions, to be discussed below, are also summarized. As before, we also simultaneously define the operational semantics of the language and assume that procedures take exactly one variable as a parameter and that no program calls an undefined procedure.

Chaos. The chaotic process can do anything whatsoever.

$$\text{div} = Obs$$

Clearly, $d(\text{div}) = t(\text{div}) = Obs$. Operationally, such an agent is always willing to progress in any store. This progress affects neither the store nor the agent's subsequent behavior:

$$\text{div} \xrightarrow{(d,d)} \text{div} \qquad (17)$$

Tells. Consider a process which immediately terminates, after augmenting the store with some constraint $c \in E$. Let us call such a process c. The resting points of such a process are clearly all stores $e \geq c$. To reach this resting point, the process can at most add c to the store. It is not hard to see that a bto f satisfies the condition that for all inputs x in its domain, $f(x) \leq x \sqcup c$ iff $\tilde{f} \sqcap \uparrow c \subseteq f$. When does such a process diverge? It must diverge iff it can engage in some sequence of interactions with the store (in which its output is bounded by c), after which it reaches a state in which if it were to output c, it would reach false:

$$c = \{f \mid \tilde{f} \sqcap \uparrow c \subseteq f, \tilde{f} \geq c\}$$
$$\cup e\{f \mid \tilde{f} \sqcap \uparrow c \subseteq f, \tilde{f} \sqcup c = \text{false}\}$$

It is easy to work through the definitions and establish that

$$d(c) = e\{f \mid \tilde{f} \sqcap \uparrow c \subseteq f, \tilde{f} \sqcup c = \text{false}\}$$
$$t(c) = \{f \mid \tilde{f} \sqcap \uparrow c \subseteq f\} \cup d(c)$$

and that c (as defined above) is a process.

The relevant axiom for the transition relation for these agents is the same as in the determinate case (Axiom 4).

Dependent choice. Consider the process $F \equiv \square_{j \in J}(c_j \to F_j)$. It has two kinds of resting points: first, the resting points d that arise because for no $j \in J$ is $d \geq c_j$, and secondly, the resting points of each F_j which are stronger than the corresponding c_j. Furthermore, the btos generating the first kind of resting point are simple: they are of the form $d! = \downarrow d$, since no output is produced by the process before it quiesces in d. On the other hand, the path followed by F in reaching a resting point of F_j stronger than c_j is the path that F_j would have followed given that the environment is willing to supply at least c_j, that is paths $f \in F_j$ such that $f = c_j \to f$. This leads us to the definition:

$$\square_{j \in J}(c_j \to F_j) = \{f \in F_j \mid f = c_j \to f, c_j \leq \tilde{f}, j \in J\}$$
$$\cup \{\downarrow d \mid \forall j \in J. d \not\geq c_j\}$$

As can be calculated, the divergences and traces of F are:

$$d(\square_{j \in J}(c_j \to F_j)) =$$
$$\{f \in dF_j \mid f = c_j \to f, c_j \leq \tilde{f}, j \in J\}$$
$$t(\square_{j \in J}(c_j \to F_j)) =$$
$$\{f \in tF_j \mid f = c_j \to f, c_j \leq \tilde{f}, j \in J\}$$
$$\cup \{\downarrow d \mid \forall j \in J. d \not\geq c_j\}$$

The combinator is monotone and continuous in each of its process arguments.

Two special cases of this operator are worth singling out. In case the index-set is singleton, dependent choice is not a form of choice at all and reduces to just the ask-combinator. That is, $c \to A$ is just dependent choice in which only one conditional is given. In terms of denotations, we get:

$$c \to F = \{f \in F \mid f = c \to f, c \leq \tilde{f}\} \cup \{\downarrow d \mid d \not\geq c\}$$

Note that for such agents, the transition Axiom 11 reduces to just Axiom 5 (Section 3).

Similarly, blind unconditional choice can also be expressed. Consider the binary combinator $\sqcap$ defined such that $F \sqcap G$ can behave either like F or like G. The decision can be made arbitrarily, even at compile-time. Thus the failures of $F \sqcap G$ should be precisely the failures of F or the failures of G. As can easily be checked, $F \cup G = \text{true} \to F \square \text{true} \to G$ as well. Therefore, $F \sqcap G$ can be defined as $\text{true} \to F \square \text{true} \to G$. Clearly, blind choice is idempotent, associative and commutative and has div as a zero element. Operationally, an agent built from blind choice satisfies the axioms:

$$A \sqcap B \xrightarrow{(d,d)} A$$
$$A \sqcap B \xrightarrow{(d,d)} B \qquad (18)$$

Parallel composition. What are the resting points of $F \wedge G$? Clearly, if c is a resting point of F and of G, then it is a resting point of $F \wedge G$. The path followed to this resting point by $F \wedge G$ can be any parallel composition of the paths followed by F and by G. Therefore, each failure in the set $F \| G$ is going to be a failure of $F \wedge G$, where

$$F \| G = \{f \cap g \in Obs \mid \tilde{f} = \tilde{g}, f \in F, g \in G\}$$

But what are the divergences of $F \wedge G$? The divergences of $F \wedge G$ arise not only from the divergences of F and of G, but also from the possibility that the two agents may engage in an infinite sequence of interactions with each answering the others asks, without demanding input from the environment at any stage. There will be no bto in $F \| G$ corresponding to such "mutual feed-back" because there is no common resting-point on this execution branch.

Capturing these possibilities for a cc language built over an arbitrary constraint system seems rather subtle. A simple formulation is possible, however, for finitary constraint systems, that is, constraint systems in which a finite element dominates only finitely many finite elements. In this case we can show:

Lemma 4.7 *If $\mathcal{D}$ is a finitary constraint system, then for every $F \in \text{NProc}(\mathcal{D})$, $dF = dtF$.*

This suggests that to determine the divergences of $F \wedge G$, it is sufficient to determine the divergences of the traces of $F \wedge G$. But this is easy: a trace of $F \wedge G$ is just a trace of F running in parallel with a trace of G, and hence the divergent traces are just $ed(tF\|tG)$. We thus get:

$$F \wedge G = F\|G \cup ed(t(F)\|t(G))$$

From these we can caculate:

$$d(F \wedge G) = ed(tF\|tG)$$
$$t(F \wedge G) = (tF\|tG) \cup ed(tF\|tG)$$

Proving continuity of this operator requires some care. The basic issue is to show that $ed(tF\|tG)$ is continuous in its arguments.

The operational transition rule for agents built with $\wedge$ is the same as in the deterministic case (Axiom 6).

Projection. d is a resting point of $\exists X F$ iff when F is initiated in $(\exists_X d)$, it reaches a resting point e such that the only new information in e (over d) is on X; that is, such that $(\exists_X e) = (\exists_X d)$. Therefore d is a resting point of $\exists X F$ iff there is an $f \in F$ such that $\exists_X \tilde{f} = \exists_X d$. The route taken by $(\exists X F)$ to reach d from true must be the route prescribed by $\exists X g$, where g is obtained from f by extending it to be a closure operator over $|D|_0$, restricted to $\downarrow d$. Thus define:

$$X\hat{\ }F =$$
$$\{g \in Obs \mid g \leq \downarrow d \cap (\exists X(f.\text{false}!)), \exists_X d = \exists_X \tilde{f}, f \in F\}$$

Now the failures of $\exists X F$ are:

$$\exists X F = X\hat{\ }F \cup \{g \leq f \mid f \in ed(X\hat{\ }F)\}$$

The divergences and traces for this process can be shown to be:

$$d(\exists X F) = \{g \leq f \mid f \in ed(X\hat{\ }F)\}$$
$$t(\exists X F) = X\hat{\ }tF \cup \{g \sqsubseteq f \mid f \in d(X\hat{\ }F)\}$$

This operator is monotone and continuous in its argument. The transition relation for $\exists X A$ is the same as in the determinate case; the transition relation must therefore be extended to agents with an internal store.

Recursion. Recursion is handled in the usual way, by taking limits of the denotations of all syntactic approximants, since the underlying domain of processes is a cpo and all the combinators are continuous in their process arguments. The diagonal elements are used to effect parameter passing (see Table 2). Operationally, procedure calls are handled as in the determinate case.

4.4 Operational Semantics

The operational semantics associates with every program and every initial store the set of all possible outputs obtainable from the store, with the caveat that if the process diverges or produces false, then every output is deemed observable. Here we use the notation P has a (c, d)-sequence to mean P has a terminal c-transition sequence with final store d.

Definition 4.3 For any program P define

$$\mathcal{O}(P) = \begin{cases} & Obs \text{ if } P \text{ has an infinite true-sequence} \\ & Obs \text{ if } P \text{ has a } (\text{true}, false)\text{-sequence} \\ & \{d \mid P \text{ has a } (\text{true}, d)\text{-sequence }\} otherwise \end{cases}$$

$\square$

Relationship with the denotational semantics. We make the connection between the operational semantics and the denotational semantics via the following theorems. The proofs are omitted in this version.

Theorem 4.8 (Adequacy) $\mathcal{O}(P) = \{d \mid \{d\} \in \mathcal{P}(P)\}$

That is, the results obtained by executing a program are identical to the resting points of the program obtained from the store **true**. Note that this is a weaker correspondence than in the determinate case, when the operational semantics was identical to the denotational semantics. The following full abstraction proof uses the notion of context previously defined for determinate programs.

Theorem 4.9 (Full abstraction) $\mathcal{P}(P) = \mathcal{P}(Q)$ iff for all contexts $\mathcal{C}[\bullet]$, $\mathcal{O}(\mathcal{C}[P]) = \mathcal{O}(\mathcal{C}[Q])$.

If the denotations of two programs P and Q are different, then there will be a $\leq$-maximal bto f in one and not in the other. It can be shown that the sequence s corresponding to such an f can be expressed in the language, which implies that the sequence s^{-1} corresponding to f^{-1} can also be expressed in the language. But then the finite bto $s^{-1} \wedge \bullet$ is a context which distinguishes the two programs. Let $F = \mathcal{P}(P)$, $G = \mathcal{P}(Q)$. Assume without loss of generality that $f \in F$ and $f \notin G$. There are two cases: $f \in dF$ and $f \in cF$. If $f \in dF$ then $s^{-1} \wedge F$ will diverge, and $\mathcal{O}(s^{-1} \wedge F) = |D|_0$. $f \notin G$ implies $s^{-1} \wedge G$ will not diverge, and therefore $\text{false} \notin \mathcal{O}(s^{-1} \wedge G)$. If $f \in cF$, then $\tilde{f} \in \mathcal{O}(s^{-1} \wedge F)$. If $\tilde{f} \in \mathcal{O}(s^{-1} \wedge G)$ then f must be a convergence of G, which violates the assumption.

4.5 Relationship between the nondeterminate and determinate semantics

We have only one set of transition rules for the determinate combinators, and the same notion of observation for the determinate and nondeterminate semantics. Therefore, the operational semantics for the determinate language and the determinate subset of the nondeterminate language are the same. Because both the determinate ($\mathcal{A}_D$) and nondeterminate ($\mathcal{A}_N$) denotational semantics are fully abstract with respect to the corresponding operational semantics, there should be some relationship between $\mathcal{A}_N(P)$ and $\mathcal{A}_D(P)$. Consider the two determinate agent-equivalence classes C_D and C_N induced by $\mathcal{A}_D$ and $\mathcal{A}_N$, respectively. Because the nondeterminate language has more contexts with which to tell apart agents than the determinate language, C_D should be a coarsening of C_N, and we should therefore be able to recover a determinate program's determinate denotation from its nondeterminate denotation.

Definition 4.4 An element $F \in \text{NProc}$ is *determinate* iff

1. $f \in cF$, $F \in \text{NProc}$ and $c > \tilde{f}$ implies $f.c\star \notin tF$

2. $f \in cF$, $g \in tF$ and $\tilde{g} = \tilde{f}$ implies $g \in cF$.

Let DNProc be the subset of determinate processes of NProc. $\square$

Henceforth when we say *determinate*, we mean that we have an agent in NProc that satisfies the determinacy condition and not an element of the syntactic class of determinate processes. We, of course, would like the denotation of agents built from the determinate combinators to be determinate:

Theorem 4.10 $\mathcal{A}_N(A)$ *is determinate if A is constructed using the determinate combinators.*

We are now ready to define DN, which associates with $F \in \mathtt{DNProc}$ a corresponding element in $\mathtt{DProc}$, the domain used for the denotational semantics of determinate agents in Section 3.

Definition 4.5 $DN(F) = \{\tilde{f} \mid f \in cF\} \cup \{false\}$, for $F \in$ $\mathtt{DNProc}$. $\square$

Theorem 4.11 $DN(\mathcal{A}_N(A)) = \mathcal{A}_D(A)$ *for all agents A constructed from the determinate operators.*

We prove this theorem by first showing that $DN(\mathcal{A}_N(A))$ is a closure operator. We then show by structural induction that the theorem holds for finite agents built using the determinate combinators. We prove the theorem for recursively defined agents by showing that DN is monotone and continuous.

5 Conclusion and Future work

This paper presents a comprehensive treatment of the specification-oriented approach to the semantics of programs written in concurrent constraint programming languages. This treatment includes programs built using recursion. By formalizing a general notion of constraint system, we cleanly separate the semantics of the programming language combinators from the semantics of the underlying data domain. This separation allows us to uniformly address the semantics of a wide variety of concurrent constraint programming languages with a single general framework. These languages include, among others, the concurrent logic programming languages and Kahn data-flow networks.

Our work brings into sharp focus the seamntic complexity caused by having nondeterminacy in the cc languages. The determinate semantics need only record the stores at which a process quiesces – there is no need to maintain any intermediate process state information. The nondeterminate semantics, on the other hand, must record both the stores in which a process may quiesce, and, for each such store, the possible computation paths to that store. It is interesting that finitariness plays a key role in the determinate semantics but not in the nondeterminate semantics.

We make the connection between the determinate semantics and the nondeterminate semantics by defining an operator that extracts the determinate denotation of a program built with the determinate combinators from its nondeterminate denotation. We also present an equational axiomatization that is complete for finite programs built with the determinate combinators.

This paper also presents a single transition system for both the determinate and nondeterminate languages. This transition system uses diagonal elements and local stores to eliminate messy variable renaming operations.

There are many directions for future research. These include foundational concerns, such as are addressed here, implementation issues and applications. We intend to pursue all these issues in the coming months. In this section we only mention the semantic issues.

We have by no means exhausted the range of interesting combinators that are available in the determinate cc languages. For example, the *glb* operator on agents is also available, and provides a sort of determinate "disjunction".

Some of these operators will be treated in the complete version of this paper. A useful line of investigation is to try to characterize "all sensible combinators" that one may use. Here general results from category theory may help.

There are a variety of different semantics corresponding to different notions of observations. We would like to develop a semantics for the indeterminate case that is not based on viewing divergence as chaos. This would be like Plotkin's powerdomain treatment of indeterminate imperative languages [Plo76]. In subsequent work we plan to develop proof systems for safety and liveness properties of cc programs based on these models. In a related paper we are developing the closely related safety model and an axiomatization of equality for it.

We also believe that it is possible to develop a theory of higher-order determinate cc programming languages. There are interesting connections to be made with other theories of higher-order concurrent processes [BB90,JP90,Mil90] and also with classical linear logic. It appears that concurrent constraint languages may be related to the proof nets introduced by Girard in his discussion of the proof theory of linear logic. If this connection were successful it would exhibit concurrent constraint programs as arising from linear logic via a Curry-Howard isomorphism.

Acknowledgements This research was supported in part by DARPA contract N00014-87-K-0828, NSF grant CCR-8818979 to Cornell University and an NSERC grant to McGill University. We gratefully acknowledge discussions with Seif Haridi, Tony Hoare, Radha Jagadeesan, Mark Josephs, Ken Kahn, John Lamping, Keshav Pingali and Gordon Plotkin. The debt our treatment owes to Mark's development of receptive processes should be clear to anyone who has read his paper. None of them should be held responsible for any remaining errors.

References

[ANP89] Arvind, Rishiyur Nikhil, and Keshav K. Pingali. I-structuers: data-structures for parallel computing. *ACM Transactions on Principles of Programming Languages*, 11(4):598–632, October 1989.

[BB90] G. Boudol and G. Berry. The chemical abstract machine. In *Proceedings of the 17th Annual ACM Symposium on Principles of Programming Languages*, pages 81–94. ACM, 1990.

[CM88] Mani Chandy and Jay Misra. *Parallel Program Design—A foundation*. Addison Wesley, 1988.

[dBP90a] F. S. de Boer and C. Palamidessi. A fully abstract model for concurrent constraint logic languages. In *Proceedings of CONCUR '90*, 1990.

[dBP90b] F. S. de Boer and C. Palamidessi. A fully abstract model for concurrent constraint programming. June 4 1990.

[DL86] Doug DeGroot and Gary Lindstrom, editors. *Logic Programming: Functions, Relations and Equations*. Prentice Hall, 1986.

[FT89] Ian Foster and Steve Taylor. *Strand: New concepts in parallel programming*. Prentice Hall, 1989.

[GCLS88] Rob Gerth, Mike Codish, Yossi Lichtenstein, and Ehud Shapiro. A fully abstract denotational semantics for Flat Concurrent Prolog. In *LICS 88*, 1988.

[Gir87] J.-Y. Girard. Linear logic. *Theoretical Computer Science*, 50:1–102, 1987.

[Gir89] J.-Y. Girard. *Proofs and Types*, volume 7 of *Cambridge tracts in Theoretical Computer Science*. Cambridge University Press, 1989. Translated and with appendices by Y. Lafont and P. Taylor.

[GKK+80] G.Gierz, K.H.Hoffman, K.Keimel, J.D.Lawson, M.Mislove, and D.S.Scott, editors. *A compendium of continuous lattices*. Springer-Verlag Berlin Heidelberg New York, 1980.

[GL90] M. Gabbrielli and G. Levi. Unfolding and fixpoint semantics of concurrent constraint logic programs. Technical report, University of Pisa, 1990.

[GMS89] Haim Gaifman, Michael J. Maher, and Ehud Shapiro. Reactive behavior semantics for concurrent constraint logic programs. In *North American Logic Programming Conference*. MIT Press, October 1989.

[HMT71] Leon Henkin, J. Donald Monk, and Alfred Tarski. *Cylindric Algebras (Part I)*. North Holland Publishing Company, 1971.

[Hoa89] C.A.R. Hoare. A theory of conjunction and concurrency. Oxford PRG, May 1989.

[Hoa90] C.A.R. Hoare. Let's make models. In *Proceedings of CONCUR 90*, August 1990.

[JL87] Joxan Jaffar and Jean-Louis Lassez. Constraint logic programming. In *Proceedings of the SIGACT-SIGPLAN Symposium on Principles of Programming Languages*, pages 111–119. ACM, January 1987.

[Jos90] Mark B. Josephs. Receptive process theory. Technical report, Programming Research Group, Oxford University, July 1990.

[JP90] R. Jagadeesan and P. Panangaden. A domain-theoretic model of a higher-order process calculus. In M. S. Paterson, editor, *The Seventeenth International Colloquium On Automata Languages And Programming*, pages 181–194. Springer-Verlag, 1990. Lecture Notes In Computer Science 443.

[JPP89] R. Jagadeesan, P. Panangaden, and K. Pingali. A fully abstract semantics for a functional language with logic variables. In *Proceedings of IEEE Symposium on Logic in Computer Science*, pages 294–303, 1989.

[Kah74] G. Kahn. The semantics of a simple language for parallel programming. In J.L. Rosenfeld, editor, *Proceeedings of IFIP Congress 74*, pages 471–475., August 1974.

[KYSK88] S. Kliger, E. Yardeni, E. Shapiro, and K. Kahn. The language fcp(:,?). In *Conference on Fifth Generation Computer Systems*, December 1988.

[Lev88] Giorgio Levi. Models, unfolding rules and fixpoint semantics. In *Proceeedings of the Fifth International Conference and Symposium on Logic Programming, Seattle*, pages 1649–1665, August 1988.

[Lin85] Gary Lindstrom. Functional programming and the logical variable. In *Proceedings of the Twelfth ACM Symposium on Principles of Programming Languages*, pages 266–280, January 1985.

[LS86] J. Lambek and P. Scott. *An introduction to higher-order categorical logic*, volume 7 of *Studies in Advanced Mathematics*. Cambridge University Press, 1986.

[Mah87] Michael Maher. Logic semantics for a class of committed-choice programs. In *4th International Conference on Logic Programming*. MIT Press, May 1987.

[Mil90] R. Milner. Functions as processes. In M. S. Paterson, editor, *The Seventeenth International Colloquium On Automata Languages And Programming*, pages 167–180. Springer-Verlag, 1990. Lecture Notes In Computer Science 443.

[MPW89] R. Milner, J. G. Parrow, and D. J. Walker. A calculus for mobile processes. LFCS Report ECS-LFCS-89-85, University of Edinburgh, 1989.

[MR97] M. Makkai and G. Reyes. *First order categorical logic*, volume 611 of *Lecture Notes in Mathematics*. Springer-Verlag, 197.

[OH86] E.-R. Olderog and C.A.R. Hoare. Specification-oriented semantics for communicating processes. *Acta Informatica*, 23:9–66, 1986.

[Plo76] G.D. Plotkin. A powerdomain construction. *SIAM J. of Computing*, 5(3):452–487, September 1976.

[Ros88] A. W. Roscoe. An alternative order for the failures model. Technical Report Technical Monograph PRG-67, Programming Research Group, Oxford University, July 1988.

[Sar85] Vijay A. Saraswat. Partial correctness semantics for cp($\downarrow$,|, &). In *Proceedings of the FSTTCS Conference*, number 206, pages 347–368. Springer-Verlag, December 1985.

[Sar88] Vijay A. Saraswat. A somewhat logical formulation of CLP synchronization primitives. In *Proceedings of LP 88*. MIT Press, August 1988.

[Sar89] Vijay A. Saraswat. *Concurrent Constraint Programming Languages*. PhD thesis, Carnegie-Mellon University, January 1989. To appear, Doctoral Dissertation Award and Logic Programming Series, MIT Press, 1990.

[Sco76] Dana S. Scott. Data types as lattices. *SIAM*, 5(3):522–587, 1976.

[Sco82]   Dana S. Scott. Domains for denotational seman-
            tics. In *Proceedings of ICALP*, 1982.

[SKL90]   Vijay A. Saraswat, Ken Kahn, and Jacob Levy.
            Janus: A step towards distributed constraint
            programming.   In *Proceedings of the North
            American Conference on Logic Programming*,
            October 1990.

[SPRng]   Vijay A. Saraswat, Prakash Panangaden, and
            Martin Rinard. What is a constraint?   Tech-
            nical report, Xerox PARC, forthcoming.

[SR90]   Vijay A. Saraswat and Martin Rinard.   Con-
            current constraint programming. In *Proceedings
            of Seventeenth ACM Symposium on Principles
            of Programming Languages, San Fransisco*, Jan-
            uary 1990.

[Tar56]   A. Tarski.   *Logics, semantics and meta-
            mathematics*. Oxford University Press, 1956.
            Translated by J.H. Woodger.

Chapter 7:
More Innovative Approaches to Parallel Programming

This chapter describes approaches to parallel programming that have not yet become accepted but have properties that make them of interest. Some are not really programming languages (yet), but rather they are models or abstract machines. Compared to the languages discussed in the earlier chapters of this book, these languages generally tend to have been designed with stronger semantics, directed toward software construction and correctness. Also, there is a general realization that the level of abstraction provided by a parallel-programming language should be higher than the typical abstraction level of languages designed in the past decade. This need for a higher abstraction level is no doubt partly due to the growing reality of massive parallelism.

The languages covered in this chapter can be divided into two groups. In the first, programs are built from predefined structures chosen because they have good implementation properties, are common in applications, or both. Building programs from such predefined structures both restricts and benefits programmers. On the one hand, programmers cannot write arbitrary programs but rather can write only those programs that are compositions of the predefined structures. On the other hand, the structures abstract away from issues such as the number of processors in the target architecture, the decomposition of the computation into threads, and the communication within a structure.

The predefined structures are called *skeletons* in a functional setting and *data parallelism* in an imperative setting. Skeletons may be chosen to implement particular control structures or common algorithms, or they may be based on particular data types. The Bird-Meertens Formalism is a general way of building skeletons for data types. The first paper included in this chapter, "Architecture-Independent Parallel Computation," by Skillicorn, presents the skeletons for join or concatenation lists.

The second paper included here, "A Methodology for the Development and the Support of Massively Parallel Programs," by Danelutto et al., describes the Pisa Parallel Programming Language (P^3L), an algorithmic skeleton language. The skeletons it provides are chosen from those that seem to have been useful for parallel programming. These include farm and pipeline skeletons. A sophisticated implementation has been built that is capable of mapping these skeletons to different hardware configurations. The skeleton approach is popular at the moment with skeletons based on *bags/multisets* [BAN91], skeletons based on *sets* [FLY93], and other algorithmic skeletons [COL89], [DAR93]. For example, Gamma [BAN91], [CRE91] defines skeletons over bags. The correspondence is hard to see, because Gamma consciously dispenses with the global skeleton structure and emphasizes the operations being applied. The Gamma view is based on a chemical analogy in which the elements of a bag are regarded as molecules in a solution. The solution can be reduced by applying an operation that selects two elements, applies some function to them, and then places the result in the same or another bag.

The third paper included in this chapter, "Bulk Synchronous Parallel Computing," by McColl, describes Bulk Synchronous Parallelism (BSP), an approach related to the skeletons approaches. In BSP, the structured operations are single threads of a characteristic length that depends on the size of the target architecture. These threads contain at most a single global communication action. Computations are arranged in *supersteps*, each of which is a collection of these threads. A superstep does not begin until all the global communications initiated in the previous superstep have been completed (so that there is an implicit barrier synchronization at the end of each superstep). Computations can be efficiently implemented if the time taken to deliver a set of global communication actions is the same as the computation time of each superstep. BSP can be understood as a complexity model, because a computation that fails to efficiently execute can still be analyzed to give its actual runtime.

The last two papers included in this chapter discuss two second-generation parallel-programming languages in the imperative style, both of which are concerned with composing parallel programs to produce larger programs while preserving the properties of the original programs.

The first of these papers, "Productive Parallel Programming: The PCN Approach," by Foster, Olson, and Tuecke, describes Program Composition Notation (PCN). PCN programs consist of collections of procedures that have an internal structure in the Occam style (that is, parallel, sequential, or choice collections of statements). In PCN, communication is handled by single-use variables, which may be written once within their scope but may be read multiple times. (If the write has not yet occurred, read blocking takes place.) Streams can be implemented by recursive procedure calls. PCN includes higher level structuring tools: arrays of communication variables, sets of processes and an associated virtual topology for reuse, and structured sets of cells (which start to resemble skeletons). There are also annotation features—built-in functions to determine topology, number of processors, and location of a particular piece of code—that allow procedures to modify their actions according to implementation context.

The second of the final two papers here, "The Derivation of Compositional Programs," by Chandy and Kesselman, describes Compositional C++. Compositional C++ contains many of the same ideas as does PCN but in an object-oriented framework that forms a superset of C++. Three constructors—*par*, *parfor*, and *spawn*—can be used to structure code. Again, communication uses single-use variables, called *sync variables*, and the same syntax as constants. Unlike in PCN, threads in Compositional C++ can share other variables, but the final value of a variable that is written by multiple threads is guaranteed only to be one of the possible values. Logical processor objects allow code to be grouped to preserve locality and to provide a name space.

References cited

[BAN91]   J.P. Banâtre and D. Le Metayer, "Introduction to Gamma," in *Lecture Notes in Computer Sci.—Research Directions in High-Level Parallel Programming Languages*, J.P. Banâtre and D. Le Metayer, eds., Vol. 574, Springer-Verlag, New York, N.Y., June 1991, pp. 197–202.

[COL89]   M. Cole, *Algorithmic Skeletons: Structured Management of Parallel Computation*, Research Monographs in Parallel and Distributed Computing, Pitman, London, United Kingdom, 1989.

[CRE91]   C. Creveuil, "Implementation of Gamma on the Connection Machine," in *Lecture Notes in Computer Sci.—Research Directions in High-Level Parallel Programming Languages*, J.P. Banâtre and D. Le Metayer, eds., Vol. 574, Springer-Verlag, New York, N.Y., June 1991, pp. 219–230.

[DAR93]   J. Darlington et al., "Parallel Programming Using Skeleton Functions," *Lecture Notes in Computer Sci.—Proc. Parallel Architectures and Languages Europe (PARLE '93)*, Vol. 694, Springer-Verlag, New York, N.Y., 1993.

[FLY93]   S. Flynn Hummel and R. Kelly, "A Rationale for Parallel Programming with Sets," *J. Programming Languages*, Vol. 1, 1993, pp. 187–207.

Architecture-Independent Parallel Computation

David B. Skillicorn

Queen's University at Kingston

Parallel computers have failed to make a major impact on mainstream computation, despite the fact that commercial products have been available for almost a decade. A substantial performance/price advantage over conventional supercomputers, and even large uniprocessors, has not been enough to convince users to move from a sequential to a parallel mode of computation.

An examination of the state of the art in parallel computing suggests an explanation. Different classes of parallel architectures require radically different paradigms for describing and executing computations. In addition, both practitioners and theoreticians have specialized along architectural lines. There is no obvious winner among these architectures; it is hard to move applications from one class to another; and many potential users are unwilling, on the present evidence, to make a computer acquisition decision with long-term implications.

There is currently no way to develop software for parallel computers and expect it to have a long lifetime. Software developed for uniprocessors has turned out, rather surprisingly, to have a very long lifetime indeed. A great deal of software that was written more than 20 years ago is still in use. By contrast, developers of software for parallel computers do not expect their software to have a very long life span; they are often resigned to substantially reworking their programs with the advent of the next generation of computers.

Existing parallel languages are almost all tied to some particular architectural class. Even when the software environ-

Locality-based computation, the foundation for an architecture-independent programming language grounded in the Bird-Meertens formalism, shows that architecture-independent parallel programming is possible.

ment seems superficially the same (some variant of C or Fortran, perhaps), the underlying mechanisms for communication and synchronization are often substantially different. In some cases, software must be substantially modified to take full advantage of, or even to execute on, a larger configuration of the same kind of multiprocessor. Such software is not portable in any serious sense.

Because the paradigms and patterns of program execution for various parallel architectures differ, programmers today must approach parallel programming in ways that are architecture dependent. The standard repertoires of algorithms and program fragments for each of the various architecture classes have very little in common. Moving from one architecture class to another very often means learning to design and program all over again. Thus, programmers are no more "portable" than software.

Software engineering techniques for developing parallel programs have not yet been developed. The present generation of languages requires programmers to be aware of, and explicitly handle, either the degree of physical parallelism, or communication, or both. Programmers must be aware of the kind of architecture on which their software will run, and often the number of processors, their storage capacity, and their configuration. Formal techniques for managing the development of software in this environment must necessarily be complex.

The most popular approach to software engineering for uniprocessors is to begin with a set of requirements, develop a program, and then show that the resulting program satisfies the requirements. The structure of the program is not implicit in the requirements, and it is the programmer's job, using a repertoire of techniques and experience, to decide how the requirements might best be met. It is questionable whether, even in the sequential case, this approach is better than a transformational one, in which programs are derived by algebraic or algorithmic transformation from their specifications. In a parallel environment, the transformational approach seems much better suited, since we do not already have a repertoire of standard techniques, and proofs of requirement satisfaction are harder to obtain.

Another major problem with the current state of parallel computing is the lack of a theory that relates the complexity of algorithms to the complexity of programs running on actual machines. We have forgotten how deeply we make use of the fact that Turing machines are universal. Therefore, an implementation of an algorithm on one manufacturer's uniprocessor will differ in speed by no more than a constant factor from that on another's. In the parallel world, we have no such guarantees. The most popular complexity models, the PRAM (Parallel Random Access Machine) model and the Boolean circuit model, both omit important properties of physical architectures. The result is that prospective purchasers of a specific parallel computer must face the fact that their intended applications may run slower than benchmarks by a nonconstant factor. Should the prospective purchasers decide to buy a particular style of computer, they won't be assured that a new development might not bring a new computer to market that would be better than the existing one by a nonconstant factor. It is no wonder that users have, by and large, held back from buying parallel computers.

The lack of a relevant complexity theory has also made it difficult to assess exactly how much progress has been made in algorithm design. Algorithms developed for different machine classes cannot easily be compared, and the point at which a real improvement has occurred is not always clear.

Progress in bringing parallel computing into the mainstream can only be made by addressing all of these issues. There is some urgency about the problem. For the time being, the speed of uniprocessors continues to increase, parallelizing compilers make it possible to exploit some parallelism in existing sequential software on computers with moderate parallelism, and there is a vast amount of existing sequential software. We expect that these factors will allow the current pattern of sequential software development to continue for a few years. However, it seems likely that both hardware improvements and parallelizing compiler improvements will be subject to diminishing returns. In addition, the continuing high cost of uniprocessors relative to parallel computers will force software developers to change to an environment that can capture substantial parallelism from the start.

Experience suggests that when such a

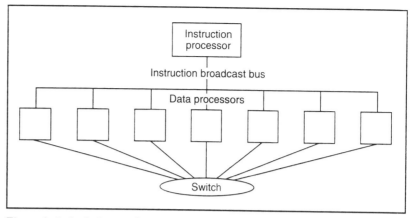

Figure 1. A single instruction, multiple data computer.

switch occurs, the first viable approach will quickly become the standard. It is important that it should be the right one — one that can provide a growth path for software development for many years. One of the challenges facing computer science researchers is to develop this approach.

In this article, I will consider four major parallel architecture classes:

- single instruction, multiple data or SIMD computers,
- tightly coupled multiple instruction, multiple data or tightly coupled MIMD computers,
- hypercuboid computers, and
- constant-valence MIMD computers.

Other, more specialized, architectures are possible, but the four classes listed above cover all general-purpose parallel computers.

A SIMD computer (see Figure 1) consists of a single instruction processor that broadcasts each instruction to a set of data processors. Each data processor has its own memory and is connected by a switch to the other data processors. Thus, a single instruction stream acts on a large number of data streams. The important characteristic of this architecture class is that only one action can take place at a given time. Even coding instructions as data and triggering them from the instruction processor can't significantly weaken this restriction, as I will demonstrate.

A tightly coupled MIMD computer (see Figure 2) consists of a set of processors

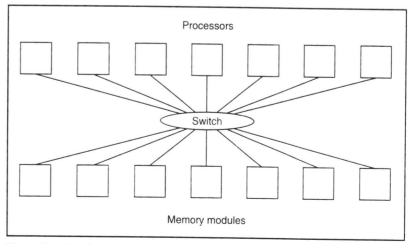

Figure 2. A tightly coupled multiple instruction, multiple data computer.

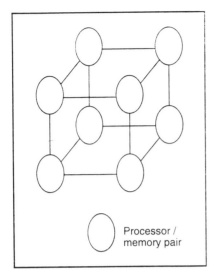

Figure 3. A hypercuboid MIMD computer.

connected to a set of memory modules by a switch. Each processor can execute its own thread of instructions, either synchronously with the other processors or asynchronously, and can access any memory location through the switch. Processors cannot communicate with each other except by writing to locations that can then be read by others. The important property of this architecture class is that, at least until optical technology has developed further, there is considerable latency in the switch. If the number of processors is p, then the switch depth (and, hence, latency) is $\Omega(p)$. Attempts by more than one processor to read from the same location (in fact, a location in the same module) will fail.

A hypercuboid computer (see Figure 3) is loosely coupled, that is, it consists of processor/memory pairs connected by a communication network. Each processor controls its local memory and can only access a location in the memory of another processor by requesting it to read the value and communicate it, or by sending it a value and asking for it to be stored. Hypercuboid architectures have a communication topology in which the number of links per processor grows as the logarithm of the number of processors in the computer. The hypercube is the best known example in this class. The diameter (that is, the number of links that a message must traverse between most distant processors) is logarithmic in the number of processors.

A constant-valence MIMD computer (see Figure 4) is like a hypercuboid computer, except that the number of links per processor is a small constant. Similarly, the diameter of the communication network is logarithmic in the number of processors. The chief difference between this class and the hypercuboid is the restricted capacity for communication caused by the sparsity of communication links. As I will show, this difference is crucial to performance. Further description of architecture classes and their characteristics can be found in an earlier article.[1]

The remainder of this article

• reviews Valiant's argument[2] that the PRAM model is universal over tightly coupled and hypercube systems, but not over constant-valence-topology, loosely coupled systems — thus showing precisely how the PRAM model is too powerful to permit broad universality;

• discusses ways in which a model of computation can be restricted to become universal over less powerful architectures;

• introduces the Bird-Meertens formalism and shows how it is used to express computations in a compact way;

• shows the surprising result that the Bird-Meertens formalism is universal over all four architecture classes — the main result of the article — and shows that nontrivial restrictions of functional programming languages exist that can be efficiently executed on disparate architectures;

• discusses how the Bird-Meertens formalism is the basis for a programming language and shows that it is expressive enough to be used for general programming; and

• reviews other models and programming languages with architecture-independent properties.

Universal models

Valiant[2] carried out a careful analysis of the universality of the PRAM model over the four architecture classes described above.

The PRAM model is an abstract machine consisting of p processors, each of which can, in unit time, carry out a local memory access, a global memory access, and a standard instruction. It is thus an approximation to a tightly coupled MIMD computer, but one that ignores the complications of memory and switch. The PRAM memory is considered to be a single, shared memory accessed through a zero latency switch (see Figure 5).

Figure 4. A constant-valence MIMD computer.

The sequence of steps executed by a single PRAM processor is called a thread. The number of time units a thread takes to execute is exactly the number of steps it contains. Because the only way a dependency between threads can be implemented is by one thread writing to memory and another reading the stored value, a dependency requires two-unit time steps. This is indicated by a two-unit arrow from one thread to another (see Figure 6).

A particular computation may be scheduled in many ways using different amounts of parallelism. Each schedule produces a trace consisting of threads. In what follows, we assume that the schedule chosen is as compact as possible, that is, it uses as little time and as few processors as possible. Thus, we assume, without loss of generality, that each thread contains a step at each time. For a computation of size n, we can characterize its parallelism and execution time by considering the width and length of its trace.

Suppose that the trace has $p(n)$ threads and $t(n)$ steps. By our assumption of compactness, the trace forms a $t(n)$ by $p(n)$ rectangle. We say that the cost of the PRAM computation is $t(n) \cdot p(n)$, representing the total amount of resources that must be used.

We define a computation model to be *universal* over an architecture class if there is a nontrivial architecture in that class that can emulate computations with time-parallelism products of the same order as their costs in the model. For example, the PRAM model would be universal over a particular architecture if a PRAM computation taking time $t(n)$ and $p(n)$ processors could be executed on that architecture in time $t(n)$ on $p(n)$ processors, or in time $2t(n)$ on $p(n)/2$ processors.

Emulation on tightly coupled computers. Let us consider the PRAM model of computation implemented on a variety of architectures, beginning with the tightly coupled MIMD class. For this class, the switch is the performance bottleneck. Crossbar switches are very expensive in hardware, and optical switches are still highly experimental. Conventional dynamic switches require a traversal time logarithmic in the width of the switch, so that a p processor system has an $\Omega(\log p)$ cost for each global memory access.

If we consider a straightforward implementation of this computation model on such an architecture (with $p(n)$ processors), we incur a time penalty, because each of the global accesses that takes unit

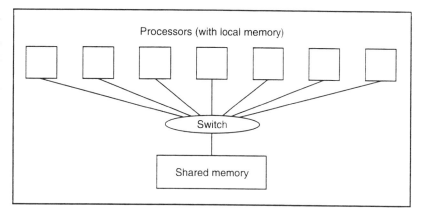

Figure 5. A PRAM machine.

time in the model takes logarithmic time on the real machine. Thus, the computation will take $t(n) \log p(n)$ time units, increasing the time-parallelism product by a factor of $\log p(n)$. Hence, this emulation is not universal. In fact, this example shows that we could not have defined a stronger form of universality in terms of execution time alone, since any real implementation incurs nonunit-time delays for references to distant data.

Fortunately, we can still construct a time-parallelism optimal simulation by reducing the number of processors to compensate for the increased memory latency. We reduce the number of processors to $p(n)/\log p(n)$ and use each processor to execute $\log p(n)$ threads of the computation in a kind of prescheduled multitasking. Each processor executes the first step of its first thread, then the first step of the second thread, and so on. After executing the first step of $\log p(n)$ threads, it executes the second step of the first thread, the second thread, and so on (see Figure 7). The elapsed time between successive steps of the same thread is $O(\log p(n))$ while the latency of the switch is

$$\log \left(\frac{p(n)}{\log p(n)} \right) < \log p(n)$$

Thus, ignoring potential contention in the switch, this emulation executes in time $t(n) \log p(n)$ using $p(n)/\log p(n)$ processors, giving an optimal time-parallelism product. This lower bound on switch traversal can be achieved by a result of Mehlhorn and Vishkin,[3] which shows that memory hashing can spread the memory references uniformly with high probability. This makes contention in the switch rare.

Notice that, to achieve this result, more parallelism must exist in the computation than in the machine, a property that Valiant calls *parallel slackness*.[4] The virtual parallelism of the computation must be much larger than the physical parallelism used to execute it. This really means that it doesn't help to use extra hardware for a computation — a thousand-way parallel algorithm can only make good use of a hundred-way parallel computer.

Unfortunately, this class of architectures does not seem to be a good candidate for long-term development. The problem lies in the scalability of the switch. Unless optical interconnects make a revolutionary

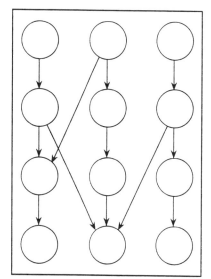

Figure 6. Three threads showing dependencies.

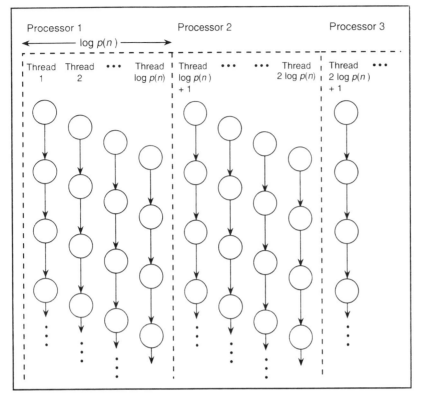

Figure 7. Multitasking of threads onto physical processors.

difference, today's estimate of the maximum possible switch size is about 10,000 × 10,000. As existing architectures are within an order of magnitude of this size, long-term prospects do not seem attractive.

Emulation on hypercuboid computers. Let us now consider emulating PRAM computations on a loosely coupled multiprocessor where the number of communication links from each processor grows as the logarithm of the number of processors. We call such systems *hypercuboid*, since the hypercube is the best known example of the class. Each processor has its own local memory, but can only access the data in the memories of remote processors by using a network of communication links.

The global references in our computation model must be transformed into messages to other processors that will not necessarily be adjacent. Hence, messages might travel through a number of intermediate communication links. We call the maximum number of links traversed the *effective diameter d*. By a theorem of Bokhari and Raza,[5] the diameter of any connected graph can be reduced to logarithmic by adding at

most one new edge per vertex. There is thus little point in considering any static communication topology that has a diameter worse than logarithmic in the number of processors; such a topology could always be improved by adding only a single extra communication link to each processor. So, even a path topology could have its diameter reduced to logarithmic and its valence increased only to three. We therefore assume that in practical systems d is bounded above by $\log p$.

A direct emulation of the PRAM model will result in the same increase in execution time as for the tightly coupled implementation because unit-time global references take logarithmic time on the real machine. We use the same multitasking technique to reduce the number of processors, scheduling the steps just as before. The time between successive steps of the same thread is once again $\log p(n)$, and thus enough time exists for references to the opposite extremity of a $p(n)/\log p(n)$ processor machine to complete. The argument that this lower bound can be achieved in the presence of contention depends on two probabilistic results:

- memory hashing, to spread references uniformly; and
- two-phase randomized routing.[2]

Two-phase randomized routing channels a message from A to B by first sending it from A to some randomly chosen processor C by the straightforward shortest route, and then sending it from C to B, again by the shortest route. The total distance travelled does not exceed twice the diameter of the network; this strange procedure reduces the probability of contention to an arbitrarily small amount. On the hypercube, it guarantees to deliver $\log p(n)$ permutations in time $\log p(n)$ with overwhelming probability. The total time taken for the emulation is $t(n) \log p(n)$ with parallelism $p(n)/\log p(n)$, so that again we have a universal emulation. Parallel slackness is again required in the computation.

This architecture class is also problematic with respect to scalability. The number of links per processor depends on the size of computer in which it is embedded. Thus, it is not possible to build a scalable computer without replacing the processors whenever the system size is doubled.

Emulation on constant-valence computers. Let us now turn to loosely coupled, fixed-valence topology multiprocessors. In such computers, each processor has only a fixed number of communication links. Hence, such computers can be built as arbitrary size ensembles of the same basic processor. As before, we assume that the network diameter is at most logarithmic in the number of processors.[5]

A simple counting argument suffices to show that the restricted connection structure of such architectures must prevent universal emulation on them. Suppose we have a p processor machine, that there are α communication links per processor, and that the effective communication diameter (that is, number of link traversals) of messages is d. In a single instruction step, as many as pd message traversal requirements may be generated. Of course, these requirements are partly obligations for the future, as they must be satisfied on subsequent steps. The number of link slots available to transmit messages during a single step is $p\alpha$. Now d is logarithmic in the number of processors while α is a small constant depending on the processor design. Therefore, on average, the communication system will not be able to deliver messages as quickly as they are generated. To compensate, the processors must be slowed by at least a factor of d/α.

310

We use the same multitasking approach to schedule the steps of our computation model. Global references take time at least logarithmic in the number of processors extended by a factor of d/α, giving a total execution time of

$$t(n) \cdot \log p(n) \cdot \frac{d}{\alpha}$$

on $p(n)/\log p(n)$ processors. The lower bound on communication time can be achieved for the cube-connected-cycles topology, using memory hashing and two-phase randomized routing. However, universal emulation is clearly not possible for this class of architectures.

The class of constant-valence topology MIMD computers is of great practical interest because computers in the class are scalable since the neighborhoods of each processor are homogeneous. Unlike the two classes previously considered, this class contains computers with extremely large numbers of processors.

Emulation on SIMD computers. Let us consider the fourth architecture class, the SIMD computers. Simulating our PRAM computation on a SIMD computer is difficult. Using a local table, a SIMD machine can simulate a MIMD machine by decoding each instruction broadcast into an instruction to execute. This broadcast instruction can be considered an index into the table; the table entries are then the instructions themselves. The question is whether such a simulation can be carried out without loss of universality. The general belief is that this cannot be so (it has the status of a folk theorem), but I have been unable to find an existing proof. The following theorem shows that universality cannot be maintained, except in the trivial case. It is based on the extra uniformity that a SIMD computer requires (a similar proof based on interprocessor communication is probably possible). The proof has the advantage that it applies even if the PRAM processors compute entirely independently.

Theorem: An arbitrary PRAM computation cannot be simulated on a SIMD architecture without increase in the time-parallelism product, except for the trivial simulation on a one-processor SIMD machine.

Proof: We assume that a SIMD architecture has a bounded bandwidth communication channel that broadcasts from the (single) instruction processor to the data processors. Call this bandwidth x. Let IS be the cardinality of the instruction set of the data processors. Then x is bounded above by $\log IS$.

Suppose the PRAM calculation uses p processors. Then, there are IS^p possible steps in the PRAM calculation. Suppose the PRAM calculation is simulated by a SIMD architecture with m processors. Without loss of generality, we can assume that $m \leq p$ since a PRAM computation that forces absolute dependencies between successive steps can always be constructed; such a program cannot make use of more than p processors. Each step of the PRAM calculation is simulated by p/m steps of the SIMD machine, with each set of m operations chosen arbitrarily. There are IS^m possible different configurations of m of the PRAM operations, so that each SIMD step requires broadcasting $\log IS^m$ bits. With bandwidth x, this takes time

$$\frac{\log IS^m}{x}$$

Thus, the total time to simulate one step of the PRAM computation is

$$\log IS^m \frac{p}{mx}$$

and the time-parallelism product for the simulation is

$$\text{time–parallelism product} = \log IS \cdot \frac{mp}{x}$$

The time-parallelism product of the step of the PRAM computation is p.

Assuming that $x = \log IS$ (the usual way SIMD machines are designed), we see that the slowdown is the expected m; hence, when $m = 1$, the simulation remains universal, but it is suboptimal for all larger values.

The single step of the PRAM computation can be extended to an arbitrary number of steps; and a factor of s appears in both of the calculations above. Hence, a full $\log IS^m$ bits are needed to handle all possible IS^m combinations. A PRAM computation long enough to use all possible combinations no matter how the m are chosen can always be constructed.

This proof does not depend on any properties of the data processors used or any encoding of the instructions. It is based solely on the information flow across the instruction processor/data processor boundary. If the data processors are powerful enough to execute instructions stored as data, with direction from the instruction processor broadcasting fetch, decode, and execute, then the machine is best regarded as a MIMD computer and other arguments apply.

The class of SIMD architectures is also of long-term interest because computers in the class scale well; the only potential bottleneck is the fan-out from the instruction processor.

This shows that the PRAM model is universal over the classes of tightly coupled and hypercuboid multiprocessors. The PRAM model is not universal over constant-valence topology multiprocessors and SIMD computers. Unfortunately, this is as bad as it could be: Those architecture classes that can optimally emulate don't scale; those classes that do scale force a suboptimal emulation.

Restricted computation models

The results in the previous section show why the PRAM model cannot be made universal over all four architecture classes. On the one hand, it requires frequent communication (possibly on every step); on the other hand, many diverse operations can take place simultaneously on different processors. The first creates problems in emulating the PRAM on communication-poor architectures; the second creates problems for SIMD architectures. A model universal over all four classes will have to be more restricted than the PRAM model, limiting communication richness and imposing more regularity on simultaneous steps.

A weaker model is not necessarily a bad thing. It was decided long ago that a sequential von Neumann machine's capability to treat instructions as data was not worth the problems it caused in software development and execution. Most von Neumann machines might as well be considered as Harvard architectures. Much the same reasoning was used to restrict imperative languages to a small set of control structures and to insist that programs be developed in a modular way.

There are many ways in which the PRAM model of computation might be weakened. There are two ways to treat the problems caused by communication: reduce the frequency of communication or reduce the distance each message travels. These suggest different, and largely incompatible, new models.

Glossary

Concurrent-read PRAM: One in which simultaneous reads from the same memory location are allowed in unit time. It is usually implemented by replicating the value on its way from the memory to the processors.

Concurrent-write PRAM: One in which simultaneous writes to the same memory location are allowed in unit time. The actual value stored may vary: It may be a randomly chosen member of the set of values written, the result of applying an associative operation to the set of values, or the value from the lowest numbered processor participating.

Cube connected cycles: An interconnection topology that has many of the properties of the hypercube but only requires constant valence. Imagine a hypercube of dimension d. d links converge on each corner. A cube connected cycles topology is obtained by removing the corners and replacing them with a cycle of size d.

First-order functional programming: Programming with functions that may take only data as their arguments. Many dataflow languages are first order.

FP/FL: Languages designed by Backus et al. They are built using first- and second-order functions. Much program transformation can be done using identities that are variable free; that is, they are identities of the functions only.

KIDS: Kestrel Interactive Development System, an algorithm development system built at the Kestrel Institute. It requires minimal user direction to derive algorithms of a number of common kinds: divide-and-conquer, dynamic programming, etc.

Loosely coupled MIMD computer: One in which each processor has its own local memory and is connected to other processor-memory pairs by an interconnection network. There is no direct access by one processor to another's memory.

Memory hashing: A technique for allocating variables to memory locations or modules such that, probabilistically, there is little chance of collisions during typical access patterns. It is based on uniform hashing functions.

Model of computation: An abstract but computable description of a computation. It usually corresponds to an abstract machine that can execute the model directly.

OBJ: A language based on order-sorted equational logic. Program code consists of equations that are interpreted as rewrite rules. Rewriting is done modulo commutativity and associativity and user-defined evaluation strategies may be defined. This provides a very flexible evaluation mechanism that can emulate other programming techniques.

Parallel slackness: The property of having much more virtual parallelism in a computation than is available on the physical machine executing it. Its presence often allows latency to be hidden.

PRAM: Parallel Random Access Machine, a popular computation model based on an abstract multiprocessor consisting of processors connected to a shared memory by a switch. In unit time, each processor can access its local memory or registers, access the shared memory, and perform a standard operation.

Second-order functional programming: The programming language contains (first-order) functions and data, but also functions that may take other functions as arguments. Usually the set of second-order functions is fixed.

SIMD computer: One in which a single instruction processor controls a set of data processors that simultaneously execute the operation broadcast by the instruction processor. The data processors are interconnected so that they can permute data among themselves.

Tightly coupled MIMD computer: One in which there is a large shared memory that is equally accessible to all processors. Because of the need to arbitrate the access to the shared memory, processors are not as independent as in loosely coupled MIMD computers.

Two-phase randomized routing: A routing algorithm that probabilistically reduces contention in static interconnection networks. It works by choosing a random destination for each message, routing it from the source processor to that random processor by a deterministic algorithm, and then routing it on to its destination using the same deterministic algorithm. This at most doubles the path length taken and spreads the load evenly across the communication paths.

Universal: A computation model is said to be universal over an architecture class if it can be simulated on that class without increasing the time-processors product required.

VLIW: Very long instruction word architectures use small fixed amounts of parallelism by constructing an instruction thread that contains a number of concurrent subthreads. This amount of parallelism can be extracted from ordinary sequential code at compile time using techniques rather like horizontal microcode compaction.

XPRAM: A variant of the PRAM suggested by Valiant. References to shared memory are counted as taking unit time but can only occur on every Lth step in each processor.

Valiant has proposed the bulk synchronous parallel model, or XPRAM, a model which reduces the frequency of communication. It corresponds to a PRAM model in which nonlocal communication is constrained to occur no more frequently than every L step in each processor. Choosing L to be the size of $\log p(n)$ reduces the communication requirements enough to permit a universal emulation on the constant-valence topology architectures. *A fortiori*, universal emulations remain possible for tightly coupled and hypercuboid architectures.

The XPRAM can be regarded as a PRAM in which the granularity of the steps has increased to L. The instruction set of the XPRAM consists of all threads of length L from the original PRAM. However, the structure of the computation now depends on the size of the target machine. Using a larger machine means choosing a larger L and, hence, recasting the algorithm so that global communication is less frequent. This seems unsatisfactory and hard to implement. The kind of decisions required seem too difficult for a programmer, although they could conceivably be incorporated into a compiler. For example, work in compiling for VLIW (very long instruction word) architectures suggests that it is possible to recast algorithms for small values of L, but the technique will not work for arbitrary-sized L.[6] If L is pragmatically bounded above by 10, computers are bounded to about a thousand processors, small even by today's standards. The memory allocation required is also quite unusual. There is a considerable advantage in locality of reference in a single processor, but memory hashing is required for interprocessor reference. Also, the XPRAM model does not address the problem of emulation on SIMD architectures.

The second way of restricting the computation model is to reduce the distance over which communication takes place. I call this *locality-based* computation. Under this model of computation, nonlocal references can only be to threads that are close under some metric, in fact within some constant distance. Such a computation model can be universal over constant-valence topology multiprocessors, because the effective diameter d is a constant. As a result, it becomes possible to use only a small (constant) degree of multiplexing to hide latency — only constant parallel slackness is required. This allows more effective use of hardware.

First- and second-order functional programming are two attractive forms of locality-based computation. The appropriateness of first-order functional programming can be seen by regarding a computation as a dataflow graph consisting of nodes, representing functions, and arcs, describing the flow of data from one function to another. If the functions have only a small number of arguments and each produces only a single result, then the nodes are of low valence and can be mapped onto a constant-valence topology without "stretching" any of the arcs by more than a small amount. Hence, locality is always guaranteed.

Locality-based computation using second-order functions is even more attractive. The arguments to second-order functions must be functions that have some similarities. For our purposes, the similarities we are interested in are consistent communication patterns and uniform computation steps. If we can find a set of second-order functions such that each requires only constant locality, then the set can be used as a model of computation that will be universal over constant-valence topology multiprocessors and, therefore, over tightly coupled and hypercuboid multiprocessors as well. If the set of second-order functions has appropriate regularity, then we can consider emulations on SIMD computers as well.

The Bird-Meertens formalism[7] provides exactly such a set of second-order functions, although they were developed with rather different goals in mind. In the next section,

I introduce this formalism, show that universal emulations over constant-valence and SIMD systems are possible, and discuss the expressiveness of the formalism.

The Bird-Meertens formalism

The Bird-Meertens formalism consists of a set of theories built on a base algebra with unary and binary functions. Each theory captures the behavior of a particular class of data structures. The theory of lists has been well developed and some work has been done on the theories of trees and arrays.

A theory adds to the base algebra a set of second-order functions and laws that relate them. A program consists of a composition of functions, in much the same style as FP. The laws provide a set of meaning-preserving transformations that can be applied for optimization or regarded as rewrite rules in the style of OBJ.[8] The Bird-Meertens formalism thus owes something to APL and to the treatment of lists in conventional functional languages.

The theory of lists adds the following second-order functions to the base algebra: map (*), reduce (/), directed reduce ($\twoheadrightarrow$), accumulate ($/\!\!/$), prefix (//), filter ($\lhd$), *inits*, *tails*, and cross product (×). If f is a unary function, $\oplus$ a binary function written in infix notation, and lists are indicated by brackets, then we can define *map* applied to f by

$$f * [a, b, c, ...] = [fa, fb, fc, ...]$$

The function *reduce* is defined by

$$\oplus/[a, b, c, ..., x] = a \oplus b \oplus c \oplus ... \oplus x$$

assuming that $\oplus$ is associative, so that bracketing is not needed on the right hand side. If $\oplus$ is not associative, we can define a directed reduce by

$$\oplus \twoheadrightarrow [a, b, c, ..., x] = (((a \oplus b) \oplus c) ... \oplus x)$$

The *accumulate* function defines a prefix computation over an operator that need not be associative. It is written $/\!\!/$ and is defined by

$$\oplus /\!\!/_e [a, b, c, ..., x] = [e, e \oplus a, (e \oplus a) \oplus b, ..., (...((e \oplus a) \oplus ...) \oplus x]$$

An associative version of *accumulate* called *prefix* can be defined by

$$\oplus // [a, b, c, ..., x] = [a, a \oplus b, ..., (...(a \oplus ...) \oplus x]$$

The *filter* operation provides selection. If p is a Boolean predicate then

$$p \lhd [a, b, c, ..., x]$$

selects those elements of the list for which p is true. Thus, its result is a (possibly empty) list.

The function *inits* computes the initial segments of a list and returns them as a list. Hence,

$$inits [a, b, c, ..., x] = [[\,], [a], [a, b], ..., [a, b, c, ..., x]]$$

The function *tails* computes the final segments of a list, that is, *inits* of the reverse of a list.

The cross product operator forms the list of cross products of elements of two lists so that

$$[a, b, ..., m] \times_\oplus [n, o, ..., z] = [a \oplus n, a \oplus o, ..., a \oplus z, b \oplus n, ..., m \oplus z]$$

I illustrate the Bird-Meertens style with a simple example; many more examples, together with their derivations, can be found in references in the "Further reading" section. The *maximum segment sum* problem has been regularly discussed in programming literature. It can be stated as: Given a list of integers, find the contiguous sublist with maximum sum. Clearly, the following computation

$$mss = \uparrow / \cdot +/* \cdot segs$$

where $\uparrow$ is the binary maximum operator, + is integer addition, and *segs* computes all of the contiguous sublists of a list, meets this specification. The contiguous sublists of a list can be computed in the way implied by the following definition, in which $+\!\!\!+$ is the binary list catenation operator,

$$segs = +\!\!\!+ / \cdot tails * \cdot inits$$

This computation finds the maximum segment sum by computing all of the contiguous sublists of the given list, summing the elements of each, and then selecting the maximum of those sums. This is clearly a computationally expensive solution to the problem.

The laws of the theory of lists can be used to rewrite the solution; after a nontrivial derivation, the following solution results

$$mss = \uparrow / \cdot \otimes \ \nleftrightarrow_0$$

where

$$a \otimes b = (a + b) \uparrow 0$$

The new version generates many fewer intermediate values and can be computed in two pipelined passes over the list. It uses the fact that, if the running sum falls below zero, then the corresponding sublist cannot be part of the maximum sum segment. The faster algorithm is not obvious, but is derivable by standard transformations. Some insight is required, but the process seems susceptible to automation. For example, the Kestrel Interactive Development System (KIDS)[9] can develop programs from specifications with minimal user input about the kind of algorithm that is appropriate — divide-and-conquer, dynamic programming, and so on.

Demonstrating universality

To show that the second-order functions are universal over constant-valence topology multiprocessors, we must show that the time-parallelism product of an emulation is no worse (asymptotically) than the equivalent PRAM calculation, and that communication is sufficiently local that communication links are not saturated. In the following discussion, assume that lists are stored in a kind of normal form in contiguous processors, one element in each. Also assume that each list is of length $O(p)$ for a p-processor system, corresponding to our assumption that at least $p(n)$ processors were available to execute PRAM computations. Each processor is aware of the length of the list. In each of the following implementations, this information is sufficient to permit clean termination of each function.

Here, I give a case analysis for each of the second-order functions.

Map: The computation of a map requires each processor to apply a given function to the list element it holds. This can be done in constant time if we assume that the function is treated as part of the program, that is, it does not have to be broadcast at execution time. No interprocessor communication is required.

Reduce: The PRAM time complexity of reduce is logarithmic in the size of the list. I show that the same time complexity can be achieved using the following technique: A reduction can be carried out in a cube

---

The Kestrel Interactive Development System can develop programs from specifications with minimal user input about the kind of algorithm that is appropriate — divide-and-conquer, dynamic programming, and so on.

---

connected cycle network by first doing the reduction in each cycle. This takes time linear in the cycle length, that is, $\log p$. The remaining steps of the reduction can be done through dimension-by-dimension collapse. All of the values in one hyperplane are transmitted to the other parallel hyperplane, the $\oplus$ operation is performed at each corner, and the process is repeated in another dimension. Changing dimensions requires a shift around each of the cycles. All of the communication takes place with nearest neighbors in the topology.

Directed reduce: The PRAM complexity of a directed reduction is linear in the size of the list. It can clearly be implemented on the constant-valence multiprocessor in linear time, using only nearest neighbor communication, provided a Hamiltonian path exists. (A Hamiltonian path passes through every vertex in the graph exactly once. An example of a graph without such a path is a binary tree).

Accumulate: The accumulate function uses exactly the same communication pattern as the directed reduce, except that a copy of the partial result is left at each processor.

Prefix: The parallel implementation of prefix is due to Ladner and Fisher[10] and has a PRAM complexity that is logarithmic in the size of the list. In a constant-valence topology multiprocessor, their approach requires some nodes to transmit a logarithmic number of messages to others.

A constant locality parallel prefix can be computed in a cube-connected cycle topology as follows: First, compute the prefixes in each cycle of a cube connected cycles network. Then, use the following hypercube prefix algorithm. Each processor (with the

---

result of a prefix from a cycle) holds two values, the sum of all the values in its current hypercube and its own partial sum (that is, the prefix value). Matching hypercubes are recursively merged into a larger dimension hypercube by having corresponding corners exchange their total sum, computing a new total sum, and those processors in the "upper" hypercube using the total sum from the other half to compute new partial sums. The hypercube part of the algorithm is clearly logarithmic, as is the initial prefix at each corner, for an overall logarithmic algorithm.

Filter: The filter operation returns a list in which those elements that do not satisfy the predicate have been removed. Its PRAM complexity is therefore logarithmic since, after elements have been deleted, those that remain must establish their new position in the list. On the constant-valence topology, the same operations must be done and take the same amount of time. However, one extra step, moving the values to contiguous processors, must also be done. The determination of new position can be calculated as

$$+ \ \nleftrightarrow_0 \ (\text{if } p \text{ then } K_1 \text{ else } K_0)$$

where K_i is the constant i function.

Moving the values to their correct positions may require arbitrary data movements. However, the destinations of each element of the list are unique, so the routing required is a permutation. Using two-phase randomized routing, an arbitrary permutation can be realized in logarithmic time in a network such as cube connected cycles. The use of two-phase randomized routing only occurs during filter operations. Each filter operation begins with a logarithmic time prefix operation; hence, repeated use of two-phase randomized routing is separated by a logarithmic time gap. This provides sufficient time to guarantee that successive routing steps will not interfere with each other. Thus, we can maintain an overall logarithmic time for the operation.

Inits: The PRAM complexity of inits is clearly linear since a linear number of processors must generate a quadratic amount of data. It can be computed on the constant-valence topology by circulating one copy of the list from left to right along a Hamiltonian path and adding the newly arrived element to the list being constructed at each processor. This takes linear time.

Tails: The tails operation can be computed in the same way as inits, except that the shift is from right to left.

Cross product: The cross product of two

lists, each of which is in normal form, can be computed by circulating one list around a Hamiltonian cycle and forming products at each processor on each step. This takes time linear in the length of the lists and requires only nearest neighbor communication. The PRAM complexity of the operation is clearly linear.

Thus, the requirements for optimal evaluation on a constant-valence topology multiprocessor are the existence of a Hamiltonian cycle, the capability to do a tree-structured reduction in logarithmic time, and the capability to deliver an arbitrary permutation in logarithmic time. The second requirement is almost trivial because it amounts to requiring a log depth spanning tree of finite valence (which can simulate a binary spanning tree with no more than constant slowdown), and any interesting topology will have this property.

Both tightly coupled and hypercuboid multiprocessors are much less restricted than constant-valence topology architectures. Therefore, these results apply equally to those architecture classes.

The SIMD implementations of the second-order functions are no more complicated than the constant-valence topology implementations. In fact, the SIMD architecture is more powerful, since the requirement for locality is removed. It requires a certain regularity or uniformity in the computation because of the restriction that all processors must execute the same instruction at each step. The second-order functions we have been discussing all possess the required uniformity.

The details of the implementation of each of the functions on SIMD computers follow. We assume that the interprocessor topology is at least as rich as a constant-valence multiprocessor, so that communication patterns take the same amount of time as before. We need only show that processors are either executing the same operation or are idle during each step of the computation.

Map: As before, map can be applied in constant time and requires no communication.

Reduce: A reduction can be carried out by the obvious tree-structured algorithm in which half the processors participate for the first step, a quarter for the next step, and so on. The complete reduction is done after log n steps.

Directed reduce: A directed reduction requires only a single processor to be active on each time step; hence, it takes the

obvious linear amount of time.

Accumulate: The accumulate operation is done in the same way as a directed reduction.

Prefix: The parallel prefix algorithm described above can be easily adapted to a SIMD architecture and still takes logarithmic time.

Filter, inits, tails: As before, these can be done using prefix computations.

Cross product: The same technique used for constant-valence computers can be used, giving a linear time algorithm.

I have shown that the Bird-Meertens formalism is universal over a diverse class of architectures, including computers that have limited communication or require uniformity of action. A computation model so restricted might not might have been expected to be powerful enough to be useful as a programming tool. The surprising result of this work is that such a universal model can be powerful enough to program most applications in a natural, although novel, way.

Benefits of the Bird-Meertens theory

Knowing that the Bird-Meertens formalism is a computation model that is universal over four important classes of parallel architectures, it should also be clear that the Bird-Meertens formalism can be executed by uniprocessors and that many of its functions can exploit vector architec-

tures. Thus, it is truly an architecture-independent programming language. It addresses many of the problems raised at the beginning of this article.

A natural question you might ask is whether the formalism is expressive enough or whether programmers will find it too restrictive. Making this case would require more space than is practical here, but interested readers can read the extensive variety of papers discussing applications. While this does require learning a new way of thinking about parallel computation, those who have used it seem to find no difficulty. In fact, several nonobvious improvements on existing algorithms have been discovered.

The choice of second-order functions is critical. Spivey has shown[11] how the basic set of second-order functions on lists arise as adjunctions between appropriate categories. Because such adjunctions are unique, all algebraic properties of list functions are captured by the laws that arise from the adjunctions. Thus, we can be sure that all algebraic properties of lists have been captured by these laws.

Software written in a language that is universal over a wide range of architectures is portable when it is written. But it also has a potentially long life span because it can be moved onto new hardware platforms as they are developed. Programmers also are less committed to a particular architecture class because they write in much the same way for any architecture.

The Bird-Meertens formalism also addresses some of the difficulties of software engineering for parallel architectures. In fact, it was developed with software engineering goals in mind, as an environment in which to do transformational program development. This approach postulates the ability to write down an initial solution that manifestly meets a given requirement as I did with the maximum segment sum problem. In fact, it may be little more than stating the requirements carefully. This solution can then be transformed, using the laws, which are actually algebraic identities, as meaning-preserving rewrite rules. This continues until a sufficiently efficient implementation is derived. Considerable experience with human derivation has been accumulated, and there seems to be no reason why the process could not be at least partially automated. I am investigating this possibility.

There is no guarantee that transformations will preserve the execution complexity of functions. It seems sensible to define new second-order functions whenever we can build implementations for them that are faster than the corresponding transformed functions would be. For example, a left accumulate can be defined in terms of a left reduction

$$\oplus /\!\!/_e = \otimes /\!\!/_e$$

where

$$x \otimes a = x \,+\!\!\!+\, [\text{last } x \oplus a]$$

but this definition is not computationally interesting since we know how to implement the left accumulate with the same parallel time complexity as the reduction. Obviously, this creates new problems since we cannot be certain that we know all useful transformation rules. Insight will be required to notice when some new composition admits a fast implementation. There are many interesting research problems here.

The analysis of the performance behavior of each of the second-order functions can be used to form the basis of a consistent complexity theory over different architectures. It can also be used to control program transformations, so that it is clear what an efficient solution actually is. Second-order functions such as reduce have recursion embedded within them, but it isn't visible to the programmer. However, when a cost measure is applied to functions such as reduce, the result is a first-order recursive function for which it is difficult to find general closed form solutions. We have shown that the complexity of the second-order functions is asymptotically the same as the PRAM versions, but the constants are almost always larger. Thus, it is interesting to consider architecture-directed optimizations that would help to reduce the practical disadvantages of the emulations. Many interesting research questions remain.

Other architecture-independent languages

Attempts to find architecture-independent computation models or programming languages take two approaches: restricting the PRAM model by requiring the use of new primitives; or removing restrictions such as scheduling from the PRAM model.

Models that restrict the PRAM are easier to implement because their demands on the underlying hardware are more predictable. Thus, providing performance guarantees for such models is usually possible. At first glance, it seems paradoxical that a model is restricted by adding primitives, but performance gains are achieved by restricting programmers to using the new primitives rather than all of the flexibility of the original model. For example, adding a structured *if* and *while* to an imperative language is a restriction of general programming, even though it involves adding new language constructs.

The first restriction I will consider is the addition of concurrent read or concurrent write at the same memory location. These can be regarded as parallel read or write primitives. As with all such primitives, these are added because they can be efficiently implemented. On a tightly coupled MIMD computer, the paths through the switch from each processor to a fixed memory location form a tree. If the internal nodes of this tree can do simple computations, they can merge requests for reads from the same location and then distribute the data when it returns from memory. Writes to the same location can be merged on their way through the switch using any of a number of rules: keep one value and discard the others, apply an associative operation to the two values and transmit the result, and so on. Thus, with the addition of suitable (quite expensive) hardware, concurrent read and write can be implemented at the same time cost as ordinary memory access that is logarithmic in the number of processors.

Another primitive that can be added to the PRAM model is the *scan*, suggested by G. Blelloch (see "Further reading"). A scan is essentially a parallel prefix. Again, in a tightly coupled MIMD computer, this operation can be implemented by the switch in time logarithmic in the number of processors.

A.G. Ranade has suggested a further restriction of the PRAM model (see "Further reading"). He describes a new primitive called *multiprefix* that generalizes *scan*. Suppose that some set of k processors references a variable A, the processors are ordered, and $\oplus$ is a binary operation. If the initial value of A is a, then the execution of the multiprefix $MP(A, v_i, \oplus)$ by processor i results in it acquiring the value $a \oplus v_1 \oplus v_2 \oplus ... \oplus v_i$ and the variable A ends up with the value $a \oplus v_1 \oplus ... \oplus v_k$. Ranade shows that the multiprefix operation will terminate (with overwhelming probability) in $\log p(n)$ steps. Thus, on a tightly coupled MIMD computer, it is no more expensive in time than memory reference. The Bird-Meertens formalism can be regarded as an extension of this approach to a set of primitives that is in some sense complete while still being efficiently implementable.

The second approach is to build models stronger than the PRAM in which the programmer must say less about scheduling and communication. Such models are harder to implement because the programmer provides less information. But, of course, the programmer's job is easier for the same reason.

Macro-dataflow is a popular model of this kind. It is stronger than the PRAM model because the programmer no longer needs to specify the order of execution of parts of the program, and there is no longer any explicit memory. Instead, scheduling is inferred at runtime by the presence of arguments ("firing rule"), and memory is replaced by tokens traversing arcs. Dataflow machines attempt to create execution schedules dynamically as a program executes. Doing this efficiently is the major challenge of this approach.

Another programming language, or perhaps abstract machine model, is W.J. Dally's parallel machine interface (see "Further reading"). The PMI consists of a set of mechanisms that can be efficiently supported by the underlying parallel computers while being rich enough to allow programming in a number of suitable styles. The mechanisms act as an abstract machine for which higher software layers can be targeted, decoupling the software development process from the underlying implementation.

The abstract machine is considered to consist of a number of nodes, each of which can execute tasks. Tasks have their own local memories, called segments. Segments contain the entire context of a task, including a flag indicating whether they are available to run, and memory locations are tagged with their full/empty status. Tasks on the same node can access the segments of other tasks.

Communication and synchronization are both implemented by a single *send* primitive that transfers a block of data to another node, places it in a segment, and flags the segment as ready to execute. Thus, messages can trigger actions on remote nodes. These actions can mimic typical *receive* operations, and they can also suspend or resume other tasks on the destination node.

The PMI approach cannot provide any guarantees about the performance of a computation on a range of implementation architectures. However, it is possible to compute the complexity of a computation on each individual architecture by examining the implemented cost of the primitive.

Parallel languages that require even less

of the programmer have also been suggested. One of the best known is Linda, which is perhaps best considered as a memory abstraction that may be used in many programming languages. Thus, C-Linda, Ada-Linda, and so on can all be built on the same abstraction. Linda provides the abstraction of a shared, content-addressable memory that can be accessed by any process with equal ease. Both scheduling and communication are handled by the system. Programmers need only specify dependencies. The memory is called tuple space, and the entities it contains are called tuples.

Four access mechanisms are provided:

- *in* selects, removes, and returns a tuple from the tuple space based on the number, types, and supplied values provided in the call; missing values are filled in from the values in the tuple;
- the primitive *read* selects and copies a tuple from the tuple space (so that the tuple is left in the tuple space for subsequent accesses);
- the primitive *out* places a tuple in the tuple space; and
- the primitive *eval* gets a tuple from the tuple space, treats it as executable code, and schedules it for execution.

This abstraction is very powerful because of its capability to access data based on partial descriptions and because of the capability to start new tasks with little overhead. Storage, synchronization, and communication are all managed by the same mechanism. In addition, tuple space might survive the execution of a single program; that is, it has some of the characteristics of a file.

However, the power of the abstraction creates problems for the implementer, particularly on a loosely coupled architecture. If each tuple exists only once in the tuple space, then accesses to it from other processors are necessarily slow; if the tuple is replicated, then it is hard to implement the semantics of *in* because *in* must guarantee that all copies other than the one returned are destroyed. The simulation of a large-content addressable memory, particularly one that may be accessed by a variety of different key patterns, is also challenging and creates substantial overhead. Thus, although Linda provides a very pleasant environment for the programmer, and one that makes portability straightforward, it does so at the expense of any guarantee about performance.

Linda also makes it difficult to capture fine-grained parallelism. For instance, the obvious implementation of +/*a* by

```
in(a, x)
in(a, y)
out(a, x+y)
```

fails because of the potential deadlock when the number of processors is as large or larger than the number of elements of the list. This seems unsatisfactory.

Another approach that requires no explicit control of scheduling or communication is K.M. Chandy and J. Misra's Unity and its relatives (see "Further reading"). A Unity program consists of a loop around a block of guarded statements. On any iteration of the loop, a statement whose guard evaluates to *true* is executed. The choice of statement is made nondeterministically. Such a program can be executed by a parallel computer by executing all statements whose guards are true in parallel. This simulates multiple iterations of the loop. Unity was developed as a language for reasoning about computation rather than executing computation. Whether Unity is implementable at any practical cost is not clear.

However, a related approach called *action systems* has been considered as an executable language. For example, R.J.R. Back shows how a sequential program in the formalism can be refined to a parallel program suitable for either shared-memory or loosely coupled architectures (see "Further reading"). The refinement preserves total correctness, so that the attractive reasoning properties can be retained even while operational notions such as parallelism are integrated. An implementation on a transputer system with reasonable performance exists.

The somewhat surprising result that a nontrivial computation model exists that is universal over four major classes of parallel architectures (tightly coupled, SIMD, hypercuboid, and constant-valence topology multiprocessors) provides the basis for an architecture-independent programming language. Programs developed in this language can be moved from machines in one architectural class to machines of another class without reprogramming and without paying performance penalties of more than constant factors. Thus, this new model provides the flexibility of Linda, but provides stronger guarantees about performance. Stronger results may yet be obtained, depending on progress in exploiting program optimization. This question is being investigated.

The programming language for this new model is closely related to the Bird-Meertens formalism. This relationship makes it possible to demonstrate that the language is quite expressive, since extensive algorithm development has been done within that formalism. Categorical results also increase confidence that the limited set of second-order functions included in the language is rich enough to capture all properties of general lists. In addition, these results provide a large set of algebraic identities that can be used for optimization. ■

Acknowledgments

Discussions with Bill McColl, Gaétan Hains, Laurie Hendren, and Kieran Herley greatly helped me with the content and presentation of this article, and I am grateful to them for their help. I also thank members of the Programming Research Group at the University of Oxford in England for their hospitality during my stay as a visiting researcher. The Natural Sciences and Engineering Research Council of Canada supported this work.

References

1. D.B. Skillicorn, "A Taxonomy for Computer Architectures," *Computer*, Vol. 21, No. 11, Nov. 1988, pp. 46-57.

2. L.G. Valiant, "General-Purpose Parallel Architecture," Tech. Report TR-07-89, Computer Science Dept., Harvard Univ., 1989.

3. K. Mehlhorn and U. Vishkin, "Randomized and Deterministic Simulation of PRAMs by Parallel Machines with Restricted Granularity of Parallel Memories," *Acta Informatica*, Vol. 21, 1984, pp. 339-374.

4. L.G. Valiant, "Optimally Universal Parallel Computers," *Proc. Royal Soc.*, 1987.

5. S.H. Bokhari and A.D. Raza, "Augmenting Computer Networks," in *Proc. Int'l Conf. Parallel Processing*, IEEE Computer Soc., Aug. 1984, pp. 338-345.

6. A. Aiken and A. Nicolau, "Optimal Loop Parallelization," in *Proc. SIGPlan 88: ACM Conf. on Programming Language Design and Implementation*, R. Wexelblat, ed., 1988, pp. 308-317.

7. R.S. Bird, "Algebraic Identities for Program Calculation," *The Computer J.*, Vol. 32, No. 2, Feb. 1989, pp. 122-126.

8. J.A. Goguen and T. Winkler, "Introducing OBJ3," Tech. Report SRI-CSL-88-9, Computer Science Lab., SRI Int'l, Aug. 1988.

9. D.R. Smith and M.R. Lowry, "Algorithm Theories and Design Tactics," in *Math. Program Construction*, Springer-Verlag

Lecture Notes in Computer Science 375, June 1989, pp. 379-398.

10. R.E. Ladner and M.J. Fisher, "Parallel Prefix Computation," *J. ACM*, Vol. 27, 1980, pp. 831-838.

11. J.M. Spivey, "A Categorical Approach to Theory of Lists," in *Math. Program Construction*, Springer-Verlag Lecture Notes in Computer Science 373, June 1989, pp. 399-408.

Further reading

Ahuja, S., et al., "Matching Languages and Hardware for Parallel Computation in the Linda Machine," *IEEE Trans. Computers*, Vol. 37, No.8, Aug. 1988, pp. 921-929.

Back, R.J.R., "A Method for Refining Atomicity in Parallel Algorithms," in *Parle 89, Parallel Architectures and Languages Europe*, Springer Lecture Notes in Computer Science 366, June 1989, pp. 199-216.

Back, R.J.R., and K. Sere, "Stepwise Refinement of Action Systems," in *Math. Program Construction*, Springer Lecture Notes in Computer Science 375, June 1989, pp. 115-138.

Backus, J., "Can Programming be Liberated from the von Neumann Style: A Functional Style and Its Algebra of Programs," *Comm. ACM*, Vol. 21, No. 8, Aug. 1978, pp. 613-641.

Backus, J., et al., "FL Language Manual, Parts 1 and 2," Tech. Report RJ7100, IBM Almaden Research Center, Oct. 1989.

Bird, R.S., "A Calculus of Functions for Program Derivation," Oxford Univ. Programming Research Group Monograph PRG-64, 1987.

Bird, R.S., "An Introduction to the Theory of Lists," in *Logic of Programming and Calculi of Discrete Design*, M. Broy, ed., Springer-Verlag, 1987 pp. 3-42.

Bird, R.S., "Lectures on Constructive Functional Programming," Oxford Univ. Programming Research Group Monograph PRG-69, 1988.

Blelloch, G., "Scans as Primitive Parallel Operations," in *Proc. Int'l Conf. Parallel Processing*, CS Press, Los Alamitos, Calif., Order No. 783, Aug. 1987, pp. 355-362.

Chandy, K.M., and J. Misra, *Parallel Program Design: A Foundation*, Addison-Wesley, 1988.

Dally, W.J., "Universal Mechanisms for Concurrency," in *Parle 89, Parallel Architectures and Languages Europe*, Springer-Verlag Lecture Notes in Computer Science 365, June 1989, pp. 19-33.

Meertens, L.G.L.T., "Algorithmics — Towards Programming as a Mathematical Activity," in *Proc. Dutch Center for Math. and Computer Science (CWI) Symp. Math. and Computer Science*, North-Holland, 1986, pp. 289-334.

Ranade, A.G., Fluent Parallel Computation, PhD thesis, Yale Univ., 1989.

Valiant, L., "A Bridging Model for Parallel Computation," *Comm. ACM*, Aug. 1990, pp. 103-111.

David B. Skillicorn is an associate professor in the Department of Computing and Information Science at Queen's University, Kingston, Ontario, Canada. His research interests are in parallelism, spanning architectures, languages, and compilers.

Skillicorn received a BSc in 1978 from the University of Sydney, Australia, and a PhD in 1981 from the University of Manitoba, Canada. He is a member of the IEEE Computer Society and the ACM.

Readers can write to Skillicorn at the Department of Computing and Information Science, Queen's University, Goodwin Hall, Kingston, Ontario, Canada K7L 3N6, e-mail skill@qucis.queensu.ca.

A methodology for the development and the support of massively parallel programs

Marco Danelutto [a,b], Roberto Di Meglio [a], Salvatore Orlando [a,b],
Susanna Pelagatti [a] and Marco Vanneschi [a]

[a] *Dipartimento di Informatica, Università di Pisa, Corso Italia 40, Pisa, Italy*
[b] *Pisa Science Center, Hewlett Packard Laboratories, Corso Italia 115, Pisa, Italy*

Abstract

Danelutto, M., R. Di Meglio, S. Orlando, S. Pelagatti and M. Vanneschi, A methodology for the development and the support of massively parallel programs, Future Generation Computer Systems 8 (1992) 205–220.

The most important features that a parallel programming language should provide are *portability, modularity*, and *ease of use*, as well as *performance* and *efficiency*. Current parallel languages are only characterized by some of these features. For instance, most of these languages allow programmers to efficiently exploit the massively parallel target machine. Unfortunately, the estimation of the performance of each application is usually made by the programmer, without the support of any tool. Moreover, the programs produced by using such languages are not portable or easily modifiable.

Here, we present a methodology to easily write efficient, high performance and portable massively parallel programs. The methodology is based on the definition of a new explicitly parallel programming language, namely P^3L, and of a set of compiling tools that perform automatic adaptation of the program features to the target architecture hardware. Target architectures taken into account here are general purpose, distributed memory, MIMD architectures. These architectures provide the scalability and low cost features that are necessary to tackle the goal of massively parallel computing.

Following the P^3L methodology, the programmer has just to specify the kind of parallelism he is going to exploit (pipeline, farm, data, etc.) in the parallel application. Then, P^3L programming tools automatically generate the process network that implements and optimizes, for the given target architecture, the particular kind of parallelism the programmer indicated as the most suitable for the application.

Keywords. Massive parallelism; optimization tools; MIMD architectures; high level languages.

1. Introduction

Most of the existing massively parallel applications developed for general purpose, distributed memory, MIMD machines are built of a mix of two kinds of code:

code that is necessary to implement *that* particular algorithm the programmer has in mind, and

code that is necessary to *adapt* the particular algorithm the programmer has in mind to the specific hardware that he is going to use.

Correspondence to: M. Danelutto, Dipartimento di Informatica, Università di Pisa, Corso Italia 40, Pisa, Italy.

The former kind of code, that in the following will be indicated with the name *true algorithmic code*, has mainly to cope with aspects such as sequential coding and parallelism structuring. The latter kind of code, henceforth called *machine dependent code*, has to cope with aspects such as interprocess and interprocessor communication handling, load balancing and process to processor mapping. In this context, *machine dependent code* does not mean code written by using instructions that are peculiar to a given machine. Conversely, it is meant to be a kind of code that takes into account the specific architecture in terms of number of processors, interconnection network topology, etc.

This dual nature of massively parallel application code leads to several important consequences when writing parallel programs using existing message-passing parallel languages:

- the parallel application code is *hard to write* as the programmer is forced to take into account the physical structure of the machine; in fact, the programmer is charged to write both the pure algorithmic code and the machine dependent code;
- the resulting application code *is not portable*, even over slightly different MIMD architectures; the machine dependent code may turn out to be useless moving from a given architecture to another one, or it may be the case that it turns out to be not sufficient;
- the machine dependent code, which should be automically optimized by means of compiling tools to guarantee both portability and performance, *cannot be easily recognized* mainly because it is mixed with the true algorithmic code.

Moreover, it has been observed that most of the massively parallel programs actually use a restricted set of *patterns* to exploit parallelism [12,16,18]. Thus, the process graph of massively parallel applications turns out to be *highly regular* and characterized by specific performance properties. This regularity is an essential feature of massively parallel programming. As an example, it can be used to improve the performance of a parallel application by transforming it into *locality of communications*. Applications exploiting just local communications can achieve higher performance onto architectures that have a limited interprocessor communication bandwidth. Yet, regularity can only be exploited if it can be recognized within the application code.

Within the *Pisa Parallel Processing Project* (P^4, a joint project of the Hewlett Packard Pisa Science Center and of the Department of Computer Science of the University of Pisa [13]), we are developing a *methodology* for the design and support of massively parallel programs. The methodology is aimed to overcome some of the typical problems found in massively parallel programming, which are strongly related to the machine-dependent/algorithmic code mix described above, namely

- portability
- automatic optimizability
- performance
- efficiency.

In particular, the methodology is based on the definition of two main components [1,2,8]:

- at high level, explicitly parallel programming language for massive parallel computing (*Pisa Parallel Programming Language*, P^3L), which provides as primitives a well defined, restricted set of parallelism exploitation patterns [8,11];
- a set of compiling and optimizing tools, which deals with all the machine dependent features in order to achieve performance and efficiency along with portability, reusability and maintainability of P^3L programs [9];

P^3L is built out of a sequential part and of a set of constructors for the exploitation of parallelism. This set includes constructors modeling standard parallelism patterns such as pipelining, processor farms and data parallelism. These constructors are provided as *language primitives*. P^3L applications can be written by using the sequential part of the language to describe the sequential portions of the algorithm, and the constructor set to model their parallel structure.

Thus the overall structure of a P^3L application turns out to be a hierarchical composition of constructors structuring portions of code which are either sequential or already structured by means of other constructors. This kind of composition is strictly functional and we are going to develop formal techniques to prove composition properties in the style of those developed in [6] for the Unity system or of those developed in [4] for functional programs.

This kind of approach to massively parallel programming has two main advantages:

- the programmer is not forced to take into account machine dependent features, thus achieving both portability and easy programmability goals;
- the regular, hierarchical application structure can be used by the compiling/optimizing tools to efficiently map (i.e. to implement) P^3L programs onto different MIMD target architectures.

The design of an efficient set of compiling/optimizing tools for P^3L is crucial to the success of the overall massively parallel programming methodology. Once the programmer has established the logical structure of the parallel application, the tools are charged to efficiently implement application code onto the target machine.

On the one hand, this implies that the compiling/optimizing tools have a deep knowledge of the target architecture. In other words, both the hardware structure of the machine and the costs associated with each basic machine mechanism (process creation, inter-process communication, etc.) are exposed to the tools.

On the other hand, the tools have to provide efficient solutions for problems such as mapping and load-balancing, which, in the general case, turn out to be NP-hard [5]. In our case, efficient heuristics and/or exact algorithms can be devised to address these issues, due to the usage of a *restricted* set of parallel constructors whose *performance properties* (concerning mapping, load balancing, scheduling, communication overlapping and so on) can be analytically modeled. Taking into account the results obtained by using these analytical models along with the specific features of the target architecture, the compiling/optimizing tools can choose one of the possible implementations, achieving the goals of maximizing performance and/or effciency. Finally, this restricted set of constructors is characterized by *semantic properties* that are essential for modular software development and correctness proofs.

2. P^3L

The main goals in the language design have been massive parallelism (vs. small scale parallelism), general purpose (vs. special purpose programming languages), portability (vs. specific machine architecture orientation), and efficiency, intended both as high performance and as efficiency in the (hardware and software) resource usage.

P^3L is a parallel language that forces the programmer to use a well defined set of patterns, in order to achieve parallelism exploitation. This is the most innovative feature of the language. It comes from the observation that massively parallel applications always exploit some kind of structured parallelism. While such a parallelism can be classified as pipeline, farm, geometric, and algorithmic, it is possible to recognize within the independent control flows generated during a parallel application execution a regular structure

obtained by hierarchically composing those patterns of parallelism.

P^3L is built of two main components [9]:
- a *sequential part*, which is used to write the sequential parts of the parallel application;
- a *set of parallelism exploitation patterns*, henceforth called *constructors*, which is used to compose both sequential and parallel parts of the application code in a *structured, hierarchical* way.

The sequential part of the language can be implemented choosing anyone of the current sequential programming languages. In the current version of P^3L, we choose a subset of C++ [7], just because of the large number of tools that is available for this language. The sequential part of the language is completely encapsulated into the parallel part of P^3L. C++ code is used to describe the behaviour of the sequential parts of the parallel application, but all the other parallel features of P^3L do not rely upon the concepts proper of C++. As an example, parameter passing between P^3L constructors of an application are handled by linguistic constructs that are external to the sequential C++ kernel.

The parallel part, i.e. the set of constructors, is used to deal with all those features related to parallelism exploitation. In this set, we included patterns that can be used to model:
- *pipelines* [14,15], by means of the `pipe` constructor;
- *iterative* and *recursive computations*, by means of the `loop` constructor;
- *process farms* [17], of different kinds, by means of the `farm` constructor;
- *vector processing* and *data parallel* computations, by means of the `geometric` constructor;
- *tree structured computations*, by means of the `tree` constructor.

The model of parallel application assumed by P^3L is a communicating process model, i.e. the application code generated by the P^3L compiling tools, starting from plain P^3L code, is a collection of communicating sequential processes. These processes are scheduled for execution according to a data-flow model, i.e. a process always waits for some input data and starts running as soon as the complete set of its input data is ready. However, the programmer does not specify, in the source code, this process structure. It is derived by the P^3L compiling tools. He has only

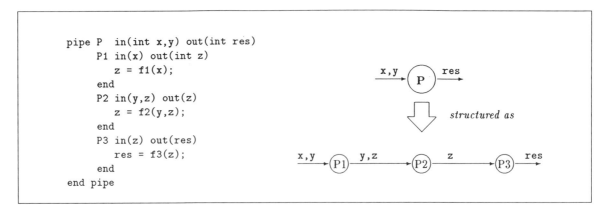

```
pipe P  in(int x,y) out(int res)
    P1 in(x) out(int z)
        z = f1(x);
    end
    P2 in(y,z) out(z)
        z = f2(y,z);
    end
    P3 in(z) out(res)
        res = f3(z);
    end
end pipe
```

Fig. 1. Pipe constructor.

to specify the kind of parallelism he wants to exploit. He specifies it by using a composition of parallelism exploitation constructors and sequential code.

Let us outline now the syntax and semantics of the constructors included in the language. For each constructor, we show an example of application code along with the corresponding process network, which points out the channels between the processes and the data to be transmitted.

Pipeline. *Figure 1* shows a typical pipe constructor.

Looking at the code, we can notice the constructs in(...) and out(...). They stand for the input and the output parameter lists of every P^3L constructors. For instance, in(int x,y) out(int res) are the parameters of the whole

pipe constructor P. The pipe constructor P comprises three stages, namely P1, P2 and P3. In this case the stages are sequential portion of code, but, in the general case, they may be parallel P^3L constructors. This assumption applies also to the other P^3L constructors. The functions computed by the three stages are $f1(\ )$, $f2(\ )$ and $f3(\ )$, respectively. Each stage Pi, $i \in \{1, 2, 3\}$, describes a process P_i, having specific input and output parameter lists, and executing its own sequential code each time it will be scheduled. In general, every process P_i starts working onto data incoming (as a result) from process P_{i-1}, and delivers its computed results to process P_{i+1}. As soon as process P_i delivers its results to the next pipeline process, it can begin a new computation on a new set of input data. In particular, the process corresponding to the first

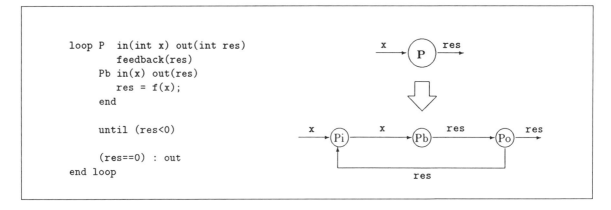

```
loop P  in(int x) out(int res)
        feedback(res)
    Pb in(x) out(res)
        res = f(x);
    end

    until (res<0)

    (res==0) : out
end loop
```

Fig. 2. Loop constructor.

stage of the pipeline (P_1 in the example above) starts executing its code on the data incoming to the whole `pipe` constructor, while data computed by the process corresponding to the last stage (P_3 in the example above) are returned as output of the whole `pipe` constructor.

It is worth noticing that in the above pipeline, the input parameter y is not consumed by the first stage of the pipe, but is read by process P_2 to compute function $f2(\ )$. Thus, y must go through process P_1 without being updated.

Loop. A typical loop structure is shown in *Fig. 2.* A `loop` constructor encapsulates a process (either sequential or parallel) and models iterative (recursive) computations. In this case, the encapsulated process is sequential, and is called `Pb`. It is executed first onto the data incoming to the constructor (specified in `in(int x)`). This means that the assignment `res=f(x)` is executed. Then the `until` Boolean condition is evaluated (`res<0` in the example above). If it is true, the execution of the constructor is terminated and the *output* data set (`res`) is delivered over the constructor output channel. Otherwise, the *feedback* data set is assumed as the new `loop` input and the execution is iterated. Only in this case, the guard condition (`res==0):out` is evaluated. This guard is optional. If the guard is true, before re-executing the loop, the *output* data set is output over the loop output channel.

On the right side of the code, we have shown the corresponding process network. Processes P_i

and P_o are compiler-generated, and their functioning reflects the behaviour illustrated above. P_i has to provide the merge between the data flowing over the loop input channel (x), and the data coming from the feedback input channel (`res`). Notice the feedback channel, which goes from P_o to P_i. Moreover, P_i has to activate the execution of process P_b, sending the input data x to it. If the loop works in pipeline, and P_i accepts input data (x) even when the previous loop computations are in progress, thus the problem of identifying the various computations must be addressed. Process P_o receives the output data `res` from P_b, and checks the Boolean conditions illustrated before, providing the necessary support to the feedback and the output channel activities.

Pure farm. A typical pure farm has the structure shown in *Fig. 3.*

When this farm constructor is executed, a number of *workers*, whose code corresponds to the sequential constructor `w`, are activated ($\{W_1, \ldots, W_n\}$ in the process network of *Fig. 3*). Each of these workers is able to compute the function $f(\ )$, as specified by the corresponding sequential code. The number of workers is determined by the P^3L compiling tools, on the basis of the specific architectural parameters. The goal that the tools have to achieve is the balance of the computational load between the workers involved.

The processes P_e and P_c are the *emitter* and the *collector* of the farm, respectively. The for-

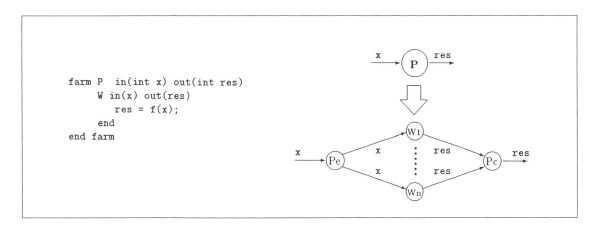

Fig. 3. Farm constructor.

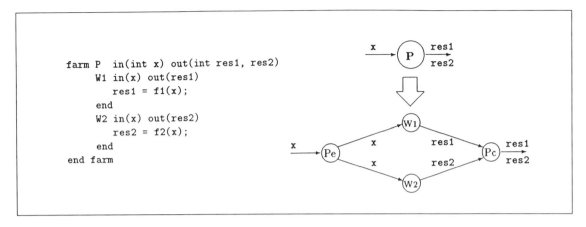

```
farm P  in(int x) out(int res1, res2)
     W1 in(x) out(res1)
         res1 = f1(x);
     end
     W2 in(x) out(res2)
         res2 = f2(x);
     end
end farm
```

Fig. 4. MISD farm constructor.

mer selects a worker to which the incoming data will be sent. The latter reorders the data produced by the various workers.

The farm constructor provides parallelism between distinct activations. In other words, there exists parallelism only if P receives a stream of input data. However, if the input data of the worker process is a data-partition of the input data of the whole farm constructor, then more workers must be activated to compute the output data of the farm. Each of these workers receives a partition of the input data of the farm. If this is the case, the output data of each worker must also be a data-partition of the output data of the whole farm. As an example of data partition, an

int basic type data-partitions an int[] array type.

MISD farm. The typical MISD farm is shown in *in Fig. 4.*
When the MISD farm is executed, the input data set, namely in(int x), is passed to *all* the process workers, i.e. W_1 and W_2. The results res1 and res2 of these computations are delivered as result of the whole MISD farm. In general, the function computed by a MISD farm is $x_i \rightarrow f_1(x_i), \ldots, f_n(x_i)$, if $f_i( )$ is the function computed by the ith worker of the farm.

Looking at the process network above, notice that process P_e has to broadcast the input data

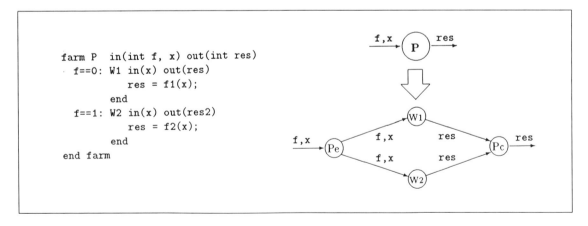

```
farm P  in(int f, x) out(int res)
   f==0: W1 in(x) out(res)
           res = f1(x);
         end
   f==1: W2 in(x) out(res2)
           res = f2(x);
         end
end farm
```

Fig. 5. Dedicated farm constructor.

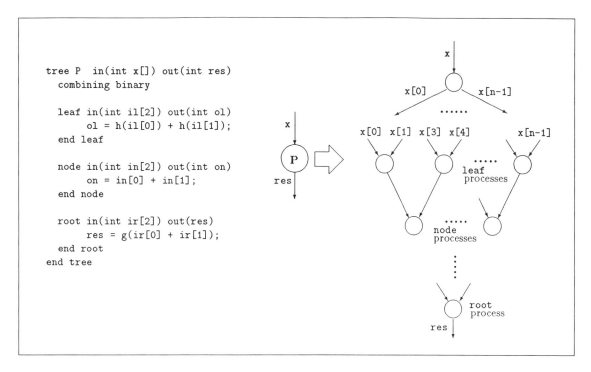

```
tree P  in(int x[]) out(int res)
  combining binary

  leaf in(int il[2]) out(int ol)
       ol = h(il[0]) + h(il[1]);
  end leaf

  node in(int in[2]) out(int on)
       on = in[0] + in[1];
  end node

  root in(int ir[2]) out(res)
       res = g(ir[0] + ir[1]);
  end root
end tree
```

Fig. 6. Tree constructor.

set to all the workers, while process P_c has to collect and order the data computed by all the workers.

Dedicated farm. The typical dedicated farm is illustrated in *Fig. 5*.

In this case the execution of each worker on a portion of the input data set of the whole constructor is conditioned by some *guards*. The input data of the constructor are processed by all those workers whose guards are satisfied. In the dedicated farm above, the guards are Boolean conditions on a portion of the input data set, namely f==0 and f==1. Logically, the emitter process (P_e in the corresponding process network) has to broadcast the input data to all the workers (W_1 and W_2), while the collector process (P_c) has to wait for the computation results from the workers, and has to return them as result of the whole farm.

Tree. An example of the tree constructor is shown in *Fig. 6*.

This tree constructor computes the following function of the vector $x = \langle x_0, \ldots, x_{n-1} \rangle$, (*n even*):

$$f(x) = g\left(\sum_{i=0}^{n-1} h(x_i) \right).$$

This kind of tree is called combining binary, as the resulting process network is a binary tree where data flow from the leaves to the root of the tree. If the tree had been declared as distributing binary, data would flow from the root to the leaves of the tree.

Notice that we have declared three kinds of processes, denoted by three distinct keywords of the language: *leaf*, *node* and *root*. They correspond to the three kinds of processes composing the tree. Since the tree has been declared as *binary*, each of of these processes will receive as input a 2-element vector of int, and will return as output an int value. The number of levels of this process tree is not specified by the programmer (see the process network shown on the right side of the code), but is derived by the compiling tools on the basis of the incoming data, i.e. on the basis of the dimensions of the input vector x.

325

Geometric. The code of *Fig. 7* corresponds to a geometric constructor whose topology is a *mesh*. This means that the *logical* interconnection network between the processing nodes onto which the various processes are to be mapped is a toroidal mesh.

First, the programmer has to define the topology that he wants to use (e.g. vector, array, mesh). Then, he must specify the data partitions (of the input/output data sets) to be mapped onto the various processing nodes of the topology chosen. For this purpose, some specific variables, called *free variables,* must be used. *i and *j are examples of this kind of variables. If n and m are the lengths of the two dimensions of the array x[][], the range of *i goes from 0 to $n-1$, while the range of *j goes from 0 to $m-1$. Finally, the code of each process must be defined. Notice that the data passed as input data set to each process denoted by the pair (*i, *j) are allocated ei-

ther to the same processing node, or to neighboring nodes with respect to the specific topology. On the other hand, the data set modified by each process, i.e. its output data set, has to be allocated onto the same processing node. In other words, only local data can be written to by every process. The topology dimension can either be inferred by the P^3L compiling tools or explicitly stated by the programmer, as in the example above.

As regards the algorithm computed by the code of *Fig. 7*, it computes a new array int res[][] from an initial array in x[][]. Specifically, the generic process (i, j) updates an element res[i][j] of the output array res. The computation performed by the process consists of a function $f(\ )$ applied to the element x[i][j] of the initial array (this elements is local to the process), and to other four elements of the array (these elements are allocated to the four neigh-

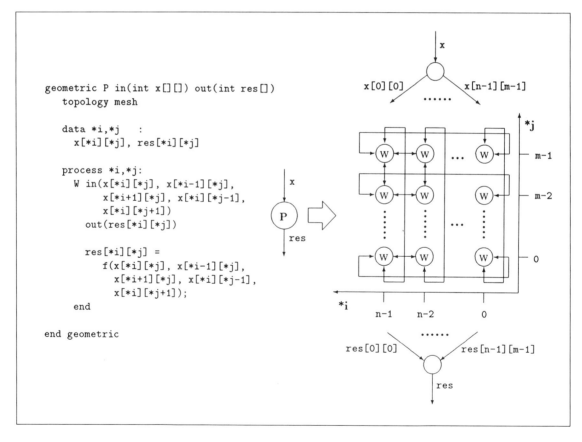

Fig. 7. Geometric constructor.

326

bours of the processing node onto which process (i, j) was mapped).

3. A simple application

Consider the following problem:

We want to implement a *function server* server such that it computes two specific functions, $f1(\ )$ and $f2(\ )$ onto a stream of input data $x_1, \ldots, x_k, \ldots$ Each stream item is a pair in which the first element indicates the name of the function that has to be applied to the second element of the pair ($x_i = \langle f_x, data_i \rangle$). The probability that a request for function $f1(\ )$ appears onto the input data stream is equal to the probability that a request for $f2(\ )$ appears. The computation of $f1(\ )$ takes much more time than the computation of $f2(\ )$ (say $10 \times$). It is known that function $f1(\ )$ can be decomposed in three pipeline stages, while function $f2(\ )$ cannot be split into stages. We want to have a parallel implementation of server written in P^3L.

The P^3L programmer, looking at the problem, has to devise which is, or are, the proper constructors that can be used to exploit *all* the parallelism implicit in the problem. He is not required to try to optimize the solution with respect to a given hardware machine, as this is exactly the job of the P^3L compiling tools.

At the very beginning, in the coding process, the programmer looks at the problem specification and he should be able to decide which kind of parallelism he wants to exploit. In the example, at this point, he should be able to decide that the following kinds of parallelism are worthwhile to be exploited:

farm parallelism to achieve parallel computation of functions $f1(\ )$ and $f2(\ )$;

pipeline parallelism, to parallelize the computation of the different steps of $f1(\ )$; this because from the problem specification it is known that $f1(\ )$ can be pipelined;

farm parallelism to achieve parallel computation of function $f1(\ )$ over different input data;

farm parallelism in the execution of $f2(\ )$ over different input data, as this is the only way he can enhance the throughput of a function which cannot be pipelined.

At this point, he can write the code, which turns out to look like the following:

```
#define F1 (1)
#define F2 (2)
```

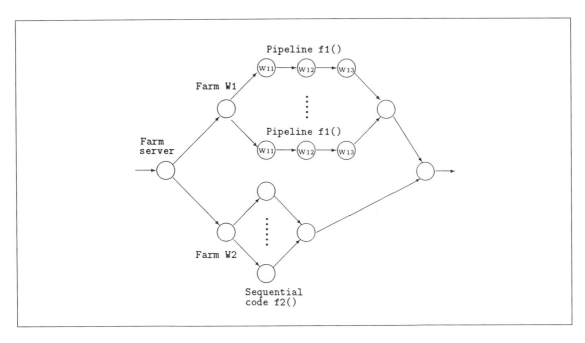

Fig. 8. Process structure for the example application.

327

```
farm W1 in(int datain) out(int result-
out)
  pipe
    W11 in(datain) out(int stage1)
      {sequential code for the first
      stage of f1}
    W12 in(stage1) out(int stage2)
      {sequential code for the second
      stage of f1}
    W13 in(stage2) out(resultout)
      {sequential code for the last
      stage of f1}
  end pipe
end farm

farm W2 in(int x) out(int resx)
  {sequential code for f2}
end farm

farm server in(int fun, data)
              out(int result)
  fun=F1: W1(data,result);
  fun=F2: W2(data,result);
end farm
```

This is all the code that the programmer has to write in order to implement a parallel function server. The process structure that will be created by the P^3L compiling tools is depicted in *Fig. 8*. It is worthwhile to note that, to obtain the same structure with any other parallel programming language, the programmer would have been forced to explicitly write the code for each process, the channel linking, the interprocessor communications and so on.

Notice also that in P^3L it is possible to define farm structures without explicitly specifying the number of workers at the source code level (this is the case for both the farm computing $f1( )$ and the farm computing $f2( )$). The most suitable number of workers (taking into account the characteristics of the target architecture) will be decided by the P^3L compiling tools.

4. The P^3L compiler

Once the programmer has specified all the kinds of parallelism he wants to exploit in the application, the P^3L compiling tools start transforming the original program until the optimized object code for the target machine is produced.

Notice that this approach is the opposite with respect to that usually followed in automatic parallelizing tools. Often, the programmer is requested to write code which is very similar to the sequential one. Then a set of parallelizing tools starts analyzing that code and produces automatically, some kind of parallel code.

In P^3L, the programmer writes the application code specifying *all* the parallelism he wants to exploit. Tools compile the program optimizing it for a specific architecture. However, they do not introduce any kind of parallelism exploitation but those patterns provided by the programmer. Yet, as the programmer specifies a *logical* pattern for parallelism exploitation, tools can perform significant optimizations onto the program, once the target architecture is known.

The P^3L compiler is built of a *front-end*, analyzing the source code and producing the internal representation of the program, a *middle-end*, performing target architecture specific optimizations, and a *back-end*, generating the object code of the application for a given target machine.

Actually, the back-end does not compile into a specific language. The P^3L compiler relies upon the existence of an abstract machine that exposes the hardware features in a suitable way. Within the P^4 project, this abstract machine is called P^3M [3]. This machine provides a set of mechanisms such as interprocess and interprocessor communication, interprocess synchronization, process scheduling and process-to-processor mapping directives, shared memory emulation, etc. Each one of these mechanisms is provided to the P^3L compiler along with its *time cost*. This cost obviously depends upon the target architecture features. Furthermore, the abstract machine provides the P^3L compiling tools with an abstract view of the machine architecture, mainly its topology, the amount of memory available at each node and the kind of processing elements included in each node.

The peculiar part of the P^3L compiling tools is the middle-end. Middle-end works on internal program representations. It is built out of a set of co-routines: the *process graph handler*, the *mapper* and the *load balancer*.

The process graph handler performs local optimizations onto the process graph, once this has been built by the first phase of the compiler middle-end, or once the mapper (or the load balancer) has built a new process graph derived from the composition of simpler process graphs.

The mapper chooses from a library of *weighted* possible mapping schemas the most suitable one. Here *weighted* means that, in the library, a *time cost* is associated with each mapping. The mapper uses the information provided by the abstract machine to make clever choices.

The load balancer tries to balance the load on each one of the processing elements involved in the computation. Like the mapper, the load balancer heavily uses the information provided by the abstract machine to achieve static load balancing.

In the next sections, the mapper and load balancer details will be discussed with respect to the example presented in Section 3.

4.1 The mapper

Once a program such as that of Section 3 has been transformed into an internal representation by the front-end, the mapper starts considering the mappings included in the *mapping library*. This library holds different mappings schemas related to the P^3L constructors and to different classes of architectures, along with a measure of their *costs*. These costs are in general defined as functions of a set of parameters that are provided by the underlying abstract machine. As an example, the cost of a mapping schema can be a function of either the network bandwidth or the context switching cost on the processing elements.

Suppose that the P^3L compiler has to map the server example onto a 2D-mesh architecture.

Let us consider the farm constructor. In the mapping library, there will be some mapping schemas for the farm constructor onto a 2D-mesh. Suppose that they are those presented in *Fig. 9*. In the figure, the single circles represent processors where routing processes or farm emitter (collector) processes have to be allocated. The double circles represent processor where farm workers have to be allocated.

In this case, let us suppose that the cost functions of the four mapping schemas depend upon

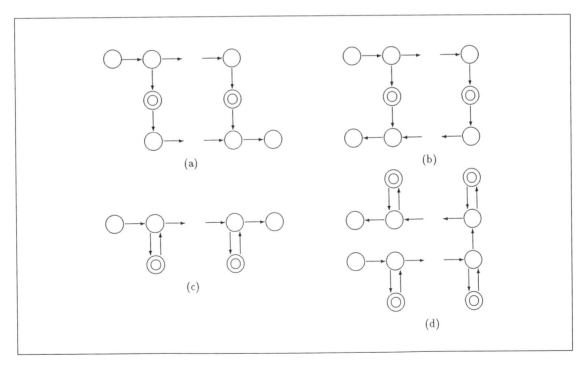

Fig. 9. Mapping schemas for the farm constructor onto a 2D-mesh architecture.

the following parameters:

τ_w that represents the time cost of a single job processed by one of the workers;

τ_e that represents the time cost for the emission of a single job by the emitter process for a generic worker process;

τ_c that represents the time cost for the collection of the results of a single job by the collector;

τ_p that represents the time cost spent in traversing one of the processors holding the routing processes (for the job distribution).

All these parameters are related to the characteristics of the hardware (as exposed by the abstract machine) and to the application structure.

The mapper evaluates the cost functions of these mapping schemas and decides which is the best one.

The assumptions stated here about the existence of such cost functions are not unrealistic. We studied the farm constructor [10] and we came up with some analytical formulation for these functions. For instance, for the mapping schemas shown in *Fig. 10(a)* or *(b)*, if we suppose that $\tau_p \geq \tau_e$ and $\tau_p > \tau_c$, the total execution time $\mathcal{T}_{\mathrm{ex}}$ can be expressed as

$$\mathcal{T}_{\mathrm{ex}} = \begin{cases} \tau_e + 2(n_w + 1)\tau_p + \dfrac{n_t}{n_w}\tau_w + \tau_c \\ \quad \text{if } n_w\tau_p \leq \tau_w \\ \tau_e + (n_t + n_w + 1)\tau_p + \tau_w + \tau_c \\ \quad \text{if } n_w\tau_p \geq \tau_w \text{ or } n_t \leq n_w, \end{cases} \quad (1)$$

where n_w is the number of workers and n_t is the number of jobs to be processed.

In the same way we can express the speedup function for the same mappings as

$$\mathcal{S}p = \begin{cases} \dfrac{n_t\tau_w}{\tau_e + 2(n_w + 1)\tau_p + \dfrac{n_t}{n_w}\tau_w + \tau_c} \\ \quad \text{if } n_w\tau_p \leq \tau_w \\ \dfrac{n_t\tau_w}{\tau_e + (n_t + n_w + 1)\tau_p + \tau_w + \tau_c} \\ \quad \text{if } n_w\tau_p \geq \tau_w \text{ or } n_t \leq n_w, \end{cases} \quad (2)$$

where $n_t\tau_w$ is the sequential execution time of the same sequence of tasks.

Furthermore, by means of this analytical modelling we can derive the maximum number of workers (n_w^{opt}) that can be included in a farm

without saturating the hardware communication bandwidth. Such number is derived from the speedup formula, supposing to know the values of τ_p, τ_e, τ_c and τ_w and to have a large number of tasks to be processed. In fact by deriving (1) and (2) we obtain

$$n_w^{\mathrm{opt}} = \frac{\tau_w}{\tau_p}.$$

Thus, the mapper not only decides which kind of mapping schema has to be used but also how many workers have to be included in the farms computing $f1(\ )$ and $f2(\ )$.

The mapping schemas that are included in the mapping library have been extensively studied with analytical techniques. Each of them represents some kind of 'best choice' mapping of a given constructor onto a given architecture.

4.2 Process graph handler

Once the mapper has devised a proper mapping for all the constructors belonging to the source code, the process graph handler optimizes the composition of such mappings.

In our case, the mapper decides that a mapping schema such as that of *Fig. 9(a)* can be used for farms. Now it has to be decided how to 'glue together' the three farms implementing the parallel function `server` (the one for $f1(\ )$, the one for $f2(\ )$ and the one for the overall `server`).

Process graph handler looks at another library where constructor mapping transformations are stored, i.e. possible transformations of mappings that do not alter the cost of the mapping but only its schema. An example of the information stored in such a library can be the following: schema (a) of *Fig. 9* can be transformed in schema (b) without modifying its time costs.

Such transformations turn out to be useful to optimize the mapping of a constructor composition.

In our case, the process graph optimizer will eventually find out the mapping of *Fig. 10*. In *Fig. 10*, E_1, E_2, E_s (C_1, C_2, C_s) represent processors where the farm emitter (collector) processes as been allocated ($f1(\ )$, $f2(\ )$ and `server` emitters, respectively). Double circles represent processors where farm worker processes have been allocated, as usual.

4.3. Load balancing

Static load balancing is performed at the P^3L compiling tools level in order to match architecture dependent and program process graph features.

As already stated, the P^3L programmer inserts code in the program that only states the *kind* of parallelism that has to be exploited, not its exact amount. Then, other routines of the P^3L compiling tools specify the missing *numerical parameters* such as the number of workers in the farm.

Such load-balancing routines try to make these parameters match the features of the underlying architecture, once that the overall process graph has been correctly dimensioned. This means, for instance, that it tries to enhance the efficiency achieved in the hardware resource usage by the program.

In our example, the mapper devises both the number of workers that has to be included in the farm computing $f1(\ )$ and the number of $f2(\ )$ workers. These numbers are computed using the analytical results briefly outlined in Section 4.1. Furthermore, the mapper is always assumed to have enough resources available to generate the maximum useful number of farm processes.

The amount of computing resources devised by the mapper can turn out to be unavailable for two main reasons:

- even if the machine is large enough to match the program requirements, yet, due to machine multiprocessing, an insufficient amount of resources is allocated to the program execution;
- the machine is not big enough with respect to the resources required by the program.

In both cases, the load balancer is called to transform the process structure generated by the mapper in such a way that the new process struc-

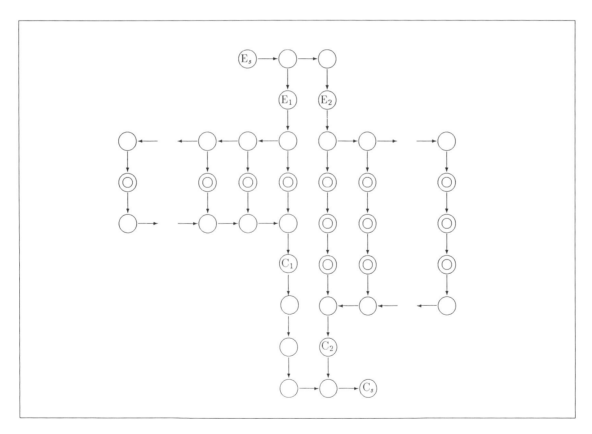

Fig. 10. Mapping of the example application onto a 2D-mesh architecture.

ture matches the actual machine configuration. In order to achieve this goal, the load balancer can take a set of choices:

(a) it can group a set of processes and schedule them onto a single physical node, in a multiprocessing environment; the processes grouped can be either 'user' processes (e.g. farm workers) or 'system generated' processes, such as the emitter or the collector farm process or the routing ones.

(b) it can vary some of the parameters devised by the mapping tool, such as the number of workers assigned to a farm. As the amount of resources assigned by the mapper is always the maximum with respect to the speedup achieved, then the parameters affected by the load balancer can only be made smaller.

In our example, the load balancer will eventually compute the times τ_{W1} and τ_{W2} that are spent in the computation of a single application $f1(x)$ and $f2(x)$ starting from the times $\tau_{w_{11}}$, $\tau_{w_{12}}$, $\tau_{w_{13}}$ and $\tau_{w_{f2}}$.

Once these times have been computed, the load balancer can take some decisions such as:

- Group onto the same node some of the processes that perform routing depicted in *Fig. 3*. Process C_1 can be moved up one position and process C_s can be allocated onto the node immediately below the one where process C_2 is allocated. This is an optimization of type (a) (referring to 'system generated' processes). (See *Fig. 11*.)

- Let us suppose that the time costs that have been computed for the pipeline stages are such that $\tau_{w_{11}}$ is bigger than the sum of the time costs of the other two stages. In this case, processes W_{12} and W_{13} can be allocated onto the same node without increasing the time cost of the overall pipeline. This is an optimization of type (a) (referring to 'user' processes).

- Looking at the time costs of the two farms computing $f1(\ )$ and $f2(\ )$, the load balancer can find out that $\tau_{w1} \gg \tau_{w2}$ and can decide to reduce the resources allocated to the execution of the second farm. This reduction can be achieved by either reducing the parameter n_{w_2} or grouping some of the worker processes of W_2 onto a single node. This is an optimization of type (b).

Once these optimizations have been performed, the process graph handler can be called again if

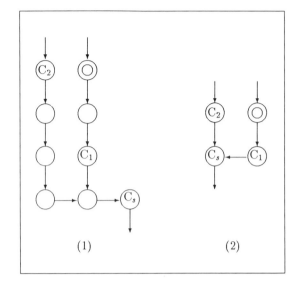

Fig. 11. Load balancer optimizations.

the load balancer has heavily modified the process graph structure.

All the optimizations performed by the load balancer described in this section do not produce any improvement in the performance of the parallel program. They only affect the efficiency in the hardware usage.

Other kind of load balancing will be taken into account later on in the P^4 project. As an example, dynamic load balancing will be taken into account to efficiently implement some particular kinds of process farms, where workers have different loads depending on the problem data.

5. Conclusions

Here, we have discussed a new approach to massively parallel architecture programming.

The key idea of this new approach is that the programmer is only required to specify the kind of parallelism he wants to exploit within the parallel application. All the other stuff needed to implement a parallel computation, such as devising a proper process graph, setting up interprocess communication structure or optimizing the implementation with respect to a particular hardware architecture, is completely in charge of the language compiling tools.

This approach allows portability to be achieved along with performance, efficiency and easy program writing.

In this paper we briefly outlined the P^3L programming language. Then we have gone through a working example trying to illustrate the techniques employed in the compiling tools construction. We have not been very formal, but the intended meaning has been to give a general overview of the work we have made around P^3L.

Our first studies on this approach to programming massively parallel applications have already produced interesting results, and much more work is currently under way in the University of Pisa and the Pisa Science Center in order to create a complete programming environment for distributed memory, general-purpose MIMD architectures.

We are currently developing a prototype implementation of a first version of the language, in order to test the approach and the mapping and load balancing heuristics. Analytical techniques are being applied to define cost formulas for all constructors included in P^3L, and at the same time different formal techniques are being considered in order to develop a suitable proof system for the correctness of P^3L programs.

References

[1] F. Baiardi, M. Danelutto, M. Jazayeri, S. Pelagatti and M. Vanneschi, Architectural models and design methodologies for general-purpose highly-parallel computers, in: *Proc. IEEE CompEuro '91 – Advanced Computer Technology, Reliable Systems and Applications* Bologna, Italy (May 1991).

[2] F. Baiardi, M. Danelutto, R. Di Meglio, M. Jazayeri, M. Mackey, S. Pelagatti, F. Petrini, T. Sullivan and M. Vanneschi, Pisa parallel processing project on general-purpose highly-parallel computers, in: *Proc. COMPSAC '91* (Sep. 1991).

[3] F. Baiardi, M. Jazayeri, M. Mackey, F. Petrini and M. Vanneschi, P^3M: An abstract architecture for massively parallel machines, in: *Workshop on Abstract Machine Models for Highly Parallel Computers*, Leeds, UK (Apr. 1991).

[4] R.S. Bird, Lectures on constructive functional programming, in: M. Broy, ed., *Constructive Methods in Computing Science*, NATO ASI Series, 1988, International Summer School directed by F.L. Bauer, M. Broy, E.W. Dijkstra and C.A.R. Hoare.

[5] T.L. Casavant and J.G. Kuhl, A taxonomy of scheduling in general-purpose distributed computing systems, *IEEE Trans. Software Engrg.*, 14 (2) (Feb. 1988) 141–154.

[6] K.M. Chandy and J. Misra, *Parallel Program Design: A Foundation* (Addison-Wesley, Reading, MA, 1988).

[7] S.C.D. and K.T. Stark, *Programming in C + +* (Prentice Hall Software Series, Englewood Cliffs, NJ, 1989).

[8] M. Danelutto, R. Di Meglio, S. Pelagatti and M. Vanneschi, High level language constructs for massively parallel computing, in: *ISCIS VI, Sixth Internat. Symp. on Computer and Information Sciences* (Elsevier, Amsterdam, 1992) (to appear).

[9] M. Danelutto, S. Pelagatti and S. Orlando, P^3L, The Pisa Parallel Programming Language, Technical Report HPL-PSC-91-27, Hewlett Packard Laboratories, Pisa Science Center (Italy), 1991.

[10] M. Danelutto, S. Pelagatti and M. Vanneschi, An analytical study of the processor farm, Technical Report HPL-PSC-91-22, Hewlett Packard Laboratories, Pisa Science Center (Italy), 1991.

[11] M. Danelutto, S. Pelagatti and M. Vanneschi, High level languages for easy massively parallel programming, Technical Report HPL-PSC-91-16, Hewlett Packard Laboratories, Pisa Science Center (Italy), 1991.

[12] A.J.G. Hey, Experiments in MIMD parallelism, in: *PARLE 1989 (LNCS 365, Springer, Berlin, 1989).*

[13] M. Jazayeri and M. Vanneschi, Pisa Parallel Processing Project: An Introduction, Technical Report HPL-PSC-90-1, Hewlett Packard Laboratories, Pisa Science Center (Italy), 1990.

[14] C.T. King, W.H. Chou and L.M. Ni, Pipelined data-parallel algorithms: part I-Concept and modeling, *IEEE Trans. Parallel Distributed Syst.* 1 (4) (Oct. 1990).

[15] C.T. King, W.H. Chou and L.M. Ni, Pipelined data-parallel algorithms: Part II-Design, *IEEE Trans. Parallel Distributed Syst.* 1 (4) (Oct. 1990).

[16] H.T. Kung, Computational models for parallel computers, in: *Scientific Applications of Multiprocessors* (Prentice Hall, Englewood Cliffs, NJ, 1989).

[17] D. May, R. Stepherd and C. Keane, Communicating process architecture: Transputers and occam, in: P. Treleaven and M. Vanneschi, eds., *Future Parallel Computers*, Vol. 272 of *Lecture Notes in Computer Science* (Springer, Berlin, 1987) 35–81.

[18] D.B. Skillicorn, Architecture-independent parallel computation, *IEEE Comput.* (Dec. 1990) 38–50.

Marco Danelutto received the 'Laurea' degree cum laude and the Ph. D. degree in Computer Science from the University of Pisa in 1984 and 1989, respectively.

He is currently a researcher at the Department of Computer Science, University of Pisa.

He is involved in the research activity of the Hewlett Packard Pisa Science Center, where he is leading the P^3L resarch group.

His research interests include parallel execution of functional programs, fine grain parallelism exploitation through instruction level parallelism, massively parallel, variable grain parallel machine design and formal tools for program verification.

Roberto Di Meglio received the Laurea degree cum laude in Computer Science from the University of Pisa in 1990.

He is currently a Ph. D. student at the Department of Computer Science of the University of Pisa and is also involved in the research activity of the Hewlett Packard Pisa Science Center on the P^4 project.

His main research interests are in the area of parallel languages, methodologies for software development on massively parallel architectures, artificial intelligence and computer graphics.

Salvatore Orlando received a Laurea degree cum laude and a Ph. D. degree in computer science from the University of Pisa in 1985 and 1990, respectively.

He is currently a research fellow at the Hewlett Packard Pisa Science Center, where he is involved in the research activity of the P^3L group.

His research interests include parallel languages, medium-fine grain parallelism exploitation, optimizing and parallelizing static tools, synchronous execution models for parallel architectures, parallel algorithm design and implementation, and fault-tolerant parallel systems.

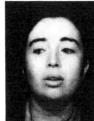

Susanna Pelagatti received the Laurea degree cum laude in Computer Science from the University of Pisa in 1987.

She is currently a Ph. D. student at the Department of Computer Science, University of Pisa, and she is involved in the research activity of the Hewlett Packard Pisa Science Center, where she cooperates with the P^3L group.

Her current research interests include mapping and modelling of concurrent programs, methodologies and languages for massively parallel architectures.

Marco Vanneschi graduated in Electronic Engineering at the University of Pisa in 1970. In 1973, he joined the University of Pisa, Department of Computer Science, as assistant professor in Computer Architecture. Since 1980, he has been full professor in Computer Science at the same department.

His research activity is in the context of computer architecture at several abstraction levels. Specific activities have been: microprogramming and microprogrammable machine architecture, architectural models and performance evaluation of pipeline machines, concurrency models, data-flow languages and architectures, multiprocessor architectures, concurrent languages, distributed systems and fault-tolerance.

For several years, he has been leading the parallel computer architecture group at the Department of Computer Science, University of Pisa, working on models, languages and tools for highly parallel machines.

He is author of more than 70 papers published in international journals and conference proceedings, and of three books on computer architecture, microprogramming and concurrent programming respectively.

BULK SYNCHRONOUS PARALLEL COMPUTING

W F McColl

Programming Research Group,
Oxford University,
11 Keble Road,
Oxford OX1 3QD,
England.

Email: `mccoll@prg.oxford.ac.uk`

Abstract

Bulk synchronous parallel architectures offer the prospect of achieving both scalable parallel performance and architecture independent parallel software. They provide a robust model on which to base the future development of general purpose parallel computing systems. In this paper we discuss some of the current issues involved in the development of parallel systems which support both fine grain concurrency and global memory models. We describe the BSP and PRAM models, and demonstrate how they can be efficiently realised on distributed memory parallel architectures.

1.1 Introduction

For most of the 1980s, low level hardware considerations have been the main driving force in parallel computing. Rapid progress in VLSI technology has permitted the development of a wide variety of distributed memory multicomputer architectures (Athas and Seitz 1988, INMOS Limited 1988, Seitz 1985, Seitz 1990, Whitby-Strevens 1985). These systems consist of a set of general purpose microprocessors connected by a sparse network, e.g. array, butterfly or hypercube. The relatively low speed and capacity of such networks forces the programmer to think in terms of a model in which one has multiple private address spaces connected in some complex way, e.g. in a hypercube structure, with explicit message passing by the programmer (Hoare 1985, Hoare 1991, Jones and Goldsmith 1988) for all non-local memory requests. The key to algorithmic efficiency in such systems is the careful exploitation of network locality. By minimising the number of nodes through which a message has to travel one can substantially improve efficiency. Despite the programming difficulties inherent in this approach, a large amount of scientific and technical applications software has been developed for such systems. In positive terms, this work has demonstrated conclusively that for many important applications, scalable parallel performance can be achieved in massively parallel systems (Gustafson 1988a, Gustafson 1988b), despite the reservations expressed by Amdahl (Amdahl 1967). However, in this message passing approach, most of the effort in software development tends to be devoted to the various low level process mapping activities which need to be performed to achieve efficiency. Besides being extremely tedious in many cases, this usually produces software which cannot easily be adapted to another architecture. In a world of rapidly changing parallel architectures, this architecture-dependence has proved to be a major weakness, and it has inhibited the growth of the field beyond the area of scientific research.

An alternative approach, which has been extensively pursued by computer science researchers in the last decade, is to make software the driving force. A variety of approaches of this kind have been investigated. They differ in terms of the type of programming language considered, e.g. functional (Bird and Wadler 1988, Hudak 1989, Hudak *et al.* 1991) , single assignment, logic, mostly functional, and in the computational model which they adopt, e.g. graph reduction, rewriting, dataflow. However, they share a number of similarities, particularly in comparison to the framework proposed in this paper. One example of this approach is where one starts by noting that a high level functional language (Bird and Wadler 1988, Hudak 1989, Hudak *et al.* 1991) (if properly used) can often expose a large amount of implicit parallelism in a computational problem. The decision to work with a functional language, for reasons of architecture-independence, naturally leads to a decision to adopt, say, graph reduction as the model of parallel computation. The technological (hardware) goal is then to develop a scalable massively parallel architecture for graph reduction (Peyton Jones 1989). This "software first" approach has a great deal of merit given that hardware is changing rapidly and that the cost and time required to produce software makes architecture-independence in software a major goal. Unfortunately, however, the amount of progress which has been made on the development of efficient parallel architectures for graph reduction, dataflow or rewriting has not been particularly impressive so far, despite much effort. The experiences of the last decade suggest that, in the pursuit of efficiency, it is often necessary to compromise some of the elegance and simplicity of such approaches. To a large extent, this has already happened in dataflow implementations of functional languages, e.g. the implementation of Id (Nikhil 1991) on Monsoon (Papadopolous and Traub 1991). Modern dataflow architectures (Iannucci 1988, Iannucci 1990, Nikhil and Arvind 1989, Nikhil *et al.* 1991, Papadopolous and Traub 1991) are in many important respects quite close to those described in this paper. For example, they must achieve latency tolerance through multithreading since, in the dataflow model, memory accesses are *split transactions* (Nikhil *et al.* 1991). (In the dataflow model, a read may be requested before the value is computed.)

A third alternative is to have some model of parallel computation as the driving force. Around 1944, von Neumann produced a proposal (Burks *et al.* 1946, von Neumann 30 June 1945) for a general purpose stored-program sequential computer which captured the fundamental principles of Turing's work (Turing 1936) in a practical design. The design, which has come to be known as the "von Neumann computer", has served as the basic model for almost all sequential computers produced from the late 1940s to the present time. As noted in (Hennessy and Patterson 1990), "The paper by Burks, Goldstine and von Neumann ((Burks *et al.* 1946)) was incredible for the period. Reading it today, one would never guess this landmark paper was written more than 40 years ago, as most of the architectural concepts seen in modern computers are described there." For an account of the principles of modern general purpose sequential (i.e. von Neumann) computer design, see (Hennessy and Patterson 1990). For sequential computation, the stability of the von Neumann model has permitted the development, over the last three decades, of a variety of high level languages and compilers. These have, in turn, encouraged the development of a large and diverse software industry producing portable applications software for the wide range of von Neumann machines available, from personal computers to large mainframes. The stability of the underlying model has also allowed the development of a robust complexity theory for sequential computation, and a set of algorithm design and software development techniques of wide applicability. General purpose sequential computing based on the von Neumann model has developed vigorously over the last four decades. The widespread adoption of the model has not proved to be a harmfully constraining influence, in fact, it has been quite the reverse. A variety of hardware approaches have flourished within the framework provided by the model. The stability it has provided has been invaluable for the development of the software industry.

No single model of parallel computation has yet come to dominate developments in parallel computing in the way the von Neumann model has dominated sequential computing (Gear 1991, Valiant 1990a, Valiant 1990b). Instead we have a variety of models such as VLSI systems, systolic arrays and distributed memory multicomputers in which, as we have noted, the careful exploitation of network locality is crucial for algorithmic efficiency. We will use the generic term "special purpose" to refer to this type of parallel computing. In (McColl 1993c) we describe a number of aspects of the work which has been done in recent years on the design, analysis, implementation and verification of such special purpose parallel computing systems. A major challenge for contemporary computer science is to determine the extent to which general purpose parallel computing can be achieved. The goal is to deliver both scalable parallel performance and architecture independent parallel software. (Work on special purpose parallel computing (McColl 1993c), and on architectures for declarative languages (Hudak 1989,

Hudak *et al.* 1991, Nikhil 1991, Nikhil and Arvind 1989, Nikhil *et al.* 1991, Papadopolous and Traub 1991), having demonstrated that either of these alone can be achieved.)

Can we identify a robust model of parallel computation which offers the prospect of achieving the twin goals of general purpose parallel computing - scalable parallel performance and architecture-independent parallel software ?

Success in this endeavour would permit the long overdue separation of software and hardware considerations in parallel computing. This separation would, in turn, encourage the growth of a large and diverse parallel software industry, and provide a focus for future hardware developments.

The achievement of these goals would have profound consequences for the future development of both the computing industry and the academic subject of computer science. Given this fact, one might suspect that this issue would be central to much of the current research in parallel computing. However, at present, relatively little work is being done with these goals directly in mind. Much of the practical work in massively parallel computing today is concerned with the development of scientific applications software, without particular regard for the development of a credible strategy which would permit portability of that software as new architectures appear.

The current situation in parallel computing is remarkably chaotic when compared with that of sequential computing. With no agreed model to provide a focus for technological innovation, parallel hardware suppliers continue to develop, and attempt to market, systems with widely differing characteristics. Those people with the unenviable task of choosing a parallel system for their organisation are faced with the prospect of investing substantial resources in the purchase of such a machine, and in the development of software for it, only to find that the software quite quickly becomes obsolete. At the present time, the MFLOP performance of the processors used in parallel systems is increasing rapidly. Unfortunately, this is not being matched by corresponding increases in communications performance. This rising imbalance is likely to further increase the difficulty of achieving architecture-independence in software. An important general message of the results in this paper is that architecture-independence is more likely to be achieved in those parallel systems which invest more substantially in communications performance than in processor performance. It is striking that relatively few of the commercial parallel systems being produced today seem to reflect this basic idea.

The current chaos in parallel computing has led many to conclude that the answer to the above question, on the prospects for agreement on a model, is no. Advocates of "heterogeneous parallel computing" (Kung 1991) take as their starting point the idea that no convergence on a model is likely to take place. They argue that a wide variety of designs which are to some extent "special purpose" will continue to be produced and marketed, and that the primary function of parallel computing should be to develop languages and communications networks for the coordination of these ensembles of devices. It is again striking that many in computing have already accepted the inevitability of this rather pessimistic scenario, especially as no serious theoretical impediments to the achievement of the goals of general purpose parallel computing have yet been identified, despite much effort to find them. One can contrast this with the situation in complexity theory where the ideas of NP-completeness have demonstrated in a precise way that many desirable goals in terms of algorithmic performance, for problems in AI, scheduling, optimisation etc. are unlikely to be achievable and that we must, in some way, limit our expectations. There is no compelling evidence that general purpose parallel computing, as described above, cannot be achieved. We can be reasonably confident that, as future hardware developments alone fail to significantly increase the market for parallel systems, the manufacturers of those systems will see it as in their interests to seek convergence on a model, rather than to seek to avoid it. A major goal for computer science today is to develop the ideas and techniques which will provide the required solutions when that change in thinking comes about.

In this paper we will describe one way possible way forward for parallel computing, based on the bulk synchronous parallel (BSP) model of computation (Valiant 1990a). While we believe that this approach has many strengths, we would not want to argue that it is the only viable approach. Two alternatives, which merit serious consideration, are the actor model (Agha 1990) and the dataflow model (Iannucci 1988, Iannucci 1990, Nikhil 1991, Nikhil and Arvind 1989, Papadopolous and Traub 1991). The most fundamental difference between these two approaches and the BSP model is that they both have at their core the idea of local (usually pairwise) synchronisation events, whereas the BSP model, as well as various PRAM (Gibbons and Spirakis 1993, JáJá 1992, Valiant 1990b, Vishkin 1991b) and data parallel models (Blelloch 1990, Hillis and Steele Jr 1986), have the idea of global barrier synchronisation as the basic mechanism. Another significant difference is that in the BSP, PRAM and data parallel approaches there is usually tight control of ordering and scheduling by the programmer. In contrast, a major attraction of the dataflow approach is that the programmer is freed from consideration of such issues. Although we have stressed the differences between these various approaches, there is reason to believe that, at the architectural level, the BSP, PRAM, actor and dataflow models will require a number of similar mechanisms for efficient implementation, in particular, high performance global communications, uniform memory access, and multithreading to hide network latencies. It is perhaps not unreasonable to summarise the current situation with respect to these various approaches as follows. Work on the actor and dataflow models is much more highly developed in the areas of programming languages and methodologies than it is in the area of algorithm design, analysis and complexity. In contrast, for the BSP and PRAM models we have a highly developed set of techniques for the design and analysis of algorithms, but we do not yet have an established framework for the programming of such systems.

1.2 Parallel Random Access Machine

Various idealised models of parallel computation have been used in the study of parallel algorithms and their complexity. Of these, the most widely studied has been the parallel random access machine. A *parallel random access machine (PRAM)* consists of a collection of processors which compute synchronously in parallel and which communicate with a common global random access memory. In one time step, each processor can do (any subset of) the following - read two values from the common memory, perform a simple two-argument operation, write a value back to the common memory. There is no explicit communication between processors. Processors can only communicate by writing to, and reading from, the common memory. The processors have no local memory other than a small fixed number of registers which they use to temporarily store the argument and result values. In a *Concurrent Read Concurrent Write (CRCW) PRAM*, any number of processors can read from, or write to, a given memory cell in a single time step. In a *Concurrent Read Exclusive Write (CREW) PRAM*, at most one processor can write to a given memory cell at any one time. In the most restricted model, the *Exclusive Read Exclusive Write (EREW) PRAM*, no concurrency is permitted either in reading or in writing. The CRCW PRAM model has a large number of variants which differ in the convention they adopt for the effect of concurrent writing. Three simple examples of such conventions are : two or more processors can write so long as they write the same value, one of the processors attempting to write will succeed but the choice of which one will succeed will be made nondeterministically, the lowest numbered processor will succeed (assuming some appropriate numbering.) In other CRCW models (Ranade 1989) one might have the possibility of concurrent writing in which the memory location is updated to the sum of the written values, or to the minimum of the written values. An important characteristic of the PRAM model is that it is a one-level memory (or shared memory) model, i.e. all of the memory locations are uniformly far away from all of the processors, the processors have no local memory and there is no kind of memory hierarchy based on ideas of network locality. These simplifying properties of the PRAM model have made it extremely attractive as a robust model for the design, analysis and comparison of algorithms, and we now have a large set of PRAM algorithms for important problems (Gibbons and Spirakis 1993, JáJá 1992, Kruskal *et al.* 1990, Vishkin 1991b).

In discussing the complexity of PRAM algorithms we normally refer only to the parallel time complexity and the number of processors required. However, the communication complexity of PRAM algorithms, in a simplified setting, has also been studied by a number of researchers, see, for example (Jung *et al.* 1989, Papadimitriou and Ullman 1987, Papadimitriou and Yannakakis 1990). In their work, the computational problem to be solved is modeled as a dag, with nodes corresponding to the functions computed and arcs corresponding to functional dependencies. The task is to efficiently schedule the dag on a p processor parallel system which may have a large local memory at each processor, i.e. to assign each node of the dag to one or more processors in the system which will compute that node. A schedule must satisfy the constraint that a node can only be computed at a given time step if its predecessors have been computed in previous time steps. Communication complexity is captured in an obvious way. If node v depends on node u, i.e. there is an arc from u to v in the dag, and u, v are computed in distinct processors then that arc is said to be a communication arc. The communication complexity c of a given schedule is simply the number of communication arcs in the dag. This measure captures an important practical cost in the implementation of parallel algorithms on a multiprocessor system, i.e. the total message traffic generated. A number of important results have been obtained for this model, showing tradeoffs between the time required for a parallel computation and the total number of messages which must be sent. Algorithms for scheduling dags have also been developed. Such work may provide a theoretical basis for the future development of software tools which efficiently schedule shared memory parallel algorithms for implementation on distributed memory architectures.

Aggarwal, Chandra and Snir (Aggarwal *et al.* 1990) have also studied the communication complexity of PRAM algorithms. They consider the design of efficient algorithms for a model called the *local memory PRAM*, or *LPRAM*, which also captures both the communication and computation requirements of PRAM algorithms in a convenient way. An LPRAM is a CREW PRAM in which each processor is provided with an unlimited amount of local memory. Processors can simultaneously read from the same location in the global memory, but two or more are not allowed to simultaneously write into the same location. The input variables are initially available in the global memory, and the outputs must also be eventually there. The multiprocessor is a synchronous MIMD machine. In order to model the communication delay and computation time, it is convenient to restrict the machine such that, at every time step, the processors do one of the following :

- In one communication step, a processor can write, and then read a word from global memory.

- In a computation step, a processor can perform a simple operation on at most two values that are present in its local memory.

A computation is represented as a dag, and a schedule for a dag consists of a sequence of computation steps and communication steps. At a computation step each processor may evaluate a node of the dag; this evaluation can only take place at a processor when its local memory contains the values corresponding to all of the incoming arcs. After the computation step is completed the values for the outgoing arcs are held in the local memory. At a communication step, any processor may write into the global memory any value that is presently in its local memory, and then it may read into its local memory a value from the global memory. They analyse a number of important problems, in terms of the two LPRAM complexity measures, parallel time (number of computation steps) and communication delay (number of communication steps).

A major issue in theoretical computer science since the late 1970s has been to determine the extent to which the PRAM and related models can be efficiently implemented on physically realistic distributed memory architectures. A number of new routing and memory management techniques have been developed which show that efficient implementation is indeed possible in many cases (McColl 1993a, Valiant 1990a, Valiant 1990b). The efficient implementation of a single address space on a distributed memory architecture requires an efficient method for the distributed routing of read and write requests, and of the replies to read requests, through the network of processors. Consider the problem of packet routing on a p-processor network. Let an *h-relation* denote the routing problem where each processor has at most h packets to send to various points in the network, and where each processor is also due to receive at most h packets from other processors. We are interested in the development of distributed routing methods in which the routing decisions made at a node at some point in time are based only on information concerning the packets that have already passed through the node at that time. Using *two-phase randomised routing* (Valiant 1990b) we can show the following

Theorem 1.2.1 *With high probability, every 1-relation can be realised on a p processor cube-connected-cycles, butterfly, 2D array and hypercube in a number of steps proportional to the diameter of the network.*

Theorem 1.2.2 *With high probability, every (log p)-relation can be realised on a p processor hypercube in $O(log\ p)$ steps.*

Proofs of Theorems 1.2.1 and 1.2.2 can be found in (Valiant 1990b). (In addition to such theoretical results, randomised routing has also been shown, in many studies, to work extremely well in practice.) In order to show that we can efficiently simulate a shared address space on a distributed memory architecture we also need to show that we can deal with the problem of "hot spots", i.e. where a large number of processors simultaneously try to access the same memory module. One very effective method of uniformly distributing memory references, which has now been widely studied, is to hash the single address space. A detailed technical account of the role of hashing in achieving efficient general purpose parallel computing on a distributed memory architecture can be found in (Valiant 1990b). We will only mention here the following two results which demonstrate that certain distributed memory architectures can efficiently simulate PRAMs. Let $EPRAM(p,t)$ [$CPRAM(p,t)$, $HYPERCUBE(p,t)$, $COMPLETE(p,t)$] denote the class of problems which can be solved on a p processor EREW PRAM [CRCW PRAM, hypercube, completely connected network, respectively] in t time steps.

Theorem 1.2.3. ((Valiant 1990b))
With high probability, $EPRAM(p \log p, t/\log p) \subseteq HYPERCUBE(p,t)$.

Theorem 1.2.4. ((Karp *et al.* 1992))
With high probability,
$CPRAM(p \log \log p \log^* p, t) \subseteq COMPLETE(p, t \log \log p \log^* p)$.

Theorems 1.2.3 and 1.2.4 show that PRAM algorithms with a degree of parallel slackness can be implemented on distributed memory architectures in a way which is optimal in terms of the processor-time product.

Definition 1.2.5 *An m processor algorithm, when implemented on an n processor machine, where $n \leq m$, is said to have a parallel slackness factor of m/n for that machine.*

Parallel slackness is an idea of fundamental importance in the area of general purpose parallel computing. If parallel algorithms and programs are designed so that they have more parallelism than is available in the machine, then the available parallel slackness can be effectively exploited to hide the kind of network latencies one finds in distributed memory architectures. The only requirement is that the processors provide efficient support for multithreading and fast context switching (Blumofe 1992, Nikhil *et al.* 1991, Papadopolous and Traub 1991). Latency tolerance via multithreading is likely to be more effective on large scale general purpose parallel computing systems than the use of complex caching schemes for latency reduction.

The idea of exploiting parallel slackness can even be carried over into the area of sequential computing. Much effort in recent years has been devoted to the development of complex heuristic techniques for the efficient prefetching of values from memory in sequential computations. A radical alternative to this approach is, instead, to design parallel algorithms for implementation on sequential machines. The parallel slackness of the algorithm can then be exploited to achieve efficient prefetching. For more on this topic, see (Vishkin 1991a, Vishkin 1992).

We have seen then that by achieving a degree of parallel slackness in program designs one can provide significant opportunities for the effective scheduling of those programs, by the programmer or by a compiler, to hide the various kinds of latencies which arise in both sequential and parallel computing. In recent years, parallel slackness, or overdecomposition, has come to be recognised as crucial, not only for efficient implementation of PRAM like models (Karp *et al.* 1992, McColl 1993a, Valiant 1990a, Valiant 1990b), but also for dataflow models (Nikhil *et al.* 1991). The prospects for "autoparallelising" sequential code, which may be regarded as the extreme opposite of this approach, appear very bleak indeed.

A general design principle which emerges from these studies is, therefore, that one should aim, at all times, to produce algorithms and programs which have more parallelism in them than is available in the machine. In the future we can expect to see the development of a variety of programming languages for general purpose parallel computing. A clear message from the above discussion is that such languages must permit, and indeed encourage, the development of programs which demonstrate a high degree of fine grain concurrency. The GL programming language (McColl 1993b) is being developed with these ideas in mind.

1.3 Bulk Synchronous Parallel Computer

For a detailed account of the BSP model, and of the various routing and hashing results which can be obtained for it, the reader is referred to (Valiant 1990a, Valiant 1992a, Valiant 1992b). We concentrate here on presenting a view of (i) how a bulk-synchronous parallel architecture would be described, and (ii) how it would be used. A *bulk-synchronous parallel (BSP) computer* consists of the following :

- a set of processor-memory pairs

- a communications network that delivers messages in a point-to-point manner

- a mechanism for the efficient barrier synchronisation of all, or a subset, of the processors

There are no specialised combining, replication or broadcasting facilities. If we define a time step to be the time required for a single local operation, i.e. a basic operation on locally held data values, then the performance of any BSP computer can be characterised by the following four parameters :

- p = number of processors

- s = processor speed, i.e. number of time steps per second

- l = synchronisation periodicity, i.e. minimal number of time steps between successive synchronisation operations

- g = (total number of local operations performed by all processors in one second) / (total number of words delivered by the communications network in one second)

The parameter l is related to the network latency, i.e. to the time required for a non-local memory access in a situation of continuous message traffic. The parameter g corresponds to the frequency with which non-local memory accesses can be made; in a machine with a higher value of g one must make non-local memory accesses less frequently. More formally, g is related to the time required to realise h-relations in a situation of continuous message traffic; g is the value such that an h-relation can be performed in gh steps.

A BSP computer operates in the following way. A computation consists of a sequence of parallel *supersteps*, where each superstep is a sequence of steps, followed by a barrier synchronisation at which point any memory accesses take effect. During a superstep, each processor has a set of programs or threads which it has to carry out, and it can do the following :

- perform a number of computation steps, from its set of threads, on values held locally at the start of the superstep
- send and receive a number of messages corresponding to non-local read and write requests

The BSP computer is a two-level memory model (McColl 1993a), i.e. each processor has its own physically local memory module; all other memory is non-local, and is accessible in a uniformly efficient way. By uniformly efficient, we mean that the time taken for a processor to read from, or write to, a non-local memory element in another processor-memory pair should be independent of which physical memory module the value is held in. The algorithm designer / programmer should not be aware of any hierarchical memory organisation based on network locality in the particular physical interconnect structure currently used in the communications network. Instead, performance of the communications network should be described only in terms of its global properties, e.g. the maximum time required to perform a non-local memory operation, and the maximum number of such operations which can simultaneously be in the network at any time. The complexity of a superstep S in a BSP algorithm is determined as follows. Let L be the maximum number of local computation steps executed by any processor during S, h_1 be the maximum number of messages sent by any processor during S, and h_2 be the maximum number of messages received by any processor during S. The cost of S is then $max\{l, L, gh_1, gh_2\}$ time steps. (An alternative is to charge $max\{l, L + gh_1, L + gh_2\}$ time steps for superstep S. The difference between these two costs will not, in general, be significant.) When g is small, e.g. $g = 1$, the BSP computer corresponds closely to a PRAM, with l determining the degree of parallel slackness required to achieve optimal efficiency. For a BSP computer of this kind, i.e. with a low g value, we can use hashing to achieve efficient memory management (Valiant 1990a). The case $l = g = 1$ corresponds to the idealised PRAM, where no parallel slackness is required. In designing algorithms for a BSP computer with a high g value, we need to achieve a measure of *communication slackness* by exploiting thread locality in the two-level memory, i.e. we must ensure that for every non-local memory access we request, we are able to perform approximately g operations on local data. To achieve architecture independence in the BSP model, it is therefore appropriate to design parallel algorithms which are parameterised not only by n, the size of the problem, and p, the number of processors, but also by l and g. The following example of such an algorithm appears in (Valiant 1990a). The problem is the multiplication of two $n \times n$ matrices A, B on $p \leq n^2$ processors. The standard $O(n^3)$ sequential algorithm is adapted to run on p processors as follows. Each processor computes an $(n/p^{1/2}) \times (n/p^{1/2})$ submatrix of $C = A.B$. To do so it will require $n^2/p^{1/2}$ elements from A and the same number from B. For each processor we thus have a computation requirement of $O(n^3/p)$ operations, since each inner product requires $O(n)$ operations, and a communications requirement of $O(n^3/p)$ for the number of non-local reads, since $p \leq n^2$. If we assume that both A and B are distributed uniformly amongst the p processors, with each processor receiving $O(n^2/p)$ of the elements from each matrix, then the processors can simply replicate and send the appropriate elements from A and B to the $2p^{1/2}$ processors requiring them. Therefore, we also have a communications requirement of approximately $n^2/p^{1/2} = O(n^3/p)$ for messages sent. We thus have a total parallel time complexity of $O(n^3/p)$, provided $l = O(n^3/p)$ and $g = O(n/p^{1/2})$. An alternative algorithm, given in (Aggarwal *et al.* 1990), that requires fewer messages altogether, can be implemented to give the same optimal runtime, with g as large as $O(n/p^{1/3})$ but with l slightly smaller at $O(n^3/p \ log \ n)$.

The BSP model can be regarded as a generalisation of the PRAM model which permits the frequency of barrier synchronisation to be controlled. By capturing the network performance of a BSP computer in global terms using the values l and g, the model enables us to design algorithms and programs which are parameterised by those values, and which can therefore be efficiently implemented on a range of BSP architectures with widely differing l and g values. It therefore provides a solution to the problem posed at the start of the paper. We have a simple and robust model which permits both scalable parallel performance and a high degree of architecture independence in software. Its simplicity also offers the prospect of our being able to develop a coherent framework for the design and analysis of parallel algorithms.

The use of the parameters l and g to characterise the communications performance of a BSP computer contrasts sharply with the way in which communications performance is described for most distributed memory architecture on the market today. We are normally told many details about local network properties, e.g. the number of communications channels per node, the speed of those channels, the graph structure of the network etc. The way in which such descriptions emphasise local properties of the network, rather than its global properties, reflects the fact that most of those machines are designed to be used in a way where network locality is to be exploited. Those customers who have highly irregular problems, for which such exploitation is much more difficult, are often much less impressed by such machines when they are told about the global performance of the network in situations where network locality is not exploited. A major feature of the BSP model is that it lifts considerations of network performance from the local level to the global level. We are thus no longer particularly interested in whether the network is a 2D array, a butterfly or a hypercube, or whether it is implemented in VLSI or in some optical technology. Our interest is in global parameters of the network, such as l and g, which describe its ability to support non-local memory accesses in a uniformly efficient manner. As an aside, we note that it might be an interesting and instructive exercise to benchmark the various parallel architectures available today, in terms of such global parameters.

In the design and implementation of a BSP computer, the values of l and g which can be achieved will depend on (i) the capabilities of the available technology, and (ii) the amount of money that one is willing to spend on the communications network. As the computational performance of machines, i.e. the performance captured by p and s, continues to grow, we will find that to keep l and g low it will be necessary to continually increase our investment in the communications hardware as a percentage of the total cost of the machine. A central thesis of the BSP and PRAM approaches to general purpose parallel computing is that if these costs are paid, then parallel machines of a new level of efficiency, flexibility, and programmability can be obtained. On the basis of Theorems 1.2.1 and 1.2.2 we might expect to be able to achieve the following values of l and g for a p processor BSP computer, by using the network shown.

Network	l	g
2D Array	$O(p^{1/2})$	$O(p^{1/2})$
Butterfly	$O(log\ p)$	$O(log\ p)$
Hypercube	$O(log\ p)$	$O(1)$

These estimates are based entirely on the asymptotic degree and diameter properties of the graph. In a practical setting, the use of techniques such as wormhole routing (Leighton 1992, Seitz 1990), rather than store and forward routing, would also have a significant impact on the values of l and g which could be achieved.

In the BSP model described above, communication is point-to-point. There are no specialised combining, replication or broadcasting facilities.

In contrast to this, it has often (Abolhassan *et al.* 1991, Ranade 1989) been proposed that one should use more complex (and costly) routing networks, containing combining hardware, in order to efficiently support a much broader class of communications (and, in some cases, that one should even support simple forms of computation, e.g. the computation of prefix sums, within the "router"). In a recent paper, Valiant (Valiant 1992a) describes a mechanism for recirculating messages in a simple point-to-point routing network so that the added functionality of a network with combining hardware, for arbitrary communication patterns, can be efficiently achieved by the more basic device. There would not appear, therefore, to be a very strong case for modifying the architectural requirements of the BSP model in this direction.

Although we have described the BSP computer as an architectural model, one can also view bulk synchrony as a programming model or, indeed, as a kind of programming methodology. The essence of the BSP approach is the notion of the superstep and the idea that the input/output associated with a superstep (or reading/writing, depending on how one views it) is performed as a global operation, involving a whole set of individual sends and receives. Viewed in this way, a "BSP program" is simply one which proceeds in phases, with the necessary global communications taking place between the phases. The BSP approach can, therefore, be regarded as a programming methodology which is applicable to all kinds of parallel architecture, e.g. shared memory multiprocessors, distributed memory architectures, or networks of workstations. (The values of g in such different forms of architecture would, of course, vary enormously.) It would appear then, that the BSP approach provides a consistent, and very general, framework within which to develop portable parallel software for the wide range of parallel architectures which are likely to emerge in the future.

1.4   Challenges

In the previous sections we have seen that there are a variety of theoretically and practically efficient solutions to the problem of supporting a single address space on a distributed memory architecture. In this section we briefly describe some of the main issues which need to be addressed in the future in order to continue the development of this framework for general purpose parallel computing based on fine grain concurrency in a shared address space.

1.4.1   *Architecture*

Most distributed memory architectures are based on conventional microprocessors (Hennessy and Patterson 1990). We need alternative processor designs which can support a very large number of lightweight threads simultaneously, and can provide fast context switching, message handling, address translation, hashing etc. (Boothe and Ranade 1992, INMOS Limited 1988, Whitby-Strevens 1985). If such designs are not produced then we may find that the processors, and not the communications network, will be the bottleneck in the system.

We need to continue to develop improved networks for communication (Dally 1990, Leighton and Maggs 1989) and synchronisation (Birk *et al.* 1989, Kruskal *et al.* 1988). There is currently great emphasis in parallel computing on various "Grand Challenge" applications in science and engineering. While not doubting the importance of these applications, we would suggest that perhaps the most important challenge for parallel architectures at the present time is to develop systems for which global "inefficiency parameters", such as l and g in the BSP model, are as low as possible. The use of optical technologies may prove to be extremely important in this respect (McColl 1993a). In focusing our attention on the reduction of global parameters such as l and g, we should note that it may not necessarily be cost-effective to try to obtain the extreme case of the PRAM, where l and g are both 1. At any given point in time, the capabilities and economics of the technologies available will determine the most cost-effective values of such parameters. An important advantage of the BSP model (Valiant 1990a) over the PRAM (Abolhassan *et al.* 1991, Ranade 1989) is that it provides an architecture-independent framework which allows us to take full advantage of whichever values of l and g are the most cost-effective at a given point in time.

Large general purpose parallel computer systems will inevitably suffer hardware faults of various kinds during their operation. We need to develop efficient techniques which can provide a degree of fault tolerance for processors, memories, and communications links. An interesting approach to this problem is to use the idea of information dispersal (Lyuu 1992, Rabin 1989), where a space efficient redundant encoding of data is used to provide secure and reliable storage of information, and efficient fault tolerant routing of messages. Other approaches to the problems of fault tolerance are described in (Kedem *et al.* 1991, Shvartsman 1991).

The communications architecture of the Inmos T9000 transputer has been designed to support the kind of high performance global communications required to efficiently implement BSP computer systems.

1.4.2 *Algorithms*

Although the potential for automating memory management via hashing is a major advantage of the BSP model, the BSP algorithm designer may wish to retain control of memory management in the two-level memory to achieve higher efficiency, e.g. on a BSP computer with a high value of g. A systematic study of direct bulk-synchronous algorithms remains to be done. Some first steps in this direction are described in (Bisseling and McColl 1993, Gerbessiotis and Valiant 1992, Valiant 1990a).

1.4.3 *Languages and Software*

The PRAM model was developed to facilitate the study of parallel algorithms and their complexity. In that context it has proved to be extremely useful. However, as we have pursued the design and implementation of parallel architectures based on the PRAM model, it has become clear that we have no well developed framework for the programming of such architectures. This can be contrasted with other approaches to general purpose parallel computing such as the actor and dataflow models, where there has been an intensive effort to develop a programming framework, although rather less on the investigation of parallel algorithms and their complexity. It is vital for the success of the approach described in this paper that we develop programming languages and methodologies for the kinds of parallel architectures proposed. Of the various challenges mentioned, this is perhaps the most important, and in many respects the most difficult one. The apparent unwillingness of many programmers of parallel machines to use anything other than minor variants of the sequential languages FORTRAN and C is widely perceived to be a major impediment to the continuing development of parallel computing. Another impediment is, of course, the "dusty decks" of old FORTRAN codes which many organisations are unwilling, or unable, to abandon. Many new parallel programming languages have been proposed and rejected over the last decade or so. Nevertheless, we must continue to seek a programming model which will provide a means of achieving the architecture-independence sought, while permitting scalable parallel performance on the kinds of architectures described. Some preliminary work in this direction can be found in (McColl 1993b). It is to be hoped that as such a programming framework is developed we will also be able to provide a strategy for the migration of the dusty decks to the new architectures.

1.5 Other Approaches

A large number of approaches are currently being proposed as the basis of a framework for general purpose parallel computing. In this paper I have presented the case for the BSP/PRAM approach. In this section I will briefly mention, and comment on, some of these other approaches. Perhaps the most conservative of the alternatives is SIMD or data parallelism. Although a number of interesting algorithms have been developed for such architectures (Blelloch 1990, Hillis and Steele Jr 1986, Steele Jr and Hillis 1986) , the model does not appear to be sufficiently general, even when extended to its SPMD form. Another conservative approach is simply to continue with architectures based on message passing across a fixed set of channels (Hoare 1985, Hoare 1991, Jones and Goldsmith 1988). Although such a model is adequate for the development of many special purpose parallel systems, and for low level systems programming, it does not appear to offer enough in terms of architecture-independence. An approach related to message passing which appears to be more attractive is the actor model (Agha 1986), which we might think of as message passing using names rather than a fixed set of channels. The names are first class objects and can be passed in messages. The graph of possible interactions between actors can thus change dynamically. The actor model provides a convenient framework for concurrent object-oriented programming (Agha 1990). Dally has developed an interesting parallel architecture, called the J Machine (Dally *et al.* 1989, Dally and Wills 1989), which supports the actor model.

The dataflow model has evolved considerably over the last decade. Modern designs for dataflow architectures (Iannucci 1988, Iannucci 1990, Nikhil and Arvind 1989, Nikhil *et al.* 1991, Papadopolous and Traub 1991) emphasise the importance of ideas such as efficient multithreading and the exploitation of parallel slackness, in the same way as the PRAM architectures do. There are, of course, major differences between the two approaches in terms of synchronisation control, scheduling control etc. It is not yet clear whether the freedom which the dataflow model offers the programmer has a cost to be paid in terms of scalable parallel performance.

Other approaches to general purpose parallel computing which have been suggested in recent years include asynchronous PRAMs (Cole and Zajicek 1989, Gibbons 1989), block PRAMs (Aggarwal *et al.* 1989), hierarchical PRAMs (Heywood 1991), the LogP model (Culler *et al.* 1993), tuple space (Carriero and Gelernter 1989), graph reduction (Peyton Jones 1989), rewriting, and shared virtual memory.

1.6 Conclusion

The goals of general purpose parallel computing are to achieve both scalable parallel performance and architecture-independent parallel software. Despite much effort to find them, no serious theoretical impediments to the achievement of these goals have yet been found. We have argued that the BSP computer is a robust model of parallel computation which offers the prospect of achieving both requirements. The main challenge at the present time is to develop an appropriate programming framework for the BSP model.

Two other models which appear to offer the required architecture-independence are the actor and dataflow models. The most fundamental difference between these two approaches to parallel computing and the BSP, PRAM and data parallel models, is that they both have at their core the idea of local (usually pairwise) synchronisation events, whereas the BSP, PRAM and data parallel models have the idea of global barrier synchronisation as the basic mechanism. Another significant difference is that in the BSP, PRAM and data parallel approaches there is usually tight control of ordering and scheduling by the programmer. In contrast, a major attraction of, for example, the dataflow approach, is that the programmer is freed from consideration of such issues. It is not yet clear whether the actor and dataflow models can offer the same scalability in parallel performance as we have demonstrated can be obtained for the BSP model. It is also unclear at present whether they can offer a convenient framework for the investigation of parallel algorithms and their complexity. Nevertheless, by virtue of their attractiveness in programming terms, they merit serious consideration.

Although we have stressed the differences between these various approaches, there is reason to believe that, at the architectural level, the BSP, PRAM, actor and dataflow models will require a number of similar mechanisms for efficient implementation; in particular, high performance global communications, uniform memory access, and multithreading to hide network latencies.

REFERENCES

F Abolhassan, J Keller, and W J Paul. On the cost-effectiveness of PRAMs. In *Proc. 3rd IEEE Symposium on Parallel and Distributed Processing*, pages 2–9, 1991.

A Aggarwal, A K Chandra, and M Snir. On communication latency in PRAM computations. In *Proc. 1st Annual ACM Symposium on Parallel Algorithms and Architectures*, pages 11–21, 1989.

A Aggarwal, A K Chandra, and M Snir. Communication complexity of PRAMs. *Theoretical Computer Science*, 71:3–28, 1990.

G Agha. *Actors : A Model of Concurrent Computation in Distributed Systems*. MIT Press, Cambridge, MA, 1986.

G Agha. Concurrent object-oriented programming. *Communications of the ACM*, 33(9):125–141, September 1990.

G M Amdahl. Validity of the single processor approach to achieving large scale computing capabilities. In *Proc. AFIPS Spring Joint Computer Conference 30*, pages 483–485, 1967.

W C Athas and C L Seitz. Multicomputers : Message-passing concurrent computers. *IEEE Computer*, 12(8):9–24, August 1988.

R S Bird and P Wadler. *Introduction to Functional Programming*. Prentice Hall, 1988.

Y Birk, P B Gibbons, J L C Sanz, and D Soroker. A simple mechanism for efficient barrier synchronization in MIMD machines. Research Report RJ 7078, IBM Research, October 1989. Also appears in Proc. 1990 IEEE International Conference on Parallel Processing, Volume II Software, pages 195-198.

R H Bisseling and W F McColl. Scientific computing on bulk synchronous parallel architectures. Technical report, Shell Research (KSLA, Amsterdam) and Programming Research Group, Oxford University, 1993. (In preparation).

G E Blelloch. *Vector Models for Data-Parallel Computing*. MIT Press, Cambridge, MA, 1990.

R D Blumofe. Managing storage for multithreaded computations. Technical Report (M.Sc. Thesis) MIT/LCS/TR-552, Laboratory for Computer Science, Massachusetts Institute of Technology, September 1992.

B Boothe and A Ranade. Improved multithreading techniques for hiding communication latency in multiprocessors. In *Proc. 19th Annual International Symposium on Computer Architecture*, pages 214–223, 1992.

A W Burks, H H Goldstine, and J von Neumann. *Preliminary discussion of the logical design of an electronic computing instrument. Part 1,*

Volume 1. The Institute of Advanced Study, Princeton, 1946. Report to the U.S. Army Ordnance Department. First edition, 28 June 1946. Second edition, 2 September 1947. Also appears in *Papers of John von Neumann on Computing and Computer Theory*, W Aspray and A Burks, editors. Volume 12 in the Charles Babbage Institute Reprint Series for the History of Computing, MIT Press, 1987, 97-142.

N Carriero and D Gelernter. How to write parallel programs: A guide to the perplexed. *ACM Computing Surveys*, 21(3):323–358, September 1989.

R Cole and O Zajicek. The APRAM : Incorporating asynchrony into the PRAM model. In *Proc. 1st Annual ACM Symposium on Parallel Algorithms and Architectures*, pages 169–178, 1989.

D Culler, R M Karp, D A Patterson, A Sahay, K E Schauser, E Santos, R Subramonian, and T von Eicken. LogP: Towards a realistic model of parallel computation. In *Proc. 4th ACM SIGPLAN Symposium on Principles and Practice of Parallel Programming*, pages 1–12, May 1993.

W J Dally and D S Wills. Universal mechanisms for concurrency. In E Odijk, M Rem, and J-C Syre, editors, *Proc. PARLE 89 : Parallel Architectures and Languages Europe. LNCS Vol.365*, pages 19–33. Springer-Verlag, 1989.

W J Dally, A Chien, S Fiske, W Horwat, J Keen, M Larivee, R Lethin, P Nuth, and S Wills. The J-Machine : A fine-grain concurrent computer. In G X Ritter, editor, *Proc. Information Processing 89*, pages 1147–1153. Elsevier Science Publishers, B. V., 1989.

W J Dally. Network and processor architecture for message-driven computers. In R Suaya and G Birtwistle, editors, *VLSI and Parallel Computaion*, pages 140–222. Morgan Kaufmann, San Mateo, CA, 1990.

C W Gear, editor. *Computation and Cognition. Proceedings of the First NEC Research Symposium*. SIAM Press, 1991. Panel Session - The Future of Parallelism, pages 153-168.

A V Gerbessiotis and L G Valiant. Direct bulk-synchronous parallel algorithms. Technical Report TR-10-92 (Extended version), Aiken Computation Laboratory, Harvard University, 1992. Shorter version appears in Proc. 3rd Scandinavian Workshop on Algorithm Theory, July 8-10, 1992. LNCS Vol. 621, pp 1-18, Springer-Verlag.

A M Gibbons and P Spirakis, editors. *Lectures on Parallel Computation*, volume 4 of *Cambridge International Series on Parallel Computation*. Cambridge University Press, Cambridge, UK, 1993.

P B Gibbons. A more practical PRAM model. In *Proc. 1st Annual ACM Symposium on Parallel Algorithms and Architectures*, pages 158–168, 1989.

J L Gustafson. Development of parallel methods for a 1024-processor hypercube. *SIAM Journal on Scientific and Statistical Computing*, 9(4):609–638, July 1988.

J L Gustafson. Reevaluating Amdahl's Law. *Communications of the ACM*, 31(5):532–533, May 1988.

J L Hennessy and D A Patterson. *Computer Architecture : A Quantitative Approach*. Morgan Kaufmann, San Mateo, CA, 1990.

T H Heywood. A practical hierarchical model of parallel computation. Technical Report SU-CIS-91-39, School of Computer and Information Science, Syracuse University, November 1991.

W D Hillis and G L Steele Jr. Data parallel algorithms. *Communications of the ACM*, 29(12):1170–1183, December 1986.

C A R Hoare. *Communicating Sequential Processes*. Prentice Hall, 1985.

C A R Hoare. The transputer and occam : A personal story. *Concurrency : Practice and Experience*, 3(4):249–264, August 1991.

P Hudak, S Peyton Jones, and P Wadler, editors. Report on the Programming Language Haskell - A Non-Strict, Purely Functional Language. Version 1.1 , 1991.

P Hudak. Concept, evolution, and application of functional programming languages. *ACM Computing Surveys*, 21(3):359–411, 1989.

R A Iannucci. Toward a dataflow/von Neumann hybrid architecture. In *Proc. 15th Annual International Symposium on Computer Architecture*, pages 131–140, 1988.

R A Iannucci. *Parallel Machines : Parallel Machine Languages*. Kluwer Academic Publishers, Dordrecht, 1990.

INMOS Limited. *Transputer Reference Manual*. Prentice Hall, 1988.

J JáJá. *An Introduction to Parallel Algorithms*. Addison-Wesley, 1992.

G Jones and M Goldsmith. *Programming in occam 2*. Prentice Hall, 1988.

H Jung, L Kirousis, and P Spirakis. Lower bounds and efficient algorithms for multiprocessor scheduling of dags with communication delays. In *Proc. 1st Annual ACM Symposium on Parallel Algorithms and Architectures*, pages 254–264, 1989.

R M Karp, M Luby, and F Meyer auf der Heide. Efficient PRAM simulation on a distributed memory machine. In *Proc. 24th Annual ACM Symposium on Theory of Computing*, pages 318–326, 1992.

Z M Kedem, K V Palem, A Raghunathan, and P G Spirakis. Combining tentative and definite executions for very fast dependable parallel computing. In *Proc. 23rd Annual ACM Symposium on Theory of Computing*, pages 381–390, 1991.

C P Kruskal, L Rudolph, and M Snir. Efficient synchronization on multiprocessors with shared memory. *ACM Transactions on Programming Languages and Systems*, 10(4):579–601, 1988.

C P Kruskal, L Rudolph, and M Snir. A complexity theory of efficient parallel algorithms. *Theoretical Computer Science*, 71:95–132, 1990.

H T Kung. New opportunities in multicomputers. In C W Gear, editor, *Computation and Cognition. Proceedings of the First NEC Research*

Symposium, pages 1–21. SIAM Press, 1991.

F T Leighton and B M Maggs. Expanders might be practical: Fast algorithms for routing around faults on multibutterflies. In *Proc. 30th Annual IEEE Symposium on Foundations of Computer Science*, pages 384–389, 1989.

F T Leighton. *Introduction to Parallel Algorithms and Architectures : Arrays, Trees, Hypercubes*. Morgan Kaufmann, San Mateo, CA, 1992.

Y-D Lyuu. *Information Dispersal and Parallel Computation*, volume 3 of *Cambridge International Series on Parallel Computation*. Cambridge University Press, Cambridge, UK, 1992.

W F McColl. General purpose parallel computing. In Gibbons and Spirakis (1993), pages 337–391.

W F McColl. GL : An architecture independent programming language for scalable parallel computing. Technical Report 93-072-3-9025-1, NEC Research Institute, Princeton, June 1993.

W F McColl. Special purpose parallel computing. In Gibbons and Spirakis (1993), pages 261–336.

R S Nikhil and Arvind. Can dataflow subsume von Neumann computing? In *Proc. 16th Annual International Symposium on Computer Architecture*, pages 262–272, 1989.

R S Nikhil, G M Papadopolous, and Arvind. *t : A killer micro for a brave new world. Computation Structures Group Memo 325, Laboratory for Computer Science, Massachusetts Institute of Technology, July 1991.

R S Nikhil. Id - Language Reference Manual. Version 90.1. Computation Structures Group Memo 284-2, Laboratory for Computer Science, Massachusetts Institute of Technology, July 1991.

C H Papadimitriou and J D Ullman. A communication-time tradeoff. *SIAM Journal on Computing*, 16(4):639–646, August 1987.

C H Papadimitriou and M Yannakakis. Towards an architecture-independent analysis of parallel algorithms. *SIAM Journal on Computing*, 19(2):322–328, 1990.

G M Papadopolous and K R Traub. Multithreading : A revisionist view of dataflow architectures. In *Proc. 18th Annual International Symposium on Computer Architecture*, pages 342–351, 1991.

S L Peyton Jones. Parallel implementation of functional programming langauges. *The Computer Journal*, 32(2):175–186, 1989.

M O Rabin. Efficient dispersal of information for security, load balancing, and fault tolerance. *Journal of the ACM*, 36(2):335–348, April 1989.

A G Ranade. Fluent parallel computation. Ph.D. Thesis, Department of Computer Science, Yale University, May 1989.

C L Seitz. The Cosmic Cube. *Communications of the ACM*, 28(1):22–33, January 1985.

C L Seitz. Concurrent architectures. In R Suaya and G Birtwistle, editors, *VLSI and Parallel Computaion*, pages 1–84. Morgan Kaufmann,

San Mateo, CA, 1990.

A A Shvartsman. Achieving optimal CRCW PRAM fault-tolerance. *Information Processing Letters*, 39(2):59–66, 1991.

G L Steele Jr and W D Hillis. Connection Machine Lisp : Fine-grained parallel symbolic processing. In *Proc. ACM Conference on Lisp and Functional Programming*, pages 279–297, 1986.

A M Turing. On computable numbers, with an application to the Entscheidungsproblem. *Proceedings of the London Mathematical Society. Series 2*, 42:230–265, 1936. Corrections, *ibid.*, 43 (1937), 544-546.

L G Valiant. A bridging model for parallel computation. *Communications of the ACM*, 33(8):103–111, 1990.

L G Valiant. General purpose parallel architectures. In J van Leeuwen, editor, *Handbook of Theoretical Computer Science : Volume A, Algorithms and Complexity*, pages 943–971. North Holland, 1990.

L G Valiant. A combining mechanism for parallel computers. Technical Report TR-24-92, Aiken Computation Laboratory, Harvard University, November 1992.

L G Valiant. Why BSP computers? Technical Report TR-26-92, Aiken Computation Laboratory, Harvard University, November 1992. To appear in Proc. 7th International Parallel Processing Symposium, April 1993.

U Vishkin. Can parallel algorithms enhance serial implementation? Technical Report UMIACS-TR-91-145, Institute for Advanced Computer Studies, University of Maryland, 1991.

U Vishkin. Structural parallel algorithmics. In J Leach Albert, B Monien, and M Rodriguez Artalejo, editors, *Proc. 18th International Colloquium on Automata, Languages and Programming, LNCS Vol.510*, pages 363–380. Springer-Verlag, 1991.

U Vishkin. Methods in parallel algorithmics and who may need to know them? In T Ibaraki, Y Inagaki, K Iwama, T Nishizeki, and M Yamashita, editors, *Algorithms and Computation, Third International Symposium, ISSAC 92, LNCS Vol. 650*, pages 1–4. Springer-Verlag, December 1992.

J von Neumann. *First draft of a report on the EDVAC*. Moore School of Electrical Engineering, University of Pennsylvania, 30 June 1945. Contract No. W-670-ORD-4926 between the United States Army Ordnance Department and the University of Pennsylvania. Reprinted in *Papers of John von Neumann on Computing and Computer Theory*, W Aspray and A Burks, editors. Volume 12 in the Charles Babbage Institute Reprint Series for the History of Computing, MIT Press, 1987, 17-82.

C Whitby-Strevens. The transputer. In *Proc. 12th Annual International Symposium on Computer Architecture*, pages 292–300, 1985.

Productive Parallel Programming: The PCN Approach

IAN FOSTER, ROBERT OLSON, AND STEVEN TUECKE

Mathematics and Computer Science Division, Argonne National Laboratory, Argonne, IL 60439

ABSTRACT

We describe the PCN programming system, focusing on those features designed to improve the productivity of scientists and engineers using parallel supercomputers. These features include a simple notation for the concise specification of concurrent algorithms, the ability to incorporate existing Fortran and C code into parallel applications, facilities for reusing parallel program components, a portable toolkit that allows applications to be developed on a workstation or small parallel computer and run unchanged on supercomputers, and integrated debugging and performance analysis tools. We survey representative scientific applications and identify problem classes for which PCN has proved particularly useful. © 1992 by John Wiley & Sons, Inc.

1 INTRODUCTION

After many years as academic curiosities, computers combining hundreds or thousands of powerful microprocessors have overtaken vector processors and become essential tools for scientists and engineers. Unfortunately, the programming of these parallel supercomputers is still immensely time consuming. Frequently, many months of effort are required to develop, validate, and tune parallel codes; apparently minor algorithmic changes can take weeks. These factors severely limit the productivity and creativity of those using these advanced machines.

A clear need exists for tools that reduce the cost of program development to more manageable levels. Good software engineering practice tells us that these tools should possess three characteristics: (1) a *notation* that permits us to *program smarter*, by lessening the gap between our conception of a problem solution and its eventual implementation; (2) support for *code reuse* that allows us to *program less*, by reusing old code when solving new problems; and (3) a *toolkit* that permits us to *program faster*, by reducing the effort required to find errors, adapt programs to different architectures, etc.

In this article, we introduce PCN, a parallel programming system with these characteristics. PCN has been developed over the past 3 years at Argonne National Laboratory and the California Institute of Technology (Caltech). It features a simple concurrent language (Program Composition Notation), facilities for reuse of sequential and parallel code, and a toolkit supporting compilation, debugging, and performance analysis. Important benefits of the approach include the ability to rapidly prototype complex concurrent algorithms, particularly those involving dynamic communication or computation structures; application portability, which permits programs developed on a workstation to move to networks of

Received February 1992
Revised March 1992

workstations and to parallel supercomputers with little change; the ability to incorporate existing Fortran and C code into parallel programs; and support for the reuse of parallel program structures in different applications.

PCN is not the solution to all programming problems. A disadvantage for some programmers is the need to learn a new programming language. Others are uncomfortable with a high-level approach, preferring to program parallel computers at the lowest level possible. In addition, the PCN system is research software and, as such, not yet as sophisticated as conventional sequential programming systems. Nevertheless, it has already been used successfully to develop applications and to teach parallel programming to undergraduates. We expect it to prove useful to many users and for many purposes.

Rather than an academic exposition of PCN, this article provides an informal introduction to its capabilities and an analysis of the experiences of those using it to address substantial programming problems. By conveying the flavor of the approach and indicating the classes of problems for which it appears particularly appropriate, we hope to stimulate our readers to experiment with PCN in their own applications. The latest version of both the software and detailed documentation can be obtained by anonymous FTP from the directory pub/pcn at info.mcs.anl.gov.

The rest of this article is divided into five parts. These provide an overview of the approach, a description of the programming language, a discussion of the techniques used to reuse existing code, a description of the programming tools, and a survey of representative applications.

2 APPROACH

The focus of the PCN approach to parallel programming is the development of programs by the *parallel composition* of simpler components, in such a way that the resulting programs preserve properties of the components that they compose. In particular, deterministic compositions of deterministic components should themselves be deterministic: the result of such computations should never depend on the order in which components are scheduled for execution. Similarly, the result computed by a program should be independent of how its components are mapped to processors. This compositional property is critical to both the development of robust applications and the reuse of existing code.

The PCN language is carefully designed to realize compositionality. In particular, it requires that concurrently executing components interact by reading and writing special single-assignment or *definitional* variables. A definitional variable is initially undefined and can be assigned at most a single value. If a component attempts to read an undefined variable, execution of that component is suspended until the variable is defined. Hence, the result of a computation can never depend on the time at which read and write operations occur.

This focus on parallel composition and definitional variables leads to the following approach to parallel program design. A problem is decomposed into a large number of subproblems and a process is created for each subproblem. PCN code is written to organize the exchange of data between these processes and to coordinate their execution. Existing *software cells* and *templates* may be integrated into the program; these define sets of processes that implement commonly used operations such as parallel reductions or transforms. Finally, the mapping of the processes to the processors of a parallel computer is specified; this can alter performance but not the result computed.

The PCN compiler is optimized for efficient execution of programs that create many processes and that communicate and synchronize via definitional variables. It ensures that process creation, scheduling, termination, and migration are extremely inexpensive operations: typically a few tens of instructions. (Process migration incurs an additional cost proportional to the size of a process's data.) Read and write operations on definitional variables are implemented in terms of pointer operations within a single address space and message passing between address spaces. Processes are scheduled for execution so as to overlap computation and communication. Data structures are created dynamically and deallocated either when the process in which they are defined terminates (in the case of local variables) or when they are no longer accessible (in the case of definitional variables shared by several processes).

Components composed by PCN programs can be written in PCN or in sequential languages such as Fortran and C. In the latter case, existing code and compiler technology can be reused. Programs that do not use Fortran common or C global data can be composed in exactly the same way as PCN programs. If programs do use common/global data, then certain restrictions apply, as the use of common/global data violates the requirement that programs only communicate via definitional variables. This issue is discussed in Section 4.1.

3 NOTATION

Programming is rarely easy, but an appropriate notation can make it less difficult. As Whitehead [1] observed of mathematics: "By relieving the brain of all unnecessary work, a good notation sets it free to concentrate on more advanced problems." In parallel programming, a good notation should express concurrency, communication, synchronization, and mapping straightforwardly and clearly. It should also discourage nondeterminism, just as a mathematical notation avoids ambiguity.

The programming notation used in the PCN system is Program Composition Notation (PCN). PCN extends sequential programming with two simple ideas—concurrent composition and single-assignment variables—and defines how these ideas interact with conventional sequential constructs [2, 3]. The PCN system also incorporates two additional constructs—virtual topologies and port arrays—that allow the definition and reuse of parallel program structures called cells and templates [4].

Our description of the PCN language is divided into five parts. These describe in turn the constructs used to specify concurrency, communication and synchronization, nondeterminism, mapping, and composition of process ensembles.

3.1 Concurrency

Syntax is similar to that of the C programming language. A program is a set of procedures, each with the following general form ($k,l \geq 0$).

```
name(arg₁, . . . , argₖ)
declaration₁; . . . ; declarationₗ;
block
```

A block is a call to a PCN procedure (or to a procedure in a sequential language such as Fortran or C), a composition, or a primitive operation such as assignment. A composition is written { op block₁, . . . , blockₘ}, $m > 0$,

where op is one of "‖" (parallel), ";" (sequential), or "?" (choice), indicating that the blocks block₁, . . . , blockₘ are to be executed concurrently, in sequence, or as a set of guarded commands (a sort of parallel case statement, with each block being a condition/action pair), respectively.

A parallel composition specifies opportunities for parallel execution but does not indicate how the composed blocks (which can be thought of as lightweight processes) are to be mapped to processors. The techniques used to specify mapping are described below.

3.2 Communication and Synchronization

Statements in a parallel composition communicate and synchronize by reading and writing special single-assignment or *definitional* variables. (Conventional, or *mutable*, variables are also supported, but can be used only within sequential blocks.) Definitional variables are distinguished by a lack of declaration, are initially undefined, can be written (defined) once using the primitive operator =, and once written cannot be modified. (An attempt to overwrite a definitional variable is flagged as a runtime error.) A process that requires the value of an undefined variable suspends until the required data are available. This provides a dataflow model of computation, with execution order within parallel compositions determined by availability of data.

Processes that share a definitional variable can communicate regardless of their location in a parallel computer. For example, in the parallel composition {‖ producer(x), consumer(x)}, the two procedure calls producer(x) and consumer(x) can use x to communicate, whether they are executing concurrently on one processor or in parallel on two processors.

Consider the following definitions for producer and consumer. The producer defines its parameter to be the string ''hello,'' hence communicating this value to any process that shares that variable (in the composition in the previous paragraph, this is consumer). The consumer is defined in terms of a choice composition. The two guarded commands define tests on the parameter v (v == ''hello'' and v != ''hello'') and the actions that are to be performed if these tests succeed (calls to the procedures greet() or ignore(v), respectively). Hence, the procedure consumer suspends until v has a value and then executes one of the two procedures.

```
producer(u)
{|| u = ''hello''}

consumer(v)
{ ? v == ''hello'' -> greet(),

    v != ''hello'' -> ignore(v)
}
```

Stream Communication

A shared definitional variable would not be very useful if it could only be used to exchange a single value. Fortunately, simple techniques allow a single variable to be used to communicate a *stream* of values [5]. A stream acts like a queue: the producer places elements on one end, and the consumer(s) take them off the other.

Stream communication is achieved by the incremental construction of linked list structures. The technique makes use of a data type called the *tuple*. A tuple is represented by zero or more terms enclosed in parentheses, for example { } (the empty tuple) or {head, tail} (a two-tuple). The *match* operator ?= is used to access a tuple's components. For example, x ?= {msg, xt} checks whether x is a two-tuple and, if so, defines msg and xt to be references to its two components.

Imagine a producer and a consumer sharing a variable x. The producer defines x to be a two-tuple containing a message and a new definitional variable (x = {msg, xt}). The consumer matches x ?= {msg, xt} to access both the message and the new variable. These operations both communicate msg to the consumer and create a new shared variable xt that can be used for further communication. This process can be repeated arbitrarily often to communicate a stream of messages from the producer to the consumer. The stream is closed by defining the shared variable to be the empty tuple.

The following program implements this protocol. The stream_producer generates n messages, calling produce to generate each message, and then closes the stream. The stream_consumer consumes messages until the stream is closed, calling greet or ignore to process each incoming message. Note that both procedures are defined recursively. For example, the producer generates one message (by defining u to be the

tuple {msg, u1}) and then calls itself recursively to produce further messages. Recursion is often used in PCN because it allows the introduction of an unbounded number of new definitional variables; the PCN compiler is designed to compile such programs efficiently, and in fact translates recursive procedures into iterative code. Explicit iterative constructs are also available: these are described in a subsequent section.

```
stream_producer(n, u)
{ ? n > 0 ->
        {|| produce(n, msg),
            u = {msg, u1},
            stream_producer(n-1, u1)
        },
    n == 0 -> u = {}
}

stream_consumer(v)
{? v ?= {msg,v1} ->
    {|| { ? msg == ''hello'' -> greet(),
            msg != ''hello'' -> ignore(msg)
    },
        stream_consumer(v1)
    }
}
```

3.3 Nondeterminism

The use of definitional variables as a communication mechanism avoids errors due to time-dependent interactions. Race conditions, in which the result of a computation depends on the time at which a process reads a variable, cannot occur: a consumer of a variable always suspends until the variable has a value, and then computes with a value that cannot change.

Nevertheless, it is sometimes useful to be able to specify nondeterministic execution, particularly in reactive applications. PCN also allows the specification of nondeterministic actions, but in a tightly controlled manner. Only if the conditions associated with two or more actions in a guarded command are not mutually exclusive is execution nondeterministic. For example, the following procedure merges two input streams (in_stream1 and in_stream2) into a single output stream (out_stream). Note that the two streams are not mutually exclusive: as guards are executed concurrently, messages can be received from either input stream, in a time-dependent manner.

```
merge(in_stream1, in_stream2, out_stream)
{ ?
```

```
in_stream1 ?= {msg, more_in1} ->
    {||
              out_stream = {msg, more_out},
        merge(more_in1, in_stream2, more_out)
    }
in_stream2 ?= {msg, more_in2}->
    {||
              out_stream = {msg, more_out},
        merge(in_stream1, more_in2, more_out)
    }
}
```

PCN programs in which conditions are mutually exclusive are guaranteed to be deterministic. This is an important property that greatly simplifies parallel programming. (The reader might be concerned about the possibility of writing conditions which are mistakenly not mutually exclusive. In practice, this has not proved to be a problem.)

Two potential sources of nondeterminism that are not prevented by PCN are concurrent I/O operations and concurrent access to Fortran common or C global data by Fortran or C procedures composed by PCN. The latter issue is discussed in Section 4.1.

3.4 Mapping

Parallel compositions define concurrent processes; shared definitional variables define how these processes communicate and synchronize. Together with the sequential code executed by the different processes, these components define a concurrent algorithm that can be executed and debugged on a uniprocessor computer. However, we do not yet have a parallel program: we must first specify how these processes are to be mapped to the processors of a parallel computer. Important features of PCN are that the mapping can be specified by the programmer, and that the choice of mapping affects only the performance, not the correctness, of the program. The following language features are used when writing code to define mappings.

Information Functions

When defining mappings, we sometimes require information about the computer on which a process is executing. This information is provided by the primitive functions topology(), nodes(), and location().

topology(): Returns a tuple describing the type of the computer, for example, {''mesh'',16,32} or {''array'',512}.

nodes(): Returns the number of nodes in the computer.
location(): Returns the location of the process on the computer.

Location Functions

Mapping is specified by annotating procedure calls with system- or user-defined *location functions*, using the infix operator ''@''. These functions are evaluated to identify the node on which an annotated call is to execute; unannotated calls execute on the same node as the procedure that called them. For example, the following two procedures implement the location functions node(i) and mesh_node(i,j), which compute the location of a procedure that is to be mapped to the ith node of an array and the (i,j)th node of a mesh, respectively. Note the use of a match (?=) to access the components of the mesh topology type. The percent character, ''%'', is the modulus operator.

```
function node(i)
{|| return( i%nodes() ) }

function mesh_node(i, j)
{ ? topology() ?= {''mesh'', rows,
                                cols} ->
      return( (i*rows + j)%nodes() ),
    default -> error()
}
```

The following composition uses the function node(i) to locate the procedure calls p(x) and c(x).

```
{|| p(x) @ node(10), c(x) @ node(20)}
```

Location functions are often used in an iterative construct called a *quantification* to create a computation that executes on many processors. A quantification has the general form

```
{ op i over low..high :: block},
```

and specifies that block should be executed once for each i in the range low..high, either concurrently (if op = ||) or sequentially (if op = ;).

The following two procedures use quantifications and the location functions defined previously to execute the procedure work in every node of an array and mesh, respectively. For example, a call to array on a 1024-processor computer will create 1024 instances of work(), one per processor. (In practice. we may choose to use a more efficient tree-based spawning algorithm on a large machine.)

```
array()
{|| i over 0..nodes()-1 ::
        work() @ node(i)
}

mesh()
{ ? topology() ?= {''mesh'', rows,
                             cols} ->
        {|| i over 0..rows-1 ::
            {||j over 0..cols-1 ::
                    work() @
                            mesh_node(i, j)
            }
        },
    default -> error()
}
```

Virtual Topologies and Map Functions

The ability to specify mapping by means of location functions would be of limited value if these mappings had to be specified with respect to a specific computer. Not only might this computer have a topology that was inconvenient for our application. but the resulting program would not be portable.

PCN overcomes this difficulty by allowing the programmer to define mappings with respect to convenient *virtual topologies* rather than a particular physical topology. A virtual topology consists of one or more virtual processors or *nodes*, plus a type indicating how these nodes are organized. For example. 512 nodes may be organized as a one-dimensional array. a 32×16 mesh. etc.

The embedding of a virtual topology in another physical or virtual topology is specified by a system- or user-defined *map function*. A map function is evaluated in the context of an existing topology; it returns a tuple containing three values: the type of the new embedded topology. the size of the new topology. and the function that is to be used to locate each new topology node in the existing topology. For example. the following function embeds a mesh of size rows×cols in an array topology: the mapping will be performed with the location function node provided previously. (The location function is quoted to indicate that it should not be evaluated.) Note that the map func-

tion does not check whether the new topology "fits" in the old topology. It is quite feasible to create a virtual topology with more nodes than the physical topology on which it will execute.

```
function mesh_in_array(rows, cols)
{ ? topology ?= {''array'', n} ->
    {|| type = { 'mesh'', rows, cols},
       size = rows*cols,
       map_fn = 'node()',
       return( {type, size, map_fn} )
    },
    default -> error()
}
```

We use the annotation submc to specify the map functions that will generate the virtual topologies used in different components of a program. For example. if the mesh procedure specified previously is to be executed on an array computer. we may invoke it as follows.

```
mesh()
    @ submc(mesh_in_array(rows,cols))
```

Virtual topologies and map functions allow us to develop applications with respect to a convenient and portable virtual topology. When moving to a new machine. it is frequently possible to get adequate performance with just a naive embedding of this virtual topology. For example. our applications invariably treat all computers as linear arrays. regardless of their actual topology. and nevertheless achieve good performance. If communication locality were important (e.g.. if we moved to a machine without cut-through routing). we would probably have to develop a map function that provides a more specialized embedding. This can generally be achieved without changing the application code.

3.5 Port Arrays

Recall that individual processes communicate by reading and writing shared definitional variables. as in the composition {|| producer(x), consumer(x)}. The *port array* provides a similar mechanism for use when composing sets of processes.

A port array is an array of definitional variables that has been distributed evenly across the nodes of a virtual topology. A declaration ''port P[N];'' creates a port array P with N elements. distributed blockwise across the nodes of the vir-

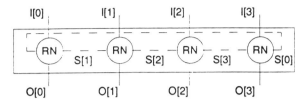

FIGURE 1. Ring pipeline cell.

tual topology in which the port array is declared. Elements of a port array are accessed by indexing, in the same way as ordinary arrays: the elements can be used as ordinary definitional variables.

The following procedure, a variant of the `array` procedure given earlier, uses port arrays for two purposes: first, to provide each `ring_node()` process with definitional variables for use as input and output streams; and second, to establish internal communication streams between neighboring processes, so that each process has two streams, one shared with each neighbor. The `i`th node of this structure is given elements `I[i]` and `O[i]` of the two port arrays `I` and `O` passed as parameters, so as to allow communication with the outside world, and two elements of the local port array `S`. As in the C programming language, the dimension of an array passed as an argument is not specified.

```
ring(I, O)
port S[nodes()], I[], O[];
{|| i over 0..nodes()-1 ::
      ring_node(I[i], O[i], S[i],
      S[(i+1)%nodes()]) @ node(i)
}
```

The process structure created by a call to this procedure in a four-processor virtual topology can be represented as follows, with the solid lines indicating external port connections and the dotted lines internal streams. The box separates the internals of the process structure from what is visible to other processes. The `ring_node` procedure executed by each process can use the four definitional variables passed as arguments to communicate with other processes (see Fig. 1).

4 REUSE

The ability to reuse existing code is vital to productive programming. The PCN system supports two forms of reuse: reuse of sequential code writ-

ten in C or Fortran, and reuse of parallel code written in PCN. The former is important when migrating existing sequential applications to parallel computers; the latter is becoming increasingly important as our parallel code base grows.

4.1 Sequential Code: Multilingual Programming

A simple interface allows sequential code (currently, Fortran and C are supported) to be integrated into PCN programs as procedure calls, indistinguishable for most purposes from calls to PCN procedures. Sequential procedures can be passed definitional and mutable data, but suspend until definitional data is available and hence never deal with incomplete information. Sequential procedures can modify only mutable variables.

A deficiency of the Fortran interface is that no special allowance is made for "common" data. Each physical processor has a single copy of all common data declared in an application's Fortran code, and every process on a processor has access to that data. Hence, while PCN data structures are encapsulated in processes to prevent concurrent access, the same protection is not provided for common data. It is the programmer's responsibility to avoid errors due to concurrent access. Experience shows that programmers deal with this problem in one of two ways. (1) If an application is of moderate size, or is being developed from scratch, they often choose to eliminate common data altogether. This may be achieved by allocating arrays in PCN and passing them to the different Fortran programs. Although this approach requires substantial changes to the application, the bulk of the existing Fortran can be retained, and the full flexibility of PCN is available to the programmer. (2) If substantial rewriting of an application is not possible, programmers maintain common data in its usual form and use PCN to organize operations on this data in a way that avoids nondeterminate interactions. Although certain operations are then more difficult (e.g., process migration is complicated, and the programmer must check for race conditions manually), other benefits of the PCN approach still apply.

The interface to sequential programming languages means that we do not need to throw away the many years of investment in sequential code and compiler development when moving to parallel computers. Fortran and C are good sequential languages but are less well suited to parallel programming. Experience suggests that PCN is a good parallel language; nevertheless, it cannot compete with Fortran and C in code base and compiler technology. *Multilingual programming* permits us to take the best from each approach, using PCN for mapping, communication, and scheduling, and Fortran and C for sequential computation.

4.2 Parallel Code: Cells and Templates

Cells

Our approach to the reuse of parallel code is based on what we term a *software cell*: a set of processes created within a virtual topology to perform some distinct function such as a reduction or a mesh computation, and provided with one or more port arrays for communication with other program components.[4] We have already seen several examples of cells: for instance, the procedure `ring` in the preceding section implements a cell that performs ring pipeline computations.

The interface to a PCN cell consists simply of the port arrays and definitional variables that are its arguments. A cell definition does not name the processors on which it will execute, the processes with which it will communicate, or the time at which it expects to execute. These decisions are encapsulated in the code that composes cells to create parallel programs: a virtual topology specifies the number and identity of processors, port arrays specify communication partners, and the PCN compiler handles scheduling. As we will see in subsequent examples, the simplicity of this interface allows cells to be reused in many different contexts.

Templates

The `ring` cell would be more useful if the code to be executed at each node could be specified as a parameter. This is possible, and in this case we refer to the cell definition as a *template*, as it encodes a whole family of similar cells. For example, the following is a template version of `ring`. The procedure to be executed is passed as the parameter `op`, which is quoted in the body to indicate that it is used as a variable.

```
ring(op, I, O)
port S[nodes()], I[], O[];
{|| i over 0..nodes()-1 ::
```

```
    'op'(I[i], O[i], S[(i+1)%nodes()],
        S[i]) @ node(i)
}
```

This template invokes the supplied procedure with four definitional variables as additional arguments. For example, if `op` has the value `nbody(p)`, then a procedure call `nbody(p, d1, d2, d3, d4)` (`d1..d4` being the variables from the port array) is invoked on each node of the virtual topology. All parameters to `op` must be definitional variables; it is the programmer's responsibility to ensure that the number and type of these parameters match `op`'s definition.

Example

We illustrate how cells and templates are composed to construct complete applications. We make use of the ring template and also the following simple input and output cells: `load` reads values from a file and sends them to successive elements of the port array P; `store` writes to a file values received on successive elements of port array Q. Both use the sequential composition operator to sequence I/O operations.

```
load(file, P)
port P[];
{ ; i over 0..nodes()-1 ::
        read(file, stuff),
        P[i] = stuff
}

store(file, Q)
port Q[];
{ ; i over 0..nodes()-1 ::
        write(file, Q[i])
}
```

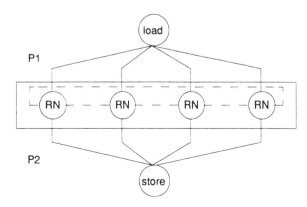

FIGURE 2. N-body program.

We compose the three cells to obtain a program `main` that reads data from `infile`, executes a user-supplied function in the ring pipeline (e.g., a naive N-body algorithm), and finally writes results to `outfile`. Note that although we use a parallel composition, data dependencies will force the three stages to execute in sequence. However, if `load` were to output a stream of values rather than a single value per node, then the three stages could execute concurrently, as a pipeline.

```
main(param, infile, outfile)
port P1[nodes()], P2[nodes()];
{|| load(infile, P1),
    ring(nbody(param), P1, P2),
    store(outfile, P2)
}
```

Data flows from `load` to `ring` via port array `P1` and from `ring` to `store` via port array `P2`. This is illustrated in Figure 2, which shows the process structure created in a four-node topology.

The complete program executes in an array topology (``main(if,of) in array()'')and will create a ring with one process per node of that topology.

5 TOOLS

The high-level nature of the PCN language requires a sophisticated compiler (to achieve efficient execution on sequential and parallel computers) and a specialized debugger (to keep track of multiple concurrent processes). These tools are integrated with other components to form a toolkit that supports debugging, performance tuning, and integration of Fortran and C code, and that allows programs to be executed on a wide variety of parallel computers and workstation networks.[3] In this section, we describe four components of this toolkit: compiler, network implementation, parallel debugger, and performance analysis tools.

5.1 Portable Compiler and Runtime System

We summarize the techniques used to translate PCN programs into executable code, so as to provide some insights into the efficiency of the PCN implementation.

The PCN compiler implements both the PCN language and the constructs introduced to support reuse of parallel code. It translates PCN programs to a machine-independent, low-level form that is linked with both object code for sequential language procedures and a small runtime system, to produce an executable program. The compiler is responsible for generating code to perform specialized operations such as creating processes, suspending processes, terminating processes, and generating messages: the runtime system routes incoming messages, schedules executable processes, and manages the heap on which are allocated process records, program data, etc.

The compiler and runtime system have been carefully designed to optimize the creation, scheduling, migration, and termination of lightweight processes. A process with n arguments is represented by a process record that occupies $n + 2$ words of memory, with n of these words containing pointers to arguments: hence, processes can be created, scheduled, or descheduled in a few tens of instructions. A process is migrated to another processor by communicating the process record and the data structures accessible from this process record. Thus, the cost of migration is primarily the cost of transferring its data, and processes with little data can be migrated extremely cheaply. The low cost of scheduling means that the runtime system is able to schedule idle tasks when waiting for the results of remote communication operations. That is, it automatically overlaps computation and communication operations.

The compiler does not currently optimize the performance of pure PCN code, which may execute 5 to 10 times slower than equivalent Fortran or C code. As PCN applications typically spend much of their time executing Fortran or C, this has not been a serious difficulty. (The profiling tools described below can be used to identify bottlenecks: if necessary, PCN procedures can be rewritten in Fortran or C to improve performance.) Future compilers will improve PCN performance, allowing a larger proportion of applications to be written in PCN.

A novel aspect of the compiler is a programmable source transformation system, incorporated as an optional stage in the compiler pipeline, after the parser and before the encoder. Programmers can use this facility to implement application-specific extensions to the PCN language. For example, the transformation system has been used to implement specialized composition operators that generate self-scheduling computations [6].

5.2 Network Implementation

The network implementation of PCN (net-PCN) allows users to treat a set of workstations as a parallel computer. Programs developed for multiprocessors and multicomputers can be run without modification on networks, although because of higher communication costs, algorithms must normally be more coarse-grained to execute efficiently.

Net-PCN can run on any machine that supports the TCP communication protocol. Hence, a single computation can in principle run on several workstations of a particular type, several workstations of differing types, several processors of a multiprocessor, or a mix of workstations and multiprocessor nodes. Currently, we require that all processors involved in a computation employ common representations for the basic PCN data types (characters, integers, and double-precision floats). In the future, type conversions will be performed automatically, allowing PCN programs to run transparently on arbitrary networks.

A useful component of net-PCN is a utility program called host-control, which provides facilities for managing a network computation. This utility allows the user to inquire about the status of nodes available to net-PCN, add and delete nodes, and execute programs [7].

5.3 PDB: A Parallel Debugger

Debugging tools that assist in the location of logical errors are, of course, a critical component of any programming system. PCN's unconventional language constructs, in particular its lightweight processes and dataflow synchronization, require specialized debugging support. This is provided by the PCN symbolic debugger, PDB.

The major difference between PCN and conventional sequential programming languages is that in PCN programs, many threads of control (processes) can be active at one time. Hence, PDB not only provides conventional debugger features, such as the ability to interrupt execution and examine program arguments, but also permits the user to examine enabled and suspended processes, identify definitional variables for which values have yet to be produced, and control the order in which processes are scheduled for execution.

A common error in PCN programming is for one program component not to produce a value required by another component. This results in a *deadlock* situation, in which all processes are suspended waiting for data. This situation can be detected by PDB. The programmer can examine the set of suspended processes and identify variables for which no values have been produced.

5.4 Understanding Performance

In parallel computing, where performance is critical and often nonintuitive, it is important to provide tools to assist in the identification of *performance errors*. Two such tools, Gauge and Upshot, have been integrated into PCN.

Gauge

Gauge is an execution profiler: it collects information about the amount of time that each processor spends in different parts of a program [8]. It also collects procedure call counts, message counts, and idle time information. Three properties of Gauge make it particularly useful: profiling information is collected automatically, without any programmer intervention; the overhead incurred to collect this information is small, typically much less than 1%; and the volume of data does not increase with execution time. A powerful data exploration tool permits graphical exploration of profile data. The use of Gauge is illustrated in a subsequent section.

Upshot

Upshot is a trace analysis tool that can provide insights into the fine-grained operation of parallel programs [9]. Upshot requires that the programmer instrument a program with calls to event logging primitives. These events are automatically recorded and written to a file when a program runs. A graphical trace analysis tool allows the programmer to examine temporal dependencies between events. Like any trace-based tool, Upshot suffers from scaling problems. However, it can be useful when used in a controlled manner, to examine local phenomena identified as problematic by Gauge.

6 APPLICATIONS

PCN has been used in substantial programming projects that have produced programs used to further scientific research on the world's fastest computers. For example, the first two applications operational on the 528-processor, 30 Gflops Intel

367

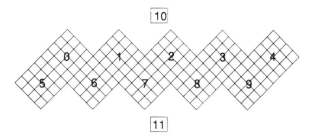

FIGURE 3 Icosahedral mesh domain decomposition.

Touchstone Delta system—a geophysical modeling code and a fluid dynamics code—were both PCN programs [10, 11]. Here, we describe one of those programs, survey other representative applications, and identify factors that appear to favor the use of PCN for programming projects.

6.1 Icosahedral Climate Modeling Code

This application implements a numerical method proposed for use in climate models, a second-order, conservative control volume method on an icosahedral-hexagonal grid. The code was developed to permit detailed studies of both the method's accuracy and the long-term behavior of fundamental modes of the atmospheric circulation. The code integrates existing Fortran and C code into a parallel framework implemented in PCN.[10]

An icosahedral-hexagonal grid can be structured as $10\,n \times n$ meshes plus two separate polar points. The parallel algorithm decomposes each mesh into c^2 submeshes, giving $10\,c^2 + 2$ subdomains, two with one point and the rest with $(n/c)^2$ points. Communication must be performed to obtain values from neighboring subdomains during integration. The design of an efficient mapping is complicated by the irregular domain. On some parallel computers, it may be desirable to place two or more subdomains on the same processor.

Implementation

The development of the parallel code is simplified if mapping is specified with respect to a virtual topology with the same shape as the problem domain [4]. We define an `ico_mesh` topology containing 10 $c \times c$ meshes and two polar processors (Fig. 3) and map functions `rhombus(i)` and `pole(i)` that embed subtopologies corresponding to a single mesh or pole in an `ico_mesh`. These functions are defined as follows. They lo-

cate rhombus i on nodes $ic^2 .. (i+1)c^2 - 1$ and pole j on node $10c^2 + j$ of an `ico_mesh` topology.

```
function rhombus(i)
{? topology() ?= {''ico_mesh'', c}, i >= 0,
    i < 10 ->
  {|| type = {''mesh'',c,c},
    size = c*c,
    map_fn = 'add_offset(i*c*c)',
    return( {type, size, map_fn} )
  },
  default -> error()
}


function pole(i)
{? topology() ?= {''ico_mesh'', c}, i >= 0,
    i < 2 ->
  {|| type = {''mesh'',1,1},
    size = 1,
    map_fn = 'add_offset(10*c*c+i)',
    return( {type, size, map_fn} )
  },
  default -> error()
}


function add_offset(offset,i)
{|| return( i + offset ) }
```

The following sketch of the top-level code for this application shows how mapping is expressed in terms of the icosahedral topology. Ten calls to a `mesh` template are used to set up a mesh cell inside each rhombus, two calls to `poleop` set up the polar computations, a call to a `reduce` cell establishes a global reduction structure (used for computing global minimums), and the `interconnect` procedure establishes communication streams between the various cells. For brevity, we omit the definitional variables representing communication streams.

```
sphere()
{|| {|| i over 0..9 ::
        mesh(...) @ submc(rhombus(i))
  },
  poleop(...) @ submc(pole(0)),
  poleop(...) @ submc(pole(1)),
  reduce(...),
  interconnect(...)
}
```

The `mesh` procedure used to create a single mesh is essentially the same as that outlined in Section 3.4. As the code executed within a subdomain is derived from the original Fortran and C, and a global reduction library is available, the only code that must be developed specifically for this application is the `interconnect` procedure and some interface code. To give an impression of

```
step(args,tau,tmax,dt,subrhombus,streams,to_r)
double subrhombus[];
{ ?
    tau < tmax ->
    { ;
        {|| /* Compute ''local_dt'' */
          find_local_dt(subrhombus,local_dt),
           /* Check old ''dt'' ok for this time step */
          { ? local_dt < dt -> error() },
           /* Initiate computation of ''new_dt'' */
          to_r = {{''min'',local_dt,new_dt},to_r1}
           /* Exchange data with neighbors */
          communications(streams,subrhombus,streams1)
        },
        pre_filter(args,subrhombus),
         /* Compute on grid, using old ''dt'' */
        update_grid(args,dt,tau,subrhombus),
        post_filter(args,subrhombus),
         /* Proceed to next time step, passing ''new_dt'' */
        step(args,tau+dt,tmax,new_dt,subrhombus,streams1,to_r1)
    },
    default -> terminate(args,subrhombus)
}
```

FIGURE 4. Main driver program.

what the interface code looks like. we include in Figure 4 the main driver executed for each subrhombus. Conceptually, this alternates communication and computation. However, there are some subtleties. For example, the code communicates with a reduction cell to determine a global time step (Δt) consistent with the CFL condition. The use of the new Δt is delayed for one iteration so as to permit overlapping of the communication required for the reduction with other computation. This is achieved by using dt as Δt in the current step, and passing new_dt to the recursive call to step for use as Δt in the next step.

Experiences

The parallel code was developed in collaboration with the mathematician who wrote the original sequential code. He provided advice to the undergraduate intern who wrote the parallel program. and assisted with various enhancements to the numerical method. We were fortunate in that the Fortran code used common storage only for constants: storage for program data was allocated by a C driver. This meant that we could reuse much of the Fortran without change. In addition, once we had set up the constants in the common storage on each processor, we were free to map processes to processors in any way we wanted. The complete code totals 1,400 lines Fortran. 870 lines C, and 750 lines of PCN. The relatively large amount of PCN code reflects the fact that a number of enhancements to the sequential code were implemented in PCN rather than Fortran. due to the greater ease of programming in the higher-level language.

The parallel program was developed. debugged. and refined on a Sun workstation. The resulting code was moved to a 26-node Sequent Symmetry shared-memory computer for performance studies and from there was ported with only minor changes to a 192-node Symult s2010 mesh. 64-node Intel iPSC/860 hypercube. and 528-node i860-based Intel Touchstone Delta mesh. The changes were due primarily to use of a different I/O structure on the Delta, and a need to work around certain deficiencies in the Delta's file system (since corrected). This portability allowed us to obtain scientific results within 1 week of the Delta's being installed at Caltech in May 1991: applications developed with other technologies were not operational until weeks or even months later.

Profile and trace data provided by Gauge and Upshot allowed us to identify mapping and load

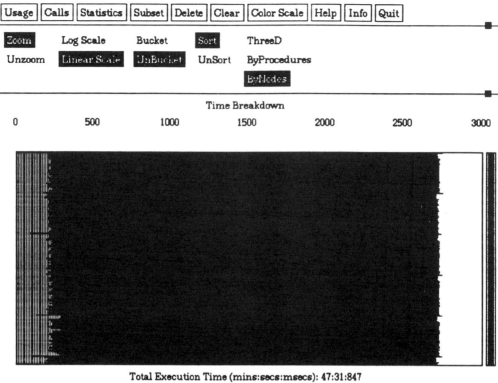

Total Execution Time (mins:secs:msecs): 47:31:847
Total Reductions: 2785082505
Total Suspensions: 3553936826

FIGURE 5 Gauge performance display: time breakdown.

balancing problems in early versions of our program. One problem was that a too-coarse-grained decomposition of the Fortran code gave the PCN compiler too little opportunity to overlap computation and communication. The result was much idle time. A more fine-grained implementation was easily achieved in a few hours' work; this gave the good performance results reported below.

An example of a load imbalance is illustrated in Figure 5. This is a Gauge histogram display of summary data for a run on 492 Delta processors, with each pixel in the vertical dimension representing a processor and shading distinguishing time spent idle (light) and busy (dark). (About 260 processors are visible.) A slight load imbalance is evident: it appears that the processors handling location (0,0) in each rhombus are spending more time computing than other processors. Other Gauge facilities allowed us to isolate the Fortran routine in which the load imbalance occurs, at which point it was easily corrected by modifying the Fortran code. We claim that without Gauge it would have been difficult to correct this load imbalance (or even, perhaps, to suspect its existence).

Good parallel efficiencies are achieved on all four parallel computers. On the Delta, we obtain approximately 2.5 Gflops (5 Mflops per processor) and 80% efficiency relative to the pure Fortran code running on a single i860 processor, for a problem size of N = 56 (approximately 150-km resolution). This compares favorably with other applications, which have typically achieved 3 to 6 Mflops/processor. Tuning of the sequential Fortran and improvements to the Delta compiler are expected to further improve overall performance.

The parallel code uses a simple embedding of the icosahedral mesh that is not specialized for either hypercube or mesh topologies. This mapping does not attempt to cluster neighboring icosahedral mesh nodes but simply allocates nodes in the icosahedral mesh to consecutive nodes in the underlying computer. It is specified as follows.

```
function icosahedron(c)
{|| type = {''ico_mesh'', c},
   size = 10*c*c+2,
   map_fn = `node()',
   return( {type, size, map_fn} )
}
```

Because parallel efficiency is so good. we have not been motivated to explore alternative mappings of the icosahedral mesh. (Some tinkering with the mapping did not appear to generate significant improvements: this is probably to be expected, given that cut-through routing in the Symult and Delta reduces the importance of communication locality.) Nevertheless. the use of the icosahedral virtual topology leaves us with the option of exploring alternatives in the future. if either improvements in per-node performance increase relative communication costs, or the code is ported to a machine on which locality is more important. One potentially interesting mapping would fold the whole icosahedral mesh structure (locating two or more nodes per processor) so as to reduce message latency. Of course, this can be achieved without changing the application code.

6.2 Application Survey

Most applications developed to date are. like the icosahedral code, scientific in nature: almost all use PCN to organize the parallel execution of pre-existing Fortran or C code. Although they solve a wide variety of problems, many can be structured in terms of one or more of a small number of basic cells and templates. We describe some representative examples, indicating the structures used in the implementations. We also give code sizes when this information is available to us.

Mesh Structures

The structure of many different mesh-based applications can be captured in one- or two-dimensional mesh templates. A two-dimensional mesh template forms a building block for both the icosahedral code and another climate modeling code based on overlapping stereographic meshes (3,800 lines C. 640 lines PCN) [10]. Other mesh-based applications include a computational fluid dynamics code developed by Harrar *et al.* for computing Taylor-vortex flows. based on a torus structure [11] (5.300 lines Fortran. 900 lines PCN); a finite-element code for simulating flow in Titan rocket engines (9,000 lines Fortran, 180 lines PCN): and a parallel implementation of the mesoscale weather model MM4 (15.000 lines Fortran, 250 lines PCN). Work is under way to build a version of MM4 in which the mesh template performs dynamic load balancing.

Ring Structures

Cells similar to the ring structure presented in Section 4.2 form the basis for several applications. A code for computing nonlinear dynamics properties of extended climate simulations uses an algorithm similar to that used for naive N-body simulations of molecular dynamics (250 lines Fortran. 170 lines PCN). Essentially the same algorithm and structure have also been used in programs for computing molecular interactions and covariances between bases in genetic sequences (the latter is 500 lines C. 800 lines PCN). Similar structures are used in a parallel implementation of the spectral transform method used in climate modeling (7.400 lines Fortran. 370 lines PCN).

Tree Structures

Tree and butterfly structures are used in many codes to perform parallel reductions. A good example of a code based entirely on a tree structure is one developed by Wright to solve two-point boundary value problems [12] (700 lines Fortran. 50 lines PCN). This algorithm dynamically creates a process tree: data is produced at the leaves. flows up the tree to the root (being reduced at each node), and then back down to the leaves to yield the final solution [3]. The code is defined with respect to a tree virtual topology: the map function that defines this topology specifies how the complete structure is embedded in a parallel computer. Note that it is the low cost of process creation and migration in PCN which makes this dynamic formulation of the algorithm (which proved to be particularly convenient) feasible.

Self-Scheduling Structures

A self-scheduling program incorporates code to dynamically map tasks to idle processors: although this approach introduces additional overhead relative to a static schedule. it is essential for some very dynamic problems. Self-scheduling programs can be constructed easily in PCN because of the simplicity of process migration [6]. (The global address space provided by the compiler means that processes can be migrated as data structures.) Self-scheduling applications include codes for aligning genetic sequences, computing phylogenetic trees. and predicting protein structure. (Computational biology is a rich source of applications for self-scheduling techniques because of the frequent use of heuristics.) An application under development at Argonne schedules tasks to ring structures (each involving several processors) rather than to individual processors. An interesting aspect of all these codes is that the scheduling code can be separated from the application-specific code in a distinct scheduling cell. Alternative scheduling cells can be substituted without changing the application: typically the scheduling structure is specified in 20 to 100 lines of code.

Genetic Algorithms

Genetic optimization algorithms maintain a population of candidate solution vectors and apply simulated natural selection to improve the quality of this population. One approach to parallelizing these algorithms is to maintain multiple populations, with periodic exchanges of individual vectors. Our PCN implementation of a parallel genetic algorithm is parameterized with the initialization, mutation, and mating operators that define a genetic algorithm. The PCN code handles all aspects of execution on a parallel computer, using a *router* cell for asynchronous communication of selected individuals between populations and a *reduction* cell for computing global values when checking for termination. The PCN code totals 500 lines: applications developed with this code have added anything from a few hundred lines of C to 6,000 lines of Fortran.

6.3 Discussion

As this brief survey shows, PCN applications span a wide range, from the simple and straightforward to the sophisticated and complex. The amount of PCN code incorporated in the various programs depends both on the complexity of the parallel algorithms and the extent to which PCN was used for algorithm development in addition to porting.

It is probably too early to draw firm conclusions regarding the merits of the approach. However, we can make a few observations concerning user reactions. We find that programmers perceive a substantial benefit from the use of PCN (and frequently become ardent advocates of the technology) when their programming problem has one or more of the following characteristics.

1. A complex communication structure, or a need to overlap computation and communication.
2. A need for load balancing.
3. Dynamic computation, communication, or mapping structures.

4. A need for portability and scalability.
5. Initial performance errors that are corrected by using Gauge.
6. An interest in exploring algorithmic alternatives: e.g., different stencils, reduction strategies, communication algorithms, or mappings.
7. An ability to reuse existing cells and templates.

In contrast, programmers working with simple, regular problems (such as one-dimensional decompositions with static mapping) find it hard to justify the inevitable learning curve associated with a new approach to programming.

7 CONCLUSIONS

The ability to develop parallel programs quickly and easily is becoming increasingly important to many scientists and engineers. Although we cannot expect parallel programming to become easy, we can avoid unnecessary difficulties by using appropriate tools. In this article, we have described tools that take us several steps beyond the low level facilities commonly available on parallel supercomputers. A simple concurrent programming notation allows us to express complex parallel algorithms without unnecessary contortions. Interfaces to sequential languages allow us to reuse existing Fortran and C code. Support for cells and templates allows us to define and reuse parallel program structures. Compiler, debugging, and performance analysis tools reduce the labor associated with program development and provide portability over a wide range of machines.

PCN has already been used to develop substantial applications; other application projects are under way. Optimizing compilers are being developed, with particular emphasis on the requirements of fine-grained computers. Libraries of software cells and templates are being developed to support fluid dynamics, geophysical modeling, and computational chemistry; similar libraries can and should be developed for other areas of computational science.

ACKNOWLEDGMENTS

This work is a collaborative effort involving research groups at Argonne and Caltech. As such, it owes a great debt to many individuals. Steve Taylor leads the research at Caltech. Mani Chandy has contributed to the language definition. Sharon Brunett and Dong Ling are responsible for compiler development. Gauge and Upshot were developed by Carl Kesselman and Ewing Lusk, respectively. I-liang Chern and Steve Hammond helped develop the icosahedral grid application.

This research was supported at Argonne by the National Science Foundation's Center for Research on Parallel Computation under Contract NSF CCR-8809615 and by the Applied Mathematical Sciences subprogram of the Office of Energy Research, U.S. Department of Energy, under Contract W-31-109-Eng-38.

REFERENCES

[1] A. Whitehead. *An Introduction to Mathematics.* Oxford, England: Oxford University Press, 1958.

[2] C. Chandy and S. Taylor. *An Introduction to Parallel Programming.* Boston, MA: Jones and Bartlett, 1991, pp. 1–228.

[3] I. Foster and S. Tuecke. *Parallel Programming with PCN,* Technical Report ANL-91/32, Argonne National Laboratory, 1991.

[4] I. Foster. *Information hiding in parallel programs,* Preprint MCS-P290-0292, Argonne National Laboratory, 1992.

[5] I. Foster and S. Taylor. *Strand: New Concepts in Parallel Programming.* Englewood Cliffs, NJ: Prentice-Hall, 1989, pp. 1–333.

[6] I. Foster. "Automatic generation of self-scheduling programs," *IEEE Trans. Parallel and Distributed Systems,* vol. 2, no. 1, pp. 68–78, January 1991.

[7] R. Olson. *Using host-control,* Technical Memo ANL/MCS-TM-154, Argonne National Laboratory, 1991.

[8] C. Kesselman. *Integrating Performance Analysis with Performance Improvement in Parallel Programs,* Technical Report UCLA-CS-TR-91-03, UCLA, 1991.

[9] V. Herrarte and E. Lusk. *Studying parallel program behavior with Upshot,* Technical Report ANL-91/15, Argonne National Laboratory, 1991.

[10] I. Chern and I. Foster, "Design and parallel implementation of two methods for solving PDEs on the sphere," *Proc. Conf. on Parallel Computational Fluid Dynamics,* Stuttgart, Germany: Elsevier Science Publishers B.V., 1991, pp. 83–96.

[11] H. Harrar, H. Keller, D. Lin, and S. Taylor, "Parallel computation of Taylor-vortex flows," *Proc. Conf. on Parallel Computational Fluid Dynamics,* Stuttgart, Germany: Elsevier Science Publishers B.V., 1991, 193–206.

[12] S. Wright. *Stable parallel algorithms for two point boundary value problems,* Preprint MCS-P178-0990, Argonne National Laboratory, and *SIAM J. Sci. Statistical Comput.,* 1992 (in press).

The Derivation of Compositional Programs

K. Mani Chandy and Carl Kesselman *
California Institute of Technology
Pasadena, California 91125, USA
mani@vlsi.caltech.edu, carl@vlsi.caltech.edu

Abstract

This paper proposes a parallel programming notation and a method of reasoning about programs with the following characteristics:

1. Parallel Composition The notation provides different forms of interfaces between processes; the more restrictive the interface, the simpler the proofs of process composition. A flexible interface is that of cooperating processes with a shared address space; proofs of programs that use this interface are based on non-interference [OG76] and temporal logic [Pnu81, CM88, Lam91]. We also propose more restrictive interfaces and specifications that allow us to use the following *specification-conjunction* rule: the strongest specification of a parallel composition of processes is the conjunction of the strongest specifications of its components. This rule is helpful in deriving parallel programs.

2. Determinism A process that does not use certain primitives of the notation is guaranteed to be deterministic. Programmers who wish to prove that their programs are deterministic are relieved of this proof obligation if they restrict their programs to a certain subset of the primitives.

1 Parallel Composition

VLSI is an example of parallel programming as Chuck Seitz asserts. The success of VLSI is due in part to a hierarchy of interfaces for composing circuits: from composing transistors to form memory units, to composing microprocessors to form multicomputers. A designer putting transistors together has to be concerned with issues such as parasitic capacitance. A designer putting microprocessors together works with a more restrictive interface that does not deal with such details; the interface is such that a microprocessor behaves as a microprocessor regardless of the circuits to which it is connected. Composing transistors and composing microprocessors are both instances of parallel composition; the interfaces between transistors is different from the interfaces between microprocessors, and therefore, the ways of reasoning about compositions of transistors is different from the ways of reasoning about compositions of microprocessors.

What is the analogy to composing processes? There are situations where we may want to employ flexible interfaces between concurrent processes and other situations in which we want to use more restrictive interfaces between processes. In general, more restrictive interfaces allow for simpler proof techniques and more flexible interfaces can provide more efficiency. We propose a notation and methods of reasoning about programs that allow programmers to design different kinds of interfaces between concurrent processes. Programmers can balance flexibility on the one hand with ease of reasoning on the other, in designing their own interfaces.

A very flexible interface between concurrent processes is where processes share variables, and use atomicity and **await** commands [OG76]; in this case methods of reasoning are based on non-interference [OG76] or temporal logic and its derivatives [Pnu81, CM88, Lam91]. More restrictive interfaces and specifications allow us to use the powerful specification-conjunction rule for reasoning about parallel composition.

Consider a simple example that illustrates the problem of interfaces between concurrent processes.

Example The process p:

```
do x = 0  →  x := x+2   []    x = 1 →  x := -1 od
```

satisfies the specification: $(x = 0) \rightsquigarrow (x \geq 2)$, if $x = 0$ at any point in its computation, then at a later point in its computation $x \geq 2$.

The same specification is satisfied by the process q:

```
do ((x = 0) ∨ (x = 1))  → x := x + 1 od
```

The parallel composition of p and q, p‖q, does not satisfy the specification, because q can change the value of x from 0 to 1, and then p can change the value of x to -1, after which x remains unchanged.

The parallel composition of processes, all of which have a common specification R, may not satisfy specification R, because the shared-memory interface between processes is flexible and allows one process to "interfere" with the proof of another [OG76]. Later, we define more restrictive interfaces and specifications that permit simpler proofs.

1.1 Processes

We define processes in terms of transition systems [Pnu81, Lam91, CM88]. A system is a set $\mathcal{P}$ of processes and a set $\mathcal{G}$ of global variables. A process is (i) a set L of *local variables*, (ii) a set G of *shared variables* where $G \subseteq \mathcal{G}$, (iii) the *initial values* of its variables $L \cup G$, and (iv) a set of atomic *actions*. The name space of local variables of a process is local to the process; by contrast, the name space of shared variables is global to the system.

A state of a process is defined by the values of the variables of the process. (Program counters or other methods of representing the locus of control are treated as variables, as in [CM88].) The initial state of a process is given by the initial values of its variables.

An action is a binary relation on states of the process. We shall say that an action A takes a process from a state S to a state S' if and only if $(S, S') \in A$. An action A is *executable* in a state S if there exists an S' such that A takes the process from S to S',

1.2 System States and Transitions

The state of a system is a tuple of states of its component processes where the values of shared variables are consistent among all processes, i.e., if v is shared by p and q, and $v = v'$ in the state of process p in the tuple, then $v = v'$ in the state of process q in the tuple as well.

The initial state of a system is a tuple of initial states of its component processes if the values of shared variables are consistent in the tuple. If initial shared-variable values are inconsistent, the initial system state is undefined.

Transitions between system states are labeled with actions of component processes. There exists a transition labeled A from a system state S to a system state S' if and only if there exists a transition A in a component process p such that

1. values of all variables other than those referenced by p are identical in S and S', and

2. action A takes the values of variables referenced by p from their values in S to their values in S'.

1.3   Computations

A *computation* of a process p is an initial state S_0 of the process, and a sequence of pairs (A_i, S_i) where $i > 0$ and action A_i takes the process from process-state S_{i-1} to process-state S_i, and the sequence satisfies the following *fairness rule*:

For all infinite computations, if action B is executable at some point in the computation then there is a later point in the computation at which either B is executed or B is not executable.

B is executable in $S_i \Rightarrow$
$\quad (\exists j : j > i : (A_j = B) \vee (B \text{ is not executable in } S_j))$

A *terminal* process-state is a state S such that all actions of the process are disabled in S. A *maximal computation* of a process is either an infinite computation or a computation that ends in a terminal state.

System computations, terminal system states, and maximal computations of systems are defined in the same way as for processes (except that system states replace process states in the definitions).

1.4   Process Properties and Open Systems

A conventional definition of process *properties* is as follows:

Closed-System Definition of Properties
A property R of a process p is a predicate on maximal computations of p where all maximal computations of p satisfy R.

With this definition, $p\|q$ does not have a property common to both p and q. How can we define process properties so as to use the following rule:

> *A property of p is a property of $p\|q$, for all processes q?*

An obvious solution is to redefine properties in a somewhat unconventional way:

Open-System Definition of Properties

R is a property of p if and only if for all processes q, R is a predicate on maximal computations of $p\|q$, and R holds for all maximal computations of $p\|q$.

The conventional definition of process properties is sometimes referred to as the *closed-system* definition, and the alternative definition is called an *open-system* definition; this nomenclature is because the conventional definition defines properties of a process executing in isolation, whereas the alternative definition defines properties of a parallel composition of a process with some arbitrary "environment."

Relative Advantages of Open and Closed Systems

The primary disadvantage of the open-system definition is that the properties that we can prove about open-systems are weak. To prove a property of a process p we have to consider computations of p executing concurrently with q, for *all* processes q. So, we are forced to consider processes that the designer of p had no intention of composing with p. For instance, we cannot prove that a multiplier circuit multiplies because it can be connected to a megavolt power supply that fries the multiplier!

The primary disadvantage of the closed-system definition is that we do not enjoy the benefits of specification-conjunction. When we wish to prove properties about the parallel composition of processes we use noninterference [OG76] or prove properties from the *text* of the component programs [CM88] as opposed to the preferred mode of composing specifications without regard to program text.

2 The Proper Interface Approach

An approach that enjoys some of the advantages of both open and closed systems is the *proper interface* approach. We define a *proper* interface (or protocol) by which processes cooperate. We restrict attention to process composition in which the interface between processes is proper; we call composition with proper interfaces *proper composition*. We define process properties as for open systems, but we restrict attention to proper interfaces:

Proper-Interface Definition of Properties

A property of a process p is a predicate on maximal computations of $p\|q$, that holds for all maximal computations of $p\|q$, for all q *such that the interface between p and q is proper*.

Are the properties we can prove, using proper interfaces, too weak to be useful? That depends on the definition of proper interfaces — the more flexible the interface, the weaker the properties.

One of the advantages of hardware modules is that engineers have developed a set of proper interfaces. A hardware module is specified in terms of its inputs and outputs for a proper interface. When hardware modules are composed, the designer proves that the interfaces are proper (and this is usually straightforward) and then the designer can use specification-conjunction. Design is simplified greatly by being able to assert that the output of a multiplier circuit is the product of its inputs, regardless of the circuits with which the multiplier is composed, provided that the interfaces are proper. The designer of a multiplier circuit does not have to be concerned about the circuit being connected to a megavolt power supply because such an interface is not proper. The designer has to be concerned, however, with *all* possible environments with proper interfaces.

A problem with concurrent programming is that we do not usually specify software processes in terms of standard interfaces with clearly defined inputs and outputs; and we define process properties in terms of closed systems; and, therefore, we cannot use specification-conjunction to prove properties of concurrent programs. A proper-interface approach is particularly helpful in designing libraries of processes, all of which use the same interface.

2.1 A Collection of Proper Interfaces

For an open-systems specification, we specify an interface of a process in terms of the outputs of the process and the outputs of the environment of the process. The form of outputs (messages, shared-variables,...) is not important at this stage. There are many ways of designing interfaces, but to simplify design we will design processes and proper interfaces that satisfy the following rules.

Rule 1: An action is one of the following three types:

1. **Inputs:** The action reads shared variables as input and (possibly) reads or modifies local variables.

2. **Outputs:** The action modifies shared variables as output and (possibly) reads or modifies local variables.

3. **Internal:** The action does not reference shared variables.

The output actions and internal actions of a process are nonblocking because they depend only on the state of the process (and are otherwise independent of the state of the system).

Rule 2:   If an input action B is executable at some point in a computation, then it remains executable until it is executed.

$$(B \text{ is executable in } S_i) \land (B \neq A_{i+1}) \Rightarrow (B \text{ is executable in } S_{i+1})$$

This rule disallows probes [Mar85] and other nonmonotonic operators on inputs. A probe checks whether an input is present and takes some action if there is no input; this action can be disabled when an input arrives. But, according to the rule, if an action is executable, it must remain executable until the action is taken.

This rule also prohibits a process from changing an earlier output value; a process can *add* to its earlier output but it cannot change its earlier output. Thus, we have an ordering relation on the "length" of outputs and inputs. For now, assume that outputs and inputs are sequences of values. We can consider other data structures such as trees, provided "length" is defined properly, but this is not central to our discussion.

Rule 3:   An input of a process is a prefix of an output of at most one process.

If an input to a process were an output of two or more processes, we would have to deal with interference between processes writing to the same input.

The input to a process may not equal the output from a process because of delays in transmission; hence, we require the input to be an initial subsequence of the output.

An output can feed an arbitrary number of inputs. If x is a process output, and y and z are process inputs, we can have:
$(x \text{ is a prefix of } y) \land (x \text{ is a prefix of } z)$

Consider the example, given earlier, of processes p and q sharing a variable x, where though both p and q have a property R, the parallel composition $p\|q$ does not have property R. What are the inputs to p? One definition is that the inputs to p are the sequence of values of x prior to actions by p; these are the sequence of values of the shared variable, projected on p's computation. A definition of the outputs of q are the values of x at the termination of actions of q. But, with this definition, the rules for inputs and outputs are not satisfied! One process can modify x with no impact on the computation of the other process. There seems to be no convenient way to define inputs and outputs so that the input of one process is a prefix of the output of the other.

Next we propose a few proper interfaces that satisfy the rules.

2.2 Examples

Modify Privileges   At most one process has the privilege of modifying a shared variable. The modify-privilege for a shared-variable can be passed between processes; the methods by which privileges are passed is not important at this point in the discussion. An input of a process p, and an output of a process q is the sequence of values of a shared variable at the points in the computation at which the modify-privilege for the shared variable is passed from q to p.

Single-Assignment   Associated with each shared variable x is a boolean x.assigned which is initially false. When a value is assigned to x, the boolean x.assigned becomes true — i.e., a postcondition to every assignment to x is x.assigned.

A value can be assigned to a shared variable at most once in a computation; therefore, if the precondition to an assignment to x is x.assigned holds, then the postcondition is that error holds, where error is a boolean that indicates whether an error has occurred.

The booleans x.assigned cannot appear in the program text. Note that rule 2 prohibits testing whether a variable is unassigned.

The execution of a process reading an unassigned shared variable is suspended until the variable is assigned a value. Each shared variable referenced by a process is either an input or an output variable of the process, and a shared variable is an output variable of at most one process.

An output (input) of a process is the value (if any) assigned to an output (input) variable of the process

Computations of unbounded length are achieved by using data structures, such as lists, of unbounded length.

Message Passing   The shared variables are first-in-first-out channels. The state of a channel is a queue of messages. The length of the queue is unbounded. A channel is empty initially. At most one process can send messages on a channel (append to the queue) and at most one process can receive messages on a channel (delete from the queue). Sending is nonblocking — i.e. the executability of a send action of a process p depends only on the state of p. Receives are blocking — a receive on a channel is executable only if the channel is nonempty. Probes are not permitted: a channel cannot be tested to determine if it is empty.

An output of a process p is the sequence of messages that p sends on a channel. An input of a process p is the sequence of messages received by p on a channel.

The privilege to send messages, and to receive messages, on a channel can also be sent from one process to another [FC92].

2.3 Reasoning about Programs

A property of a process is a temporal logic formula, and the only rule we have for parallel composition is: if R is a property of p then R is a property of $p\|q$, for any q such that the interface between p and q is proper.

Because, we have an ordering on the lengths of inputs and outputs, an operator that is useful is *establishes* [CT91]. Let R be a predicate on process states. Process p *establishes* R if and only if for all maximal computations of $p\|q$, where q is any process such that the interface between p and q is proper, there exists a suffix of the computation such that R holds for each state of the suffix.

In temporal-logic terms, p establishes R means "eventually always R."

The proof that establishes is conjunctive is straightforward [CT91].

$(p \text{ establishes } R) \wedge (p \text{ establishes } T) \Rightarrow (p \text{ establishes } R \wedge T)$
$(p \text{ establishes } R) \wedge (q \text{ establishes } T) \Rightarrow (p\|q \text{ establishes } R \wedge T)$

The following example illustrates the use of *establishes*.

Consider a single-assignment interface. Process p has inputs x and output y. Process q has inputs x and y and output z. The body of p is: y = x+1 and the body of q is z = x*y

We can prove:

p establishes (x.assigned $\Rightarrow$ y.assigned $\wedge$ y = x+1)
q establishes ((x.assigned $\wedge$ y.assigned) $\Rightarrow$ z.assigned $\wedge$ z = x*y)

Using specification-conjunction and predicate calculus:

$p\|q$ establishes
((x.assigned $\Rightarrow$ y.assigned $\wedge$ z.assigned $\wedge$ y = x+1 $\wedge$ z = x*y)

The use of *establishes* simplifies proofs of parallel composition with proper interfaces. The operator *establishes* was proposed within the context of the PCN theory. Here, we observe that the same constructs can be extended to other proper interfaces.

3 Determinism

We can prove that if each process in a parallel composition is deterministic, and the parallel composition satisfies our 3 rules for proper interfaces, then the parallel composition is deterministic as well: Different executions of the parallel composition produce identical output.

4 Programming Languages and Proper Composition

Next, we consider language support for the design of families of interfaces for parallel composition. We wish to support flexible interfaces with which we use closed-systems specifications and we also wish to support more restrictive interfaces with which we use proper-interface specifications.

We have based our research on the C++ programming language [ES90]. A major objective of C++ is to provide a language framework for constructing program libraries with well defined, compiler enforced interfaces. These features, along with its widespread, use motivated our choice of C++. Our design methodology is supported by C++ augmented by small number of simple extensions. We call the resulting language Compositional C++ or CC++. A detailed discussion of CC++ can be found in [CK92].

Parallel composition in CC++ is provided by parallel blocks (equivalent to parbegin/parend) and a parallel loop construct. Any statement can appear in a parallel block; blocks can be nested. The execution of a parallel block terminates when all statements in the block terminate.

A generalization of the single assignment rule is used to synchronize operations between statements executing in parallel. Primitive data types can be declared to be synchronization or sync objects. A process reading an uninitialized sync object suspends until the object is initialized by an assignment. Multiple initialization of the same variable is an error. CC++ generalizes single assignment variables in that *user-defined* data types can also be made sync. The designer of the data type has complete control over the semantics of user defined sync objects and the operations that can be performed on such a data object.

In C++, one can associate a function with a user-defined data type; such a function can only be applied to an object of the appropriate type. These functions control the manner in which a data type can be used. Such functions are commonly invoked through a pointer to an object of that data type. If a pointer to an object is a global variable of a system, invoking a function through such a pointer corresponds to a remote procedure call. If a reference to an object is shared by more than one statement in a par block, nondeterministic execution can result. As part of the interface specification for a data type, we can indicate that the operations of a function take place atomically.

5 The Relationship between CC++ and Logic Programming

In our work, we have focused on language mechanisms that facilitate the design of interfaces for parallel composition. The design of CC++ draws ideas from a wide range of parallel programming languages.. These include data flow languages with single-assignment variables [TE68, Ack82], remote procedure calls [TA90], message passing [Sei91], actors [Agh86], concurrent logic programming [FT90, Ued86, Sha86] and compositional languages, particularly PCN [CT91]. While a range of comparisons are possible, the following discussion will focus on the relationship between CC++ and concurrent logic programming languages.

A "pure" logic program has a declarative reading. Such a program does not presuppose any ordering on the actions the program performs. The execution of a program produces a consistent set of variable bindings. As long as the bindings are consistent between program components, the order in which the bindings are determined is not specified. Thus, the conjunction and disjunction operators in a logic program can be viewed as specifying a parallel composition. Clearly, in a pure logic program, one that does not utilize predicates with side effects, all compositions are proper. One may write an open-system specification for a program component, however, that specification is restricted to use only logical variables. If predicates with side effects are used (i.e. such as cut, input/output, assert), then the specification must be weakened.

The situation in the committed choice languages such as Strand [FT90], FCP [Sha86], GHC [Ued86] or Parlog [Gre87] is not as clear cut. In these languages, only one solution path is explored, there is no backtracking or or-parallel search. In order to control which solution path is followed, modify access to variables is restricted. A consequence of read only variables is that the programmer has additional proof obligations, or the open-system specification is weakened. For example, a procedure can deadlock if the environment with which it is composed does not follow an appropriate resource acquisition protocol.

Concurrent logic programming languages provide the safety net that all programs written in such a language conform to the protocol of a proper declarative composition. By contrast, CC++ places the burden of designing interfaces and their proofs on the programmer. We observe, however, that in many large scale parallel programs, efficiency and system concerns dictate that some parts of the program be written in an imperative programming language. Indeed multilingual programming using a concurrent logic programming language as the interface had been proposed as a useful parallel programming paradigm [FO90, FO91, FT90, CT91] and most logic programming languages include "foreign language" interfaces. However, once foreign language components are introduced into a system, the tasks of designing interfaces and their proofs falls back onto the user.

It is important to recognize that a sync variable in CC++ is a pure single assignment variable and not a logical variable. In particular, the assignment x = y suspends until y has a value; variable-to-variable assignments are not made. Consequently, structured sync data behaves more like an I-Structure [AT80] from the dataflow language Id [Ack82] than a tuple from a logic programming language. The use of single assignment variables in place of logical variables has the advantages that assignment semantics are completely consistent with C++, and that pointer dereferencing is not required prior to variable use. The disadvantage is that some concurrent logic programming techniques, such as the short circuit technique [Tak89] become sequentialized. This is not a significant drawback, however, because termination of parallel blocks is easily determined.

CC++ has many ideas in common with the parallel programming language PCN [CT91] which in turn draws heavily from committed choice concurrent logic programming languages such as Strand [FT90]. There are, however, fundamental differences between them. These include:

- CC++ provides a general shared memory model. This includes having pointers to data objects.

- PCN permits x = y as an equality. CC++ treats all assignment operators as assignment of value.

- Remote procedure call is a primitive operation in CC++.

- There are no nondeterministic language constructs in CC++ as opposed to PCN. Nondeterminism in CC++ is obtained through interleaving of atomic actions.

- The emphasis in CC++ is on the development of families of interfaces and proofs. PCN provides a single-assignment interface and proof theory.

6 A Programming Example

To demonstrate how CC++ supports parallel program design through proper interfaces, we present a simple example. The parallel program we wish to construct is a producer/consumer system. The producer process produces a sequence of values. The values are processed in order by a consumer process. Both the producer and the consumer execute in parallel. One of the advantages of CC++ is that the parallel code is quite similar to the sequential C++ code that solve the same problem. The primary difference is the use of sync variables and the introduction of parallel blocks.

We will solve this problem using three different interfaces: i) a declarative interface, ii) a modify-privileges interface, and iii) a message passing interface.

Figure 2 shows how a producer/consumer program is constructed using a declarative interface. The sequence of values is passed from the producer to the consumer on a list. The list structure, whose declaration is shown in Figure 1, is declared so that both the value being placed on the list, and the pointer to the next cell of the list are sync. The producer iterates, creating new list cells, initializing their values and setting the next field of the previous cell to point to the newly created cell. The consumer is passed a sync pointer to a list cell. It cannot proceed until that pointer is assigned a list cell. Furthermore, the value field of the list cell cannot be used until it is initialized. Within the main routine, the producer and consumer execute in parallel.

The modify-privileges interface is essentially the same as the declarative interface. The only difference is that the value field of the list cell is *not* sync. The modify-privileges interface protocol requires that shared values can only be modified by the procedure with modification privileges. Modify privileges are passed from the producer to the consumer when the sync next

```
// The value of the list element and the pointer to the
// next list cell are both sync variables

struct list {
  sync T value;
  struct list * sync next;
}
```

Figure 1: The list structure used to pass data between a producer and a consumer.

pointer is initialized. Thus we must ensure that the value component of the list is initialized before the next pointer is set.

Our final example is a message passing interface. In a message passing interface, we must have an entity to send a message to. Therefore, we will define the producer and consumer as user defined types. We associate a set of functions with each user defined type. Thus the produce function can be applied to a variable of type producer, while the insert_queue and consume operations can be applied to a variable of type consumer. The consumer also has a get_queue operation which is only accessible to variables of type consumer.

The main program creates a producer and consumer variable and applies the produce and consume operations to the producer and consumer respectively. The producer inserts a data value directly into the queue of the consumer by calling applying the insert_queue operation. The consumer then extract the data values and processes them. The operations on the queue must be made atomic to prohibit insert_queue and get_queue operations from occurring simultaneously.

References

[Ack82] William B. Ackerman. Data flow languages. *Computer*, 15(2):15–25, feb 1982.

[Agh86] Gul Agha. *ACTORS: A Model of Concurrent Computation in Distributed Systems*. MIT Press, 1986.

[AT80]   Arvind and R.E. Thomas. I-Structures: An efficient data structure for functional languages. Technical Report TM-178, MIT, 1980.

[CK92]   K. Mani Chandy and Carl Kesselman. Compositional C++: Compositional parallel programming. Technical Report Caltech-CS-TR-92-13, California Institute of Technology, 1992.

[CM88]   K. Mani Chandy and Jayadev Misra. *Parallel Program Design*. Addison-Wesley, 1988.

[CT91]   K. Mani Chandy and Stephen Taylor. *An Introduction to Parallel Programming*. Bartlett and Jones, 1991.

[ES90]   Margaret A. Ellis and Bjarne Stroustrup. *The Annotated C++ Reference Manual*. Addison-Wesley, 1990.

[FC92]   Ian Foster and K. Mani Chandy. Fortran M: Modular Fortran for parallel programming. Technical report, Argonne National Laboratory, 1992.

[FO90]   Ian Foster and Ross Overbeek. Experiences with bilingual parallel programming. In *The Proceedings of the Fifth Distributed Memory Computer Conference*, 1990.

[FO91]   Ian Foster and Ross Overbeek. Bilingual parallel programming. In *Proceedings of the Third Workshop on Parallel Computing and Compilers*. MIT Press, feb 1991.

[FT90]   Ian Foster and Stephen Taylor. *Strand: New Concepts in Parallel Programming*. Prentice Hall, 1990.

[Gre87]   Steve Gregory. *Parallel Logic Programming in PARLOG*. International Series in Logic Programming. Addison-Wesley, 1987.

[Lam91]   Leslie Lamport. Temporal logic of actions. Technical report, DEC-SRC, 1991.

[Mar85]   Alain J. Martin. The Probe: An addition to communication primitives. *Information Processing Letters*, 20:125–130, April 1985.

[OG76]   S. Owicki and D. Gries. An axiomatic proof technique for parallel programs I. *Acta Informatica*, 6(1):319–340, 1976.

[Pnu81]   Amir Pnueli. The temporal semantics of concurrent programs. *Theoretical Computer Science*, 13:45–60, 1981.

[Sei91]   Charles Seitz. *Developments in Concurrency and Communication*, chapter 5, pages 131–200. Addison Wesley, 1991.

[Sha86]   Ehud Shapiro. Concurrent Prolog: A program report. *IEEE Computer*, 19(8):44–58, August 1986.

[TA90]   B. H. Tay and A. L. Ananda. A survey of remote procedure calls. *ACM Operating Systems Review*, 24(3), July 1990.

[Tak89]   Akikazu Takeuchi. How to solve it in Concurrent Prolog. Unpublished note., 1989.

[TE68]   L. Tesler and H. Enea. A language for concurrent processes. In *Proceedings of AFIPS SJCC*, number ANL-91/38, 1968.

[Ued86]   Kazunori Ueda. Guarded horn clauses. In *Logic Programming '85*, pages 168–179. Springer-Verlag, 1986.

```
producer(list * sync * ptr) {
    // A producer iterates allocating a new list cell, storing the pointer to
    // it into the sync next pointer from the previous iteration and
    // initializing the value field of the list cell.
    list * tmp;          // tmp is a pointer to a list cell
    while (1) {
        tmp = new list;                        // Allocate a new list cell
        tmp->value = producer_value();         // Initialize the value being produced
        (*ptr)->next = tmp;                    // Pass modify privileges
        ptr = & (tmp->next);        // Get a pointer to the next field
    }
}


consumer(list * sync ptr) {
    // Iterate over the list created by the consumer. Because they
    // are both sync, we have to wait for both the value and the
    // next pointer to be initialized before continuing.
    while (1) {
        consume_value(ptr-> value);
        ptr = ptr->next;
    }
}


main() {
    list * sync X;
    // Run the producer and consumer in parallel. The consumer waits for
    // the list pointer X to be assigned a value. The producer is passed
    // a non-sync pointer to the list so that it dosn't have to wait.

    par { producer(& X); consumer(X); }
}
```

Figure 2: A producer/consumer example using a declarative interface.

```
// Produce a value by sending it directly to the consumer
struct producer {
  produce(consumer * ptr) {
      while (1) { ptr->insert_queue(producer_value()); }
  }
}


// A consumer is a user defined data type with three operations associated with
// it.
struct consumer {
  atomic insert_queue(T); // Insert a value into the consumers queue
  void consume(list sync * ptr) // Consume the values put in the queue
     {
       while (1) { consume_value(get_queue()); }
     }
private:
   atomic T get_queue();   // Extract a value from the queue.
}

main() {
  producer P;                     // Create a producer object
  consumer C; // Create a consumer object

   // Start the producer and consumer
  par { P.produce( &C ); C.consume(); }
}
```

Figure 3: A producer/consumer example using a message passing interface.

Bibliography

S.G. Akl, *The Design and Analysis of Parallel Algorithms*, Prentice-Hall, Inc., Englewood Cliffs, N.J., 1989.

P. America, "POOLT: A Parallel Object-Oriented Language," in *Object-Oriented Concurrent Programming*, A. Yonezawa and M. Tokoro, eds., MIT Press, Cambridge, Mass., 1987, pp. 199-220.

G.R. Andrews and F.B. Schneider, "Concepts and Notations for Concurrent Programming," *ACM Computing Surveys*, Vol. 15, No. 1, Mar. 1983, pp. 3–43.

Arvind, R.S. Nikhil, and K.K. Pingali, "I-Structures: Data Structures for Parallel Computing," *ACM Trans. Programming Languages and Systems*, Vol. 11, No. 4, Oct. 1989, pp. 589–632.

T. Axford, *Concurrent Programming: Fundamental Techniques for Real-Time and Parallel Software Design*, John Wiley & Sons, Inc., New York, N.Y., 1989.

J. Backus, "Can Programming Be Liberated from the Von Neumann Style? A Functional Style and Its Algebra of Programs," *Comm. ACM*, Vol. 21, No. 8, Aug. 1978, pp. 613–641.

R.J.R. Back, "A Method for Refining Atomicity in Parallel Algorithms," *Lecture Notes in Computer Sci.—Proc. Parallel Architectures and Languages Europe (PARLE '89)*, Vol. 365, Springer-Verlag, New York, N.Y., 1989, pp. 199–216.

R.J.R. Back, "Refinement Calculus Part II: Parallel and Reactive Programs," Tech. Report 93, Depts. of Computer Sci. and Math., Abo Akademi, Abo, Finland, 1989.

R.J.R. Back and K. Sere, "Stepwise Refinement of Action Systems," in *Lecture Notes in Computer Sci.—Mathematics of Program Construction*, Vol. 375, Springer-Verlag, New York, N.Y., June 1989, pp. 115–138.

R.J.R. Back and K. Sere, "Deriving an Occam Implementation of Action Systems," Tech. Report 99, Depts. of Computer Sci. and Math., Abo Akademi, Abo, Finland, 1990.

H.E. Bal, "A Comparative Study of Five Parallel Programming Languages," *Future Generation Computer Systems*, Vol. 8, Nos. 1–3, July 1992, pp. 121–135.

C.R. Banger, "Arrays with Categorical Type Constructors," *Proc. Workshop Arrays (ATABLE '92)*, 1992, pp. 105–121.

C.R. Banger, *The Categorical Construction of Arrays*, doctoral thesis, Dept. of Computing and Information Sci., Queen's Univ., Kingston, Canada, 1993.

R.E. Benner, J.L. Gustafson, and R.E. Montry, "Development and Analysis of Scientific Application Programs on a 1024-Processor Hypercube," Tech. Report SAND 880317, Sandia Nat'l Laboratories, Albuquerque, N.M., 1988.

M. Ben-Ari, *Principles of Concurrent and Distributed Programming*, Prentice-Hall Int'l, Englewood Cliffs, N.J., 1989.

D.P. Bertsekas and J.N. Tsitsiklis, *Parallel and Distributed Computation: Numerical Methods*, Prentice-Hall, Inc., Englewood Cliffs, N.J., 1989.

S. Brawer, *Introduction to Parallel Programming*, Academic Press, New York, N.Y., 1989.

A. Brogi and P. Ciancarini, "The Concurrent Language Shared Prolog," *ACM Trans. Programming Languages and Systems*, Vol. 13, No. 1, Jan. 1991, pp. 99–123.

B. Chapman, P. Mehrotra, and H. Zima, "Programming in Vienna Fortran," *Scientific Programming*, Vol. 1, No. 1, Fall 1992, pp. 31–50.

J. Crichlow, *An Introduction to Distributed and Parallel Computing*, Prentice-Hall, Inc., Englewood Cliffs, N.J., 1988.

W.J. Dally and D.S. Wills, "Universal Mechanisms for Concurrency," *Lecture Notes in Computer Sci.—Proc. Parallel Architectures and Languages Europe (PARLE '89)*, Vol. 365, Springer-Verlag, New York, N.Y., 1989, pp. 19–33.

M. Danelutto, S. Pelagatti, and M. Vanneschi, "High Level Languages for Easy Massively Parallel Computing," Tech. Report HPL-PSC-91-16, Hewlett-Packard Pisa Sci. Center, Pisa, Italy, 1991.

P. de la Torre and C.P. Kruskal, "Towards a Single Model of Efficient Computation in Real Parallel Machines," *Lecture Notes in Computer Sci.—Proc. Parallel Architectures and Languages Europe (PARLE '91)*, Springer-Verlag, New York, N.Y., 1991.

D. Feldcamp and A. Wagner, "Parsec: A Software Development Environment for Performance Oriented Parallel Programming," in *Transputer Research and Applications 6*, S. Atkins and A. Wagner, eds., IOS Press, Amsterdam, The Netherlands, May 1993, pp. 247–262.

G. Fox et al., *Solving Problems on Concurrent Processors*, Prentice-Hall, Inc., Englewood Cliffs, N.J., 1988.

J. Gibbons, *Algebras for Tree Algorithms*, doctoral thesis, Programming Research Group, Oxford Univ., Oxford, United Kingdom, 1991.

J.A. Goguen and T. Winkler, "Introducing OBJ3," Tech. Report SRI-CSL-88-9, Computer Sci. Laboratory, SRI Int'l, Aug. 1988.

J. Goguen et al., "The Rewrite Rule Machine 1988," Tech. Monograph PRG-76, Programming Research Group, Computing Laboratory, Oxford Univ., Oxford, United Kingdom, 1989.

C.A.R. Hoare, *Communicating Sequential Processes*, Prentice-Hall Int'l Series in Computer Sci., Prentice-Hall, Inc., Englewood Cliffs, N.J., 1985.

R.W. Hockney and C.R. Jesshope, *Parallel Computer: 2 Architecture, Programming, and Algorithms*, 2nd ed., IOP Pub. Ltd., Pa., 1988.

J. Jaja, *An Introduction to Parallel Algorithms*, Addison-Wesley Pub. Co., Reading, Mass., 1992.

A.H. Karp, "Programming for Parallelism," *Computer*, Vol. 20, No. 5, May 1987, pp. 43–57.

R.M. Karp and V. Ramachandran, "Parallel Algorithms for Shared-Memory Machines," in *Handbook of Theoretical Computer Science, Vol. A*, J. van Leeuwen, ed., Elsevier Sci. Pub., New York, N.Y., and MIT Press, Cambridge, Mass., 1990.

J.R. Larus, B. Richards, and G. Viswanathan, "C**: A Large-Grain, Object-Oriented, Data-Parallel Programming Language," Tech. Report TR1126, Univ. of Wisconsin-Madison, Madison, Wisc., Nov. 1992.

E. Lust et al., *Portable Programs for Parallel Processors*, Holt, Rinehart & Winston, New York, N.Y., 1987.

G. Malcolm, *Algebraic Data Types and Program Transformation*, doctoral thesis, Rijksuniversiteit Groningen, The Netherlands, Sept. 1990.

J. Meseguer and T. Winkler, "Parallel Programming in Maude," in *Lecture Notes in Computer Sci.—Research Directions in High-Level Parallel Programming Languages*, J.P. Banâtre and D. Le Metayer, eds., Vol. 574, Springer-Verlag, New York, N.Y., June 1991, pp. 253–293.

R. Milner, *Communication and Concurrency*, Prentice-Hall, Inc., Englewood Cliffs, N.J., 1989.

T. More, "On the Development of Array Theory," tech. report, IBM Cambridge Scientific Center, 1986.

A. Osterhaug, ed., *Guide to Parallel Programming on Sequent Computer Systems*, 2nd ed., Prentice-Hall, Inc., Englewood Cliffs, N.J., 1989.

M.J. Quinn, *Designing Efficient Algorithms for Parallel Computers*, McGraw-Hill, New York, N.Y., 1987.

R.K. Raj et al., "Emerald: A General-Purpose Programming Language," *Software: Practice & Experience*, Vol. 21, No. 1, Jan. 1991, pp. 91–118.

A.G. Ranade, *Fluent Parallel Computation*, doctoral thesis, Yale Univ., New Haven, Conn., 1989.

E. Schonberg, M. Gerhardt, and C. Hayden, "A Technical Tour of Ada," *Comm. ACM*, Vol. 35, No. 11, Nov. 1992, pp. 43–52.

D. Shasha and M. Snir, "Efficient and Correct Execution of Parallel Programs That Share Memory," *ACM Trans. Programming Languages and Systems*, Vol. 10, No. 2, Apr. 1988, pp. 282–312.

P. Singh, *Graphs as a Categorical Data Type*, master's thesis, Dept. of Computing and Information Sci., Queen's Univ., Kingston, Canada, 1993.

D.B. Skillicorn and W. Cai, "A Cost Calculus for Parallel Functional Programming," Tech. Report 92-329, Dept. of Computing and Information Sci., Queen's Univ., Kingston, Canada, 1992.

D.B. Skillicorn, "Categorical Data Types," *Proc. 2nd Workshop Abstract Models Parallel Computation*, Oxford Univ. Press, New York, N.Y., 1994.

D.R. Smith and M.R. Lowry, "Algorithm Theories and Design Tactics," in *Lecture Notes in Computer Sci.—Mathematics of Program Construction*, Vol. 375, Springer-Verlag, New York, N.Y., June 1989, pp. 379–398.

D.R. Smith, "Structure and Design of Global Search Algorithms," *Acta Informatica*, 1993.

L. Snyder, "Synopsis of Orca, a Simple Language Implementation of Phase Abstractions," *Proc. Workshop Languages, Compilers and Run-Time Environments Distributed Memory Multiprocessors*, *ACM SIGPLAN Notices*, Vol. 28, No. 1, Jan. 1993, pp. 40–43.

J.M. Spivey, "A Categorical Approach to the Theory of Lists," in *Lecture Notes in Computer Sci.—Mathematics of Program Construction*. 375, Springer-Verlag, New York, N.Y., June 1989, pp. 399–408.

D. Szafron et al., "Enterprise: An Interactive Graphical Programming Environment for Distributed Software," 1991 (available by ftp from cs.ualberta.ca).

P.C. Treleaven, D.R. Brownbridge, and R.P. Hopkins, "Data-Driven and Demand-Driven Computer Architecture," *ACM Computing Surveys*, Vol. 14, No. 1, Mar. 1982, pp. 93–143.

C.-W. Tseng, *An Optimizing Fortran D Compiler for MIMD Distributed-Memory Machines*, doctoral thesis, Rice Univ., Houston, Tex., Jan. 1993 (also published as Tech. Report Rice COMP TR-93-199, Rice Univ., Houston, Tex., Jan. 1993).

D. Whiddett, *Concurrent Programming for Software Engineers*, John Wiley & Sons, Inc., New York, N.Y., 1987.

S.A. Williams, *Programming Models for Parallel Systems*, John Wiley & Sons, Inc., New York, N.Y., 1989.

D.S. Wills, "Pi: A Parallel Architecture Interface for Multi-Model Execution," Tech. Report AI-TR-1245, MIT Artificial Intelligence Laboratory, Cambridge, Mass., 1990.

Subject Index

Italicized page numbers indicate pages in the reprinted papers. The name in parentheses is the name of the first author of the paper.

Bolded page numbers indicate pages in the introductory material of each chapter.

Author Index

About the Authors

David B. Skillicorn

David B. Skillicorn has been a member of the Department of Computing and Information Science at Queen's University in Kingston, Canada, since 1982. Currently, he is a professor in this department. His research interests are general-purpose parallel computation and programming models.

Skillicorn received a BSc (Hons) degree in pure mathematics from the University of Sydney, Australia, in 1977 and a PhD degree in computer science from the University of Manitoba, Canada, in 1981. He is a member of the IEEE Computer Society and the ACM.

Skillicorn may be contacted at Department of Computing and Information Science, Queen's University, Goodwin Hall, Kingston, K7L 3N6 Canada; fax: (613) 545-6513; e-mail: skill@qucis.queensu.ca.

Domenico Talia

Domenico Talia has been working in the area of parallel architectures and distributed systems since 1983. Currently, he is a senior researcher fellow of the parallel computing team at CRAI (Consorzio per la Ricerca e le Applicazioni di Informatica) in Rende, Italy. His research interests are parallel architectures, distributed systems, and concurrent programming languages.

Talia studied physics at the University of Calabria, Italy. In 1982, he was awarded a 3-year Formez Fellowship at CRAI. He is a member of the IEEE Computer Society and the ACM.

Talia may be contacted at CRAI, Località S. Stefano, I-87036 Rende, CS, Italy; fax: +39 (984) 446044; e-mail: dot@crai.it.

IEEE Computer Society Press Titles

AUTHORED BOOKS

Advances in ISDN and Broadband ISDN
Edited by William Stallings
(ISBN 0-8186-2797-2); 272 pages

Advances in Local and Metropolitan Area Networks
Edited by William Stallings
(ISBN 0-8186-5042-7); 448 pages

Advances in Real-Time Systems
Edited by John A. Stankovic and Krithi Ramamritham
(ISBN 0-8186-3792-7); 792 pages

Architectural Alternatives for Exploiting Parallelism
Edited by David J. Lilja
(ISBN 0-8186-2642-9); 464 pages

**Artificial Neural Networks —
Concepts and Control Applications**
Edited by V. Rao Vemuri
(ISBN 0-8186-9069-0); 520 pages

**Artificial Neural Networks —
Concepts and Theory**
Edited by Pankaj Mehra and Banjamin Wah
(ISBN 0-8186-8997-8); 680 pages

**Artificial Neural Networks—
Forecasting Time Series**
Edited by V. Rao Vemuri and Robert D. Rogers
(ISBN 0-8186-5120-2); 220 pages

**Artificial Neural Networks—
Oscillations, Chaos, and Sequence Processing**
Edited by Lipo Wang and Daniel L. Alkon
(ISBN 0-8186-4470-2); 136 pages

**Autonomous Mobile Robots:
Perception, Mapping and Navigation — Volume 1**
Edited by S. S. Iyengar and A. Elfes
(ISBN 0-8186-9018-6); 425 pages

**Autonomous Mobile Robots:
Control, Planning, and Architecture — Volume 2**
Edited by S. S. Iyengar and A. Elfes
(ISBN 0-8186-9116-6); 425 pages

Branch Strategy Taxonomy and Performance Models
Written by Harvey G. Cragon
(ISBN 0-8186-9111-5); 150 pages

Bridging Faults and IDDQ Testing
Edited by Yashwant K. Malaiya and Rochit Rajsuman
(ISBN 0-8186-3215-1); 128 pages

**Broadband Switching:
Architectures, Protocols, Design, and Analysis**
Edited by C. Dhas, V. K. Konangi, and M. Sreetharan
(ISBN 0-8186-8926-9); 528 pages

**Cache Coherence Problem in Shared-Memory Multiprocessors:
Hardware Solutions**
Edited by Milo Tomasevic and Veljko Milutinovic
(ISBN 0-8186-4092-8); 448 pages

Codes for Detecting and Correcting Unidirectional Errors
Edited by Mario Blaum
(ISBN 0-8186-4182-7); 224 pages

**Communication and Computer Networks:
Modelling with Discrete Time Queues**
Written by Michael E. Woodward
(ISBN 0-7273-0410-0); 280 pages

**Computer-Aided Software Engineering (CASE)
(Second Edition)**
Edited by Elliot Chikofsky
(ISBN 0-8186-3590-8); 184 pages

Readings in
Computer-Generated Music
Edited by Denis Baggi
(ISBN 0-8186-2747-6); 232 pages

Computer Algorithms: Key Search Strategies
Edited by Jun-ichi Aoe
(ISBN 0-8186-2123-0); 154 pages

Computer Arithmetic II
Edited by Earl E. Swartzlander, Jr.
(ISBN 0-8186-8945-5); 412 pages

**Computer Communications:
Architectures, Protocols, and Standards (Third Edition)**
Edited by William Stallings
(ISBN 0-8186-2712-3); 360 pages

**Computer Graphics Hardware:
Image Generation and Display**
Edited by H. K. Reghbati and A. Y. C. Lee
(ISBN 0-8186-0753-X); 384 pages

Computer Graphics: Image Synthesis
Edited by Kenneth Joy, Nelson Max, Charles Grant,
and Lansing Hatfield
(ISBN 0-8186-8854-8); 380 pages

Computer Vision: Principles
Edited by Rangachar Kasturi and Ramesh Jain
(ISBN 0-8186-9102-6); 700 pages

Computer Vision: Advances and Applications
Edited by Rangachar Kasturi and Ramesh Jain
(ISBN 0-8186-9103-4); 720 pages

Current Research in Decision Support Technology (IS Series)
Edited by Robert W. Blanning and David R. King
(ISBN 0-8186-2807-3); 256 pages

Decision Fusion
Written by Belur V. Dasarathy
(ISBN 0-8186-4452-4); 300 pages

Digital Image Warping
Written by George Wolberg
(ISBN 0-8186-8944-7); 340 pages

Readings in
Distributed Computing Systems
Edited by Thomas Casavant and Mukesh Singhal
(ISBN 0-8186-3032-9); 632 pages

**Distributed Computing Systems:
Concepts and Structures**
Edited by A. L. Ananda and B. Srinivasan
(ISBN 0-8186-8975-0); 416 pages

Distributed Mutual Exclusion Algorithms
Edited by Pradip K. Srimani and Sunil R. Das
(ISBN 0-8186-3380-8); 168 pages

Distributed Open Systems
Edited by Frances Brazier and Dag Johansen,
(ISBN 0-8186-4292-0); 192 pages

Digital Image Processing (Second Edition)
Edited by Rama Chellappa
(ISBN 0-8186-2362-4); 816 pages

For further information call toll-free 1-800-CS-BOOKS or write:

IEEE Computer Society Press, 10662 Los Vaqueros Circle, PO Box 3014,
Los Alamitos, California 90720-1264, USA

IEEE Computer Society, 13, avenue de l'Aquilon,
B-1200 Brussels, BELGIUM

IEEE Computer Society, Ooshima Building, 2-19-1 Minami-Aoyama,
Minato-ku, Tokyo 107, JAPAN

IEEE Computer Society